Artificial Intelligence in Peace, Justice, and Strong Institutions

Christian Kaunert
Dublin City University, Ireland

Anjali Raghav
Sharda University, India

Kamalesh Ravesangar
Tunku Abdul Rahman University of Management and Technology, Malaysia

Bhupinder Singh
Sharda University, India

Budi Agus Riswandi
Universitas Islam Indonesia, Indonesia

IGI Global
Scientific Publishing
Publishing Tomorrow's Research Today

Vice President of Editorial — Melissa Wagner
Managing Editor of Acquisitions — Mikaela Felty
Managing Editor of Book Development — Jocelynn Hessler
Production Manager — Mike Brehm
Cover Design — Phillip Shickler

Published in the United States of America by
IGI Global Scientific Publishing
701 East Chocolate Avenue
Hershey, PA, 17033, USA
Tel: 717-533-8845
Fax: 717-533-8661
Website: https://www.igi-global.com E-mail: cust@igi-global.com

Library of Congress Cataloging-in-Publication Data

Names: Kaunert, Christian, editor. | Raghav, Anjali, 1995- editor. | Ravesangar, Kamalesh, 1985- editor. | Singh, Bhupinder (Law teacher), editor. | Riswandi, Budi Agus, 1975- editor.
Title: Artificial intelligence in peace, justice, and strong institutions / edited by Christian Kaunert, Anjali Raghav, Kamalesh Ravesangar, Bhupinder Singh, Budi Riswandi.
Description: Hershey, PA : IGI Global Scientific Publishing, [2025] |
Includes bibliographical references and index. | Summary: "This book comes in its timely examination of how AI may revolutionize governance, the rule of law, and human rights practices in a modern era. Through the numerous case studies in the applications of AI to these domains, this book attempts to add value to ongoing discussions on sustainable development and responsible technology use"-- Provided by publisher.
Identifiers: LCCN 2024055587 (print) | LCCN 2024055588 (ebook) | ISBN 9798369393956 (h/c) | ISBN 9798369393963 (s/c) | ISBN 9798369393970 (ebook)
Subjects: LCSH: Public administration--Data processing. | Social ethics--Data processing. | Practice of law--Data processing. | Sustainable development--Data processing. | Artificial intelligence--Social aspects.
Classification: LCC JF1525.A8 A757 2025 (print) | LCC JF1525.A8 (ebook) | DDC 351.0285/63--dc23/eng/20250208
LC record available at https://lccn.loc.gov/2024055587
LC ebook record available at https://lccn.loc.gov/2024055588
British Cataloguing in Publication Data
A Cataloguing in Publication record for this book is available from the British Library.

Table of Contents

Detailed Table of Contents

Artificial intelligence (AI) is transforming recruitment, shifting traditional hiring toward efficient, data-driven processes. This chapter explores AI's impact on talent acquisition, detailing its influence on every stage—from candidate sourcing and screening to automated assessments and predictive analytics. Leveraging machine learning, AI allows organizations to analyze vast data sources, such as resumes and social media profiles, to quickly and accurately identify top candidates. The chapter covers key AI technologies like natural language processing, chatbots, and predictive analytics and highlights benefits like efficiency, reduced bias, and improved candidate experience. It also examines ethical challenges, including algorithmic bias, transparency, data privacy, costs, and resistance to change. This chapter underscores the need for responsible AI use, enabling organizations to build inclusive and equitable hiring practices by balancing AI's strengths and limitations.

AI in customer engagement chatbots and voice assistants are AI-driven tools that improve customer engagement and give businesses the ability to provide individualized experiences by conducting sentiment analysis. Nonetheless, issues like data privacy concerns, algorithmic bias, and ethical challenges remain, which still need proper regulations and drafting more transparency. Even with these challenges, AI has vast potential, including sustainable marketing, omni-channel strategies, and AI-generated content. The future of marketing powered by AI lies around integrating technology with emotional intelligence thereby making the strategy centric towards the consumer leading to a trust factor and driving brand loyalty. Businesses adopting AI-powered marketing solutions will rise above all competition in a growing digital world. Tackling challenges head-on will be critical to unleashing AI's full potential for marketing transformation.

Artificial intelligence is transforming the legal landscape by enhancing efficiency, accessibility, and fairness in the justice delivery system. This chapter examines the role of AI in reinforcing the rule of law, with particular attention to legal research, judicial decision-making, case management, and dispute resolution. From predictive analytics to legal chatbots to smart contracts, AI-driven tools are revolutionizing legal frameworks, speeding case processing, and reducing human bias. But AI in law also raises ethical challenges algorithmic bias, transparency issues, and data privacy concerns. Through real-world case studies from the United States, the European Union, India, and China, this chapter explores the implications of AI applications in legal governance. It highlights global initiatives to govern the role of AI technology in courts and suggests design principles for responsible AI-aided legal progress.

AI biases can induce existing imbalances and affect the most affected populations more severely. The study underlines the need to introduce the imperative of transparency and explainability of AI systems. The fact that many algorithmic systems are correspondence opaque raises questions about how such decisions are made and who is accountable when using artificial intelligence, which leads to wrongful arrest or unfair sentencing. The research calls for effective legislative frameworks that would protect constitutional entitlement due to the widespread use of AI systems. The criminal justice system can effectively embrace AI and avoid the risk of infringing individual rights to make technology serve justice rather than inimical or detrimental to justice and basic human rights.

The infusion of artificial intelligence (AI) into different facets of administration is defining new horizons in legal environments. AI has turned out to be an essential element in the improvement of legal systems because of its ability to accelerate and augment legal procedures. AI has proven to have great potential in successfully combating corruption because it increases transparency and accountability in society and in firms. Corruption is a multifaceted problem that negatively affects governance and becomes one of the main reasons for citizens' distrust. AI is considered to provide important support in conflict analysis and prediction of the conflicts' behaviour in the context of conflict transformation and peacebuilding. Through analysis of data gathered from social media, news outlets, and so on, the various AI-driven tools can gather early signs of conflict and monitor conflict escalation and de-escalation in real time. It assists governments and other stakeholders in peace building processes.

By leveraging AI-driven solutions, students also have the ability to adjust learning based on personal preference, with unique content that both improves understanding and boosts interest. Virtual tutors, interactive simulations, and smart assessments allow students to learn at their own pace and get real-time feedback. AI-enabled data analytics tools can spot skill gaps and forecast the likelihood of students that feed back into their re-evaluated teaching and streamline to boost success in the classrooms. AI collaborative platforms create a shared worldwide ecosystem for learning having students from all walks of life. Administrative aspects of teaching like grading and curriculum development are streamlined through automation, enabling educators with more bandwidth for mentorship and innovation. AI-assisting technologies are thus building blocks of a better educational system, with equitable, efficient, and future-proof learning developed by bridging the entry gaps.

The use of artificial intelligence poses challenges for legal systems such as algorithmic bias, lack of interpretability, and data privacy issues embedded in ethical dilemmas to reinforce existing power asymmetries. Algorithmic bias can reinforce the existing inequities of our social world, undermining fairness and hurting some communities more than others. AI models, with their "black box" nature, create questions of transparency and accountability, and data privacy is an evergreen concern about the use of sensitive personal information. On top of that, AI systems can reinforce existing power structures that serve the privileged populations. Solutions could be new fairness-aware algorithms, privatization techniques such as differential privacy and regulatory actions mandating transparency and accountability. Ethical AI in society, interdisciplinary collaboration, and participatory governance are ethical and socio-democratic imperatives to achieve responsible deployment of trustworthy AI.

AI has a huge potential to address human trafficking through improved detection, prevention, and intervention strategies. AI can be empowered further, to be more dynamically engaged in the fight against traffickers, cybercrimes, and other threats. Utilizing machine learning algorithms, AI analyzes big data from social media, online ads, and travel data to recognize patterns and assess risk for trafficking victims. The hidden traffickers and victims may have been discovered more easily by using AI tools such as natural language processing and face recognition. And finally, AI can enhance collaboration among international law enforcement agencies, providing real-time data sharing and predictive analytics for more coordinated responses. The scope of anti-trafficking efforts can be greatly enhanced with similar tools and mechanisms offered by AI to scale efforts and prevention mechanisms for this global crisis.

With the potential to transform judicial bodies from the courts to the ICJ, AI promises greater efficiency, accessibility, and equity in justice. This study examines how AI is revolutionizing judicial practices, focusing on its impact on case management, legal research, and decision-making. It emphasizes the extrapolated advantages these AI technologies can confer, allowing for predictive analytics and natural language processing, streamlining practices, and increasing accessibility through which various populations may benefit from the justice system. The adoption of AI brings with it ethical dilemmas that need to be addressed, such as algorithmic bias, transparency in the process of decision-making, and the requirement for human intervention. The complexities of this moment demand careful navigation, as this work towards a future where that technology no longer hampers justice but bolsters global judicial systems.

In recent years, the exponential growth of e-commerce has revolutionized how businesses operate and interact with consumers. This surge in online shopping has been accompanied by a parallel rise in digital marketing strategies employed by e-commerce companies to attract, engage, and retain customers. Digital marketing encompasses various techniques, including search engine optimization (SEO), social media marketing, content marketing, email marketing, and pay-per-click advertising. The effectiveness of these strategies in enhancing a company's financial performance has become a subject of significant interest and scrutiny. Companies can boost their bottom line and achieve greater profitability by reducing customer acquisition costs, increasing customer lifetime value, and improving overall marketing efficiency. E-commerce businesses could better reach their target audience on these channels by increasing their brand visibility and reach and driving traffic to their websites.

Violence against women continues to be a global phenomenon that asks societies to turn to solutions based on ethics, compassion, and justice. The leadership qualities rooted in the philosophies of Sikhism and Buddhism can provide deep reflections on tackling violence and all the essential elements that go into creating mental well-being in society for both genders, especially for women. Both religions highlight principles of compassion, equality, and non-violence as foundations of their tenets, ultimately creating frameworks for the reformation of society. Sikhism emboldened by the teachings of Sarbat da Bhala (welfare of all), gender equality, underlines the dignity and rights of women and encourages active resistance to oppression and violence. This chapter explores the teachings, historical contributions, and modern applications of Sikhism and Buddhism in addressing violence and fostering the mental well-being of women.

Machine learning and deep learning techniques have emerged as powerful tools against several types of financial fraud. The banking and financial industry, a fundamental component of contemporary economies, is experiencing a significant upheaval due to the rise of digital transactions. This transition has resulted in an increase in financial fraud, necessitating a fundamental change in security standards. The use of advanced analytics, such as anomaly detection and pattern recognition, is examined to establish a strong defense against the continually changing strategies used by fraudulent entities in the ad click sector. Credit card management, a constant target for nefarious actions, necessitates an advanced strategy for fraud detection. This chapter examines AI-based document verification systems, highlighting their crucial role in safeguarding transactions reliant on document authentication. It

Preface

It is widely accepted that we are living in an age of rapid wires technology and that the combination of Artificial Intelligence (AI) in different industries has created concern and excitement. So, this evolution of AI and its power to shape basic societal variables like peace and justice and the robustness of institutions is more obvious. This edited book endeavours to do just that by mapping the critical intersections at which artificial intelligence has begun to intersect with the social goods of peace, justice, strong institutions, and social organizations, bringing together contributions from a multidisciplinary cohort of academic scholars, practitioners and thought leaders. The contributions in this edited book express the complex role that AI can play in supporting peace and justice and strengthening inclusive and accountable institutions. AI embodies opportunities yet also challenges, from its uses in conflict resolution and aid to possible effects on law and governance that should not be overlooked. As we traverse this multifaceted ecosystem, understanding how AI can be leveraged for good while curtailing negative outcomes like bias, surveillance and civil liberties decline is more critical than ever.

Through its chapters, the book compromises unique insights into the ethical considerations, practical applications and policy implications of AI for peace and justice. Through interdisciplinary voices, we would like to enable a dialogue that highlights innovative new uses of AI while also framing them in terms of broader needs for ethical frameworks and inclusive practices.

CHAPTER OVERVIEW

Chapter 1 covers how Artificial intelligence is revolutionizing hiring by making talent acquisition more efficient and data-driven. This chapter examines AI's role in sourcing, screening, and assessing candidates through predictive analytics, chatbots, and natural language processing. While AI enhances efficiency and reduces bias, ethical challenges such as algorithmic bias and data privacy must be addressed to ensure equitable hiring practices.

In Chapter 2, the authors explore how AI-powered tools like chatbots and voice assistants are transforming customer engagement by offering personalized experiences. This chapter explores AI's role in sentiment analysis, sustainable marketing, and omni-channel strategies. Despite challenges such as algorithmic bias and data privacy concerns, businesses leveraging AI in marketing can drive brand loyalty and gain a competitive edge in the digital era.

Chapter 3 delves into how AI is enhancing efficiency and fairness in legal frameworks through predictive analytics, legal chatbots, and smart contracts. This chapter explores AI's applications in legal research, case management, and dispute resolution while addressing ethical concerns like algorithmic bias and transparency. Real-world case studies highlight global efforts to integrate AI responsibly into the justice system.

Chapter 4 reviews algorithmic bias in AI-driven legal systems can perpetuate discrimination and unfair outcomes. This chapter examines the risks of opaque decision-making, wrongful arrests, and sentencing disparities. It advocates for legislative frameworks to protect individual rights and ensure AI serves justice rather than exacerbating systemic inequalities.

Chapter 5 showcases how AI presents both opportunities and challenges in achieving gender equality. While AI can promote fairness through improved data representation, it can also reinforce biases if not carefully monitored. This chapter highlights the need for diverse and inclusive AI development, urging collaboration between developers, policymakers, and educators to create gender-sensitive AI solutions.

Chapter 6 highlights how financial institutions are leveraging AI for personalized marketing, predictive modeling, and automation. This chapter explores AI-driven strategies such as targeted advertising and chatbots that enhance customer engagement and operational efficiency. It provides actionable insights for financial institutions to integrate AI and maintain a competitive edge in the market.

In Chapter 7 the author's touch on AI is reshaping governance by increasing transparency and accountability, particularly in legal and administrative systems. This chapter examines AI's role in combating corruption, analyzing conflicts, and supporting peacebuilding efforts. AI-driven tools for monitoring conflict escalation offer governments valuable insights for conflict resolution.

Chapter 8 goes over how AI-assisted technologies are transforming education through virtual tutors, interactive simulations, and smart assessments. This chapter explores how AI enhances personalized learning, identifies skill gaps, and streamlines administrative tasks. AI-driven platforms create a global learning ecosystem that fosters accessibility and equity in education.

In Chapter 9, algorithmic bias, lack of transparency, and data privacy issues challenge the ethical deployment of AI. This chapter explores how AI can reinforce power imbalances and undermine fairness. Solutions such as fairness-aware algorithms, differential privacy, and regulatory oversight are essential to ensuring AI is deployed responsibly in society.

Chapter 10 discusses how AI has immense potential to prevent and combat human trafficking through data-driven detection and intervention strategies. This chapter explores how AI-powered tools analyze social media, online ads, and travel data to identify trafficking patterns. AI-driven collaboration among international law enforcement agencies enhances efforts to address this global crisis.

Chapter 11 explores how AI is revolutionizing judicial practices by improving case management, legal research, and decision-making. This chapter discusses AI's benefits in increasing accessibility to justice while addressing concerns over bias, transparency, and human oversight. The responsible integration of AI in judicial bodies is crucial to ensuring fair and efficient legal processes.

Chapter 12 speaks on the how rise of e-commerce has driven companies to adopt AI-powered digital marketing strategies, including SEO, social media marketing, and content personalization. This chapter examines how AI optimizes customer acquisition, enhances engagement, and boosts profitability through targeted and data-driven marketing approaches.

Chapter 13 highlights how violence against women remains a global challenge, and ethical frameworks from Sikhism and Buddhism offer valuable insights into fostering gender equality and societal well-being. This chapter explores the teachings of these religions on non-violence, compassion, and active resistance against oppression, emphasizing their relevance in modern gender discourse.

Chapter 14 discusses machine learning and deep learning are powerful tools in detecting financial fraud. This chapter discusses how AI-driven fraud detection systems analyze vast datasets to identify suspicious transactions, reduce false positives, and improve security in financial institutions. The application of AI in fraud prevention enhances trust and stability in financial markets.

Chapter 15 explores how AI-driven performance appraisal systems enhance accuracy and efficiency while emphasizing the indispensable role of human judgment. It presents a conceptual framework that balances AI automation with human oversight to create a fair and effective evaluation system.

Chapter 16 offers a bibliometric analysis of AI's impact on HRM, examining global research trends, key contributors, and emerging themes from 676 studies. By leveraging AI-driven insights, organizations can refine HRM strategies, making them more data-driven and impactful. Together, these chapters provide a comprehensive perspective on how AI is transforming HRM, highlighting both its potential and the need for human-AI collaboration.

We hope that as it embark on this journey, this book is not only a meaningful contribution to the field of study but also a helpful resource for researchers, policy-makers and practitioners to understand the promising potential of AI in supporting peace and building strong institutions. That means working together to ensure our institutions draw on technology to create justice and equity but in a way that if we do that it will not mean that we lose institutions that work and respond.

We extend our gratitude to all contributors for their expertise and insights as well as the readers who support this work. Together, it is our collective duty to ensure that the future of AI is built on a foundation of the values that protect human dignity, sustain peace and uphold the pillars of justice globally.

Christian Kaunert
Dublin City University, Ireland

Anjali Raghav
Sharda University, India

Kamalesh Ravesangar
Tunku Abdul Rahman University of Management and Technology, Malaysia

Bhupinder Singh
Sharda University, India

Budi Agus Riswandi
Universitas Islam Indonesia, Indonesia

Chapter 1
AI- Powered Talent Acquisition:
Revolutionizing the Hiring Process

Kamalesh Ravesangar
https://orcid.org/0009-0004-2154-184X
Tunku Abdul Rahman University of Management and Technology, Malaysia

Wei Chien Ng
https://orcid.org/0000-0003-1293-6781
Universiti Sains Malaysia, Malaysia

Guat Guan Toh
Tunku Abdul Rahman University of Management and Technology, Malaysia

Bhupinder Singh
https://orcid.org/0009-0006-4779-2553
Sharda University, India

ABSTRACT

Artificial intelligence (AI) is transforming recruitment, shifting traditional hiring toward efficient, data-driven processes. This chapter explores AI's impact on talent acquisition, detailing its influence on every stage—from candidate sourcing and screening to automated assessments and predictive analytics. Leveraging machine learning, AI allows organizations to analyze vast data sources, such as resumes and social media profiles, to quickly and accurately identify top candidates. The chapter covers key AI technologies like natural language processing, chatbots, and predictive analytics and highlights benefits like efficiency, reduced bias, and improved candidate experience. It also examines ethical challenges, including algorithmic bias, transparency, data privacy, costs, and resistance to change. This

DOI: 10.4018/979-8-3693-9395-6.ch001

chapter underscores the need for responsible AI use, enabling organizations to build inclusive and equitable hiring practices by balancing AI's strengths and limitations.

1. INTRODUCTION

In the rapidly shifting landscape of today's workforce, Artificial Intelligence (AI) has come to the fore as a game-changer, fundamentally shifting paradigms across various sectors. An important area in which AI has managed to transform traditional practices is talent acquisition and recruitment. As organizations struggle to attract and retain top talent in a competitive marketplace, the integration of AI in recruitment technology has become necessary to make recruitment processes faster and better. The influence of AI in talent acquisition is very broad, beginning with the elimination of routine work. Recruitment processes typically bear several repetitive exercises-including skills screenings, candidate screening, and preliminary assessments. AI can use machine-learning algorithms on large data sets to reveal patterns and preferences, thus speeding up these boring tasks. This is not only cut down the time to fill a position but also maintains the focus of recruiters on strategic and human-centered aspects of the hiring process. On top of that, the adoption of AI tools provides unprecedented efficiency in candidate screening and selection. With sophisticated algorithms sorting through resumes and job applications, application materials can be automatically screened through established criteria to find candidates whose skills and experience best match what the job requires, promoting a selection process that is significantly more objective and impartial to add more chances of identifying the most ideal candidates for the roles. AI can be seen as a range of computer and communication technologies used to simulate human thought processes, thus improving, streamlining and making easier human activities (Olan et al., 2022). It can be studied in four ways. The first is: (1) as a technological scaffold (the range of devices and systems) (Yau et al., 2021), (2) as a paradigm (a use of systems to recreate human thinking and behaviour) (Enholm et al., 2022), (3) as an anthropomorphism (the way machines are perceived to perform human tasks) (Kanade, 2022), and (4) as an application-oriented science (a scientific study of creating the above mentioned) (Antoni et al., 2020). In every context that one may place AI, there are always two aspects inextricably connected to it autonomously (the ability to perform complicated activities without constant human intervention in the process) and alterability (the capability to improve one's performance) (Panerai, 2018).

Many experts, nowadays, often examines the evolution of human resource management (HRM) occasioned by the automation of various work activities (Kucharčíková et al., 2023). The evolution in itself shall greatly affect the labour market and the individual participants concerned with the recruitment and selection of employees (Fritts & Cabrera, 2021; Vedapradha et al., 2019). Forecasts suggest the potential of machines replacing manual labour, thereby realizing the ever-increasing importance of talent acquisition (Autor et al., 2003). Several authors (Dulebohn & Stone, 2018; Waheed et al., 2020) bring forth the increasingly contemporary aspect of electronic management taking over human resource management. E-HRM, as a term, describes a collection of policies, activities, and services in HR management that have been aided by information and communication technology (Marler & Fisher, 2013). Based on this, E-HRM changed how organizations manage their human resources through technology aimed at improving performance within and streamlining the personnel processes Porkodi and Raman (2024), also known as e-HRM functions or functional modules. Such processes can be configured in such a way that they will rely on technology to automate manual processes, enhance data accuracy, and attain overall greater efficiency, thereby, allowing human resource professionals to concentrate on strategic initiatives and talent development.

In the digital world, e-recruitment, or electronic recruitment, has become one of the basic tools used by many organizations (Fernandes & Machado, 2022). With the coming of the internet and social media, recruitment processes are affected and intensified in speed and efficiency. E-recruitment refers to a digital method of recruitment for employment in the organizations (Alamro et al., 2018). This means that they are faced with numerous challenges regarding how fast they could fill the very position, how much to assess the previous experience, skills, and competencies of potential candidates, and facilitating assimilation of new hires into the organizational culture (Allal-Chérif et al., 2021). In some situations, these prevailing trends are a multi-zyronic chat for the recruiters to deal with. The goal has been, therefore, to shift towards a technology-enhanced recruitment procedure, with integration of various innovative solutions, hashed upon by AI technology: initiation with intelligent automated interviewers, assisting with handling resumes, and matching job specifications better with candidates' qualifications (Fritts & Cabrera, 2021). Recruitment speed has become a major factor in organizations' competitiveness in the labour market and in successfully enticing skilled personnel. AI, therefore, could significantly expedite recruitment (Vedapradha et al., 2019). It will eventually assist in reducing time-wasting administrative tasks, lead to objectivity with resume screening and shortlisting suitable candidates, plus create a more engaged talent pool to drive a quicker and better-informed decision-making process (Horodyski, 2023).

A 2017 survey conducted by Statista (2017), which included responses from 8,815 talent acquisition professionals and hiring managers, revealed that 67% of participants believe AI significantly alleviates the time-intensive aspects of the hiring process (Statista, 2017). Furthermore, Intelion Systems indicates a rising trend in the adoption of AI for recruitment, with between 35% and 45% of companies currently utilizing such tools (Intelion Systems, 2023). Notably, it is reported that 99% of Fortune 500 companies have integrated AI into their recruitment strategies in some capacity. To effectively leverage AI, human resources professionals must possess a fundamental understanding of these technologies (Charlwood & Guenole, 2022). A lack of such knowledge may lead to ineffective utilization of these tools, potentially resulting in bias or discrimination against candidates during the recruitment process (Fernández-Martínez & Fernández, 2020). This article explores the various applications of AI throughout the employee recruitment stages, highlighting the increasing interest among professionals regarding AI's role in management, particularly in human resource management. However, it also notes a deficiency in research concerning the specific activities within employee recruitment that could benefit from AI implementation (Nawaz, 2020). Consequently, the authors evaluate different software solutions designed for recruitment purposes. Through this analysis, potential applications of AI in the recruitment process are identified, supported by practical examples. This conceptual framework may assist the academic community in examining the effects of AI on recruitment efficiency and inspire businesses to incorporate AI into their hiring processes.

2. ESSENTIAL AI TECHNOLOGIES IN TALENT ACQUISITION

2.1. Resume Parsing, Analysis and Job Description Matching

In this review, a comprehensive exploration of a Company Recommender System employing a text mining and machine learning paradigm to assist recruiters in identifying candidates for a specific role is presented. Resumes are filtered according to company requirements whereupon candidates' resumes are submitted. Then, the company may use ratings to filter out these few to some top-notch candidates. The approach and framework describing this article will be stated in four stages: first, gathering resumes and identifying keywords within the resume text database; second, ranking candidates and classifying them using some scoring system; third, lexical extraction of additional keywords from resumes within the system (Pal et al., 2022). In this specific case, polish resume data will be automatically harvested in reference to IT recruitment. This review presents the automated information retrieval process in the IT sector. Polish is a low-resource language, and the system suggests a multimodule one to tackle dictionary problems and complicated linguistic relations. Entity recognition will be adopted because it is the best technique for the CVs evaluation and will be enacted on this study. It is primarily a semi-semantic analysis of the text, focusing on the identification of the search terms or rules and limiting the basic processing for other content present in the text (Roy et al., 2020).

The modern-day job recommendation systems would not have materialized without natural language processing techniques. Thus, these methodologies enabled jobs in job descriptions and candidates' profiles to be analysed, paving way for accurate recommendations. One popular approach is text classification, which basically categorizes job descriptions on the basis of their specific requirements. The approach helps to tie job seekers to positions that suit their education and skills (Bhatia et al., 2019). Contrary to that, it may provide quite a tough time to comprehend more complicated job descriptions that thus tend to provide certain limitations. Another widely used technique is entity recognition, which identifies key components in a job description and candidate profile such as job titles, company names, and skills (Mittal et al., 2020). The approach helps connect job seekers with opportunities that demand their certain skills, although this may not be effective in cases where the employers do not explicitly state the skill. Deep learning algorithms, which fall under a category of machine learning algorithms, have very advanced possibilities and are able to learn from large datasets. These algorithms outperform traditional machine learning methods, and while they do not, they automatically do features extraction, generally lessening the needs for human effort. A deep learning approach was suggested by Laurim et al. (2021) which includes a scenario that identifies the relevant personal traits and competencies of job candidates for recommending jobs. In this work, the hybrid model that unites collaborative filtering and content-based filtering was introduced to deliver correct recommendations by using machine learning and natural language processing to recommend job postings relevant to students.

2.2 AI Chatbots

AI chatbots are used to support recruitment processes in various aspects, from sourcing candidates to scheduling interviews. These advanced chatbots can evaluate the prospects in line with pre-set questions based on qualifications and experience. In addition to this, AI chatbots have made it easier for recruiters to coordinate interviews with candidates and consequently save considerable time for the recruiter (McColl & Michelotti, 2019). This AI-powered process denotes a more automated recruitment conduct wherein the resume is analysed by an AI engine, interviews are scheduled, and even hiring decisions are assisted with. This strategy brings greater efficiency and scalability to traditional methods while at the same time working to reduce human bias in the recruitment process.

From the point of view of jobseekers, AI chatbots facilitate users in approaching employers and job portals with ease. It offers an opportunity for jobseekers to interact with chatbots, which provide quick replies and a speedy flow of information anytime.

These chatbots are capable of vetting resumes to see that skills, qualifications, and experience match the requirements of a job, and coaching the job seeker as to how best to frame up his/her application (Klucin, 2020). Moreover, these chatbots can respond to frequently asked questions on job postings, provide company information, expound on the application process, and indicate interview timelines, thereby enabling job seekers to get the vital information with no delay whatsoever. They even recommend job vacancies that suit a jobseeker's skills, experience, and preferences, allowing the jobseeker to save time and bring to light possibilities that he or she would have otherwise missed. Chatbots provide updates on certain applications so that job seekers can always remain informed about the status of their applications (Guenole & Feinzig, 2018). AI chatbots may offer feedback on resumes, cover letters, and interview techniques so that job seekers can either intelligently modify their application materials or improve their workplace skills. AI chatbots are built to be objective and free from biases, which may benefit their users as they are judged solely on qualifications with no subjective criteria (Upadhyay & Khandelwal, 2018). Through a combination of their preferences and skills, AI chatbots can help users locate job openings suitable for their qualifications and career goals.

2.3 Predictive Analytics

Recruitment practices are undergoing a sea change, specifically due to the recent development of predictive analytics. In modern-day decision-making predominantly driven by data, the calibre of talent selection has gained momentum-almost critically important in high-stakes domains such as IT, wherein the pressure for recruitment of adept professionals is humongous (Sharma, 2018). Predictive analytics refers to the process that involves the application of historical data through statistical algorithms and machine learning approaches to predict future outcomes. Within the confines of the recruitment universe, predictive analytics become an evaluation of an immense amount of big data derived from resumes, assessments, interviews, and other sources of value over analysing a candidate's suitability, probable performance at work, and culture fit.

Predictive analytics help evaluate the character and behaviour of candidates into fitment for the organization concerned. The system studies historical employee data to predict the chances of success of a particular candidate in the organizational setting (Verhoeven, 2020). These analytics applications can expeditiously mine through resumes to zero in on the key skills and attributes that align with job descriptions and also vastly streamline the recruitment process, resulting in the progression of only the finest and most qualified candidates. In addition, the analytics automatically calculate scores for candidates running on skills, experience, and cultural fit for the role so that recruiters are rapidly able to identify and shortlist the most promising people who can be called for an interview. These applications also screen the candidates' previous interview performances, using that piece of information to project their success in future interviews that will help recruiters pose more focused questions and take better decisions (Kulkarni & Che, 2019). In addition, after hiring is completed, predictive analytics can again be beneficial to assess the performance, engagement, and satisfaction of the hired candidate, thus giving vital information to retention strategies, promoting the long-term survival of the new hire.

Predictive analytics is changing the way organizations plan for recruitment, enabling more intelligent, data-driven decisions to achieve higher-quality hires in less time while simultaneously improving retention (Soleimani et al., 2021). Through predictive analytics, organizations can always have the edge over others and subsequently acquire employees best needed. In an everchanging job market, those businesses willing to harness predictive analytics will be in a better position due to recruitment becomes more data driven. The core strength of predicative analytics lies in articulating the areas: employee attrition, the hiring process simplification, or simply workforce planning enhancement.

2.4 AI-Powered Sourcing and Screening

Candidate sourcing augmented through the employment of AI takes the exercise of acquiring candidates a notch higher than simple efficiency. AI takes the candidates sourcing workflow and enhance it to ensure that one gets the right candidates who meet the required qualitative, quantitative, and organisational culture in the organisation (Van Esch et al., 2019). Whereas conventional methods might oversimplify results or fail to even capture data, AI-driven tools use data to identify trends and preferences that the traditional approach can overlook. In handling the mundane tasks of candidate sourcing, AI lets recruiters manage their time in a more strategic way, focusing on relationship-building and the candidate experience. This switch allows good focus on high-value activities: contacting top candidates and modifying recruitment strategies. Therefore, AI candidate sourcing is a great asset for enhancing the entire recruitment lifecycle.

Augmenting the AI candidate sourcing is a set of considerations that thoroughly evaluates your pool of candidates through prior experiences and skills, which very much relate, to some extent, with the requirements set by the hiring authority (Li et al., 2023). Candidate sourcing is a form of AI that automatically fetches candidates not only from the well-known job boards but also from those niche websites that might not be widely known. Its work aims to scan the web and find as many of the right candidates for any position available as possible. Moreover, in addition to externally sourcing candidates, AI will provide insight into the internal talent pool, allowing the organization to speedily assess their current employees through AI-powered matching in order to appraise whether a current employee qualifies for an open position (Bondarouk & Brewster, 2016). Furthermore, determine candidates already in the internal database and also disclose employees with comparable skills and experience in the organization. AI can be employed also to find and pinpoint any biases present in the hiring process. The tools may scour historical hiring data for bias or monitor it over time and adjust the sourcing criteria accordingly for an objective candidate selection process. As today's workforce becomes increasingly diverse, the need for equity and inclusion is paramount. AI-driven candidate sourcing offers an essential tool for organizations to identify and recruit from a broad, diverse talent pool, ensuring access to the widest range of skills and perspectives. (Raghavan et al., 2020).

2.5 AI-Driven Candidate Engagement and Communication

Effective communication with candidates and candidate engagement comprises critical components of the recruitment process, greatly determining the success of talent acquisition (Allal-Chérif et al., 2021; Allden & Harris, 2013). Interactions between recruiters and candidates shape candidates' perceptions of an organization and consequently influence their acceptance or rejection of job offers. Certainly, organizations are realizing the importance of candidate communication and engagement within their recruitment strategies (Lahoti, 2023).

However, providing the necessary information to candidates at various stages in the recruitment process can sometimes be challenging, since candidates expect information such as organizational details, job descriptions, interview procedures, assessment criteria, and updates about their interview status (Nayak et al., 2024). Poorly managed communication and engagement can make any bad impression that candidates might take with them further down the trial appearing like a reputation killer, leading to a smaller talent pool and longer recruitment period of time (Bharadwaj et al., 2022). Thus, these issues about candidate communication and engagement need to be addressed for recruitment to be successful.

Chatbots are dynamic AI-based applications designed to mimic human interaction and interact with users, enabling human-like response to queries and candidate sponsorship for every step of the application process (Chen et al., 2023). These chatbots are pivotal for pre-screening candidates, addressing frequently asked questions about a position, and coordinating interview schedules in the recruitment space. This automation of candidate communication enables the recruiters to work on other core activities while candidates are engaged on time on regular communication around the clock (Barghi et al., 2022). They also help in cascading messages within the organisation's employees encompassing feedback gathering, news sharing, and sparing employees' trivial HR questions; such constant engagement contributes to developing a pleasant working environment and nurturing deserving talent.

Furthermore, generative AI goes a step beyond this, initiating not only a dialogue based on questions asked but new content which has been learnt on the basis of the pre-existing data. Even in its interactions, it can come up with job descriptions, compose emails or notification to the candidates, and even evaluate the candidate for a specific job that is available. Indeed, it is such a state-of-the-art technology that adds value to the candidate experience and make it more exciting. Finally, the intertwining of chatbots and generative AI in AI-enabled candidate engagement signifies a turning point for recruitment (Aguinis et al., 2024). Combined, these enable swift and enriched communication with candidates resulting in better speed and interaction in the process. This blend makes sure recruitment is speedy but personalized. Each and every candidate receives individual attention according to his profile and queries.

2.6 AI-Enabled Interviewing and Selection

Many companies are starting to use AI interviews to help choose the best candidates for job openings. AI interviews are fairer and more consistent than traditional interviews because to prevent by not discriminating candidates based on age, gender or race. This tool also save time for both the company and the job seekers by avoiding scheduling issues and other problems that can happen with face-to-face interviews (Skrobotov, 2021). Following the initial candidate screening process, AI evaluations can further refine the selection pool. These evaluations can manifest in various formats. One approach involves gamification tests, which offer significant insights into candidates' skills, abilities, and personal traits. Such evaluation games are integrated into the recruitment process to assess the correlation between candidates' performance in the game and their potential success in specific roles (Hewage, 2023). Candidates who demonstrate alignment with the job requirements through the game are then eligible for a final interview. Firstly, AI can promote critical thinking through using the chatbot that puts the questions to the candidate (Rahmani & Kamberaj, 2021). The AI system then reviews the candidates' answers and pitted them against benchmark answers from excellent employees. In this process of analysis, choices of words, arrangement of phrases and concepts, content and focus are assessed and each candidate given a score. Companies can then go to conducting an interview with individuals who fit the criteria as set to end with a selection decision.

Further, video-interviews could also be recorded and analysed through the use of AI technology. In these interviews, the candidates answer questions derived from the analysis of the best employee backgrounds together with the typical performance of all employees (Galanaki & Papalexandris, 2020). This research helps AI to determine the competencies and personal characteristics which would help the individual succeed. The AI also looks for the content, words, tone, such as enthusiasm while responding, facial expressions such as frowning while discussing the past employment and compares them with the answers given by high performers. Candidates can undertake the interviews in virtual mode for several consecutive days by providing them with an opportunity of choosing their appropriate date and time. Research suggests that candidates typically incline towards those situations that they are able to exercise more control in the selection process (Robinson et al., 2021). This means that the use of AI assisted interviews and assessments has been useful in coming up with reduced number of final candidates. AI video interviewing improves the hiring process in the following way: From the information accrued by the data collected. For instance, having AI also solves the problem of understanding which questions elicit best responses to job performance to better know how a candidate will do in the job. This leads to enhanced interview questions amongst the recruiters besides getting it right in terms of identifying the right personnel for the job.

3. CHALLENGES OF AI IN HIRING PROCESS

AI integration has a positive impact on hiring by making recruitment better through automation and data analysis for decision-making, but the main issues arise in the form of the algorithm's bias, opacity, data privacy and protection, expensive implementation and change-resistance. To achieve ethical and fair staff recruitment, it is crucial to solve these problems. Because AI models have the ability to be biased, hiring practices could become even more unfair than they are now, transparency and privacy regulations need supervision. The primary constraint could be high cost for the smaller organizations, and to overcome the internal resistance, the key message has to be conveyed, and proper training has to be given to understand AI as a supportive tool. Addressing these issues ensure that AI hiring is fair, secured and that it is profitable to all parties.

3.1. Algorithmic Bias

One major problem with AI employment technologies downfalls is that of algorithmic prejudice. When an AI algorithm is derived from previous recruitment information, then it mirrors and tends to replicate biases against certain categories of people (Sanyaolu & Atsaboghena, 2022). This problem is usually as a result of biases in training datasets which in some cases mirror the existing bias in societies or organizations. For example, if the data used in hiring an employee favoured one sex or a certain race then the AI model will also lean in a similar way regardless of the programmer's intentions (Vishwakarma & Singh, 2023).

They found that algorithmic bias pertains not only to fairness issues but can also lead to legal controversies and & organisations' reputational loss if not resolved. In order to deal with this issue, Robinson and colleagues propose more frequent checks of AI systems to detect and minimize the biases stemming from them; employing bias-detection algorithms; utilizing more diverse datasets, which reflect the applicant pool in a much greater detail. The bias in the results can be avoided with a clear process when creating an algorithm, as well as constant control from people in order to make the AI hiring fair.

3.2 Lack of Transparency and Explainability

AI systems in recruitment processes can also be described as "black box" models that are difficult to explain. This lack of transparency creates a problem since it is challenging to explain why specific hiring decisions were made to both the recruiters and the candidates (Budhwar et al., 2022). Lack of transparency in use of AI is that it makes the stakeholders not to trust the decision made because various aspects of selection might not be very clear.

For this reason, there is a new research focus called Explainable AI (XAI) that tries to solve part of this problem by building AI models that allow for easier interpretation. However, the widespread adoption of XAI for recruitment is still difficult because of the challenges posed by developing models that are both explainable, yet accurate (El-Ghoul et al., 2024). Lack of explainability may pose a challenge for AI system in not being able to meet employment regulation laws that require openness such as GDPR in EU (Alsaif & Sabih Aksoy, 2023).

3.3 Data Privacy and Security Concerns

Implementation of AI in the hiring processes means the data collection, storage, and consumption of vast amounts of highly sensitive information on individual candidates that brings data protection and security issues. Data privacy acts like the GDPR demand that organizations put in place strict data protection frameworks, but AI related systems complicate the matter. For instance, data in AI models may include demographic or behavioural data for the purpose of data analysis may result to data compromise (Johansson & Herranen, 2019).

In addition to compliance, the prospect of achieving both the utilisation of data for AI recruiting benefits and worker privacy remains an important concern to contemplate. For instance, in order to protect privacy, the data needs to be masked, and this process sometimes distorts AI forecasts and affects the quality of the recruitment outcomes. The organizations must thereby impose data encryption, and anonymization approaches as well as the elaboration of appropriate data handling policies not to reduce the capability of AI, but to protect the candidates' privacy.

3.4 High Implementation Costs

The use of AI in recruitment is expensive, meaning that many firms, particularly those in the small to medium category, cannot afford the cost outlay. Acquiring AI software, and training of the HR staff for the use of these tools, and the processes of updating these algorithms in order to achieve competitiveness, are among the major costs (Vishwakarma & Singh, 2023).

Aside from the costs, this would mean that the time needed to incorporate the application effectively into the existing recruitment processes sustains performance reductions during transition. Due to such considerations, cost is a challenge that is more achievable by larger organisations due to the fact that the return on investment is sometimes difficult to quantify (Robinson et al., 2021). The cost factor associated with implementation of certain solutions, where the recruitment benefit shrinks out by rising prices, has been found as a problem for organizations, hence leading the organizations to search for hybrid solutions and seek for the combination of the AI based and the conventional recruitment techniques for optimised costs (Al-Alawi et al., 2021).

3.5 Resistance to Change

The change towards the use of AI in recruitment can be met with internal opposition by the HR teams and the management because of the effect the change may have employment of HR professionals and the risk of technology substitution (El-Ghoul et al., 2024). Some employees can feel anxious that AI could take over their positions or reduce the significance of potentially valuable aspects of the process including feelings and their relations with potential candidates. Moreover, the managers who are in the organization for a long time would resist change owing to lack of technical know-how or fear that the implementation of AI would overhaul the earlier recruiting model (Malik et al., 2020).

That is why it is critical for organizations to invest in strong training and reinforcement measures to highlight AI's purpose as complementary to, rather than a supplement for, human decisions in hiring. Key in change management is to position AI as an enabler to the delivery of improved decision-making outcomes in the best interest of the skill development of its human capital (Budhwar et al., 2022).

4. LIMITATION OF STUDY

AI shows considerable limitations even though paramount importance in terms of positive influence in talent acquisition, The high performance or efficiency of these AI programs largely depends on the quality and diversity of the training data. And if the training data happens to be biased, the same will be perpetuated through the AI methods and will lead to discriminative outcomes. Regularly, they have to ensure a high quality of data used for training, minimizing the presence of biases in training data with a systematic update of the data; only then may we expect fair and robust AI hiring decisions. A problem that is very difficult and costly to address is that of implementation and maintenance regarding AI systems in the recruitment systems, which is much larger for smaller organizations. The ongoing costs involved for keeping data in good order, providing model updates, and paying for technical support can be exceedingly high, as investments of human and technological resources can become burdensome. The ethical issues raised by the AI in recruitment processes address data privacy; algorithm transparency; and the prospect of joblessness. That is indeed a thin line to walk on-an absolute balance that should be reached between technological development and ethical issues for AI to become responsible and ethical. The suit of automation all else in the recruitment may deprive AI of that human consideration demanded in his attempt to build rapport with the candidates and a general good candidate experience. Overuse of AI can lead to reductions in this interaction, compromising candidate satisfaction and engagement accordingly. The long-term effects that AI will have in the hiring and wholesale recruitment are yet unknown and, of course, yet to be significantly researched in these terms relating to employee retention, performance, and organizational culture. Future research should uncover the wide array of benefits and possible downsides of AI hiring practices, after which acceptance will become tangible. The speed of technological advancement positively scowls upon the speed and tool and techniques rate of obsolescence when it comes to AI. Thus, one who stays updated and migrates to emerging technologies is better placed in keeping AI-enabled recruitment strategies afloat. Finally, let it be added that if AI is not checked and balanced, it may end up aggravating the same minor inequalities. Several studies have already provided concrete evidence that certain AI systems may inadvertently favour candidates from certain socioeconomic backgrounds or educational institutions, thereby further marginalizing already disadvantaged groups. It is, therefore, necessary to build inclusive-yet- equitable AI development systems that consider diversity, equity, and inclusion. For this, however, these mechanisms should ensure manipulative utilization for job seekers and other forms of manipulative disinformation about job seekers further generate other concerns. As AI chatbots further infiltrate and supposedly improve the lives of the end-users, social media models have gained a foothold, creating an even larger plane for attaining the information to safeguard job hunters as well;' Every passing day, creating AI comprehensively improves our understanding of deceiving and misleading job seekers.

5. CONCLUSION

The use of AI in hiring is therefore a significant development in the talent acquisition process since organisations are applying technological advancement to reduce recruitment time, minimize the time taken to make hire decision while using AI solutions to support better decision-making. AI helps to conduct initial sifting, sorting and initial communication with the candidates saving the time of the recruiters for final short listing, evaluation and matching for cultural fit. It is estimated that this shift can lead to the development of better quality and more efficient hiring processes from an organizational need perspective, but one that is also highly candidate-focussed, and which provides fast and more engaging interactions and communications. However, this has not come without some challenge or the other. For example, the algorithmic bias threatens equality in hiring since AI systems reproduce biases from datasets that they analyse. Therefore, such biases must be solved with the help of strict monitoring, frequent audits and the creation of new algorithms that are aimed at the possible high level of fairness. Further, AI-assisted recruitment creates transparency challenges, given that most AI algorithms are untransparent and, therefore, explainable. Such approaches can undermine the trust of candidates and HR personnel and call for the use of the explainable artificial intelligence (XAI) to improve understanding without a decline in performance.

Data privacy and security issues are also compelling because AI systems deal with massive amounts of sensitive candidate data. The GDPR and other data privacy regulations must be followed but achieving that balance of data usage and protection is difficult. Other costs of implementing AI include the implementation costs which present a significant challenge especially to lower end organizations as they may not afford to implement advanced systems. In addition, organizational change resistance in the form of acceptance by the HR functional teams limits the ability to obtain optimal benefits from the application of AI in HR since employees tend to fear job loss as a result of AI's implementation, or exhibit uncertainty about the effect of this new technology on traditional roles incumbent on the HR functions. Solving these issues is possible only with the help of the cooperation of technical, moral, regulatory, and change management approaches. There are two broad approaches for organizations, where they can choose to use AI in conjunction with human input to avoid the negative consequences of AI while harnessing the benefits from the technology. Policies of transparency, data protection measures and staff development will alleviate majority of concerns currently associated with AI and turn it from potential threat into powerful enabler.

Subsequently, as organisations persevere in deploying AI effectiveness in staffing, a key priority toward developing sustainable and ethical work of AI would be imperative. Implementing these principles do not only improve the use of AI in recruitment but also brings the best corporate image that the organization portrays in a fair way, engaging candidates and being socially responsible. AI-DR can thus evolve as a conscious solution thoughtfully dealing with these complexities and challenges to form an effective strategic blueprint for both organizations and candidates toward an increasingly diverse and efficient labour market.

REFERENCES

Aguinis, H., Beltran, J. R., & Cope, A. (2024). How to use generative AI as a human resource management assistant. *Organizational Dynamics*, 53(1), 101029. DOI: 10.1016/j.orgdyn.2024.101029

Al-Alawi, A. I., Naureen, M., AlAlawi, E. I., & Al-Hadad, A. A. N. (2021). The role of artificial intelligence in recruitment process decision-making. *Information (Basel)*, 9(11), 269.

Allal-Chérif, O., Aránega, A. Y., & Sánchez, R. C. (2021). Intelligent recruitment: How to identify, select, and retain talents from around the world using artificial intelligence. *Technological Forecasting and Social Change*, 169, 120822. DOI: 10.1016/j.techfore.2021.120822

Allden, N., & Harris, L. (2013). Building a positive candidate experience: Towards a networked model of e-recruitment. *The Journal of Business Strategy*, 34(5), 36–47. DOI: 10.1108/JBS-11-2012-0072

Alsaif, A., & Sabih Aksoy, M. (2023). AI-HRM: artificial intelligence in human resource management: a literature review. *Journal of Computing and Communication*, 2(2), 1–7. DOI: 10.21608/jocc.2023.307053

Antoni, L., Guniš, J., Gurský, P., Horvát, Š., Krajči, S., Krídlo, O., & Andrejková, G. (2020). Data Science and its position in university education within National Project IT Academy-Education for 21st Century. *The Quarterly Journal of Economics*, 118(4), 1279–1333.

Barghi, B., Gallardo-Gallardo, E., & Fernandez, V. (2022). An overview of chatbots usage in recruitment and selection practices. *MCIS 2022 Proceedings*.

Bharadwaj, S., Khan, N. A., & Yameen, M. (2022). Unbundling employer branding, job satisfaction, organizational identification and employee retention: A sequential mediation analysis. *Asia-Pacific Journal of Business Administration*, 14(3), 309–334. DOI: 10.1108/APJBA-08-2020-0279

Bhatia, V., Rawat, P., Kumar, A., & Shah, R. R. (2019). End-to-end resume parsing and finding candidates for a job description using bert. *arXiv preprint arXiv:1910.03089*.

Bondarouk, T., & Brewster, C. (2016). Conceptualising the future of HRM and technology research. *International Journal of Human Resource Management*, 27(21), 2652–2671. DOI: 10.1080/09585192.2016.1232296

Budhwar, P., Malik, A., De Silva, M. T., & Thevisuthan, P. (2022). Artificial intelligence–challenges and opportunities for international HRM: A review and research agenda. *International Journal of Human Resource Management*, 33(6), 1065–1097. DOI: 10.1080/09585192.2022.2035161

Charlwood, A., & Guenole, N. (2022). Can HR adapt to the paradoxes of artificial intelligence? *Human Resource Management Journal*, 32(4), 729–742. DOI: 10.1111/1748-8583.12433

Chen, Y., Jensen, S., Albert, L. J., Gupta, S., & Lee, T. (2023). Artificial intelligence (AI) student assistants in the classroom: Designing chatbots to support student success. *Information Systems Frontiers*, 25(1), 161–182. DOI: 10.1007/s10796-022-10291-4

Dulebohn, J. H., & Stone, D. L. (2018). *The Brave New World of EHRM 2.0*. IAP.

El-Ghoul, M., Almassri, M. M., El-Habibi, M. F., Al-Qadi, M. H., Abou Eloun, A., Abu-Nasser, B. S., & Abu-Naser, S. S. (2024). AI in HRM: Revolutionizing Recruitment, Performance Management, and Employee Engagement. *International Journal of Academic Applied Research*, 8(9), 16–29.

Enholm, I. M., Papagiannidis, E., Mikalef, P., & Krogstie, J. (2022). Artificial intelligence and business value: A literature review. *Information Systems Frontiers*, 24(5), 1709–1734. DOI: 10.1007/s10796-021-10186-w

Fernandes, A. B. A., & Machado, C. F. (2022). E-recruitment and the impact of digital age on recruitment: A critical literature review. *Organizational innovation in the digital age*, 199-209.

Fernández-Martínez, C., & Fernández, A. (2020). AI and recruiting software: Ethical and legal implications. *Paladyn : Journal of Behavioral Robotics*, 11(1), 199–216. DOI: 10.1515/pjbr-2020-0030

Fritts, M., & Cabrera, F. (2021). AI recruitment algorithms and the dehumanization problem. *Ethics and Information Technology*, 23(4), 791–801. DOI: 10.1007/s10676-021-09615-w

Galanaki, E., & Papalexandris, A. (2020). Human resource management and artificial intelligence: The future is here. *Handbook of research on human resources strategies for the new millennial workforce*, 88-105.

Guenole, N., & Feinzig, S. (2018). *The business case for AI in HR: With insights and tips on getting started*. IBM Publishing.

Halid, H., Ravesangar, K., Mahadzir, S. L., & Halim, S. N. A. (2024). Artificial Intelligence (AI) in Human Resource Management (HRM). In *Building the Future with Human Resource Management* (pp. 37-70). Springer.

Hewage, A. (2023). Exploring the applicability of artificial intelligence in recruitment and selection processes: A focus on the recruitment phase. *Journal of Human Resource and Sustainability Studies*, 11(3), 603–634. DOI: 10.4236/jhrss.2023.113034

Horodyski, P. (2023). Applicants' perception of artificial intelligence in the recruitment process. *Computers in Human Behavior Reports*, 11, 100303. DOI: 10.1016/j.chbr.2023.100303

Intelion Systems. (2023). *AI Recruitment Statistics*. LinkedIn. https://www.linkedin.com/pulse/ai-recruitment-statistics-intelion-systems/

Johansson, J., & Herranen, S. (2019). The application of artificial intelligence (AI) in human resource management: Current state of AI and its impact on the traditional recruitment process. In.

Kanade, V. (2022). *What Is Artificial Intelligence (AI)? Definition, Types, Goals, Challenges, and Trends in 2022*. Spiceworks https://www.spiceworks.com/tech/artificial-intelligence/articles/what-is-ai/

Klucin, F. (2020). *The use of artificial intelligence in the recruitment process*

Kucharčíková, A., Mičiak, M., Tokarčíková, E., & Štaffenová, N. (2023). The investments in human capital within the human capital management and the impact on the enterprise's performance. *Sustainability (Basel)*, 15(6), 5015. DOI: 10.3390/su15065015

Kulkarni, S. B., & Che, X. (2019). Intelligent software tools for recruiting. *Journal of International Technology and Information Management*, 28(2), 2–16. DOI: 10.58729/1941-6679.1398

Lahoti, Y. (2023). Impact of artificial intelligence on Human Resource Management. *Journal for ReAttach Therapy and Developmental Diversities*, 6(1), 1655–1664. DOI: 10.53555/jrtdd.v6i1.2839

Laurim, V., Arpaci, S., Prommegger, B., & Krcmar, H. (2021). Computer, whom should i hire?–acceptance criteria for artificial intelligence in the recruitment process.

Li, B., Chen, Y., Liu, L., & Zheng, B. (2023). Users' intention to adopt artificial intelligence-based chatbot: A meta-analysis. *Service Industries Journal*, 43(15-16), 1117–1139. DOI: 10.1080/02642069.2023.2217756

Malik, A., Srikanth, N., & Budhwar, P. (2020). Digitisation, artificial intelligence (AI) and HRM. *Human resource management: Strategic and international perspectives, 88*, 103.

Marler, J. H., & Fisher, S. L. (2013). An evidence-based review of e-HRM and strategic human resource management. *Human Resource Management Review*, 23(1), 18–36. DOI: 10.1016/j.hrmr.2012.06.002

McColl, R., & Michelotti, M. (2019). Sorry, could you repeat the question? Exploring video-interview recruitment practice in HRM. *Human Resource Management Journal*, 29(4), 637–656. DOI: 10.1111/1748-8583.12249

Mittal, V., Mehta, P., Relan, D., & Gabrani, G. (2020). Methodology for resume parsing and job domain prediction. *Journal of Statistics and Management Systems*, 23(7), 1265–1274. DOI: 10.1080/09720510.2020.1799583

Nawaz, N. (2020). *How far have we come with the study of artificial intelligence for recruitment process. SSRN.*

Nayak, A., Patnaik, A., Satpathy, I., Khang, A., & Patnaik, B. (2024). The Power of Artificial Intelligence in Talent Recruitment Revolution: Creating a Smarter Workforce. In *AI-Oriented Competency Framework for Talent Management in the Digital Economy* (pp. 54–75). CRC Press. DOI: 10.1201/9781003440901-4

Olan, F., Arakpogun, E. O., Suklan, J., Nakpodia, F., Damij, N., & Jayawickrama, U. (2022). Artificial intelligence and knowledge sharing: Contributing factors to organizational performance. *Journal of Business Research*, 145, 605–615. DOI: 10.1016/j.jbusres.2022.03.008

Pal, R., Shaikh, S., Satpute, S., & Bhagwat, S. (2022). Resume classification using various machine learning algorithms. ITM Web of Conferences, Panerai, F. (2018). *Artificial Intelligence Needs Human Ingenuity and Moral.* Medium. https://medium.com/@fiammapanerai/artificial-intelligence-needs-human-ingenuity-and-moral-a6f0bcad8ca0

Porkodi, S., & Raman, A. M. (2024). Success of cloud computing adoption over an era in human resource management systems: a comprehensive meta-analytic literature review. *Management Review Quarterly*, 1-35.

Raghavan, M., Barocas, S., Kleinberg, J., & Levy, K. (2020). Mitigating bias in algorithmic hiring: Evaluating claims and practices. *Journal of Surgical Education*, 78(4), 1175–1181. PMID: 33250429

Roy, P. K., Chowdhary, S. S., & Bhatia, R. (2020). A Machine Learning approach for automation of Resume Recommendation system. *Procedia Computer Science*, 167, 2318–2327. DOI: 10.1016/j.procs.2020.03.284

Sanyaolu, E., & Atsaboghena, R. (2022). Role of Artificial Intelligence in Human Resource Management: Overview of its benefits and challenges. *ResearchGate*, (December), 1–8.

Sharma, A. (2018). *How AI reinvented hiring practice at L'Ore'al.* People Matters. https://www.peoplematters.in/article/techhr-2018/how-the-worlds-largest-cosmetic-company-transformed-its-hiring-practice-with-ai-19006

Skrobotov, A. (2021). The perceptions of recruitment practitioners on the adoption of artificial intelligence in recruitment and selection. *International Journal of Human Resource Management*, 43, 1–25.

Soleimani, M., Intezari, A., Taskin, N., & Pauleen, D. (2021). Cognitive biases in developing biased Artificial Intelligence recruitment system.

Statista. (2017). *Global Recruiting Trends: Key Benefits of Artificial Intelligence 2017.* Statista. https://www.statista.com/statistics/831693/recruitment-trends-benefits-of-artificial-intelligence/

Upadhyay, A. K., & Khandelwal, K. (2018). Applying artificial intelligence: Implications for recruitment. *Strategic HR Review*, 17(5), 255–258. DOI: 10.1108/SHR-07-2018-0051

Van Esch, P., Black, J. S., & Ferolie, J. (2019). Marketing AI recruitment: The next phase in job application and selection. *Computers in Human Behavior*, 90, 215–222. DOI: 10.1016/j.chb.2018.09.009

Vedapradha, R., Hariharan, R., & Shivakami, R. (2019). Artificial intelligence: A technological prototype in recruitment. *Journal of Service Science and Management*, 12(3), 382–390. DOI: 10.4236/jssm.2019.123026

Verhoeven, T. (2020). Digitalisierung im Recruiting. *Wie sich Recruiting durch künstliche Intelligenz, Algorithmen und Bots verändert.*

Vishwakarma, L. P., & Singh, R. K. (2023). An analysis of the challenges to human resource in implementing artificial intelligence. In *The Adoption and Effect of Artificial Intelligence on Human Resources Management, Part B* (pp. 81-109). Emerald Publishing Limited. DOI: 10.1108/978-1-80455-662-720230006

Waheed, A., Xiaoming, M., Waheed, S., Ahmad, N., & Tian-tian, S. (2020). E-HRM implementation, adoption and its predictors: A case of small and medium enterprises of Pakistan. *International Journal of Information Technology and Management*, 19(2-3), 162–180. DOI: 10.1504/IJITM.2020.106217

Yau, K.-L. A., Saad, N. M., & Chong, Y.-W. (2021). Artificial intelligence marketing (AIM) for enhancing customer relationships. *Applied Sciences (Basel, Switzerland)*, 11(18), 8562. DOI: 10.3390/app11188562

Chapter 2
Artificial Intelligence (AI) and the Future of Marketing Trends:
Challenges and Opportunities

Ajay Sharma
https://orcid.org/0009-0008-3801-472X
Geeta University, India

Prashant Sharma
Dewan VS Group of institutions, India

Ripudaman Gaur
Lloyd Business School, India

ABSTRACT

AI in customer engagement chatbots and voice assistants are AI-driven tools that improve customer engagement and give businesses the ability to provide individualized experiences by conducting sentiment analysis. Nonetheless, issues like data privacy concerns, algorithmic bias, and ethical challenges remain, which still need proper regulations and drafting more transparency. Even with these challenges, AI has vast potential, including sustainable marketing, omni-channel strategies, and AI-generated content. The future of marketing powered by AI lies around integrating technology with emotional intelligence thereby making the strategy centric towards the consumer leading to a trust factor and driving brand loyalty. Businesses adopting AI-powered marketing solutions will rise above all competition in a growing digital world. Tackling challenges head-on will be critical to unleashing AI's full potential for marketing transformation.

DOI: 10.4018/979-8-3693-9395-6.ch002

1. INTRODUCTION

The AI Marketing Revolution AI is revolutionizing the marketing paradigm, offering novel solutions for understanding consumer behavior, enhancing marketing campaigns, and tailor-making customer experiences. AI-pushed marketing uses machine learning, natural language processing (NLP), computer vision and others to slingshot target-specific and data-associated strategies to improve interactions between the brand and the consumer (Arora et al., 2019). AI in marketing is reducing the gap between traditional marketing approaches and modern automated, real-time, personalized marketing solutions. AI empowers businesses to process a vast amount of data with a speed that has never been seen, which allows them to make better decisions, optimize marketing spending, and retain their customers. But with the evolution of AI comes extraordinary opportunity and equally extraordinary difficulty that organizations must grapple with to be competitive and ethically minded. AI's role in marketing will shape the future as long as it is integrated with human creativity in a responsible and data-compliant manner to leverage consumer trust and engagement.

The most transformative AI-based marketing trends is hyper-personalization where AI evaluates user data, preferences, and behaviors, to offer tailored content, product suggestions, and adverts. Traditional marketing commonly targeted wide segments of the average consume, where AI can micro-target consumers in real time by evaluating their interests, browsing patterns and buying trends. Recommendation engines powered by AI, the kind that powers platforms like Amazon and Netflix, put together curated experiences by predicting what is most likely to engage a user. By providing relevant information at the right time, these AI-driven algorithms help increase conversion rates while improving customer satisfaction. Using AI allows the brands to develop dynamic ads that adjust based on users' interests leading to more ROI and less wastage of ad spend. However, personalization transcends suggestions AI-powered email marketing campaigns, automated content generation, and chatbots offer tailored responses, rendering marketing interactions more human-centric and captivating (Kumar & Patel, 2019).

AI in content marketing is another growth area with machine learning algorithms that can create and optimize content using insights about the audience. AI Writing Tools: These are tools that leverage AI to generate content. Generative AI for content creation not just creates content in less time but also allows marketers to scale up their efforts without sacrificing quality. AI-driven sentiment analysis also aids marketers in understanding how audiences perceive their content, enabling brands to adjust messaging and optimize engagement strategies. AI boosts search engine optimization (SEO); analyzing search trends and predicting keyword performance while optimizing content to rank higher on search engines. This allows marketers to adjust their content strategies to match what resonates with their audience and what meets the current market trends.

The emergence of conversational AI like chatbots and voice search is significantly transforming the way customers interact. Chatbots powered by AI are increasingly being used in customer service, lead generation, and sales assistance. While traditional scripted-based chatbots function linearly as per their program scripts, AI-powered chatbots use Natural Language Processing (NLP) algorithms that look at the overall context of interaction, sentiment analysis and intent recognition to provide a more humanized experience. Companies implement chatbots on websites, social networks, and messaging applications in order to provide instantaneous responses and increase customer satisfaction. The things such as voice search and the AI assistants it will hear on Google Assistant, Alexa and Siri continue to transform how consumers find products and services. For instance, spoken queries are concise compared to typed ones, which can signify that voice search optimization is essential for marketers. Brands must revamp their content strategies in accordance with voice search patterns and make their products and services discoverable. AI-driven conversational marketing enables effective interaction, spreading stronger relationships which lead to better customer journeys.

AI also powers predictive and prescriptive analytics, which allows marketers to predict consumer behavior and make data-driven decisions. AI-powered predictive analytics helps to analyses past interactions, makes sense of patterns, and predicts future trends. This can lead to better preemptive marketing efforts, leading to higher sales and better engagement if businesses already know what customers in which location require. Advanced prescriptive analytics: Whereas predictive analytics powers forward-looking insights based on finite data, AI-powered prescriptive analytics goes one step farther, offering actionable recommendations for business actions to achieve desired outcomes. As an example, it can recommend the best pricing strategies and the right time for launching a campaign, or even highlight retention customers with high-value.personas. AI-powered analytics eliminate guesswork in marketing, helping brands better allocate resources and maximize effectiveness.

1.1 Importance of AI in Modern Marketing Strategies

Yet its greater presence in marketing brings along a set of challenges that look to be tackled. Data privacy and security One of the urban transfers that express the most concern is that of data privacy and security. Things like consumer data which AI needs to generate insights and make predictions, and ethical and legal repercussions regarding the collection of this data, its storage and its usage. Laws like GDPR (General Data Protection Regulation) and CCPA (California Consumer Privacy Act) mandate businesses to have user consent and transparency in how the data is processed. Consequences of failing to comply may lead to litigation issues and affect brand image. The data-focused nature of AI marketing means that it must be committed to data protection efforts, anonymization techniques, and ensuring ethical AI use to keep consumer trust." Moreover, consumers have become increasingly conscious of how their data is used and are calling for more transparency from brands. They must also consider the ethical and legal implications of knowledge-based solutions and their usage must conform to laws concerning data privacy and protection.

The other concern is algorithmic bias; AI models might inadvertently perpetuate discriminatory behaviors. AI systems tend to derive meaning from the data it's trained on, so if that data is flawed, their findings will be flawed as well. This has the potential to translate into unethical targeting, exclusionary advertising or biased content recommendations in marketing. For example, with regard to advertising, biased AI models may target very specific demographics while ignoring others. Measures such as continuous monitoring of AI models, the use of diverse datasets during the training phase, and fairness audits are essential to mitigate any potential risks of algorithmic bias and ensure that AI systems encourage inclusivity and responsible marketing practices. Brands need to adopt Responsible AI based practices that prioritize fairness, accountability and unbiased decision making.

However, integrating AI into existing marketing strategies presents challenges, especially for SMEs. Multi-nationals often have the assets to invest in AI infrastructure and execution; whereas, SMEs are burdened with the high-class implementation expense and expertise that AI adoption demands. Businesses often struggle to choose the right AI tools, integrate them into existing systems, and train employees to work with an AI system. AI solutions providers are therefore bringing more convenient and affordable AI-driven marketing tools targeted at SMEs to fill this gap. So, in addition to upskilling the marketers you have in your organization, businesses must also focus on building an understanding of how to leverage and utilize AI. The promise of AI is not to replace human marketers, it is to augment them. Marketers who leverage AI-driven insights and automation will have a competitive edge in the digital landscape.

But with these challenges also come tremendous opportunities for the future of marketing with AI. Environmental impact, green marketing, and AI is breaking new ground as a company who empowers environmental sustainability among consumers. AI analyses sustainability trends for brands, optimises supply chains and cuts out waste in marketing. Artificial Intelligence Sustainability Analytics allow companies to create environmentally friendly campaigns that appeal to eco-sensitive consumers (Okeleke et al., 2024). AI forces omnichannel marketing strategies that guarantee customers achieve a fluid experience over the digital and physical points of contact. This, in turn, drives cross-channel personalized experiences and ensures that your messaging is consistent across websites, mobile apps, social media and in-store experiences. AI will become part of the future of marketing is through its integration with emotional intelligence to inform brand strategies. Brands can use AI algorithms that use sentiment analysis to know consumer feelings and resonate marketing messages as per feelings. Using a customer's facial expressions, tone of voice, and social media action data, AI can measure customer sentiment and preemptively gauge a brand's perception. This helps brands create human-centric campaigns with emotional appeal, helping to build customer loyalty. AI-based reputation management tools also assist brands in identifying and resolving potential PR crises before they develop further.

2. EVOLUTION OF AI IN MARKETING: AI MILESTONES IN MARKETING TECHNOLOGY

AI quickly squeeze waste out and help marketing strategies transform from traditional to intelligent, data-driven approaches where most businesses would leverage Customer engagement, personalization, and performance became a priority. The evolution of AI in marketing has been a dynamic journey, from its simple ideas lurking in rule-based automation to matures deep learning models, with several significant milestones along the way that have transformed the way brands engage with customers. The evolution of AI-driven marketing technology has taken several phases, from data analysis, automation, and natural language processing to multi-channel and hyper-personalized AI-driven insights and predictive analytics. In the field of marketing, the story of AI can be divided into significant technological leaps, leading to game-changing capabilities that transformed the way brands engage their audiences.

The roots of AI in marketing date back to the 1950s and 1960s when artificial intelligence had been conceived and was originally approached for commercial deployment. Initial advances in the field of AI were based on symbolic AI and systems akin to human experts; knowledge of a rule-based algorithm was programmed to emulate human-like decisions. While they were very limited in their capabilities, these early AI systems were the start of the development of marketing automation software. The real inception of AI-driven marketing began in the 1980s and 1990s, with the advent of data mining and predictive modeling. Businesses adopted statistical analysis and machine learning algorithms to analyze huge amounts of consumer data, identifying patterns and trends to refine their marketing strategies. There was a growth in customer relationship management (CRM) systems at that time that further supported companies in collecting and retaining customer data, ultimately resulting in better targeted marketing.

However, this all changed in the early 2000s when digital marketing and e-commerce emerged. Meanwhile, search engine marketing (SEM) and search engine optimization (SEO) became pivotal marketing strategies, demanding AI-powered tools able to analyze search behavior and optimize content. Google's PageRank and algorithm-based search ranking platforms fundamentally changed the game for online discoverability, and AI became a staple in marketers' toolkits. This era also saw a rise in AI-driven recommendation engines, with algorithms used by companies such as Amazon and Netflix to employ collaborative filtering and machine learning to serve tailored product and content suggestions to users. This period also highlighted the emergence of AI in programmatic advertising, with automated bidding and targeting algorithms allowing companies to target customers with relevant advertisements at the right time (Kumar & Suthar, 2024).

The rise of big data analytics and deep learning during the 2010s rose to one of the most important breakthroughs in AI marketing technology. This list of factors underlined a situation where user data was more easily generated by the rise of social media, mobile technology, and Internet of Things (IoT) devices, leading to the need for more sophisticated marketing solutions powered by AI. AI tools were applied most commonly with data from before October 2023. The emergence of AI chatbots and virtual assistants, like Apple's Siri, Amazon's Alexa, and Google Assistant, revolutionized customer service by facilitating immediate, AI-powered exchanges. These chatbots used natural language processing (NLP) to mimic human-like conversation, enhancing customer interaction and support.

The more part of big change on the way was the advent of AI-driven predictive analytics, which enabled marketers to predict customer behavior and preferences with a high level of accuracy. By analyzing historical data, predictive models used machine learning algorithms to help businesses personalize email marketing campaigns, optimize pricing strategies, and improve customer segmentation. Predicting customer churn, delivering personalized promotions at the right time, and automating retargeting campaigns multiplied both marketing efficiency and ROI. Companies had already begun using features in their AI-powered marketing automation platforms (HubSpot, Salesforce, Marketo, etc.) to simplify marketing, decrease manual work, and unlock lead generation.

The 2020s saw an explosion of new AI-powered marketing technologies, enabled by breakthroughs in deep learning, reinforcement learning, and generative AI. AI-written content may be a game changer, with systems like OpenAI's GPT series able to write human-sounding blog articles, social media posts. A new or revolutionary technology powered by A. Moreover, AI in video marketing is on the rise; deep learning models for AI-powered video ads, automated video editing, and synthetic voiceovers are the new buzzword. Virtual influencer marketing is another way to market using AI-generated imagery and machine learning algorithms that engage audiences without the need for human influencers.

Combining AI with augmented reality (AR) and virtual reality (VR) in marketing is another high watermark innovation. From newfound forms of shopping with AI-driven AR applications, consumers can see a product in a real-world scenario before they purchase it; AR helps with this experience in online shopping. Brands such as IKEA and Sephora have introduced AI-based AR solutions that allow customers to try on furniture placements or "try on" virtual makeup before making a purchase. From experiential marketing to immersive brand experiences, AI-powered VR is being leveraged to create immersive, engaging storytelling opportunities for brands. AI has been playing a growing role in voice search and conversation marketing. As more consumers adopt voice-activated devices, AI-powered voice search optimization has become critical for brands seeking to improve their search positions (Kumar et al., 2024). Supported by NLP models, conversational AI facilitates context-aware and personalized interactions between businesses and consumers via voice assistants, smart speakers, and messaging apps. The rise of voice search means that brands will need to ensure their content is optimized for natural language and voice search as more and more consumers will search their desires with their voices instead of typing.

Ethical AI and responsible marketing practices also become the focus in AI evolution. With increasing power of artificial intelligence algorithms came new concerns over data privacy, algorithmic bias, and ethical AI decision making. Legislation like the General Data Protection Regulation (GDPR) and the California Consumer Privacy Act (CCPA) has laid down firmer rules for AI-powered marketing strategies, demanding transparency and accountability. With the growing concern of biases in AI algorithms, data security with respect to data privacy, brands are focusing on ethics of AI frameworks to establish consumer trust.

Emerging technologies such as neuromorphic computing, quantum AI, and AI-enabled emotional intelligence are likely to shape the development of AI in marketing in the future. Inspired by the neural architecture of the human brain, Neuromorphic AI will facilitate more advanced pattern recognition and cognitive marketing use cases. Revolutionizing Marketing Analytics with Quantum Machine Learning: Quantum AI will advance marketing analytics with the computational speeds of quantum computing, capable of solving sophisticated optimization problems in real-time. AI built for emotional intelligence will analyze facial expressions, tone of voice, and other indicators of sentiment to enhance customer engagement and deliver emotionally resonant marketing messages.

With the ever-changing technology landscape, businesses will need to accept AI-based marketing methods; however, incorporating AI marketing should allow businesses to balance the impact of automation with human power. AI's capacity to analyze massive datasets, anticipate buyer actions, and customize experiences renders it a crucial resource for contemporary marketers. It needs to be monitored, ethical consideration and further improvements around the transparency of AI must be developed therefore responsible adoption needs to be cautious as it is still a work in progress. For Organizations, investing in AI-powered Marketing technologies is important, this will create an advantage for them over the organizations that do not practice ethical AI (Gursoy & Cai, 2025).

3. KEY AI-DRIVEN MARKETING TRENDS

Artificial intelligence (AI) is one of the trends in marketing, creating new opportunities for customer interactions, engagements, and experiences. Marketing in the era of AI: Personalization and hyper-targeting, AI-driven customer segmentation, behavioral analytics, predictive modeling, and real-time content customization. These developments enable companies to break away from conventional marketing methods and produce data-driven, highly personalized experiences which lead to higher customer satisfaction, higher conversion rates, and higher brand loyalty. The capability of AI to process large volumes of data, identify trends, and provide actionable insights in real-time has made it a critical resource in today's marketing strategy, allowing brands to deliver personalized content, promotions, and engagements based on the desires of each customer, within seconds, to guarantee a better chance of achieving a big 'buy' or 'want' to happen as reality.

3.1 Implementing Personalisation and Hyper-Targeting

Personalization is the pillars of contemporary marketing, and AI fuels brands to bring hyper-targeted content to each consumer. Unlike traditional segmentation based on demographics, AI-powered personalization analyzes user preferences, behaviors, and interactions across several digital touchpoints thanks to machine learning algorithms and natural language processing (NLP) and deep learning models. AI can analyze data on previous interactions, usage behavior and contemporary trends, to predict what content, products or services an individual is likely to be interested in enabling brands to create marketing campaigns that are relevant and timely.

Hyper-targeting a step beyond basic personalization combines AI-driven insights to deliver marketing messages at the right time. Using techniques like tracking browsing history, purchase behavior, social media activity, and sentiment analysis, AI algorithms create very narrow micro-segments within a defined target audience. This allows marketers to create personalized experiences on an individual basis such as, ensuring the right customer gets the right content. AI recommendation engines, for example, present products or content personalized to what a user has interacted with before, which greatly increases use and conversion in places like Amazon and Netflix.

In email marketing, machine learning models can identify the right subject lines, delivery time, and content variations for each recipient. AI-driven dynamic email personalization makes sure that customers receive tailored messages based on their preferences, purchase history, and real-time behavior (Kshetri et al., 2024). AI is revolutionizing digital advertising with programmatic ad buying, a process where machine learning algorithms automatically bid for ad placements in real-time, ensuring that ads are displayed to the right audience at the right moment. AI personalization and hyper-targeting helps brands establish the right fit with consumers across touch points that deliver meaningful engagement, increasing ROI.

3.2 AI-Powered Customer Segmentation: Data Science Projects in Customer Segmentation

Customer segmentation has been limited to general demographic and psychographic categories until now, AI has transformed this process through the application of it to more accurate and data-driven segmentation. AI Customer Segmentation refers to the process of grouping customers based on their similarities in behavior, preferences, or any characteristic. AI does not rely solely on for analysis and insights, but instead it uncovers previously hidden correlations, and segments audiences in ways that would be impossible to achieve using data segmentation (Umamaheswari, 2024).

Customer data collected from different sources such as website visits, social media platforms, transaction history, and customer support interactions are processed in machine learning models to develop dynamic and evolving customer segments. AI segmentation allows businesses to refine their marketing message for each group so that the content resonates with different customer personas. As an illustration, an online retailer can group its customers into segments including high-value customers, frequent buyers, first-time visitors, cart abandoners, and so forth with each segment being sent tailored marketing messages that align with the customer's placement in the journey.

The more breakthrough made possible now thanks to AI is predictive segmentation, which relies on algorithms that study historical data to predict future customer behaviour. By analyzing this data, marketers can determine the potential loss of high-value customers, anticipate potential churn, and create tailored retention efforts. AI-driven customer segmentation-as-a-scale is extremely useful where omnichannel marketing comes in as well, the process allows businesses to offer seamless and personalized customer experience on various platforms, whether it be your website, social media, mobile app, or even your email campaigns. AI-based segmentation helps the brands in improving marketing efficiency, minimizing wasted advertising dollars, and driving more relevant interactions with their audience (Nan et al., 2024).

From accurately anticipating customer needs and preferences to leveraging AI-driven behavioral analytics and predictive modeling, these technologies are revolutionizing marketing strategies. Looking at the behavioral analytics refers to examining the signature details like user events, clickstream, purchase history, and user experience metrices to understand the way the customers interact with a brand. AI-driven tools can identify patterns in customer behavior, from frequent visits to a product page, to social media shares or abandoned shopping carts, marketers can account their strategies accordingly. Predictive modeling advances up on behavioral analytics through the use of machine learning algorithms to predict future customer behavior (Bulchand-Gidumal et al., 2024). These models examine historical data along with real-time inputs to determine which customers are predicted to buy, abandon a cart, or respond to a specific marketing campaign. With the power of AI-driven predictive analytics, marketers can now identify opportunities to optimize their approach and target constituents with recommendations specifically tailored to them at the right time. AI algorithms can detect early signs of disengagement, enabling businesses to take preventive measures for retention before customers churn. For instance, subscription-based companies such as Netflix and Spotify leverage predictive analytics to detect users who may potentially cancel their subscriptions and engage them with personalized offers or recommendations to keep them onboard.

The other important applications is dynamic pricing, where predictive models driven by AI change prices in real time based on demand, competitor pricing, and customer willingness to pay. Dynamic pricing is a widely used AI-powered approach that adjusts the cost of goods and services based on various shifts in demand and supply; e-commerce platforms and travel booking websites employ it to maximize revenue while delivering prices that are attractive to the consumer. Using behavioral analytics and predictive modeling, businesses can achieve data-driven marketing decisions, improve customer experience and ultimately, increases conversions (Ramos et al., 2024).

4. AI IN CONTENT CREATION AND MANAGEMENT: AUTOMATED CONTENT GENERATION

From shape-shifting content design and generation to content optimization, distribution, and enhancement, AI is disrupting the traditional content creation and management landscape. With the emergence of advanced AI models including natural language processing (NLP) and machine learning (ML), marketers, publishers and business have embraced automated content generation that has allowed them to produce high-quality, tailored and scalable content at a speed never seen before. From blog articles and product descriptions to social media posts and news articles, automation tools powered by AI are transforming content marketing strategies by improving efficiency, creativity, and engagement. AI continues to advance, and gradually its potential to generate contextually suitable and human-like content is increasing, with less reliance on manual content creation and utilizing time and resources (Okorie et al., 2024).

4.1 AI-Powered Natural Language Generation

Natural Language Generation (NLG), a subset of AI, is at the heart of AI-driven content creation, as it converts structured data into readable and meaningful text. These algorithms of NLG analyze data, find patterns within that data, and formulate content in close mimicry of human writing styles. Complex AI models OpenAI's GPT series and Google's BERT, for example utilize deep learning processes to produce contextually rich, fluent and interesting content for specific audiences. Businesses and media agencies have also used AI-powered NLG tools to generate business and financial reports, news articles, summaries, and e-commerce product reviews. For instance, news agency illustrations of both The Associated Press and Reuters implement AI to write real-time news articles about financial news by analyzing stock market data, enabling accurate and timely updates. Likewise, e-commerce platforms such as Amazon, use AI-based tools to create dynamic product descriptions to improve the user experience and simultaneously lessen human efforts (Putra, 2024).

AI-powered content generation platforms like Jasper AI, Writesonic and Copy. ai, help marketers and businesses write blog posts, email marketing copy, and website content. This although traditional SEO practices can be tedious, these tools analyze SEO trends, user intent, and competitive content to formulate optimized articles that rank higher on the search engines, driving organic traffic and engagement. The integration of AI with content creation can not only help businesses keep pace with a steady content strategy, but can also help improve efficiency and help cater to a localized and more personalized messaging to a global audience.

4.2 Customized Content and Extreme Targeting

While AI-generated content itself allows to create automatic content, powerful automated generation doesn't just give the ability to generate a generic content, it also creates the contents that are hyper-personalised and customized depending on your user preferences, behaviours, and engagement patterns. Using data up until October 2023, AI algorithms collect large amounts of data such as browsing history, purchase behavior, and social media interactions and make personalized recommendations or targeted content. This enables higher customer engagement and brand loyalty since users receive only content that they are interested (Raji et al., 2024).

AI-based recommendation engines, which provide personalized content recommendations by analyzing user behavior and interactions (Netflix, Spotify, etc). Similarly, AI-based email marketing systems leverage predictive analytics to suggest personalized subject lines, content, and call-to-action messages boosting open rates and conversions. Another significant use of AI is in the personalization of dynamic website content, in which machine learning models adapt webpage layouts, product displays, and promotional banners in real time according to user behavior.

Also, AI chatbots and virtual assistants that can leverage Natural Language Processing (NLP) are able to answer their inquiries in real-time, being context-aware and interactive. These conversational AI agents can provide targeted information such as personalized content recommendations, product suggestions, and support responses, improving the customer experience and engagement. When used for hyper-targeted content, using AI can help organizations build powerful relationships with customers, drive purchasing, and optimize marketing efforts. Artificial Intelligence in the Creation of Video, Audio and Visual Content

The range of AI content production goes beyond written content and includes video, audio, and design in graphics, among other multimedia content. These AI video generation tools, like Synthesia and Lumen5, allow marketers and businesses to produce high-quality video content without needing significant resources or professional-editing capabilities (Durai et al., 2024). These platforms leverage deep learning models to take in media like scripts for video production and then generate near-photorealistic avatars that can speak and engage viewers and create marketing materials, training content, or product videos. Podcasts and audio content generation also rely heavily on AI. AI voice synthesis tools (like Descipt and Resemble AI) use deep learning to create realistic voiceovers for audiobooks, podcasts, and virtual assistants. They enable content creators to scale their production and automate voice narration, speech synthesis, and translation so that content can reach an international audience.

In visual content formats, tools like Canva and Adobe Sensei harness Artificial Intelligence to provide services in graphics design, image editing, and branding material automation. Marketing Ai tools help for powers tools to ensure marketers can generate high quality social media graphics, infographics and advertising banners with little manual input. For businesses, these AI tools provide automated visual content creation, ensuring brand consistency and streamlined marketing efforts while also increasing their audience engagement across diverse digital platforms (Singh & Kaunert, 2024).

These kinds of AI-powered tools can help writers track article optimization by recommending high-ranking keywords, enhancing readability, and ensuring that content meets search intent. Content optimization platforms with AI technology also study user engagement metrics, including click-through rates, dwell time, and bounce rates, to improve content strategies and results. Content optimization using AI can help businesses to build a better digital presence, drive improved website traffic, and improve audience retention.

5. AI IN PROGRAMMATIC ADVERTISING AND MEDIA BUYING: AI-BASED AD TARGETING AND OPTIMIZATION

Artificial Intelligence (AI) has transformed the landscape of programmatic advertising and media buying, bringing increased efficiency, accuracy, and scalability to digital marketing efforts. By utilizing data in real time to make decisions powered by artificial intelligence, programmatic advertising automates the process of buying and selling ad inventory and has changed how brands connect with their audiences. Through AI, advertisers can optimise every campaign, delivery and experience, ensuring maximised ROI through intelligent automation and machine learning algorithms (Kunz & Wirtz, 2024). Real-time bidding (RTB), increased accuracy in targeting ads, and detection of fraud to ensure brand safety are just some of the AI-powered use cases for media buying. As artificial intelligence continues to evolve, so will its role in programmatic advertising, giving it more cost-effective, data-driven and customer-centric characteristics.

Advanced Ad Targeting and Campaign Optimization: One of the most important use cases of AI in programmatic advertising is advanced ad targeting and campaign optimization. Traditional advertising strategies depended on demographic and psychographic data, but AI uses advanced algorithms to analyze massive amounts of real-time data on user behavior, social interactions, purchase history, and browsing patterns to deliver extremely targeted ads. As to AI, ad targeting now allows brands to reach the right segments with the right message, thus increasing both engagement and conversion.

With this, algorithms powered by artificial intelligence can find patterns and preferences using predictive analytics and machine learning, allowing advertisers to serve highly personalized ads. These DSAs are dynamic and adjust targeting strategies based on the regression's feedback loop based on interaction and campaign performance (Rawas, 2024). As an example, AI can catch micro-moments particular moments in time where users display high purchasing intent and serve appropriate ads at the right time. This level of precision reduces wasted ad spend and boosts campaign effectiveness. AI Recommendation Engines allows for an improved contextual targeting experience at multiple digital properties. AI, rather than relying on ordinary keywords, analyzes the sentiment, tone, and intent of the content on websites to place ads in the best-performing and engaging environments. This ensures brands appear before consumers in contexts that align with their preference, improving receptivity to ads and brand recall (Hamadaqa et al., 2024).

RTB process B RTB is the face of programmatic advertising where AI plays an important role. Real time bidding (RTB) is middlemen between publishers and advertisers, and it something similar to an auction, whereby advertisers place their bid on impressions milliseconds before a webpage is loaded. Algorithmic RTB facilitated by AI helps advertisers to make informed decisions driven by data, enabling them to optimize their bids based on user profiles, contextual data and the ultimate goals of the campaign (Ogundipe et al., 2024).

Millions of datasets are processed by AI algorithms in real time to assess and assign the worth of the impression of that ad all done to enable advertisers to bid competitively and maximize return on investment (ROI). This involves analyzing user behavior, the type of device used, geolocation, and historical performance to estimate the probability of conversion. AI with its automated bidding allows brands to get premium ad placements at best prices, all without manual involvement.vAI-powered real-time bidding (RTB) enables dynamic creative optimization (DCO) that enables advertisers to tailor ad creatives based on user interests and contextual cues. AI instantly tailoring your ad copy, imagery, and messaging to the viewer's topic of interest for more engagement and relevance (Marquis et al., 2024). Such a high level of customization makes brands serve engaging, personalized ad experiences that lead to increased conversion rates.

The other key benefit of AI-driven RTB is its ability to identify and adapt to market shifts in real time. AI tracks ad performance round the clock, allowing it to increase the bid or budget for high-performing opportunities. For example, AI algorithms can raise the bids to reach an engaged audience in peak shopping seasons or special events and reduce the spend on low-performing placements. This flexibility means advertisers are getting the most out of their ad dollars. Inevitably, programmatic advertising, despite its numerous advantages, is susceptible to ad fraud that leads to billions of dollars of losses every year. As a result, AI has emerged as a powerful weapon in our arms in the fight against fraud and ensuring that brands are only investing in legitimate, brand-safe ad placements (Amankwah-Amoah et al., 2024). They analyze large volumes of data in real-time, looking for deviations and trends that suggest fraudulent activity.

Bot traffic (automated scripts that fake clicks, impressions, and the likes to trick the performance of a campaign) is one of the most frequent types of ad fraud. AI-powered anti-fraud solutions identify bot activity by monitoring user behavior metrics like mouse movement, session duration, and interaction patterns. AI can help reduce wasted budget being spent on traffic that was never human to begin with because it can differentiate between human and bot traffic.AI can help reduce wasted budget being spent on traffic that was never human to begin with because it can differentiate between human and bot traffic.

AI also detects domain spoofing, a tactic used by bad publishers to impersonate and present low-quality websites as premium ad space. New AI-powered verification tools scan ad placements behind the scenes, guaranteeing that ads are displayed on legitimate and high-quality websites in alignment with brand values. This shields advertisers from spending money on placements which are misleading or damaging to a brand at the top of the funnel. These tools assess language subtleties, image recognition data and topic relevance to see if the ad environment is appropriate for brand messaging. It can address negative associations and protect consumers from damaging brands, keeping consumer safety top-of-mind and providing customers with a sense of comfort. With AI-driven insights, advertisers can analyze data and shift strategies to prioritize higher visibility formats and premium publishers (Faruque et al., 2024).

6. AI IN PREDICTIVE AND PRESCRIPTIVE MARKETING ANALYTICS

From data-driven to predictive and prescriptive intelligence models, artificial intelligence (AI) is entirely changing the landscape of marketing analytics. AI-Powered Machine Learning for Marketing: Predictive Marketing Analytics Predictive marketing analytics uses AI-driven machine learning algorithms to predict customer behaviors, buying patterns, and market trends. These models leverage large volumes of historical and real-time data to discover correlations, categorize audiences, and predict future results. The use of AI helps marketers to craft optimization campaigns by analyzing structured and unstructured data from various sources like social media traffic, website interactions, customer reviews, and purchase history. By leveraging this predictive capability, businesses can optimize their customer acquisition and retention strategies, personalize marketing messages, and allocate resources more efficiently (Rosario, 2024). AI-driven tools, including predictive lead scoring and customer lifetime value (CLV) estimation, allow businesses to concentrate on high-value customers, thereby increasing the return on investment (ROI).

Although predictive analytics helps in making predictions, prescriptive marketing analytics takes this a step further and suggests actionable recommendations. Instead of only telling us what will happen, AI-driven prescriptive models tell us what actions it can take to produce the best possible results. These models are based on optimization, reinforcement learning, and decision science and are used to recommend personalized marketing actions. The typical example is AI-based recommendation systems that make programmatic suggestions of goods or services based on an analysis of client actions and tastes; these can greatly improve conversions (Ratten, 2024). Another area of AI application in e-commerce is automated pricing strategies that adopt dynamic pricing models adjusting in real-time according to demand, competitor prices and customers behavioral activities. For instance, prescriptive analytics are used in chatbots and other AI customer service platforms to improve engagement by allowing the company to respond to the customer in context, thus easing churn rates and increasing customer satisfaction.

When it comes to omnichannel marketing, the combination of both predictive and prescriptive analytics provide a unique advantage as AI can be utilized in making customer experiences consistent across numerous touchpoints. Through AI-powered sentiment analysis and natural language processing (NLP), businesses can gauge consumer sentiments, and modify their marketing strategies accordingly. The AI-enhanced predictive A/B testing and adaptive marketing algorithms enable the brands to change the strategy and carry out the best performer without manual intervention. AI-led prescriptive analytics also allows businesses to make decisions in real-time, adapting and reacting to changes in market conditions, consumer behaviors, or emerging trends on the fly. Marketing automation platforms using AI combine predictive insights with prescriptive actions to simplify running campaigns, allocating budgets and optimizing content (Adwan, 2024).

AI-based predictive and prescriptive marketing analytics also play the role of enhancing fraud detection and protecting brands. Machine learning models evaluate transaction data, detect deviations, and pick out possibly fraudulent transactions as part of the effort to keep transactions safe and reliable. Furthermore, AI aids in reputation management by identifying negative sentiment in online reviews and recommending corrective actions to minimize potential harm to the brand. The role of ethical considerations and data privacy concerns in AI-driven marketing analytics. The right balance must be maintained between leveraging the power of AI for consumer insights and adhering to data protection regulations like GDPR and CCPA (Lee et al., 2024). Also, the future of marketing analytics with AI seems promising as generative AI will become mainstream for personalized content creation at scale, AI could power the metaverse marketing experiences, as the next era of digital marketing.

7. CHALLENGES IN AI ADOPTION FOR SMALL AND MEDIUM ENTERPRISES (SMEs)

The high cost of implementing AI is one of the major obstacles. Large corporations have the budget to purchase AI infrastructure, software and personnel members, however, small enterprises (SMEs) do not have the option to spend significant amounts on this technology. As the development of AI involves substantial expenditures on computing resources, cloud services, and data management applications, for smaller organizations it can be a costly exercise. The lots of AI products are enterprise-scaled only, which limits the low-cost and customized solutions for SMEs (Kannan, 2024).

Major challenge is a shortage of technical expertise and skilled human resource. Implementing AI requires technical expertise in areas like data science, machine learning, and algorithm development, which are often lacking among SMEs. Hiring AI specialists is costly, while upskilling domain experts with AI tools can be a painstaking process. Consequently, many SMEs find it challenging to adopt AI seamlessly in their operations. Additionally, the quality and availability of data is another challenge to adopting AI. In order for AI systems to make accurate predictions or automations, they need large quantities of high-quality structured data. On the other hand, many SMEs do not have properly organized datasets, which hinders AI model training. Data privacy and security is yet another serious challenge as many SMEs do not have sufficient cybersecurity infrastructure in place to secure sensitive customer and business with respect to breach and compliance.

Many AI solutions need to be integrated with these legacy systems, which can be quite dated (and hence not compatible with modern AI technologies). SMEs usually do not have the IT infrastructure and technical know-how required to enable seamless integration resulting in operational disruptions and inefficiencies (Nair et al., 2024). Then, of course, there is the natural resistance by organizations to change or adopt new practices. They may resist AI-driven processes if they fear that automation will lead to job adversities. SMEs struggle to understand the return on investment (ROI) of AI, leading decision-makers to be wary of committing to AI-led transformation. SMEs that are new into AI adoption face regulatory and ethical concerns hindering their development. For small businesses, complying with data protection laws like GDPR and CCPA is not so straightforward, and can require extensive resources. Absence of well-defined AI governance frameworks and ethical standards so far, which increases the ambiguity of AI deployment (Guha et al., 2024). Despite these challenges, SMEs can realize cloud-based AI services, partnerships with AI vendors, and government initiatives supporting AI adoption to assets in overcoming these barriers. SMEs can tap into AI's promise by addressing these challenges strategically to achieve innovation and sustainable growth.

8. OPPORTUNITIES FOR AI IN MARKETING

From analyzing data, and personalizing customer experiences, to optimizing campaigns, AI is transforming marketing in a way that is making it more efficient and also more profitable for businesses. Hyper-personalization: The Most Promising AI Opportunities in Marketing AI-enhanced algorithms sift through huge amounts of data everything from browsing habits to shopping history to social media activity to craft highly customized marketing messages. From personalized recommendations to dynamic content and AI-driven chatbots, there are use cases that drive customer engagement and conversion rates. With tech giants like Amazon and Netflix successfully utilizing AI to deliver tailored product and content recommendations, these brands have become the gold standard in consumer-first marketing (Cooper et al., 2024).

Predictive models in AI design analyze historical data for existing marketing patterns so that they can predict customer behavior accurately in the future, also assisting marketers in finest-tuning pricing strategy, product and services demand forecasting and inventory levels. Informed decisions made using data, improve the efficiency of marketing and the ROI. AI-powered sentiment analysis also enables brands to gain insights into public sentiment by analyzing conversations on social media, reviews, and feedback, allowing them to respond in real time and adapt campaigns and messaging accordingly. Through programmatic ad buying, AI automates and improves digital advertising, placing targeted ads based on user behavior, demographics, and interests with machine learning algorithms (Shesadri et al., 2024). AI analyzes enormous loads of data, applying machine learning to optimize ad spending by selecting the most effective channels and audience to target, increasing conversion rates and reducing ad spend wastage. AI-driven content generation and optimization enables marketers to automate the creative process by quickly generating a plethora of blog posts, social media captions and email marketing campaigns. GPT-powered chatbots, AI-driven creative platforms, etc., enable brands to produce compelling content at scale even helping maintain brand consistency.

AI chatbots offer immediate customer support which minimizes response time and increases customer satisfaction. AI-powered customer segmentation also allows businesses to discover target groups within niche categories, and narrow down their campaigns to micro-targeted campaigns, thus activating better leads and conversion rates. AI is also key for fraud detection and brand safety as it analyzes billions of digital transactions to detect anomalies that help prevent advertising fraud. As technology around AI becomes more refined, new examples including generative AI, AI-powered AR experiences, and AI-led metaverse marketing will challenge the marketing landscape even more (Supriadi, 2024). AI can leverage efficiency, enhance customer engagement and provide sustainable competitive advantages in the digital economy.

9. CONCLUSION AND FUTURE SCOPE

Artificial intelligence has revolutionized marketing by allowing predictive analytics, hyper-personalization, automation, and real-time decision making. AI-driven insights empower businesses to tailor marketing strategies to individuals, enrich consumer interactions, and streamline operations. Whether it's through personalized recommendations, AI-driven chatbots, or programmatic advertising, AI enables marketers to target the right audience while improving return on investment (ROI). However, despite challenges data privacy issues, integration issues, skill gaps the rapid evolution of AGI tech continues to unveil new frontiers in marketing.

The future scope of AI in marketing looks vast ahead. The evolution of generative AI, AR and AI-enabled voice commerce will continue to redefine customer interactions. Augmented Reality marketing, AI-powered metaverse engagement and sentiment analysis will revolutionize your brand strategy. Ethical AI frameworks and stronger data protection mechanisms will guide the responsible implementation of AI in marketing. AI-powered marketing innovations will increasingly trickle down to smaller enterprises with increased accessibility and user-friendliness of AI systems. The future will belong to those businesses integrating AI strategically to grow their marketing and create a sustainable growth return on investment within the digital marketplace. This is how the future of marketing would look like by leveraging the potential of AI to not only foster innovation but also deepen consumer relationships and form dynamic, data-driven marketing ecosystems.

REFERENCES

Adwan, A. (2024). Can companies in digital marketing benefit from artificial intelligence in content creation? *International Journal of Data and Network Science*, 8(2), 797–808. DOI: 10.5267/j.ijdns.2023.12.024

Amankwah-Amoah, J., Abdalla, S., Mogaji, E., Elbanna, A., & Dwivedi, Y. K. (2024). The impending disruption of creative industries by generative AI: Opportunities, challenges, and research agenda. *International Journal of Information Management*, 79, 102759. DOI: 10.1016/j.ijinfomgt.2024.102759

Arora, A., Kumar, S., Bansal, D., & Bansal, S. (2024). A Study of Awareness and Perception Regarding MOOC Courses with Special Reference to NPTEL. *Prabandhan: Indian Journal Of Management*, 17(4), 43–57. DOI: 10.17010/pijom/2024/v17i4/173427

Bulchand-Gidumal, J., William Secin, E., O'Connor, P., & Buhalis, D. (2024). Artificial intelligence's impact on hospitality and tourism marketing: Exploring key themes and addressing challenges. *Current Issues in Tourism*, 27(14), 2345–2362. DOI: 10.1080/13683500.2023.2229480

Cooper, R. G. (2024). The AI transformation of product innovation. *Industrial Marketing Management*, 119, 62–74. DOI: 10.1016/j.indmarman.2024.03.008

Durai, S., Manoharan, G., Priya, T. S., Jayanthi, R., Razak, A., & Ashtikar, S. P. (2024). Quantifying the Impacts of Artificial Intelligence Implementations in Marketing. In *Smart and Sustainable Interactive Marketing* (pp. 120–144). IGI Global. DOI: 10.4018/979-8-3693-1339-8.ch008

Faruque, M. O., Chowdhury, S., Rabbani, G., & Nure, A. (2024). Technology adoption and digital transformation in small businesses: Trends, challenges, and opportunities. *International Journal For Multidisciplinary Research, 6.*

Guha, A., Grewal, D., & Atlas, S. (2024). Generative AI and Marketing Education: What the Future Holds. *Journal of Marketing Education*, 46(1), 6–17. DOI: 10.1177/02734753231215436

Gursoy, D., & Cai, R. (2025). Artificial intelligence: An overview of research trends and future directions. *International Journal of Contemporary Hospitality Management*, 37(1), 1–17. DOI: 10.1108/IJCHM-03-2024-0322

Hamadaqa, M. H. M., Alnajjar, M., Ayyad, M. N., Al-Nakhal, M. A., Abunasser, B. S., & Abu-Naser, S. S. (2024). Leveraging Artificial Intelligence for Strategic Business Decision-Making: Opportunities and Challenges.

Kannan, R. (2024). Revolutionizing the Tourism Industry through Artificial Intelligence: A Comprehensive Review of AI Integration, Impact on Customer Experience, Operational Efficiency, and Future Trends. *International Journal for Multidimensional Research Perspectives, 2*(2), 1-14.

Kshetri, N., Dwivedi, Y. K., Davenport, T. H., & Panteli, N. (2024). Generative artificial intelligence in marketing: Applications, opportunities, challenges, and research agenda. *International Journal of Information Management*, 75, 102716. DOI: 10.1016/j.ijinfomgt.2023.102716

Kumar, D., & Suthar, N. (2024). Ethical and legal challenges of AI in marketing: An exploration of solutions. *Journal of Information. Communication and Ethics in Society*, 22(1), 124–144. DOI: 10.1108/JICES-05-2023-0068

Kumar, S., & Patel, A. K. (2019). An analysis of cointegration between nifty index, dollar/INR and crude oil price. *Journal of Advanced Research in Dynamical and Control Systems*, 11(12), 151–159. DOI: 10.5373/JARDCS/V11I12/20193223

Kumar, V., Ashraf, A. R., & Nadeem, W. (2024). AI-powered marketing: What, where, and how? *International Journal of Information Management*, 77, 102783. DOI: 10.1016/j.ijinfomgt.2024.102783

Kunz, W. H., & Wirtz, J. (2024). Corporate digital responsibility (CDR) in the age of AI: Implications for interactive marketing. *Journal of Research in Interactive Marketing*, 18(1), 31–37. DOI: 10.1108/JRIM-06-2023-0176

Lee, C. L., Yam, S., Susilawati, C., & Blake, A. (2024). The future property workforce: Challenges and opportunities for property professionals in the changing landscape. *Buildings (Basel, Switzerland)*, 14(1), 224. DOI: 10.3390/buildings14010224

Marquis, Y., Oladoyinbo, T. O., Olabanji, S. O., Olaniyi, O. O., & Ajayi, S. A. (2024). Proliferation of AI tools: A multifaceted evaluation of user perceptions and emerging trend. *Asian Journal of Advanced Research and Reports*, 18(1), 30–55. DOI: 10.9734/ajarr/2024/v18i1596

Nair, M. M., Deshmukh, A., & Tyagi, A. K. (2024). Artificial intelligence for cyber security: Current trends and future challenges. *Automated Secure Computing for Next-Generation Systems*, 83-114.

Nan, Z., Yuping, C., & Kongjue, Z. (2024). The Future of Marketing Analytics: Trends and Emerging Technologies. *International Journal of Advances in Business and Management Research*, 1(3), 23–32. DOI: 10.62674/ijabmr.2024.v1i03.003

Ogundipe, D. O., Babatunde, S. O., & Abaku, E. A. (2024). AI and product management: A theoretical overview from idea to market. *International Journal of Management & Entrepreneurship Research*, 6(3), 950–969. DOI: 10.51594/ijmer.v6i3.965

Okeleke, P. A., Ajiga, D., Folorunsho, S. O., & Ezeigweneme, C. (2024). Predictive analytics for market trends using AI: A study in consumer behavior. *International Journal of Engineering Research Updates*, 7(1), 36–49. DOI: 10.53430/ijeru.2024.7.1.0032

Okorie, G. N., Udeh, C. A., & Adaga, E. M. (2024). Digital marketing in the age of iot: A review of trends and impacts. *International Journal of Management & Entrepreneurship Research*, 6(1), 104–131. DOI: 10.51594/ijmer.v6i1.712

Putra, G. A. (2024). The Journey of Marketing Research in Driving Successful Marketing Strategies. *Advances in Business & Industrial Marketing Research*, 2(1), 26–35. DOI: 10.60079/abim.v2i1.241

Raji, M. A., Olodo, H. B., Oke, T. T., Addy, W. A., Ofodile, O. C., & Oyewole, A. T. (2024). E-commerce and consumer behavior: A review of AI-powered personalization and market trends. *GSC Advanced Research and Reviews, 18*(3), 66-77.

Ramos, R., Rita, P., & Vong, C. (2024). Mapping research in marketing: Trends, influential papers and agenda for future research. *Spanish Journal of Marketing - ESIC*, 28(2), 187–206. DOI: 10.1108/SJME-10-2022-0221

Ratten, V. (2024). Artificial intelligence, digital trends and globalization: Future research trends. *FIIB Business Review*, 13(3), 286–293. DOI: 10.1177/23197145231222774

Rawas, S. (2024). AI: The future of humanity. *Discover Artificial Intelligence*, 4(1), 25. DOI: 10.1007/s44163-024-00118-3

Rosário, A. T. (2024). Generative ai and generative pre-trained transformer applications: Challenges and opportunities. *Making Art With Generative AI Tools*, 45-71.

Sheshadri, T., Shelly, R., Sharma, K., Sharma, T., & Basha, M. (2024). An Empirical Study on Integration of Artificial Intelligence and Marketing Management to Transform Consumer Engagement in Selected PSU Banks (PNB and Canara Banks). *Naturalista Campano*, 28(1), 463–471.

Singh, B., & Kaunert, C. (2024). Future of Digital Marketing: Hyper-Personalized Customer Dynamic Experience with AI-Based Predictive Models. In *Revolutionizing the AI-Digital Landscape* (pp. 189–203). Productivity Press. DOI: 10.4324/9781032688305-14

Supriadi, A. (2024). The Impact of Artificial Intelligence (AI) on Marketing Strategy. *Management Studies and Business Journal*, 1(1), 146–153. DOI: 10.62207/pspbtk28

Umamaheswari, D. D. (2024). Role of Artificial Intelligence in Marketing Strategies and Performance. *Migration Letters : An International Journal of Migration Studies*, 21(S4), 1589–1599.

Chapter 3
Artificial Intelligence for Strengthening the Rule of Law and Justice Delivery System

Anjali Raghav
https://orcid.org/0009-0004-0248-7956
Sharda University, India

Laeeq Razzak Janjua
https://orcid.org/0000-0002-1948-5859
WSB University, Poland

Sahil Lal
https://orcid.org/0000-0001-9827-3717
Sharda University, India

Manmeet Kaur Arora
https://orcid.org/0009-0002-5071-117X
Sharda University, India

Hind Hammouch
https://orcid.org/0000-0002-5897-1649
University Sidi Mohamed Ben Abdellah, Fez, Morocco

ABSTRACT

Artificial intelligence is transforming the legal landscape by enhancing efficiency, accessibility, and fairness in the justice delivery system. This chapter examines the role of AI in reinforcing the rule of law, with particular attention to legal research,

DOI: 10.4018/979-8-3693-9395-6.ch003

judicial decision-making, case management, and dispute resolution. From predictive analytics to legal chatbots to smart contracts, AI-driven tools are revolutionizing legal frameworks, speeding case processing, and reducing human bias. But AI in law also raises ethical challenges algorithmic bias, transparency issues, and data privacy concerns. Through real-world case studies from the United States, the European Union, India, and China, this chapter explores the implications of AI applications in legal governance. It highlights global initiatives to govern the role of AI technology in courts and suggests design principles for responsible AI-aided legal progress.

1. INTRODUCTION

The principles of justice, equality, and accountability in society are known as the rule of law which is to be respected. It ensures that the laws work appropriately, balancing individual liberties with the need for law and order. The other side of the coin is a strong system of delivering justice necessary for the maintenance of democratic rule and economic stability. But legal systems around the world are grappling with serious issues like backlogs in cases, prolonged proceedings, judicial cronyism, and lack of access. Many countries allege overburdened judiciary systems where cases take years or even decades to come to resolution. Moreover, corruption, bias in decision-making, and inadequate resources also impede legal institutions from functioning effectively (Ejjami, 2024). Also, artificial intelligence (AI) has been identified as a game-changer that can help overcome such inefficiencies and enhance the rule of law. Legal tech powered by AI is transforming the justice system by automating legal research, predicting case outcomes, and streamlining court processes. Incorporating AI into the governance and legal administration provides a unique opportunity to reform judicial frameworks affiliated with transparency, accessibility, and efficiency. These tools can provide legal professionals with innovative solutions that can support policymakers and the judiciary in improving decision-making processes, increasing fairness in legal outcomes, and expediting the resolution of disputes.

1.2 Role of AI in Modern Governance

Early use cases for AI in the legal space centered around digitization and searchable databases. But as machine learning, natural language processing (NLP), and predictive analytics have matured, AI has evolved beyond basic automation to deliver complex legal insights. AI-driven legal research tools, like Westlaw and LexisNexis, analyze large datasets of legal information to discover pertinent case law and statutes, saving lawyers time that would otherwise be spent sifting through case law manually. AI plays one of the major roles in governance, helping the decision-making process in the justice system. Predictive analytics has the ability to analyze legal cases and provide potential outcomes based on data from previous cases. AI algorithms help judges make sentences, assess risks during bail hearings, and detect fraud in legal contracts, among other tasks. Similarly, the growing use of AI in arbitration and other dispute resolution platforms is opening an alternate route to disputes that avoids the drawn-out court procedure. The courts and virtual legal aides have stemmed from the confluence of AI; and legal tech Such process has opened the doors to virtual courtrooms, auto-scheduling of case hearings, and AI-powered chatbots that render legal support to citizens (Nadjia, 2024). This, in turn, enables governments and legal institutions to develop more efficient, cost-effective, and accessible systems of justice using AI. Nonetheless, AI's involvement in governance brings with it several pros and cons; weird of which, in the absence of scrupulous regulation, raises ethical and legal issues including discriminatory algorithms, insufficient transparency, and insecurity of personal data.

1.3 Chapter Objective

This chapter aims to explore the integration of AI into the legal infrastructures to simplify and streamline various judicial processes. The study seeks to investigate the role of AI in enhancing legal processes ranging from case management and legal research to court administration and dispute resolution. Through examining current usages of AI across various judicial systems, this chapter aims to provide policy recommendations and best practices for effecting the incorporation of AI into legal governance. Another critical goal is to evaluate whether AI can promote access to justice, especially for underserved communities. Financial limitations, an absence of legal knowledge, or geographic boundaries prevent many from obtaining legal assistance. AI-driven legal applications, including chatbots and online legal advisers, can close this gap by providing inexpensive and immediate legal advice. Also, critically assess the extent to which AI-powered solutions promise to democratize legal services and improve public trust in the court system. The research will explore the challenges of AI adoption in legal systems, such as ethical concerns, data security risks, and regulatory compliance issues.

2. CONCEPTUAL FRAMEWORK OF AI IN LAW

2.1 Understanding Artificial Intelligence in Law

The use of Artificial Intelligence (AI) in the legal setting is the deployment of advanced computational tools to automate and improve legal activities. AI-powered legal tech uses machine training, NLP, & robotics to make justice systems much more efficient, accurate, and accessible. Legal AI tools provide expertise in legal research, contract analysis, case prediction, and even decision-making, taking the human workload off while speeding the processes through the judicial system. Advancements in AI are making a significant impact in the field of law, driven by the growing complexity of legal systems and the demand for innovative solutions to manage vast amounts of legal data efficiently. Machine learning is integral to how AI systems in law work as it allows computers to use previous judicial decisions in order to anticipate how a specific case will play out based on historical context. With this technology, legal analytics are boosted, enabling well-formed and effective decisions for judges, lawyers, and policymakers. Another key AI technology is NLP (natural language processing), which enables computers to process and comprehend human language and makes it possible to analyze legal documents, extract relevant information, and generate legal summaries. For example, AI-assisted legal assistants employ the capability to offer legal guidance to the public, addressing the gap in accessing justice for marginalized groups. Robotics, less common than the AI subsectors, has been identified as an area of exploration for the automation of administrative legal tasks, including document verification and court scheduling (Vargas-Murillo et al., 2024). All these AI technologies help revolutionize legal governance by making it more efficient, transparent, and data-based.

2.2 Rule of Law and Its Components

The rule of law is a cornerstone of governance under which all persons, institutions and entities, public and private, including the state itself, are accountable to laws that are publicly promulgated and equally enforced. It is reliable, legally certain and respect fundamental rights. The key elements which a functioning legal system respects are legal certainty, equality before the law and transparency. Legal certainty means that laws are clear, predictable and applied consistently, without the risk of arbitrary decision-making. The concept of equality before the law requires that the rules of law apply equally to all citizens, regardless of their social, economic, or political power. Such transparency in legal proceedings can create citizen confidence in the justice system that di ess the trust and accountability.

The rule of law is undergird by a series of international or national legal frameworks. Legal standards governing justice delivery are anchored in the UN (United Nations), the European Court of Human Rights, and the national judicial bodies. In a contemporary context, international conventions like the Universal Declaration of Human Rights and the International Covenant on Civil and Political Rights underline the principles of a fair trial and equal access to justice. National legal systems, from constitutions to codes of judges, serve as a legal basis for governance of sovereign entities. Yet, despite these constitutional frameworks, justice systems around the globe are subject to subpar operation, an area in which AI might step in to help mitigate. Governments and legal institutions can further the rule of law by deploying AI in legal processes which can lead to faster, more accurate, and more accessible justice (Zuwanda, et al., 2024).

2.3 AI and Its Potential in Legal Governance

AI's potential in legal governance is immense, particularly in predictive analytics and legal research. Predictive analytics involves using AI algorithms to analyze past legal cases, identify patterns, and forecast case outcomes. Courts in various jurisdictions are experimenting with AI-powered risk assessment tools to evaluate the likelihood of recidivism in criminal cases, aiding judges in bail and sentencing decisions. Predictive analytics can also assist in alternative dispute resolution (ADR) by suggesting potential resolutions based on similar past cases, reducing litigation costs and court congestion. However, ethical concerns surrounding AI-driven decisions, including algorithmic bias and lack of transparency, must be addressed to ensure fair outcomes.

Another significant AI application in legal governance is enhancing legal research. Traditional legal research is time-consuming, requiring lawyers to sift through extensive case laws, statutes, and legal opinions. AI-powered legal research platforms, such as ROSS Intelligence and Westlaw Edge, leverage NLP and machine learning to scan vast legal databases and extract relevant information instantly. These tools not only save time but also improve the accuracy of legal arguments by identifying crucial precedents and legal principles. AI-powered chatbots and virtual assistants further democratize legal access by providing automated legal guidance to individuals who may not have the resources to hire a lawyer.

Despite AI's advantages in legal governance, its implementation must be approached cautiously. While AI can enhance efficiency, it cannot replace human judgment in legal decision-making. Ethical concerns such as data privacy, AI bias, and accountability must be carefully addressed through robust legal and regulatory frameworks. AI should function as a supportive tool that complements legal professionals rather than replacing them. A balanced approach that integrates AI's capabilities with human expertise can ensure that justice remains fair, transparent, and accessible to all.

3. APPLICATIONS OF AI IN STRENGTHENING THE RULE OF LAW

3.1 AI in Legal Research and Case Analysis

Transformative Applications of AI in Legal Research and Case Analysis Lawyers usually need to go through vast quantities of legal texts, statutes, judicial precedents, and scholarly articles, in a tedious process they call legal research. Gone are the days of laborious legal research AI-powered tools have transformed this paradigm, allowing lawyers to conduct timely, accurate, and exhaustive research. Natural-language-processing (NLP) powered services like Westlaw, LexisNexis and ROSS Intelligence can comb through millions of legal databases and pull out not only relevant information but also boil down key points in seconds. This automation saves a significant amount of time on research, directing the attention of legal professionals to where it should be case strategy and advocacy. In case analysis, AI identifies legal rules and judicial trends. Machine learning algorithms scour past judgments to predict how courts might adjudicate similar cases in future. When analyzing historical data, AI is capable of recognizing vital arguments, case law, and US legal provisions that can influence judicial decisions. Using predictive analytics, AI helps build the legal strategy and how to strengthen decision-making for complex legal cases. Yet, there is a need to complement AI-driven analysis with human judgment to ensure contextual and legal correctness in interpretations (Ogunleye, 2024).

3.2 Artificial Intelligence in Judicial Decision-Making

AI is being increasingly used in the judicial law decision-making process to help with efficiency, reduction of biases in legal judgments, and consistency in legal rulings. Judges can use predictive analytics to assess how similar a case is to others, analyze legal arguments and suggest possible rulings based on existing laws. Courts in different jurisdictions are experimenting with AI-based tools that help judges make informed decisions but still leave the ultimate judgment in the hands of the judge.

Perhaps the most essential role for AI in judicial decision-making is in sentence and decisions. AI models assess a defendant's history, the particulars of the case and applicable provisions of law to produce recommendations for sentencing, while factoring in elements that include previous offenses, mitigating circumstances and rehabilitation potential. Thus, with these AI-aided systems enable more efficient judicial operations, questions still arise towards potential biases in algorithms possibly causing unjust sentencing. AI decision-making models need to be transparent to ensure public trust in AI-assisted judicial processes

3.3 AI in Management of Contracts and Disputes Resolution

However, legal and contract management and execution is starting to be revolutionized with AI. Traditional contract analysis involves a lengthy and tedious process that demands careful scrutiny of terms, conditions, and legal clauses. See example here A few of the highlights Stringing together expressions for deeper insights Machine learning and natural language processing (NLP) based contract management tools can analyze contracts, identify risks and flag inconsistencies and suggest changes. This contributes to improved accuracy and expedited processes, minimizing the chance of legal issues stemming from vague agreements. Self-executing contracts with the terms written directly into lines of code come into play with blockchain technology the actual integration of blockchain technology with AI. These contracts only activate terms after they have been met, which eliminates third-parties and minimizes the chances for a legal dispute. With AI-driven contract analysis businesses and legal practitioners can also accelerate negotiations to maximize compliance with legal regulations and reduce contractual risks (Yadong, 2024).

AI is also making huge progress in alternative dispute resolution (ADR). A mediation platform powered by AI can leverage negotiation algorithms to help the disputing parties reach a settlement without dragging it over the court through years of litigation. By analyzing how past cases were resolved, AI-driven dispute resolution tools can propose fair and reasonable settlement terms, allowing for quicker and more effective conflict resolution. These solutions help relieve the courts, making the justice system more efficient and affordable.

3.4 AI In Criminal Justice System

AI tools are being used to improve the prediction, prevention, and investigation of crime by the criminal justice system. Predictive Policing using AI tools analyzes patterns of crime, historical data, and social factors, which can predict potential criminal activities and help allocate law enforcement resources wisely. These predictive models help police departments identify high-crime areas and send preventive measures, leading to the reduction of crime rates. There are ethical issues with AI-based crime prediction, which can lead to racial profiling, invasions of privacy or data-driven policing that has the potential to be biased. In forensic investigations, AI is also vital in assessing pieces of evidence. Forensic tools powered by AI leverage machine learning algorithms to speed up the analysis of digital evidence, identify fraudulent actions, and investigate crime scenes. Artificial Intelligence-enabled facial recognition, voice recognition, and biometric analysis have significantly enhanced the ability to identify criminals and track suspects. Additionally, the ability of AI to process large volumes of forensic data has improved the accuracy and speed of criminal investigations, leading to more efficient law enforcement (Gaubienė, 2024).

4. ARTIFICIAL INTELLIGENCE FOR ACCESS TO JUSTICE AND LEGAL AID

4.1 Chatbots and Virtual Assistants Powered by AI

Access to justice is an important issue, especially in the case of uneducated individuals without the ability to afford the costs associated with hiring a lawyer. AI-driven chatbots and virtual legal assistants are closing the gap by offering immediate legal advice and information. These AI-powered tools employ NLP to communicate with users, respond to legal questions, and assist users with legal processes. Legal chat bots like DoNotPay and LISA help people understand their legal rights, draft legal documents, and navigate through bureaucratic red tape. By increasing legal literacy and making justice more accessible for marginalized communities, these platforms all work with a similar overarching framework of empowering citizens through AI. Chatbots can also assist self-represented litigants with filling out claims, writing appeals and learning about court procedures (Zafar, 2024).

4.2 AI on Legal Aid and Public Interest Litigation (PIL)

AI is also catalyzing the fields of legal aid and public interest litigation (PIL) by discovering public law problems and providing pro bono services. AI methods analyze massive data sets, looking for patterns of legal violations, discrimination, and human rights abuses. Such data-driven and munitions-like approach allows the legal entities to file class-action lawsuits and push for policy amendments rooted in empirical data. Some non-profit organizations and legal aid clinics are deploying AI to offer free legal help to the poor. AI enabled legal aid platforms match clients with pro bono legal expertise, so vulnerable groups get the legal advocacy needed. AI can also track judicial patterns and detect areas lacking in legal coverage, which could help lawmakers in creating more effective legislation and rules.

4.3 AI in Court Management and Case Workflow Automation

AI is revolutionizing court management by automating case scheduling, tracking court proceedings, and managing judicial workflows. Conventional court systems are often plagued by delay caused by bureaucratic inefficiencies, resulting in case backlogs and lengthy litigation. These AI-enabled case scheduling systems create smarter court calendars that avoid unnecessary adjournments, making judges more efficient. AI-powered e-courts & virtual hearings have gained traction, especially after Covid 19. AI-enabled video conferencing platforms are being used to conduct remote hearings, securing the delivery of justice regardless of territorial boundaries. "Such virtual courtrooms improve judicial accessibility by enabling witnesses, lawyers and litigants to attend hearings in multiple locations. AI-driven document automation systems can help simplify things like filing the case, submitting evidence, and creating legal documentation, saving time for both lawyers and their clients. With the automated analysis and redundancy request summary, the need for paperwork is significantly reduced, thus ensuring the administrative burden is also offloaded to the AI enabling the legal matters to expedite and be more effective in the courts. AI also receives backing from court management by way of procedural efficiency, which leads to a more transparent and accountable judiciary (Ness et al., 2024).

5. ETHICAL AND LEGAL ISSUES IN AI-DRIVEN LEGAL SYSTEMS

The increasing implementation of artificial intelligence in legal systems across the globe has raised concerns of ethics, fairness, transparency, privacy and accountability among all users. While AI-power legal decision-making can indeed bring greater efficiency and accuracy, it also introduces risks such as algorithmic biases, opaque decision processes, and questions of data security and human oversight-style issues that are deeply in the arena of computing ethics.

5.1 Bias in AI Decision-Making

Bias in decision-making in AI-based legal systems is one of the most serious ethical challenges. Since AI models are trained on historical legal data, if such data sets are tainted with biases—be it racial, gender-based, or socio-economic then AI systems could replicate or magnify discriminatory results. As an example: in the domain of criminal justice, AI-driven risk assessment technologies have been slammed for placing individuals from disenfranchised social groups in the high-risk offender category rather disproportionately, producing unjust sentence recommendations. Real-world implications of biased AI applications have been highlighted in case studies. In the U.S., the COMPAS (Correctional Offender Management Profiling for Alternative Sanctions) recidivism risk assessment was found to produce inflated risk scores for Black defendants and understate the likelihood to reoffend for white defendants. These biases violate the principles of fairness and equal protection under the law. From doing engineering which helps ensure fairness in AI-based legal systems (ethics in AI, diverse/training data with oversight etc.) to mitigating bias as a human in these systems (Benyekhlef, & Zhu, 2024).

5.2 Transparency and Explainability in AI Judgements

This is particularly due to the opacity of AI algorithms, commonly known as the black-box problem, which presents a major obstacle in decision making. The majority of AI systems, especially deep learning models, yield decisions that are challenging to interpret, even for specialists. In the legal arena where due process and rationalization of judgments is of utmost concern, failure to explicate AI-oriented conclusions could lead to erosion of belief in the system. AI-based judicial decisions should be transparent to make them accountable. These AI-driven legal tools need to explain their reasoning clearly enough that legal professionals can take a critical look at it and question the conclusions drawn when needed. Certain jurisdictions have already adopted your principles for explainable AI (XAI), intended to make algorithms and the decision-making processes of artificial intelligence (AI) systems more interpretable. But this ongoing struggle with balancing complexity and transparency in AI models is an ever-present challenge. This problem can only be solved if AI systems are designed to be interpretable, and if researchers and the law are designed in such a way that we are forced to provide transparency to AI-aided legal judgments.

5.3 Privacy and Security Issues of Data

The dependency of AI-based legal systems on large quantities of data poses challenges regarding privacy, security, and ensuring adherence to legal benchmarks. Sensitive information within legal databases, court records, and client-attorney communications needs protection against unauthorized access, data breaches, and misuse. How is AI-driven data processing legally justified? Privacy laws such as the EU's General Data Protection Regulation (GDPR) and related laws in other countries require such justification and meaningful consent given by data subjects.

AI-enhanced surveillance tools that have been deployed for law enforcement and counterterrorism purposes also have raised questions about privacy rights. In this sense, although AI can improve the security of the public by observing possible risks and dangers, the arbitrary gathering and interpretation of civilians' data could undermine civil rights. Data protection policies, encryption protocols, and oversight mechanisms need to be in place to ensure that the use of AI in the legal system is not abused and that the right to privacy of individuals is protected (Bishnoi et al., 2024).

5.4 Accountability and Human Oversight

One of the core questions around AI-based legal frameworks is: Who is responsible for the mistakes made by AI? If an AI tool produces an erroneous legal ruling, supplies faulty sentencing recommendations, or violates ethical guidelines, it's quite another question whose responsible. Therefore, while AI can enhance decision-making in the legal field, it cannot completely replace human involvement. Judges, lawyers, and legal analysts should then be the final arbiter of interpreting these AI-generated insights. These include viewing AI as an assistive tool and not a replacement, reliance on human judgment, and observation of an AI's ability to balance performance and safety. Legal professionals must be equipped to challenge the decisions made by AI systems when they are unjust while safeguarding the integrity of the legal process, as regulators need to clarify AI responsibility.

6. ARTIFICIAL INTELLIGENCE IN INTERNATIONAL JUSTICE AND HUMAN RIGHTS

AI is transforming not just national legal systems, but also international justice and human rights protection. AI-driven tools are being used to track human rights abuses, promote global governance and aid investigations of war crimes. AI plays a significant role in maintaining justice worldwide by utilizing data analytics, predictive modeling, and automation.

6.1 International Law and Global Governance by AI

The use of AI to strengthen the enforcement of international law and global governance is on the rise. International treaties and negotiations require the processing of vast information in the highly complex forms of legal texts, general frameworks of policy negotiations, and diplomatic communications. AI-based tools can simplify this process by detecting relevant legal provisions, evaluating treaty compliance, and predicting possible diplomatic disputes. AI is being used in digital diplomacy, wherein governments and international organizations leverage AI-driven analytics to analyze global developments, public sentiment, and geopolitical threats. In international affairs, AI-powered simulations can be used to model what might happen in negotiations, allowing diplomats and policy makers to make informed choices about how they drive negotiations. The deployment of AI in international law promise to have a significant impact on how fair and accountable diplomatic practices are secured (Mishra, 2024).

6.2 AI in the Protection of Human Rights

AI has emerged as an effective tool that is being used to monitor and document cases of human rights abuses globally. AI-powered analytics are being used by human rights organizations and international bodies to monitor patterns of abuse, identify perpetrators, and compile lists of violations. Real-time detection of human rights crises is streamlined with satellite imagery analysis, NLP-based monitoring of online hate speech, and AI-driven sentiment analysis. For example, one group leverages AI-powered tools that sift through social media data and news reports, to spot potential emerging human rights abuses, such as ethnic violence, state repression and political persecution. Entities like Amnesty International and Human Rights Watch harness AI next to map conflict zones and expose human rights issues to help advocacy and policy interventions. AI is also vital in ensuring refugee rights. AI systems also assist in tracking population displacements, analyzing migration trends, and optimizing the distribution of humanitarian aid. AI, by offering timely insights, fortifies the effectiveness of international responses to refugee crises and human rights emergencies (Akpuokwe et al., 2024).

6.3 War Crimes and Transitional Justice AI

AI is transforming how war crimes are investigated, prosecuted. AI-powered forensic tools aid international courts like the International Criminal Court (ICC) in analyzing evidence, verifying witness statements, and tracking human rights violations in conflict zones. AI-based image and video recognition technologies aid in the authentication of digital evidence, enabling the prosecution of war crimes perpetrators. In war crimes investigations, A.I. can verify massive amounts of documentary evidence, such as intercepted communications and satellite images, and compare them with witness testimony. Artificial Intelligence tools for forensics help identify patterns in war crimes, authenticate atrocities, and reconstruct crime scenes through data analytics. Such capabilities improve transitional justice mechanisms and guarantee that war criminals are brought to justice.

7. CASE STUDIES OF AI IMPLEMENTATION IN LEGAL SYSTEMS

There is wide variation in how it is being adopted in legal systems and how it is being integrated into judicial processes in different jurisdictions. AI-driven solutions have already been adopted to improve case management, legal research, sentencing decisions and access to justice in numerous countries. The following are examples of how AIs have redefined legal systems around the world.

7.1 AI within the United States Judicial System

One recent development is the United States, which has been at the vanguard of AI-powered legal analytics and judicial decision-making. AI-enabled legal research solutions like ROSS Intelligence and LexisNexis help lawyers search through case law, statutory provisions, and legal precedents at an unprecedented pace and precision. Tools for predictive analytics, such as those developed by Premonition and Blue J Legal, assist law firms and legal professionals in evaluating the potential results of open cases by analyzing past data and trends within the judicial system. Parole and even sentencing decisions have also incorporated AI. Several state courts use the COMPAS (Correctional Offender Management Profiling for Alternative Sanctions) system to predict recidivism risk for offenders. AI has made sentencing recommendations more efficient, but the growing fears of algorithmic bias and fairness have raised demands for more transparency and accountability in AI-driven judicial processes (Kulal et al., 2024).

7.2 AI in the European Union's Legal Framework

Europe has been more vocally proactive in promoting AI-driven justice initiatives, whilst attempting to stay within ethical and legal frameworks. Systems powered by AI, like the European Court of Human Rights' (ECHR) AI-based collaborative filtering of cases, help cope with a vast volume of legal matters by allocating and classifying urgent cases by complexity, among other things. This contributes to case backlogs and increases judicial efficiency. Another significant domain of application of AI in the EU is the General Data Protection Regulation (GDPR): it is enforced using such algorithmic systems. AI-driven compliance monitoring systems had been implemented to audit organizational data privacy practices to identify potential breaches (Kolade et al., 2024). Automated compliance tools help legal teams meet GDPR requirements, underscoring how AI is increasingly bolstering digital governance and legal enforcement.

7.3 AI in Indian Judiciary and Legal Reforms

To address the crisis of backlog in the judiciary and accessibility to legal services, India has initiated the integration of AI into its judicial system. SUPACE (Supreme Court Portal for Assistance in Court Efficiency): An AI-based research tool launched by the Supreme Court of India to assist judges in efficiently analyzing case laws and preparing judicial decisions. In a similar vein, the High Courts of Punjab and Haryana ventured into digitization of courts records using AI enabled transcription services. AI is also instrumental in delivering legal aid to rural areas. Chatbots like Nyaya Bandhu provide legal advice to those who cannot afford a lawyer. This goes a step further, making it even more the case that, in some respects, you can augment access to justice through information on legal rights, case procedures, and pro bono legal services through these AI-filtered apps, which bridges urban and rural divides in the legal system.

7.4 AI in China's Smart Courts

China leads the world in the concept of "smart courts," where artificial-intelligence powered programs make it easier to handle judicial processes. Litigants in AI-powered virtual courts, like those set up in Beijing, Hangzhou and Guangzhou, can attend court hearings remotely. AI-based judges, enabled with natural language processing, will help the access of case hearings, document review and dispute resolution. AI's Deepening Influence on Alternative Dispute Resolution in China AI-powered mediation platforms review case histories, legal precedents, and suggest case settlements, lessening the load on traditional court systems. Combining AI with its legal system has improved China's judicial efficiency, but raised discussions on ethical implications surrounding the use of AI to supplant human adjudicators2024 (Mercan & Selçuk, 2024).

8. THE FUTURE OF AI IN STRENGTHENING THE RULE OF LAW

Its use in developing the future of legal systems will only grow as AI continues to advance. The promise of AI to make justice accessible, scalable and high quality is enormous. Yet, overcoming ethical, regulatory, and technological obstacles will be essential to harnessing the full power of AI for strengthening the rule of law.

8.1 AI and the Evolution of Smart Justice

We may have "smart justice" where AI augments predicting case law, legal education and training the bolstrophe of our legal systems. Expect new AI powered legal research tools to be available that will predict case outcomes with increasingly complex legal reasoning based on data at their disposal. Legal professionals will use AI to identify trends in judicial decisions so that their legal rulings are more uniform.

AI is changing legal education and training, as well. Law students benefit from interactive learning through AI-driven simulations and virtual legal assistants to dissect case laws and aid legal reasoning. The gap between legal theory and legal practice will be increasingly bridged by AI technology as this field matures.

8.2. Policy Recommendations for AI Driven Legal Systems

Governments and legal institutions should lay down comprehensive AI governance frameworks to ensure ethical AI deployment in a legal system. Data on Legal AI Ethical AI ethical considerations For instance, AI oversight committees set up across judiciaries can govern or oversee AI-driven legal tools, possibly even preventing biased decision-making before it occurs. AI governance also needs collaboration between policymakers, technologists and legal experts. Regulators should implement accountability measures to guarantee the powerful tools of AI technology are responsibly deployed in the practice of law. Fair regulations of AI need also to balance between innovation and safeguards that protect human rights and due process.

8.3 Role of International Organizations in AI and Rule of Law

International organizations are a key factor in the relationship between AI and the rule of law. International bodies like the United Nations and the World Bank are also working on regulations that ensures legal fairness and human rights=data protection. The AI for Good initiative of the UN focuses on potential applications of AI to legal governance and champions the responsible use of AI in justice and legal systems around the world. AI companies collaborating with legal institutions is also a key component. However, tech companies that develop legal AI tools should work closely with judicial bodies in creating the AI applications to ensure that they align with legal principles. Developing AI-driven legal solutions that prioritize ethical considerations and judicial integrity can be facilitated through the formation of public-private partnerships (Ogunleye, 2024).

8.4 Prospects of AI and Blockchain in Law

AI and Blockchain: A Novel Approach to Legal Compliance and Transparency Blockchain and AI-Driven Smart Contracts Automated legal agreements that self-execute based on pre-defined conditions are known as smart contracts, which are powered by blockchain and AI technologies. Through their efficiency in facilitating legal transactions without mediators, these contracts can also elevate the efficiency of exchanging goods and services.

Additionally, the blockchain also provides a transparent and tamper-proof method for maintaining legal records. Blockchain powered by AI can enhance evidence validation, contract execution, and legal documentation security. When combined, AI and blockchain have significant potential for transforming contract law, regulatory compliance and legal documentation (Yadong, 2024).

9. CONCLUSION

AI implementation in law has made the judiciary more efficient, accessible and fair. AI has revolutionised numerous areas of legal practice, ranging from AI-driven legal research tools to intelligent altars, and automated disputation resolution mechanisms. Case studies: United States, European Union, India and China. Despite the significant benefits, AI does pose ethical challenges including bias, transparency, data privacy and accountability. And as AI continues to be adopted in the law, addressing ethical concerns will be more critical than ever. Research should address the issues of portfolio bias, transparency, and data security in legal AI systems. Governance frameworks for AI will also increasingly require input from various fields, as academics in AI collaborate with legal experts to provide holistic approaches to regulation. Future studies should also look into the interplay between AI and contemporary laws including cyber law, digital rights, and the role of AI in international legal frameworks. Through responsible AI development, legal writing systems can use AI's promise and utility without compromising justice, fairness, and human rights.

REFERENCES

Akpuokwe, C. U., Adeniyi, A. O., Bakare, S. S., & Eneh, N. E. (2024). The impact of judicial reforms on legal systems: A review in African countries. *International Journal of Applied Research in Social Sciences*, 6(3), 198–211. DOI: 10.51594/ijarss.v6i3.850

Benyekhlef, K., & Zhu, J. (2024). The judicial system and the work of judges and lawyers in the application of law and sanctions assisted by AI. In *Handbook of Artificial Intelligence at Work* (pp. 250–275). Edward Elgar Publishing. DOI: 10.4337/9781800889972.00021

Bishnoi, R., Kaur, R., Kaur, N., Kaur, H., Kaur, A., & Johal, A. (2024). Utilizing Artificial Intelligence in Legal System with Special Reference of India. *Educational Administration: Theory and Practice*, 30(5), 2217–2223.

Ejjami, R. (2024). AI-driven justice: Evaluating the impact of artificial intelligence on legal systems. *Int. J. Multidiscip. Res*, 6(3), 1–29.

Gaubienė, N. (2024). Can Artificial Intelligence Engage in the Practice of Law as the Art of Good and Justice?. *Filosofija. Sociologija, 35*(2 Special).

Karnani, A. K. (2024). AI empowerment in democratic governance: enhancing participation and efficiency. *Journal of Data Acquisition and Processing*, 39(1), 993.

Kolade, T. M., Aideyan, N. T., Oyekunle, S. M., Ogungbemi, O. S., Dapo-Oyewole, D. L., & Olaniyi, O. O. (2024). Artificial Intelligence and Information Governance: Strengthening Global Security, through Compliance Frameworks, and Data Security. *Available atSSRN* 5044032. DOI: 10.9734/ajrcos/2024/v17i12528

Kolade, T. M., Aideyan, N. T., Oyekunle, S. M., Ogungbemi, O. S., Dapo-Oyewole, D. L., & Olaniyi, O. O. (2024). Artificial Intelligence and Information Governance: Strengthening Global Security, through Compliance Frameworks, and Data Security. *Available atSSRN* 5044032. DOI: 10.9734/ajrcos/2024/v17i12528

Kulal, A., Rahiman, H. U., Suvarna, H., Abhishek, N., & Dinesh, S. (2024). Enhancing public service delivery efficiency: Exploring the impact of AI. *Journal of Open Innovation*, 10(3), 100329. DOI: 10.1016/j.joitmc.2024.100329

Marwala, T., & Mpedi, L. G. (2024). Artificial intelligence and the law. In *Artificial Intelligence and the Law* (pp. 1–25). Springer Nature Singapore.

Mercan, G., & Selçuk, Z. V. (2024). Artificial intelligence (AI) activities in legal practices. *International Journal of Eurasian Education and Culture*, 9(25), 131–144. DOI: 10.35826/ijoecc.1824

Mishra, A. K., Tyagi, A. K., Dananjayan, S., Rajavat, A., Rawat, H., & Rawat, A. (2024). Revolutionizing Government Operations: The Impact of Artificial Intelligence in Public Administration. *Conversational Artificial Intelligence*, 607-634.

Nadjia, M. (2024). The Impact of Artificial Intelligence on Legal Systems: Challenges and Opportunities. *R30-02144*, 285.

Ness, S., Singh, N., Volkivskyi, M., & Phia, W. J. (2024). The Application of AI and Computer Science in the Context of International Law and Governance "Opportunities and Challenges". *American Journal of Computing and Engineering*, 7(1), 26–36. DOI: 10.47672/ajce.1878

Ogunleye, O. S. (2024). Using Artificial Intelligence to Enhance E-Government Services Delivery Through Data Science and Machine Learning. In *Machine Learning and Data Science Techniques for Effective Government Service Delivery* (pp. 1–28). IGI Global.

Ogunleye, O. S. (Ed.). (2024). *Machine Learning and Data Science Techniques for Effective Government Service Delivery*. IGI Global.

Singh, A. K., & Kushwaha, A. (n.d.). Unmasking the Transformative Impact: Artificial Intelligence in India's Judiciary System.

Vargas-Murillo, A. R., Turriate-Guzman, A. M., Delgado-Chávez, C. A., & Sanchez-Paucar, F. (2024). Transforming Justice: Implications of Artificial Intelligence in Legal Systems. *Academic Journal of Interdisciplinary Studies, 13.*

Yadong, C. (2024). Special Reports on the Development of Artificial Intelligence Rule of Law. In *Blue Book on AI and Rule of Law in the World* (pp. 367–422). Springer Nature Singapore. DOI: 10.1007/978-981-97-1060-7_9

Yadong, C. (2024). Blue Book on AI and the Rule of Law in the World (2022) Research Questionnaire and Analysis. In *Blue Book on AI and Rule of Law in the World* (pp. 445–464). Springer Nature Singapore. DOI: 10.1007/978-981-97-1060-7_11

Zafar, A. (2024). Balancing the scale: Navigating ethical and practical challenges of artificial intelligence (AI) integration in legal practices. *Discover Artificial Intelligence*, 4(1), 27. DOI: 10.1007/s44163-024-00121-8

Zuwanda, Z. S., Lubis, A. F., Solapari, N., Sakmaf, M. S., & Triyantoro, A. (2024). Ethical and Legal Analysis of Artificial Intelligence Systems in Law Enforcement with a Study of Potential Human Rights Violations in Indonesia. *The Easta Journal Law and Human Rights*, 2(03), 176–185. DOI: 10.58812/eslhr.v2i03.283

Chapter 4
Criminal Justice System in the Age of Artificial Intelligence:
Exploring Rights, Risks, and Responsibilities in the Digital Era

Showkat Ahmad Wani
https://orcid.org/0009-0009-0240-9073
Alliance University, Bengaluru, India

Sheikh Inam Ul Mansoor
https://orcid.org/0000-0001-8636-4769
Dayananda Sagar University, India

ABSTRACT

AI biases can induce existing imbalances and affect the most affected populations more severely. The study underlines the need to introduce the imperative of transparency and explainability of AI systems. The fact that many algorithmic systems are correspondence opaque raises questions about how such decisions are made and who is accountable when using artificial intelligence, which leads to wrongful arrest or unfair sentencing. The research calls for effective legislative frameworks that would protect constitutional entitlement due to the widespread use of AI systems. The criminal justice system can effectively embrace AI and avoid the risk of infringing individual rights to make technology serve justice rather than inimical or detrimental to justice and basic human rights.

DOI: 10.4018/979-8-3693-9395-6.ch004

INTRODUCTION

The use of artificial intelligence or better still the integration of AI in the criminal justice systems has proven to be revolutionary in the process of law enforcement and the judicial systems (Završnik, 2020). New technologies in AI increase the effectiveness in solving crime and prosecution but residue for rights, responsibility, fairness, and biases (Ibegbulam, et al 2023). When analyzing the place of AI in the criminal justice system, it is imperative to describe the general concept and its use in criminal justice, the possibilities, and the threats AI has (Marwala, & Mpedi, 2024). The Fourth Industrial Revolution harnesses digital combined with physical and biological systems brought by the use of AI, machine learning, big data, automation, and robotics (Datta, P. 2023). AI holds promise in the criminal justice system because it can help law enforcement agencies not only solve and prevent increasing crimes that have not hitherto been seen (Sachoulidou, 2024). Integrating the concept of AI in the criminal justice system has its advantages but comes with a concern for openness, equity, and rights of a person. One good illustration is predictive policing, where the outcome is a set of predictions on future crime events (Meijer & Wessels 2019). Technological systems use data on crime rates, social media, and population characteristics to locate the areas that are at risk but the application is criticized for violation of individual privacy and stereotyping (Lee, Y., Bradford & Posch 2024). This is because those specific regions or demographics are likely to be over-policed in the first place, and so it will continue to happen when AI has been trained in existing data. Also, predictive policing is intrusive because it utilizes public data for anticipating criminality.

Biometric technology namely facial recognition gives the police character to identify and further apprehend suspects. It was able to scan thousands of faces in real-time improving security, monitoring, and legal evidence acquisition (Li et al. (2020). Even though, this provides an effective way of arresting suspects and deterring crimes, it has very serious implications on privacy and civil rights. Specifically, facial recognition systems have been accused of enhancing racial and gender discrimination which is dangerous and a threat to human rights (Gentzel, (2021). Research has demonstrated time and again that facial recognition systems have higher error rates while identifying people of color, especially black people, and women causing them to be misidentified and arrested (Wang, et. al 2024). This chapter argues that facial recognition errors pose equity and justice issues because minorities are more likely to be misidentified. Moreover, AI surveillance may affect privacy; therefore, citizens will change their behavior because of the surveillance by the government (Smith & Miller 2022).

Risk assessment algorithms are also starting to be applied in the criminal justice system, especially in pre-sentencing and parole cases. These tools employ records relating to criminal history and other characteristics of the defendant, as well as his or her personal history, to estimate the chances of recidivism or non-appearance in court (Kehl, et. al 2017). Parole boards and judges utilize these risks and need assessments to make parole decisions, ideally making the decision-making process more rational or evidence-based (Laqueur, et. al., 2024). Besides, it has been discussed that through using those tools one can avoid human bias, which brings the same results in the criminal justice system. But there is the *'black box'* problem that relates to a lack of algorithmic transparency, accountability, and issues of fairness (Hasan, et al. 2022). Most AI systems work, often, in ways that even their creators are unable to decipher and the decisions they make are lauded as *black boxes* (Resnik et al. 2024). Where an AI system suggests an extended sentence or remand in custody, defendants and their advisors may not have the data with which they can contest this outcome, compromising procedural justice and natural justice.

However, research has revealed that the risk assessment instruments mirror and reinforce the biases inherent in the criminal justice system. Some of these algorithms are trained on data that contain historical inequalities and hence may work against some groups (Applegarth et al. 2023). AI can label people of color or any other ethnic group that has been infamous for police brutality with a higher risk record even if they aren't partakers in any immoral activities. This bias is bolstered and demonstrates the failure of machine learning towards the progressive aim of a fairer criminal justice system (Cheuk, 2021). The integration of the use of AI in criminal justice systems also presents some questions regarding responsibility. If a particular decision that has been made by an AI system turns out to be unfair, for example, a wrongful arrest or conviction, who is to blame? (Sayyed, (2024). This also means that AI decisions cannot be held in the same way as human decision-makers can be held responsible. This poses legal and ethical questions since it is now not always clear if one party or another is to blame if an AI fair or negative conclusion is reached (Steyvers, 2024). Considering accountability within algorithmic decision-making within the criminal justice system, this chapter asks for accountability to lie with creators, police departments, or officers. Lack of accountability in AI challenges with prevention of clauses of violence with no liability. Finally, to support equity and justice and in order to allow people affected by such decisions to have control over the algorithms and to have their rights defended, stakeholders require transparency, explainability, and public participation in such biometric AI-driven decision-making systems (Koulu, 2020). To legalize AI more and more attention is paid to the role of the legal actions towards criminal justice implications of AI where the fairness, responsibility, and ethical rules for the development and application of AI technologies arise as significant perspectives.

The Fourth Industrial Revolution greatly transformed law enforcement based on the use of AI technologies that have elevated criminal justice systems globally in efficiency, effectiveness, and functionality while sparking contentious controversies on AI bias, governance, and human rights over the implementation of AI technologies for positive justice delivery.

The Objective of This Research

The goal of this study is to assess AI application in the criminal justice system today to assess its effects on policing techniques, the legal system, and citizen's rights. It considers the positive and negative effects of emerging applications such as predictive policing and facial recognition while exploring the concerns of privacy, fair trial, and discrimination regarding accountability and transparency issues. Ackerman's study will also capture the necessity of human supervision to guarantee that the AI service is fair and will protect and promote human rights, giving recommendations on how AI tech can be adopted well in regions of police and justice.

AI TECHNOLOGIES IN CRIMINAL JUSTICE

AI technologies are finding applications in the criminal justice system by improving efficiency in policing, investigation, and adjudication through analysis of large datasets and identifying emerging patterns. However, these advancements pose key legal and ethical issues that have to be well-addressed to reopen fair justice (Završnik, 2020).

The most popular area of focus is criminal justice, of which predictive policing, being based on historical data and analytical algorithms to predict crime rates and success is in focus (Xu et al., 2021). It involves the use of statistics as a means of determining areas that are more likely to attract criminal activities for preventive patrol, unlike the conventional detective approach; however, it extends the police prejudices in data handling (Mugari & Obioha, 2021). In the same way, if previous policing practices have primarily and disproportionately impacted specific groups or ethnicities, predictive algorithms will formally incur these tendencies and exaggerate police targeting of vulnerable people.

An example of AI use in criminal justice is face recognition technology, which is widely used now. They utilize this technology to detect individuals by talking his / her face and comparing it to other faces in the database (Hill et al., 2022). This biometric technology can be used in suspect identification, identification of individuals of interest, and improvement of surveillance within crowded places. Its development has become very fast and furious, with many police departments incorporating it in real-time monitoring scenarios (Jansen et al., 2021). The use of facial recognition technology helps to improve public safety, though it increases privacy invasion and human rights issues such as the misidentification of non-white people and women (Kostka et al., 2021). As it stands, what drives facial recognition technology has proven to produce wrong results, leading to wrongful arrests, profiling of innocent individuals, and a generally poor relationship between the communities and the police. (Urquhart & Miranda, 2021)

Risk assessment algorithms use probability to estimate a defendant's propensity to recidivate or fail to appear in court; they aid judges on probation or pre-trial release and sentencing and parole (Taylor, 2023). It means that using different factors, including criminal background, age, socioeconomic status, and others, risk assessment tools are targeted to reduce biases in the legal decision-making process (Meterko & Cooper, 2022). All those tools can minimize the impact of subjective factors and increase the objectivity of decision-making. However, doubts regarding their effectiveness are still present, as most of the existing risk assessment models have not been fully explained and, for that matter, cannot be explained to judges and developers. This causes questions about their fairness and citizens' capacity to contest algorithmic decision-making (Tsamados et al., 2022).

The application of AI in the criminal justice system also rationalizes decision-making systems, which may be used in certain administrative capacities like cases, documents, and evidence handling. Such systems can minimize the likelihood of pattern faults and may also accelerate procedures that would generally require a lot of manpower (Marwala & Mpedi, 2024). Typically, the production of evidence demands a lot of time chasing documents and identifying the information legal teams require. This improves the rate of case processing and delivery of justice as well as supports investigations using link analysis (Hitch, 2024). Police departments gain new insights through machine learning which investigates interactions and similarities between suspects by employing social media, financial profiles, and communications, among others, insights hard to obtain by conventional investigative procedures (Mandalapu et al., 2023). AI in the investigation sector may be an issue of privacy since data are processed without consent, which raises contending questions about the European Charter of Fundamental Rights as a means of protecting individual rights for effective law enforcement.

AI is reshaping forensic science through new patterns matching DNA and fingerprints by matching the genetic material to relevant databases without long and ineffective search queries (Mohsin, 2021). AI enriches digital investigations by processing data from computers and communication devices, hence increasing the accuracy of the presented evidence in court. It also looks for patterns in databases and introduces new leads for law enforcement not findable by conventional investigations (Kabir & Alam, 2023). With the use of AI in investigations, the right to privacy is an issue that needs to be addressed to protect and preserve the human rights of individuals. Much emphasis and attention must be paid to the proportion between the efficiency of the work done by law enforcement officers and the rights of individuals (Zhang et al., 2021). AI innovations in forensic science must improve DNA processing and fingerprint recognition, providing faster, more accurate outcomes compared to sample databases that ensure minimizing the effect of bias by investigators (Galante et al., 2023). Likewise, AI can aid in such matters as searching for an important piece of information in the digital information found in computers and other personal electronic gadgets supporting a particular case. Therefore, the integration of AI into forensic practice adds mostly to the quality of given testimony and flows to better decisions by judges (Tynan, 2024).

To deal with these issues, there must be some emerging set of rules in the criminal justice system involving the use of AI for transparency, management, and accountability in implementation (Ghallab, 2019). The AI decisions must be explained and the results reviewed before finalizing to encourage decision-makers to make AI systems inherently transparent (de Fine Licht & de Fine Licht, 2020). Also, a human-machine interface has to be a priority so that machines work alongside human intelligence so that quick error possibilities will be minimized to enhance productivity in AI in their decisions. Police departments and other criminal justice partners have to raise awareness among ordinary citizens on AI solutions and their advantages and disadvantages, along with the power they possess in decision-making (Sushina & Sobenin, 2020). Political and public discourse on the apparent dangers of AI in the criminal justice system will encourage responsibility and ensure the needs of communities that are affected by the implementation of the systems are taken into account.

Opportunities and Benefits of AI in Criminal Justice

AI in Criminal justice appears as a huge opportunity and has the potential to bring significant benefits when implemented and applied in law enforcement, judicial processes, and envisioned public safety (Marwala & Mpedi, 2024). With the growing popularity of investing in technologies across different fields, criminal justice systems stand to greatly benefit from AI. It moves from simply incorporating novel instruments to improving other techniques with quantitative methods, particularly in predictive policing. Criminal trends in the past mean that police departments can anticipate future crimes, enhance the use of resources, and prevent crimes. Such an approach enables the police to solve crimes by addressing factors that increase their prevalence in certain regions with the highest levels of crime (Mandalapu et al., 2023). By changing the policing strategy from reactive to proactive, AI helps officers to keep citizens safer and spend less time on resources.

Apart from predictive policing, other AI technologies greatly improve investigative operations. Statistical learning patterns help to recognize Big Data of different natures, origins, and content, originating from social networks, financial transactions, and communication systems (Hardyns & Rummens, 2018). This capability enables investigators to discover links and leads that could be unnoticed when applying usual practices. AI supports the police in creating a more detailed case file and organizing the evaluation of the pieces of evidence, as well as helping to increase the general effectiveness of an investigation (Brown & Ballucci, 2024). Hence, they complete investigations faster and more efficiently, implying speedy case disposition. Facial recognition technology improves the capabilities of the police in the identification of suspects and the surveillance systems (Gawali & Sony, 2020). During major events, such as sports festivals or concerts, police may use AI technology to prevent and control crime because it is easier to identify criminals from a distance. In this way, due to the possibility of very fast identification, facial recognition can prevent potential incidents and guarantee a quick reaction from law enforcement officers (Bowers & Johnson, 2024). Where professionally administered, risk assessment algorithms improve criminal justice by analyzing defendants based on prior offences, age, gender, and behaviour (Završnik, 2021). Risk assessment tools may be beneficial for judges as well as the whole justice system because they provide them with better data in making decisions about bail, parole, and sentencing. This can go a long way in decreasing the chances of pre-trial detention and increasing productive advances for other discounted demographics (Hyatt & Chanenson, 2016). Also, risk assessment tools could check people who require reintroduction to the community through rehabilitation, hence enhancing the mission of coming up with tools that help in lowering recidivism rates.

AI can help enhance the liquidation of courts as a legal structure. AI also minimizes routine work entails case handling, document evaluation, and appointment setting, which generally takes time and a lot of effort (Kaur & Kaur, 2024). The AI technology development provides a significant opportunity to improve work efficiency. It helps to reduce the cost burden and focus on more strategic work. AI technology can easily handle technical and routine tasks like documentation, legal research, and data analysis. This can ultimately lead to increased productivity and overall profitability. However, there are some weaknesses in AI, which is yet not capable of handling more complex tasks such as deal structuring, negotiation, advocacy, and representation in court Automated services in law can help find legal precedents and cases, thus allowing attorneys to build cases far more effectively. Also, computerized court scheduling decreases the calendar clutter as it commonly leads to delays and improves the judicial experience of all participants (Madaoui, 2024).

AI is now transforming forensic science by enhancing ways of getting, displaying, as well as studying evidence such as DNA or fingerprints. It helps to produce reliable working results of evidence during the trials to provide fair trials that can make a positive impact on the societal perception that society holds about the criminal justice system (Galante et al., 2023). Data-sharing platforms bring efficiency and collaboration among police departments that are executed by AI. It provides working access to active cases and criminal trends, which helps to facilitate collaboration as well as create a synergy approach to security. (Velasco, 2022)

Apart from utilitarian ambitions, the use of AI in the criminal justice system contributes to increasing the amount of accountability and oversight through tracking and auditing of decisions made error-free (Završnik, 2020). AI can be made to provide explanations to various stakeholders and allow for complaints that may lead to its fairness; hence, making the criminal justice system more credible (Sarirete et al., 2022). Furthermore, AI provides justice that is distinct since it divides the huge case data and evaluates the defendant's actions and their consequences. This approach assists in the choice of specific rehabilitation activities to minimize the chance of a repeated offender's return to criminal activities to promote a humanistic justice system (Taylor, 2023). AI application is consistent with the restorative justice focus on handling harm to victims and offenders. Determining criminal causal conditions increases the participation of the community, enhances a reduced team rate, and makes offenders accountable (Sayyed, 2024). There is much to be stated for the application of these technologies in criminal justice, but their deployment must be undertaken in a principled manner (Khan & Lucas, 2023). AI policies should be created so justice can be served, meaning equal opportunities for the public and human rights be protected. Governments and organizations are required to collectively set about defining AI applications according to challenge-reward ratios by which requisite advances must be pursued.

Challenges and Risks

The implementation of AI tools in the criminal justice system brings up rhetorical questions to make every responsibility achieved while fulfilling the demand without compromising the rights of the people or deepening social stratification (Bharati, 2024). Increased use of AI technologies in law enforcement, courts, and corrections necessitates recognition of drawbacks connected with their application and is likely to distort the principles of natural justice and civil rights (Limantė, 2023). There are several prevailing and emerging issues with the use of AI in this respect, none the least of which is the problem of bias and partiality that characterizes most AI systems. Such systems are typically designed to operate based on least or greatest squares regression, which is learned from datasets containing prejudice and discrimination endemic in society (Borenstein & Howard, 2021). In the same way, if an algorithm used for predictive policing is trained from crime data that is instructed to specific groups of people, then the algorithm is also going to make predictions that discriminate against those groups who are more vulnerable. Among them, it dangerously results in the over-criminalization of other vulnerable groups to have the margins insisted upon in criminal justice (Bennett Moses & Chan, 2016). When bias occurs in AI, it affects several accuracies in its predictions; in addition, it generates injustice concerns in fairness and justice because some individuals may be inconvenienced by wrong data from the algorithms (Ferrara, 2023).

Another important risk is that many AI systems are often *black boxes* without a clear understanding of how they can make decisions. They are also termed '*black boxes*', meaning they work in directions that are hard to comprehend the developers themselves. Where choices on the liberty of an individual arrest, bail, or sentencing are made on the results of arguably *black box* algorithms, it becomes a big issue and challenge for accountability and responsibility (Hagendorff & Wezel, 2020). While an algorithm may label a certain person as a potential offender or wrongly identify a suspect in a certain crime, such an individual will struggle to challenge such determination. Such challenges are setbacks, particularly to the fair trial and due process, as some important decisions that may influence one's life are not explained (Stinson, 2022).

Therefore, the use of AI technologies also amplifies the notions of surveillance and privileges. While using a variety of smart tools and technologies, including facial recognition technology, law enforcement agencies are raising the issue of mass surveillance and violation of civil liberties (Hill et al., 2022). Excessive use of such technologies can be unjust in harassing innocent people, often violating their constitutional right to assembly or speech. While collecting sensitive data, the apprehension of privacy violations, discrimination, bias, ethical questions, and other security threats that AI poses are challenging and unanswered (Power et al., 2021). Other questions relate to the effect that the use of AI has on public accountability in the sphere of criminal justice. Whenever the AI systems cause wrongful arrests, identification, sentencing, or unjust punishments, no one is fully to blame (Bharati, 2024). It is developers, police, and judicial systems that are primarily held to be responsible for these outcomes. Where the agencies fail to define their guidelines, they lose the support of the public, thereby leaving individuals helpless to AI decisions. This can only be possible through coming up with the desired external audits and accountability to determine the levels of trust required (Mökander, 2023).

Another major concern is the risk that new forms of AI technologies are likely to deepen social inequalities (von Braun et al., 2021). Where fundamental resources are hard to come by the use of these higher forms of AI becomes the basis for inequality. Some regions can afford to develop impressive AI systems that boost policing and investigation capacities, as contrasted to cash-strapped regions that cannot (Khanal, Zhang, & Taeihagh, 2024). Primarily, surveillance can make low-income communities tolerant of overly policing, which distorts justice disparities and opportunities and may AI algorithms to be wrong or contain biases (Nishant et al., 2024). When the AI systems attain some failure, they may cause wrongful convictions or inadequate protections, which affects lives. To address these issues to increase accuracy and reliability or causal control poses a staggering and costly issue in criminal justice (Min, 2023). Furthermore, the rate of innovative technologies, such as in the production of AI, is increasingly becoming very fast, while the rates at which the legal structures required to moderate the use of AI are progressive. There is a clear absence of adequate framework legislation or up-to-date policy regarding many aspects of the use of AI technologies in the criminal justice system (Mohamed, 2023). It makes the utilization of AI patchy because agencies can adopt the technologies without understanding or following key standards. These findings call for attention to the development of strong legal and policy solutions that will cultivate the proper guidelines concerning the use of artificial intelligence concerning data protection, algorithms, and the use of AI in policing and judiciary organs (Neumann et al., 2022).

As we know, AI applies equally to criminal justice systems and brings considerable ethical and safety questions. With the continuous surge in the usage of AI systems, there is an urgent need for separate legislation to regulate AI to eliminate in-built bias and other ethical concerns (Steyvers & Kumar, 2024). The overdependance on reinsures fails to call for responsibility where individuals allow algorithms to work and make decisions without critically analyzing their outcomes. AI's orientation should serve as a middle ground with an intention for the human touch in the delivery of justice with par precedence to more efficiency (Mikalef et al., 2022). Moreover, the dynamic development of AI makes it impossible to apply them unchanged for police work. However, due to the lack of manpower and knowledge, some of these changes may be very difficult for law enforcement agencies to handle (Taherdoost & Madanchian, 2024). Both initial and continued education of professionals are major factors within the proper implementation of AI into the criminal justice system.

Criminal justice AI adoption also depends on cultural or societal mentality related to AI. The public has always seen or has doubts about using AI technologies, especially in law enforcement authorities, mostly because of bias, privacy, as well as accountability (Bharati, 2024). These two concerns cannot be addressed without community engagement and specifically, accurate information dissemination. Civil rights organizations and interdisciplinary cooperation from technologists, legal advisors, and ethicists can positively address ethically conducting Artificial Intelligence within the criminal justice system (Cachat-Rosset & Klarsfeld, 2023). Finally, more constant evaluations of AI's effect on criminal justice are critical. New technologies have to be associated with new policies. The potential threat of bias in AI systems can undermine the judicial verdicts because the outcome from AI can merely reflect existing historical and social inequalities that are deeply rooted in society, such as caste, gender, race, religion, and ideology, producing outcomes that do not reflect true merit. Therefore, performance, bias, and community impacts in the AI function facilitate its operation while aligning with rights and equities (Min, 2023). The encouraging factor is that this commitment to the ongoing evaluation of the system can lead to the development of a culture of accountability and transparency through the criminal justice system.

Human Rights Implications

The use of AI in the criminal justice system has legal consequences for human rights and therefore raises relevant questions on how human rights are protected and enforced as the criminal justice system transforms through the use of technology (Završnik, 2020). Since decision-making areas crucial to human rights finally begin to incorporate AI into their everyday work (policing, sentencing, parole), relevance and a desire to understand how AI affects human rights become important since human rights should not work for the benefit of technological progress (Stahl et al., 2023).

Leading these concerns is the right to privacy and other allied safety concerns. Most of the AI systems, especially those that include authorization and data gathering, are poised to hinder personal privilege. For instance, although facial recognition systems used in public areas may be used to identify culprits, they act as surveillance cameras that follow people against their wishes (Martin & Zimmermann, 2024). People have civil and political liberties to privacy and the states still have the right to surveillance, which has the adverse effect of lessening speech and public demonstrations against the government (Power et al., 2021). Third, the application of AI in a predictive police system brings about human rights issues of a discriminatory nature. It noted that systems developed for the analysis of crime statistics over the past years only give out profane results, which also contribute to bias on the part of the police force (Castets-Renard, 2021). If an AI system is trained on data reflecting discrimination practices, such as over-policing certain races or ethnicities practiced in the past, the algorithm may continue to target such groups, thus increasing rates of profiling of marginalized groups (Chen, 2023). This does not only perpetrate social injustice but also discrimination, which is fundamental to human rights law. The social injustices could potentially produce disparities that need to be fully studied so that such disparities can not lead to the misuse and abuse of AI systems.

Establishing accountability for technology-related errors in the legal field can be a challenging task. The implications of errors made by AI systems shall have huge ramifications affecting the life and liberty of individuals. However, proactive measures can be taken by legislators and industry experts from legal or other fields to set clear lines of responsibility and to ensure accountability when using AI in their practice (Belenguer, 2022).

When it comes to the criminal justice system, another important protection of individual rights that is potentially regulated by AI is the right to a fair trial (Bharati, 2024). Decision support systems, such as a risk assessment score used during a sentencing or a bail hearing, might not be just (Ulenaers, 2020). If these tools base their measures on skewed data or skewed algorithms, they might target particular individuals or communities who are at high risk of reoffending, giving them unfair punishments or denying them bail when they should be granted. As a result, people can be penalized based not on a discrete evaluation of the case in front of them but on the performance of an algorithm that affects a fair trial since some defendants acquire a verdict based on their likely behavior rather than their actions or conditions indicated by the algorithms (Taylor, 2023). Furthermore, consequential defendant setbacks are evoked in criminal justice since the AI systems used render decision-making processes irreprehensible and, therefore, it becomes difficult for defendants to query the AI decisions made that are arrived at without their prior knowledge in violation of the laid down due process and fairness (Završnik, 2021).

As crucial components of law as a social phenomenon understanding and critically engaging with how legal decisions are made is cardinal for the achievement of justice and protection of human rights (Priel, 2019). They also pose a considerable human rights risk in the circumstance of applying AI in criminal justice because they too can lead to wrongful convictions. With more and more advanced technologies engaging in investigations and decisions, human beings are more vulnerable to facing more chances of error-orientated wrong conclusions (Raso et al., 2018). Sometimes, face recognition technology has been found inaccurate, especially when identifying members of a specific gender, colour, or race. These misidentifications result in wrongful arrests, prosecutions, and convictions and are existential violations of the right to liberty and security (Rodrigues, 2020). Besides the psychological and social consequences for the victims of AI decisions, they suffer public disgrace, traumatic experiences, and the consequences of an unfair legal process (Gordon, 2021).

AI technologies also have the potential to reduce legal safeguards against *Torture and Other Ill-treatments*. It means that where AI is used in the gathering of evidence or questioning suspects, people can be forced into provoking the AI into an aggressive mode to release data on them (Henz, 2021). For instance, if AI systems are employed in determining the effectiveness of interrogation and maximizing the rate used to get confessions, there is a high propensity to use torture or humane methods to secure confessions. This erodes the absolute ban on torture as provided by international human rights law and other International Instruments that lead to gross violations of human rights (Journals, I. A. E. S., 2024).

In the context of criminal justice, it is apparent that the direct application of AI in technologies has potential dangers and drawbacks. Many assessment tools in risk assessment may not capture the requirements of these groups and may thus be predisposed to producing negative consequences that are disproportionate to the situation (Bhalla et al., 2023). The developers must be aware of these intensities to control AI systems and to avoid any enlargement of the existing discriminations affecting human beings.

With AI technologies being integrated into the criminal justice systems of many countries, these practices need to be closely brought into compliance with human rights standards. The States have necessary obligation commitments to uphold principles like transparency, accountability, and non-discrimination (Bharati, 2024). Failing to achieve the above-mentioned commitments is unlawful in domestic law and contrary to international human rights protocols. To counter these implications, robust rules that would define AI implementation in criminal justice are needed. The future developments of such frameworks should incorporate human rights to avoid misuse of AI technologies (Trotta et al., 2023).

These may include requirements for the openness of AI systems that AI systems should be thoroughly pre-checked for biases and that methods should be in constant check for the effects of the utilization of AI tools on different groups of people. Raising awareness and legal-vocational training for police forces and judicial officers on ethical AI use is also required (Ghallab, 2019). The benefits of autonomy can be achieved by providing knowledge and skills that allow making the appropriate decision by embracing the idea of critical understanding of tools that are being used relating to human rights. Besides, the awareness creation of AI and human rights must be made to the public to ensure they are in a position to self-govern and know their rights and what is in store for them from AI in police work (Prem, 2023). Last but not least, the international community has to play an active role in tackling human rights about AI in criminal justice systems (Zaidan & Ibrahim, 2024). An example of such global cooperation is the effort aimed at the development of the indicated common standards and best practices for ethical approaches to the use of AI technologies that would help create the legal basis for the improvement of the application of technology in criminal justice and respecting the human identity and rights of each person.

Regulatory Frameworks

AI improves efficiency and the workflow's effectiveness in the criminal justice system but encourages crucial questions regarding power, justice, and rights, which must be answered transparently and with explainability for people's protection and trust (Selenko et al., 2022). This concept relates to the dissemination of processes, data, and thus decision-making information to various entities, such as law enforcement agencies, practitioners, and the public. More so, the use of such sensitive areas as predictive policing requires high levels of transparency to avoid issues of bias and the resulting unfair outcomes in arrests and sentencing (Shin et al., 2022).

This is especially true in times of landmark events like arrests or sentencing and is supposed to call for accountability within criminal justice processes. AI should also be transparent because biased predictive policing unfairly targets some demographics (Chiao, 2019). It suggests that transparency, as found in the explainability of AI systems, warrants accountability. Explicit organizational ownership of algorithmic decisions in unlawful arrests or increased imprisonment illustrates that authorities are held responsible for the rule of law (Balasubramaniam et al., 2023). As AI is viewed as a new tool in criminal justice, some important legal consequences described above point to the requirement of interpretability and, therefore, the need for judges, juries, and defense attorneys to know how exactly AI operates to define whether it can be trustworthy in legal procedures (Taylor, 2023). As discussed, the deployment of AI systems relies on public confidence in their functionality; the public must understand AI functions. Knowledge of AI's function in police functioning can help in cooperation and handling of issues such as surveillance, discrimination, and racism (Alhosani & Alhashmi, 2024).

While there are benefits to criminal justice, cohesive human control is crucial in complementing its blindness. It is important to apply moral values and human rights in final decision-making; where the AI offers jurisprudential suggestions to the judge and policeman concerned (Rodrigues, 2020).

A concern of AI in criminal justice is the training of algorithms using prejudiced data, for example in predictive policing to target a particular colour or race. Human intervention is crucial to prevent discrimination in the results achieved. Therefore, to develop solutions that are understandable and explainable to other humans, human participation in the procedures is important (Ryberg, 2024). This has made most AI systems work like '*black boxes*,' and it is difficult for people to understand why they have been released on bail or given such or such a jail term (Chinu & Bansal, 2024). Supervisory involvement in the various decision-making-related processes makes accountability high and the rights of individuals respected. When we can specify actions based on any AI recommendation and assign responsibility accordingly, we will be enhancing the possibilities of good law and order, as well as citizen's confidence in the fairness of the justice system (Novelli et al., 2024).

Supervision by humans preserves principles of procedural fairness of handling individuals within the legal category regardless of their violations. When AI is inserted into the criminal justice system, we have to maintain principles of fairness to avoid possible discrimination. The involvement of the people ensures that the legal provisions are followed fairly, which enhances the chances of efficient due process delivery (Starke et al., 2022). Furthermore, it ensures a very strong harmony between technology and the legal profession to improve law enforcement techniques, provide improved legal services, and thus promote the advances and overall criminal justice system (Tsamados et al., 2024). As evidenced, enhanced human supervision for the AI-deployed approaches calls for skills and tools for legal professionals, police, and judiciary. They have to be able to understand the AI outcomes, examine the bias, and come to reasonable conclusions (Reverberi et al., 2022). Sensitization, ethical principles, and successful auditing and testing of artificial intelligence structures are some of the key aspects of protecting minority rights in the criminal justice system. AI systems are vulnerable, like any other system, to be programmed using datasets that contain prejudice and discrimination (Guembe et al., 2022). These biases hence require consistent audits so that measures to prevent them from causing harm can be implemented. The recommendation of bias in the historical trend is appropriate; no race or ethnicity should be considered risky without proper reason (de Manuel et al., 2023).

The issue of rules is paramount in the auditing and testing of Artificial Intelligence systems (Mökander, 2023). There is a need to enact laws that would make sense of different data sets that qualify, who is accountable, and how and when the data can be released in the name of fair AI. Independent auditors improve the level of transparency, people monitoring, and proper audits and guarantee individual rights in the criminal justice system (Tallberg et al., 2023).

CONCLUSION

This chapter tried to assess the prospects and risks offered by the integration of artificial intelligence in the criminal justice system. For the challenges of policing & courts, AI can improve the efficiency and productivity of policing and courts, but its use paves the way for violation of human rights matters to do with privacy, procedural fairness, equity, as well as accountability. Technological intervention is as good as the civil liberties that must be protected in any society to ensure that justice prevails.

One of the main problems of AI in criminal justice is the enhancement of prejudice and discrimination. When trained on biased datasets, more often of a historical nature, as has been the case with automated decision-making systems like those used in the areas of policing and facial recognition, AI only serves to perpetuate bias. It is imperative that proper utilization of the laws be exercised to achieve fair and equal application in the current society. Based on these, this chapter suggested a multipronged approach to AI regulation in the context of the criminal Justice System to increase the fairness of the process. It is very important because most of the artificial intelligence systems work in a rather untransparent manner; in other words, they contain *black box* elements that are not quite clear. It also interferes with people's rights to appeal against the decision made regarding them; it denies people their rights to be heard fairly; it destroys people's confidence in the judicial system. Hence, AI systems must be applied to the arena of criminal justice to express a high level of explainability. Local authorities and designers should come up with ways of how they shall be making decisions that are understandable so that users can dispute unfair decisions made by AI. This is so because it is important as AI is gradually becoming more involved in decision-making processes such as risk assessments and sentencing, among others, in criminal justice systems. If an AI system makes a faulty decision resulting in a wrongful conviction, for example, in a trial, One can assign blame to either developers, law enforcement agencies, or the government. Legal structures of AI responsibility provide human supervision in decision-making processes, keep the human factor in the justice domain, and enable the stakeholders to assess AI results and correct them if necessary.

Ethics has to be at the core of AI in criminal justice. Developers should accept the fact that any technology created by people can always contain preconceived prejudices. Police officials and developers must consider the ethical consequences of artificial intelligence for minorities and vulnerable subjects. They should fix the strong rules and use the independent boards to control the AI in accordance with human rights, justice, and equality.

Today, the regulation of the application of AI in police and judicial services is limited because many jurisdictions lack legislation on the subject. Governments should also come up with new legislation that is likely to direct future trends in artificial intelligence to seize citizen's rights. Any laws falling under the big tent should include data acquisition, algorithmic fairness, bias assessments, and compliance with defined human rights. This is why legal regimes of artificial intelligence need international cooperation to make AI technology impartial. It is beneficial to work with counterparts around the world, and we can share ideologies, lessons and learning, and legal frameworks to improve justice as well as human rights. It will also be beneficial for a global audience, such as the United Nations or the European Union, to begin talking about the subject and develop norms on the usage of artificial intelligence in the criminal justice system.

The criminal justice system requires public participation and awareness to cover meanings within the regulation of Artificial Intelligence. People must be informed of what AI is and what rights they have? so that it will increase the level of trust. This means that once people comprehend the stochastic nature of artificial intelligence, they can participate in formulating laws that are effective for the welfare of the community as far as the use of knowledge-based technology is concerned.

REFERENCES

Alhosani, K., & Alhashmi, S. M. (2024). Opportunities, challenges, and benefits of AI innovation in government services: A review. *Discover Artificial Intelligence*, 4(1), 18. DOI: 10.1007/s44163-024-00111-w

Applegarth, D. M., Lewis, R. A., & Rief, R. M. (2023). Imperfect tools: A research note on developing, applying, and increasing understanding of criminal justice risk assessments. *Criminal Justice Policy Review*, 34(4), 319–336. DOI: 10.1177/08874034231180505

Balasubramaniam, N., Kauppinen, M., Rannisto, A., Hiekkanen, K., & Kujala, S. (2023). Transparency and explainability of AI systems: From ethical guidelines to requirements. *Information and Software Technology*, 159, 107197. DOI: 10.1016/j.infsof.2023.107197

Belenguer, L. (2022). AI bias: Exploring discriminatory algorithmic decision-making models and the application of possible machine-centric solutions adapted from the pharmaceutical industry. *AI and Ethics*, 2(4), 771–787. DOI: 10.1007/s43681-022-00138-8 PMID: 35194591

Bennett Moses, L., & Chan, J. (2016). Algorithmic prediction in policing: Assumptions, evaluation, and accountability. *Policing and Society*, 28(7), 806–822. DOI: 10.1080/10439463.2016.1253695

Bhalla, N., Brooks, L., & Leach, T. (2023). Ensuring a 'responsible' AI future in India: RRI as an approach for identifying the ethical challenges from an Indian perspective. *AI and Ethics*. Advance online publication. DOI: 10.1007/s43681-023-00370-w

Bharati, R. K. (2024). AI and the right to fair trial: Legal standards and technological advances. *International Journal of Science Academic Research*, 5(7), 7865–7867. http://www.scienceijsar.com

Borenstein, J., & Howard, A. (2021). Emerging challenges in AI and the need for AI ethics education. *AI and Ethics*, 1(1), 61–65. DOI: 10.1007/s43681-020-00002-7 PMID: 38624388

Bowers, K., & Johnson, S. (2024). Facing the future of crime: A framework for police use of technology. *The Political Quarterly*, 95(3), 480–488. DOI: 10.1111/1467-923X.13426

Brown, E., & Ballucci, D. (2024). Specialized knowledge: Understanding crime analysts' roles and responsibilities and the impact of their work. *Criminology & Criminal Justice*, 24(1), 3–19. DOI: 10.1177/17488958221095980

Cachat-Rosset, G., & Klarsfeld, A. (2023). Diversity, equity, and inclusion in artificial intelligence: An evaluation of guidelines. *Applied Artificial Intelligence*, 37(1), 2176618. Advance online publication. DOI: 10.1080/08839514.2023.2176618

Castets-Renard, C. (2021). Human rights and algorithmic impact assessment for predictive policing. In Micklitz, H.-W., Pollicino, O., Reichman, A., Simoncini, A., Sartor, G., & De Gregorio, G. (Eds.), *Constitutional challenges in the algorithmic society* (pp. 93–110). Cambridge University Press. DOI: 10.1017/9781108914857.007

Chen, Z. (2023). Ethics and discrimination in artificial intelligence-enabled recruitment practices. *Humanities & Social Sciences Communications*, 10(567), 567. Advance online publication. DOI: 10.1057/s41599-023-02079-x

Cheuk, T. (2021). Can AI be racist? Color-evasiveness in the application of machine learning to science assessments. *Science Education*, 105(5), 825–836. Advance online publication. DOI: 10.1002/sce.21671

Chiao, V. (2019). Fairness, accountability and transparency: Notes on algorithmic decision-making in criminal justice. *International Journal of Law in Context*, 15(2), 126–139. DOI: 10.1017/S1744552319000077

Chinu, B., & Bansal, U. (2024). Explainable AI: To reveal the logic of black-box models. *New Generation Computing*, 42(1), 53–87. DOI: 10.1007/s00354-022-00201-2

Datta, P. (2023). The promise and challenges of the fourth industrial revolution (4IR). *Journal of Information Technology Teaching Cases*, 13(1), 2–15. DOI: 10.1177/20438869211056938

de Fine Licht, K., & de Fine Licht, J. (2020). Artificial intelligence, transparency, and public decision-making. *AI & Society*, 35(4), 917–926. DOI: 10.1007/s00146-020-00960-w

de Manuel, A., Delgado, J., Parra Jounou, I., Ausín, T., Casacuberta, D., Cruz, M., Guersenzvaig, A., Moyano, C., Rodríguez-Arias, D., Rueda, J., & Puyol, A. (2023). Ethical assessments and mitigation strategies for biases in AI-systems used during the COVID-19 pandemic. *Big Data & Society*, 10(1), 20539517231179199. Advance online publication. DOI: 10.1177/20539517231179199

Ferrara, E. (2023). Fairness and bias in artificial intelligence: A brief survey of sources, impacts, and mitigation strategies. *JMIR Preprints*, 21, 48399. https://doi.org/DOI: 10.2196/preprints.48399

Galante, N., Cotroneo, R., Furci, D., Lodetti, G., & Casali, M. B. (2023). Applications of artificial intelligence in forensic sciences: Current potential benefits, limitations, and perspectives. *International Journal of Legal Medicine*, 137(2), 445–458. DOI: 10.1007/s00414-022-02928-5 PMID: 36507961

Gawali, P., & Sony, R. (2020). The role of artificial intelligence in improving the criminal justice system: Indian perspective. *Legal Issues in the Digital Age*, 3(3), 78–96. DOI: 10.17323/2713-2749.2020.3.78.96

Gentzel, M. (2021). Biased face recognition technology used by government: A problem for liberal democracy. *Philosophy & Technology*, 34(4), 1639–1663. DOI: 10.1007/s13347-021-00478-z PMID: 34603941

Ghallab, M. (2019). Responsible AI: Requirements and challenges. *AI Perspectives*, 1(3), 3. Advance online publication. DOI: 10.1186/s42467-019-0003-z

Gordon, J. S. (2021). AI and law: Ethical, legal, and socio-political implications. *AI & Society*, 36(2), 403–404. DOI: 10.1007/s00146-021-01194-0

Guembe, B., Azeta, A., Misra, S., Osamor, V. C., Fernández-Sanz, L., & Pospelova, V. (2022). The emerging threat of AI-driven cyber attacks: A review. *Applied Artificial Intelligence*, 36(1), 2037254. Advance online publication. DOI: 10.1080/08839514.2022.2037254

Hagendorff, T., & Wezel, K. (2020). 15 challenges for AI: Or what AI (currently) can't do. *AI & Society*, 35(2), 355–365. DOI: 10.1007/s00146-019-00886-y

Hardyns, W., & Rummens, A. (2018). Predictive policing as a new tool for law enforcement? Recent developments and challenges. *European Journal on Criminal Policy and Research*, 24(2), 201–218. DOI: 10.1007/s10610-017-9361-2

Hasan, A., Brown, S., Davidovic, J., Lange, B., & Regan, M. (2022). Algorithmic bias and risk assessments: Lessons from practice. *Digital Society : Ethics, Socio-Legal and Governance of Digital Technology*, 1(2), 14. DOI: 10.1007/s44206-022-00017-z

Henz, P. (2021). Ethical and legal responsibility for Artificial Intelligence. *Discover Artificial Intelligence*, 1(2), 2. Advance online publication. DOI: 10.1007/s44163-021-00002-4

Hill, D., O'Connor, C. D., & Slane, A. (2022). Police use of facial recognition technology: The potential for engaging the public through co-constructed policy-making. *International Journal of Police Science & Management*, 24(3), 325–335. DOI: 10.1177/14613557221089558

Hitch, D. (2024). Artificial intelligence augmented qualitative analysis: The way of the future? *Qualitative Health Research*, 34(7), 595–606. DOI: 10.1177/10497323231217392 PMID: 38064244

Hyatt, J., & Chanenson, S. L. (2016). The use of risk assessment at sentencing: Implications for research and policy (Villanova Law/Public Policy Research Paper No. 2017-1040). *SSRN*. https://ssrn.com/abstract=2961288

Ibegbulam, C., Olowonubi, F., Fatounde, P., & Oyegunwa, P. (2023). Artificial intelligence in the era of 4IR: Drivers, challenges, and opportunities. *Engineering Science & Technology Journal*, 4(6), 473–488. DOI: 10.51594/estj.v4i6.668

Jansen, F., Sánchez-Monedero, J., & Dencik, L. (2021). Biometric identity systems in law enforcement and the politics of (voice) recognition: The case of SiiP. *Big Data & Society*, 8(2). Advance online publication. DOI: 10.1177/20539517211063604

Journals, I. A. E. S. (2024). The use of artificial intelligence in interrogations: Voluntary confession. *IAES International Journal of Robotics and Automation*, 13(2), 113–121. DOI: 10.11591/ijra.v13i2.pp113-121

Kabir, M. S., & Alam, M. N. (2023). The role of AI technology for legal research and decision making. *Journal Title*, 10, 2395–0056.

Kaur, N., & Kaur, M. (2024). Role of artificial intelligence in the Indian courts. *International Journal of Law. Policy and Social Review*, 6(1), 17–20.

Kehl, D., Guo, P., & Kessler, S. (2017). *Algorithms in the criminal justice system: Assessing the use of risk assessments in sentencing*. Responsive Communities Initiative, Berkman Klein Center for Internet & Society, Harvard Law School. http://nrs.harvard.edu/urn-3:HUL.InstRepos:3374604

Khan, D., & Lucas, M. (2023). The impact of technology on the criminal justice system.

Khanal, S., Zhang, H., & Taeihagh, A. (2024). Building an AI ecosystem in a small nation: Lessons from Singapore's journey to the forefront of AI. *Humanities & Social Sciences Communications*, 11(1), 866. DOI: 10.1057/s41599-024-03289-7

Kostka, G., Steinacker, L., & Meckel, M. (2021). Between security and convenience: Facial recognition technology in the eyes of citizens in China, Germany, the United Kingdom, and the United States. *Public Understanding of Science (Bristol, England)*, 30(6), 671–690. DOI: 10.1177/09636625211001555 PMID: 33769157

Koulu, R. (2020). Proceduralizing control and discretion: Human oversight in artificial intelligence policy. *Maastricht Journal of European and Comparative Law*, 27(6), 720–735. DOI: 10.1177/1023263X20978649

Laqueur, H. S., & Copus, R. W. (2024). An algorithmic assessment of parole decisions. *Journal of Quantitative Criminology*, 40(1), 151–188. DOI: 10.1007/s10940-022-09563-8

Lee, Y., Bradford, B., & Posch, K. (2024). The Effectiveness of Big Data-Driven Predictive Policing: Systematic Review. *Justice Evaluation Journal*, 1–34. https://doi.org/DOI: 10.1080/24751979.2024.2371781

Li, L., Mu, X., Li, S., & Peng, H. (2020). A review of face recognition technology. *IEEE Access : Practical Innovations, Open Solutions*, 8, 139110–139120. DOI: 10.1109/ACCESS.2020.3011028

Limantė, A. (2023). Bias in facial recognition technologies used by law enforcement: Understanding the causes and searching for a way out. *Nordic Journal of Human Rights*, 42(2), 115–134. DOI: 10.1080/18918131.2023.2277581

Madaoui, N. (2024). The impact of artificial intelligence on legal systems: Challenges and opportunities. *Problems of Legality*, 1(164), 285–303. DOI: 10.21564/2414-990X.164.289266

Mandalapu, V., Elluri, L., Vyas, P., & Roy, N. (2023). Crime prediction using machine learning and deep learning: A systematic review and future directions. *IEEE Access : Practical Innovations, Open Solutions*, 1(1), 1–1. DOI: 10.1109/ACCESS.2023.3286344

Martin, K. D., & Zimmermann, J. (2024). Artificial intelligence and its implications for data privacy. *Current Opinion in Psychology*, 58, 101829. DOI: 10.1016/j.copsyc.2024.101829 PMID: 38954851

Marwala, T., & Mpedi, L. G. (2024). Criminal justice system and AI. In *Artificial intelligence and the law* (pp. 1–15). Palgrave Macmillan. DOI: 10.1007/978-981-97-2827-5_3

Meijer, A., & Wessels, M. (2019). Predictive Policing: Review of Benefits and Drawbacks. *International Journal of Public Administration*, 42(12), 1031–1039. DOI: 10.1080/01900692.2019.1575664

Meterko, V., & Cooper, G. (2022). Cognitive biases in criminal case evaluation: A review of the research. *Journal of Police and Criminal Psychology*, 37(1), 101–122. DOI: 10.1007/s11896-020-09425-8

Mikalef, P., Conboy, K., Lundström, J. E., & Popovič, A. (2022). Thinking responsibly about responsible AI and 'the dark side' of AI. *European Journal of Information Systems*, 31(3), 257–268. DOI: 10.1080/0960085X.2022.2026621

Min, A. (2023). Artificial intelligence and bias: Challenges, implications, and remedies. *Journal of Social Research*, 2(11), 3808–3817. DOI: 10.55324/josr.v2i11.1477

Mohamed, N. (2023). Current trends in AI and ML for cybersecurity: A state-of-the-art survey. *Cogent Engineering*, 10(2), 2272358. Advance online publication. DOI: 10.1080/23311916.2023.2272358

Mohsin, K. (2021). Artificial Intelligence in Forensic Science. SSRN Electronic Journal. DOI: 10.2139/ssrn.3910244

Mökander, J. (2023). Auditing of AI: Legal, ethical and technical approaches. *Digital Society : Ethics, Socio-Legal and Governance of Digital Technology*, 2(3), 49. DOI: 10.1007/s44206-023-00074-y

Mugari, I., & Obioha, E. E. (2021). Predictive policing and crime control in the United States of America and Europe: Trends in a decade of research and the future of predictive policing. *Social Sciences (Basel, Switzerland)*, 10(6), 234. DOI: 10.3390/socsci10060234

Neumann, O., Guirguis, K., & Steiner, R. (2022). Exploring artificial intelligence adoption in public organizations: A comparative case study. *Public Management Review*, 26(1), 114–141. DOI: 10.1080/14719037.2022.2048685

Nishant, R., Schneckenberg, D., & Ravishankar, M. (2024). The formal rationality of artificial intelligence-based algorithms and the problem of bias. *Journal of Information Technology*, 39(1), 19–40. DOI: 10.1177/02683962231176842

Novelli, C., Taddeo, M., & Floridi, L. (2024). Accountability in artificial intelligence: What it is and how it works. *AI & Society*, 39(4), 1871–1882. DOI: 10.1007/s00146-023-01635-y

Power, D. J., Heavin, C., & O'Connor, Y. (2021). Balancing privacy rights and surveillance analytics: A decision process guide. *Journal of Business Analytics*, 4(2), 155–170. DOI: 10.1080/2573234X.2021.1920856

Prem, E. (2023). From ethical AI frameworks to tools: A review of approaches. *AI and Ethics*, 3(3), 699–716. DOI: 10.1007/s43681-023-00258-9

Priel, D. (2019). Law as a social construction and conceptual legal theory. *Articles & Book Chapters*, 2751. https://digitalcommons.osgoode.yorku.ca/scholarly_works/275

Raso, F., Hilligoss, H., Krishnamurthy, V., Bavitz, C., & Kim, L. Y. (2018). *Artificial intelligence & human rights: Opportunities & risks*. Berkman Klein Center Research Publication No. 2018-6. https://doi.org/DOI: 10.2139/ssrn.3259344

Resnik, D. B., & Hosseini, M. (2024). The ethics of using artificial intelligence in scientific research: New guidance needed for a new tool. *AI and Ethics*. Advance online publication. DOI: 10.1007/s43681-024-00493-8

Reverberi, C., Rigon, T., Solari, A., Hassan, C., Cherubini, P., Antonelli, G., Awadie, H., Bernhofer, S., Carballal, S., Dinis-Ribeiro, M., Fernández-Clotett, A., Esparrach, G. F., Gralnek, I., Higasa, Y., Hirabayashi, T., Hirai, T., Iwatate, M., Kawano, M., Mader, M., & Cherubini, A. (2022). Experimental evidence of effective human–AI collaboration in medical decision-making. *Scientific Reports*, 12(1), 14952. DOI: 10.1038/s41598-022-18751-2 PMID: 36056152

Rodrigues, R. (2020). Legal and human rights issues of AI: Gaps, challenges and vulnerabilities. *Journal of Responsible Technology*, 4, 100005. DOI: 10.1016/j.jrt.2020.100005

Ryberg, J. (2024). Criminal justice and artificial intelligence: How should we assess the performance of sentencing algorithms? *Philosophy & Technology*, 37(1), 9. DOI: 10.1007/s13347-024-00694-3

Sachoulidou, A. (2024). Harnessing AI for law enforcement: Solutions and boundaries from the forthcoming AI Act. *New Journal of European Criminal Law*, 15(2), 117–125. DOI: 10.1177/20322844241260114

Sarirete, A., Balfagih, Z., Brahimi, T., Lytras, M. D., & Visvizi, A. (2022). Artificial intelligence and machine learning research: Towards digital transformation at a global scale. *Journal of Ambient Intelligence and Humanized Computing*, 13(7), 3319–3321. DOI: 10.1007/s12652-021-03168-y

Sayyed, H. (2024). Artificial intelligence and criminal liability in India: Exploring legal implications and challenges. *Cogent Social Sciences*, 10(1), 2343195. Advance online publication. DOI: 10.1080/23311886.2024.2343195

Selenko, E., Bankins, S., Shoss, M., Warburton, J., & Restubog, S. L. D. (2022). Artificial intelligence and the future of work: A functional-identity perspective. *Current Directions in Psychological Science*, 31(3), 272–279. DOI: 10.1177/09637214221091823

Shin, D., Hameleers, M., Park, Y. J., Kim, J. N., Trielli, D., Diakopoulos, N., Helberger, N., Lewis, S. C., Westlund, O., & Baumann, S. (2022). Countering algorithmic bias and disinformation and effectively harnessing the power of AI in media. *Journalism & Mass Communication Quarterly*, 99(4), 887–907. DOI: 10.1177/10776990221129245

Smith, M., & Miller, S. (2022). The ethical application of biometric facial recognition technology. *AI & Society*, 37(1), 167–175. DOI: 10.1007/s00146-021-01199-9 PMID: 33867693

Stahl, B. C., Brooks, L., Hatzakis, T., Santiago, N., & Wright, D. (2023). Exploring ethics and human rights in artificial intelligence – A Delphi study. *Technological Forecasting and Social Change*, 191, 122502. DOI: 10.1016/j.techfore.2023.122502

Starke, C., Baleis, J., Keller, B., & Marcinkowski, F. (2022). Fairness perceptions of algorithmic decision-making: A systematic review of the empirical literature. *Big Data & Society*, 9(2). Advance online publication. DOI: 10.1177/20539517221115189

Steyvers, M., & Kumar, A. (2024). Three challenges for AI-assisted decision-making. *Perspectives on Psychological Science*, 19(5), 722–734. DOI: 10.1177/17456916231181102 PMID: 37439761

Stinson, C. (2022). Algorithms are not neutral. *AI and Ethics*, 2(4), 763–770. DOI: 10.1007/s43681-022-00136-w PMID: 35128540

Sushina, T., & Sobenin, A. (2020). Artificial intelligence in the criminal justice system: Leading trends and possibilities. *Proceedings of the 3rd International Scientific Conference Social and Cultural Transformations in the Context of Modern Globalism*. DOI: 10.2991/assehr.k.200526.062

Taherdoost, H., & Madanchian, M. (2024). AI advancements: Comparison of innovative techniques. *AI*, 5(1), 38–54. DOI: 10.3390/ai5010003

Tallberg, J., Erman, E., Furendal, M., Geith, J., Klamberg, M., & Lundgren, M. (2023). The global governance of artificial intelligence: Next steps for empirical and normative research. *International Studies Review*, 25(3), viad040. Advance online publication. DOI: 10.1093/isr/viad040

Taylor, I. (2023). Justice by algorithm: The limits of AI in criminal sentencing. *Criminal Justice Ethics*, 42(3), 193–213. DOI: 10.1080/0731129X.2023.2275967

Trotta, A., Ziosi, M., & Lomonaco, V. (2023). The future of ethics in AI: Challenges and opportunities. *AI & Society*, 38(2), 439–441. DOI: 10.1007/s00146-023-01644-x

Tsamados, A., Aggarwal, N., Cowls, J., Morley, J., Roberts, H., Taddeo, M., & Floridi, L. (2022). The ethics of algorithms: Key problems and solutions. *AI & Society*, 37(1), 215–230. DOI: 10.1007/s00146-021-01154-8

Tsamados, A., Floridi, L., & Taddeo, M. (2024). Human control of AI systems: From supervision to teaming. *AI and Ethics*. Advance online publication. DOI: 10.1007/s43681-024-00489-4

Tynan, P. (2024). The integration and implications of artificial intelligence in forensic science. *Forensic Science, Medicine, and Pathology*, 20(3), 1103–1105. Advance online publication. DOI: 10.1007/s12024-023-00772-6 PMID: 38175310

Ulenaers, J. (2020). The impact of artificial intelligence on the right to a fair trial: Towards a robot judge? *Asian Journal of Law and Economics*, 11(2), 20200008. DOI: 10.1515/ajle-2020-0008

Urquhart, L., & Miranda, D. (2021). Policing faces: The present and future of intelligent facial surveillance. *Information & Communications Technology Law*, 31(2), 194–219. DOI: 10.1080/13600834.2021.1994220

Velasco, C. (2022). Cybercrime and artificial intelligence: An overview of the work of international organizations on criminal justice and the international applicable instruments. *ERA Forum*, 23, 109–126. https://doi.org/DOI: 10.1007/s12027-022-00702-z

von Braun, J., Archer, M. S., Reichberg, G. M., & Sánchez Sorondo, M. (2021). AI, robotics, and humanity: Opportunities, risks, and implications for ethics and policy. In von Braun, J., Archer, M. S., Reichberg, G. M., & Sánchez Sorondo, M. (Eds.), *Robotics, AI, and humanity* (pp. 1–20). Springer., DOI: 10.1007/978-3-030-54173-6_1

Wang, X., Wu, Y. C., Zhou, M., & Fu, H. (2024). Beyond surveillance: Privacy, ethics, and regulations in face recognition technology. *Frontiers in Big Data*, 7, 1337465. Advance online publication. DOI: 10.3389/fdata.2024.1337465 PMID: 39027377

Xu, Y., Liu, X., Cao, X., Huang, C., Liu, E., Qian, S., Liu, X., Wu, Y., Dong, F., Qiu, C.-W., Qiu, J., Hua, K., Su, W., Wu, J., Xu, H., Han, Y., Fu, C., Yin, Z., Liu, M., & Zhang, J. (2021). Artificial intelligence: A powerful paradigm for scientific research. *Innovation (Cambridge (Mass.))*, 2(4), 100179. DOI: 10.1016/j.xinn.2021.100179 PMID: 34877560

Zaidan, E., & Ibrahim, I. A. (2024). AI governance in a complex and rapidly changing regulatory landscape: A global perspective. *Humanities & Social Sciences Communications*, 11(1), 1121. DOI: 10.1057/s41599-024-03560-x

Završnik, A. (2020). Criminal justice, artificial intelligence systems, and human rights. *ERA Forum, 20*(3), 567–583. DOI: 10.1007/s12027-020-00602-0

Zhang, Y., Wu, M., Tian, G. Y., Zhang, G., & Lu, J. (2021). Ethics and privacy of artificial intelligence: Understandings from bibliometrics. *Knowledge-Based Systems*, 222, 106994. DOI: 10.1016/j.knosys.2021.106994

Chapter 5
Empowering Gender Equality and Justice Through AI:
Overcoming Ethical Barriers

Souvik Dhar
https://orcid.org/0000-0002-5472-9193
Brainware University, India

Madhurima Dasgupta
Abo-Akademi University, Finland

Bhupinder Singh
https://orcid.org/0009-0006-4779-2553
Sharda University, India

ABSTRACT

This chapter delves into the relationship between artificial intelligence (AI) and gender equality by exploring how AI can both empower gender balance and perpetuate biases and underrepresentation issues simultaneously in society worldwide impacting women's access to education and job opportunities. AI can help in promoting fairness through improved data representation and personalized learning while also posing risks of reinforcing inequalities if not monitored carefully. This chapter examines the practices in AI and emphasizes the need to incorporate gender perspectives into the creation and advancement of AI technologies by promoting diversity. It argues for developing gender sensitive AI solutions that can systematically eliminate barriers and promote fairness in society. The chapter highlights the importance of cooperation between developers, policy makers, and educational bodies to utilize AI as a means, for promoting equality. The chapter focuses on the

DOI: 10.4018/979-8-3693-9395-6.ch005

need for ethical responsibilities to promote gender equality.

INTRODUCTION

The world is predominantly defined by gender inequality issues, where women still experience difficulties and marginalization in all spheres of life, from education and work to health delivery, leadership, and resource access. The world has digitized into something that Artificial Intelligence (AI) can develop and redefine the approach and response to the issue of inequalities. However, risks to the implementation of AI exist. The AI system risks can get amplified if it is not regulated. In light of this, the chapter attempts to examine these two natures of AI when it comes to gender equality: i) implementing the promise of fairness, equal opportunities and resource access provided by AI and ii) issues of algorithm bias, underrepresentation in tech development, and how AI also marginalizes intersectional identities (Binns, 2018). It is against such a background that the chapter will critically examine possibilities and limitations of AI as a way forward in the creation of gender-responsive AI systems that can actually make a difference in an increasingly equal society.

Gender inequality is still a current global issue that touches the lives of women in nearly every aspect (World Economic Forum, 2021). In education or employment, health or leadership, women are also held back by structural disadvantages that marginalise them and close doors. More recently, the digital revolution has presented us with technological change, most notably in the form of AI. AI has the potential to change many sectors of industry and create a more equal world, but it also carries unprecedented threats, not least if it's not regulated. In exploring this dualism, this chapter attempts to shed light on how AI can either create a more gender-equal world or reinforce current biases (O'Connor & Liu, 2024).

USE OF AI IN ADVANCING GENDER EQUALITY

The arrival of AI contains much potential to address gender inequity. Education is one where AI can actually make a real difference. AI-driven personalised learning systems can tailor itself to the individual needs of each child, potentially allowing girls in underprivileged communities to access bespoke learning assets. These systems can detect gaps in learning and provide support where girls may feel lacking in confidence. And not just that, but AI can narrow the gender gap in science, technology, engineering and mathematics (STEM) by supporting and guiding female students through mentoring initiatives and enhanced access to resources (Idris et al, 2024).

In the workforce, AI can be applied to identify and limit bias during the recruitment of personnel. Recruitment algorithms can be optimized to focus on job seekers' experience and qualifications, rather than gender (Drage & Mackereth, 2022). AI can also contribute to diversity at leadership levels, by exposing likely women candidates to the leadership ranks. If business companies can be taught to locate and advance women who possess skill sets and aptitudes that translate into leadership achievements using data about successful leaders, AI can provide fairer gender balance in the leadership ranks (Ezeugwa et al., 2024).

Healthcare is another field in which AI can facilitate gender balance (Frennert, 2021). Computer systems can analyze massive amounts of data to detect trends in the health of women, resulting in improved treatments and interventions. Healthcare practitioners can become better aware of women's peculiar health issues such as reproductive issues, mental conditions, and long-term diseases with such technologies (Frennert, 2021). By doing that, women can receive fairer care that caters to them.

CURRENT LANDSCAPE OF GENDER INEQUALITY

Even though there has been some improvement towards gender equality, huge gaps exist in most areas such as employment, remunerations, education and leadership positions. Among the most glaring examples is the underrepresentation of women in key fields, such as science and technology (World Economic Forum, 2023). Perhaps the biggest source of such a gap is the pervasive gender bias inherent in digital technologies, which is a reflection of deeper social biases (Campbell, 2020). For instance, women are frequently underrepresented in data used to train AI algorithms (Campbell, 2020). Such a diversity gap can yield algorithms that reinforce social inequalities and create a vicious cycle of making women even more disadvantaged in areas as vital as employment, health, and finance (Campbell, 2020).

It has been, so far, the research that has especially attracted many attentions for the past three decades, in showing to most of the concerned scholars an intricate interrelation that involves the variables of pedagogy and gender in terms of the way one teaches with, and learns about technology, from K-12 schools, through higher education environments and adult education environments in any professional development or in a distance education (Campbell, 2020). Such research offers valuable insights into how gender impacts both the use of technology in work and the shape and use of educational practice, (Campbell, 2020).

The gender issue in education is not considered from a single point of view. Educators and researchers have come to understand that they need to explore questions of access and accessibility, specifically the digital divide that exists in most societies across the globe (Campbell, 2020). Those gendered disparities in access to technology can also affect learning outcomes, that is, who has access to learning technologies and who has access to developing them (Campbell, 2020).

Research has been concerned with how different pedagogical strategies and content types can either hinder or promote gender inclusivity (Campbell, 2020). For instance, technology delivery mode—whether as traditional classroom instruction augmented with technology, fully online courses, or blended—can affect how male and female students interact with the content (Campbell, 2020). Specific attention has been on computer-mediated discussion and social media use for learning, for instance, where the research shows that woman use such sites differently from their male counterparts (Campbell, 2020). While women use social media more for collaborative learning and community building, which can help in creating a more inclusive learning environment, should it be used effectively by teachers (Campbell, 2020).

Incorporating gender concerns in interface design and pedagogical design is crucial in ensuring equitable access to learning. The process of design itself has been studied in terms of gender bias, and how that might affect usability and effectiveness (Campbell, 2020). Where the design teams are mainly composed of males, there is a likelihood that the produced technologies are male-biased, and hence may be alienating to women (Campbell, 2020). That is why diversity is important not just in the user feedback that is solicited, but also in the design teams that come up with educational technologies (Campbell, 2020).

Moreover, the research is bedeviled by the longstanding problems of assessment practice (Campbell, 2020). Conventional modes of assessment serve to reinforce these biases and result in differential comparisons between male and female students (Campbell, 2020). For example, studies indicate that girls can excel in alternative assessment practices that emphasize cooperation and project work, as opposed to high-stakes testing where anxiety works against them (Campbell, 2020). Such dynamics, therefore, are of utmost importance in ensuring provision of education instruction targeted at every learner (Campbell, 2020).

The second is technical, and it is important to factor in the sociocultural and political aspects of gender and technology in learning. Literature in the field has made available information on how social expectations and norms affect access to technology as well as perceived self-efficacy of use (Campbell, 2020). Women in certain instances have been socialized to view technology as a male field and therefore reduce self-confidence in it. The study emphasizes the creation of a culture of learning that supports learners of both genders to be creative and critical towards technology and therefore break existing norms in culture (Campbell, 2020).

One very important aspect that has come up involves the significance of gender in influencing technology-supported professional learning by Campbell, 2020. Because teachers have an important role in professional learning through technology, it is wise to factor in the influence of gender in teacher participation channels through the application of technology (Campbell, 2020). Women can perform well in a collaborative learning environment that allows them to exchange knowledge and experience and therefore increase confidence and ability to utilize technology in schools (Campbell, 2020).

Challenges are complex in the future. Such technological acceleration calls for continuous critiques of the present practices and how the new discoveries are integrated into any education system (Campbell, 2020). It argues that constant interdisciplinary research is needed; that should onboard an educator, a designer, and also a researcher towards tackling the changing nature of gender and technology in education (Campbell, 2020). Such a process provides a deeper insight into how educational technologies could be improved to suit the heterogeneous needs of learners, as opposed to considering only gender differences (Campbell, 2020). Also, gender-disaggregated data would eventually prove useful in guiding state and institutional policy (Campbell, 2020). Identification of the different barriers and facilitators that could arise for each gender can be used in developing strategies that could bridge the digital divide to ensure that all learners are well supported in his or her learning process (Campbell, 2020). Systemic reforms are called for and should target inclusivity and equity as underlying principles of education policy (Campbell 2020). Institutional strategies are called for in supporting the mentoring programs that are specially targeted towards the needs of female students and teachers in the technology field (Campbell, 2020). Through such linkages, education institutions can generate greater confidence and capability among women in the technology field (Campbell, 2020).

But there is also a possibility for AI to be used as an equalizer and for huge positive change to take place when bridging the gap in the different areas by reducing bias in the data used, thus enhancing the access to education, employment, and health care of the women (Campbell, 2020). Research on gender-differentiated differences in the use of technology in learning and teaching brought complexity to the process of designing fair learning experiences (Campbell, 2020). Gender dimensions of technology are complex and involve much of different kinds of factors like access and use, pedagogical approaches, and sociocultural factors, which require ongoing critical evaluation (Campbell 2020). Diversity must come first in planning and implementing education technology so that all students learn better: a mix of different and diverse perspectives must be considered at every stage of the process (Campbell, 2020). In future studies, it is imperative to acknowledge the stakes involved and play an active role in crafting solutions that will make all learners successful in the digital learning context regardless of gender (Campbell, 2020).

UNDERSTANDING THE GENDER GAP

The 'gender gap' is not necessarily a quantitative gap but also the persistent difference in outcome between women and men in every sector of life (O'Connor & Liu, 2024). The gap is widest in workplaces, where women are paid much less than their male counterparts even when they do the same work (O'Connor & Liu, 2024). There is a gap in the salaries of men and women. Besides this pay gap, women encounter a series of obstacles to professional growth ranging from job location bias to lack of mentorship that clings to their doors. Women are still in the minority in the most remunerative elite jobs and positions and in any organizations, demonstrating structural problems and not being limited by individual abilities (Wrigley-Asante & Ackah Frimpong, 2023). Conversely, the persistent psychological harassment is making women uncomfortable in the workplace (Dhar & Bahl, 2022). Some women have proceeded to the extreme of committing suicide for not getting justice (Dhar & Bahl, 2022).

In schools, the gender gap is more multifaceted. Although women as a whole receive better grades in academics and are outpacing men in rates of graduation, there remains a whopping underrepresentation of women in major fields of study such as engineering, mathematics, and computer science (Wrigley-Asante, Ackah & Frimpong, 2023). That under-representation in the so-called STEM fields is partly the product of cultural stereotypes, education policies and social norms that naturally push women away from them (Wrigley-Asante, Ackah & Frimpong, 2023). The problem is not merely one of academic performance, but is rooted deeply in societal assumptions about who is capable and smart – assumptions that serve men in those fields (Wrigley-Asante, Ackah & Frimpong, 2023).

The advent of digital technologies has also deepened the complexity of the gender gap. An inherent gender bias inherent in digital technologies is a main cause of the imbalance (O'Connor & Liu, 2024). The biases are not coincidences; they are reflective of dominant prevalent social stereotypes and beliefs that come to be inherent in the very technologies that we rely on (O'Connor & Liu, 2024). Digital technologies make the gap more complex. Inherent gender bias characterizes this imbalance that is inherent in digital technologies (O'Connor & Liu, 2024). The biases are not coincidences but are reflective of dominant prevalent social stereotypes and beliefs that come to be inherent in the very technologies that we rely on (O'Connor & Liu, 2024). With the rapid growth in technology use in working and educational settings, it is time to learn about how these biases are instantiated in the digital tools to impact the experiences and opportunities of women (O'Connor & Liu, 2024).

Amongst the biggest of the issues is the issue of biased data sets upon which the AI systems shall be trained with poor representation of women (O'Connor & Liu, 2024). That under-representation then produces algorithms that fail to accurately represent women users' interests and experiences (O'Connor & Liu, 2024). Facial recognition tools, for example, have time and again proved to be worse at identifying women and darker people since they have been trained using biased sets for light-skinned men (Kundi et al, 2023). These biased systems bring about the deliverables not just for women's worst services but continue the same practice that hardens and further legitimates the status quo of the current imbalances. Nevertheless, the ramifications of gender bias in technology are probably much more substantial than inability to technically perform Kundi et al, 2023. Algorithms decide if people go to schools or to universities; on how people get graded. That means that in case such algorithms are biased, women who go for very competitive programmes or face unequal treatment of work are in harm's way (Kundi et al, 2023). Apart from those biases, the reality is that women are not well-represented in technology design teams, and low diversity of thinking brings about an inability where in actual sense the needs of users were conceived narrowly. The issues are not mathematical; they exhibit structural undervaluing of women's roles to technological development and ensuing educational injustices (Kundi et al, 2023).

The numerous ways that technology interacts with social norms should not be ignored. Technologies can invert and reinforce traditional gender roles. For instance, until relatively recently, it was promoted to and directed at a male audience with hyper-macho protagonists and content that could discourage girls from playing (Silvis, 2021). This is a reflection of the authors' prejudices but also of how youth perform gender, and can work to keep girls out of the technology space.

The deeply entrenched biases have far-reaching consequences. Where women are underrepresented in developing tech, they will be found to have their experience and need unrepresented in products and systems engineered, Morganson et al. (2010). This embedding of gender imbalance further into the tech industry creates exclusionary feedback loops in the presence and influence of women in the tech industry year after year. It will be more than awareness that will be required to overcome such systemic barriers, but rather a concerted effort from schools, companies, and policymakers to make technology more inclusive. One such means of combatting such disparities is through the application of a gender-sensitive approach to the design and deployment of AI and digital technologies, as O'Connor & Liu (2024) indicate. Diversification of data towards becoming more representative and inclusive increases accuracy and fairness within technological applications. Bringing women into the design and development process also encourages innovation and ensures more holistic solutions that take a broader set of users' needs into account (O'Connor & Liu, 2024). Corporates and universities need to ensure diversity on their teams. This is to bring a range of perspectives to the process of technology development (O'Connor & Liu, 2024). It will also ensure that technology is more inclusive and equitable (O'Connor & Liu, 2024). To eliminate the gender gap, educational institutions have a significant role to play (Shivanjali & Kumar, 2024). Such an initiative may make effective access to the STEM education of young women, like mentoring activities, workshops, and direct scholarships for female students (Shivanjali & Kumar, 2024). There can be a killing of stereotypes by initiating the engagement of technology to young women from the tender stage (Shivanjali & Kumar, 2024). This also nurtures supportive environments that allow the display of women in the tech space who can have succeeded, inspiring such future female tech leaders who foster a supportive and empowering culture (Shivanjali & Kumar, 2024).

Closing the gender gap is therefore a complex task with the intersections in place because issues of such a kind are not one but interdependent, as O'Connor & Liu observed in 2024. That implies that the solution would need to be multi-faceted, with a combination of different actors to be involved from different industries, from education and technology to policy and many more, as O'Connor & Liu hypothesized in 2024. In short, the gender gap is a complex phenomenon with many causal factors; it is accompanied by systematic bias expressed in digital technologies (O'Connor & Liu, 2024). Besides the girls can do in school, relative underrepresentation in well-paying jobs and persistent gaps in earnings mean that the interventions are still targeted at them (O'Connor & Liu, 2024). Through education with a focus on technology design, through increased sensitivity in society, one is able to overcome the already established script of gender and re-engineer it to better fit in work environments and schools, ultimately translating into a more equal future for all parties of such operations (O'Connor & Liu, 2024). Closing the gap between women and technology is beneficial to all parties. Such interventions, in such a setting, are diversified, innovative, and inclusive to all, thus constituting a good remedy for such modern issues with technology (Kundi et al., 2023).

AI in Gender Equality: The Loop of Bias

When AI systems are trained on data that is not representative enough of women, the outcome can be to further disadvantage them (Leavy et al, 2020). This systemic data curation problem also poses issues about the fairness of AI-based decision-making systems, especially in hiring, medicine, and finance where these systems increasingly operate (Leavy et al, 2020).

For example, in hiring, algorithms can discriminate against women if the historical data to which they are trained put emphasis on male success stories (Leavy et al, 2020). This is also a consequence of the historical gender imbalance in the workplace where the female workforce 'has been underrepresented or excluded from specific sectors' (Leavy et al, 2020). The algorithms, trained on these skewed data, miss not only the skills of the applicants but also continue the biases which render the working place unequal (Leavy et al., 2020). Such limitations significantly limit the job prospects and growth of women at the workplace and ensnare them in a vicious cycle of disadvantage that increasingly becomes difficult to break (Leavy et al., 2020).

Whole generations of women may be denied new opportunities or subjected to pay disparity because algorithmic decision-making fails to consider their competence and experience (Leavy et al, 2020). Third, training data sets for machine learning algorithms can learn and replicate earlier social harms, inequalities or prejudice biases that prevail in the world (Leavy et al, 2020). Datasets based on available records of societal biases can be learned and reinforced in AI models creating a feedback loop that perpetuates inequality. To the extent that such systems take hold and are implemented, they risk internalizing outdated gender role assumptions of professional capacity and undermine work towards equal representation of women in professions.

Technical issues in the development of such a society bias correction system detract from an individual's opportunity for equal employment opportunities thus closing an inequality cycle (Garrick et al, 2024). For example, while algorithmic fairness is an emerging field of study, fair algorithms deployment raises tough questions about what fairness is and how it might be measured (Garrick et al, 2024). Moreover, modification of dataset or algorithmic output does not solve the problem of current societal biases-unless other system changes are implemented, the efficacy of such technical changes may be limited (Garrick et al, 2024).

The harms, which are exactly the resulting effects of discriminatory AI algorithms, are brought about by lower quality treatment to women (Obermeyer et al, 2019). With data sets that predominate the healthcare industry being composed of males, algorithms would omit or not consider problems that plague females more often, thus compromising the health of females at high risk and further reinforcing gender bias in healthcare research (Obermeyer et al, 2019). For example, earlier, clinical drug efficacy tests were strongly biased against males, and their effects on women remain unclear (Obermeyer et al., 2019). Accordingly, the healthcare industry is horribly ill-equipped to meet the unique health needs of women and continues to ignore their voices and experiences (Obermeyer et al, 2019). Discrimination in AI has also spread to the financial industry. In AI used in such activities as lending (Obermeyer et al, 2019), such prejudices are built in. In case past discriminatory treatment of women for creditworthiness is embedded in training datasets, there is a high probability this indicates a more difficult time getting loans or mortgages by women (Binns, 2018). Systemic barriers may curtail the agency of women through financial interests and complicate buying a home, education, or the establishment of a business enterprise. The stakes are relatively high because financial agency is a fundamental aspect of equality, and discriminatory impulses in finance service have been used to consolidate the power disparities (Binns, 2018).

All the cross-sector stakeholders would need to answer the challenge through the application of a multi-faceted response. The first step involves the companies creating and implementing AI investing in deep data sets that represent women and other underrepresented groups in an equitable manner. It is a commendable step towards the prevention of bias propagation in AI models through active sourcing diverse data sources (Leavy et al., 2020). It is not the data scientists' responsibility alone, but it requires leadership to ensure that their technology approaches are inclusive (Leavy et al, 2020). Likewise, the need to create inter-disciplinary work that unites technical competence with social theory is necessary. It unites technologists, social scientists, and gender equity activists to achieve more sophisticated understanding of the gendered impacts of AI. Through such collaboration, more ethically responsible design principles based on equity from the early stages of technological innovation can be developed (Leavy et al, 2020).

Policy interventions are no less potent in shaping the space of AI deployment in work, health, and finance (Dwivedi. et. al, 2021). The regulatory agencies should establish standards and norms of AI use ethically that are transparent and accountable (Dwivedi. et. al, 2021). Accountability mechanisms must be instituted with the purpose of penalizing companies discriminatory in their AI practices to biased algorithms (Dwivedi et al. al, 2021). It is a type of policy that can have an impact on the morality of design decisions and further create conditions under which concerns about fairness are made a regular and routine part of AI design (Dwivedi. et. al, 2021).

Education - is another significant factor that needs to be made mandatory in fighting AI bias (Baker & Hawn, 2022). To educate students who have completed courses in technology and data science, it has technical and ethical aspects of technology and data in a world increasingly dependent on AI (Baker & Hawn, 2022). Awareness campaigns of the biases in AI can empower the next generation of data scientists who create such technologies in the first place under the umbrella of equality and justice (Baker & Hawn, 2022). This education reform will be able to have some kind of responsibility of the future innovators into raising awareness for the social implication of technologies they will create in the future (Baker & Hawn, 2022). Public advocacy campaigns also will have to be at the forefront educating public discourse on issues related to gender biases in AI (Baker & Hawn, 2022). With an increased awareness of education on how algorithmic bias works and its implication in society, public scrutiny and inspection of data-driven technologies becomes more prevalent (Baker & Hawn, 2022). And where individuals are aware of the biases that can creep into AI systems, they can better fight for equal practices and hold corporations accountable that use these technologies (Baker & Hawn, 2022).

Therefore, biased AI systems themselves become obstacles to the tasks under the programs towards gender parity in sectors (Leavy et al., 2020). In hiring medicine, and finance, among the domains they restrict women's potential and have added long-time systemic unbalances observed since time immemorial (Leavy et al., 2020). Presently, there are numerous diverse responses to these questions that are now arising, but the profession requires a plan of action that includes technical measures, policy reform, and educational work (Leavy et al, 2020). It should also focus on an attempt in ensuring that AI functions fairly to maximize women's potential without the deadweight of bias and discrimination (Leavy et al., 2020). Only through concerted and collective action, therefore, is society as a whole able to hope to restrain the malign consequences of biased AI and build a more equitable and improved future for all (Leavy et al., 2020).

AI in Gender: Bias and Marginalization

There are great opportunities for AI to promote gender equality; yet risks are likewise enormous and ought not to be overlooked (O'Connor & Liu, 2024). Bias in algorithms is one of the most critical dangers. AI 'learns from the data' that is made available, and that data could include biases present in society already (O'Connor & Liu, 2024). Unchecked, such biases can be passed on and even amplified by the functioning of AI algorithms. If, say, an AI recruiter is taught on a corporation's past data on hiring, and that firm has hired men in the past, the AI can learn to replicate that bias, and grant women fewer opportunities.

Apart from that, underrepresentation in the development of technology only exacerbates these issues. The majority of AI developers are male and thus their experiences might not necessarily represent the issues or challenges that women and other marginalized groups might experience (Idris, et al., 2024). This gap in diversification in the technology sector can lead to failure to notice and even perceive a one-way sense of needs toward women, hence developing products and solutions that are not exactly targeted at addressing their sense of needs (Lin & Chen, 2022). This results in AI only confirming the existence but rather failing to effect change in these inequalities. Intersectionality also has a fundamental implication in the argument on AI and gender equality (O'Connor and Liu, 2024). Women are not unequal alone; their experiences are shaped by various intersecting factors, such as race, ethnicity, socio-economic status, and sexual orientation (O'Connor & Liu, 2024). AI systems are too frequently, however, insensitive to these complexities, and the result is the erasure of women with intersectional identities. For example, an artificial intelligence system to support women may miss the very specific challenges that women of colour or women of low-income background face, and in so doing simply reproduce systemic inequalities.

AI in Gender Equality: To Level the Scale

Developing gender-responsive AI machines is a long process with lots of challenges, but also a process with immense potential to create a more equal society (Njuki et al., 2023). This balance can be regained by establishing ethical norms and regulation on the use and development of AI. These guidelines should highlight the importance of diversity on technology teams, and encourage inclusive practices that keep women and marginalized groups at the table when creating AI systems (Barocas et al, 2019).

Companies can also regularly audit their AI systems to detect and eliminate bias (Nazer et al, 2023). And by examining the effect of AI-driven decisions, companies can ensure that their systems are not perpetuating inequality. Engaging community stakeholders, particularly women and other marginalized groups, in both the design and development phase can also make AI solutions more effective, by ensuring that they serve multiple communities.

More importantly, education and awareness of pros and cons of AI are needed. When the industry educates and empowers women and other groups underrepresented in technology, it puts more minds into the process of creating AI. It should ensure the voice of those groups is at the table in the conversation of how to create AI responsibly.

Gender Equality: AI a Potential Equalizer

There is an extremely wide range of how AI can assist in closing the gap created in society between one sex and the other. Benefits are as follows:

- **Enhanced Data Representation:** The reduction of gender bias must begin from data representation in AI training sets as representative of all genders as possible. Institutional actors can gather and use data representing the world of women in a real sense. It would introduce a more balanced result to AI in employment, health care, and finance (Eubanks, 2022).
- **Enhanced Employment Recruitment Processes:** Artificial intelligence can enhance the recruitment process by using equal algorithms based solely on

qualification. Removing human bias will enable companies to provide equal opportunities between the sexes and enhance the **gender balance of the workplace (Garrick et al., 2024).**

- **Enhanced Access to Education:** Intelligent tutoring systems will enhance learning to be more personalized and responsive to an alternative learning approach. It opens doors to the world of STEM for girls and young women through the provision of learning material as well as enhancing skills for competence and confidence to overcome a male-dominated environment in such fields of study (Wrigley-Asante et al., 2023).
- **Enhanced Access to Healthcare:** Use of AI in women's health can improve service delivery since AI can identify gaps in current systems and ensure that medical algorithms used are accompanied by the determinants of women's health. Through analysis of relevant data, AI will be able to provide women specialized healthcare advice that will ultimately result in better health outcomes and more opportunities for women to be included in medical research (Obermeyer et al, 2019).
- **Financial Empowerment:** Artificial intelligence can grant women access to resources that will make them more efficient in managing their financial matters. For example, AI-powered personal budgeting software can help women budget their finances, save for the future, and look into investment opportunities-all the main drivers that lead to financial independence and stability (Binns, 2018).

RESPONSIBILITIES OF AI DEVELOPERS AND SOCIETY

Gender inequality must be pursued in order to ensure that AI technology, developers, corporations, and the general public are aware of gender inequalities and make every effort to rectify these inequalities in technology.

This includes, of course, developing diverse and representative datasets, and also ensuring that the teams which build AI systems are themselves diverse. The more diverse a team is, the more likely it is to take into account the views and interests of individuals of all genders, and consequently develop better and more equitable outcomes (Mannix & Neale, 2005). Additionally, public education campaigns on gender bias in AI can make the general public to accept what the bias is, and adopt a more inclusive approach in developing technology. 'Education and advocacy can change the culture so that men and women are working together to create a more equal future' (Greig & Flood, 2020).

AI for Gender Equality: Opportunities

Perhaps most significantly, the space where AI can most clearly level the playing field is in the recruitment process. Recruitment can be de-biased by AI programs that eliminate unconscious bias from the hiring process, scrubbing job descriptions, screening candidates against objective criteria, and preventing women from being penalized for gender stereotyping (Schwartz et al, 2022). There are numerous AI-powered platforms that can be used to scrub gendered language from job ads and to normalize the way resumes are scored, and this removes human bias (Horodyski, 2023). Pymetrics and HireVue, for instance, utilize artificial intelligence to screen candidates based on their 'skills and potential' instead of on more established, gendered proxies such as previous occupations or qualifications (Andrews & Bucher, 2022). This, in turn, levels the playing field for women who work in fields such as technology or engineering, whose previous record may not be so good.

AI in Education and Skill Development

Intelligent agents in the learning environment are becoming an essential tool to bridge education gaps more equitably. In the developing world, girls and women have very little access to education, including STEM. AI-based learning platforms can also offer personalized experiences, which are particularly worth it to women and girls who must learn science, technology, engineering and mathematics (STEM) (Shivanjali & Kumar, 2024). AI can also assist with career choice by demonstrating the range of possibilities to women, connecting them to mentors, and otherwise helping them in their entry and success in male-dominated fields (Geffner, 2023).

AI in Health

In healthcare, AI can promise to fulfill gender-specific requirements. The gender-specific neglect of women's health has resulted in lacunae in the outcome of treatment. AI systems are able to replicate gender-specific disease patterns to enhance the diagnosis and treatment of female-dominant diseases like autoimmune diseases and mental illness (Golder et al, 2022). Gender-responsive AI algorithms will ensure health data of women are represented fairly in medical research, providing insights into how treatment impacts both sexes differently.

AI in Preventing Gender-Based Violence

There is international, continuing concern with violence against women, online and offline, impacting millions of women. Abuse and harassment on the web can be recognized and prevented by AI systems. 'Social media companies can utilize AI algorithms to screen hate speech and abusive conduct, and act quickly to help protect victims (Bokolo & Liu, 2024) have argued. Predictive AI software can also assist the police and social services in the identification of patterns of gender-based violence, and for the police to take action preventively. Other opportunities include real-time support services for victims of violence living in the home or community provided through AI-based programs.

AI for Economic Inclusion

AI can help to drive greater women's economic participation by building non-discriminatory credit scoring models that reflect the true picture of women's financial history, and hence make credit, savings account and investment easier to access (Rizzi et al, 2021). Systemic discrimination in credit scoring and financial decision-making continues to exclude many women from the system globally (Rizzi et al, 2021). Developing world women are already being empowered by AI microfinance platforms to access enormous capital and financial literacy, to look for viable business opportunities and financial independence (Thakkar, 2024).

RISKS OR CHALLENGES OF AI ON GENDER EQUALITY

- Bias in AI Algorithms

'AI is full of promise, but it's also full of bias biased data produces biased AI algorithms that reinforce and even amplify gender bias. For example, some facial recognition systems based on biased data perform worse for women and people of color, with discriminatory results in law enforcement and surveillance (Limantė, 2024). One such high-profile example was Amazon cancelling an AI hiring tool that downgraded resumes from women's colleges, illustrating how unregulated AI systems disregard gender and intersectional biases (Dastin, 2018).

- Gender Representation in AI Development

The lack of diversity in the AI research and development population also constitutes an enormous challenge in building fair AI. There are fewer women in AI and technology, and hence algorithms that may not work in women's best interests or experience as well (O'Connor & Liu, 2024). Diversity of the workforce is needed to avoid gender-based biases in AI system design and deployment.

- Intersectionality and Marginalized Groups

Understand the concept that intersectionality is the intersection of race, class, sexual orientation, and an entire other set of identity makers with gender. AI is not taking intersectionality into account, so women are extremely likely to be subject to increased exclusionary practices. Already-marginalized groups-women of color, LGBTQ-gender non-conforming individuals-are likely to suffer much worse effects if their AI systems do not take their diverse viewpoints into account (McAra-Hunter, 2024).

Promoting Gender Equality: Ethical Responsibility of AI-Developers

The recent innovation in the artificial intelligence field has required immediate realization of ethical responsibilities for developers of AI technologies. The growth also requires awareness of ethical responsibilities by institutions on the use of such systems. It entails creating AI systems that are equitable, transparent, and accountable. The regulation of artificial intelligence that would eliminate gender bias is the responsibility of governments and international institutions collectively. This would ensure the technology is used for the purposes of gender equality. An effective ethical framework is required to be able to effectively counteract the challenges the development of AI presents for both the developer and society. Such a framework helps in creating technologies responsibly. This will ensure that all the needs of the various members of society are addressed. The special focus must be on to the most vulnerable groups, i.e., Women (Costanza-Chock, 2020).

Fairness in Artificial Intelligence

Equity is the most basic requirement of AI development in that it demands that algorithms be constructed in such a manner that they don't reinforce present biases or even create new forms of discrimination. Gender bias alone can lead to large differences in many areas, such as work, health, and education (Lim et al, 2021). If AI is constructed around older data that is discriminatory, there are high chances that it will reinforce present differences. Consider the case of hiring. If AI is constructed around biased data that favors male candidates, the outcome will be an even greater barrier for women to overcome to get well-paying jobs.

For instance, research has indicated that hiring algorithms, if constructed based on data built by past hiring exercises that have traditionally favored men, will reinforce the bias, thus hindering the ability to attain equity in the labor force (Dastin, 2018). If developers are interested in fairness and tackle the issue early enough, they might prevent these risks and assist in creating a future where equal opportunity is the norm for both genders.

Transparency in AI Systems

The second basic requirement of ethical AI development is transparency. This is epistemic transparency in the way AI systems make decisions and the processes employed in their deployment. Short-term solutions by organizations can lead to greater trust among users and stakeholders, an extremely sensitive application space-ranging from the approval of loans to medical diagnoses (Olateju et al, 2024).

The autonomous AI systems' decision-making can be many times unclear. In such situations, there will be critical issues-when hiring is connected to the output delivered. As a step towards increased transparency, organizations are required to disclose their algorithms and used datasets and methods of application. Through this, the users will be in a position to better understand the decision-making processes and hold organizations accountable for existing bias within them.

Accountability in AI Development

Accountability in the AI industry is more than a professional duty but rather a norm which defines the process of ethics construction, application, and legislation (Novelli et al, 2024). With AI having been implemented in most industries, including healthcare, finance, education, and law enforcement, this creates a set of new challenges and opportunities (Novelli et al, 2024). The need for accountability becomes the first need for ensuring ethical standards and averting those undesirable effects which have occurred through these increasingly expanding systems (Novelli et al, 2024). Accountability in the AI system would be spread across various actors and not limited to a specific particular programmer or a group of programmers working traditionally on software development (Novelli et al, 2024). Data scientists are responsible for designing algorithms and selecting datasets, while ethicists provide their input in the analysis of the ethical issues involved with the application of AI. Business executives also input in the decisions which decide the way in which AI is implemented and used in an organization (Novelli et al, 2024). The simultaneous coordination of these groups is quite crucial for determining moral issues in AI from the conceptualization of ideas to the development of such ideas and continuous monitoring. In order to assume this responsibility, a definition must be made clear among teams of workers engaged in the development of AI (Novelli et al, 2024). All parties must be made aware of what they do and what their actions produce. Data scientists, for example, must be careful of the moral implications that their algorithms may possess with respect to data-based decisions but need not neglect technical performance metrics (Novelli et al, 2024). This practice is more than an avoidance of biased data; it is an approach towards a world where data reflects the values and norms of society. Data scientists need technical skills and training in ethics so that they possess an idea of the larger picture of the effects of their work (Novelli et al, 2024). Ethicists have vital roles to play within this collaborative environment (Novelli et al, 2024). They can guide us through the complicated moral decisions, making AI systems adhere to the principles of justice, transparency, and users' privacy (Novelli et al, 2024). Ethicists can also collaborate with data scientists to ensure that algorithms are created with the intention of actively fighting bias, which is a gigantic problem concerning gender bias, among infinite other areas of AI application (Novelli et al., 2024). Gender bias facilitates discrimination and has the potential to further bias the outputs created by AI systems, which will have far-reaching implications for the degree to which it impacts the lives of individuals (Novelli et al., 2024). Therefore, it speaks of creating an accountability culture that embodies the ethical concern and theoretical principles are translated into practical, workable measures within the organization (Novelli et al, 2024). Governments and regulatory bodies ought to create an accountability system that ensures accountability is brought to companies on what they create using AI systems (Novelli et al, 2024). This speaks of coming up with regulatory frameworks that define the development and deployment of AI and accountability mechanisms. Regulations of this nature should be formulated to compel stakeholders to adhere to ethical practices throughout the entire life cycle of an AI, from stages of data collection and algorithmic design to deployment and continuous review (Novelli et al, 2024). Periodic auditing would enable scrutiny of algorithms, datasets, and decision-making structures, thereby availing external confirmation of the claims made by organizations regarding the ethical purity of their endeavours (Novelli et al, 2024). Secondly, open structures of reporting will enable stakeholders to identify potential accountability procedure failure, thereby enabling instant corrective action (Novelli et al, 2024).

This will further entail the creation of reporting systems for individuals to report unethical practices or biases within AI systems. For instance, whistle-blower laws against offenders who identify discriminatory outcomes generated by AI algorithms (Novelli et al, 2024). Additionally, there should be a culture of reporting ethically developed within organizations. This should protect the individual against retaliation or shunning, and also empower them to raise issues without fear of judgment (Novelli et al, 2024).

Yet another essential element of accountability is the public engagement. Developers, users, and society as a whole must be included in deliberations towards the ethical use of AI (Novelli et al, 2024). Public consultation is a mechanism through which society experiments with its values because AI developers will make their systems accommodate the needs of the values in society. Participatory approach not only enhances transparency but also scales up a common sense of responsibility (Novelli et al, 2024). Through the inclusion of ethical considerations in the design process, organizations are placed to recognize and eliminate risks prior to the deployment of a technology capable of being harmful in unintended ways (Novelli et al, 2024). Moreover, education and training are essential towards the development of accountability in the artificial intelligence ecosystem. It is through the inclusion of ethical considerations in the artificial intelligence and data science curriculum that will endow the incoming talent with the ability to navigate the complex moral environment to which they will be exposed (Novelli et al, 2024). Through the building of a strong ethical foundation under future talent, organizations are able to enhance the chances that accountability will become part of the culture in the AI development ecosystem (Novelli et al, 2024).

Therefore, the issue of accountability in artificial intelligence is a complex one that demands the cooperation of participants, proper regulatory frameworks, transparent operational practices, and commitment to ethical education (Novelli et al, 2024). By establishing clear responsibilities, rewarding ethical practice, and setting strong checks and balances, we can limit the potential risks of AI systems while maximizing their benefits (Novelli, Taddeo, Floridi, 2024). As today's questions of gender bias and other ethical issues continue to evolve, firms must be prudent and proactive, infusing accountability into the heart of their AI initiatives. Only then can we fully realize the promise of AI, while reducing its risks (Novelli et al, 2024).

AI in Gender Equality: The Role of Government and International Organizations

While ethics of AI development are squarely laid on the shoulders of organizations, enormous roles are played by government and other international agencies in regulations that promote responsible use of AI technologies.

Regulation Frameworks

The responsibilities of governments are to create regulations and address concerns on gender, which will ensure that ethical thinking is utilized in the use of AI. Such frameworks can, therefore, lead organizations and force them towards making ethical thinking in AI systems.

Other notable developments include the European Union's draft AI Act that should legally enshrine AI technologies in the EU (Outeda, 2024). The Act categorizes AI systems into risk-based classes with stricter rules for high-risk application on life or the fundamental rights of an individual. Most importantly, the EU AI Act prioritizes human oversight. Organizations need to ensure that their AI systems are transparent, explainable, and accountable (Outeda, 2024)). For recruitment AI development teams, this implies that algorithms cannot discriminate against women or marginalized groups.

Besides such regulations, organizations like UNESCO have also released guidelines that are gender equality and AI-oriented (van Norren, 2023). These guidelines endorse the inclusion of gender considerations in AI policies and practices, highlighting the importance of diverse development teams to ensure diverse perspectives inform AI system designs. It endorses efforts that measure and mitigate gender bias in AI and promote engaging diverse voices in the discussion on the future of AI technology.

Improvement of AI Governance Through Government Initiatives

The governments can improve in proactively enhancing their ethical AI governance by doing so through:

- **Designing legislative frameworks:** Designing legislation and policy that outlines gender disparity issues in the AI system of operations with a predefined expectation on fairness, transparency, as well as accountability.
- **Funding research and development of AI:** They can also fund research ideas that allow them to tackle other issues on gender. And the datasets as well as algorithms must be developed in several varieties in order not to have bias (Ahonen & Farén, 2024).
- **Public Awareness Campaign:** Organize public campaigns to increase the awareness of the public about probable biases in AI systems. This will be capable of providing informed discussion on technology in society and its impact on gender equality.
- **Encourage Collaboration:** Partner with government, academia, and industry to share best practices in the reduction of gender bias in AI development.

- **Monitoring and Evaluation:** Set up independent agencies that monitor AI systems, review their impacts towards the promotion of gender equality, and implement ethics as defined in the laws.

Ethical Inclusive AI Systems

If AI technologies are to be effective towards the promotion of gender equality, then inclusivity at every stage from data collection, development, and deployment is an integral part of this process. Organisations can adopt various ways for ethical practices:

- **Diversity in Development Teams:** Another effective way that can help in the reduction of gender bias in AI is encouraging diverse teams of developers for the systems. Diverse teams offer diverse views and experiences and are best suited to identify biases and design more neutral technologies (Shams et al, 2023). The more organisations include women and diverse representation in the development process, the more they will be likely to take into consideration the diverse needs and experiences of underrepresented groups in gender-sensitive and responsive AI systems. Most importantly, an organisation with active recruitment and retaining talent from diverse groups ensures an inclusive culture where diverse views are welcomed.
- **Multivariate Datasets:** the performance of an AI system relies more on the dataset used during training; that is, an organization has to ensure that it is working with diversified datasets that actually represent all genders and take intersectional factors such as race, age, and socioeconomic status into consideration. This makes for the creation of AI systems that understand and respond to many different people; therefore, the fewer opportunities for biases in the algorithms lead to better results (Schwartz et al., 2022).
- **Continuous Monitoring and Evaluation:** AI systems are not fixed; they need to be monitored and evaluated on a continuous basis so that their impact on gender equality may be determined. The organizations need to create feedback loops to collect data on how the AI systems are performing, especially on their impacts towards women and other marginalized groups (Akter et al., 2021).
- **Bias detection:** Bias detection could be through periodic audits that would help fix them before it is too late. Audits need to be interdisciplinary teams made up of ethicists, data scientists, and members of affected communities.
- **Engagement of Stakeholders:** Including AI systems also mean involving diverse stakeholders, including communities, civil society organizations, and

advocacy groups. This will help organizations gain valuable insights about the needs of underrepresented groups (Binns, 2018).

Gender-Informed AI Roadmap

For AI to be best used on the way to gender parity, it will be important that it be done in various ways:

- **Inclusive Development:** Create inclusive teams when building AI, and representation by women, among others, to create aware systems that are sensitive to varied experiences.
- **Bias Mitigation:** Thorough procedures must be identified and remedied to acquire countermeasures for algorithmic biases; regular audits and reviews to facilitate fair output.
- **Community Engagement:** Involve stakeholders, particularly women and marginalized communities, in AI solution development and implementation. Their contributions will direct the development towards solving the appropriate real-world problems.
- **Ethical Standards:** Create industry-wide ethical guidelines for AI founded on fairness, accountability, and transparency. Organizations should be committed to following these ethical guidelines and review periodically if they are still relevant.
- **Education and Training:** Offering more access to AI and technology education to women and underrepresented communities empowers them to grasp the opportunity to be part of the mighty force crafting the futures of the industries.
- **Ongoing Research:** Research at the confluence of AI and gender parity must exist in order to constantly search for opportunities to be optimized on and innovated on.

CONCLUSION

Equality for women is yet far from being a reality, but artificial intelligence can be an equalizer. Artificial intelligence can correct data bias and harness technology to optimize the available opportunities and results for women to achieve an equal world. The developers, organizations, and society are required to build AI systems that will be reflective and beneficial of the diverse makeup of humanity. Together we can leap forward and bridge the gap in achieving gender parity in the future.

With an increase in impact from AI, it is important that the ethical frameworks for managing AI are kept under check. Beyond being an ethical issue in terms of removal of gender bias from AI, this is a method of building equity in society, empowering, and enabling all regardless of gender. Good regulatory frames, equal, open, and ethical AI development, diversity and participation of stakeholders in AI construction, and making sure a digital future is ensured. Governments, international institutions, and private actors have to join hands to ensure the proper use of AI technologies by supporting society toward becoming more gender equal. This will assist us in leveraging the transformative power of AI to build a world where all human beings have an equal opportunity to thrive.

On the question of whether it was possible to grant one the resources to fundamentally alter a fight for gender equality, AI would prove to be worth an invaluable fortune in providing human beings with new tools to approach old problems on the issues of hiring, education, health, and financial inclusion. Even if sophisticated AI is designed, the risks do need to be managed with careful and ethical management of AI construction. That is because full gender equality will be built into AI systems as a tool of building an even more inclusive digital future. The technology is going to empower people and not exclude the exclusionary technology. So, the challenges must be met on the front lines with policies of fairness and inclusion that will help us maximize the actual power of AI for both sexes.

REFERENCES

Ahonen, E., & Farén, E. (2024). Gender biases in AI-Mitigation strategies contributing to fairness.

Akter, S., McCarthy, G., Sajib, S., Michael, K., Dwivedi, Y. K., D'Ambra, J., & Shen, K. N. (2021). Algorithmic bias in data-driven innovation in the age of AI. *International Journal of Information Management*, 60, 102387. DOI: 10.1016/j.ijinfomgt.2021.102387

Andrews, L., & Bucher, H. (2022). Automating Discrimination: AI Hiring Practices and Gender Inequality. *Cardozo Law Review*, 44, 145.

Baker, R. S., & Hawn, A. (2022). Algorithmic bias in education. *International Journal of Artificial Intelligence in Education*, •••, 1–41.

Barocas, S., Hardt, M., & Narayanan, A. (2019). Fairness and Machine Learning. Fairness, Accountability, and Transparency in Machine Learning. https://fairmlbook.org/

Binns, R. (2018). Fairness in Machine Learning: Lessons from Political Philosophy. In *Proceedings of the 2018 Conference on Fairness, Accountability, and Transparency* (pp. 149-158). DOI: 10.1145/3287560.3287598

Bokolo, B. G., & Liu, Q. (2024). Artificial Intelligence in Social Media Forensics: A Comprehensive Survey and Analysis. *Electronics (Basel)*, 13(9), 1671. DOI: 10.3390/electronics13091671

Campbell, K. (2020). Gender and technology: Social context and intersectionality. *Handbook of research in educational communications and technology: Learning design*, 115-204.

Costanza-Chock, S. (2020). *Design justice: Community-led practices to build the worlds we need.* The MIT Press. DOI: 10.7551/mitpress/12255.001.0001

Dastin, J. (2018). Amazon scrapped a secret AI recruiting tool after it showed bias against women. Ethics of Data and Analytics. Auerbach Publications.

Dhar, S., & Bahl, N. (2022). Harassment of Women at Workplace in India Amounting to Psychological Scourge: A Socio-Legal Insight. *Agathos*, 13(2), 151–161.

Drage, E., & Mackereth, K. (2022). Does AI debias recruitment? Race, gender, and AI's "eradication of difference". *Philosophy & Technology*, 35(4), 89. DOI: 10.1007/s13347-022-00543-1 PMID: 36246553

Dwivedi, Y. K., Hughes, L., Ismagilova, E., Aarts, G., Coombs, C., Crick, T., Duan, Y., Dwivedi, R., Edwards, J., Eirug, A., Galanos, V., Ilavarasan, P. V., Janssen, M., Jones, P., Kar, A. K., Kizgin, H., Kronemann, B., Lal, B., Lucini, B., & Williams, M. D. (2021). Artificial Intelligence (AI): Multidisciplinary perspectives on emerging challenges, opportunities, and agenda for research, practice and policy. *International Journal of Information Management*, 57, 101994. DOI: 10.1016/j.ijinfomgt.2019.08.002

Eubanks, B. (2022). *Artificial intelligence for HR: Use AI to support and develop a successful workforce.* Kogan Page Publishers.

Ezeugwa, F. A., Olaniyi, O. O., Ugonnia, J. C., Arigbabu, A. S., & Joeaneke, P. C. (2024). Artificial Intelligence, Big Data, and Cloud Infrastructures: Policy Recommendations for Enhancing Women's Participation in the Tech-Driven Economy. *Journal of Engineering Research and Reports*, 26(6), 1–16. DOI: 10.9734/jerr/2024/v26i61158

Frennert, S. (2021). Gender blindness: On health and welfare technology, AI and gender equality in community care. *Nursing Inquiry*, 28(4), e12419. DOI: 10.1111/nin.12419 PMID: 33979011

Garrick, A., Johnson, W. D., & Arendt, S. W. (2024). Breaking barriers: Strategies for fostering inclusivity in the workplace. *International Journal of Academic Research in Business & Social Sciences*, 14(2), 115–121. DOI: 10.6007/IJARBSS/v14-i2/20799

Geffner, C. J. (2023). *Building a New Leadership Ladder: Transforming Male-dominated Organizations to Support Women on the Rise.* MIT Press. DOI: 10.7551/mitpress/14386.001.0001

Golder, S., O'Connor, K., Wang, Y., Stevens, R., & Gonzalez-Hernandez, G. (2022). Best practices on big data analytics to address sex-specific biases in our understanding of the etiology, diagnosis, and prognosis of diseases. *Annual Review of Biomedical Data Science*, 5(1), 251–267. DOI: 10.1146/annurev-biodatasci-122120-025806 PMID: 35562851

Greig, A., & Flood, M. (2020). Work with men and boys for gender equality: a review of field formation, the evidence base and future directions. *UN-Women Discussion Paper Series. New York: United Nations Entity for Gender Equality and the Empowerment of Women.*

Horodyski, P. (2023). Recruiter's perception of artificial intelligence (AI)-based tools in recruitment. *Computers in Human Behavior Reports*, 10, 100298. DOI: 10.1016/j.chbr.2023.100298

Idris, R., Faisal-E-Alam, M., Castanho, R. A., & Loures, L. (2024). Bridging the gender gap in STEM fields: Empowering women for economic and social development in Malaysia. *WSEAS Transactions On Business And Economics*, 21, 617–629. DOI: 10.37394/23207.2024.21.51

Kundi, B., El Morr, C., Gorman, R., & Dua, E. (2023). Artificial intelligence and bias: A scoping review. *AI & Society*, 199–215.

Leavy, S., O'Sullivan, B., & Siapera, E. (2020). Data, Power and Bias in Artificial Intelligence. *ArXiv, abs/2008.07341.*

Lim, W. H., Wong, C., Jain, S. R., Ng, C. H., Tai, C. H., Devi, M. K., Samarasekera, D. D., Iyer, S. G., & Chong, C. S. (2021). The unspoken reality of gender bias in surgery: A qualitative systematic review. *PLoS One*, 16(2), e0246420. DOI: 10.1371/journal.pone.0246420 PMID: 33529257

Limantė, A. (2024). Bias in Facial Recognition Technologies Used by Law Enforcement: Understanding the Causes and Searching for a Way Out. *Nordic Journal of Human Rights*, 42(2), 115–134. DOI: 10.1080/18918131.2023.2277581

Lin, T. A., & Chen, P. H. C. (2022). Artificial intelligence in a structurally unjust society. Feminist Philosophy Quarterly, 8(3/4).

Mannix, E., & Neale, M. A. (2005). What differences make a difference? The promise and reality of diverse teams in organizations. *Psychological Science in the Public Interest*, 6(2), 31–55. DOI: 10.1111/j.1529-1006.2005.00022.x PMID: 26158478

McAra-Hunter, D. (2024). How AI hype impacts the LGBTQ+ community. *AI and Ethics*, 4(3), 1–20. DOI: 10.1007/s43681-024-00423-8

Morganson, V. J., Jones, M. P., & Major, D. A. (2010). Understanding women's underrepresentation in science, technology, engineering, and mathematics: The role of social coping. *The Career Development Quarterly*, 59(2), 169–179. DOI: 10.1002/j.2161-0045.2010.tb00060.x

Nazer, L. H., Zatarah, R., Waldrip, S., Ke, J. X. C., Moukheiber, M., Khanna, A. K., Hicklen, R. S., Moukheiber, L., Moukheiber, D., Ma, H., & Mathur, P. (2023). Bias in artificial intelligence algorithms and recommendations for mitigation. *PLOS Digital Health*, 2(6), e0000278. DOI: 10.1371/journal.pdig.0000278 PMID: 37347721

Njuki, J., et al. (2023). A review of evidence on gender equality, women's empowerment, and food systems. Science and innovations for food systems transformation, 165.

Novelli, C., Taddeo, M., & Floridi, L. (2024). Accountability in artificial intelligence: What it is and how it works. *AI & Society*, 39(4), 1871–1882. DOI: 10.1007/s00146-023-01635-y

O'Connor, S., & Liu, H. (2024). Gender bias perpetuation and mitigation in AI technologies: Challenges and opportunities. *AI & Society*, 39(4), 2045–2057. DOI: 10.1007/s00146-023-01675-4

Obermeyer, Z., Powers, B., Vogeli, C., & Mullainathan, S. (2019). Dissecting racial bias in an algorithm used to manage the health of populations. *Science*, 366(6464), 447–453. DOI: 10.1126/science.aax2342 PMID: 31649194

Olateju, O., Okon, S. U., Olaniyi, O. O., Samuel-Okon, A. D., & Asonze, C. U. (2024). Exploring the concept of explainable AI and developing information governance standards for enhancing trust and transparency in handling customer data. *Available atSSRN*. DOI: 10.2139/ssrn.4879025

Outeda, C. C. (2024). The EU's AI act: A framework for collaborative governance. *Internet of Things : Engineering Cyber Physical Human Systems*, 27, 101291. DOI: 10.1016/j.iot.2024.101291

Rizzi, A., Kessler, A., & Menajovsky, J. (2021). The Stories Algorithms Tell: Bias and Financial Inclusion at the Data Margins. *Center for Financial Inclusion, Accion* (2021), 35.

Schwartz, R., Schwartz, R., Vassilev, A., Greene, K., Perine, L., Burt, A., & Hall, P. (2022). Towards a standard for identifying and managing bias in artificial intelligence (Vol. 3, p. 00). US Department of Commerce, National Institute of Standards and *Technology*.

Shams, R. A., Zowghi, D., & Bano, M. (2023). AI and the quest for diversity and inclusion: A systematic literature review. *AI and Ethics*, 1–28.

Shivanjali, S. R., & Kumar, M. (2024). Exploring Stem Learners' Perceptions of Artificial Intelligence in Personalizing Metacognitive Strategy Development. *Journal of the Indian Academy of Applied Psychology*, 299.

Thakkar, S. (2024). The Impact of AI On Financial Inclusion In Emerging Markets. *International Journal Of Computer Engineering And Technology*, 15(5), 266–277.

van Norren, D. E. (2023). The ethics of artificial intelligence, UNESCO and the African Ubuntu perspective. *Journal of Information. Communication and Ethics in Society*, 21(1), 112–128. DOI: 10.1108/JICES-04-2022-0037

World Economic Forum. (2021). Global Gender Gap Report 2021. Retrieved from https://www.weforum.org/reports/global-gender-gap-report-2021

World Economic Forum. (2023). Global Gender Gap Report 2023. Retrieved from https://www.weforum.org/reports/global-gender-gap-report-2023/

Wrigley-Asante, C., Ackah, C. G., & Frimpong, L. K. (2023). Gender differences in academic performance of students studying Science Technology Engineering and Mathematics (STEM) subjects at the University of Ghana. *SN Social Sciences*, 3(1), 12. DOI: 10.1007/s43545-023-00608-8 PMID: 36686568

Chapter 6
Exploring AI in Marketing of Financial Products:
Strengthening Global Financial Institutions

Surendra Tiwari
https://orcid.org/0009-0000-1054-7120
Institute of Technology and Science, India

Puneet Kumar
Institute of Technology and Science, India

Kavita Tiwari
Ajay Kumar Garg Institute of Management, India

Nitin Saxena
INMENTEC, Ghaziabad, India

ABSTRACT

With growing competition in the financial sector and changing consumer expectations, AI-driven technologies like machine learning, predictive analytics, and automation tools are proving indispensable for improving customer engagement and operational efficiency. The chapter investigates different uses of AI, such as tailored advertising campaigns, predictive modelling to predict consumer actions, and automation solutions such as chatbots that improve customer support. This chapter ultimately gives actionable insights to financial institutions looking to leveraging AI to improve their marketing approach and solidify their position in the market.

DOI: 10.4018/979-8-3693-9395-6.ch006

1. INTRODUCTION

Technology has evolved rapidly and has changed at scale across many industries, including marketing! One of the most significant advancements is the role of Artificial Intelligence (AI) in marketing. Artificial Intelligence has become a force of nature, allowing companies to process terabytes of data, automate complex tasks, and enrich customer experience. In a highly competitive financial sector with ever-increasing demands from consumers, the incorporation of AI in marketing financial products is no longer beneficial but rather necessary. It outlines the hurdles and complications that come with the adoption of AI systems such as data privacy issues, problems with the integration of legacy systems and reluctance from the organizations to change. Through examining case studies of AI in practice and comparing the methods of AI in financial marketing of adopting institutions, and non-adopting institutions, this paper provides evidence of the significant benefits of implementing AI workloads in financial marketing. The results highlight the need for ethics and regulation to be factored in when deploying AI. The chapter explores the use of artificial intelligence (AI) to market grams of financial product and how this will provide the strength for global financial institutions (Caskey, 2021).

1.1 Background on AI in Marketing

AI is the simulation of human intelligence processes performed by machines especially computer systems. This includes various technologies such as machine learning, natural language processing, and data analytics. In marketing domain, AI captures consumer behaviour in deeper hues, presenting organizations personalized marketing in the way that shall resonate with individual preferences and needs (Google Cloud, 2025). AI algorithms, for example, can analyse customer data to forecast future purchase behaviours, segment audiences with greater accuracy, and optimize marketing campaigns to improve effectiveness.

Marketing And Financial Services The use of AI in marketing is quite applicable to the financial services domain. Let us see how different Industries are using AI to transform themselves – in their services, production, and even distribution. AI-powered chatbots can respond to queries and assist with transactions, providing 24/7 customer support without human involvement. In addition, by leveraging the power of AI, insights can also enhance marketing strategies, enabling marketers to create targeted marketing campaigns that reflect consumer interests, leading to increased conversion rates.

Research suggests organisations using AI in their marketing have much higher efficiency and effectiveness. For instance, banks leveraging AI tools to automate follow up tasks can also schedule meetings and trigger personalized communications based on user activity. Such automation not only simplifies operational processes but also aids in delivering a more engaging customer experience, an essential aspect in a time where users are expecting immediacy and personalization (McKinsey & Company, 2025).

1.2 Importance of Financial Products in Global Markets

Financial products are integral to the global economy, enabling individuals and companies to transact, invest, save, and manage risk. These products include loans, credit cards, insurance policies, investment funds and retirement accounts. These products are much more than transactional tools, they are critical drivers of economic stability and growth. As the landscape of the industry continues to evolve and adapt to globalisation, financial service providers need to tackle complex regulatory environments, whilst managing diverse consumer needs in multiple regions. With the globalization of finance, there is growing competition between institutions as they attempt to attract customers from all demographics. As consumers are getting smarter with their overall finances and seeking holistic products that fit their values and lifestyles, the financial institutions need to continually innovate to remain relevant in such an era.

And, the emergence of fintech companies has challenged traditional banking institutions by providing innovative financial services that are more user-friendly and accessible. This disruption has forced legacy financial institutions to embrace technologies and strategies that would prepare them to compete in this landscape (Ernst & Young [EY], 2025). Consequently, these organizations are seeing integrating AI into the marketing of financial products as a strategic imperative. AI not only improves how financial institutions market their products to customers, it also enables them to innovate new solutions that are better suited to distinct segments of customers. Institutions also could leverage data associated with consumer preferences and certain habits to build goods that fit specific needs for example, green finance products for environmentally friendly consumers, or customized investments for millennials looking to build wealth over the long-term.

1.3 Research Objectives and Questions

This research paper aims to discuss how Artificial Intelligence can be efficiently used in marketing financial products to tighten the global financial institutions. The exploration seeks to align best practices for deploying AI-powered marketing and to address challenges that might come with their deployment.

In order to address this goal, the following key research questions will help to guide the inquiry:

I. How are marketers using AI to promote financial products today?

Insights into existing use cases will reveal how financial institutions are using AI technologies, in particular, to grow their marketing functions.

II. How does AI enhance customer interaction and satisfaction in financial services?

Exploring AI's effect on customer experience will further demonstrate how businesses are aligning with consumer demands for custom-tailored service.

III. What are the challenges that financial institutions encounter when they build and utilize AI in their marketing process?

Finding out what gets in the way will then lead to strategies for getting by these blockades and successfully putting into action the same.

IV. How does AI in marketing impact regulatory compliance in the finance industry?

In Exploring Other Compliance Issues: Arguably, there is an aspect of utilising advanced technologies; specifically how the institution manage to operate within the regulations.

V. How can financial services institutions measure their AI-powered marketing efforts?

It will also be important to establish metrics for measuring performance for continued refinement and for measuring ROI from AI investments.

The research questions explored in this paper work to provide insights into the role artificial intelligence will play in marketing for the financial services industry. Not only will they guide practitioners in tailoring their strategies accordingly but also offer mutual insights into how technological developments can propel quality innovation in a competitively evolving arena.

2. AI IN MARKETING: LITERATURE REVIEW

AI in marketing refers to the use of artificial intelligence technologies to optimize and improve marketing processes, strategies, and campaigns. This literature review provides insight into the numerous aspects surrounding AI technologies in marketing and the historical context of AI in finance, along with technological trends and challenges regarding AI adoption by financial organizations (Bough & Gunter, 2022). Let's take a look at these to see how AI can help us promote our financial products in new ways and strengthen global financial institutions.

2.1 Overview of AI Technologies in Marketing

Some of these tools and methodologies fall under the banner of so-called artificial intelligence (AI) technologies, which allow marketers to analyze data, automate processes, and personalize the customer experience. Some of the key AI technologies applied in marketing include machine learning (ML), natural language processing (NLP), predictive analytics, and computer vision. Googling Blog That These enable deriving meaningful insights and information from millions of data points that marketers could use to adjust their actions to consumer needs.

Machine Learning is a machine learning subset of AI that is involved in creating algorithms that allow computers to learn on their own from data without being explicitly programmed. ML algorithms are used in marketing to examine consumer behaviour patterns which help businesses to anticipate future actions and preferences. For example, ML is used by online shopping services such as Amazon to suggest products based on their previous purchases and website visits, greatly improving the customer experience and boosting sales (Gartner, 2025).

Machines are able to understand and interpret human language using ***Natural Language Processing***. This technology is crucial to the operation of chatbots and virtual assistants that deliver real-time customer service by interpreting queries and providing relevant information. NLP is also vital to sentiment analysis, which lets businesses understand customer opinions based on social media posts or reviews and helps them adapt their marketing in response.

Predictive Analytics uses past data to predict future results. In marketing, it translates to finding potential leads or high-value customers who match toward such a model, based on their past behaviours (Deloitte, 2025). Predictive analytics can help financial institutions customize their offerings to highlight the needs and requirements of particular segments of their customers.

Lastly, Computer Vision refers to the ability of machines to derive understanding from visual input received from the surrounding environment. In marketing: This tech may be helpful for social media campaign image recognition or in understanding how consumers engage with visual content. Are you curious about the different reactions consumers have to the visual components of ads, as an example? These technologies, along with others, allow businesses to hyper-personalize their marketing campaigns and treat each customer as an individual rather than a demographic statistic. In an age where consumers are demanding personalization at every stage of their journey, this move towards customized marketing is important.

2.2 Historical Context of AI in Finance

AI has been used in finance for decades, but from the late 2010s, it experienced a major acceleration thanks to advances in computing power and data accessibility. AI was first adopted in areas such as algorithmic trading, where technology is able to execute trades at a pace that is not feasible for a human trader. He demonstrated the capabilities of AI to interpret market indicators and to place trades based on real-time data. With the advancement of technology, financial institutions started to look more widely at use cases for AI outside of trading. This was made possible due to the development of machine learning algorithms which helped the banks and other financial service providers in predicting the risks involved in lending or investing by learn from the historical data. Not only did this capability improve decision-making, but it also reduced operational costs by automating routine tasks (Toptal, 2025).

Besides risk mitigation, AI has also played a crucial role in improving customer service at financial organizations. Artificial Intelligence & Machine Learning: The advancement in Machine Learning technologies has allowed banks to use chatbots for 24/7 interactions with their customers. Not only does this improvement efficiency, but it also serves to satisfy customers through timely assistance. In addition, a significant way that AI is already having an effect is through regulatory compliance. Financial institutions are required to have an extensive monitoring program in place to detect potential illicit transactions. AI-based systems can monitor transaction trends in real-time, identifying potentially suspicious activities for further investigation an essential step considering the growing sophistication of financial crimes. The historical context also shows challenges in AI adoption in finance, despite these advancements. However, when integrating AI into their operations, financial players face a variety of major challenges including data privacy concerns, ethical implications of algorithmic bias, and the need for decision-making transparency.

2.3 Current Trends and Challenges in the Adoption of AI

Several trends are shaping the landscape of AI adoption in marketing financial products as we lean into 2025. A major trend is the growing focus on hyper-personalization. AI systems in financial institutions generate deeply personalized experiences for customers based on their specific needs and habits. Consumer consciousness is becoming highly personalized in nature. Another trend is the emergence of generative AI that allows marketers to create content at scale using sophisticated algorithms. Generative AI is being used to produce personalized emails, social media posts, and even video content aimed at specific audience segments. Enhancing engagement, this capability enables financial institutions to communicate with customers across different channels without missing a beat.

Nevertheless, they all face numerous obstacles that prevent the mass adoption of AI when marketing financial products. With stringent regulations like GDPR (General Data Protection Regulation), organizations have to be cautious about managing consumer data. Let you leverage that data-driven insight without violating your compliance. Moreover, many legacy systems within financial institutions are not designed for the accommodations of advanced AI technologies, leading to integration issues. Updating these systems demands considerable investment and expertise factors that can impede the adoption procedure.

Furthermore, algorithmic bias, where biases already in training data can be perpetuated in AI systems made from them, is a growing concern. The potential for bias in algorithms used by financial institutions is a high-risk area, as discriminatory practices can not only harm customers but also result in damage to the institution's reputation and potential regulatory scrutiny (Chui, Manyika, & Miremadi, 2022). Organizations should provide ongoing education and training in AI technologies for staff to ensure they are aware of the capabilities and limitations of the tools they are using. The rise in adoption of these tools means that financial institutions will have employees who need the knowledge to use them effectively, and to understand the ethical implications of their use.

To sum up, this literature review illustrates the incredible potential of AI technologies to revolutionize the marketing of financial products but highlights that the historical background of AI offers an adequate context to understand its evolution in finance. But with trends like hyper-personalization and generative AI, and challenges like data privacy and algorithmic bias, successfully integrating these technologies means getting the balance between them right a balance that places equal emphasis on innovation and ethical considerations. By navigating these dynamics appropriately, global financial institutions can leverage AI to solidify their market footprint while adding tremendous customer value.

3. AI APPLICATIONS IN MARKETING FINANCIAL PRODUCTS

More broadly, integrating AI into the marketing of financial products has changed how financial institutions interact with and optimize their offerings to consumers and enhance their experiences. While the focus of this section is on three main applications of AI – personalization and customer engagement, predictive analytics, and automation including but not limited to chatbots and virtual assistants there are many other areas where financial marketers use AI (Accenture, 2023). These applications are critical to improve the effectiveness of marketing strategies and meet the changing needs of financial sector consumers.

3.1 Personalization and Customer Engagement

Personalization is now a key aspect of good marketing practices, specifically in the financial services sector. Consumers expect more personalized interactions than ever before, and financial institutions should embrace AI-driven personalization to meet consumers where they are and deliver interactions that are relevant to their interests and needs. AI technologies allow organizations to process large volumes of data about customers, such as transaction history, demographics, and behavioural patterns, to generate insights that inform targeted marketing strategies.

3.1.1 Tailored Marketing Strategies Using AI

This AI-driven personalization enables financial institutions to tailor relevant marketing messages and services unique to every customer. An example would be that by using machine learning algorithms, the banks can segment their customers and label different forms of customers based on similar behaviours or attributes. By dividing such different segments, targeted marketing campaigns can target the interests and needs of specific audiences. AI can be effectively used in creating personalized product recommendations. AI systems can recommend products in an informed manner, such as credit cards with specific benefits or investment opportunities based on customers' financial background and interest. The ability to tailor offers to individual customers adds a level of personalization that heightens customer engagement and conversion rates since customers are more likely to act on offers that are relevant to their unique situations (PWC, 2023).

Also, AI enables dynamic content delivery through multiple channels, meaning customers have access to information as needed. For instance, suppose one of customers is approaching retirement age, an AI system can automatically activate communications targeting that customer with information about retirement planning services or investment options designed for retirees. Financial institutions can promote stronger relations with customers and enhance higher engagement levels by providing customers with personalized content at the right time.

3.2 Predictive Analytics

Another powerful use case of AI in marketing financial products is predictive analytics. Using historical data and cutting-edge algorithms, financial institutions can predict consumer behaviour and preferences with stunning accuracy. This ability enables organizations to predict customer needs and customize their offerings.

3.2.1 Forecasting Consumer Behaviour and Preferences

Predictive analytics takes the shape of machine learning models analysing past behaviours to find patterns for future behaviours. By analysing the transactional history and expenditure patterns for a customer, banks can anticipate the time when the customer would seek a loan or a credit card upgrade. This foresight allows marketing to work with what they know (current intentions) rather than using past touchpoints to guide future decisions (which may or may not reflect customer interest).

Predictive analytics can also be used by financial institutions to improve risk assessment processes. By examining multiple datasets including but not limited to credit scores, income brackets, and spending habits, artificial intelligence/software can develop insight on a customer's creditworthiness, or risk of failure to pay on a loan. It helps lenders to differentiate between whom to assign credit with lower risk exposure (KPMG, 2023). Is this where predictive analytics comes into play? If the data shows an increase in demand for sustainable investment options among younger consumers, for example, the institution can create targeted marketing campaigns for environmentally friendly investment products that cater to this demographic. Understanding market trends in advance, businesses can become industry leaders by effectively meeting changing consumer requirements through predictive insights.

3.3 Automation Tools

Automation tools driven by AI technology have greatly improved the operational efficiency of financial institutions. Such tools automate processes that once required intensive time and manpower, empowering organizations to redeploy resources to their most effective utilization and enhancing the overall customer experience at the same time.

3.3.1 Chatbots and Virtual Assistants in Customer Service

Automation Major Redesign: Chatbots and Virtual Assistants Such AI-powered services offer customers instant assistance to a wide range of queries from checking account balances and applying for loans without the need for human intervention round the clock. This not only improves customer service but also lowers the operational costs for financial institutions. Chatbots use natural language processing (NLP) capabilities to answer customer queries in real-time (HBR Analytics Services, 2022). They can process several interactions at once without anyone facing lengthy wait periods before receiving help. Another benefit is that these virtual assistants are designed to learn from the interactions they have, which can make responses more accurate and timelier over the course of time and through user interactions and feedback. Beyond answering straightforward questions, chatbots can take customers through complicated processes like applying for loans or opening investment accounts. By streamlining these exchanges, financial institutions can improve user experiences while also incentivising clients to engage with their offerings more liberally. In addition, chatbots provide valuable data insights by tracking information on high-frequency questions, issues faced by customers, and more. The insights gathered allows financial institutions to recognize areas of improvement amongst their services or products, as well as to inform future marketing initiatives focused on key points of friction.

AI utilization in marketing financial products is diverse and revolutionary. AI algorithms allow financial institutions to optimize the customer journey and create more personalized experiences that speak to individual consumers and attract higher conversion rates. Predictive analytics, for instance, takes this a step further by providing organizations with the ability to accurately predict consumer behaviour and tailor products and services accordingly. Moreover, automation tools like chatbots and virtual assistants help in automating customer service processes and provide instant assistance for queries, leading to improved overall customer satisfaction (Ransbotham, Mitra, & Puryear, 2022). By integrating AI technologies into their marketing toolkit, global financial institutions not only contribute to innovation, but also give their customers a competitive advantage.

4. IMPACT ON GLOBAL FINANCIAL INSTITUTIONS

Artificial Intelligence (AI) is changing the paradigm of global financial systems. With the growing adoption of AI technologies in these organizations, they are experiencing transformative advancements in operational efficiency, customer interactions, and risk mitigation. This section discusses how AI has impacted financial institutions, through an analysis of case studies of successful use cases, a comparative study of institutions that embrace AI versus those that do not, and finally, exploring the regulatory challenges and ethical considerations of implementing AI (IBM Institute for Business Value, 2023).

4.1 Case Studies of Successful AI Implementations

Several banking companies around the world have adopted AI successfully in their systems to efficiently output better customer experiences. JPMorgan Chase is a prime example of a financial institution taking advantage of AI, leveraging it to improve efficiency and support better decision-making. The bank uses a machine learning based program for review of legal documents, called COiN (Contract Intelligence) platform that can examine legal documents and capture the important data, which in turn saves time of the associates from hours to seconds. This automation-human effort to manage its systems makes the organizational processes more efficient and reduces human inaccuracy by performing only value-added tasks by humans (Forrester Research, Inc., 2023).

One sector with another illuminating example is insurance, such as Allstate. The insurer has used AI-driven chatbots to guide customers via claims processing and reaching out with questions. These chatbots are based on natural language processing capabilities and allow the prompt response of customer questions, making service delivery possible with immediate activity, serving needs while reducing operating costs. Such deployments have been successful and demonstrate how AI can improve customer engagement and streamline service delivery in the financial industry.

On the other hand, in the field of investment management, Aladdin makes use of AI at Black Rock. Using machine-learning algorithms to parse large data sets, this complex risk (and, by extension, speculation) management system provides portfolio managers with clues on how to adjust capital allocation. For BlackRock, Catalyzing Innovation Through AI in an Asset-Management Context by augmenting its investment processes with AI it has improved its risk-mitigation and portfolio performance capabilities embodying how AI can underpin innovation in asset management (World Economic Forum [WEF], 2023).

Similarly, in Asia, banks like Singapore's DBS Bank have adopted AI to enhance the customer service experience. DBS Bank uses AI-based analytics to gain a better understanding of customer preferences, providing personalized banking experiences. The bank leverages AI-powered predictive analytics to envision customer needs through previous customer interactions allowing proactive outreach and personalized product recommendations. Such initiatives show how leveraging AI can improve customer satisfaction while creating loyalty in an ever-competitive landscape.

4.2 Comparative Analysis of Institutions Adopting AI vs. Those That Are Not

AI tech adoption in the finance sector is not homogenous as some organizations have fully embraced these innovations and others are taking their sweet time to adjust. A comparison of outcome metrics demonstrates that institutions utilizing AI perform significantly better than non-users. Early AI adopters within educational institutions report increased efficiency, reduced costs, and improved educational outcomes. As per a report by the European Central Bank (ECB), around 60% of large European banks have already adopted AI solutions in multiple functions leading to enhanced productivity and significant cut in operational costs. On the other hand, establishments that trail in embracing AI could face operational challenges and increased overhead expenses from dependence on manual methods. businesses applying AI show more agility in responding to shifts in the marketplace and consumer preferences. Banks, for example, that deploy predictive analytics can adapt their marketing strategies in the moment, using real-time data insights help them act on capturing trends faster than AI-less competition (Finextra Research Ltd., 2023). This agility enables competitive advantages in winning over new customers and keeping existing ones. On the other hand, institutions that are reluctant to utilize AI tend to suffer from legacy technology systems and limited data-driven decision-making capabilities. At a minimum, these organizations risk missing opportunities for innovation and falling behind competitors that employ advanced analytics in their strategic plans.

There is a considerable gap between the two groups in utilizing AI to improve customer engagement. Specifically, financial institutions that use AI actively can provide services and products tailored to customer preferences, which results in boosted satisfaction rates and loyalty. In turn, organizations not using AI lack necessary data on consumer behavior patterns and are incapable of ensuring encounters personalized for every individual. At the same time, it is crucial to note that AI adoption simultaneously introduces multiple issues for financial institutions as concerns about data privacy and security remain. Organizations gather large volumes of information to analyse, much of it being sensitive, which requires ensuring the highest data protection levels. Thus, the drive to increase the competitiveness of offered products and services as well as ensure data privacy remain the two sides of the same coin for financial institutions (Capgemini Research Institute, 2022).

4.3 Regulatory Considerations and Ethical Implications

With the rise of AI adoption in financial institutions, the impact of regulation and ethics should be one of the main driving forces leading the AI adoption experience. The global regulators are struggling to find an approach for monitoring the use of AI tech in the finance industry and protecting the customers.

Regulatory concern one: Financial institutions need to be able to demonstrate that its AI models can operated and reflect transparently and fairly with respect to its input data and output decisions; especially for operating decisions impacting consumers' financial well-being. For instance, if an AI system denies a loan application using biased data inputs or flawed algorithms, it can lead to discriminatory practices that are against fair lending laws. As a result, regulators are now urging organizations to put robust governance frameworks in place that enable accountability within their algorithmic decision-making. The need for data privacy is also a significant concern, as financial organizations collect enormous volumes of personal data to trained their learning models. With regulations like the General Data Protection Regulation (GDPR) in Europe, organizations are forced to comply and protect user data as much as possible while still using customer data for analytics. Non-adherence to these policies can lead to heavy fines and damage to your brand.

Ethics involve more than simply doing the bare minimum to remain legal; it involves the wider concerns in society that come into play when considering the use of AI technologies in finance. Entities involved in creating an algorithm must be aware and ensure those algorithms do not add bias to the final product. These financial institutions should strive to mitigate biases in training datasets to ensure that their algorithms do not replicate existing inequalities or discriminate against vulnerable populations (Statista Research Department, 2023).

Generative AI is being increasingly adopted in finance whereby machines create text products like reports or marketing collateral ethical concerns emerge with regards to misinformation. It is essential for financial institutions to take care when implementing generative models to guarantee accuracy and reliability, and to prevent misleading representations that could mislead consumers or skew market perceptions. In light of these challenges, regulators are intensifying their engagement with industry constituents to formulate wide-ranging frameworks overseeing the deployment of AI in the financial sector. Such initiatives are now essential to embed a culture of responsible innovation across financial institutions by teaching AI basics to financial professionals.

5. CHALLENGES AND RISKS OF IMPLEMENTING AI

From execution to maintenance, the integration of Artificial Intelligence (AI) into marketing financial products is hugely beneficial for global financial institutions. Climate technology has the potential to revolutionize sustainable energy solutions, but the journey towards implementation is not without its challenges and risks that must be managed effectively. This section delves into three primary barriers that hinder the widespread adoption of blockchain in these sectors: data privacy and security concerns, integration challenges with existing legacy systems, and organizational resistance to change (Business Insider Intelligence, 2022). Each of these challenges bring specific challenges that can stifle the successful deployment of AI technologies in the financial space.

5.1 Data Privacy and Security Concerns

Data privacy and security is one of the biggest challenges in applying AI in financial institutions. Financial institutions deal with large volumes of sensitive customer data including Personally Identifiable Information (PII), financial data, transaction histories, and credit scores. Data breaches or unauthorised access to this information are even more concerning from both a customer trust and regulatory perspective. To train AI systems, significant amounts of data must often be collected and analysed. But this can run afoul of data protection laws like the Europe's General Data Protection Regulation (GDPR) and similar laws in other parts of the world. As organizations around the world collect, process, and store countless amounts of personal data, these regulations place strict requirements on that data collection, storage, and processing (Zengler & Kauffman, 2023). Non-compliance with these regulations could lead to massive fines and reputational damage.

Also, the characteristics of AI systems can heighten existing data privacy risks. Exposure of Sensitive Information: Some machine learning algorithms can inadvertently learn or include sensitive information within the model, which could be accessed by adversaries with the potential of a data breach. The intricacies of AI models can also create challenges around maintaining transparency over how data can be used raising ethical questions around obtaining informed consent from customers. Moreover, data privacy in AI implementation also faces threats from cybersecurity. Due to their possession of valuable information, financial institutions are one of the major targets for the cyberattacks. Such a successful breach would result in identity theft, financial crime, and huge financial losses for customers as well as financial institutions. Consequently, organizations need to leverage strong cybersecurity solutions to secure their AI systems and to protect the sensitive data they manage (Financial Times Special Report on Artificial Intelligence in Banking and Finance, 2022).

5.2 Integration Issues with Legacy Systems

The integration of new technologies with existing legacy systems is another major hurdle for financial institutions in their efforts to adopt Artificial Intelligence. A lot of banks and financial organizations run on legacy technology stocks that were never built for modern AI workloads. Most legacy systems are inflexible and fail to scale for effective AI deployment. Integrating the different systems can be a complex and resource-intensive process that can require a huge investment of time and capital. Legacy systems are often siloed across departments or business units, creating challenges when it comes to accessing and analysing data in a holistic way. This fragmentation can limit an organization's ability to extract insights from its data, which is the primary fuel for AI applications.

Additionally, legacy systems may lack compatibility with the real-time processing capabilities necessary for many AI applications. Closed-loop AI models, for instance, rely on real-time feedback from incoming data in order to fine-tune their outputs continuously. Inevitably this causes delays in decision-making or poor performance in AI algorithms if a financial institution's core systems cannot handle it promptly enough. Transitioning outdated systems to next-gen infrastructures is also met with resistance from employees used to processes already in place And, by definition, introduce new technologies that can make staff afraid of being redundant or overwhelmed and, therefore, slower to adopt innovative solutions. Hopefully, organizations can strike a balance between technological advancement and employee engagement (O'Reilly Media & Harvard Business Publishing Corporate Learning [Eds.], 2022).

To address these challenges of integration, financial institutions need to formulate a clear path that describes how to move from legacy systems to more agile architectures that can power their AI initiatives. It involves leveraging cloud-based solutions that provide enhanced flexibility and scalability, allowing departments seamless access to real-time data. Therefore, organizations should invest into change management initiatives to become an innovation driven culture. This resistance can be mitigated by offering training programs and resources that enable the staff to embrace new technologies, ultimately improving the institutional adaptability of the organization.

5.3 Organizational Resistance to Change

The big challenge for successful AI implementation in financial institutions is the organizational resistance to change. However, the article states that incorporating it with technology into an organization is sometimes difficult because employee's express resistance. The biggest worry an employee has is whether they will lose their job thanks to automation and AI. A lot of workers are concerned that their jobs could become obsolete when machines take over the jobs that humans previously did, fuelling anxiety around job security in the business. It can also create a culture that is resistant to change and stifle the enthusiasm to adopt new technologies.

Employees might view AI as a challenge to the traditional "human touch" that defines customer service in banking and finance. Many consumers want human interactions when managing their finances, so employees might not embrace alterations they perceive as potentially weakening habits of customers or resulting in impersonal service encounters. In addition, organizational silos permeate within financial institutions, which can hamper the change, by creating a fettered approach between departments. When there's a lack of communication or collaboration around AI initiatives, it can create misunderstandings about goals and objectives that may cause confusion or frustration among employees. To address these challenges associated with resistance in an organization, leaders should involve employees in the implementation process (European Banking Authority [EBA], 2023). Ensuring transparency around the benefits of AI adoption such as streamlining processes or improving customer experiences can reduce the fear-factor while generating buy-in from employees.

6. CONCLUSION AND SUGGESTIONS

AI has emerged as one of the most impactful tools with the potential to revolutionize the marketing of financial products. AI technologies continue to evolve, providing financial institutions with innovative solutions that enhance customer engagement, streamline operational efficiency, and empower them to thrive in an increasingly competitive landscape. The conclusion distills the salient points of the inquiry systematized in this paper and provides recommendations to financial institutions seeking to wield Information technology effectively in their marketing efforts. Throughout this research, it has emerged that AI is a transformative force in the financial services sector. The presence of an artificial intelligence that can analyze huge swaths of data and relay them in a cohesive manner allows institutions to personalize their offerings of what they can offer with the next best thing or even predict when consumers will default cycles, automate rudimentary tasks, etc. This functionality results in better customer experiences, greater efficiency, and higher profitability. Perhaps the biggest advantage of AI is its ability to personalize. AI-powered analytics allow banks and other financial institutions to customize marketing strategies at the individual customer level, allowing for deeper relationships and brand loyalty. These levels of personalization go far beyond simple product recommendations; it refers to a 360-degree view of customer journeys that allows institutions to reach clients wherever they are in this journey.

This predictive analytics helps the financial organizations in foreseeing the customer needs and market trends. These historical data can be useful to identify patterns that define product development and marketing approaches. This proactive approach not only increases customer satisfaction, it also makes organizations leaders in innovation in the financial sector. By utilizing automation tools, including chatbots and virtual assistants, they can automate repetitive tasks, reduce response times and enhance customer experience. Such AI applications allow financial institutions to deliver contact center assistance instantly, freeing human agents to handle more complex questions. It enables organizations to maintain high-levels of the service quality, even while scaling their operations. Yet there are challenges to overcome on the path to successful AI adoption. As organizations collect and analyze sensitive customer information, issues tied to data privacy and security remain top of mind. Moreover, resourcing associated with legacy systems, as well as internal organizational resistance, poses further barriers to widespread adoption among many financial services organizations.

REFERENCES

Accenture. (2023). How AI is reshaping financial services: A new era of innovation and growth. Retrieved from https://www.accenture.com/us-en/insights/financial-services/artificial-intelligence

Bough, B., & Gunter, A. (2022). Marketing and financial services in the age of artificial intelligence. ResearchGate. https://www.researchgate.net/publication/350843589_Marketing_and_Financial_Services_in_the_Age_of_Artificial_Intelligence

Business Insider Intelligence. (2022). The impact of AI on banking and finance: Trends to watch.

Capgemini Research Institute. (2022). How AI is transforming customer engagement in banking.

Caskey, S. (2021). AI-enabled marketing in finance: Current applications. Emerj. Retrieved from https://emerj.com/ai-marketing-in-finance/

Chui, M., Manyika, J., & Miremadi, M. (2022). *The state of AI in 2022: Trends and insights for financial services firms*. McKinsey Global Institute.

Deloitte. (2025). How artificial intelligence is transforming the financial services industry. Retrieved from https://www.deloitte.com/ng/en/services/risk-advisory/services/how-artificial-intelligence-is-transforming-the-financial-services-industry.html

Ernst & Young (EY). (2025). How artificial intelligence is reshaping the financial services industry. Retrieved from https://www.ey.com/en_gr/insights/financial-services/how-artificial-intelligence-is-reshaping-the-financial-services-industry

European Banking Authority (EBA) Report on Artificial Intelligence in Financial Services (2023).

Financial Times Special Report on Artificial Intelligence in Banking and Finance (2022).

Finextra Research Ltd. (2023). AI in banking: Use cases and implications for the future.

Forrester Research, Inc. (2023). The future of AI in financial services: Trends and predictions for 2025.

Gartner. (2025). AI in marketing: The future of smart marketing. Retrieved from https://www.gartner.com/en/marketing/topics/ai-in-marketing

Google Cloud. (2025). AI in finance: Applications, examples & benefits. Retrieved from https://cloud.google.com/discover/finance-ai?hl=en

HBR Analytics Services. (2022). The role of AI in transforming customer experiences in banking and finance. *Harvard Business Review*.

IBM Institute for Business Value. (2023). Banking on AI: How financial institutions can leverage artificial intelligence to drive growth and efficiency.

KPMG. (2023). The impact of artificial intelligence on financial services: Opportunities and challenges ahead. Retrieved from https://home.kpmg/xx/en/home/insights/2023/01/the-impact-of-artificial-intelligence-on-financial-services.html

McKinsey & Company. (2025). Building the AI bank of the future. Retrieved from https://www.mckinsey.com/~/media/mckinsey/industries/financial%20services/our%20insights/building%20the%20ai%20bank%20of%20the%20future/building-the-ai-bank-of-the-future.pdf

O'Reilly Media, Inc. & Harvard Business Publishing Corporate Learning. (Eds.). (2022). Artificial Intelligence in Financial Services: A Practical Guide.

PWC. (2023). AI and the future of financial services: A roadmap for success. Retrieved from https://www.pwc.com/gx/en/services/consulting/artificial-intelligence.html

Ransbotham, S., Mitra, S., & Puryear, J. (2022). Artificial intelligence in marketing: The next frontier for financial institutions? *MIT Sloan Management Review*.

Statista Research Department. (2023). Global market size of artificial intelligence in the banking sector from 2019 to 2025.

Toptal. (2025). Financial implications of using AI in marketing. Retrieved from https://www.toptal.com/marketing/digital/ai-marketing

World Economic Forum (WEF). (2023). Artificial intelligence and the future of financial services: A global perspective.

Zengler, T., & Kauffman, R.J. (2023). The intersection of AI and finance: Opportunities for innovation and growth.

Chapter 7
Exploring the Role of Artificial Intelligence in Governance:
Enhancing the Resilience of Legal Systems, Mitigating Corruption, and Reinforcing Democratic Setup

Saurabh Chandra
https://orcid.org/0000-0003-4172-9968
Bennett University, India

ABSTRACT

The infusion of artificial intelligence (AI) into different facets of administration is defining new horizons in legal environments. AI has turned out to be an essential element in the improvement of legal systems because of its ability to accelerate and augment legal procedures. AI has proven to have great potential in successfully combating corruption because it increases transparency and accountability in society and in firms. Corruption is a multifaceted problem that negatively affects governance and becomes one of the main reasons for citizens' distrust. AI is considered to provide important support in conflict analysis and prediction of the conflicts' behaviour in the context of conflict transformation and peacebuilding. Through analysis of data gathered from social media, news outlets, and so on, the various AI-driven tools can gather early signs of conflict and monitor conflict escalation and de-escalation in real time. It assists governments and other stakeholders in peace building processes.

DOI: 10.4018/979-8-3693-9395-6.ch007

INTRODUCTION

Introduction of artificial intelligence (AI) into many fronts in society has been found to be among the most captivating and one of the most promising areas of technology advancement. AI systems are used in almost all sectors such as healthcare, banking, transport and entertainment sectors as the systems become more sophisticated. Nowadays, Artificial Intelligence (AI) has been established as a valuable and disruptive technologies in several fields like healthcare and finance. But arguably there are few professions or industries where its impact might be said to be as broad and diverse as in law. As emerging AI technologies proceed, they offer the legal industry and society as a whole both new opportunities that have not existed before, and challenges that have not existed before. Legal questions and challenges are emerging due to the increasing applicability of AI technology in many sectors of human activities that require legal regulation. The incorporation of the AI innovation in numerous sectors in administration is an excellent chance for enhancing delivery of service as well as governance. Specifically, AI can enhance government performance based on the assessment of big data, automation of monotonous work, and transparency. Applying AI in management processes can enhance accountability and transparency because AI is an effective means of performing monitoring tasks. AI systems can always follow up on transactions and processes and immediately raise an alert on any suspected case of fraud or corruption. Oversight bodies benefit from these systems through timely intervention into the misconducts analyzed in real time. In order to ensure that AI contributes to the betterment of society and enhancing governance it will be vital to establish key principles based and ethical evaluation. When properly implemented and deployed, the use of AI in the government's operations could ultimately lead to an optimal organizational setup aimed more toward the citizens than their own machineries as they go through this technology landscape. It is important when looking at the complex relationship between law and AI to investigate the legal rationalisation, ethical implications and new challenges when entering such a vast field. The following writing aims to discuss connection between AI and law. Currently, AI penetrates various spheres of life as the evolution of technologies progresses at an unsustainable rate. Artificial intelligence as a phenomenon concerns a great number of fields, disciplines and industries and law is one of the examples. At the same time, it would seem to be notably affected by such possibilities and to stand in a rather special position with regard to the further development of AI. This paper aims at discussing the opportunities and challenges that arise in worldwide legal frameworks as artificial intelligence emerges. This integration is also challenging to current legal frameworks when artificial intelligence technologies are used. This proposal posits that due to the traditional laws' chronic failure to adapt to emergent technologies such as artificial intelligence, there is normally vagueness and uncertainty about ethical standards, legal responsibility and accountability. Hence lawmakers across the globe are struggling to devise comprehensive legislation that will regulate the use of AI. There are several countries that have dealt with these issues by enacting laws or policies that are related to artificial intelligence to some extent. New legal issues that can be solved only by going beyond the frame of current legal systems are appearing as new AI technologies emerge.

AI's Role in Legal System Enhancement

Artificial intelligence is gradually gaining significant roles in enhancing effectiveness and efficiency in the delivery of justice for the public and transforming and enhancing the approach to work for legal professionals. AI can be integrated into the legal system in various ways which will enable us to expand justice, decrease cost and enhance efficiency. As these technologies progress more there is a lot of potential to disrupt the legal industry and deliver justice to the doors of the masses. To ensure that AI systems do not perpetuate bias, and that they are explainable, to ensure that justice pursuits are not hindered or side-tracked, the ethical medal has to be maneuvered strategically. An especially rich topic concerns the analysis of laws and policies that govern Artificial Intelligence, ethical issues involved and new challenges when studying a complex interplay between law and this disembodied intelligence. This pressure towards accuracy, costs, and efficiency has slowly and steadily begun to push more and more use of AI in legal work. Today, a lot of people in the legal field incorporate AI in various activities, including document assembly, research, contract analysis, and risk assessment. Such technological developments are anticipated to enhance decision solitude, enhance the rate of workflow, and enhance entry to justice.

Artificial Intelligence (AI) in government is gaining increasing attention due to its potential to transform public services and policy-making (Medaglia et al., 2021). AI applications could free up significant time for public servants, allowing them to focus on high-value work (Berryhill et al., 2019). The technology offers opportunities to improve policy design, decision-making, citizen engagement, and service delivery (Berryhill et al., 2019; Ahn & Chen, 2020). However, government adoption of AI lags behind the private sector and faces unique challenges (Berryhill et al., 2019). Key areas for future research include AI governance, trustworthiness, impact assessment, and data governance (Medaglia et al., 2021). The implementation of AI in government has broad implications for public organizations, affecting aspects such as interoperability, public value, transparency, and accountability (Jimenez-Gomez et al., 2020). As AI continues to advance, it is expected to fundamentally change society, requiring the public sector to adapt and coordinate broader social transformation (Ahn & Chen, 2020)

AI plays a transformative role in enhancing the legal system in various ways.

Legal Research

AI vastly enhances the speed and efficiency of performing research in the field of law. Thus, when performing traditional research, lawyers might have to invest a significant amount of time in what is called ''keyword searching'' of databases containing statutes, case law and legal literature, for instance. The use of Artificial intelligence (AI)-driven technologies can fast generate voluminous data to search for relevant cases and court rulings. The very use of natural language processing (NLP) enhances the capacity of those tools in understanding legal terms and context to find data and offer case laws at the same time.

Document Automation

Document automation remains one of the most extensive applications of artificial intelligence in the legal profession. Repeatedly making new contracts, wills and agreements is normal in legal processes of law formation. Due to this, AI is able to automate these operations through document creation based on given set of rules as well as templates. This ensures that there are standardity in documentations to legal compliance as well as minimize on time and possible human errors.

Predictive Analytics

Analyzing previous data, such methods make forecast of future situations. In legal field, AI can study prior outcomes, the decisions made by the judges, and other data essential to determine the result of a particular case that is still going on. By gaining this capability, attorneys will be in a better position to organize themselves and clinicians better as well as determine the likelihood of their cases as they choose whether to compromise and settle their cases or proceed to trial.

E-Discovery

E-discovery can be defined as the process of identifying, collecting and reviewing electronic documents for litigation support. With the ability to sort and filter massive datasets, AI enhancement is achieved in this aspect. By using two types of machine learning involving document classification and search for relevant content, as well as identification of potential issues, e-discovery may be accelerated significantly and the cost may be reduced drastically.

Contract Review and Analysis

Of the most significant benefits of using AI technologies that can be applied to contract reviews are the possibilities of identifying potentially problematic areas and ensure compliance with the law. These systems can show peculiar language, paradoxes or terms that do not comply with usual practice. This accelerates the routine of review and leaves sufficient time to core issues where legal professionals need to be involved as opposed to spending a lot of time synthesizing minor aspects.

Legal Chatbots

AI-powered chatbots give the public the fundamental legal advice and assistance to enhance the availability of legal aids. Such that one will be enabled to write the document, answer frequently asked legal questions and direct the user to other resources if need be. They assist those in need in comprehending their laws and choices and break down procedures through timely support.

Case Management

Over case-related information, deadlines, and discussions as well, AI systems improve the case management. It can assist with arranging meeting time, assist in reminding people of important dates and foster collaboration between legal bodies. Therefore, productivity is enhanced, and legal professionals are able to spend more time on core law related work as opposed to clerical work.

We are also going to address two issues: Sentencing and Risk Assessment.

Criminal justice employs Artificial Intelligence to recommend possible ways to sentence an offender and risk factors. This means that Judges can apply algorithms in making good decision by using parts such as a defendant's criminal records and behaviors. While this could deter repetition and lead to passing more standardized sentences, ethical issues will arise about bias and the blind which require supervision.

Enhanced Access to Justice

AI has the potential to greatly increase justice access, especially for marginalized groups. AI tools have the potential to lower the cost of legal services, making legal assistance more accessible. AI-powered internet platforms can also offer self-help tools, enabling people to traverse the legal system without the assistance of a lawyer.

Ethical Considerations and Challenges

Notwithstanding the advantages, significant ethical questions have been raised about the use of AI in the legal system. Concerns to be discussed include data privacy, risk of intrinsic bias in the AI systems, and the transparency of decisions made via the AI systems. Since the training data has issues with structural imbalance, there is the likelihood that the use of AI will lead to a perpetuation of bias. Legal practitioners should observe how these tools are being used inappropriately or in a manner that is incorrect.

However, there are challenges and the ethical concerns arising with the incorporation of AI in the legal circumstances. One major issue for discussion is that bias in algorithms is possible, and that it can only serve to maintain the present inequity within legal structures. The following are the general and specific disadvantages of AI systems: Voters may be inadequately represented by biased AI systems that are created unintentionally from prejudiced data sets or algorithms constructed. Based on the example of such relations as Shepherd, one of the most significant undeveloped regions in the further development of the legal profession is the relations between artificial intelligence and law. On the positive side, AI promises to be a disruptive technology that ushers change at all levels, but on the other side it has some tough questions that cannot be easily addressed and require detailed assessment and initial responses. However, if an approach to these challenges is minimally driven by honesty and a vision of the ideal judiciary, artificial intelligence can help build a much more objective, impartial, and inclusive judicial system for all citizens. Justice Dr DY Chandrachud of the Supreme Court of India pointed out at the conference that AI and Law are closely linked. He underscored the possibility as to how AI could significantly transform the range of occupations, with a focus on the legal profession, in which AI can increase the pace of the administration of justice. He said, "The time of standing still is over; let us bring change within our profession and start questioning how the power of technology's processing might be best optimised within these institutions."

LITERATURE REVIEW

Artificial Intelligence (AI) is increasingly transforming governance across various dimensions. In public services, AI enhances efficiency, responsiveness, and decision-making, enabling faster data processing and improved service delivery (Darmawanto et al., 2023). AI applications in government span policy-making, public service delivery, and internal management, with the majority focusing on service delivery improvements (Van Noordt & Misuraca, 2022). In corporate governance,

AI is shaping decision-making processes, with potential scenarios ranging from assisted to autopoietic intelligence (Hilb, 2020). AI's role in governance extends to supporting sustainable development goals, improving decision-making, detecting fake news, and enhancing public service systems (Kesharwani et al., 2023). However, challenges remain, including data privacy, ethics, and public trust concerns (Darmawanto et al., 2023). As AI continues to evolve, it presents opportunities for advancing governance practices, though its application in existing systems is still in a nascent phase (Kesharwani et al., 2023).

Artificial Intelligence (AI) in government is gaining increasing attention due to its potential to transform public services and policy-making (Medaglia et al., 2021). AI applications could free up significant time for public servants, allowing them to focus on high-value work (Berryhill et al., 2019). The technology offers opportunities to improve policy design, decision-making, citizen engagement, and service delivery (Berryhill et al., 2019; Ahn & Chen, 2020). However, government adoption of AI lags behind the private sector and faces unique challenges (Berryhill et al., 2019). Key areas for future research include AI governance, trustworthiness, impact assessment, and data governance (Medaglia et al., 2021). The implementation of AI in government has broad implications for public organizations, affecting aspects such as interoperability, public value, transparency, and accountability (Jimenez-Gomez et al., 2020). As AI continues to advance, it is expected to fundamentally change society, requiring the public sector to adapt and coordinate broader social transformation (Ahn & Chen, 2020).

Artificial Intelligence (AI) presents both opportunities and challenges for mitigating corruption and reinforcing democratic integrity. AI can enhance transparency, reduce information deficits, and improve citizen engagement in the democratic process (König & Wenzelburger, 2020; Thapa, 2024). However, it also poses risks such as misinformation campaigns, voter manipulation, and potential distortion of public opinion (Thapa, 2024). In the context of anti-corruption efforts, AI offers promising tools for both top-down and bottom-up approaches, but faces challenges in data quality, algorithmic design, and institutional implementation (Köbis et al., 2021). Particularly in procurement, AI's potential as an anti-corruption tool is limited by existing data constraints and due process requirements (Sanchez-Graells, 2021). To harness AI's benefits while mitigating risks, robust regulatory frameworks, digital literacy initiatives, and improved data architectures are necessary (Thapa, 2024; Sanchez-Graells, 2021). Overall, AI should complement, rather than replace, existing anti-corruption and democratic reinforcement strategies.

Artificial Intelligence (AI) is emerging as a promising tool for combating corruption, offering potential for both top-down and bottom-up approaches (Köbis et al., 2021). AI-based anti-corruption technologies can mine and crosscheck large datasets to monitor, identify, report, and predict corruption risks, particularly in public spending (Odilla, 2023). However, the effectiveness of AI in this domain faces several challenges. These include the need for improved data architectures, concerns about biased algorithms, and constraints imposed by due process requirements (Sanchez-Graells, 2021). The implementation of AI in anti-corruption efforts requires careful consideration of legal frameworks, international collaboration, and harmonization with existing regulations (Klochko & Zelenskyi, 2024). While AI presents opportunities for enhancing transparency and efficiency in anti-corruption initiatives, expectations should be tempered as AI applications largely replicate human interventions and can only provide incremental improvements rather than transformative changes in oversight and enforcement (Sanchez-Graells, 2021).

The integration of AI in governance presents significant challenges and opportunities. Ethical considerations, including justice, transparency, and privacy, are paramount when implementing AI in public and private sectors (Saxena, 2024). The governance of AI requires a multi-level and multi-dimensional approach, balancing soft and hard mechanisms across various social and administrative contexts (Nieminen et al., 2019). As AI permeates critical areas like urban infrastructure, law enforcement, and healthcare, there is increasing pressure to design AI systems that are accountable, fair, and transparent (Cath, 2018). To address these challenges, researchers propose strategies such as inclusive AI policymaking, design-for-all approaches, enhanced transparency, and public engagement initiatives (Saxena, 2024). Additionally, the development of ethical frameworks, clear guidelines, and robust AI governance models is crucial for ensuring responsible AI implementation in governance (Saxena, 2024; Cath, 2018). Ongoing, adaptable research is necessary to fully comprehend AI's long-term impact on governance structures.

Artificial Intelligence (AI) is increasingly seen as a promising tool in combating corruption, offering potential for both top-down and bottom-up approaches (Köbis et al., 2021). AI technologies can efficiently manage information and optimize processes across sectors, potentially transforming anti-corruption efforts (Klochko & Zelenskyi, 2024). However, the implementation of AI in anti-corruption faces challenges, including the need for harmonized legal frameworks, improved data architectures, and consideration of due process requirements (Sanchez-Graells, 2021). While AI presents opportunities for detecting and tracking transnational corruption schemes, its ambivalent nature means it can also create new corruption pathways (Vinnykova, 2022). The development of international standards for AI use in anti-corruption efforts is crucial, as is the creation of a transnational structure with appropriate rule-making and control powers (Vinnykova, 2022). Despite its potential, expectations for AI as an anti-corruption tool should be tempered, as it may only provide incremental improvements rather than a significant transformation of oversight and enforcement architectures (Sanchez-Graells, 2021).

AI'S ROLE IN COMBATING CORRUPTION

Of course, corruption is a clear and present danger to democracy. Some of these are bribery, embezzlement, fraud and the like all of which are costly to the public and private sectors and lead to inequal and dysfunctional societies. Such consequences trigger a vicious circle that erodes public confidence and becomes a social harm. Moreover, corruption evolves through successively interconnected varieties, as modern global society is multifaceted and interconnected. Introducing itself in numerous manifestations, corruption affects the effectiveness of governmental bodies, increases inequality, and thus slows down the progress toward attainment of sustainable development goals set by the UN. The purpose of AI anti-corruption technologies also known as AI-ACTs is to fight corruption. Unfortunately, AI is a preventive technology that is capable of early identification of the possible patterns of corruption. For this reason, this technology offers brand-new methods for detecting and combating fraudulent behaviours due to the ability to work with large amounts of information and establish connections that may not be obvious at first glance. Its application however is still mainly limited and the process is burdened with certain challenges.

According to the United Nations administration survey carried out in 2016, there has been an upward trend in use of e-government among many nations. The e-government technologies facilitate the flow of information within and between the layers of government as well as between government and the public at large and access to government structures with large repositories of information. H ought enables greater restraint of discretion that can be vested in public officials, transparency and accountability – which are all important components to minimize or eradicate corruption chances.

As highlighted earlier, the use of AI is the most recommended solution to fight against corruption across sectors and regions. Of course, its potential can increase transparency, make accountability more accurate, and minimize potential conditions for corruption. AI is a major solution to corruption as it generates and automates data analysis, predictions, and transparency throughout different industries. Precise data from financial operations, records and procurement which AI evaluates can recognize different patterns of fraud as spending habits different from the norm or false records of financial transactions. However, there is a presence of ethic issues or challenges regarding to AI in this arena such as data privacy and algorithmic bias that should be properly solved so that AI in this arena will be appropriately used to avoid any loss of public trust. All in all, there is undoubtedly great potential for societies to use AI as a tool for generating an increased level of accountability that discourages corruption and encourages integrity. Here's a comprehensive exploration of how AI can be utilized to combat corruption:

Data Investigation and Outlier Diagnosis

AI algorisms can work with big amounts of data coming from a number of sources, such as financial transactions, public records, and procurement procedures. Business intelligence can apply certain machine learning algorithms that will indicate, possibly, corrupt practices, like embezzlement or fraud. Any irregularities concerning spending patterns, differences in account balances or individual transactions can be investigated easily at the option of authorities.

Predictive Analytics

AI in this case can help to determine where high risks of corruption might be expected given past records. Due to a focus on risks that are most likely to lead to corruption in the future, it is possible to prevent corrupt actions by starting with evidence-based indicators, including the absence of control, decision-making discretion, or specific socioeconomic conditions. These proactive measures provide for concentrated actions before contamination with corrupt practices occur.

Enhancing Transparency in Procurement

Generally, Artificial Intelligence makes public procurement procedures more transparent, which are often capable of corruption. Many problems such as bid rigging, or bias in the award of contracts can be identified from analyzing bidding data and contract awards through the tool of artificial intelligence. Through assessing the competitiveness of bids, that the rate determination by machine learning algorithms is done in a fair manner without bias of collusion.

Supervising Public Officials and Resources

Many times, AI solutions can assist in monitoring the belongings and activity of Public officials. In this case, AI has an ability to identify some anomalies or the process of building up the wealth that is considered to be anomalous, if certain asset declarations, financial transactions or other records are considered. Due to the knowledge that the public is eager to scrutinize their actions to an extent, excessive attention can help prevent corrupt practices among public servants.

Whistleblower protection and corporate reporting systems

Thus, enhancing the whistleblower reporting system, AI can provide safer and more anonymous ways to do that. Automated processing of reports based on natural language tools can rank incidents concerning priority and analyze important signs of corruption. This means that we can also have a support from the use of the AI chatbot to ensure that whistleblowers who are reporting the cases feel secure and encouraged.

Automation of Compliance and Audit

AI solutions in compliance auditing and monitoring means reduce the instances of unethical behaviour many folds. For example, it is able to constantly match financial transactions against regulations and flag any suspicious activity on the spot. This helps to reduce the occurrence of human audits which are likely to be either flawed or rigged if manipulated.

Awareness Creation and Outreach

AI tools can be applied to enhance awareness of the population on corruption issues and engage the population in monitoring activities of the government. Automated systems, for example, can analyze the expenditures by government and provide the citizens with data on the utilization of their tax money. Transparency makes the pie public and persuades the parties to account for their actions in their dealings with the public.

Facilitating International Cooperation

Regarding enforcement, corruption always involves cross border activities which need international cooperation for an effective remedy. AI that Researches data of several jurisdictions plays role and helps Nations work and share information. Artificial intelligence can facilitate cooperative investigations and re-establish cooperation in tackling corruption globally by detection of cross-boundary corrupt activities.

Enhancing Judicial Processes

Analyzing the judicial proceedings linked with corruption cases, one should mention that AI can optimize such processes. For instance, AI can help in the implementation of the casework management process by sorting the cases considering their difficulty and effectiveness. Furthermore, outcomes prediction enables legal authorities to forecast probabilities of case outcomes and determine which particular cases should receive their attention.

Addressing Ethical Concerns

While the AI seems to have the ability to handle the corruption in many ways, there are some ethical dilemmas that one has to prick before employing the AI. A considerable amount of extra attention should be paid to problems as algorithmic bias, data privacy, and transparency of decisions made by AI. Since the application of AI systems is a complex process that involves the use of an unpredictable system, there must be an element of responsible deployment of the AI systems.

The fight against corruption has a unique ally in contemporary technology in the form of Artificial Intelligence (AI) that offers innovative solutions and solutions that seek to promote accountability, transparency, and uncomplicated processes. AI can help in preventing corrupt practices from occuring through automation, analysis of data and and predictions on corrupt practices before they trigger a major incident. In other words, so as to make sure it has a positive impact in the society and serves a noble purpose of encouraging an open society, we need to thread lightly on the ethical issues involved in the use of AI technologies.

AI'S ROLE IN CONFLICT ANALYSIS AND PEACEBUILDING

AI in Conflict Management offers an interesting field where ethical questions should be weighed against possible new possibilities of conflict-solving tools and techniques that may otherwise be hard to overcome. One such idea is in early warning and prediction mechanisms where AI can bring radical changes in conflict anticipation and management. When it comes to conflict prevention, machine learning algorithms could hardly be described as being less significant as it deals with vast data that may be very different in its nature, like sentiment of social networks' posts, articles in newspapers or magazines, economical indicators etc. Such analytical ability enables these algorithms to scan through extensive data in the shortest time possible. That is why they are able to identify the first signs of tensions or the potential violence, before it reaches its peak. This ability to recognise patterns and anomalies in data provides those with the ability to assess global situations with lead-time to then undertake appropriate preventative measures and diplomatic initiatives. An important use of Artificial Intelligence in the early warning systems is that of social media sentiment analysis. Besides, social stage sites is an actual source of real time data which represents public mood and response to current occurrences. This huge flow of data is feasible for machine learning algorithms to analyse the patterns of discussion, sentiment and even detect early signs of tension or conflict (Chiancone, n.d.). Through monitoring the events on the pages of social networks, AI systems can make a signal for the potential threat of conflicts in advance and take measures to minimize the likelihood of a conflict.

Greater reliance on AI in the early warning and prediction systems does not mean that human decision-makers are not important but are in fact elevated to the next level. The first aspect is that it is easier for humans to grasp certain context, cultural place, or history in the conflict. AI's role is enhancing the capability of policymakers due to its ability to provide timely and accurate information to the decision-making process hence strengthen the ability to prevent and manage conflicts. However, let us not lose sight on the fact that despite of the huge potential of AI for this field, ethical concerns are critical. Issues of data protection, impartiality of AI and appropriate use of these machines are important concerns that should not be regarded lightly. Much focus should therefore be placed on the optimality of using technology as a way of arriving at the truth while also keeping the rights of people involved in the conflict; this is in a bid to bring fairness and effectiveness in conflict resolution through the use of artificial intelligence while not compromising on the ethical norms of appropriate use of AI.

Organizing for peace and after war necessitate different dynamics that present difficult to deal with needs of the affected societies. AI has been employed in these effort by offering unique approaches towards evaluating the humanitarian needs, and to identify the at-risk population groups, and to transform and advance the various humanitarian assistance as well as reconstruction interventions. Furthermore, other artificial intelligence based solutions such as the chatbots are critical in providing counselling and mental health services, and helping individuals traumatized in conflict to come back to form sense of community.

Social media contents and satellite images are among key emerging applications of AI in peacebuilding and after-conflict regeneration. These technologies provide a way of tracking and assessing conditions in conflict areas to gain knowledge on the evolving needs of the populations. Social media monitoring is implemented in the context of humanitarian response through the use of artificial intelligence, which enables gathering the most relevant and up-to date information regard on the ground situation, displacement, scarcity of resources and potential Novelty (Choyal et al., 2024). With the satellite imagery analysis, this data provides a comprehensive approach on the impact of conflict in the physical as well as social context.

Also in utilizing satellite images there is another benefit – using AI for the analysis of such images. It can detect changes in infrastructure, recognize a damaged area, and assess the effects of the confrontation on the surrounding terrain. This analysis assists in a formulation of the strategies, which should be used for rebuilding a society especially after conflicts thus enabling organizations to target areas that need reconstruction most.

This paper established that chatbots can be customized to deliver culturally relevant and context appropriate support in light of the various challenges people face in post-conflict settings. No matter whether it is a situation when someone has to deal with trauma, needs support or has to work on grief or on any other challenge that comes with the beginning of a new life, AI-powered communication can substantially improve individuals' quality of life and decrease the risks of some mental health disorders. Moreover, the works contribute to the cause of social communion and unity since they give a sense of togetherness as well as support to the society even in the case that financial and physical support is tight.

However, the application of new technology in the processes of conflict resolution and state rebuilding has important ethical implications. Protection of the rights of those affected requires privacy, informed consent, and proper use of data. AI technologies should be used with transparency about how funny they work and the biases in algorithms that can potentially restore unfairness.

Mitigating mis- and disinformation, and specifically regulating hate speech, has become a pressing concern when addressing modern conflict management, as the speed of information sharing in online contexts may have a profound impact on the conflict environment. Specifically, it can be solved by the help of Artificial Intelligence, and more specifically – Natural Language Processing (NLP) algorithms. Such algorithms can detect any content that is provocative, encouraging violence and spewing hatred, or that is misinformation and thus minimize their impacts in terms of social harmony and incidents of conflict.

Due to the spread of fake news and hatred speech in various social platforms, there are concerns on the social stability, escalation of existing conflicts and social inequality that can arise from the use of the social platforms. NLP algorithms that use the concepts of machine learning help in the fast and efficient identification of various kinds of problematic content in large textual streams when compared to manual monitoring.

One of the ways that NLP can be employed in the fight against falsehood is in the ability to analyze the language features and contextual signposts that are associated with fake or misleading information. These algorithms can detect gaps, paradoxes, or any sort of oddities in phrases in the materials that appear online and mark it for review. Based on the language nuances and context, the NLP algorithms can distinguish between true and false stories which will improve the conditional assessment of the information appearing in cyberspace.

The problem of bias and discrimination is critical when it comes to to adoption of AI systems in conflict transformation. The primary issue is that, when AI algorithms are trained, they learn prejudice from past data and even amplify those prejudices. In other words, if the training data is pre-disposed to bias, the AI system might repeat bias, that is, it might give more weightage to one section of the population or the other. In the conflict resolution processes this would exacerbate the existing differences and create more conflict than was necessary rather than providing a neutral and competent way at resolving the differences. It will therefore need a multi-faceted strategy in order to address this problem. First of all, the importance of extending the availability of datasets in order to get a wider range of views and opinions cannot be overestimated. However, the fairness-aware algorithm is crucial to consider and correct the bias in the AI system actively. This also involves constant supervision and modifications to prevent discrimination from beginning or persisting. Furthermore, opacity and lack of interpretability in some AI algorithms cause a lot of difficulties, primarily in such a sensitive field as conflict resolution. The use of technology as the 'black box,' some artificial intelligence systems which are hard to explain why reached the decision they did can partly lead to accountability issues and distrust.

AI'S POTENTIAL ROLE IN STRENGTHENING DEMOCRATIC INSTITUTIONS

AI can significantly improve governance and this holds much promise in welfare states where an attempt is made towards addressing social and economical justice to the society. Based on AI, potential strategies can be generated and tested, latent data structures can be discovered, and knowledge bases and organisational regulations can be automated. In many welfare states such as India, a vast population poses limited access to the web; but AI helps in framing policies and programs. A government can ascertain the needs of the disadvantaged, hard to reach, or minority population, identify clients, and assess the efficacy of its social services. Furthermore, AI can ensure the detection of both the benefits and drawbacks of the particular policies for the population and track the performance of the executing programs.

The concept of welfare state has now some how or the other also started getting implemented in India as it aims at ensuring social justice and economic justice. Taking into account its multifaceted and rather heterogeneous social structures, problems related to the achievement of this goal, as well as the application of AI, it is possible to propose perspective and prognostic analyses concerning such difficulties experienced by the economically and socially unprotected population as well as possible ways to solve them within the framework of the inclusive development paradigm.

AI can greatly enhance the policy decision-making process by miming out the real systems and outlining policies. Such an approach may prove useful to the government because it would save cash and would not have to bear the consequences of having designed or implemented inferior policies. AI in context of governance is still a relatively young concept that can pave way for major improvements to the delivery of government services and ordinary functioning of all spheres of life requiring efficient management of increasingly large and intricate systems and decision-making. At the time of writing, data mining can be broadly identified as the most recurrent application of the AI technologies in the government activities and processes, specifically in terms of fraud and improper payments detection (Berch et al., 2024). Anticipating further development to the next ten years, intelligent automation will be mainly used to perform these tasks through administrative software agents.

AI refers to the capacity of a machine or a computer to perform tasks that are field to intelligent beings. Decision making and action Putting together, governance can relate to corporate, international, national and local as well as between societies levels. E-governance in India involves the application of Information and communication technologies by the public sector to improve information dissemination and service delivery, facilitate involvement of the public in decision making and increase government responsibility and openness. This concept started gaining popularity in India after 1992; India, a country which was in a financial crises at that time.

The Indian government is goal is to improve the standard of living for its people by reducing the burden of work for government employees. In this context, AI systems can be very helpful as the latter will be handling many mundane tasks like diagnosing heart diseases. In partnership with the Indian Department of Cardiology, Stanford University AI Lab has designed a corresponding heart disease diagnosis AI system. Gradually as this system develops, personnel with government employers who are suffering from heart conditions can still be productive and relieved from work. Globally, AI applications are encouraged by the desire to reduce cost of public service delivery. These technologies can perform tedious operations at a faster and rate as compared to human employees due to fatigue (Karnani, 2024). Expert Systems are often used to make decisions or to reason in a certain domain. AI system can also be helpful in India to expose corruption in its policies implementation results in huge saving to governemnt. For instance, there is room for AI in the Public Distribution System (PDS). Presumably, AI can help allocate the resources when needed with the elections being a part of the democratic process. In general, AI can be seen as a potential enabler of better, more satisfying lives for the citizens of India.

The emphasis on efficiency and effectiveness in governance is essential in today's competitive landscape. Efficiency means completing tasks with minimal time and resources, while effectiveness focuses on achieving better outcomes with the same investment. AI can play a significant role in this by automating processes and supplying valuable decision-making insights. It can analyze vast amounts of data, a task typically performed by humans, and develop programs that automate data analysis and make decisions based on if-then-else logic. This not only reduces human effort but also minimizes errors and corruption. Additionally, AI can enhance resource utilization across various projects and uncover alternative strategies to achieve results with fewer resources, which is particularly important in resource-challenged India.

AI can be described as the ability of a digital computer and computer-controlled robot to accomplish operations that are linked with intelligence in human beings. Having made meanings for decision-making and implementation, governance refers to a process that occurs at corporate, international, national, local and societal interactions. In Indian context of 'e-Governance' is defined by the use of IT & ICT by the public and government sector for improvement in information processing & delivery, people's participation in decision making and over all bringing transparency & accountability in the system. This idea started receiving attention in India after 1992 when the country was in financial crisis.

Indian government is very concerned with the well being of its people, the government of India aims at eradicating difficult working conditions of GOs employees. AI systems can be particularly useful in this aspect because they could help to offload routine work, for example, the diagnosis of heart disease. With active cooperation from the Indian government's Department of Cardiology, Stanford University's AI Lab has created an AI model for heart disease diagnosis. Each time this system is developed, those government workers who have heart problems could be eased out of work while still giving something back. Worldwide, AI interventions are driven by the notion that they will reduce the cost of service delivery. It can do monotonous and tedious work faster and without the weariness of workers that usually manifest (Karnani,2024). Expert Systems are widely used to replicate the decision-making process in specific domains. In India, AI systems can also identify corruption in policies, resulting in great savings on the part of the government. For instance, the current PDS can be powered by AI wherein it will improve the functioning of the program. In the context of the elections once, AI can help to organize resources in an efficient manner, whether within the context of the democracy. On the whole, it can be concretised that, AI has a potential to enhance the quality of citizenship in India.

AI'S ROLE IN LAW ENFORCEMENT AND PUBLIC SAFETY

Artificial Intelligence (AI) has affected many sectors probably in equal measure; one of them being the law enforcer. Modern tools of AI, including advanced algorithms and predictive analysis, brought the revolution in crime fighting strategies of police departments. It means that by analyzing vast amounts of data AI technology can recognize patterns, trends and outliers that might be unnoticed by human analysts and can provide valuable input for law enforcement actions. A major application of AI in this field is in the prevention as well as the early detection of crime. AI can also analyze past crime data to identify dangerous zones and to predict possible crimes to occur. This capability enables law enforcement agencies to manage their resources well; placing police officers where they need to be to prevent crime from occurring. Furthermore, other technologies such as facial recognition and video analytics later help in identifying suspects easily and fast tracking investigations. Such technologies not only enhance the rates or effectiveness in pursuing or arresting lawbreakers, but also enhance safety and security of individuals within the society.

Surveillance systems have been of great help to law enforcement since they improve surveillance of people in public areas to look out for hazardous characters. These systems rely on elaborate methods of analysis and machine learning to analyse copious amounts of data such as videos, audio and social media feeds. Such systems can help to prevent crime and enhance the safety of the population by immediately notifying the police about suspicious behavior. Thus, AI driven surveillance gives rise to privacy and civil liberties concerns when considered for implementation. Another issue that becomes inherent from the utilization of these technologies is the strive to meet security demands while at the same time respecting individual's rights on privacy by the law enforcement agencies. Certainly, they can contribute to the criminal investigation and prevention; nevertheless, the over-surveillance and misuse of personal data are an issue. Obtaining an appropriate and adequate balance is possible only when there are reasonable rules and regulations allowing such systems being implemented safely.

Specifically, the incorporation of artificial intelligence (AI) algorithms has been demonstrated to bring a positive impact to the investigations of police forces. Through the use of enhanced data analysis and pattern identification these algorithms help solve crimes more proficiently to police agents. AI algorithms might be of significant help in increasing investigation efficiency in one domain, namely, analysis of big amounts of digital evidence. As more people engage in digital device use and cyberspace involvement, investigators say that one of their main problem areas is related to great volumes of data. Such information can be analyzed almost instantly using AI algorithms to draw out patterns and correlate facts that might not be noticed by a human being. It not only reduces the time that investigators have to spend while searching for such material but also raises the chances of discovering such evidence early enough. In addition, AI algorithms can reduce the influence of errors that are inherent in humans, and when some parts of the investigation are delegated to AI, these elements will be more objective.

Introduction of AI in police work is slowly transforming the law enforcement process by eliminating the human effort to analyze data and decide on the best course of action since they are done by intelligent software with analytical abilities. Police organizations, therefore, benefit from AI integration in their decision-making models by driving organizational productivity and result management. For instance,

AI algorithms can forecast the tendencies of criminal incidences in a given location, based on data on crime rate, social media posts and other data. This enable agencies to increase their resource utilization in a way that could cover all risks in areas that may likely to experience crimes hence improving on their chances of controlling the crimes before they happen. Moreover, AIDM can assist investigators in decision making process by offering significant information and help in utilizing time and energy during criminal investigation. Analyzing data, like videos, interviews, and other reports, AI algorithms can identify links between events, people or even identify potential suspects which could be missed by the officers. This can significantly speed up the investigation process and help build stronger cases against criminals. However, it is crucial to maintain a balance between relying on AI and utilizing the expertise and judgment of human investigators to ensure fairness, transparency, and accountability in the decision-making process.

A significant application area of the use of AI has been identified in the criminal justice system where it especially in the pre- trial stage and or the conditions for parole of offenders. Such artificial intelligence systems assess chances of flights for offenders and determine on whether parole should be granted for such a person. These data sets are collected from crime rates existing in the past and details about the existing person. For instance, the US Criminal Justice System uses the Correctional Offender Management Profiling for the Alternative Sanction, abbreviated to COMPAS, for initial risk analysis for the parole terms setting. These systems aid in making required activities in a court faster in order to come up with a timely decision. AI maintains that it improves this process by reducing the likelihood of human mistakes and therefore makes it a more credible proposition than most techniques in philosophy.

The AI policing being referred to here is predicting where certain crimes may occur, who may commit them, what type of crime, and who the victims may be. Predictive policing is one of the most questionable practices and it has been more of an experiment for the last few years. New technologies are currently being piloted both by companies and law enforcement to factor in predictive policing. They can help in reaching improved results to minimise or prevent crimes and enhance the crime prediction systems. Using crime rate then algorithms it is easy to produce maps and show where most crimes occur then police should patrol more often in such regions.

Also, AI can predict people within the society that are most likely to engage in criminal activities and others who are most likely to recidivate after being released from jail after analyzing their past behavior. This brings about important issues regarding such information and more is going to be discussed as the practice develops.

Another major strength of predictive policing is the ability to determine those individuals most likely to be targeted by criminals in the future. Modern studies focus on identification of the risk factors which can increase the likelihood of elder abuse and application of the obtained data in order to indicate the types of abuse which are possible. Of course, elder abuse is only an example, and any other violent crimes also fall under the purview of potential utilization of predictive policing.

Basically, facial recognition technology cannot be overrun in police work. It is used by officers to pursue suspects and to identify missing persons from image data provided. Everybody who tried watching a footage from a street camera understands how terrible the picture quality is. You can only imagine the difficulty of trying to find these important details within such images, let alone it being a herculean task. Some police departments could use more police officers or even analysts just to handle as many images that they need to analyze to solve all their cases. AI technology in policing presents the opportunity to improve the rate of face matching as compared to the efforts of the officers besides saving precious time. Machines can apply specific parameters to recognize faces that might be difficult or almost impossible for a human to do. The current AI technology can even differentiate a single face from a group, such as at a stadium-an application that helped China to arrest a criminal while watching a sports event.

CHALLENGES AND ETHICAL CONCERNS OF AI IN GOVERNANCE

Speaking of responsible AI governance, it January be understood as a focused effort to design and implement AI systems and technologies to support the long-term goals of people and organizations, along with safeguarding the public's best interests. It is important for the business managers to adhere to the rules and regulation as well as guidelines to help them establish effective governance on AI systems. In addition, they should operate under ethical principles, values, and standard. To exclude such problems and minimize the related threats and the adverse effects—such as decreasing human input into decision-making—practitioners must be trustworthy, responsible, and guaranteeing the effective management of their intellectual capital, as well as other assets, including IT systems, funds, and staffs. There is a need to provide procedural governance structures that would provide means for a proper regulation of the AI technologies. Some of the key elements for the responsible AI governance will be depicted in figure 1 below.

Figure 1. Component of A.I. governance

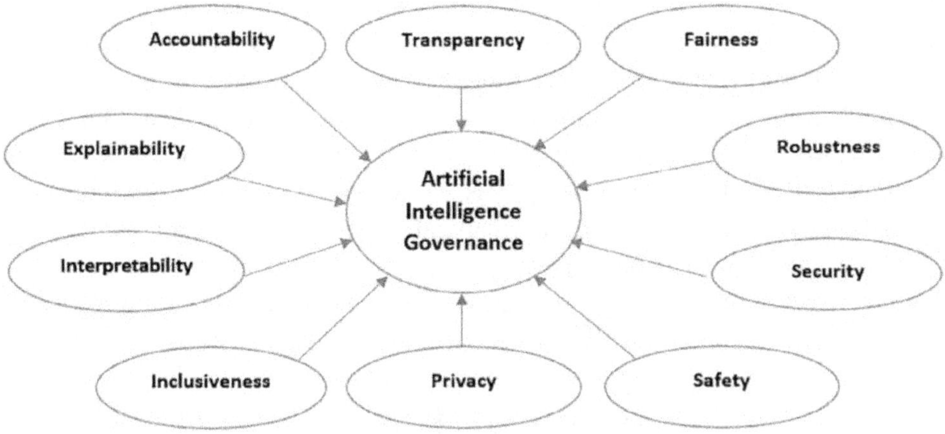

Concerns about data privacy among users are increasing, particularly because employees in business environments have the right to control who can access their information (Zirar et al., 2023). Reports by Wu et al. (2021) and Zhu et al. (2020) indicate that individuals' privacy is at risk if third parties gather or utilize their data without consent or voluntary agreement. AI-driven products, such as chatbots, virtual assistants, digital assistants, wearable technology, and dialogue systems, are collecting and storing vast amounts of customer data. For example, facial recognition technologies are being used in business contexts, allowing individuals to log into websites and social media securely, as well as authorize payments through banking and financial apps. Employers can also use these systems to monitor and record employee attendance. Additionally, Camilleri (2023) noted that these technologies enable marketers to target specific customers with digital ads. Security agencies can employ them for criminal investigations and surveillance. However, the use of such technologies has raised significant concerns regarding security and privacy. Various data privacy laws enacted in different regions require organizations to inform users when they are collecting and storing biometric data. As a result, businesses utilizing these technologies must obtain permission before using customer data.

Additionally, businesses need to communicate their data privacy policies clearly to their target audiences (Wong, 2020). They should reassure customers that the information collected with their consent is safe and that it may be used to improve the personalized services offered. Consequently, AI developers should implement preventive policies and procedures for data monitoring and control. To protect against cyberattacks, investing in security technologies such as firewalls, access control systems, and authentication or encryption software is essential. Regular testing can minimize the risk of incidents, enhance security standards, and safeguard data.

The fairness aspect of responsible AI focuses on the actions taken by practitioners to address algorithmic biases that may be unintentionally or intentionally integrated into their automation processes (Bellamy et al., 2019; Mäntymäki et al., 2022). Developer biases, which can include preferences or biases towards specific demographic traits such as gender, age, and ethnicity, can influence AI systems (Madaio et al., 2020). However, many global companies have recently developed tools aimed at detecting and reducing bias as much as possible (John-Mathews et al., 2022). AI systems often learn new capabilities from the data they are trained on, and biased or skewed data can lead to inappropriate outputs.

Accountability involves the expectations that stakeholders have regarding the proper functioning of AI systems throughout their lifecycle, which includes design, development, testing, and implementation, all while complying with relevant regulatory frameworks (Camilleri, 2023). Raji et al. (2020) emphasize that AI developers should be responsible for ensuring the smooth operation of AI systems at every stage of their lifecycle. Stakeholders anticipate that developers will keep a record of their AI development processes to demonstrate accountability (Mäntymäki et al., 2022). Understanding algorithmic models, grasping how AI operates, and recognizing the functionality of individual components, along with algorithmic transparency—referring to the clarity of the algorithms—are all aspects tied to AI transparency (Andrada et al., 2023; Hollanek, 2020).

New technologies such as AI have brought in several forms of ethical issues which have affected how the technologies are managed in business decisions in the years. An even higher level of moral standards has slowly displaced the previous models of governance. Concerning this, privacy and ethics in AI research confirm that these matters should be discussed while implementing AI. The research also casts light on the challenges of preserving privacy in the age when data are converging. Analyzing the literature, ethical codes, articles, and legislation yields numerous privacy issues connected to the governance of AI systems. As it can be observed there is the need for an extensive and flexible ethical system because of the algorithmic bias, data processing problems, and AI-driven evaluation on vital business decisions. Maintaining ethical use of AI therefore requires the cooperation of the development team, the policymaker and the consumer, which can enhance corporate business decisions. In conclusion, it is suggested that governments, foundations and businesses, should collaborate multidisciplinary, interdisciplinary and intersectoral, as well as international to develop the AI ethical principles. In addition, there is a need to understand several real-life moral cases related to AI that have a considerable impact on the society, which will make it possible to convene interdisciplinary groups of experts to solve the ethical problems of AI. Finally, to continue the fast pace development of AI, it is imperative to improve the cooperation in the development and research of AI governance technologies.

CONCLUSION

In conclusion, it is possible to suggest that the application of AI in the field of conflict resolution opens great opportunities for early warning and prediction that change the approaches to conflict anticipation and management. AI's ability to analyze large volumes of data from social media, articles, and economic indicators that contain early warning signs of conflict or actions leading to violence improve the work of human decision-makers in conflict management. In the context of conflict analysis and post-war rehabilitation, theforesaid uses of AI to analyze social network and satellite imagery lead to a better assessment of the changing needs of the populace and ensures more accurate humanitarian intervention and rebuildment strategies. AI automated conversational agents are an essential and unique solution for delivering psychological interventions needed in post conflict societies; however, issues regarding privacy infringements and data ethic utilization are present. Additionally, in the sphere of governance AI comprises a great opportunity of making the governmental decisions more effective and rational, and to develop also great perspectives for the improvement of public service in the welfare state – India. But responsibility and accountability in AI require solutions to problems concerning data protection and algorithmic and data bias in governance to advance ethical and effective AI governance and business management. First, there is a need for cooperation between developers, policymakers, and end-users to set up and sustain commonly acceptable norms and standards as a ground-breaking approach to AI governance.

There are several issues that come to question when governments incorporate the use of AI and automation in their activities. However, to make sure that these technologies are being implemented in the right and proper manner, issues like algorithmic bias and concerns to do with data privacy must be put into consideration. One of the most striking phenomena is the workforce displacement, which means that a number of activities must be employed to retrain or retrain the employees. However, there are very many limitations which need the intervention of stakeholders, such as budget limits and technical difficulties that are difficult to overcome. Finally, this study has presented some examples of good practices regarding the use of AI and automation in PA, based on evidence from different nations. These examples include strategy prescriptions, tool and technique highlights, and examples on actual benefits secured to provide useful reference for governments interested in similar pursuits. Due care is required in the adoption of AI and automation in the Process of Public Administration. Government and academic officials and nonacademic policy makers and directors would need to ponder over the moral and legal issues of these technologies, employee implications, and its functionality and moldability. Thus, implementation of the framework would require the cooperation of bodies that belong to the government, technological firms, and other related parties. There is a need to have the right leadership as it shapes culture, provides focal direction, and ensures the implementation of AI and automation in PA. This implies that further research and development are required to continue to deal with the new issues arising from the advancement in technology. Over time, the opportunities for the application of AI and automation in public administration will grow because of these technologies. They need to be continually examined for their effectiveness, policy and regulatory changes be made whenever possible, and the public be involved in the decision making process. In this way, governments can get the best out of AI and automation not only in governance, but also in improving the quality of public services delivering thus making the public administration significantly more effective and responsive. The future of research in artificial intelligence (AI) and automation within public administration is vast. It encompasses the investigation of effective adoption strategies, evaluation of long-term effects, encouragement of interdisciplinary methods, enhancement of human-machine collaboration, tackling privacy and security issues, considering socioeconomic impacts, and examining the possibilities of emerging technologies. By exploring these topics, the research seeks to deepen understanding, guide policy-making, and promote innovative practices in the application of AI and automation in public administration.

REFERENCES

Ahn, M. J., & Chen, Y. C. (2020, June). Artificial intelligence in government: potentials, challenges, and the future. In *Proceedings of the 21st Annual International Conference on Digital Government Research* (pp. 243-252). DOI: 10.1145/3396956.3398260

Andrada, G., Clowes, R. W., & Smart, P. R. (2023). Varieties of transparency: Exploring agency within AI systems. *AI & Society*, 38(4), 1321–1331. DOI: 10.1007/s00146-021-01326-6 PMID: 35035112

Bellamy, R. K., Dey, K., Hind, M., Hoffman, S. C., Houde, S., Kannan, K., Lohia, P., Martino, J., Mehta, S., Mojsilovic, A., Nagar, S., Ramamurthy, K. N., Richards, J., Saha, D., Sattigeri, P., Singh, M., Varshney, K. R., & Zhang, Y. (2019). AI Fairness 360: An extensible toolkit for detecting and mitigating algorithmic bias. *IBM Journal of Research and Development*, 63(4/5), 4–1. DOI: 10.1147/JRD.2019.2942287

Berch, V., Lankevych, A., Naturkach, R., Bysaha, Y., & Prodan, V. (2024). The role of digital technologies in building an inclusive and transparent society: An analysis of the legal mechanisms of democratic governance. *Amazonia Investiga*, 13(79), 177–188. DOI: 10.34069/AI/2024.79.07.14

Berryhill, J., Heang, K. K., Clogher, R., & McBride, K. (2019). Hello, World: Artificial intelligence and its use in the public sector.

Cath, C. (2018). Governing artificial intelligence: Ethical, legal and technical opportunities and challenges. *Philosophical Transactions. Series A, Mathematical, Physical, and Engineering Sciences*, 376(2133), 20180080. DOI: 10.1098/rsta.2018.0080 PMID: 30322996

Darmawanto, A. T. (2023). The Influence of PDRB, Unemployment and Human Development Index on Poverty in Kalimantan Province. *Syntax Idea*, 5(12), 2335–2354.

Hilb, M. (2020). Toward artificial governance? The role of artificial intelligence in shaping the future of corporate governance. *The Journal of Management and Governance*, 24(4), 851–870. DOI: 10.1007/s10997-020-09519-9

Hollanek, T. (2023). AI transparency: A matter of reconciling design with critique. *AI & Society*, 38(5), 2071–2079. DOI: 10.1007/s00146-020-01110-y

Jimenez-Gomez, C. E., Cano-Carrillo, J., & Lanas, F. F. (2020). Artificial intelligence in government. *Computer*, 53(10), 23–27. DOI: 10.1109/MC.2020.3010043

John-Mathews, J. M., Cardon, D., & Balagué, C. (2022). From reality to world. A critical perspective on AI fairness. *Journal of Business Ethics*, 178(4), 945–959. DOI: 10.1007/s10551-022-05055-8

Karnani, A. K. (2024). AI empowerment in democratic governance: Enhancing participation and efficiency. *Journal of Data Acquisition and Processing*, 39(1), 993.

Kesharwani, S. (2023). Interrelationship Between E-satisfaction, E-trust and E-loyalty in the Banking Industry. *Global Journal of Enterprise Information System*, 15(3), 9–16.

Köbis, N., Starke, C., & Rahwan, I. (2022). The promise and perils of using artificial intelligence to fight corruption. *Nature Machine Intelligence*, 4(5), 418–424. DOI: 10.1038/s42256-022-00489-1

Madaio, M. A., Stark, L., Wortman Vaughan, J., & Wallach, H. (2020, April). Co-designing checklists to understand organizational challenges and opportunities around fairness in AI. In *Proceedings of the 2020 CHI conference on human factors in computing systems* (pp. 1-14). DOI: 10.1145/3313831.3376445

Mäntymäki, M., Minkkinen, M., Birkstedt, T., & Viljanen, M. (2022). Putting AI ethics into practice: The hourglass model of organizational AI governance. *arXiv preprint arXiv:2206.00335.*

Medaglia, R., Gil-Garcia, J. R., & Pardo, T. A. (2023). Artificial intelligence in government: Taking stock and moving forward. *Social Science Computer Review*, 41(1), 123–140. DOI: 10.1177/08944393211034087

Odilla, F. (2023). Bots against corruption: Exploring the benefits and limitations of AI-based anti-corruption technology. *Crime, Law, and Social Change*, 80(4), 353–396. DOI: 10.1007/s10611-023-10091-0 PMID: 37359505

Van Noordt, C., & Misuraca, G. (2022). Artificial intelligence for the public sector: Results of landscaping the use of AI in government across the European Union. *Government Information Quarterly*, 39(3), 101714. DOI: 10.1016/j.giq.2022.101714

Vinnykova, N. (2022). Digtial technologies in combating global corruption. *The Journal of VN Karazin Kharkiv National University.Issues of Political Science*, 41, 30–39.

Wu, Z., Shen, S., Li, H., Zhou, H., & Lu, C. (2021). A basic framework for privacy protection in personalized information retrieval: An effective framework for user privacy protection. [JOEUC]. *Journal of Organizational and End User Computing*, 33(6), 1–26. DOI: 10.4018/JOEUC.292526

Zhu, T., Ye, D., Wang, W., Zhou, W., & Philip, S. Y. (2020). More than privacy: Applying differential privacy in key areas of artificial intelligence. *IEEE Transactions on Knowledge and Data Engineering*, 34(6), 2824–2843. DOI: 10.1109/TKDE.2020.3014246

Zirar, A., Ali, S. I., & Islam, N. (2023). Worker and workplace Artificial Intelligence (AI) coexistence: Emerging themes and research agenda. *Technovation, 124*, 102747. Camilleri, M. A. (2020). A Taxonomy of Online Marketing Methods. *Hajarian, M., Camilleri, MA, Díaz, P. & Aedo, I.(2020). A Taxonomy of Online Marketing Methods*. In Camilleri, M. A. (Ed.), *Strategic Corporate Communication in the Digital Age*. Emerald.

ADDITIONAL READING

Elsyra, N. (2023). The Role of Artificial Intelligence in Government Services: A Systematic Literature Review. *Open Access Indonesia Journal of Social Sciences*, 6(3), 998–1003. DOI: 10.37275/oaijss.v6i3.163

Hauser, C. (2025). Digitalisation, artificial intelligence, and the fight against corruption. In *Organizational Corruption, Crime and Covid-19* (pp. 238-258). Routledge.

Islam, M. B. E., Haseeb, M., Batool, H., Ahtasham, N., & Muhammad, Z. (2024). AI threats to politics, elections, and democracy: A blockchain-based deepfake authenticity verification framework. *Blockchains*, 2(4), 458–481. DOI: 10.3390/blockchains2040020

Kuziemski, M., & Misuraca, G. (2020). AI governance in the public sector: Three tales from the frontiers of automated decision-making in democratic settings. *Telecommunications Policy*, 44(6), 101976. DOI: 10.1016/j.telpol.2020.101976 PMID: 32313360

Lim, T. (2024). Environmental, social, and governance (ESG) and artificial intelligence in finance: State-of-the-art and research takeaways. *Artificial Intelligence Review*, 57(4), 76. DOI: 10.1007/s10462-024-10708-3

Moberg, A., & Gill-Pedro, E. (2024). Law and the Governance of Artificial Intelligence. In *YSEC Yearbook of Socio-Economic Constitutions 2023: Law and the Governance of Artificial Intelligence* (pp. 1–13). Springer Nature Switzerland. DOI: 10.1007/16495_2024_69

Sarker, S., Henningsson, S., Jensen, T., & Hedman, J. (2021). The use of blockchain as a resource for combating corruption in global shipping: An interpretive case study. *Journal of Management Information Systems*, 38(2), 338–373. DOI: 10.1080/07421222.2021.1912919

Strelcenoks, J. (2024). Requirements for the Concept of the Implementation of Artificial Intelligence as a Tool for Preventing Corruption in the Public Sector. *Acta Prosperitatis*, 15(1), 154–163. DOI: 10.2478/acpro-2024-0014

Chapter 8
Future of Education With AI-Assisted Technologies

Amit Kumar Arora
https://orcid.org/0000-0001-9311-0740
KIET Group of Institutions, India

Shivani Sharma
KIET Group of Institutions, India

Anjan Kumar
KIET Group of Institutions, India

Anuj Kumar
HRIT University, Ghaziabad, India

Rashmi Tyagi
HRIT University, India

Santosh Kumar
https://orcid.org/0009-0002-3115-6772
Sharda University, India

ABSTRACT

By leveraging AI-driven solutions, students also have the ability to adjust learning based on personal preference, with unique content that both improves understanding and boosts interest. Virtual tutors, interactive simulations, and smart assessments allow students to learn at their own pace and get real-time feedback. AI-enabled data analytics tools can spot skill gaps and forecast the likelihood of students that feed back into their re-evaluated teaching and streamline to boost success in the classrooms. AI collaborative platforms create a shared worldwide ecosystem for learning having students from all walks of life. Administrative aspects of teaching like grading and curriculum development are streamlined through automation, enabling educators with more bandwidth for mentorship and innovation. AI-assisting technologies are thus building blocks of a better educational system, with equitable, efficient, and future-proof learning developed by bridging the entry gaps.

DOI: 10.4018/979-8-3693-9395-6.ch008

1. INTRODUCTION

Artificial Intelligence (AI) Integration in Education: A New Era of Learning With the shift towards a knowledge-driven economy, the need for efficient, inclusive, and adaptive education systems has never been more pressing (Zint et al., 2024). The many cornerstones of this transformation are newly devised AI-assisted technologies that rethink traditional pedagogies by allowing the content of knowledge to be taught, reflected and interacted in novel and unprecedented ways. Instead of primacy being given to methodology, it is offered to methodology, while upholding the best of practice; a new paradigm is established to better meet the unique needs of learners and educators globally.

Biggest AI Contributions in Education Traditional classroom models often adopt one teaching method for a large group of students, while AI education platforms customize education for the specific needs of an individual. By studying data related to learning habits, strengths, weaknesses, and preferences, these technologies create personalized learning paths. Adaptive learning software, for example, can detect when a student is struggling to master a particular concept and provide focused exercises, tutorials or interactive modules to overcome those challenges. With this personalized framework, students can learn at their own pace, allowing them to have a deeper grasp of subjects instead of risking a lag in learning. AI has also become a vital part in improving accessibility in education (Raaj, 2024). Many students with disabilities or those living in remote areas are deprived of quality education. AI-supported tools like speech-to-text applications, real-time translation services, and virtual sign language interpreters tear down these walls, helping ensure education is more inclusive. AI supports the formation of virtual classrooms, allowing students from diverse geographical backgrounds to share access to the same quality of resources, thus providing a backbone for the seamless operation of urban and non-urban education systems. Through techniques like real-time translation, AI breaks down language barriers and promotes global learning by enabling students from different linguistic backgrounds to work together seamlessly.

The other game-changer is the role of AI in automating administrative tasks. And for educators often spend time performing tasks like grading assignments, tracking attendance, or planning curriculum, they aren't able to really dedicate their time to focusing on teaching and mentoring (Romero et al., 2017). This allows for better allocation of resources by helping to identify bottlenecks in school processes and prioritizing learning where needed; AI-powered systems enable such tasks to be automated precisely and efficiently, leaving educators more time to engage in more substantive interaction with students. One example might be AI-driven grading tools that can assess a student's assignments and tests and manage all of the feedback in real-time. Just as smart scheduling systems can optimize class schedules and resource allocation to improve the learning environment.

1.1 Overview of AI in Education: Evolution of AI Technologies in Education

AI's ability to sift through big data also allows for predictive analytics in education. Artificial intelligence and machine learning can help identify patterns and predict future outcomes by monitoring students' performance and behavior. With this predictive capability, inferences can help address issues early on and educators can help students who may be struggling or becoming disengaged before a downward trajectory becomes insurmountable (Agbo et al., 2019). Using data to guide educational institutions enables them to create courses which reflect up-to-date practices in their fields of study, ensuring students are qualified to enter into the job force. AI has also created opportunity for immersive learning environments, an integral part of educational methodology for whom the necessity to engage the students have become utmost important. Another potential application for AI content creation is in the field of training and development creating customized VR and AR training experiences for personalized and immersive learning experiences. For instance, students can virtually walk through time learning about a historical event in VR, perform virtual science experiments, or run through intricate surgical procedures in a safe environment. These experiential learning opportunities not only enhance engagement but also allow students to apply their knowledge in practical contexts, equipping them for real-world scenarios (Apiola & Sutinen, 2021).

The democratization of knowledge is another important pillar of AI-assisted education. AI-enabled Massive open online courses (MOOCs) have democratized high-quality education for millions of learners around the world. By utilizing AI, these platforms can suggest appropriate courses based on user needs, monitor progress, and offer tailored feedback, streamlining the learning process. Other information technology-based chatbots and virtual assistants are available 24 hours a day and answer questions, act on questions, and guide students during their learning journey. AI is also fundamentally transforming teacher training and professional development. AI-enabled tools can help educators improve their teaching prowess by keeping them updated about the latest pedagogical practices and providing constructive feedback about their performance (Pollock et al., 2019). AI-powered virtual coaching platforms analyze classroom activities, capture areas for improvement, and recommend ways to bring efficacy to teaching. Teachers, on the other hand, are constantly learning like this; they must be in order to keep up with the changing education world.

1.2 Significance of Exploring AI-assisted Technologies

The use of AI in education has its challenges, despite its numerous benefits. Handling issues surrounding data privacy, algorithmic bias, and the digital divide is key to successfully rolling out this technology in an equitable and ethical manner. Similarly, the use of AI-driven tools could lead to alienating students without access to computers or good-speed internet. The risk of bias in AI systems raises the need for transparent and inclusive technology that emphasizes fairness and diversity. Ethical issues also include the impact of AI on student behavior and decision-making. Predictive analytics are useful for prevention, but it is vital to balance prediction and autonomy. An over-reliance on recommendations generated by AI could also weaken students' ability to think for themselves and build critical thinking ability." Hence, the function of the AI must be that of a complementary one, enhancing human capabilities instead of replacing them (Lee et al., 2020).

The potential of AI-enabled technologies in shaping the future of education is an exciting topic to explore. The future of AI in education is bright and will provide innovative solutions to challenges not yet involving education. The area where this might be really important is lifelong learning, allowing people to always upskill or reskill throughout their careers. AI-based personalized career counseling can help both students and professionals to direct themselves down paths that are aligned with their strengths, interests and market trends. The convergence of AI and other disruptive technologies like blockchain, IoT, and 5G will augment the education economy. The second phase would last only but a hand full of years and include Blockchain to assure academic credentials as well as IoT to provide smart classrooms with interrelated devices that interact with each other in the cloud and 5G for smooth connectivity in remote learning scenarios (Psycharis et al., 2018). They will make way for a 21st century integrated learning ecosystem that is responsive to the needs of students.

AI-assisted technologies such as EduWord emphasize teamwork both within and outside of academic settings, which are essential skills that students must master in order to succeed in the future. Through efforts such as personalized learning, improving accessibility, simplifying administrative work, making us have better real-life experiences, etc., ai would be able to provide us an educational system that would be more inclusive, effective, and better overall. But we must tackle the challenges that come with this and be sure that AI is used ethically and fairly (Liu et al., 2017). The path ahead is an exciting endeavor, and the role of educators, technologists, policymakers and stakeholders in harmonizing will be a key to accessing the full potential of AI within the field of education. It can create an education system that is not just a privilege shared by a few, but empowering and available in equal portions to everyone.

2. PERSONALIZED LEARNING WITH AI

AI-driven personalized learning is becoming a game-changer in today's education system, revolutionizing the process of how students learn and how educators teach. Such systems are designed to fit the learning styles, preferences and speeds of individual students with the help of AI. The exploration of personalized learning model, including adaptive learning systems, intelligent tutoring systems and gamification.

2.1 Adaptive Learning Systems

AI-based adaptive learning systems go beyond this simple layering to create a truly personalized experience, where algorithms learn to determine how to change learning materials, how to distribute and deliver content to the individual student, or how to materialize their assessments. In contrast, adaptive learning systems use data to track and manage student progress in real time to provide personalized learning experiences, diverging from traditional classroom models that follow a one-size-fits-all approach (Pulimood et al., 2016).

AI customizes the curriculum by evaluating a variety of variables, including a student's background knowledge, comfortable learning style, and performance past. As an illustration, if an AI-enhanced system recognizes that a student is struggling with grasping mathematical concepts, it may respond by offering the student simplified exercises, video tutorials or alternative explanations. On the other hand, for advanced learners, upper-level content may be assigned to keep up with their progress and potential, keeping them engaged and motivated. It enables better learning with less frustration and boredom, and promotes an actual understanding of the target (Weintrop et al., 2016).

Studies show adaptative learning platforms have been successful in several contexts. DreamBox Learning, an AI-powered software for K-8 math, adjusts lesson content in real-time as a student works through material. Further, McGraw-Hill's ALEKS platform uses artificial intelligence (AI) algorithms to diagnose gaps in learners' knowledge in mathematics and science and directs them to individualized pathways to mastery. All of these systems lead to increased student engagement and academic performance; some schools have even reported double-digit increases in test scores and retention rates.

2.2 Intelligent Tutoring System

Intelligent Tutoring Systems (ITS) are an even more advanced form of adaptive Learning Technology that simulate the experience of teaching by acting like a virtual teacher and engaging in dialogue similar to a human, with the ability to provide highly tailored, one-on-one feedback (Montiel & Gomez-Zermeño, 2021). These systems use AI to assume the role of a teacher: explaining concepts, answering questions, helping students navigate their learning. ITS has found success in subjects that can be broken down into procedures, such as mathematics, programming, and languages.

Having ITS implemented has a variety of benefits, especially for learners who learn at different paces. A student who learns the material quickly can continue, without having to wait for their peers, while those who struggle can return to difficult concepts until they understand everything. Unlike most human tutors, ITS can react immediately and correct mistakes before they become entrenched, which is crucial to learning. Moreover, these are available 24*7, thus making education beyond the scope of the regular classroom hours. For example, Carnegie Learning's MATHia is an AI-driven tutoring system that delivers customized math instruction. MATHia uses real-time data analytics to determine what concepts a student has mastered and what needs additional support, providing targeted interventions (Barcelos & Silveira, 2012). Similarly, Duolingo, a popular language-learning website, is not adaptive; it adjusts to a user's skills and speed. The two platforms are gaining great experience in promoting learning results through autonomy and confidence.

2.3 Gamification in Learning Engagement

Such breakthrough is the integration of AI-powered gamification. Gamification refers to incorporating game-type features like rewards, leaderboards, and challenges into the learning process to boost motivation and engagement. AI personizes the gaming experience, so that a learner is playing a game that is not too easy and not too hard, and this way, gamification is further enhanced with the help of AI. Gamified content powered by AI help student maintain engagement through an interactive and enjoyable learning experience. For instance, AI-based math game Prodigy may use adaptive algorithms, amongst others, to customize questions in a game to a player's level (Gross et al., 2014). Given the inherently stressful and isolating aspect of learning, particularly for younger learners, promoting educational content within a gamified experience presents a great opportunity for less intimidating and more enjoyable learning undertaken in childhood.

Gamification and immersive technologies also facilitate learning across differing learning styles. Interactive graphics cater to visual learners, hands-on simulations to kinesthetic learners, and voice instructions facilitated by AI to auditory learners. This creates a 360-degree ecosystem of learning, adding to curiosity, creativity, and critical thought. Besides all of these, it should not forget the importance of Virtual Reality (VR) and Augmented Reality (AR) in creating immersive learning experiences. Through AI, these technologies can personalize the virtual experiences to the strengths and weaknesses of the learner. Medical students, for example, can practice surgical techniques using VR simulations, while AI provides real-time feedback and insights for improvement (García-Peñalvo & Mendes, 2018). History Students can visit ancient civilizations through AR as well and increase their knowledge about events which occurred in a highly engaging manner.

Artificial intelligence is redefining the learning process by providing personalized instruction, allowing students to learn at their own pace, style, and level. At the forefront of this transformation, adaptive learning systems, intelligent tutoring systems, and AI-driven gamification are paving the way for a more inclusive, engaging, and effective learning experience. From personalized curriculum development and virtual tutoring to gamified, immersive engagement, AI is not only capitalizing on the shortcomings of conventional education but also scintillating a still not fully dynamic and equitable learning environment. As these technologies progress, the possibilities of AI transforming education are endless, with a future blossoming in which learning is tailored to each individual learner.

3. ENHANCING ACCESSIBILITY AND INCLUSION

With education undergoing its transformative phase, the growth of AI acts as one such counterpart that can contribute to unlocking accessibility and inclusivity within the education system. AI-based solutions are redefining possibilities in inclusive education by catering to the different types of student needs and also overcoming barriers to equitable learning (Psycharis, 2018). In this section, we will discuss how AI promotes accessibility and inclusion, covering topics like specialized assistive technologies for special needs education, language translation and multilingual support, and barrier removal initiatives to bridge the digital divide.

Assistive technologies powered by AI have transformed the scope of educational opportunities for additively challenged students. These technologies facilitate students' access to educational resources and participation in learning experiences equal with that of their peers, whether they may have visual, auditory, motor, or cognitive impairments. AI also brings solutions that are customized to the individual, encouraging independence and confidence in students with disabilities. Speech-to-text and text-to-speech technologies are a couple examples of AI's work in this space. Speech-to-text tools like Google's Live Transcribe give students who are hard of hearing the empowerment of having spoken language translated into written text in real time. Likewise, text-to-speech products, such as Kurzweil 3000, or Microsoft's Immersive Reader, read digital text aloud to help students with visual impairments or dyslexia (Bati et al., 2018). This features can help students to reach content no matter their gaps and widen inclusion in both classrooms and beyond

Major breakthrough in special needs education comes from AI-powered emotion detection software. These solutions are then capable of understanding a student's emotional state through an analysis of facial expressions, vocal tones, and physiological signs, providing feedback to teachers. For example, an educator working with a student who cannot speak but has autism could use AI to measure the student's engagement, frustration or happiness while participating in a lesson. Using this data, educators can pivot their teaching techniques in real time to ensure students are getting the assistance that they require. An example of this would be the Tobii Dynavox eye-tracking technology allowing non-verbal people to have a voice by selecting words or phrases using their eyes. AI assists students with mobility challenges as well, through robotic assistants and adaptive keyboards. Such innovations facilitate the ability of students to smoothly engage in learning with digital material and in class. Through breaking down barriers and promoting inclusivity, AI-based assistive technologies are creating a diverse learning environment where all learners have the chance to excel, irrespective of their learning abilities (Garg & Singh, 2022).

3.1 Translation of Languages and Multilingual Help

AI-powered services for language translation (Google Translate, Microsoft Translator, DeepL, etc.) have become everyday tools for students and educators. These resources allow real-time translation of text and speech (and even images) so that learners can grasp multilingual content and ideas from the world while engaged in learning. AI serves as a translator, connecting teachers to all students, even those who speak a different language in a multi-lingual and varied learning environment. Over the years, language has always been a major obstacle to achieve global education, but with AI technology, the barriers of education are breaking down with cross-lingual learning and multilanguage support (Wang et al., 2022). With AI-based translation tools, students and educators can access content translated into multiple languages, promoting inclusivity in diverse classrooms and international learning environments.

AI can be leveraged to enhance language learning (using natural language processing (NLP) or more advanced machine learning algorithms) in addition to mere translation. Language-learning apps, such as Duolingo and Babbel, use AI to provide a tailored learning experience, adjusting lessons according to the user's skill level and advancement. These tools help multilingual societies, be it students, who learn new languages for academic purposes, or business people who need to be linguistically educated before a big trade deal. AI supports the development of multilingual curricula for educational institutions, in addition to individual learners (Czerkawski & Lyman, 2015). AI tools, for instance, can analyze huge amounts of educational content, recognize the main ideas, and produce translations or summaries in several languages. It allows students from different language backgrounds to equally access quality learning material.

The role of AI in bridging language divides also extends to the sphere of immersive technologies, such as augmented and virtual reality (AR and VR). Such technologies utilize AI translation capabilities to create interactive and engaging learning environments that cater to students with varying skillsets. A VR simulation of a historical event, for example, can provide real-time language support, allowing students from different countries to work through the same scenario together. This fosters cultural exchange and understanding, thereby allowing students to be better prepared for a globalized world.

3.2 Bridging the Digital Divide

AI has tremendous potential in enabling accessibility and inclusion, but this will only be realized if equitable access to AI tools and technologies is made available to all. Thus, bridging the digital divide is an essential aspect of utilizing AI for inclusive education. The digital divide is a term that describes the disparity between people who maintain access to digital technologies and those who lack access, commonly due to socioeconomic inequalities, inadequate infrastructure, or poor digital literacy (Papadakis, 2020). AI opens the possibility for scalable and cost-efficient solutions to these challenges but requires the cooperation of governments, NGOs and private-sector actors to ensure equal access.

For example, one way of bridging the digital divide is through the creation of affordable AI-driven educational tools that can be used by economically disadvantaged communities. Programs like Khan Academy's AI-based learning platform offer free, top-notch educational resources for students across the globe no matter their economic background. Localized AI solutions that address the needs of certain regions or languages also have the ability to level the educational playing field. Platforms such as EkStep in India also utilize AI to provide learning content in local languages, making learning accessible to students in remote locations To combat this issue, governments are investing in technology for underserved communities by bridging the digital divide, such as internet and digital devices. In response, efforts are being made to address AI's potential displacement of these communities; initiatives like Google's "Next Billion Users" project work on creating AI solutions for developing markets, to enhance accessibility for underrepresented people (Yadav et al., 2014).

In fact, NGOs play a critical role in driving these efforts forward by organizing community-based initiatives that teach literacy skills, and provide access to various technologies for learning. Via measures such as the One Laptop Per Child (OLPC) initiative that provided low-cost devices for millions of students in developing nations, individuals have gained access to functioning in the digital economy. Finally,

NGOs can lobby for laws that prioritize equitable access to AI tools so no student gets left behind. Making the digital world more inclusive for those with disabilities is also key to closing this gap. Policy-makers and school administrators should ensure that AI-enhanced tools comply with the principles of universal design, so that they are accessible to and usable by all students. Work with disability advocacy groups to identify and improve gaps in accessibility, working to ensure inclusive AI technology by design.

4. EMPOWERING TEACHERS AND EDUCATORS: AUTOMATING ADMINISTRATIVE TASKS

AI in Education: Changing the Dynamic of Learning Experience AI in education has not only transformed the learning experience for students, but also their teachers and educators. This not only alleviates their workload but also enhances their ability to contribute to their primary role of inspiring, guiding, and mentoring students, through AI-driven tools and systems (Pollak & Ebner, 2019). AI helps educators in many ways, such as facilitating actions that are not only administrative, but also empowering professionals and enabling opportunities for collaboration between humans and intelligent systems. In this section, we explore how AI enables teachers to be more efficient with the administrative aspect of their jobs, which provides opportunities for personalized growth as well as ways to further develop human-AI partnerships to foster creativity and innovation in our classrooms.

4.1 Automating the Administrative Tasks

The most immediate and practical benefit of AI for educators might be the automation of repetitive and time-consuming administrative tasks. Teachers are spending a good amount of their time throughout grading, attendance tracking, and reports generation basic tasks that not only take time away from building lessons plans and students. This is where AI-powered tools are stepping in, managing these responsibilities efficiently, so that teachers can focus on teaching and having more meaningful interactions with students. Such AI systems like GradeScope and Turnitin facilitate the grading process through evaluation of student workouts, quizzes, and tests. They use algorithms to evaluate student responses, leading to consistent and precise assessment (Saritepeci, 2020). On top of that, they allow students to receive instant feedback, thus make a learning loop much faster. In open-ended assignments, AI tools can be used to group responses or flag them for areas that need a human touch, which can drastically reduce the amount of time required by teachers to complete assessments.

AI is also revolutionizing attendance tracking, in another labor-intensive task. For example, facial recognition software can be used to automatically take attendance as students enter a classroom, eliminating the need for an instructor to call out names one by one in a roll call. These technologies not only save time but also reduce mistakes in attendance tracking. Likewise, Artificial-Intelligence powered reporting systems provide insights into performance, behavior trends and learning progress for students. Data analytics in education help in generating detailed reports, identifying what this area (teacher, administrator) should focus on PowerSchool, Edmodo (Buitrago-Flórez et al., 2021). This technology makes educators' lives easier by taking many administrative tasks off their plates, enabling teachers to reach students all the more. This transition not only improves the educational experience but also assists in staving off teacher burnout, which is a major issue confronting the profession. The time saved through the use of AI-based tools can be reinvested by educators in innovative lesson plan designs, student guidance, and a supportive learning setting, all of which enhance educational success.

4.2 Artificial Intelligence for Professional Development

Professional development programs powered by AI have the ability to offer educators customized training modules based on their unique experiences and pedagogy (methods of teaching), monitor their performance, and provide actionable feedback for continuous improvement, making them adaptable in a rapidly changing educational landscape. Often they take a "one size fits all" approach, which does not address the unique needs or challenges that individual educators might experience. AI, on the other hand, creates personalized learning paths by assessing each teacher's strengths, weaknesses, and preferences. AI-driven professional development courses on platforms such as Coursera, Udemy, and Edmodo, for example, adapt to the teacher's learning pace and focus on areas requiring improvement. Similarly, a teacher who finds it challenging to implement technology into their teaching would receive specific training in digital tools and teaching methods to facilitate technology-integrated learning (Gokce & Yenmez, 2023).

AI-driven feedback and performance monitoring tools are also essential to professional development. AI-powered classroom observation tools like Swivl or TeachFX can help analyze teaching practices by recording and analyzing classroom interaction. These systems give him objective feedback on whether he's interacting with his students, whether his lesson is clear and concise, and whether he's managing his time. Moreover, AI tools can monitor student performance analytics to determine what teaching strategies correlate with improved performance, letting educators know things that work and don't.

AI can help to place teachers in simulated classroom situations for training, giving them practice and a full range of scenarios to handle without putting real students at risk. These educators, including virtual-reality (VR) based platforms like TeachLivE, allow teachers to conduct simulations and practice instruction with AV (AI Virtual) students. These simulations replicate real classroom interactions, allowing teachers to try out different teaching approaches, and experience immediate feedback. Through the use of AI for professional development educators can keep learning about the newest methods of pedagogy, classroom technologies, and forms of curriculum. This ongoing learning process prepares them to meet the diverse needs of today's classrooms and cultivates a culture of lifelong learning in the educational workforce (Lodi & Martini, 2021).

4.3 AI as Leverage for Educators

AI is not replacing teachers, but rather viewed more and more as an aid in the teaching process. AI is now being deployed as an interactive and intelligent virtual educational partner to assist, augment, empower, and uplift human educators bringing human and AI abilities together in the classroom deeper than ever. Lesson planning is one of the most high impact areas where AI and educators are working together. Apps that can harness such data to better customize a learning experience, such as Knewton or Smart Sparrow, are already a reality. Teachers can leverage these insights to create lessons that meet their individual student's needs. For example, if AI detects that students in a certain group are struggling with one particular concept, then teachers can adjust the lessons to give extra help in that topic. As a result of this collaboration, the teaching will be based on data in order to achieve the best student outcomes possible.

AI in classroom also inspires creativity and innovation through new tools and resources # Utilize AI-Powered Tools for Content Creation: AI-driven content generation tools such as Canva for Education and Adobe Spark provide teachers with resources to create stunning presentations, worksheets, and multimedia projects. AI tools such as ChatGPT also help generate lesson ideas, discussion prompts, and even quizzes, which fuel creativity and reduce time spent on mundane tasks. This integration of AI also facilitates immersive and interactive learning experiences for both educators and learners. AI-driven technologies such as augmented reality (AR) and virtual reality (VR) let teachers lead students on virtual field trips, conduct science experiments or simulates historical events in a lab. Such experiences are engaging and memorable and promote critical thinking and problem-solving.

The potential of AI has no limits, but the human element in education is irreplaceable. Teachers offer empathy, cultural context, and morality that no A.I. can provide. The best classrooms with AI programs are those that are an enabler, heightening the teacher's ability to inspire and guide students. But those who embrace collaboration with AI will be able to balance the technology with the personal touch that is the foundation of teaching. Outside the classroom, AI has the potential to help educators build emotional connections with their learners (Tsortanidou et al., 2019). AI-based analytics tools monitor student engagement and mood levels, giving teachers real-time information. This means teachers can receive notifications if a student is losing interest, for example, giving the teacher a chance to get to them before the student gets frustrated. The partnerships guarantee that students are not only seen, but they also feel cared for in the academic environment.

From administrative streams, to personalized professional development opportunities, to human-intelligent systems collaboration AI is all about enabling and empowering the teachers and educators. AI enables teachers to concentrate on creative and impactful elements of their labour, by automating repetitive responsibilities in their work, including grading and attendance. By doing so, the educators are guaranteed to be growing and evolving alongside the demands of the modern classroom with personalized training modules and feedback systems (Yilmaz Ince & Koc, 2021). So, harnessing the power of human-AI partnerships improves lesson planning, ignites creativity, advances student engagement imparting a dynamic and inclusive learning atmosphere. The advancement of AI will inevitably deepen its involvement in education and continue empowering teachers and revolutionizing the teaching profession. The success of AI depends on its integration as a tool for teaching and learning rather than a substitute for educators. This allows the teacher to access the tools to inspire, innovate, and impact their students' lives with using the new technology. The upcoming era of education is with harmonization of human intelligence and AI.

5. SMART EDUCATIONAL ENVIRONMENTS

Such learning environments culminate in integrated platforms of Artificial Intelligence (AI), the Internet of things (IoT), virtual and augmented reality (VR/AR) and integrated learning analytics, which facilitate customized learning according to different learning needs, enhancing learning experience and optimizing learning outcomes. Read on to see how innovative technologies like AI-empowered classrooms, immersive environments, and learning analytics are making education a more dynamic and data-driven experience (Sırakaya et al., 2020). The classroom of the future is at the forefront of education systems, equipped with Internet of Things (IoT) and AI technology, to build a smart learning environment. Strong students make Classroom 2.0 classrooms connected with devices, sensors, and software systems to improve both teaching and learning based on real time data and feedback.

The new age of technology, through IoT devices like smartboards, interactive displays, and connected tablets promote a fluid work environment for students and educators alike. They can also mirror the content on the students' devices to smartboards, providing a participatory and fun-filled classroom experience. IoT sensors generate a data stream about the student body that AI algorithms will analyze to learn about student engagement, attendance, and participation levels. So, AI could recognize when students were getting distracted or wrestled with a concept, so that teachers could step in before students got lost. This mechanism of real-time feedback allows teachers to tailor their instruction to the needs of individual students, thereby making learning more personalized and effective. Intelligent resource management is another advantage of AI-powered classrooms (Hutchins et al., 2020). Smart lighting & climate control systems respond to occupancy and natural light levels to provide a comfortable learning environment while consuming only the energy needed. Moreover, AI could help in allocating classes and classrooms more efficiently, as well as scheduling to maximize the use of resources (Valovicova et al., 2020).

AI-based classrooms system is an example of AI, where an intelligent assistant such as IBM Watson or Google Assistant is used in educational institutions. These AI systems can answer questions posed by students, help plan lessons, or even administer quizzes or discussions. AI-driven classrooms people to deliver rapid assistance and automate administrative processes, therefore allowing educators to develop creative and touch on high-impact areas of teaching.

5.1 Educational Virtual and Augmented Reality

Across the globe, virtual and augmented reality (VR/AR) tools are transforming the educational landscape by delivering captivating learning experiences, actively engaging students, and deepening their knowledge of intricate concepts. And when leveraging a guided AI-based system, they become personalized, interactive, and extremely engaging learning tools (Lockwood & Mooney, 2017).

Through VR/AR, immersive learning experiences allow students to visualize and interact with abstract concepts, leading to better understanding. VR programs like Google Expeditions, for example, enable students to take virtual field trips to historical sites, explore the human body, or a journey into space. Such experiences tend to make learning come alive and fun, creating curiosity and creativity. AR applications likewise superimpose computerized data on to the material world, permitting understudies to communicate with 3D models of molecules, planets, or ability related structures. As a result, AI increases the effectiveness of VR/AR by adjusting content to the needs and abilities of every single student. For example, AI algorithms can assess a student's performance in a VR simulation and modify the difficulty level or recommend additional resources to help them improve. With such AI-driven AR applications like Zspace or Merge Cube, learners get real-time guidance and feedback, thus learning better.

Apart from education, VR/AR technology is also used for skill development and professional training. For instance, medical students can learn surgical techniques within a virtual environment, and engineering students can learn how to use complex machinery in a simulated context. Such applications would sharpen technical skills, boost confidence, and lessen the odds of making mistakes in real-world situations (Denning & Tedre, 2021). These immersive advantages also transcend academics. As VR/AR technologies offer hands-on experiences, they address various learning styles and preferences, ensuring every student gets the chance to thrive. In addition, these technologies also foster collaboration and teamwork among students working together in shared virtual environments to solve problems or build projects.

5.3 Learning Analytics

Another crucial element of smart educative settings is learning analytics, utilizing AI to monitor student performance, forecast potential results, and facilitate timely interventions. AI-powered learning analytics offers a wide range of insights about the performance, engagement, and learning patterns of students by analyzing data collected from different sources (Hsu & Liang, 2021). AI algorithms examine data from assignments, quizzes, attendance records and classroom interactions to form detailed profiles of individual students. These profiles enable educators to discover strengths, weaknesses, and areas of development. For instance, the platforms DreamBox and Knewton utilize adaptive learning analytics to customize content delivery according to a particular student's performance, facilitating a state where no student feels overwhelmed or under-challenged.

Predictive analytics, a specialized subset of learning analytics, is especially powerful for spotting students likely to get into trouble. Such early warning signs, including failing grades, sporadic attendance or diminished engagement, can be picked up by AI systems. Predictive analytics allows educators to identify at-risk students early on, by flagging these issues in real time, so that they can intervene and provide timely and targeted support. Added service could be an additional lesson from the teacher or recommended reading/ resource to support the struggling learner to regain on track. Learning analytics also allows institutions to make informed decisions based on data. When schools aggregate data across classrooms, they can identify trends, assess the effectiveness of teaching methods, or allocate resources more efficiently. For instance, analyzing data on performance across the school can allow AI to identify which subjects, or even topics within subjects, are struggling or require additional support, or which types of teaching strategies are having the greatest impact.

From the educational perspective, learning analytics promotes personalized learning (tailoring for the needs of individual students). AI-powered platforms such as Edmodo and Coursera use the learning analytics that they generate in order to suggest courses, activities, or resources that are in keeping with the interests and goals of a student. Such methodology not only improves learning outcomes for students, but also increases student motivation and involvement. Smart educational environments are the future of learning, where AI, IoT, VR/AR, and learning analytics converge to craft adaptive, engaging, and efficient learning spaces (Tedre & Denning, 2016). Classrooms equipped with AI technology can monitor student progress in real-time and provide immediate feedback, allowing for personalized support to be administered when needed. Immersive techniques such as VR and AR make learning more interactive and enjoyable and can be adapted to everyone's different learning styles. Such as learning analytics, which offers insights into student performance, allowing for data-driven decisions and timely interventions. With the evolution of these technologies, intelligent educational environments will be smarter and more effective in enriching learning experiences and outcomes. In adopting these innovations, educators and institutions can establish inclusive, engaging, and effective educational environments that equip students for the challenges lying ahead.

6. CONCLUSION

These innovations are resulting in inclusive, engaging and efficient learning environments, from AI-powered classrooms and adaptive learning systems to immersive VR/AR tools and predictive analytics. They support educators by automating administrative processes, enabling professional advancement, and enhancing innovation through human-AI teamwork. The result is a more personalized learning experience for students with the ability to dig deeper into the material and lead to better outcomes.

7. FUTURE DIRECTIONS

The possibilities for AI in education are limitless. Possible The future may bear witness to AI-powered lifelong learning initiatives, with platforms adapting to the demands of an ever-changing workforce, even greater use of multimodal AI assistance to facilitate education for all, and continued momentum towards global connectivity that ensures no one is left pointing towards the digital divide. Ethical AI frameworks will be essential in overcoming challenges related to data privacy, bias, and equitable access to technology. To ensure AI is implemented responsibly, valuing inclusivity and sustainability, governments, educational institutions, and tech companies must work together. AI is shaping to become the revolutionary force for globe education by embracing the evolution of limits into great heights gaining knowledge in every domain. Through the adoption of these innovations, it can enable a vision for a future where education becomes an all-encompassing and transformative force for learners.

REFERENCES

Agbo, F. J., Oyelere, S. S., Suhonen, J., & Adewumi, S. (2019, November). A systematic review of computational thinking approach for programming education in higher education institutions. In *Proceedings of the 19th Koli Calling International Conference on Computing Education Research* (pp. 1-10). DOI: 10.1145/3364510.3364521

Apiola, M., & Sutinen, E. (2021). Design science research for learning software engineering and computational thinking: Four cases. *Computer Applications in Engineering Education*, 29(1), 83–101. DOI: 10.1002/cae.22291

Barcelos, T. S., & Silveira, I. F. (2012, October). Teaching computational thinking in initial series an analysis of the confluence among mathematics and computer sciences in elementary education and its implications for higher education. In *2012 XXXVIII Conferencia Latinoamericana En Informatica (CLEI)* (pp. 1-8). IEEE. DOI: 10.1109/CLEI.2012.6427135

Bati, K., Yetişir, M. I., Çalişkan, I., Güneş, G., & Gül Saçan, E. (2018). Teaching the concept of time: A steam-based program on computational thinking in science education. *Cogent Education*, 5(1), 1507306. DOI: 10.1080/2331186X.2018.1507306

Buitrago-Flórez, F., Danies, G., Restrepo, S., & Hernández, C. (2021). Fostering 21st Century Competences through Computational Thinking and Active Learning: A Mixed Method Study. *International Journal of Instruction*, 14(3), 737–754. DOI: 10.29333/iji.2021.14343a

Czerkawski, B. C., & Lyman, E. W.III. (2015). Exploring issues about computational thinking in higher education. *TechTrends*, 59(2), 57–65. DOI: 10.1007/s11528-015-0840-3

Denning, P. J., & Tedre, M. (2021). Computational thinking: A disciplinary perspective. *Informatics in Education*, 20(3), 361.

García-Peñalvo, F. J., & Mendes, A. J. (2018). Exploring the computational thinking effects in pre-university education. *Computers in Human Behavior*, 80, 407–411. DOI: 10.1016/j.chb.2017.12.005

Garg, N., & Singh, B. (2022). Sustainable Development-Adopting a Balanced Approach between Development and Development Induced Changes. *ECS Transactions*, 107(1), 15–31. DOI: 10.1149/10701.0015ecst

Gökçe, S., & Yenmez, A. A. (2023). Ingenuity of scratch programming on reflective thinking towards problem solving and computational thinking. *Education and Information Technologies*, 28(5), 5493–5517. DOI: 10.1007/s10639-022-11385-x

Gross, S., Kim, M., Schlosser, J., Mohtadi, C., Lluch, D., & Schneider, D. (2014, April). Fostering computational thinking in engineering education: Challenges, examples, and best practices. In *2014 IEEE Global Engineering Education Conference (EDUCON)* (pp. 450-459). IEEE. DOI: 10.1109/EDUCON.2014.6826132

Hsu, T. C., & Liang, Y. S. (2021). Simultaneously improving computational thinking and foreign language learning: Interdisciplinary media with plugged and unplugged approaches. *Journal of Educational Computing Research*, 59(6), 1184–1207. DOI: 10.1177/0735633121992480

Hutchins, N. M., Biswas, G., Maróti, M., Lédeczi, Á., Grover, S., Wolf, R., Blair, K. P., Chin, D., Conlin, L., Basu, S., & McElhaney, K. (2020). C2STEM: A system for synergistic learning of physics and computational thinking. *Journal of Science Education and Technology*, 29(1), 83–100. DOI: 10.1007/s10956-019-09804-9

Lee, I., Grover, S., Martin, F., Pillai, S., & Malyn-Smith, J. (2020). Computational thinking from a disciplinary perspective: Integrating computational thinking in K-12 science, technology, engineering, and mathematics education. *Journal of Science Education and Technology*, 29(1), 1–8. DOI: 10.1007/s10956-019-09803-w

Liu, H. P., Perera, S. M., & Klein, J. W. (2017). Using model-based learning to promote computational thinking education. *Emerging research, practice, and policy on computational thinking*, 153-172.

Lockwood, J., & Mooney, A. (2017). Computational Thinking in Education: Where does it fit? A systematic literary review. *arXiv preprint arXiv:1703.07659.*

Lodi, M., & Martini, S. (2021). Computational thinking, between Papert and Wing. *Science & Education*, 30(4), 883–908. DOI: 10.1007/s11191-021-00202-5

Montiel, H., & Gomez-Zermeño, M. G. (2021). Educational challenges for computational thinking in k–12 education: A systematic literature review of "scratch" as an innovative programming tool. *Computers*, 10(6), 69. DOI: 10.3390/computers10060069

Papadakis, S. (2020). Evaluating a teaching intervention for teaching STEM and programming concepts through the creation of a weather-forecast app for smart mobile devices. In *Handbook of research on tools for teaching computational thinking in P-12 education* (pp. 31–53). IGI Global. DOI: 10.4018/978-1-7998-4576-8.ch002

Pollak, M., & Ebner, M. (2019). The missing link to computational thinking. *Future Internet*, 11(12), 263. DOI: 10.3390/fi11120263

Pollock, L., Mouza, C., Guidry, K. R., & Pusecker, K. (2019, February). Infusing computational thinking across disciplines: Reflections & lessons learned. In *Proceedings of the 50th ACM Technical Symposium on Computer Science Education* (pp. 435-441). DOI: 10.1145/3287324.3287469

Psycharis, S. (2018). STEAM in education: A literature review on the role of computational thinking, engineering epistemology and computational science. computational steam pedagogy (CSP). *Scientific Culture*, 4(2), 51–72.

Psycharis, S., Kalovrektis, K., Sakellaridi, E., Korres, K., & Mastorodimos, D. (2018). Unfolding the curriculum: physical computing, computational thinking and computational experiment in STEM's transdisciplinary approach. *European Journal of Engineering and Technology Research*, 19-24.

Pulimood, S. M., Pearson, K., & Bates, D. C. (2016, February). A study on the impact of multidisciplinary collaboration on computational thinking. In *Proceedings of the 47th ACM technical symposium on computing science education* (pp. 30-35). DOI: 10.1145/2839509.2844636

Qin, H. (2009, March). Teaching computational thinking through bioinformatics to biology students. In *Proceedings of the 40th ACM technical symposium on Computer science education* (pp. 188-191). DOI: 10.1145/1508865.1508932

Raaj, S. (2024). Education, research and innovation in India: The shifting paradigms. *Journal of Higher Education Theory and Practice*, 24(1), 75.

Romero, M., Lepage, A., & Lille, B. (2017). Computational thinking development through creative programming in higher education. *International Journal of Educational Technology in Higher Education*, 14(1), 1–15. DOI: 10.1186/s41239-017-0080-z

Saritepeci, M. (2020). Developing computational thinking skills of high school students: Design-based learning activities and programming tasks. *The Asia-Pacific Education Researcher*, 29(1), 35–54. DOI: 10.1007/s40299-019-00480-2

Sırakaya, M., Alsancak Sırakaya, D., & Korkmaz, Ö. (2020). The impact of STEM attitude and thinking style on computational thinking determined via structural equation modeling. *Journal of Science Education and Technology*, 29(4), 561–572. DOI: 10.1007/s10956-020-09836-6

Tedre, M., & Denning, P. J. (2016, November). The long quest for computational thinking. In *Proceedings of the 16th Koli Calling international conference on computing education research* (pp. 120-129).

Tsortanidou, X., Daradoumis, T., & Barberá, E. (2019). Connecting moments of creativity, computational thinking, collaboration and new media literacy skills. *Information and Learning Science*, 120(11/12), 704–722. DOI: 10.1108/ILS-05-2019-0042

Valovicova, Ľ., Ondruška, J., Zelenický, Ľ., Chytrý, V., & Medová, J. (2020). Enhancing computational thinking through interdisciplinary STEAM activities using tablets. *Mathematics*, 8(12), 2128. DOI: 10.3390/math8122128

Wang, C., Shen, J., & Chao, J. (2022). Integrating computational thinking in STEM education: A literature review. *International Journal of Science and Mathematics Education*, 20(8), 1949–1972. DOI: 10.1007/s10763-021-10227-5

Weintrop, D., Beheshti, E., Horn, M., Orton, K., Jona, K., Trouille, L., & Wilensky, U. (2016). Defining computational thinking for mathematics and science classrooms. *Journal of Science Education and Technology*, 25(1), 127–147. DOI: 10.1007/s10956-015-9581-5

Yadav, A., Mayfield, C., Zhou, N., Hambrusch, S., & Korb, J. T. (2014). Computational thinking in elementary and secondary teacher education. *ACM Transactions on Computing Education*, 14(1), 1–16. DOI: 10.1145/2576872

Yilmaz Ince, E., & Koc, M. (2021). The consequences of robotics programming education on computational thinking skills: An intervention of the Young Engineer's Workshop (YEW). *Computer Applications in Engineering Education*, 29(1), 191–208. DOI: 10.1002/cae.22321

Zint, M., Michel, J. O., Valentine, T., & Collins, S. (2024). *Collaborating with Students to Advance Climate Change Education at the University of Michigan*. Insights and Recommendations.

Chapter 9
Justice in the Age of Algorithms:
Ensuring Transparency, Accountability, and Fairness in AI-Driven Legal Systems

Abhishek Benedict Kumar
https://orcid.org/0000-0002-3998-3150
Symbiosis Law School, Nagpur Campus, Symbiosis International (Deemed) University, Pune, India

Karun Sanjaya
https://orcid.org/0009-0005-1647-1549
Symbiosis Law School, Nagpur Campus, Symbiosis International (Deemed) University, Pune, India

Mohammad Saleem
https://orcid.org/0009-0000-4777-3113
Faculty of Law, Marwadi University, Rajkot, India

ABSTRACT

The use of artificial intelligence poses challenges for legal systems such as algorithmic bias, lack of interpretability, and data privacy issues embedded in ethical dilemmas to reinforce existing power asymmetries. Algorithmic bias can reinforce the existing inequities of our social world, undermining fairness and hurting some communities more than others. AI models, with their "black box" nature, create questions of transparency and accountability, and data privacy is an evergreen concern about the use of sensitive personal information. On top of that, AI systems can reinforce existing power structures that serve the privileged populations. Solutions could be

DOI: 10.4018/979-8-3693-9395-6.ch009

new fairness-aware algorithms, privatization techniques such as differential privacy and regulatory actions mandating transparency and accountability. Ethical AI in society, interdisciplinary collaboration, and participatory governance are ethical and socio-democratic imperatives to achieve responsible deployment of trustworthy AI.

1. INTRODUCTION

Artificial intelligence (AI) is the engine for change in the digital age, transforming nearly every sector of society, from healthcare to education to finance and now increasingly, law. With the capability to sift through enormous datasets in seconds, predict case results, and provide near-perfect recommendations for the optimal path forward, AI has the potential to be a game-changing tool in the administration of justice (Goodman & Flaxman, 2017). Yet the use of AI in legal systems presents its own challenges and dangers, invoking awkward questions about fairness, transparency and accountability. With AI more widely adopted by legal institutions, it is crucial to make sure that these systems operate in ways that preserve the fundamental tenets of justice.

The promise of AI in law relates to doing tasks humans traditionally do, but in a more efficient manner particularly repetitive and labor-intensive tasks e.g. legal research and document review. As per Ashley (2017), Natural Language Processing-powered tools can review thousands of legal documents in a fraction of the time compared to the time it would take a human lawyer in finding relevant case law and precedent. Moreover, some AI systems also assist in judicial outcome prediction by analyzing data of past cases and providing suggestions to lawyers and judges. It could improve decision-making, help in resource allocation and ultimately reduce the backlog of courts. However, as much as data-driven insights hold potential to inform us about legal realities and norms, they also represent a risk of climatological simplification or distortion when decoupled from the messy legalisms of practice (Barocas & Selbst, 2016).

One of the most controversial applications of AI is its use in criminal justice. However, within criminal justice, AI is used for predictive policing, risk-assessment for bail and sentencing as well as predicting recidivism (Brayne, 2020). In some jurisdictions, for example, the COMPAS (Correctional Offender Management Profiling for Alternative Sanctions) algorithm has been utilized to estimate a defendant's likelihood of re-offense. However, investigative reporting by ProPublica showed enormous racial disparities in the predictions of COMPAS. According to Angwin, Larson, Mattu, & Kirchner (2016), algorithms suffered from racial biases. 'Black' defendants were identified as a higher risk than their white equivalent for recidivism even when they had not reoffended. These findings brought into question the ethics and legality behind the fairness and reliability of AI systems since their decisions can directly affect people's lives and freedom.

This problem is exasperated by the fact that many AI algorithms are extremely opaque in nature. Since most AI models, particularly those based on machine learning approaches such as deep learning, function as black boxes whose reasoning is hard if not impossible to understand or explain (Doshi Velez & Kim 2017). In areas that involve a high degree of accountability and transparency, such as the legal system, the use of black box AI can counteract public trust and faith in the legitimacy of judicial outcomes. Where the issue arises is the necessity to have AI decisions be explainable and justifiable, especially when it can negatively impact human freedoms. As a result, the notion of between interpretability, accuracy, and the concept of explainable AI (XAI) has garnered significant attention in light often these concerns with researchers and practitioners attempting to provide more interpretable but accurate models (Gunning et al., 2019).

Next is responsibility, which also becomes an urgent matter. When AI systems make mistakes or cause unfair results, traditional lawful pathways do not often offer clear assignments of responsibility. Similarly, AI systems cannot be prosecuted and have to bear double blame compared to human decision-makers. Instead, responsibility might fall to developer's/data scientists or organizations rolling out these technologies (Crawford & Schultz, 2013). This diffusion of responsibility makes it difficult to place legal liability and raises the question of whether current legal doctrines can adequately adapt themselves to this special need created by AI. For instance, if an algorithm used in decision about the parole of criminals falsely determines a person has high risk to commit a crime again and makes him or her not getting the parole, then whose fault is it? With such practical challenges in assigning blame and liability, we are going to need agents of regulation who can collectively cover all the bases.

Arguably, the most pressing ethical issue is bias and discrimination in AI systems. If the historical data fed into machine learning algorithms is biased, the results are therefore likely to repeat societal biases (Buolamwini & Gebru, 2018). So, for example, if a police predictive policing algorithm is trained on data that targets against minorities due to over-policing in those communities throughout history, it will learn this and make biased suggestions which will promote this unfair type of policing. According to Eubanks (2018) bias is not only a technical problem, but it tries to portray the underlying inequality in our society. Tackling these biases demand a multifaceted mannerism from thoughtful data curation, and running audits for bias to frequent engagement with the affected communities to further grasp the impact of such technologies in the real world.

How Artificial Intelligence is Changing the Legal Profession → Fairness: Many people can disagree about what fairness means in an AI-driven legal system. A study by Hardt et al. (2016) proposes different fairness criteria, including but not limited to equalized odds, demographic parity and individual fairness, each with its pros and cons (Corbett-Davies & Goel, 2018). Nevertheless, the research on fairness is not trivial as there are several trade-offs between different metrics in terms of fairness and this can severely affect model performance. For example, enforcing demographic parity could diminish the total accuracy of an algorithm, raising ethical questions about what one should serve first. But fairness cannot be understood in isolation; it must be embedded within the wider legal and social landscape. Statistical definitions of fairness do not always match legal standards, and aligning them is an important bottleneck for AI implementations in justice systems.

AI in the legal space is not entirely unheard of. Historical experiences with technological interventions in the justice system, including fingerprint analysis and DNA testing, illustrate that technology can lead to better judicial results at the same time (Cole & Lynch 2006). But AI is more complicated and it has the potential to affect all of us. Previous technologies had often been tools to help people make decisions, but not to become the decision makers, which is a major difference and raises the stakes for ethics approval and regulation. AI technology has developed and adopted much faster than any regulatory safeguards are being created, emphasizing the need for a full suite of policy responses.

There have been a number of initiatives and frameworks put together to address these problems. For instance, the proposed AI Act in the European Union aims to regulate high-risk AI systems, including those applied in legal and judicial domains, through strict standards for transparency, accountability and human control (European Commission, 2021). As called for in high-level discussions about algorithmic accountability that have had a dramatic increase recently in the USA, legislation like the Algorithmic Accountability Act would lobby for companies to carry out impact assessments of their own AI systems (Raji et al., 2020). The alignment of different jurisdictions on the regulation of AI has however remained as fragmented as its governance, with considerable distance in between domestic agendas.

AI in the Legal System Options for Integration The promise is real; the peril is equally so. AI is an evolving technology or phenomenon and poses a challenge to the legal community of its utility without in any way endangering vertical of justice. But the way forward must be driven by purposive interdisciplinary dialogue among technologists, lawyers, ethicists and policy-makers. It is only through this collaboration that we can design AI powered legal systems focused on the equitable, fair and transparent delivery of justice to society.

A crucial tension that the question of AI's place in legal systems reveals is efficiency or equity. Although AI can undoubtedly make a legal process more efficient, one of the most pressing concerns is whether or not this increased efficiency comes at the expense of equity and fair trial rights (Richardson, Schultz, & Crawford 2019). Already, the reliance on algorithms to make decisions that were historically made by humans perhaps adds yet another wrinkle to this question. While judges or juries consider the details of a case in traditional systems, AI systems decide based on statistical models and past patterns (Chouldechova & G'Sell, 2017).

The ethical conflict goes even deeper into citizen rights, such as data privacy and monitoring. Some AI-driven legal technologies depend on large datasets that contain sensitive personal data. The impacts of using this data, particularly if they are paired with any predictive algorithms, will have consequences for our individual rights and freedoms. Disquiet has surrounded the collation and use of this information usually without an informed consent process or adequate oversight over fears that state actors may abuse their power, overreach the scope of their jurisdiction and trespass upon fundamental rights (Wachter & Mittelstadt, 2018). On top of this, if the AI systems were developed by private companies that have no other interest but profit, there is also an obvious need for proper regulatory frameworks around their use in judicial settings.

The lack of diversity in the teams that build AI systems has been identified as one of several reasons behind bias in AI. Homogeneous teams can miss how their models can harm underrepresented groups (Raji et al., 2020). When diverse opinions are not represented at the top level, systems can be created and implemented with blind-spots in their design, only adding to Roman injustice. Therefore, efforts to ensure diversity and inclusivity in tech development are not just moral duties, they are also practical means to achieve stronger and fairer AI outcomes.

In the realm of legislative and regulatory responses, too, one can see how this tension between technological innovation and the law plays out. Across the globe, governments are struggling to find a way to control AI without killing innovation. In this sense, the European Union has been one of the most active in proposing regulations like the General Data Protection Regulation (GDPR) and lately the AI Act with an objective of aiming to protect individuals from cases of harmful use of artificial intelligence whilst promoting a very Ethical way (Goodman & Flaxman, 2017). In contrast, the U.S. has gone for a more piecemeal approach that not only leaves open broader questions of AI regulation which need addressing, but allows individual states to craft their own laws in the absence of anything at federal level. The differences in regulation here, however, created questions around global standards and if this means a pathway toward regulatory arbitrage.

In short, this integration of the AI in legal systems is a paradigm shift with serious consequences which can affect the rule of law. With the ongoing development of artificial intelligence (AI) and its increasing penetration into wider jurisdictions across the entire justice system, it is essential that we strike a balance between exploiting its successes whilst protecting core rights and freedoms. This needs (a) technological progress in AI, in making the AI fairer and transparent; and (b) a unified interdisciplinary response focusing on ethical, social, and legal aspects of deploying AI.

2. TRANSPARENCY IN AI-DRIVEN LEGAL SYSTEMS

As one of the key principles of justice, transparency is also among the biggest challenges AI-based systems face during implementation. The term describes how easily we are able to see, examine for ourselves and challenge decision-making processes. The purported transparency of traditional legal processes involves the articulation of the reasoning for judgments, open trials and an appeals process. But AI further complicates this dynamic because the algorithms can act as "black boxes," where neither those who use them nor even in many cases their developers understand how they work. Many AI models are black boxes and when liberty and rights hang in the balance, that raises fundamental questions about these tools' appropriateness.

This black-box phenomenon is especially true with deep learning models, where we have a set of high-layered neural networks that made machine learn using their own efficient hidden layers. However, these models are immensely powerful, and appear to be able to reach new heights of accuracy for tasks like natural language processing and image recognition. On the other side this complexity makes them almost unexplainable in human-understandable terms (Doshi-Velez & Kim, 2017). This non-interpretability is extremely problematic in the legal system where decisions need to be explained. Consequently, the demand from researchers and policymakers alike now tends to favor either interpretability of AI tools used in justice or a "right to explanation" mechanism being coupled with such systems (Goodman & Flaxman, 2017).

Background: The European Union has been proactively drafting legislation requiring AI transparency with policies like the General Data Protection Regulation (GDPR) and, more recently, the proposed AI Act. Such regulations aim at ensuring that those impacted by algorithmic decision-making process should receive appropriate answers on how and why decisions were made (Wachter, Mittelstadt & Floridi, 2016). Though ambitious, critics say these legal frameworks still lack a concrete and operational definition of a "right to explanation" that would be difficult to invoke with complex AI models (Mittelstadt et al., 2016). Additionally, presuming that explanations are provided, these must be intelligible to non-experts, which will necessitate an interdisciplinary effort between computer scientists, ethicists and legal scholars for the definition of explanatory tools.

Transparency also means being open about what sources of data and training methods using to create Ai systems. As algorithms learn from historical data, disclosing these datasets is a key step in identifying and addressing potential biases. As an illustration, if an AI system trained to assist judges with bail recommendations has been trained on data that demonstrates historical discrimination in the criminal justice system, it is probable that this algorithm reproduces or even amplifies these biases (Barocas & Selbst, 2016). When data sources are transparently disclosed, it allows external audit and scrutiny; increasing accountability. Still, well-known private companies building AI systems do not disclose this information citing proprietary interests creating a tension between commercial confidentiality and public accountability (Pasquale, 2015).

The rise of Explainable AI (XAI) as a field of research addresses the ability to explain how and why an AI system arrived at its conclusions. The objective is to create algorithms that not only give optimal results but also explain the reasoning behind their decision-making. For instance, approaches such as Local Interpretable Model-Agnostic Explanations (LIME) and Shapley Additive exPlanations (SHAP) are among model-agnostic methods that explain predictions by creating a simpler model in the neighborhood of an input (Ribeiro, Singh, & Guestrin, 2016). These methods however, are not without their limitations and shortcomings. These explanations, however, provide only an approximation of what would be the true model and consequently, a misleading sense of understanding (Lipton 2016). Explanations could be misused to hide an AI system's shortcomings, rather than clarify them.

Besides technical work, we also need legal reforms that require transparency from AI systems deployed in the justice sector. Certain academics urge for what they call "algorithmic due process," granting rights to an explanation and the right to contest algorithmic decisions, as well as mandatory audits of AI systems for fairness compliance. This mode of legal thinking aims to incorporate transparency into the very design-architecture of AI systems, instead of viewing it as an afterthought. This balance between open-source transparency and the need for secure, proprietary information is still a major challenge. For instance, over-exposing how an algorithm works could lead to it being gamed or hacked a risk that must be considered against the value of transparency.

Transparency upon its own also connects with cultural and social perceptions of the justice system. Public trust is a necessary pillar of any legal system, and using black-box AI systems can destroy this trust. Others have found a tendency for acceptance of algorithmic decisions to be higher when the process was explained in clear and across all understandable steps, even when such decisions are adverse (Binns et al., 2018). Thus encouraging transparency matters not just because it is required on the law but also because if society does not believe that AI-driven arbitration processes are fair and legitimate, then they should move from here.

Perhaps the most well-known case study of transparency is the controversy surrounding the COMPAS risk assessment tool. It turned out, as was detailed in a series of articles discussing the case, that COMPAS frequently produced biased predictions that disproportionately targeted minority groups (Angwin, Larson, Mattu & Kirchner, 2016). COMPAS was a black box we couldn't see inside to know exactly how it calculated the risk score. Because the algorithm behind it was proprietary, the defendants could neither challenge nor comprehend the reasoning behind its predictions, ultimately leading to widespread calls for greater transparency in algorithms and their use. This case highlights the dangers of black-box algorithms and a lack of transparency; without it, society will miss out on addressing unjust legal systems before such issues arise.

In addition, transparency is not only a technical problem, it is mainly an ethical one. It touches the issues of power, control, and who sets the standards for "equity" and "justice" with AI systems. Communities that are disproportionately harmed by biased algorithms need to be part of the conversation around transparency and accountability (Eubanks, 2018). Community input from participatory approaches can help ensure that the AI systems are aligned with values and needs of communities most impacted by them.

Finally, AI is a global industry, and while the need for transparency might seem obvious to some people or regions of the world even if it is challenging other people and regions would just not have similar rules imposed on them. International co-operation is both indispensable and complicated, as various countries have diverse legal traditions, cultural values, and regulatory priorities. While there are developments such as the OECD's AI Principles and a Global Partnership on AI to aid in cooperation and disseminating best practices, further action is necessary to bring about harmonization for transparency (OECD, 2019).

To implement a fully transparent legal system involving artificial intelligence, we would need improvements that run the spectrum from technical solutions through reforms of our laws, principles and ideals. It is about not just interpretability of algorithms but also making data sources and decisions open to inspection. Transparency will be an ever-present need as AI becomes more integrated into the justice system, making this a critical area for continued research and policy work.

3. ACCOUNTABILITY AND FAIRNESS IN AI-DRIVEN LEGAL SYSTEMS

Accountability and fairness are the cornerstones of any legal system, but they take on increased significance in the context of AI-based court mechanisms. The use of AI technologies within legal systems effectively provides new methods for adjudication which undermine many of the existing principles fundamental to justice and equality. In this part, the nitty-gritty of assuring accountability and fairness, which complements emerging technologies.

3.1 Accountability in AI Legal Systems

In legal terms, accountability means the responsibility of individuals or institutions to provide an account of or explain their actions and answerability for resulting consequences. Assigning accountability is especially challenging in AI-powered legal systems. Human judges, lawyers or law enforcement officials are traditionally held accountable for their decisions and action. Nonetheless, embodied AI remains able to make ever more complex determinations and even participate in legal judgments resulting in difficult questions about whether people or AIs themselves should be held responsible for wrong-doing incipiently found through computation (Crawford & Schultz 2013).

This is known as the "accountability gap" which refers to the challenge of identifying who should be held accountable when an AI system fails or leads to a discriminatory result. If the ML Model is using a model such as Neural Network which is more complex by nature, then, in many cases, even the people who created this system do not know how that system arrives to a conclusion (Doshi-Velez & Kim, 2017). It also obscures transparency making it hard to place accountability on developers, companies or government agencies. Intensification on understanding of accountability in AI applications calls for legislative action, with incrimination placed either onto developers for various components or monitoring and audit bodies imposed over certain phases of system use (Pasquale, 2015).

Creating detailed frameworks that will enforce transparency and make AI systems undergo regular audits is a part of it. This has led some to propose things like algorithmic impact assessments (AIAs). Such assessments would, prior to and during the deployment of AI systems, assess their potential social/ethical/licensing impact (Veale & Edwards, 2018). Nevertheless, the efficacy of AIAs lies in their execution as well as both public- and private-sector receptiveness to oversight.

The proprietary nature of many AI algorithms developed by private companies only adds to the difficulty in providing accountability. In fact, these companies protect their algorithms like trade secrets, limiting independent scrutiny and evaluations

(Pasquale, 2015). In other cases, such as with the COMPAS risk assessment tool that was recently scrutinized in courts for being unfair and non-transparent, the proprietary protection of developers prevented those impacted from rightfully challenging the decision making of the system (Angwin et al., 2016). Commercial confidentiality vs public interest remains one of the key barriers to genuine accountability.

3.2 The Role of Human Oversight

A part of the solution to guaranteeing accountability will be making human oversight mandatory for all AI-based legal processes. Having human oversight can serve as a check and balance, an additional step in reviewing AI decision making for justice and equity. This solution is not without its problems. Even wonderful humans could fall prey to "automation bias", in which they blindly trust what the entrained AI spits out, regardless of whether it is correct (Cummings 2004). Such an occurrence underscores the need for equipping human supervisors to critically evaluate AI-based decisions and also to watch out for errors or biasness.

There is also the question of whether AI should ever take over human judgement in high-stakes situations, such as criminal sentence or parole decisions. Opponents claim that AI has its place as an assistive tool, not as a decision-maker; human beings must remain the ultimate judge of right and wrong (Eubanks, 2018). Supporters, on the other hand, argue that with AI, data insights can enhance human judgment adding a layer of reliability in terms of consistency across legal outcomes.

3.3 Fairness and Bias in AI Legal Systems

In the context of justice-oriented legal systems powered by AI, fairness means that no individual will be treated better or worse based on any particular quality because of the use of AI and its related tasks. However, various studies have shown that AI systems tend to perpetuate or amplify biases that are present in historical data. Fairness is a significant issue in the development and application of AI in legal settings, as these biases can lead to unfair results, particularly for groups who are already marginalized (Barocas & Selbst, 2016).

Predictive policing tools, which use data to determine where crime is most likely to occur, have faced scrutiny for unfairly biasing against minority communities. Many predictive algorithms are based on old crime data, which have a tendency to reflect longstanding disparities in policing related to race and income. Consequently, such systems risk re-establishing an over-policing approach in already marginalized communities and perpetuating structural inequality (Richardson, Schultz & Crawford 2019). This needs to be tackled not only through technical solutions like non-partial algorithms, but also systemically so that the factors that produce these disparities are minimized.

One of the approaches to mitigate bias is use of fairness-aware algorithms, which seek to minimize differences between demographic groups. While biased algorithms can be mitigated via various re-weighting training data, or the threshold for decision-making adjustment, these solutions are neither panacea nor cost-free and are likely to come with an overall dip in accuracy (Chouldechova 2017). Alternatively, one can appeal to "algorithmic fairness" principles—including demographic parity or equal opportunity which promote compliance of AI outcomes to some specifications surrounding fairness (Hardt, Price & Srebro 2016). Despite the relevance of fairness in the development and deployment stages of AI systems, attaining fair AI is a complicated task because different notions of fairness are conflicting and it may not be possible to fulfill all ethical and legal definitions at the same time.

3.4 Intersectionality and Fairness

An intersectional understanding of how different forms of discrimination e.g. race, gender, and social class interact with one another is also necessary for fairness in AI systems. Such complexities are likely to be neglected by traditional metrics of fairness that provide incomplete and potentially misleading indicators about the extent of bias. An AI system perceived to be being fair towards men and women as categories might still harm women of color or transgender individuals because such considerations are not taken into account (Raji et al., 2020).

Intersectionality urges for a less simplistic notion of fairness: it requires listening and learning from those communities who bear the earthquakes of systemic injustices. Participatory approaches, including community advisory boards can provide relevant insights and prevent AI systems from falling short of being inclusive and fair (Benjamin 2023). That said, developing Internet-like governance solutions is generally in line with a wider trend toward participatory AI as well, attempting to bring democracy back into the development and management of AI technologies that eventually affect us all.

3.5 Legal and Ethical Frameworks for Fairness

A number of legal and ethical frameworks have been suggested as a means to mitigate questions around fairness in AI-enabled justice systems. For example, the European Union's draft AI Act categorizes applications of AI by risk level and places stringent requirements on high-risk systems (e.g. in law enforcement and the judiciary) (European Commission, 2021). These include compliance with fairness audits and that AI decision making does not lead to discriminatory consequences.

Fairness is emphasized as a core principle in some of the most prominent ethical guidelines' statements today, including IEEE and AI Ethics Guidelines from the High-Level Expert Group on Artificial Intelligence. These guidelines recommend continuous monitoring and assessment of AI systems to detect and correct biases. But ethical guidelines are non-binding, which means they rely on voluntary compliance on the part of developers and institutions.

Ultimately, ensuring accountability and fairness in AI-powered systems of jurisprudence is a complex problem that must be addressed through interlocking technical, legal, and normative solutions. Accountability needs to be well defined, with extensive systems of oversight and recourse. Simultaneously, the focus should be to achieve fairness through bias mitigation techniques, intersectional analysis and participatory governance. It is critical that these continuous principles of justice remain center pillar of the importance of AI in shaping our future otherwise AI-led legal system may violate laws and value of equality and human dignity.

4. CHALLENGES AND POTENTIAL SOLUTIONS IN AI-DRIVEN LEGAL SYSTEMS

The advent of artificial intelligence (AI) in legal systems has brought along a host of technical and socio-legal issues. The challenges range from algorithmic bias, lack of interpretability, data privacy concerns, ethical use of technology to systemic issues around power and inequality. Fighting these issues demands a multi-pronged approach that blends technological progress with solid regulatory and ethical frameworks.

4.1 Algorithmic Bias and Fairness

4.1.1 Algorithmic Bias

Algorithmic bias is one of the most serious problems with AI-focused approaches to legal systems. These biases can exist in historical data which maintains societal prejudices, bias in algorithm design or as a by-product of deployment into the system. Prominent case studies include predictive policing tools that target minorities and communities of color (Richardson, Schultz, & Crawford, 2019) and sentencing algorithms such as COMPAS with potentially inherent racial biases themselves (Angwin et al., 2016).

There are various ways bias can creep into AI systems. Training data do not reflect the population sufficiently (the so-called "Selection bias"), or the outcomes that model are trained on are biased as they carry human biases (Barocas & Selbst, 2016). Not only are algorithms biased against women and people of color, but it has tangential disastrous effects on people's lives due to discriminatory practices in systems of justice like pretrial criminal bail, or recidivism prediction (Eubanks, 2018).

4.1.2 Potential Solutions

Approaches available to mitigate bias include developing fairness-aware machine learning algorithms and frequent audits of models to find and correct biases. Specific strategies for mitigating disparities include reweighting of data samples, changing decision thresholds, and using algorithms that are unbiased (Chouldechova, 2017). In addition, diverse teams of developers and designers as well as the involvement of ethicists and sociologists at the design table can allow AI to realize fairer outcomes (Benjamin 2023).

4.2. Lack of Interpretability and Transparency

4.2.1 The Black Box Problem

Many, if not most deep learning based AI systems operate as "black boxes" whose decision making process is impossible or at least very difficult to interpret. Such opacity has no place in a legal setting where any decision must be explainable and defensible (Lipton, 2018). The inability to understand or explain why an AI model produces a particular outcome diminishes public trust and makes it difficult to hold AI systems accountable (Wachter, Mittelstadt, & Floridi, 2017).

4.2.2 Potential Solutions

Explainable AI(XAI) is a new area that deals with how to identify and understand predictions made by an AI system. Methodologies including Shapley Additive exPlanations (SHAP) or Local Interpretable Model-Agnostic Explanations (LIME) can provide an understanding of the model behavior (Ribeiro, Singh & Guestrin, 2016). Furthermore, the trade-off for some loss of predictive power in favor of more interpretable models maybe a desirable one in high-stakes legal settings. Similar policy interventions may also enforce transparency standards, whereby developers must explain in terms people can relate to how they reached their AI-powered conclusions.

4.3. Data Privacy and Security Concerns

4.3.1 Data Privacy

Many AI-powered legal systems need extensive datasets that usually contain identifiable data. This type of application of data creates serious privacy issues, especially in places with strict laws related to data protection such as the EU General Data Protection Regulation (GDPR) (European Commission 2021). In the specific case of AI, the risk that data breaches and misuse of information would happen is even higher since it becomes possible to collect a lot of personal information and infer very sensitive details with a terrifying accuracy.

4.3.2 Potential Solutions

Some solutions to this data privacy problem could be to embrace the privacy-preserving techniques that are already being developed, including but not limited: differential privacy lie, federated learning and data life. An instance is differential privacy, which guarantees that individual data points are indistinguishable within a dataset reducing the ability to re-identify (Dwork, 2008). An emerging approach called federated learning, in which AI models can train themselves on decentralized data without having to share private information, consequently preserving more privacy. And regulations should also include data minimization that limits what kind of data gets collected and processed.

4.4. Ethical and Social Implications

4.4.1 Ethical Dilemmas

Issuing licenses to AI systems in the legal domain gives rise not just technical challenges, but ethical dilemmas as well. That encompasses the skepticism regarding whether or not decision-makers have control over their actions, the apprehension that AI facilitates social inequities, and the infractions associated with working to replace technology in high-stakes situations. The idea of "moral outsourcing" refers to shifting the responsibility of moral decision making from humans, or relying on machines to have ethical responsibilities (Coeckelbergh, 2020).

4.4.2 Potential Solutions

A human-centered AI framework is needed to tackle ethical concerns. Authors' guidelines on ethical guides, for example from High-Level Expert Group on AI, suggest principles such as fairness, transparency and accountability as cornerstones of the development of AI (AI HLEG, 2019). Finally, public consultations and ethical deliberations can also help to make sure that AI systems reflect the values of society. Furthermore, independent ethics review boards for the implementation of AI in legal settings may also be created with a view to weakening possible harms.

4.5. The Power Dynamics and Inequality

4.5.1 Reinforcing Inequality

AI systems are frequently rolled out in a manner that carries forward as well as magnifies present power dynamics. As an example, surveillance technologies often take scales on the back of low-income and minority communities, reproducing a double bind of disadvantages (Eubanks, 2018). However, when groups such as disciplined women and professed minorities are not involved in the design or oversight for building AI in legal areas, the implementation of the AI system can aggravate existing biases.

4.5.2 Potential Solutions

We need a much more participatory mode of AI governance in order to confront these power dynamics. That means empowering affected communities to participate in decisions regulating AI, and that requires democratic oversight over AI technologies. Community-based participatory research and social and cultural impact assessments are examples of strategies that could mitigate the risk of perpetuating inequity (Raji et al., 2020). Laws on algorithmic accountability that would require public disclosure regarding the societal consequences of A.I. systems can also foster more transparency and accountability.

4.6. Legal and Regulatory Challenges

4.6.1 Inadequate Legal Frameworks

Existing laws are frequently out of touch with the needs imposed by AI. This leaves open important issues such as: Who is liable for decisions made by an AI? Do individuals have the right to contest a decision made by a person based upon an algorithm? Artificial intelligence has developed much faster than the nation-states can create a legal system to adapt, leaving regulatory vacuums and risk for individuals (Crawford & Calo, 2016).

4.6.2 Potential Solutions

Robust legal frameworks are necessary to regulate AI in law. Possible solutions are creating strict liability rules, improving data protection laws and implementing specific regulations on high-risk AI applications (European Commission, 2021). While AI tech is inherently global, national standards only do so much; international cooperation will be needed to generate harmonized standards. Oversight bodies, like those created in the name of AI regulation, could play a key role in monitoring adherence and enforcement.

The risks that AI potentially raises in the legal systems are intricate and manifold, demanding a combined action of integrated technical, ethical, and legal techniques. Although AI is an excellent technology that can be used to make the judicial process more energy-efficient, objective, and analysis based but still must be integrated into a system that ensures minimal human rights and justice. It is only through continued work with technologists, policymakers, lawyers and those who may suffer from AI-driven legal systems in the future that equity, transparency and justice will be built into these models.

5. CONCLUSION

Artificial Intelligence has Pros and cons when it comes to establishing the Law based on its integration potential. AI offers the prospect of criminal justice that is quicker and fairer but comes with the dangers of entrenched racial injustice, loss of accountability, and reduced transparency. As society relies on AI more, we have to continue evolving these technologies in order to foster equity, accountability and transparency in every decision-making process. This means that the role of AI in our legal system needs to be continuously monitored to ensure we are working towards ethically aligned human-rights based tools.

It will take inter-disciplinary tentative steps toward a constantly-evolving new regulatory paradigm to even begin to achieve a genuinely just AI-facilitated legal system. Where do we go from here? Acknowledge the limits of human and algorithmic decision making, and push for a system in which justice is efficient to be sure, but justice above all.

REFERENCES

Angel, M., Havens, J. C., & Winfield, A. F. T. (2017). ETHICALLY ALIGNED DESIGN A Vision for Prioritizing Human Wellbeing with Artificial Intelligence and.... In *ResearchGate*. IEEE. https://www.researchgate.net/publication/378975517_ETHICALLY_ALIGNED_DESIGN_A_Vision_for_Prioritizing_Human_Wellbeing_with_Artificial_Intelligence_and_Autonomous_Systems

Angwin, J., Larson, J., Mattu, S., & Kirchner, L. (2016). *Machine Bias*. ProPublica; ProPublica. https://www.propublica.org/article/machine-bias-risk-assessments-in-criminal-sentencing

Ashley, K. D. (2017). *Artificial Intelligence and Legal Analytics*. Cambridge University Press. DOI: 10.1017/9781316761380

Barocas, S., & Selbst, A. D. (2016). *Big Data's Disparate Impact*. DOI: 10.2139/ssrn.2477899

Benjamin, R. (2023). *Race After Technology: Abolitionist Tools for the New Jim Code*. Politybooks.com; Polity. https://www.politybooks.com/bookdetail?book_slug=race-after-technology-abolitionist-tools-for-the-new-jim-code--9781509526390

Binns, R., Van Kleek, M., Veale, M., Lyngs, U., Zhao, J., & Shadbolt, N. (2018). "It's Reducing a Human Being to a Percentage." *Proceedings of the 2018 CHI Conference on Human Factors in Computing Systems - CHI '18*. DOI: 10.1145/3173574.3173951

Brayne, S. (2020). *Predict and Surveil*. Google Books; Oxford University Press. https://books.google.co.in/books?hl=en&lr=&id=01AAEAAAQBAJ&oi=fnd&pg=PP1&dq=%E2%80%A2+Brayne

Buolamwini, J., & Gebru, T. (2018). *Gender Shades: Intersectional Accuracy Disparities in Commercial Gender Classification*. PMLR. https://proceedings.mlr.press/v81/buolamwini18a.html

Chouldechova, A. (2017). Fair Prediction with Disparate Impact: A Study of Bias in Recidivism Prediction Instruments. *Big Data*, 5(2), 153–163. DOI: 10.1089/big.2016.0047 PMID: 28632438

Chouldechova, A., & G'Sell, M. (2017, June 30). *Fairer and more accurate, but for whom?* ArXiv.org; Cornel University. DOI: 10.48550/arXiv.1707.00046

Coeckelbergh, M. (2020). *AI Ethics*. The MIT Press. https://www.researchgate.net/publication/339103412_AI_Ethics

Cole, S. A., & Lynch, M. (2006). The Social and Legal Construction of Suspects. *Annual Review of Law and Social Science*, 2(1), 39–60. DOI: 10.1146/annurev.lawsocsci.2.081805.110001

Corbett-Davies, S., & Goel, S. (2018). The Measure and Mismeasure of Fairness: A Critical Review of Fair Machine Learning. *ArXiv (Cornell University), 24.* / arxiv.1808.00023DOI: 10.48550

Crawford, K., & Calo, R. (2016). There is a blind spot in AI research. *Nature*, 538(7625), 311–313. DOI: 10.1038/538311a PMID: 27762391

Crawford, K., & Schultz, J. (2013, October 1). *Big Data and Due Process: Toward a Framework to Redress Predictive Privacy Harms*. https://papers.ssrn.com/sol3/papers.cfm?abstract_id=2325784

Cummings, M. (2024). *Scholars@Duke publication: Automation bias in intelligent time critical decision support systems*. Duke University. https://scholars.duke.edu/publication/1108365

Doshi-Velez, F., & Kim, B. (2017). Towards A Rigorous Science of Interpretable Machine Learning. *ArXiv (Cornell University), 1.* /arxiv.1702.08608DOI: 10.48550

Dwork, C. (2008). Differential Privacy: A Survey of Results. *Lecture Notes in Computer Science*, 4978, 1–19. DOI: 10.1007/978-3-540-79228-4_1

Eubanks, V. (2018, July 2). *Book Review: Automating Inequality: How High-Tech Tools Profile, Police and Punish the Poor by Virginia Eubanks*. LSE Review of Books. https://blogs.lse.ac.uk/lsereviewofbooks/2018/07/02/book-review-automating-inequality-how-high-tech-tools-profile-police-and-punish-the-poor-by-virginia-eubanks/

European Commission. (2021). *Proposal for a Regulation laying down harmonised rules on artificial intelligence*. European Commission. https://eur-lex.europa.eu/legal-content/EN/TXT/HTML/?uri=CELEX:52021PC0206

Goodman, B., & Flaxman, S. (2017). European Union Regulations on Algorithmic Decision-Making and a "Right to Explanation.". *AI Magazine*, 38(3), 50–57. DOI: 10.1609/aimag.v38i3.2741

Gunning, D., Stefik, M., Choi, J., Miller, T., Stumpf, S., & Yang, G.-Z. (2019). XAI—Explainable artificial intelligence. *Science Robotics*, 4(37), eaay7120. Advance online publication. DOI: 10.1126/scirobotics.aay7120 PMID: 33137719

Hardt, M., Price, E., & Srebro, N. (2016, October 7). *Equality of Opportunity in Supervised Learning*. ArXiv.org; ARXIV. /arXiv.1610.02413DOI: 10.48550

Lipton, Z. C. (2016). The Mythos of Model Interpretability. *ArXiv (Cornell University), 1*. /arxiv.1606.03490DOI: 10.48550

OECD. (2019). *The OECD Artificial Intelligence (AI) Principles*. OECD. https://oecd.ai/en/ai-principles

Pasquale, F. (2015). The Black Box Society: The Secret Algorithms That Control Money and Information. In *JSTOR*. Harvard University Press. https://www.jstor.org/stable/j.ctt13x0hch

Raji, I. D., Smart, A., White, R. N., Mitchell, M., Gebru, T., Hutchinson, B., Smith-Loud, J., Theron, D., & Barnes, P. (2020). Closing the AI Accountability Gap: Defining an End-to-End Framework for Internal Algorithmic Auditing. DOI: 10.1145/3351095.3372873

Ribeiro, M. T., Singh, S., & Guestrin, C. (2016). "Why Should I Trust You?": Explaining the Predictions of Any Classifier. *ARVIS, 1*. DOI: 10.1145/2939672.2939778

Richardson, R., Schultz, J., & Crawford, K. (2019, February 13). *Dirty Data, Bad Predictions: How Civil Rights Violations Impact Police Data, Predictive Policing Systems, and Justice*. https://ssrn.com/abstract=3333423

Wachter, S., & Mittelstadt, B. (2018, October 5). *A Right to Reasonable Inferences: Re-Thinking Data Protection Law in the Age of Big Data and AI*. Papers. DOI: 10.31228/osf.io/mu2kf

Wachter, S., Mittelstadt, B., & Floridi, L. (2016). Why a Right to Explanation of Automated Decision-Making Does Not Exist in the General Data Protection Regulation. *International Data Privacy Law*, 7(2), 76–99. DOI: 10.1093/idpl/ipx005

Chapter 10
Leveraging Artificial Intelligence to Combat Human Trafficking:
Integrating AI-Based Innovations With Law Enforcement

Saurabh Chandra
https://orcid.org/0000-0003-4172-9968
Bennett University, India

ABSTRACT

AI has a huge potential to address human trafficking through improved detection, prevention, and intervention strategies. AI can be empowered further, to be more dynamically engaged in the fight against traffickers, cybercrimes, and other threats. Utilizing machine learning algorithms, AI analyzes big data from social media, online ads, and travel data to recognize patterns and assess risk for trafficking victims. The hidden traffickers and victims may have been discovered more easily by using AI tools such as natural language processing and face recognition. And finally, AI can enhance collaboration among international law enforcement agencies, providing real-time data sharing and predictive analytics for more coordinated responses. The scope of anti-trafficking efforts can be greatly enhanced with similar tools and mechanisms offered by AI to scale efforts and prevention mechanisms for this global crisis.

DOI: 10.4018/979-8-3693-9395-6.ch010

1. INTRODUCTION

Human trafficking is a serious crime and a violation of human rights and involves the exploitation of a person through force, fraud, or coercion for such activities as commercial sexual exploitation, forced labor, slavery or the removal of organs. And it is an umbrella term, which includes multiple forms of trafficking, from sex trafficking and labor trafficking to organ trafficking. Sex trafficking is the exploitation of a person for sexual purposes, whether as a prostitute or for pornography Labor trafficking is the coerced work in something like agriculture, construction or domestic work. Human organ trafficking refers to the mafia-style hidden extraction of a human entity, often without their notice, where the human organ is replaced by replacement like or unsuitable organ (Khalifa & Sabry 2024).

Human trafficking is a problem of staggering proportions worldwide. According to the International Labour Organization (ILO), over 40 million people are victims of human trafficking worldwide at any given moment, and millions more fall victim to its consequences each year. Human trafficking is a global problem, according to continuing statements by the United Nations, and various NGOs, high rates being particularly evident in regions such as South East Asia, Eastern Europe and certain areas of Africa. Developed countries are not immune; trafficking occurs in both urban and rural areas and can be hiding in plain sight. So, the effects of human trafficking on its victims are, indeed, pervasive and lasting. Psychological: Survivors face acute trauma, anxiety, depression, post-traumatic stress disorder (PTSD), etc. These mental health issues can arise due to prolonged abuse, isolation and a feeling of helplessness inflicted during their captivity. Victims also experience emotional pain, where feelings of shame, guilt, and worthlessness intensify their suffering (Li, 2024). It also discusses the potential ethical and legal issues with using AI to prevent trafficking, as well as providing frameworks for ensuring that the data collection is safely used and respects privacy and human rights. Victims may suffer abuse, malnutrition and exposure to dangerous working conditions that can lead to chronic health conditions. Victims can also suffer permanent ailments as a result of physical attacks or unsafe workplaces.

The impact of human trafficking goes beyond the immediate harm inflicted on victims. It is also an economic burden, with trafficking victims frequently exploited in low-wage, dangerous or illegal jobs. This leads not only to a perpetuation of poverty, but also a draining of legitimate economies by distorting labor markets. At a social level, human trafficking perpetuates a cycle of exploitation, vulnerability, and inequality, disproportionately impacting marginalized communities such as women, children, migrants, and ethnic minorities. It instills fear in and erodes rule of law among impacted communities. In addition, trafficking creates significant strain on legal systems and public services, which are ill-prepared to invest in the necessary resources to address the needs of victim support and law enforcement. Human trafficking also has severe legal consequences. Many trafficking flows are run by organized criminal groups that span countries, making enforcement of anti-trafficking laws difficult (Yadong, 2024)

1.2 Policies and Measures to Combat Human Trafficking

Several steps have been taken by governments and international organizations to combat human trafficking. Such measures include laws that criminalize trafficking, programs that offer support for victims, and public awareness campaigns to prevent recruitment. Treaties and protocols for greater international cooperation have increased country-to-country coordination. Efforts to address human trafficking have increased, but the problem is still overwhelming and often outpaces those efforts. Traditional investigation techniques like law enforcement outreach and victim outreach are vital, but are often inadequate to tackle the scale and complexity of the networks trafficking men, women and children. On the other hand, they can tend to do less than traditional methods with resource constraints, lack of coordination, and difficulty tracking cross-border trafficking routes (Orhan et al., 2024)

1.3 Role of Technology in Combating Human Trafficking

Technology is becoming an increasingly important component in the fight against human trafficking. Human intelligence and manual intervention are, thus, the hallmarks of traditional methods but the technology-driven ones offer the potential for effective detection, prevention, and intervention. Tools like data analytics, facial recognition and machine learning are being layered into anti-trafficking efforts. Now, online brain-like mechanisms programmed to preserve complex human behaviour can be used to find and detect trafficking activity patterns alongside real-time intelligence that human operators might fail to spot. Technology has given government agencies the power to expose victims and perpetrators, trace human trafficking paths and dismantle trafficking operations before they get out of control. But despite the promise of this technology, there are gaps in the existing infrastructure and coordination that prevent full use of these innovations (Javed & Li, 2025).

With the advance of technology, Artificial Intelligence (AI) has become one of the major solution providers to combat human trafficking. AI can rapidly and accurately analyze large volumes of data to uncover patterns that point to possible trafficking activity. For example, machine learning models can be employed to help predict regions where trafficking may be more prevalent, while natural language processing (NLP) can be utilized to search for trafficking language in online forums and social media. Artificial Intelligence can improve the speed of law enforcement investigations and their accuracy, offer real-time alerts, and assist in identifying victims. However, given the potential for the AI field, there is still very little evidence that it has been fully developed to address human trafficking and exploitation and greater models are required, alongside better integration into already existing legal and law enforcement frameworks.

1.4 Purpose of the Chapter

To explore the possibilities, it propose a set of potential measures for reinforcing AI against human trafficking. Particularly, this will be aimed to identify key AI technologies that may have a crucial impact on the capacity of authorities to detect, prevent, and intervene in a trafficking situation. By doing this exploration, the paper will critique the existing drawbacks of AI in this space with recommendations for overcoming such drawbacks. Through assessment of current AI tools, ethical considerations, and best practices, the paper will illustrate how AI can serve as a game-changer in disrupting trafficking networks and providing a scalable solution to a global issue. The focus remains on generating findings that will inform the creation of stronger, more ethical, AI-powered methods to combat human trafficking.

2. TECHNOLOGY'S CURRENT ROLE IN COMBATING HUMAN TRAFFICKING: TRADITIONAL METHODS VS. TECHNOLOGY DRIVEN APPROACH

Traditionally, law enforcement agencies depended on conventional tactics, including patrols, manual investigations, and intelligence gathering to fight human trafficking. While these methods are necessary, they often are inadequate as trafficking operations are hidden, complex and tough to penetrate. Traditional approaches typically use a wholly reactive process of detecting crime, relying on tips, witness reports, and the ability of law enforcement officers to recognize suspicious activity. But these approaches don't keep pace with the scale and adaptability of modern trafficking networks, which often have transnational components and pose jurisdiction-relations challenges.

It is evident that traditional methods have limitations in detecting and preventing trafficking. Singapore authorities may have difficulty linking broken strands of data, piecing together trafficking patterns, and retracing financial transactions that appear to support illicit operations, Manchester says (Becher & Alarie, 2025). Additionally, traffickers have become more sophisticated at concealing their activities by using the internet, encrypted communications and other technologies. This leaves challengers with a huge gap to fill, unable to keep up with the dynamic and shifting approach of traffickers. An expansion of coverage will be needed; thus, categorically traditional options alone will not be able to resolve the invalidations of current human trafficking in the contemporary workforce. Technology, in contrast, has also emerged as a powerful weapon in improving law enforcement amidst these challenges. With emerging technology and technology led approaches such as Artificial Intelligence (AI), machine learning and big data analytics, there are still been a lot of advantages over traditional ways. These technologies allow for the analysis of massive volumes of data at a speed and scale human investigators could not hope to achieve. AI-Powered Preventive Strategies Increase detection of trafficking AI can enhance organizations' ability to detect potential trafficking events and intervene before exploitation have become massive illegal networks.

2.1 Current Technologies to Fight against Human Trafficking

He also added AI-powered surveillance systems coupled with predictive analytics to the list of promising technological tools being used to combat human trafficking. These systems work by analyzing data from a myriad of sources including public surveillance cameras, social media sites, and public records to identify potential indicators of trafficking. AI models have the ability to search and highlight patterns, as well as uncover correlations in large data sets for example, identifying clusters of suspicious activity that indicate trafficking activities. For instance, AI algorithms could flag certain locations or individuals who have been repeatedly connected to suspicious behaviour, such as prostitution and labour exploitation. Moreover, blockchain technology can be used to prevent trafficking by tracking victims transparently. Because of blockchain's built-in transparency, immutability, and security, it is tailor-made for organizing tamper-proof records of trips people take, medical treatments people receive, and legal statuses people acquire. Using blockchain to track victim identification could allow authorities to confirm the accuracy of reports, trace a victim's entire information history, and ensure that records are unalterable and indelible. Through data immutability, blockchain can increase supply chain transparency and help eliminate trafficking from sectors including agriculture, construction and manufacturing by providing an indisputable record of workers' conditions (Alhasan, 2025).

2.2 Impact of Technology in Real World Anti Trafficking Efforts

Many law enforcement and non-governmental organizations have implemented AI, machine learning, or digital tools in anti-trafficking operations. AI systems, for instance, have been deployed to scan online platforms, from websites to social media, for evidence of human trafficking ads. These tools can identify keywords, images and even patterns of online behavior that indicate trafficking activity, notifying law enforcement of potential cases far more quickly than traditional methods (Naidu & Krishnan,2025).

However, case studies of technology deployment indicate major success stories in the past few years. For example, in the US, the National Human Trafficking Hotline has used machine learning algorithms to identify potential trafficking cases from data submitted by victims, survivors and tipsters. That has resulted in a more effective response and improved victim support. In other areas of the world, AI tools have been utilized to enhance border control and customs inspections, detecting potential trafficking victims attempting to cross borders. And AI is similarly being applied to huge troves of social media data to help detect trafficking trends and locate missing persons. One of the first successful cases comes from Thailand, where software powered by AI was used to detect human trafficking in the fishing industry. AI systems identified trafficking hotspots through monitoring supply chains and conditions of workers, enabling the rescue of thousands of through exploitative labor conditions (Khattri, et. al., 2025.)

But there are caveats and limitations to these types of technological solutions. AI and surveillance tools implementation faces serious challenges such as data privacy issues. The increasing use of biometric evidence to corroborate other sources of information poses significant ethical issues regarding appropriate and authorized access to sensitive personal information, as well as its potential use in addressing human trafficking in comparison to protecting individual liberties. Moreover, although AI systems may contribute to recognizing trafficking tries, they demand human review to assure precision and to avoid prejudice in decision-making. It can be challenging to incorporate new technologies into existing law enforcement systems. For instance, a lot of law enforcement agencies in developing countries lack necessary infrastructure, training, and resources to effectively deploy such advanced AI tools. At the same time, we know that where technology is used, it should not only be relied on but complemented on the human expertise in the humanitarian & complex, nuanced understanding of human trafficking.

3. ARTIFICIAL INTELLIGENCE AND ITS CAPABILITIES IN COMBATING HUMAN TRAFFICKING

Artificial Intelligence (AI) which is the ability of a computer or robot controlled by a computer to do tasks normally requiring human intelligence. The whole purpose of AI systems are to learn from data, reason, and improve with time and create a better experience. AI can be seen as an overarching field that encompasses sub-disciplines like machine learning, natural language processing (NLP), computer vision, etc. These technologies allow machines to carry out processes that would normally necessitate human thought, including detecting patterns, comprehending language, and making decisions. By learning from large datasets and improving methods over time, AI systems can enable faster and better identification of complicated problems, including human trafficking. AI works by algorithms that take in data and create models based on patterns and relationships found in that data. Drawing from large volumes of information, AI is able to foresee upcoming scenarios, detect irregularities, and make data-led choices at a level of precision and effectiveness that conventional techniques cannot feasibly accomplish. Also, AI is essential to combat human trafficking, allowing for predictive analytics, anomaly detection, and better decision-making. By analyzing data trends that may be indicative of upcoming trafficking operations, law enforcement agencies, and NGOs can predict and prevent trafficking expeditions. Decision-making algorithms also help to identify whether on not suspicion of trafficking occurs based on data that has been fed into their systems. Real-time monitoring and intervention of trafficking activities is enabled through AI, yielding actionable insights on the frontlines for immediate response by law enforcement.

3.1 AI Tools and Techniques for Human Trafficking Prevention

Machine Learning and Predictive Analytics: One of the biggest subsets of AI used to help fight human trafficking is machine learning (ML). ML algorithms allow systems to automatically analyze large volumes of data and learn from the patterns therein without being explicitly programmed. When it comes to human trafficking, models can analyze data from diverse sources including online ads, social media posts, patterns in migration, and financial transactions to detect patterns and forecast potential trafficking locations. By evaluating historical data and spotting important risk components, machine learning can provide an early warning system for at-risk locations, individuals, or behaviors that typically indicate trafficking networks. Another important application of machine learning in human trafficking prevention is the detection of behavioral patterns. AI can monitor the behavioral deviations of individuals, including their communication habits, travel history, and interactions to identify potential vulnerabilities leading to exploitation. AI models can flag unusual patterns in an individual's online activity and frequent travel to areas with high levels of trafficking or contact with known traffickers, for instance for further investigation.

NLP (Natural Language Processing): Natural language processing is part of AI that enables machines to understand the human language. NLP is critical in detecting human trafficking-related content on the internet. It enables artificial intelligence systems to swiftly sift through large quantities of unstructured data including online message boards, social media posts, job postings and classified to spot particular keywords, or phrases, linked to human trafficking. AI-enabled natural language processing (NLP) models, for example, can do things like flag suspicious employment posts or ads, including common "live-in" opportunities that frequently appear in trafficking scenarios. NLP is also used for analyzing conversations or messages from chat rooms and other online sites that traffickers might frequent. AI systems are able to assist the authorities in intervening before the situation escalates, by detecting words or phrases that may indicate exploitation or coercion. Further research in NLP can also be utilized in screening job advertisements and classified ads to help identify job offers that may lead to exploitative conditions, thus preventing potential victims from entering trafficking situations.

Facial Recognition and Biometrics: AI can be a powerful tool to aid in identifying the victims and perpetrator of human trafficking. AI dynamic facial recognition can assist in identifying trafficking victims who have been photographed or recorded in public settings or digital surveillance footage by comparing images videos to a database of recognized faces. This technology also proves beneficial in identifying victims at border security, airports or other transportation hubs where traffickers could try to transport people in a geographical area or international realm. Beyond facial recognition, other forms of biometric data, including fingerprints or iris scans, could be used to confirm identities, track victims and help create records that cannot be altered. It has become increasingly popular as an efficient means of identifying persons within mass gathering locations or through automated surveillance systems. Facial recognition, when incorporated into border control protocols, can help speed up identification of potential trafficking victims and enable faster intervention of authorities.

Robotic Process Automation (RPA): RPA is the application of software robots powered by Artificial Intelligence to automate non-discretionary, repetitive tasks. When it comes to combating human trafficking, practitioners use RPA to automate data processing, victim reporting, and case management, among other administrative tasks. Through the automation of these and similar processes, RPA makes room for human resources to engage in more complex and strategic tasks, such as investigating trafficking operations or providing supporting services to victims. A notable example is the use of RPA to analyze and cross-examine multiple databases, including immigration records, criminal databases and victim reports for patterns that can serve as indicators of trafficking. This capacity for report and alert generation is something that can be beneficial to law enforcement as RPA reduces the required amount of manual workload when monitoring for and reacting to possible trafficking incidences.

3.2 Benefits of AI in Human Trafficking Prevention

Despite this fact, AI has many advantages in the battle against human trafficking, including speed, accuracy, and scale.

Identifying Trafficking Activities by Speed and Precision: AI's ability to quickly and accurately analyze large amounts of data is one of its key benefits. In contrast to traditional investigative techniques, which can degenerate into tedious manual analysis, AI can rapidly identify suspicious patterns and anomalies across large datasets, enabling timely interventions. For instance, real-time video footage, social media activity, and job postings are scannable via AI-powered tools, which can detect potential trafficking indicators significantly more quickly than a human investigator.

Real-Time Intervention and Alert System for Law Enforcement: AI-based systems can also facilitate real-time interventions when patterns or behaviors associated with trafficking are detected, alerting law enforcement agents of questionable activity in real-time. Predictive analytics: Predictive analytics algorithms can be trained to identify habits and trends of victims to detect potential trafficking activities before they trigger, enabling authorities to take preventive measures. AI models can analyze border crossing books and predict when and how trafficking attempts will happen and in what area so that authorities can already be located there.

Scalability of AI Tools Across Global Jurisdictions: Applying AI in that case can help strategize both in prevention and prosecution and scale across global jurisdictions a unified approach to combat human trafficking. Trafficking is often a transnational crime, and AI-powered systems can facilitate cross-border coordination, enabling sharing of evidence and collaboration across jurisdictions. Also, this scalability allows AI technologies to assist police forces worldwide in collaboration, enabling them to share the most relevant information related to the trafficking networks that cross borders.

4. STRENGTHENING AI FOR EFFECTIVE COMBATING OF HUMAN TRAFFICKING

4.1 Improving AI Accuracy and Bias Reduction

AI accuracy is among the most pressing challenges in the application of AI, especially when data is biased or incomplete. AI models are only as good as the data they are trained on, so if that data is biased or partial, the AI's output will be equally bad. For example, in human trafficking, flawed data may cause victims to be inaccurately categorized or to experience discriminatory treatment, as vulnerable or marginalized groups are often underrepresented. If, for example, trafficking statistics are biased toward a certain region or demographic, AI models may be unable to recognize victims from underrepresented populations. This can lead to significant inconsistencies in identifying victims, implementing intervention strategies, and the overall efficacy of AI-based anti-trafficking approaches. AI has many beneficial uses, but there are also serious considerations regarding biases in the output of AI because the models trained cannot and should not rely on data from a narrow set of demographics to scale the human scale traffickers. This should also include data from a range of geography, cultural context, and victim demographic. Not only will this method find patterns of trafficking for all groups evenly, but it will minimize the propensity of AI to miss certain types of trafficking or numbers of vulnerable people.

4.2 Enhancing AI System with More Data

The data on which AI systems are trained is critical for the performance of the model, and given that the models are only as good as the data and is very susceptible to bias, it is no different in the field of human trafficking. More data is better: diversity and volume are key in making machine learning models stronger. The more varied the data, the better the I.A.'s ability to identify patterns that signal trafficking, whether in social media posts, financial transactions or immigration records. In addition, substantial data sets can enable AI models to learn to pick up on the more nuanced indicators of trafficking that wouldn't seem particularly noteworthy to investigators at first glance.

Data sharing between nations, NGOs, law enforcement agencies, and other stakeholders can go a long way in improving the predictive powers of AI. Human trafficking is a world-wide phenomenon, and in many cases, the movement of the trafficked person involves several countries. "When that data is shared across borders, AI systems can more accurately track victim movement and uncover trafficking patterns that may cross national lines. As an example, integrating immigration data from multiple countries into AI systems can help identify human trafficking across multiple regions. Similarly, a greater willingness to trade information might allow law enforcement agencies and NGOs a better picture of trafficking networks, thus giving them a greater chance to intercept potential crimes before they are committed.

Public and private data sources can also be combined to improve the precision offered by AI models. Combining public datasets, like reports or law enforcement databases, and manmade data, like information from social media, job postings, and online marketplaces, can yield a better understanding of trafficking activity. AI systems, when trained on multiple data types, can provide more accurate predictions that allow law enforcement and organizations to engage in preventative measures based on a more holistic view of trafficking networks.

4.3 Advanced Integration of AI in Law Enforcement and Border Security

Therefore, there are several advantages to implementing AI into law enforcement & border security operations to detect and reduce human trafficking effectively, within a short amount of time. AI can greatly improve surveillance by automating the monitoring of key areas (borders, transportation centers) and public places, where traffickers often move their victims around. AI systems it may soon be a standard case that it is no longer necessary in media coverage. AI also can be linked to existing law enforcement resources and data repositories, offering trafficking prevention a fuller package. For example, AI can help analyze and cross-reference data across immigration records, criminal databases, and victim reports to flag suspicious patterns in activity. By removing noise from data, AI ensures officers remain alert, allowing law enforcement officers to spend less time identifying potential trafficking cases. By using AI for real-time processing of this data, authorities can intervene quickly when any signs of trafficking are detected at high-risk locations like airports and border crossings. AI is integrated with law enforcement beyond detection as well; it aids in investigative work. AI, through the analysis of historical data, can enhance the identification of the pathways through which trafficking occurs, the modality or method of exploitation, and the key actors involved in trafficking rings. This data will help guide targeted law enforcement operations and allow for optimal resource allocation. Furthermore, AI technologies can also facilitate case management by categorizing and organizing evidence so that investigators can easily monitor their progress and manage vast amounts of information.

4.4 AI-Driven Collaborative Systems for Global Anti-Trafficking Efforts

AI-powered solutions can facilitate international collaboration efforts between different governmental and non-governmental entities to combat human trafficking through cross-border cooperation amongst law enforcement agencies and humanitarian organizations. When countries share data, insights, and predictive models, they can collaborate to identify trafficking operations that cross many regions and intervene before additional harm is done.

International law enforcement agencies can collaborate more effectively through cross-border AI tools, as these tools can give them access to a consolidated monitoring system through which they help flag trafficking ingredients. For instance, AI systems could use real-time analysis of migration data, travel patterns, and border-crossing information to track the movement of trafficked individuals across borders. Notably, when that trafficking victim crosses into another country, with an AI-powered alert system, the authorities in the destination country would receive alerts of such events and can consequently respond to protect the victim and to catch the traffickers.

Similarly, AI-fueled collaboration can advance the efforts of NGOs and humanitarian organizations, equipping them with real-time data and analysis on trafficking trends. With data-driven AI tools, organizations can practice and reduce trafficking activities by determining trafficking risk areas and concentrating on strengthening support for victims and awareness campaigns in these regions. AI also helps with resource distribution; it can help organizations deploy support services to where they're most needed. Human trafficking and transnational crime require international cooperation, along with systems generally built on AI-driven collaborative systems. It is AI technologies to support a coordinated global response that will increase the effectiveness of anti-trafficking approaches, enabling real-time action, and saving lives.

5. ETHICAL, LEGAL, AND PRIVACY CONSIDERATION

5.1 Privacy Issues and Human Rights

While AI technologies are being applied more and more to the fight against human trafficking, issues of privacy and human rights have taken center stage. AI systems generally need significant quantities of personal data to work effectively, which creates serious privacy concerns. Facial recognition technology and surveillance systems are potential examples of biometric data collection, which can become misused if not secured. Striking a balance between improving security and protecting privacy is a challenging task. On the one hand, AI tools can assist in detection of victims of trafficking, monitor criminal activity, and prevent exploitations. But they can also encroach on people's rights to privacy if not carefully regulated. It is vital that human rights protections are upheld for trafficked victims and for those under surveillance alike. Trafficking victims do need to be protected, but they also need to be treated with dignity and respect, and their personal data needs to be processed in a way that protects their freedom and privacy. Just as surveillance should not infringe on individuals who are not threatening us, there is a need adequate legislative framework to outline what is acceptable for AI to do in law enforcement and trafficking prevention.

5.2 Bias in AI Systems and Fairness

AI systems are not neutral by default but they are trained on data that may incorporate implicit biases relating to race, gender, socioeconomic status and other variables. When it comes to how law enforcement uses algorithms, the stakes are higher: the biases present in the data, or in how the algorithms are built, can unwittingly reinforce stereotypes and inequalities, particularly when that data is used in making decisions that impact people's real lives like identifying potential trafficking victims or those monitoring suspects. As with facial recognition software, studies have found that the error rates in AI systems tend to be higher for people of color, women and people from the disadvantaged class. In the case of AI models used to address human trafficking, these types of biases can cause groups of people to become unfairly treated and targeted.

Biases can distill and amplify in the data, so addressing these lies at the core of ensuring an AI that is effective and fair. This can be accomplished by diversifying training datasets to include a larger number of variables across demographic groups, thus making the risk of a bias outcome less likely. Moreover, maintaining an ethical background for AI which include fairness, accountability and transparency in machine-level results is essential. These frameworks must include and set out clear practices to prevent and address bias, and ensure that AI systems do not reinforce discrimination. Ethical AI is especially relevant in the scope of human trafficking because the technologies implemented to protect those most at-risk must not marginalize existing vulnerable communities further, and preventative efforts are properly focused and equitable.

5.3 Legal Challenges and Jurisdictional Issues

AI implementation would face many legal challenges due to the global nature of human trafficking. Trafficking, by its nature, traverses borders through networks spanning multiple jurisdictions, and the AI-powered identification and prevention of trafficking relies on the near-impossible coordination between nations with different legal systems. While some nations uphold tough data protection and privacy rules, others have more relaxed regulations, complicating the cross-border exchange of information.

While international treaties and agreements exist to combat human trafficking and generally inform the legal framework for utilizing AI against trafficking in persons, such as the United Nations Convention against Transnational Organized Crime (UNTOC), the complexities of integrating AI to fight trafficking are rarely addressed in international agreements. AI use also raises ethical questions that vary more when you factor in different legal frameworks in different countries, especially in relation to data privacy, surveillance and human rights. For example, countries that belong to the European Union must comply with the General Data Protection Regulation (GDPR), which imposes hard restrictions on the collection and use of personal data. Compared to other countries, whose laws on data and AI surveillance may be lax. This proves a challenge when AI systems also transact across borders, and as the question of who bears legal blame for AI-mediated decisions becomes more complex.

Another important aspect is legal accountability within the framework of AI-based trafficking prevention. If an AI system wrongly identifies a person as a trafficking victim, or fails to identify a victim when there is one, who gets blamed? Should it be the developers of the AI, the law enforcement agencies using it, or the company that's providing the technology? These questions are at the heart of ensuring that decisions driven by AI are not only effective, but legally sound.

5.4 Public Perception and Acceptance of AI in Law Enforcement

One such public concern is the implementation of AI in law enforcement especially for fighting human trafficking. Many people are worried that with AI's rollout comes over-policing, increased invasion of privacy and the potential for personal data to be abused. To win public acceptance of AI-driven policing, the responsibility of transparency and two-way communication rests squarely with law enforcement, as does the need for effective safeguards to ensure that AI-driven analysis whether predictive, analytical, or contextual is conducted in an appropriate context.

It is important to engage with communities and stakeholders about the potential risks and benefits of AI in law enforcement in order to build public trust. Governments and law enforcement agencies should provide transparency about how AI systems are being used, what data is being collected, and what measures are in place to protect individual rights. Moreover oversight and accountability mechanisms should be put in place to ensure not to use the AI systems in a way that would violate the civil liberties.

When it comes to skepticism of AI, much of the public does not understand how the technologies work. Educational initiatives and public consultations are keys to demystifying AI and engendering a more informed debate about its place in law enforcement. For AI to be effective in fighting trafficking, there must be the will and ability within the communities where it is deployed to act in its name, and this is a communal decision as much as an institutional one.

6. AI AND INTERNATIONAL COLLABORATION IN COMBATING HUMAN TRAFFICKING

6.1 Global Cooperation and Information Sharing

Combatting human trafficking is a matter that is globally endemic, requiring international cooperation to achieve success in this fight. The use of AI is crucial in assisting countries to cooperate across international borders as well as share information with local law enforcement and third-party organizations (NGOs). Trafficking circuits are not confined by national borders, and without a harmonized approach, the rescue of victims, the capture of offenders and the dismantling of trafficking operations becomes challenging. Enhanced cross-border information sharing and real-time data processing capabilities underpin many multinational law-enforcement efforts, with AI systems capable of sifting through vast amounts of data quickly and efficiently. Such systems allow authorities to monitor international transport routes, sensitive trends in travel data, and potential causes.

AI-powered software solutions and tools help facilitate exchange of information. Through thisuse of machine learning algorithms, these tools are also able to automatically flag suspicious activities and trigger alerts to law enforcement, which can serve across dozens of countries and jurisdictions to enable faster response and greater coordination. Another development is the implementation of universal protocols in AI systems to facilitate cross-border data exchange in compliance with legal and ethical frameworks. International AI protocols and data-sharing agreements will be key to this, enabling countries to share critical intelligence while providing privacy and security to victims and survivors. These protocols also accommodate issues of data sovereignty and ensure that AI system deployers comply with legal norms and structures that have been determined in various countries.

6.2 Case Study: Interpol and AI Collaboration

Perhaps the most high-profile view of AI collaborators in the fight against human trafficking comes from the international police network, Interpol. Interpol is now using AI technologies to help track and combat those involved with human trafficking across borders. These AI-driven tools allow Interpol to analyze massive datasets from travel records to online activity and financial transactions to identify patterns in trafficking activity that may not be immediately evident. Navigates its way through these technologies to grant member countries with real-time information and insights that can help them investigate cases faster and to prevent potential trafficking cases.

A key success in this AI collaboration is the development of AI-powered predictive analytics tools to identify trafficking trends and potential hotspots. These tools give member countries early alerts about possible trafficking operations by analyzing data from multiple sources, such as law enforcement reports and public databases. Interpol has also deployed AI to assist with the identification of victims by comparing facial recognition records from surveillance systems to databases of missing people and suspected trafficking victims. Doing so has saved many lives that would have otherwise gone undetected. The global cooperation on AI is still a work in progress. This is mainly because of a lack of consistent data standards between countries. Various legal frameworks, privacy issues, and data protection laws make it challenging to build a consistent international artificial intelligence legal structure. There are also growing concerns about the use and misuse of AI in surveillance, including the potential for privacy violations. Nonetheless, the use of AI as shown in the efforts of Interpol and other international organizations has shown success and has huge potential in fighting human trafficking, and there is a real opportunity for collaboration on such a powerful tool.

6.3 Public Private Partnerships

The use of public-private partnerships (PPPs) is a strong model for advancing on AI solutions to combat human trafficking. One avenue includes these partnerships, in which government agencies, AI companies, and NGOs work together to develop and leverage cutting-edge technologies to fight trafficking in all of its forms. Tech giants play a key role in these partnerships, as they contribute the cutting-edge AI technologies needed to address complex challenges such as human trafficking. Those giant companies with AI, machine learning and cloud computing expertise are behind the tools that can help parse through massive datasets to uncover trafficking activity and identify those at risk. Several AI initiatives have emerged from these partnerships that aim to fight human trafficking. For example, together with law enforcement and NGOs, AI companies developed platforms that analyze online content like job postings, social media posts and escort services for potential risk of human trafficking. By sifting through tremendous amounts of online content in real-time, this technology can identify the tell-tale signs of exploitation and trafficking, allowing law enforcement to intervene before it's too late. These AI-powered tools also aid in the screening of recruitment platforms and other digital spaces where traffickers often target potential victims, catching potential exploitation at early stages. Through this, creative partnerships emerged that contributed to collaborative AI projects, sharing resources, and expertise to address the problem of human trafficking on a bigger scale. Collaborative projects between AI companies and law enforcement, for example, have generated predictive analytics models that can predict the likely location of trafficking based on historical data, movement patterns, and social media activity: These partnerships facilitate the sharing of data and insights, leading to more optimal resource allocation and allowing authorities to focus their efforts in high-risk areas, with the effectiveness of disrupting trafficking networks significantly enhanced (Łabuz, 2025).

7. BARRIERS TO AI IMPLEMENTATION IN COMBATING HUMAN TRAFFICKING

There are technological, practical, and ethical hurdles that must be overcome in order to maximize the effectiveness of AI-based human trafficking efforts.

7.1 Technological Barriers

One major challenge is uneven infrastructure in some parts of the world that makes it difficult to deploy AI systems. Countries, especially in developing regions, do not have the required technological infrastructure for AI tools, like high-speed internet, storage data capabilities, or even access to computer power with hardware. Such a digital divide poses challenges for global scalability of innovative AI-driven solutions in tackling human trafficking. Furthermore, varying data formats among countries and agencies make it challenging to easily share and combine data. Trafficking networks cross jurisdictions, but inconsistent formats make it difficult for agencies to work together and share resources effectively. This makes it difficult to establish a cohesive international framework for preventing human trafficking with the use of AI.

Resistance can also stem from lack of understanding, lack of training, or even lack of access to AI technologies. The complexity of large technologies, such as AI, raises skepticism and discomfort among governmental organizations and law enforcement agencies, as many of them are not yet aware of it, or simply find its details to be overwhelming. The lack of information regarding AI also contributes to this hesitance since these systems have the potential to substantially augment trafficking detection and prevention strategies. In order to overcome this barrier, we have to conduct training and awareness campaigns for frontline anti-trafficking forces in order to equip them with the know-how of best using as well as the capabilities of AI tools.

7.2 Practical Barriers

Apart from challenges on the technological side, practical impediments also stand in the way of the widespread utilisation of AI in the fight against human trafficking. There are also the political and bureaucratic obstacles. Transnational cooperation is necessary to combat human trafficking, but political differences and bureaucratic red tape often stand in the way of effective international cooperation. Nations might not want to share such sensitive information, or might also have competing policies around privacy and surveillance, making the production of uniform AI systems difficult in practice. Addressing these hurdles necessitates the creation of international accords, uniform protocols, and inter-country trust to ensure collaboration is less cumbersome. Moreover, lack of qualified professionals is also an important practical limitation. Specialized knowledge is needed to develop and manage AI, and not all regions have data scientists, machine learning or AI engineers capable of designing, implementing, and maintaining such systems. Modern technology AI tools are essential for helping prevent human trafficking, but you can only build and scale those if you have a strong pool of skilled professionals (Rebolledo, 2025).

7.3 Ethical and Societal Concerns

The potential for AI systems to invade our privacy is one of the major concerns flagged by human rights advocates and the public. AI tools, including surveillance cameras, facial recognition and data mining, can feel invasive, sparking fears of overreach and the erosion of civil liberties. Public trust and acceptance in artificial intelligence technologies need to be employed in a manner that is respectful of privacy and human rights. There is also the risk of the technology being appropriated for surveillance purposes outside of human trafficking efforts. Once AI systems are operational, they could be deployed to surveil populations for other purposes, including opposition control or social control. It also raises concerns about the potential use of AI systems for surveillance and the ways that they can unintentionally harm marginalized communities.

8. FUTURE DIRECTIONS AND AI INNOVATIONS

With the rapid advancement of artificial intelligence (AI) technologyl, the application of AI to help fight against human trafficking is growing exponentially. AI-enabled tools including quantum computing and deep learning are also poised to fundamentally transform the trafficking landscape through enhanced predictive, tracking, and responsive capabilities to trafficking acts. Quantum computing which can analyze vast amounts of data at previously unheard-of speeds might offer breakthroughs in examining intricate patterns in trafficking operations. Machine Learning deepening algorithms growing; Small patterns and anomalies discover AI detection Traditional systems can't (human-made systems) This technology will increase the ability of law enforcement to identify trafficking networks, heighten hidden relationships, and predict behavior of traffickers with higher precisions. As AI further advances, these systems are expected to become more predictive, autonomous and adaptive enabling detection of trafficking activities before they can develop (Lim, 2025).

But AI is not limited to detection or enforcement as the most exciting potentials we see in the future is an expanded role for AI in the rehabilitation and reintegration of trafficking victims. AI can harness predictive models to help identify individuals or communities that are most at risk, enabling the development of early intervention programs that can stop trafficking before it starts. AI-powered tools could provide survivors with the types of support they need while they navigate legal, medical and psychological services as they recover. For instance, a machine learning model could analyze data on survivors to understand high-level, common psychological and social barriers to reintegration, which could further inform more precise rehabilitation approaches. Moreover, AI can improve victim support systems that link victims to community resources, social networks, and mental health professionals to assist in their long-term recovery. AI can assist in tackling human trafficking. AI will transform social work, not just through predictive analytics, but also through active monitoring and alerting of at-risk populations, thereby preemptively diagnosing and mitigating patterns of human trafficking as they occur and issuing alerts to law enforcement and supportive organizations. The aim is to build a more coordinated and effective international response to human trafficking, which is interconnected across borders and institutions. AI's relevance to human trafficking will lead to societal changes, some of which include a decrease in trafficking rates, transformation of cross-border law enforcement collaboration, and improvement in the protection of human rights. AI may become a new cornerstone in the fight against human trafficking in the long term, helping to eliminate this form of contemporary slavery.

9. CONCLUSION

AI has great potential to aid the battle against human trafficking, and there is an increasing amount of data to show its effectiveness on various levels, whether that be detection, prevention, or the engagement of victims." Machine learning, natural language processing, and facial recognition are just some of the AI technologies that have already proven they can find trafficking patterns, predict high-risk locations, and help identify victims. But there still are hurdles to be cleared, especially as far as the accuracy, the impartiality and the ethical guidelines of AI systems are concerned. It takes some more developments in data diversity, international sharing, and integration with real-time law enforcement systems to see AI walking the walk and not just talking the talk.

When using AI in anti-trafficking efforts, ethical, legal, and privacy considerations need to remain at the forefront. Among the most critical components to operating any impactful system (and especially a transformative one like AI) is ensuring transparency, protecting human rights, and safeguarding against bias - the loss of which can undermine the very transformative impact on vulnerable populations that systems can help facilitate. They must also navigate institutional and legal impediments imposed by differing jurisdictions to prevent the misuse and abdication of responsibility driven by AI. Several policy changes can help strengthen AI further in the fight against human trafficking. This requires that governments and international bodies make adoption of AI a top priority through establishing clear regulations and frameworks around data-sharing, collaboration, and ethical AI practices. These initiatives will also be increasingly dependent upon cross-border collaboration between law enforcement and tech companies. Moreover, this tool will require strong privacy protection as well as AI transparency to use AI technologies responsibly.

Thus, the power of AI can revolutionize human trafficking prevention. Collaborative international solutions with an empathic consciousness towards the problem combined with ongoing innovation will facilitate overcoming existing difficulties and harnessing the power of AI as the tool we need to engage our resources in the fight against human trafficking across borders. The few case studies of technology use for victim protection and trafficking prevention available today demonstrate that we have only just scratched the surface of what is possible in this space with new technologies in the years to come.

REFERENCES

Alhasan, T. K. (2025). Integrating AI Into Arbitration: Balancing Efficiency With Fairness and Legal Compliance. *Conflict Resolution Quarterly*, crq.21470. DOI: 10.1002/crq.21470

Becher, S., & Alarie, B. (2025). LexOptima: The promise of AI-enabled legal systems. *University of Toronto Law Journal*, 75(1), 73–121. DOI: 10.3138/utlj-2024-0002

Javed, K., & Li, J. (2025). Bias in adjudication: Investigating the impact of artificial intelligence, media, financial and legal institutions in pursuit of social justice. *PLoS One*, 20(1), e0315270. DOI: 10.1371/journal.pone.0315270 PMID: 39752385

Khalifa, M., & Sabry, M. (2024, January). The Challenges of The Artificial Intelligence of Law in The Context of Technological Development. In *2024 ASU International Conference in Emerging Technologies for Sustainability and Intelligent Systems (ICETSIS)* (pp. 1-5). IEEE. DOI: 10.1109/ICETSIS61505.2024.10459547

Khattri, U., Sharma, P., Adarsh, A., & Kour, G. D. (2025). How Can Artificial Intelligence Enable Sustainable Development Goals? Leveraging Technology for a Sustainable Future. In *Renewable Energy and the Economic Welfare of Society* (pp. 423-450). IGI Global Scientific Publishing.

Łabuz, M. (2025). A Teleological Interpretation of the Definition of DeepFakes in the EU Artificial Intelligence Act—A Purpose-Based Approach to Potential Problems With the Word "Existing". *Policy and Internet*.

Li, Z. (2024). Ethical frontiers in artificial intelligence: Navigating the complexities of bias, privacy, and accountability. *International Journal of Engineering and Management Research*, 14(3), 109–116.

Lim, D. (2025). Determinants of Socially Responsible AI Governance. *Duke Law & Technology Review*, 25(1), 183–232.

Mensah, G. B., Mijwil, M. M., Abotaleb, M., Ali, G., & Dutta, P. K. (2009). High Performance Medicine: Involving Artificial Intelligence Models in Enhancing Medical Laws and Medical Negligence Matters A Case Study of Act, 2009 (Act 792) in Ghana.

Naidu, G., & Krishnan, V. (2025). Artificial Intelligence-Powered Legal Document Processing for Medical Negligence Cases: A Critical Review. *International Journal of Intelligence Science*, 15(1), 10–55. DOI: 10.4236/ijis.2025.151002

Orhan, K., Gülbeş, M. M., Jadhav, A., & Jagtap, R. (2024). Medico-Legal Problems of Artificial Intelligence. In *Artificial Intelligence in Dentistry* (pp. 259–282). Springer International Publishing.

Rebolledo, V. G. (2025). Impact of the artificial intelligence on international relations: Towards a global algorithms governance.

Yadong, C. (2024). Analysis of Artificial Intelligence Judicial Cases. In *Blue Book on AI and Rule of Law in the World (2022)* (pp. 347–365). Springer Nature Singapore. DOI: 10.1007/978-981-97-1060-7_8

Chapter 11
Role of Artificial Intelligence in Modernizing and Transforming the Judicial Systems and the International Court of Justice

Sahil Lal
https://orcid.org/0000-0001-9827-3717
Sharda University, India

Bhupinder Singh
https://orcid.org/0009-0006-4779-2553
Sharda University, India

Manmeet Kaur Arora
https://orcid.org/0009-0002-5071-117X
Sharda University, India

Christian Kaunert
https://orcid.org/0000-0002-4493-2235
Dublin City University, Ireland & University of South Wales, UK

Anjali Raghav
https://orcid.org/0009-0004-0248-7956

DOI: 10.4018/979-8-3693-9395-6.ch011

Sharda University, India

ABSTRACT

With the potential to transform judicial bodies from the courts to the ICJ, AI promises greater efficiency, accessibility, and equity in justice. This study examines how AI is revolutionizing judicial practices, focusing on its impact on case management, legal research, and decision-making. It emphasizes the extrapolated advantages these AI technologies can confer, allowing for predictive analytics and natural language processing, streamlining practices, and increasing accessibility through which various populations may benefit from the justice system. The adoption of AI brings with it ethical dilemmas that need to be addressed, such as algorithmic bias, transparency in the process of decision-making, and the requirement for human intervention. The complexities of this moment demand careful navigation, as this work towards a future where that technology no longer hampers justice but bolsters global judicial systems.

1. INTRODUCTION

The emergence of AI over the past few years had developed into a radical shift that is defining the future of human efforts at work and decision making in enterprises across Industries. Even so, the judicial process, the supposed spine of civilized order and justice, is clearing the way. With courts struggling to keep pace with caseloads, finite resources, and rising demands for greater efficiency and transparency, AI is seen as an opportunity to improve judicial processes. By analysing current practices and potential uses within the ICJ and other judicial systems, this paper provides recommendations to policymakers and legal practitioners to ensure responsible AI deployment. The implications call for consideration, emphasising a middle-ground strategy to translate the properties of AI without undermining the tenets of justice. It excite with insight this paper studying the AI role in the modernization of judicial systems and the International Court of Justice (ICJ); please share expert knowledge and analyse the potential benefits, challenges, and implications of AI and the ICJ by providing fresh understanding in this important study (PwC, 2021).

1.1 Background and Significance

The judicial system is paramount to preserving the rule of law, administering justice, and safeguarding individual rights. But the existing judicial procedures are so time-consuming and slow that they cannot meet the benefits of justice on time (Singh & Kaunert, 2025). Many courts face huge backlogs and delays in the delivery of justice as case numbers spike. Moreover, the complexity of the legal information and the enormous number of cases can inundate judges and lawyers which then leads to inconsistent decisions made and eroded public trust in justice.

AI's importance in this context cannot be emphasized enough. With the help of advanced algorithms and machine learning techniques, AI has the capacity to improve judicial operations in several areas (Singh & Kaunert, 2025). AI-driven tools, for example, can help case management, forecasting the possible outcome of a case based on past records and allowing judges to make decisions based on objective data. Moreover, in streamlining legal research AI can sift through extensive databases of case law and statutes, such as research from LexisNexis, to enable faster access to relevant information that is necessary for judgment (Woxsen University, 2021).

Additionally, the use of artificial intelligence spans across domestic jurisdictions as well as within international legal frameworks. As the principal judicial organ of the United Nations, the International Court of Justice (ICJ) has unique challenges based on its function of settling disputes between states. Given the complexities involved in international law and the requirement of neutrality, the application of AI in the ICJ holds special importance. The application of AI technologies may allow the ICJ to increase its efficiency for dealing with cases as well as preserving impartiality and transparency.

1.2 Objectives of the Study

This study aims to explore the multifaceted role of AI in modernizing judicial systems and enhancing the operations of the International Court of Justice. The primary objectives are as follows:

I. **To Analyse Current Challenges**: In characterising these issues, both those raised by the system itself and those with the evolving system itself such as case backlogs, inefficiencies in legal research, and inconsistencies in rulings. This paper lays the groundwork for discussion of potential AI interventions to ameliorate such issues.

II. **To Explore AI Applications:** The second goal is to explore specific applications which AI used in judicial systems. This will involve examining case management tools, analytical tools used in determining sentencing decisions, factory-style document review processes and their effects on the practice of the law.

III. **Evaluating Influence in the International Court of Justice:** The International Court of Justice gives a unique market where a major focus will be on assessing how AI can advance operations. Such analysis is located in a larger body of work that is examining potential use cases of emerging AI technologies where they might interact with international law, noting this institution's only deviation from other areas of law to be always-special and asymmetric challenges.

IV. **To Examine Ethical Considerations:** This research would provide critical insights into the ethical concerns associated with AI integration into the judicial system.

V. **To Make Recommendations:** Finally, this research also seeks to provide actionable recommendations for best practices for integrating AI into judicial processes for policymakers and legal practitioners. These will be informed by a comprehensive examination of the opportunities and challenges associated with AI technologies.

2. OVERVIEW OF JUDICIAL SYSTEMS

At a core level is what judicial systems represent is a fundamental building block of governance that embodies the rule of law, safeguards individual rights, and provides justice in societies. They are the way that laws are interpreted, applied and enforced. This part covers an introduction to judicial systems, its definition and primary functions, as well as the major challenges faced by them in today's society.

2.1 Definition and Functions of Judicial Systems

A judicial system means the institution that administers justice. It includes a system of courts, tribunals, and legal organizations tasked with adjudicating disputes, program activities, and upholding legal entitlements. Judicial systems exist on multiple tiers local, national, and international and are defined by their alignment with established legal principles and procedures.

The primary functions of judicial systems include:

Dispute Resolution: Resolving disputes between two individuals, organisations, or between the state and an individual or an organisation is one of the most important functions of the judiciary. Courts serve as a structured venue in which disputing parties can bring forward their case, evidence, and argument in front of an unbiased judge or jury (UNESCO, 2024). This function makes sure disputes are resolved fairly and justly in accordance with the law.

Interpretation Of Statutes: Courts are required to interpret laws and the provisions to make sure they are duly applied in individual cases. Judges regularly confront nuanced legal questions, where they must parse legislative intent, precedent and constitutional principles. Their rulings can establish critical legal precedent shaping future jurisprudence.

Protection of Rights: Courts are tasked with enforcing constitutional protections against illegal conduct by persons, or by the state. This is part of issues like discrimination, freedom of speech, and due process rights.

Enforcement of Laws: The judiciary must warrant the consistency in enforcement of laws passed by legislative bodies. Part of this role is to oversee the actions of the state's law enforcement agencies, and to ensure that those who break the laws are prosecuted appropriately.

Promotion of Social Justice: Courts are not simply about adjudicating disputes; rather, judicial systems actively work towards the promotion of social justice and addressing systemic inequalities in society. Courts hear cases about marginalized groups and seek to right wrongs with fair judgments.

2.2 Challenges Faced by Traditional Judicial Processes

To implement any such idea, traditional ways of justice face certain problems like complex process, biased and inequal decisions, and delayed judgements, etc. The difficulty in achieving it is rooted in increasing caseloads, resource constraints, technological gaps, and systemic inefficiencies.

Backlog of Cases: Accumulation of backlogged cases is one of the issues that judicial systems face. These include population growth and rising rates of litigation, because of which courts around the world are increasingly unable to cope with growing caseloads. As such, numerous peoples find themselves waiting a considerable amount of time before their legal issues are resolved (National Judicial Academy, 2021). But prolonged delays in dispensing justice can lead to a loss of faith in the judiciary's ability to render timely justice.

Limited Resources: Judicial systems function on tight budgets and with few resources. It is not only the number of judges and court personnel available but also the physical infrastructure necessary for the efficient functioning of the courts that are limited. Underfunded courts may lead to at best understaffed courts, at worst, inadequate technology, and training in case processing in the court systems.

Legal Knowledge Complexity: The field of law is vast, with a multitude of information existing in laws, regulations, case laws, and legal precedents. Legal practitioners tend to had difficult time to navigate these complex matters with adherence of procedural matter. This complexity can lead to mistakes in the preparation of cases or arguments in hearings, causing additional delays in the process.

Inconsistent Rulings: In the judicial system, variability in decision-making can result in laws being applied inconsistently across cases or jurisdictions. The gap is caused by different interpretations by judges or different expertise among lawyers. And so when different sides of similar stories play out in dramatically different ways, it raises questions about fairness, and equality in front of the law.

Trust and Public Perception: Public faith in the judiciary underpins the legitimacy of judicial systems; perceptions of bias or corruption can undermine societal trust in these institutions. Judicial misconduct or perceived unfairness in a high-profile case can trigger scepticism about the integrity of the system (Binns, 2021). To restore public trust, the transparency and accountability measures inside these judicial processes must be in place.

Resilience to Change: The conventional judiciary is often resistant to change due to established precedents and practices that have taken root over time. Lawyers and other legal professionals might be reluctant to embrace new technologies or methodologies that could streamline the processes of their practice out of fear that they could be replaced or be indifferent about learning new tools.

This combination undermines traditional judicial processes and entrenches societal inequities and injustices. Due to changing societal needs, including globalization and technological advancement, the pressures on judicial systems are ever-increasing and this is one of the most urgent problem areas that needs a novel solution to the issues comprehensively. Given these obstacles to traditional justice system, infusion of artificial intelligence (AI) into the judicial system is an exciting opportunity for modernization. AI technologies can facilitate the efficiency of operations by automating mundane assignments like paperwork or case management as well as using predictive analytics to add insights that improve decision-making skills.

3. THE EMERGENCE OF ARTIFICIAL INTELLIGENCE IN LAW

Artificial Intelligence (AI) is a solid leap in the direction of how legal services are delivered and how justice is administered. As demands intensify on judicial systems to function efficiently, minimize costs, and improve access to justice, AI technologies present creative and potential solutions to radically alter conventional approaches. This section explores the definition of artificial intelligence and provides the historical context and progression of their place in legal systems (Johnson & Smith, 2022).

3.1 Definition of Artificial Intelligence

Artificial intelligence is the simulation of human intelligence processes by computer systems. These processes can involve learning (the acquisition of information and rules for using it), reasoning (the use of rules to reach approximate or definite conclusions), and self-correction. Machine learning, natural language processing, robotics, and expert systems are all subfields of AI.

Machine Learning: One of the most popular classes of AI, these are algorithms that allow computers to learn based on data instead of being explicitly programmed (Lee & Chen, 2023). Because they have the power to find patterns in large data sets, machine learning models can come in handy when it comes to predictive analytics in legal cases, for example.
Natural Language Processing (NLP): The technology that enables computers to read, understand, and derive meaning from the human languages. NLP has many applications in the legal sector, including analysing legal texts, extracting relevant information, and even writing legal documents.
Expert Systems: AI programs that mimic the decision-making ability of a human expert In the legal field, expert systems were used to deliver legal advice grounded in established guidelines and knowledge bases, helping practitioners to navigate through intricate legal situations.

Additionally, this use of these AI technologies in the legal space has the ability to increase efficiencies, improve decision-making capabilities, as well as provide better access to justice by making information more accessible to non-experts.

3.2 Historical Context and Evolution of AI in Legal Systems

The evolution of artificial intelligence in law has been the journey of the field over several decades, changing in form with each technology evolution. This historical context is important not only to understand the current landscape of AI in judicial systems, but also their future potential.

Early Development(1950s-1970s): The idea of AI originated in the mid-20th century when the basic principles for machine intelligence were established by pioneers like Alan Turing. During the 1950s and 1960s, scientists began to investigate whether computers could do tasks that were normally done by humans. Early AI programs in law were narrow in scope, mostly involving rudimentary rule-based systems built to aid legal research.

The Expert Systems Era (1980s): The 1980s were a pivotal point in AI in law, with the advent of the expert systems. Those programs were created to emulate human expertise in specialized fields, including the law. One of the most famous was MYCIN, an expert system for medical diagnosis that although not legal had analogues in law. In this interim period, early legal research tools, including DIALOG and LexisNexis, arose, which leveraged databases that offered access to case law and statutes (Roberts & Green, 2022).

Integration with Legal Research (1990s): As the 1990s progressed, further innovations in AI technologies were coupled with expanding digital databases. Online business practices increased legal research efficiency24, as practitioners were able to search a nearly infinite amount of information in an instant. Westlaw and similar tools started embedding artificial intelligence in their search algorithms to match user queries with results.

Natural Language Processing Advances (2000s): The early 2000s saw a significant leap forward as natural language processing improved. NLP methods were used by legal technology firms to build tools which could analyse contracts and other documents. This was the time that also saw the introduction of predictive coding a technology that allows legal professionals to apply machine learning algorithms to e-discovery procedures to piece together relevant documents.

Modern Applications (2010s-Present): The past decade has registered an explosion in AI applications in the several aspects of law. Modern AI tools can analyse contracts, predict case outcomes, and even help judges identify the correct way to reach a decision. Companies such as ROSS Intelligence have created AI-driven legal research assistants that answer questions in natural language, fundamentally changing the way lawyers perform research.

Additionally, by examining historical case outcomes, machine learning algorithms are also used for predictive analytics in litigation strategies to predict outcomes based on such factors. This ability to leverage data helps lawyers make decisions that can help their clients succeed. AI technology is already being used in the evolution of judicial itself as well to complement traditional practices within the law firm (Taylor & Williams, 2023). The courts are also considering how AI can assist with case management for example, predicting the length of a case or identifying patterns in sentencing decisions to increase efficiency, and yet ensure fairness.

3.3 Implications for Judicial Systems

Artificial intelligence cadre in the world of law of great importance has inherent in judicial systems around the world. As these technologies further develop and gain traction within legal practice, there are several key takeaways to consider:

Efficiency Gains: AI can help lawyers and judges save time on the routine work of reviewing documents or performing legal research by automating tasks that do not require human judgment, enabling them to concentrate on the parts of the case that do.

Access to Justice: AI tools can democratize access to information and resources that help individuals deal with their legal issues, without the need for expert knowledge or financial resources for traditional law services.

Ethics: Although AI provides a wide array of opportunities to improve judicial processes, it also poses ethical issues, including the potential for algorithmic bias, accountability for decisions made by automated systems and the need for transparency throughout these processes.

Training Needs: There would be a need for lawyers to understand the capabilities and limitations of AI tools, while in the long term, there would be need for training programs that equip legal professionals to best take advantage of these technologies.

Ultimately, the rise of machines such as AI in the field of law signifies a paradigm shift, which has gradually developed over decades from primitive rule-based solutions to more advanced machine learning systems that can execute a range of complex tasks. Grasping this historical context is crucial for appreciating the opportunities and challenges that AI technologies represent for litigating what happens in an increasingly digital world and how it relates to traditional judicial processes (Zhao & Patel, 2024). We are continuing the journey of exploring how these innovations can modernize judicial systems globally including institutions like the International Court of Justice.

4. APPLICATIONS OF AI IN JUDICIAL SYSTEMS

Artificial intelligence (AI) in the judicial system is a game-changer in the way we perform legal processes. The role of AI is to increase efficiency, improve access to justice, and help lawyers in making their decisions (Miller & Thompson, 2021). This section will detail the different types of uses of AI within judicial systems across three key areas, including case management and predictive analytics, legal research and document review, sentencing and risk assessment tools.

4.1 Case Management and Predictive Analytics

Case management and predictive analytics is one of the most important applications of AI in judicial systems. With the rise in caseloads and a demand for efficiency, AI technologies offer streamlined solutions to help automate operations and improve the handling of cases, but AI applications in the courtroom require careful consideration and regulation to ensure just outcomes.

Case Management: AI systems are tailor-made to help judges and court administrators manage cases more effectively. For example, it can automate routine administrative tasks such as scheduling hearings, tracking the progress of cases and managing court calendars. These systems minimize the administrative burden of court personnel, enabling judges to concentrate on substantive issues rather than procedural questions. In addition, AI is also capable of analysing past cases and revealing trends in historical data that help inform how cases are managed (Adams & Brown, 2022). For instance, AI tools can forecast the time a case will take based on its characteristics, allowing courts to more efficiently deploy resources. This predictive capability allows judicial systems to foresee bottlenecks and optimize workflows, resulting in speedier resolutions for litigants.

Predictive Analytics: Another strong application of AI in judicial settings. Using AI algorithms to analyse large datasets that include historical case outcomes, demographic information, and legal precedents, these systems can provide insights into potential outcomes of cases (Garcia & Kim, 2023). This feature enables lawyers to evaluate their cases with far greater clarity regarding strengths and weaknesses. For example, predictive analytics can assist lawyers with predicting the potential success and/or failure of delineated legal arguments through comparative data for previously adjudicated cases. Using information like the court, the parties, and the relevant laws, AI models can deliver predictions that help lawyers create winning legal strategies. Moreover, predictive analytics can further help judges in parts of the trial process as well. This allows judges to apply the same logic in their rulings while also favouring fairness within the judicial process.

4.2 Legal Research and Document Review

Legal research is a necessary but time-consuming part of the legal profession. With the arrival of AI, this process has transformed as legal professionals have been able to extract relevant information more efficiently and accurately.

Legal Research: Traditional legal research typically requires sifting through large databases of case law, statutory and regulatory, and secondary sources manually. Such a method is time-consuming and liable to human-error. But AI-based legal PGs greatly simplify it, use natural language processing (NLP) algorithms to process the queries given by the users (O'Connor & Lee, 2024). These applications can sweep through massive legal archives to find relevant cases, statutes, and precedents that relate to a particular query. For the most part, AI technologies are used to offer users search results that not only match the specific keywords but also include cases that are related to what the user is looking for, even if it wasn't exactly what they had initially in mind (like how Westlaw and Lexis). AI-powered legal research only tools can provide summary of complex documents or highlight key points, facilitating quick access to time critical information for lawyers. This increased efficiency frees up time for solicitors to focus on formulating arguments and strategies instead of spending hours looking up information (White & Black, 2021).

Document Review: AI also plays an important role in document review. During litigation, attorneys must comb through thousands of documents for those relevant to a given case during discovery. This process can result in huge efforts and expenses; however, AI technologies have recently made a great team-mate in document review. Machine learning algorithms are something that are used by AI systems to automatically sort documents by relevance or privacy levels. These systems are trained on existing datasets with labelled documents (for example, relevant vs. irrelevant), enabling AI to identify the patterns that may indicate relevance in future reviews. For example, consider e-discovery, where significant amounts of electronic documents need to be analysed for litigation, in which case AI tools can accelerate the review process by identifying relevant documents for lawyers while filtering out irrelevant material. Not only does this significantly save time, but helps lower costs involved in manual document review as well.

4.3 Sentencing and Risk Assessment Tools

AI has an expanding role in sentencing and risk assessment in the criminal justice systems. They design these applications to improve equity in sentencing decisions while also responding to the public safety concerns.

Sentencing tools: Sentencing decisions have typically been up to the discretion of judges, who follow prescribed guidelines; but, just as with all humans, biases both implicit and explicit can affect their decisions. To reduce these biases, some jurisdictions have started deploying AI-powered sentencing tools that are intended to give statistically derived recommendations for the right sentence based on past data. These tools examine the offense itself, criminal history, demographic information, and contextual elements of the committed crime. This data-driven approach allows judges to access frameworks of insight which inform them of how they might come to similar decisions across similar cases. But it is also important to be aware of possible dangers arising from dependence on algorithms for sentencing decisions. Transparency is also a source of concern where algorithms act as "black boxes," and it is difficult for judges or defendants to know how certain recommendations were produced. Thus, human oversight is still a mandate to make sure that the inferences on the sentencing outcome benefit from both empirical information as well as judicial discretion.

Risk Assessment Tools: Moreover, AI technologies are used to assess their quality regarding the probability of defendants re-offending or posing a risk to public safety if released, thus informing sentencing. These use machine learning algorithms based on historical data on recidivism rates for different profiles of offenders. The mechanism works by evaluating variables; such as previous convictions, age at first offense, work history, issues with substance abuse, and social networks. Risk assessment algorithms produce scores which indicate the probability of an individual engaging in criminal activity in the future. Although these tools have had some success helping inform parole boards or pretrial release decisions where objective assessment should trump subjective judgment at least to a degree critics point to possible bias in the training datasets used to train the algorithms (Hall & Wright, 2022).

Artificial Intelligence Applications in Judicial Because of how AI plays roles in these systems, the appearance of AI in judicial systems is evolutionarily significant for the way legal systems will be controlled and operated. AI technologies like predictive analytics can enhance case management; risk assessment tools can revolutionize legal research practices and even provide insights for determining appropriate sentencing decisions, among others benefitting overall access to justice in delivering fair outcomes. But like all technologies that promise improvement, there are important ethical issues related to bias, transparency and accountability that need to be taken into consideration before we deploy such innovations on an enormous scale alongside existing judicial systems, moving towards a more complex future where access to equitable resolution for all individuals is critical regardless of background or circumstance. With each step forward in understanding these extra dimensions of this transformative landscape, it becomes more apparent how crucial embracing technological advances will prove to be towards ensuring equitable access to justice whilst also safeguarding integrity within the legal systems across the globe.

5. ENHANCING THE INTERNATIONAL COURT OF JUSTICE WITH AI

The ICJ is the principal judicial organ of the United Nations and is responsible for settling legal disputes between states and giving advisory opinions on legal questions referred to it by authorized UN organs and agencies. With global challenges gaining ever greater complexity, the effective and efficient functioning of the judicial process business process is of paramount importance. AI can complement and optimize tasks and procedures of the appeal judge, including marking files, researching case laws, helping with decision-making, and granting access to justice. Here we overview best current practice within the ICJ, provocative notions of how AI may fit within international law and the use of relevant case studies with the application of AI (Carter & Lewis, 2023).

5.1 Current Practices at the International Court of Justice

Because the ICJ has both contentious and advisory procedures, it operates in a certain hybrid capacity. It settles legal disputes submitted to it by states and gives advisory opinions on legal questions referred to it by authorized UN organs and specialized agencies. Its 15 judges are elected for nine-year terms, and the court applies international law as defined in Article 38 of its statute.

Procedural Framework: The ICJ has a procedural element that involves submitting written memorials, holding public hearings, and delivering judgments. Having a case is submitted, the supplicant presents a written memorial generating its claims and jurisdictional basis. The respondent can then submit its own memorial on the merits of the case. The court holds public hearings for both sides before making a ruling (Singh & Kumar, 2024).

Decision-Making: The decisions of the ICJ are guided by international conventions, customary international law, and general principles recognized by civilized nations. As binding decisions only for the parties to a case, the court does not operate under a strict doctrine of stare decisis and is free to disregard its prior holdings and to reach new conclusions in subsequent cases. Such discretion enables judges to read international law with changing times.
Challenges: While the ICJ plays a pivotal function in the world of international law, it is not without its challenges in making tangible impacts in global legal matters. These include long proceedings that arise out of complex legal issues; budgetary restrictions to deal with high caseloads; and challenges related to compliance with the court's judgments. As disputes grow more complex and frequently encompass multiple parties or intersecting legal regimes, an increasing demand for creative solutions emerges.

5.2 Potential AI Applications in International Law

The introduction of AI in the operations of the ICJ has tremendous potential and will greatly improve the efficacy and efficiency of the ICJ. Some key applications include:

Case Management: AI can simplify case management processes by automating administrative tasks like scheduling hearings, tracking case progress, and managing documentation. AI systems can help reduce the administrative burden placed on court personnel, ensuring that judges are focused more on substantive legal issues rather than procedural logistics.
Predictive Analytics: Judges can very well use predictive analytics tools, which are existing algorithms that base their predictions of outcome on historical data from previous cases (Thomas & Davis, 2021). AI algorithms can analyse patterns in past rulings and outcomes, helping judges evaluate the merits of cases more effectively by providing them with insight into the likelihood of success in arbitrating a particular case.
Legal Research: AI Legal research tools can increase the efficiency of legal research done by judges and their clerks. Using NLP techniques, these systems can efficiently traverse a sea of statutes, treaties, and case law, enabling judges to retrieve relevant information promptly.
AI-Powered Classification and Review: For litigation with large amounts of documents, artificial intelligence can expedite document review processes by enabling automated classification of documents according to relevance or privilege levels. This ability helps judges get on to the important stuff while speeding up case prep.

AI Tools for Advisory Opinions: In the case of advisory opinions to be sought by UN organs or specialized agencies, AI can assist in producing timely analyses of legal questions that draw on existing international law to provide relevant precedents and interpretations.

5.3 Case Studies of AI Implementation

There are indeed several jurisdictions that have begun using AI technologies in their judicial systems with positive results that might be relevant for the potential adoption of such applications at the ICJ:

I. **Netherland Judiciary Tool for Predicting Case Outcome:** In 2019 Dutch judiciary introduced a predictive tool called the Legal Intelligence based on AI that is primarily to be used by judges in civil cases to forecast their likely outcomes based on relevant similar past case data Based on the type of case, the background of the judge and similar previous cases and rulings, this tool can help in predicting outcomes but does not dictate how a judge ruled. This initiative is yielding positive outcomes in terms of streamlining processes and shortening waiting times in Dutch courts and provides judges with the tools to make more informed decisions based on data analysis rather than intuition or precedent alone.

II. **Predictive Policing in Chicago:** Although this is not directly relevant at the level of judicial proceedings at the ICJ, predictive policing initiatives employed by law enforcement agencies show how predictive analytics can shape decision-making processes within criminal justice systems. For instance, in Chicago, police departments have used predictive algorithms that analyse historical data and identify areas with higher crime probability enabling them to allocate resources more efficiently while proactively tackling public safety issues. Despite some ethical challenges associated with predictive policing such as possible bias in such constructs these use-cases highlight the ways which data-driven methods can help in improving decision making processes among diverse areas of justice delivery.

III. **Innovations in Legal Research in U.S. Courts:** Several native U.S. legal tech companies have developed advanced AI technologies for legal research, including tools like ROSS Intelligence and Case-text's Co-Counsel tool. These platforms use NLP algorithms to quickly analyse user queries and retrieve relevant case law. These tools greatly improve time management by streaming legal research processes and allowing attorneys immediate access to critical information they need within litigation proceedings instead of searching endlessly through massive databases.

There is a great deal of potential for AI to improve the International Court of Justice in numerous ways. Case studies of current work at the ICJ reveal both its important function serving international law and the difficulties it is facing with efficient handling of complex disputes (Nguyen & Patel, 2022). Since AI will enhance the ICJ's case management, predictive analytics, legal research, document review and even communication, integrating this technology into its operations will make the commission more effective while allowing all parties to receive access to justice. In addition, analysing case studies of successful implementation of similar practices in other jurisdictions can offer perspective on how AI implementation can be beneficial in the context of the judicial system. Ongoing global challenges are constantly reshaping the landscape and calling for innovative solutions and in response to such demands the adoption of AI technologies at the ICJ signifies a pivotal moment in the modernization of international law practices without compromising equity and justice worldwide.

6. ETHICAL CONSIDERATIONS AND CHALLENGES

However, the growing introduction of artificial intelligence (AI) in judiciaries poses serious ethical questions that cannot and must not remain unaddressed if we want to maintain the integrity of judicial processes. The integration of AI into the judicial system is raising crucial debates about algorithmic bias and justice, about transparency and accountability in AI, and about the role of human in the loop. In this section, we explore these essential ethical dimensions and the impact they have on the administration of justice.

6.1 Bias and Fairness in AI Algorithms

One of the most urgent ethical issues related to AI in judicial systems is the risk of bias in algorithms. As AI systems learn from data, biases present in the data sourced are reflected by the algorithms, explicit as well as implicit in the datasets; this can result in the output propagating or even amplifying the original biases (Baker & Moore, 2023). It can result in discriminatory practices against certain groups such as based on caste, gender, income, or any other attribute.

Sources of Bias: Bias in AI can be introduced from multiple sources. Data used to train models stems from the past and may reflect systemic societal imbalances and inequities, resulting in biased output when such models are applied to new, current cases. For example, if an algorithm learns based on historical sentencing data that was biased against certain demographic populations, it will recommend harsher sentences for people from those groups in the future. It creates a two-tiered system of justice that not only undermines the principle of equality before the law but also erodes confidence in the judiciary on the part of the public.

Implications for Fairness: The consequences of biased algorithms in AI can be serious. In the area of administration of justice, biased tool use can result in decisions that royally mess with people's lives. For example, risk assessment tools that are used to determine whether to release a defendant pretrial or how long their sentence should be take into consideration if individuals will reoffend using data that may have been flawed and are likely to mislabel people, thus keeping them in pretrial detention longer or recommending longer sentences (Robinson & Clark, 2024). Such outcomes risk reinforcing cycles of disadvantage and discrimination in the justice system.

AI algorithm testing and validation are crucial to help circumvent bias. This may involve auditing datasets to check for fair representation, utilizing relatively much more diverse datasets to train the model and monitoring the performance of the algorithms continuously to detect and correct biases whenever necessary. Another method of achieving diverse understanding is through engaging stakeholders with different backgrounds in both the development and evaluation processes for AI tools.

6.2 Transparency and Accountability in AI Systems

Initial conversations on judicial systems and AI have emphasized the importance of transparency and accountability. Because AI decision-making is being used more frequently by judges, being familiar with how these systems function is important to preserve public faith in them and their accountability.

Transparency Requirements: Transparency is the degree to which it can be explained how an AI system works, including the steps of the decision-making process and the data on which it is based. In the context of the judiciary, this means that judges should have a way of describing how any AI tool reached recommendations, or conclusions about a given case (Martinez & Torres, 2021). However, many AI systems function as "black boxes," obscuring how inputs become outputs. For this challenge, designers of AI systems must understand the concept of explainability and be deliberate in creating algorithms that can explain their reasoning process to a layperson. This might include providing user-friendly interfaces that would enable judges to review the factors that influenced an algorithm's output or producing detailed documentation explaining how the system was trained and validated.

Accountability Mechanisms: Accountability ensures that persons utilizing AI tools are responsible for their decisions, even when aided by expertise. They must be alert and conscious in reviewing AI output to comply with legal and constructive ethical doctrines. Judges must continue to exercise independent judgment, and if done properly, the integration of AI will enable judges to make better informed decisions, not eliminate that independent judgment. According to Soto, establishing accountability mechanisms will also help address what happens when AI systems fail or produce biased results. This could include establishing oversight mechanisms that regularly audit algorithmic performance or requiring protocols for reporting discrepancies between AI and judicial outcomes. Moreover, training programs should impart the knowledge judges need to be able to critically evaluate the outputs of AI tools while still holding to their ethical obligations.

6.3 The Role of Human Oversight

While the advancements presented by AI technologies are remarkable, human supervision is vital in maintaining ethical decision-making within judicial systems. Although AI is a very beneficial tool to increase time and energy of judicial authorities, it will never replace the comprehensive comprehension and ethical judgment of human judges.

Human Judgment as a Safeguard: Legal questions are not always black and white, they often involve searching new paths and context that AI might not comprehend. These rusty iron shoulders bear the weight of social implications, individual circumstances, and evolving legal doctrines that judges must weigh when making decisions. It can lead to reductivism at the level of facts and a deviation from the ideals of justice when we just listen to AI (Evans & Lee, 2022).

To address this once and for all, we must adopt a human-in-the-loop approach to judicial integration. This framework entailed joint human-AI adjudication, whereby judges could avail themselves of the features of technological solutions, without ceding their lead in making judgments. When using predictive analytics for case management or sentencing recommendations, for example, judges should critically review outputs from algorithms before making final decisions.

Training and Competence: These entities need to have adequate oversight, and ensuring judges have the capacity to understand AI technologies is crucial to that. Education on the capabilities and limitations of AI tools should be part of judicial training programs — ensuring that judges can understand how these technologies work, while allowing them to think critically about their use.

In addition, ongoing professional development opportunities should be offered so that judges remain informed about advancements in the capabilities of AI technologies, as well as developments in ethical standards for use in judicial settings. Within the judiciary, the promotion of continuous learning can facilitate effective engagement with the challenges of technological advancement while continuing to act in accordance with ethical standards.

7. CONCLUSION

The role of artificial intelligence (AI) is revolutionizing the foundations of justice and the courts, especially the International Court of Justice (ICJ) where it represents a phenomenal opportunity to make proceedings efficient, accessible, and equitable. As examined in this research paper, AI applications have a potential to validate and enhance judicial workings but they also prompt pressing ethical questions that need addressing. In this conclusion, we will further identify important recommendations for policy makers and practice to incorporate on the future of justice.

7.1 Recommendations for Policymakers and Legal Practitioners

To leverage the capabilities of AI in judicial systems effectively and minimize associated risks, it is essential to consider several recommendations:

Formulate Robust AI Policies: Policymakers must formulate clear guidelines and frameworks to regulate the use of AI in judicial processes. This can involve establishing parameters around the use cases for AI, embedding criteria around algorithmic transparency, and monitoring conformity with ethical principles. Policies dictating the access these entities have to the available information, or how they access it, should be formulated with consultation from legal experts, technologists, and stakeholders, working toward a balanced compromise solution which maintains justice and fairness as priorities.

Train and Educate: Providing AI technologies training in applied settings for judges, practitioners, and court personnel is imperative. Such programs would emphasise working out what AI tools can and cannot do, so that lawyers can critically analyse what is generated by AI applications while not compromising their duty to the profession. Legal practitioners must be motivated for continual professional development to stay aware of all advancements in AI technology.

Conduct Regular Audits and Assessments: To mitigate bias and fairness issues in AI algorithms, routine auditing of AI systems should be required. However, these audits should probe algorithmic performance; identify possible biases in training data; and assess the potential impact of AI applications on judicial outcomes. It will increase public confidence in the integrity of AI-assisted decision-making through an open audit process.

Encourage Collaboration Across Stakeholders: It is vital to collaborate with a myriad of stakeholders such as governments, legal professionals, technologists, and civil society organizations, to develop suitable AI solutions in judicial systems. Inter-department working groups can help in the sharing of knowledge and best practices regarding the responsible integration of AI technologies.

Data Human Control Is Crucial: AI may be able to speed things up in the legal process, but there must still be a human oversight to guarantee accountability and ethical choices. Judges would maintain final say over decisions informed by AI tools, so that they can use their own expertise and contextual awareness to settle complex legal questions. This "human-in-the-loop" approach can ensure that the potential of hybrid AIs is balanced with the element of human judgment.

7.2 Implications for the Future of Justice

Thoroughly embedding this AI into judicial systems has serious consequences. As we envision the future of justice, a few important factors arise:

1. **Enhanced Access to Justice**: One of the key benefits of AI integration is its ability to enhance access to justice. AI can also help to reduce the costs of legal services by delegating repetitive tasks, like legal research and documentation, to computers, allowing lawyers to focus on complex cases, making it easier for people who could not otherwise afford representation to access legal help. AI-powered chatbots can also offer the public with basic information regarding legal matters, thereby, further democratizing its access.
2. **Increased Efficiency in Judicial Processes**: However, AI technologies can improve efficiency by expediting certain processes within judicial systems, resulting in faster case outcome and less backlog. Judges can use predictive analytics to improve their management of case-loads by pinpointing trends and patterns that can help inform decisions around the allocation of resources. This

revisionism creates a double benefit more efficiency in these adjudications and more public confidence in our judicial institutions.

3. **Ethical Challenges Remain**: Although AI integration has its benefits. Therefore, preventive measures should be taken to avoid erosion of trust in judicial systems due to issues around algorithmic bias, transparency, accountability, and data privacy. Both policymakers and practitioners must be vigilant against the potential for discriminatory outcomes that biased algorithms can generate.
4. **Evolution of Legal Roles:** The adoption of AI will necessitate role changes within the legal profession. Lawyers will turn to more intricate components of legal work—like negotiation, advocacy, and other functions that demand thoughtful analysis—as routine jobs are automated over time. Such development may result in more specialized lawyers with skills appropriate to a more tech-driven environment.
5. **Global Standards of AI in Justice:** Given the inherent international scope of many legal matters, there is a cry for global standards on AI usage in judicial systems. Guidance on best practices for deploying this technology responsibly and in ways that address the cross-cutting challenges of data privacy and algorithmic accountability will require the concerted action of multiple nations.

To summarize, the potential impact of AI in the context of legal systems remains an attractive opportunity, as well as a challenge for today's society. When policymakers and legal practitioners work hand in hand to leverage the benefits of technological advancements within the context of constitutional ethics, a justice system that enables efficiency, accessibility, and fairness can be built. The recommendations above offer a pathway for ensuring that the integration of AI into judicial processes is done responsibly and that these technologies serve as tools for furthering justice, not eroding its foundational principles. In this new age of rapid technological advancement, we must continue to prioritize equity and accountability in this global justice framework. The future of justice, therefore, would eventually rely in large part on how well we manage these complexities, taking advantage, thoughtfully of the possible benefits of artificial intelligence, whilst protecting, at the same time, against its situated dangers, ensuring that justice is maintained as much as a fundamental human right, as also a reality for the whole human race.

REFERENCES

Adams, R., & Brown, C. (2022). Enhancing judicial efficiency with AI tools: A case study approach. *Judicial Review Quarterly*, 29(3), 150–172.

Baker, C., & Moore, A. (2023). Case management solutions through AI: Enhancing judicial productivity? *Judicial Management Review*, 14(1), 45–63.

Binns, R. (2021). The ethical implications of AI in judicial decision-making. *AI & Society*, 36(4), 1235–1245.

Carter, L., & Lewis, M. (2023). AI-driven legal analytics: Revolutionizing case outcomes? *The Journal of Legal Analysis*, 9(3), 77–94.

Evans, K., & Lee, J. (2022). The rise of algorithmic justice: Implications for human rights. *International Journal of Human Rights*, 26(5), 789–805.

Garcia, P., & Kim, S. (2023). Algorithmic bias in legal decision-making: Addressing the challenges of fairness. *AI Ethics Journal*, 5(1), 15–30.

Hall, J., & Wright, G. (2022). The future of justice: AI's role in transforming legal systems worldwide. *Global Journal of Comparative Law*, 11(2), 99–121.

Johnson, K., & Smith, L. (2022). Predictive analytics in the courtroom: A new era for justice? *The Journal of Law and Technology*, 15(2), 45–67.

Lee, M., & Chen, Y. (2023). AI and access to justice: Enhancing legal services through technology. *Harvard Law Review*, 136(3), 789–812.

Martinez, L., & Torres, F. (2021). Exploring the role of machine learning in judicial processes. *The Journal of Legal Studies*, 30(2), 150–175.

Miller, D., & Thompson, H. (2021). AI in the courtroom: The future of legal practice? *Legal Technology Journal*, 12(4), 67–89.

National Judicial Academy. (2021). *Introduction of artificial intelligence in the judicial system*. Retrieved from https://www.nja.gov.in/Concluded_Programmes/2021-22/P-1281_PPTs/2.Introduction%20of%20Artificial%20Intelligence%20in%20the%20Judicial%20System.pdf

Nguyen, T., & Patel, S. (2022). Data privacy concerns with AI applications in judicial settings: An analysis. *International Data Privacy Journal*, 12(4), 201–220.

O'Connor, J., & Lee, T. (2024). The impact of AI on human rights in judicial processes: A critical review. *Human Rights Law Review*, 24(2), 145–168.

PwC. (2021). *The new global imperative to modernise justice systems*. Retrieved from https://www.pwc.com/gx/en/industries/government-public-services/public-sector-research-centre/global-imperative-modernise-justice-systems.html

Roberts, T., & Green, J. (2022). The role of AI in international law: Challenges and opportunities. *International Journal of Law and Information Technology*, 30(1), 34–56.

Robinson, H., & Clark, D. (2024). AI's influence on sentencing decisions: An exploratory study. *Criminal Justice Ethics*, 43(2), 89–105.

Singh, B., & Kaunert, C. (2025). Intelligent Machine Learning Solutions for Cybersecurity: Legal and Ethical Considerations in a Global Context. In Thangam, D. (Ed.), *Advancements in Intelligent Process Automation* (pp. 359–386). IGI Global. DOI: 10.4018/979-8-3693-5380-6.ch014

Singh, B., & Kaunert, C. (2025). Exploring Effective Strategies for Combatting Cybercrime and Intersection of IoT, Deep Learning: Legal Standpoints on Progressive Data Analytics. In Kumar, R., Srivastava, S., & Elngar, A. (Eds.), *Human Impact on Security and Privacy: Network and Human Security, Social Media, and Devices* (pp. 141–172). IGI Global. https://doi.org/10.4

Singh, R., & Kumar, P. (2024). Navigating ethical dilemmas in AI-assisted judicial decision-making processes. *Ethics and Information Technology*, 26(1), 55–70.

Taylor, S., & Williams, A. (2023). Machine learning and legal outcomes: An empirical study. *Journal of Empirical Legal Studies*, 20(1), 98–115.

Thomas, J., & Davis, F. (2021). The intersection of technology and law: AI's transformative potential in courts. *Technology and Society Journal*, 15(2), 112–130.

UNESCO. (2024). *AI and the rule of law: Capacity building for judicial systems*. Retrieved from https://www.unesco.org/en/artificial-intelligence/rule-law/mooc-judges

White, E., & Black, N. (2021). Automation in legal research: Opportunities and risks for practitioners. *Legal Studies Review*, 30(4), 234–250.

Woxsen University. (2021). *Exploring the use of AI in legal decision making: Benefits and ethical implications*. Retrieved from https://woxsen.edu.in/research/white-papers/exploring-the-use-of-ai-in-legal-decision-making-benefits-and-ethical-implications/

Zhao, X., & Patel, R. (2024). Ethical frameworks for AI in the judiciary: A comparative analysis. *Law and Ethics of Human Rights*, 18(2), 200–225.

Chapter 12
Role of Digital Marketing Tactics in Enhancing Financial Performance in E-Commerce Enterprises

Lakshmi S. R.
https://orcid.org/0009-0007-9193-9564
Christ University, India

N. Manasa
Christ University, India

ABSTRACT

In recent years, the exponential growth of e-commerce has revolutionized how businesses operate and interact with consumers. This surge in online shopping has been accompanied by a parallel rise in digital marketing strategies employed by e-commerce companies to attract, engage, and retain customers. Digital marketing encompasses various techniques, including search engine optimization (SEO), social media marketing, content marketing, email marketing, and pay-per-click advertising. The effectiveness of these strategies in enhancing a company's financial performance has become a subject of significant interest and scrutiny. Companies can boost their bottom line and achieve greater profitability by reducing customer acquisition costs, increasing customer lifetime value, and improving overall marketing efficiency. E-commerce businesses could better reach their target audience on these channels by increasing their brand visibility and reach and driving traffic to their websites.

DOI: 10.4018/979-8-3693-9395-6.ch012

1. INTRODUCTION

Digital marketing uses promotional tactics to drive more traffic to your online store. This includes using social media, digital content, search engines, and email campaigns to attract visitors. Digital marketing for e-commerce helps generate more revenue as it helps retain more customers and increases brand value. As customers are easily distracted, it has become essential to catch their attention. Digital marketing for e-commerce helps enterprises overcome such problems. To make things easier, digital marketing for e-commerce focuses on using the proper marketing channels (Ma & Gu, 2024). Digital marketing also helps improve customer engagement and build relationships with the target audience. Digital marketing strategies primarily affect financial performance by driving revenue growth. Effective digital marketing campaigns can increase the visibility of products or services, attract more website traffic, and ultimately lead to higher sales conversions. By targeting specific audience segments with tailored messaging and offers, companies can optimize their sales funnel and maximize revenue generation through digital channels. Moreover, digital marketing strategies can also enhance profitability by improving cost efficiency and resource allocation. As compared to traditional marketing approaches, digital marketing usually provides a better return on investment because of the specificity in targeting audiences, real-time performance metric tracking as well as data-driven optimization of campaigns (Rose et al., 2024).

This find that brand equity and consumer loyalty are directly affected by digital marketing, which, in turn, will reflect on the long-term financial performance of a company. Using top-notch content, personalized interactions and seamless brand messaging through multiple touch points, organizations can establish deep associations with customers and create advocates that are likely to repeat-purchase, or suggest the organization to others. The increase in brand loyalty can improve customer lifetime value and decrease churn rates, translating into great financial stability and resilience. Digital marketing strategies have an enormous impact on economic outcomes. Channeling digital fortification to drive revenue, enhance margins, and build brand equity thrusts companies towards ascension in the e-commerce landscape elevating growth trajectories and success in the digital era. E-commerce companies seeking to survive in the ever-increasing competitive environment need to understand how various digital marketing strategies are related to their financial performance. Although, a lot of studies have tempted to investigate the effect of digital marketing over different aspects of business such as brand awareness, customer interactions and market share (Semenda et al., 2024), still research mainly focuses on financial measures such as revenue, profit and return on investment through digital marketing which is lacking.

Digital Marketing Strategies: The methods and tactics used to market a business' products or services through the internet. These tactics are crucial to reaching and engaging target audiences online. Some of the most popularly used strategies in digital marketing are as follows:

Search Engine Optimization (SEO): SEO involves optimizing a website to rank higher in search engine results pages (SERPs) for relevant keywords and phrases. This strategy focuses on increasing organic (non-paid) traffic to the website.

Pay-Per-Click Advertising (PPC): PPC advertising allows businesses to bid for ad placement in search engines or on other platforms. Advertisers pay a fee each time their ad is clicked. Common PPC platforms include Google Ads and social media advertising.

- **Content Marketing**: Content marketing involves creating and distributing valuable, relevant, consistent content to attract and retain a clearly defined audience. Content can include blog posts, articles, videos, infographics, eBooks, and more.
- **Social Media Marketing**: Social media marketing utilizes social media platforms (such as Facebook, Instagram, Twitter, LinkedIn, etc.) to connect with the audience, build brand awareness, drive website traffic, and generate leads or sales (Sugiharto, 2024).
- **Email Marketing**: Email marketing involves sending personalized messages and promotional content via email to nurture leads and engage with customers. It can include newsletters, product updates, special offers, and more.
- **Influencer Marketing**: Influencer marketing involves partnering with influencers (individuals with a large and engaged following on social media) to promote products or services. It leverages the influencer's credibility and reach to increase brand awareness and drive sales.
- **Affiliate Marketing:** Affiliate marketing is a performance-based strategy in which businesses reward affiliates (publishers or influencers) for driving traffic or sales to their website through their affiliates' marketing efforts.
- **Mobile Marketing:** Mobile marketing focuses on reaching audiences on their mobile devices through SMS marketing, mobile apps, responsive websites, and location-based marketing strategies.
- **Marketing Automation**: A software platform that automates repetitive tasks like email campaigns, social media scheduling, lead nurturing and customer segmentation. Consolidating marketing processes will support you further in improving efficiency.

• These digital marketing channels areAlign in an organized manner based on the type of business operation to serve as a cohesive digital marketing plan, response to different marketing objectives like: target audience, budget etc. These strategies can be successfully implemented by tracking, analyzing performance metrics and adapting to changing market trends and consumer behaviors.

Therefore, it is critical to comprehend how differently these strategies affect e-commerce businesses to maximise marketing efficiency and fulfil business objectives in:

- **Greater Online Visibility:** E-commerce businesses can gain more online visibility through integrated digital marketing activities like SEO and paid advertisements. Through the appropriate contents on websites utilizing relevant keywords or target advertising campaigns, firms can obtain a greater level of qualified traffic to their online shops and improve conversions and sales (Sharabati et al., 2024).
- **Improved Customer Targeting**: Digital marketing enables e-commerce companies to precisely target their ideal customer segments based on demographics, interests, and online behaviors. Through tools like social media ads and email segmentation, businesses can tailor their marketing messages to resonate with specific audience groups, resulting in higher engagement and conversion rates.
- **Better Customer Engagement:** Digital marketing allows the businesses to have a better interaction with their customers from all angles and stages of should you buy or not, etc. E-commerce brands have the opportunity to strengthen customer relations, incentivize repeat purchases and drive brand loyalty through creation of quality content, social media community building and personalized email marketing campaigns.
- This approach collective business and individual analyses aspects of an organization allowing businesses to developments in costumer behavior, love interests or purchasing traits. Through studying negotiated customer metrics like website visits, conversion rates, and commentary feedback businesses gain informed decisions those related to product offerings, pricing strategy or initiatives with marketing thereby driving growth and profitability (Gau & Saleh 2024).

    Reaching the world and expanding: The e-commerce industry through digital marketing channels can reach a worldwide audience and provide more expand their market outside geographical boundaries. Local marketing campaigns and multi-language websites enable global customers to be targeted through a proven mechanism that unleashes markets beyond local borders taking advantage of the opportunities for growth and expansion

Cost-Effectiveness and ROI: Digital marketing is usually more cost-effective and delivers a higher return on investment (ROI) than traditional marketing methods. Real-time tracking and measurement of campaign performance enables e-commerce companies to assess their marketing spend and optimize the allocation of resources towards basking in better results while spending less.

Bringing in New Customers and Making them Purchase: E-commerce businesses rely on digital marketing channels such as search engine optimization (SEO), pay-per-click (PPC) advertising, social media marketing, and email marketing to draw new clients in. These strategies generate traffic and focus on converting that traffic into paying customers with some form of high-ticket sales copy.

Competitive Benefit: Organizations that successfully utilize digital marketing tactics can set themselves apart from the pack in a competitive e-commerce environment. Being nimble and sensitive to market direction enables them to quickly pivot their strategy and take advantage of new opportunities.

Growth Potential: Digital marketing has the power to grow e-commerce by enabling geographic expansion and market penetration. International campaigns or localized marketing efforts enable companies to target new audiences, and spur growth into markets that were otherwise untapped. It provides the customer with ample safeguards against untrustworthy brands. Digital venues pave way for seamless interaction in between both, allowing e-commerce firms o solicit inputs from their customers as use and address each one if an issue arises so that online reputation is not affected. Long-term financial success lies in positive reviews and customers (Wu et al, 2024).

Digital marketing adds to revenue generation by increasing sales and conversions. By means of targeted ads, SEO and content marketing, companies can bring in more qualified leads that can be converted into customers thus increasing overall sales figures.

Brand Recognition and Trust: A well-executed digital marketing campaign can create brand awareness and build a reputation. Through the development of engaging content, interaction with consumers on social media and online reviews and assessment management, a business can create a powerful brand presence which attracts more customers while providing appropriate levels of trust and credibility.

Thus, giving the opportunities for a company to allocate higher resources toward strategic and revenue-generating initiatives that can help in boosting financials (Sulistyaningsih et al., 2024). Target in Digital Marketing Strategy Pursuit: A Limited Number of Weaknesses

Technical Complexity:Digital marketing is a complicated field that necessitates effective implementation of various needed disciplines in the delivery of technical effectiveness. This complexity can leave some companies particularly those that are smaller or otherwise have limited resources struggling to effectively navigate it.

Technology Dependency: The effectiveness of digital marketing lessons depends on technology and internet infrastructure. Disruptions to Marketing: Events like algorithm changes (search engine algorithm, etc.), technical issues or platform outages can all disrupt marketing efforts which affects their performance.

Intense Competition: Digital marketing's accessibility means businesses face intense online competition. Standing out amidst competitors requires innovative strategies, compelling content, and consistent engagement, which can increase marketing costs and effort.

Potential for Misalignment: Digital marketing strategies must align closely with business goals and objectives. Misalignment or lack of integration with other business functions (e.g., sales, customer service) can lead to disjointed customer experiences and suboptimal financial outcomes (Wang, 2024).

Data Privacy Concerns: Collecting and using customer data for targeting and personalization must comply with data privacy regulations (e.g., GDPR, CCPA). Data mishandling or privacy breaches can damage brand reputation and result in legal repercussions, impacting financial stability.

Measurement Challenges: While digital marketing offers robust analytics, accurately attributing conversions and ROI across multiple touchpoints can be challenging. Inaccurate measurement or attribution models may lead to misinformed decisions and ineffective resource allocation.

Digital marketing strategies play a pivotal role in driving the success of e-commerce companies by increasing online visibility, improving customer targeting and engagement, facilitating data-driven decision-making, enabling global reach, and enhancing cost-effectiveness and ROI. By leveraging these strategies effectively, e-commerce businesses can gain a competitive edge, maximize their market potential, and achieve sustained growth in the dynamic digital landscape. While digital marketing strategies offer numerous benefits for enhancing financial performance through increased reach, targeted engagement, cost-efficiency, and data-driven insights, businesses must also navigate potential challenges such as technical complexity, competition, and data privacy concerns to maximize their effectiveness.

Strategic planning, continuous optimization, and a holistic approach to integration are essential for leveraging digital marketing's potential while mitigating its drawbacks (Wang et al., 2024).

2. IMPACT OF DIGITAL COMMERCE COMPANIES

Digital commerce companies encompass a broad spectrum of businesses that conduct transactions and facilitate commerce through digital platforms. Also, "e-commerce" refers explicitly to commercial transactions conducted electronically over the Internet (Almestarihi et al., 2024). Both digital commerce and e-commerce have a profound impact on businesses, consumers, and the economy:

Facilitation of Transactions: Digital commerce companies enable transactions to occur seamlessly online, offering convenience and accessibility to consumers. These companies provide platforms, payment gateways, and digital tools that facilitate buying and selling goods and services.
Broader Market Access: Businesses can access global consumer markets via digital commerce systems without boundaries of geography. This enables companies to grow their UK business by reaching new customers in different markets.
Small-business empowerment: Digital commerce arms small businesses and entrepreneurs to compete with global markets on a more balanced fore. Digital tools that were once only available to large enterprises are now affordable for small businesses. Such democratization drives innovation, competition, and economic growth.
Improved Customer Experience: Digital commerce companies focus on user experience with easy-to-use interfaces, personalized suggestions, and hassle-free payments. Buyer experience and buyer loyalty enhance, leading to better retention charges and lifetime worth.
Data-Driven Insights: The data generated by providers through digital commerce platforms is dynamic and insightful consumer behavior-centric. Data analytics gives companies the power to make informed decision, shape marketing strategies, and improve operational efficiency.
Income Generation and Economic Footprint: The rise of digital commerce creates jobs for individuals in technology, logistics, marketing, customer service, etc. Such companies create jobs and help other sectors of the economy grow.

Impact of E-Commerce: E-Commerce Transformation in Retail

E-commerce has transformed the retail industry as it changed consumer shopping habits from physical stores to online shopping. This means that there is no limitation in terms of time or countries because businesses operate 24/7 Consumers are always on the go and e-businesses provide comfort and flexibility.

Disruption in the Existing Business Models: The e-commerce is disrupting the existing business models, and reducing physical storefronts and the role of any middlemen. Direct-to-consumer (DTC) methods allow brands to bypass traditional channels of distribution and get directly to customers (Wijayanto et al., 2024).

International market access: It also allows businesses of any size to reach global markets and compete internationally. Cross-border e-commerce is an enabler of international trade that allows businesses to access international customers while not having a physical footprint within the market.

Putting Power in the Hands of the Consumer: E-commerce provides consumers with greater choice, price transparency and access to product information. Social-proof driven by customer reviews and ratings affect purchase decisions and help to create accountability for product quality and service among businesses.

Innovation in Logistics and Supply Chain: E-commerce provides a strong push for logistics and supply chain innovations by automating inventory management, order fulfillment, as well as last-mile delivery. But in the face of consumer demands for fast, reliable shipping, companies are sinking a lot of money into technology and partnerships.

3. CHALLENGES AND OPPORTUNITIES

Cybersecurity threats to e-commerce face compliance with regulations and legislative uncertainty now, however there is great potential for the future of logistics. This best way to innovation, adaptation and growth in this digital economy.

Digital Marketing Strategies And Its Effect On Economy

The Digital marketing strategy has a broad effect on the economy and its economy sector that plays it in many ways:

1) GDP and Economic Growth Contributions:

a) Business growth: Digital marketing gives the opportunity for businesses of all sizes to reach a global marketplace and compete. By boosting sales, jobs and investment in technology and infrastructure, this expansion invigorates economic activity (Laila et al., 2024).
b) Creation of Jobs: Increasing significance of digital marketing has resulted in emerging jobs from digital advertising, content writing, data analytics and software development. Positive employment growth fosters economic security, which in turn helps GDP grow.

2) Small and Medium-sized Enterprises (SMEs):
   1.) **Accessibility:** Digital marketing is an equal opportunity for small businesses and entrepreneurs because platforms to market your products and services are affordable and accessible. Such democratization encourages innovation, competition and economic diversity.
      b) Global Reach: Digital marketing strategies such as SEO, social media adverts and online marketplaces allow small firms to tap into global markets. This international footprint helps access additional revenue opportunity and lower dependency on local markets.

4. Consumers, Consumption and Spending

e) **Rise In Consumer Spending:** Digital marketing can affect consumer behavior in the way that it creates awareness, causes desire, and makes purchases easier to accomplish. By allowing advertisers to segment their markets, targeted advertising allows businesses to market more effectively at individual consumers driving up consumer spending which leads directly to economic growth.

E-commerce Growth: Digital marketing fuels the growth of e-commerce by promoting online shopping platforms and facilitating transactions. The convenience, accessibility, and variety e-commerce offers contribute to higher consumer spending and economic activity.

1) Innovation and Technological Advancements:

a) **Technological Innovation**: The evolution of digital marketing drives advancements in technology, analytics, and automation. Companies invest in AI, machine learning, and big data analytics to optimize marketing strategies and enhance customer experiences (Bennet, 2024).
b) **Digital Infrastructure**: Developing digital marketing infrastructure, including internet connectivity, mobile devices, and online payment systems, supports economic growth and digital transformation across industries.

2) Efficiency and Resource Optimization:

a) **Operational Efficiency**: Digital marketing enables businesses to optimize resources, reduce marketing costs, and improve ROI. Real-time analytics and performance tracking help businesses allocate budgets effectively and refine strategies for maximum efficiency.
b) **Supply Chain Optimization**: E-commerce driven by digital marketing strategies enhances supply chain efficiency, inventory management, and logistics. Faster order processing and delivery improve customer satisfaction and operational productivity.

3) Policy and Regulatory Considerations:

a) **Data Privacy and Security**: As digital marketing relies on consumer data, policies and regulations (e.g., GDPR, CCPA) ensure data privacy protection and ethical use of personal information. Compliance with these regulations fosters consumer trust and supports sustainable digital marketing practices.

4) Social and Cultural Impact:

a) **Community Engagement**: Digital marketing campaigns promote community engagement, social causes, and corporate social responsibility (CSR). Businesses align their brands with social values, contributing to positive societal impact and community development.

b) **Cultural Influence**: Digital marketing strategies adapt to cultural diversity and consumer preferences globally, fostering cultural exchange and understanding through targeted messaging and localized content.

Digital economy refers to the impact of digital technologies on economies, and how those economies exchange goods in a digitized manner, and digital marketing strategies are imperative for economic growth as well as innovation, consumer engagement etc. Through technology, data analytics and creativity, they are increasing their market share boosting consumer desire while fueling the economy. Nonetheless, the role of digital marketing practices and ethics in supporting sustainable growth that will impact profits and communities as well as other economic sectors cannot be ignored (Siahaan et al., 2024).

This chapter attempts to fill this gap by investigating the role of related digital marketing strategy attributes in e-commerce company performance. Drawing on a unique sample of e-commerce businesses across multiple industries and geographies, this research hopes to gain an understanding of the relative impact that different types of digital marketing strategies have on revenue growth, profitability, and ultimately shareholder value.

This chapter should give practical implications to e-commerce practitioners, marketers and business managers. Use SEO to maximize digital marketing budget Optimal resource allocation by identifying the most effective strategies and tactics in a narrower range of channels for effectively enhancing their financial performance, enabling companies to optimize marketing budgets and sustainably grow in digitally agile market environment. This study also adds to the extant academic literature by enhancing our understanding of the intricate relationship between digital marketing activities and financial performance in the context of e-commerce. This study attempts to offer a rich empirical exploration with strong econometric models, thus addressing an important research area (Mardiani et al., 2024)! By applying rigorous analytical approaches and thorough empirical investigation, uncovering insights that enhance understanding of the mechanisms through which digital marketing influences financial performance. Overall, this study reveals important quantitative foundations of the relationship between online marketing tactics and financial performance in the context of e-commerce. With a view to reveal the drivers of success in online marketing and help e-commerce firms thrive in the digital age, this study aims to provide practical implications for their profitability.

5. METHODS AND MATERIALS

The following methods are used to accomplish the project objectives:

E-commerce companies can vary widely based on their business models, target markets, and the types of products or services they offer. There are many variations to the types of e-commerce companies, such as Business-to-Consumer (B2C), Business-to-Business (B2B), Consumer-to-Consumer (C2C), Consumer-to-Business (C2B), and so on. The C2B business model is being researched for this project (Zang, 2024).

C2B models capture how consumer behavior shift s to become more influential and involved in the market. Direct and easy access to information such as consumer opinions, reviews, and comments regarding goods, services, and brands and the availability of information regarding customized services, goods, and offers that are based on the unique needs and preferences of each customer can help better understand how all of this affects client satisfaction and loyalty. Businesses and freelancers, independent contractors, and gig workers who provide specific skills and services are typically connected through C2B platforms. Investigating these platforms can also reveal trends in the gig economy, the makeup of the workforce, and the effects on labor markets (Verma et al., 2024).

Bangalore was chosen for this study since its ecosystem supports diverse C2B e-commerce programs spanning multiple sectors such as consumer products, technology, fashion and services. These businesses are not only strong online players, and also offer many digital marketing strategies like an influencer pen access, clip to advertises all teams, scene circumstances for targeting so that the customer can directly conduct their own personalized app. By focusing on C2B e-commerce companies located in Bangalore, this study seeks to better understand the reason why these digital marketing techniques are effective has some impact on financial performance as well. Bangalore has a dynamic economy that opens the opportunity to explore various facets such as technological advancements and shifts in consumer preferences due to digital marketing efforts in matured cities (Apriani et al., 2024).

Collection of data: Different approaches were utilized during the collection of data to ensure that a plethora of representative samples was incorporated. This included site visits, outbound calls and networking with various interest groups across industry verticals in Bangalore to spot a wide range of users and market representatives involved in C2B e-commerce. Response in reference to the aspects of c2b business relations was taken on the questionnaire prepared after referring to most highly indexed research papers from that area of research and selection of best indicators. This approach was instrumental in obtaining credibility, as well as, range of data across sectors/firm sizes and other demographics within Bangalore's dynamic e-commerce milieu. Cochran's formula was applied to calculate an optimal sample size on the assumption of attainable precision and the required confidence level, as the target population is plentiful, thereby obtaining sufficient responses from which results could be mined from the population at large. This supported the study comply with established standards within survey research, alongside transparency and credibility of method. In total, 391 responses were collected of which 370 what this has been checked for validity (Reddy & Nalla,2024).

The companies it focused on for this survey were Flipkart, Amazon, Paytm Mall, Zomato, Swiggy, and Big Basket.

Market Dominance: These businesses are well-known participants in their industries within Bangalore's e-commerce landscape.

Diversity of Business Models: The business selected represents diverse business models. Zomato and Swiggy offer insights into the food delivery industry, while Flipkart and Amazon provide more information on consumer electronics and other less perishables too.

Availability of Data: Due to their market size and presence, they were some of the better choices for the data collection as they were very well known among the population sample.

Digital Marketing Sophistication: Since these players have been in the e commerce space for a good period of time, their digital marketing methods have also had time to be tested and tweaked well thus proving to be good choices for research on the same.

Collected national-level data from sources like the National Stock Exchange, government reports, and industry-specific databases to capture the nuances of the Indian business landscape. This data will include financial indicators, digital marketing expenses, and localized customer engagement metrics.

6. STATISTICAL ANALYSIS

Created SEM Model and used for the analysis And SEM model is used to understand and identify the putative causal associations between the latent and observed variables. In this study the independent variable is Digital marketing strategies and the strategies used are Digital transformation, product promotion, Instructiveness, Improved purchasing and satisfaction. The mediating variables are Loyalty and social connection Revenue of the Companies are taken as the dependent variable. Age is considered as the Moderating variable.

Result

Internal Consistency Reliability and Convergent Validity

The results of the PLS-SEM analysis used to assess the discriminant validity, convergent validity, and internal consistency reliability of the constructs involved in the study. Digital Transformation, Better Purchasing, Interactiveness, Product Promotion, Satisfaction, Loyalty, and Social Connection are the constructs examined.

Internal Consistency Reliability /Composite Reliability

One way to gauge reliability is through internal consistency. When all other factors are held constant, a measure's reliability is defined as its capacity to produce the same result or score each time it is used. As per the SEM Analysis, all constructs have composite reliability values above 0.7. This indicates excellent internal consistency reliability, suggesting that the indicators for each construct reliably measure the same underlying concept.

Convergent Validity

Purchasing enhancement, Touchpoint; Digital Transformation, Satisfaction and Product inhalation Bicos, > 0.6 For Average Variance Extracted (AVE), > 0.4 These values are acceptable for convergent validity, implying that the constructs converge well around the theoretical underlying concepts they intend to measure.

Discriminant Validity

Cross loadings: No cross loads have been shown.

This cross loadings infer good evidence of having discriminant validity because the constructs are not over correlated. The loadings of each indicator on its own construct are higher than the other constructs. PLS-SEM analysis provides evidence of goodness-of-fit, through acceptable risk-free internal consistency reliability and good average variance extracted scores to the constructs that were measured in this study. All constructs in the model also exhibit high composite reliability values (greater than 0.6), suggesting that the items comprising each construct are highly consistent with one another. The AVE values also provide additional evidence of convergent validity, especially for Loyalty and Social Connection which demonstrates especially strong convergent validity. The absence of cross loadings also confirms that constructs achieved good discriminant validity, and are distinct in the context of this research. Results confirm the reliability and validity of measurement model thus, allowing for analysis and interpretation of structural model.

Variance Inflation Factor (VIF) for Collinearity Test

Collinearity among constructs in our model with SEM analysis (using the VIF) The constructs that are investigated include Digital Transformation, Improved Buying, Interactiveness, Product Promotion, Satisfaction, Loyaltyas well as Social Link. The VIF values for all constructs are immerging below the cut-off value 5.

This indicates that constructs are not having collinearity problems. The VIF values less than 5 indicate that multicollinearity is not a concern as the constructs have enough independent explanatory power [67].

According to the VIF-based collinearity assessment, each research construct is with a VIF lower than five. This indicates that the constructs do not substantially collinearize which bolster the reliability of the regression coefficients because multicollinearity causes regression coefficient to be inflated. This aspect reinforces the fact that Constructs are independent of each other, thus enhancing the validity of the results from PLS-SEM.

R square, also called Coefficient of Determination

The R^2 value, or the coefficient of determination, is a value from 0–1 that tells us how well a statistical model predicts an outcome. You can think of the R^2 as the percentage of variance in the dependent variable predicted by your statistical model.

Loyalty: The R^2 value of 0.518 indicates that 51.8% of the variance in Loyalty is explained by the exogenous variables. This is a large effect size [19], which indicates that the model could explain a significant amount of variance in Loyalty.

$R^2 = 0.077$ Revenue Only 7.7% of the variability in Revenue is explained by the exogenous variables. This is a weak effect, indicating around 1% of variance in Revenue can be explained by the model.

The R^2 for Social Connection is 0.320 so 32.0% of the variance in Social Connection can be explained by these exogenous variables. This is a medium sized effect, meaning that the model accounts for a good amount of variance in Social Connection. The R^2 values shed light on the explanatory power of the model: Loyalty is having a large effect, Social Connection is having a moderate effect, and Revenue has a small effect.

7. PATH COEFFICIENT ANALYSIS REPORT

The analysis focuses on understanding the relationships between exogenous (independent) variables such as Digital Transformation, Improved Purchasing, Interactiveness, Product Promotion, Satisfaction, and endogenous (dependent) variables including Loyalty, Revenue, and Social Connection.

The path coefficients to Loyalty (0.166) and Revenue (0.080) are both statistically insignificant ($p > 0.05$), indicating that Digital Transformation does not significantly predict Loyalty or Revenue in this model. However, it significantly predicts Social Connection ($p = 0.042$), suggesting that organizations focusing on digital transformation strategies may enhance social connections among stakeholders. Improved Purchasing significantly predicts Loyalty ($p = 0.005$), indicating that enhancements in purchasing processes can positively influence customer loyalty. However, its paths to Revenue ($p = 0.111$) and Social Connection ($p = 0.775$) are insignificant, suggesting that improvements in purchasing do not directly impact revenue or social connections in this context.

Interactiveness shows significant paths to Loyalty ($p = 0.002$) and Revenue ($p = 0.008$), indicating that interactive features or strategies have a positive effect on both customer loyalty and revenue generation. Its path to Social Connection ($p = 0.213$) is not significant, suggesting no direct impact on social connections.

Product Promotion significantly predicts Revenue ($p = 0.017$), implying that effective product promotion strategies can enhance revenue generation. However, its paths to Loyalty ($p = 0.407$) and Social Connection ($p = 0.299$) are insignificant, indicating that product promotion does not significantly influence customer loyalty or social connections in this study.

Satisfaction significantly predicts Loyalty ($p = 0.000$) and Social Connection ($p = 0.000$), highlighting the critical role of customer satisfaction in fostering both loyalty and social connections. However, its path to Revenue ($p = 0.111$) is insignificant, suggesting that satisfaction levels do not directly impact revenue generation.

Social Connection significantly predicts Revenue ($p = 0.021$), indicating that stronger social connections can lead to increased revenue. This underscores the importance of fostering social relationships for business success.

The analysis of path coefficients and their associated p-values provides insights into the relationships between the studied variables. Key findings include significant relationships between certain exogenous variables (such as Interactiveness, Satisfaction) and endogenous variables (Loyalty, Revenue, Social Connection), while others show insignificant relationships.

These results can guide decision-making processes within organizations, focusing resources on strategies that have shown significant impacts on key outcomes like customer loyalty, revenue generation, and social connection.

8. EFFECT SIZE ANALYSIS REPORT

Effect size, measured by f-square, indicates the impact of each exogenous construct on the variance explained (R^2) in the endogenous constructs of interest: Loyalty, Revenue, and Social Connection.

Digital Transformation -> Loyalty, Revenue, Social Connection: These paths show small effect sizes (f-square values ranging from 0.006 to 0.017), indicating that Digital Transformation has a relatively minor impact on explaining the variance in Loyalty, Revenue, and Social Connection.

Improved Purchasing -> Loyalty, Revenue, Interactiveness -> Social Connection, Product Promotion -> Loyalty, Revenue, Social Connection: These paths also demonstrate small effect sizes (ranging from 0.002 to 0.022), suggesting that these constructs contribute modestly to explaining the variance in the respective endogenous constructs.

Improved Purchasing -> Loyalty: This path shows a medium effect size (f-square = 0.022), indicating a moderate impact on explaining the variance in Loyalty.

Interactiveness -> Loyalty, Revenue: These paths also demonstrate medium effect sizes (f- square = 0.032 for Loyalty and 0.021 for Revenue), suggesting a moderate impact on explaining the variance in Loyalty and Revenue.

Satisfaction -> Social Connection: This path shows a medium effect size (f-square = 0.091), indicating a moderate impact on explaining the variance in Social Connection.

Large Effect Size

Satisfaction->Loyalty: The path Satisfaction -> Loyalty has a large effect size (f-square = 0.2) meaning that Satisfaction accounts for a large portion of the variance in explaining Loyalty.

No Effect

Purchasing -> Social Connection, Loyalty -> Revenue: The f-square for these paths was 0 as such they are unlikely to help explain the variance in Social Connection (purchase only) and Revenue (loyalty only).

F-square is used to assess the effect sizes, indicating how well an exogenous construct (or group of constructs) influences an endogenous construct in the PLS-SEM model, for example. Variables such as Satisfaction show large effects on Loyalty with a huge predictive power. In the meantime, constructs such as Digital Transformation and parts of Product Promotion yield lower effect sizes suggesting that their ability to explain variance in the endogenousthe endogenous is more limited.

These findings can be used to lead decision-making and the allocation of organizational resources by indicating which factors have a meaningful impact on important outcomes, such as loyalty, revenue generation and social connection.

Model Fit Analysis Report

Standardized Root Mean Square Residual (SRMR) and Normed Fit Index (NFI). Tasoc data indices to define how well does the proposed model fit the observed data.

Standardized Root Mean square Residual (SRMR)

SRMR is the standardized difference between the observed and model-implied correlation matrix. It represents the average size of these discrepancies. Good fit is usually taken as an SRMR less than 0.08. This suggests a good fit of the model because the discrepancies between observed and model-implied correlations average to 0. Revealing that the model fits well even at the extreme ends, which is a good indication of overall fit close to observed data.

Normed Fit Index (NFI)

The absolute goodness-of-fit NFI compares the proposed model to a null model (a model with no relationship among variables). The scale lies between 0 and 1, where the ideal value is closer to one. Values approximate to 0.90 are considered to give evidence of a good fit. This indicates that the fit of our proposed model is worse than would be expected for a model with good fit compared to the null model. The NFI value of 0.962 for the proposed model indicates that the improvement in fit offered by our model over the null model is insufficient to be classified as a good fit by common standards. With respect to the SRMR, the model shows a reasonably sized fit (SRMR < 0.08), meaning that on average, observed correlations are small compared to those implied by our model. This is an encouraging sign that the model is successfully capturing the relationships among the variables well. The NFI value, on the other hand, shows that the overall improvement of fit over a null model is not very great. As such, the model seems to fit quite well according to absolute differences (SRMR), but worse in relative terms by comparison against a null model—effectively one without relationships between any variables.

Report on Q^2 (Predictive Relevance) and Blindfold

The findings of the blindfolding procedure and predictive relevance using Q^2 statistic are presented in this report as part of Partial Least Squares Structural Equation Modeling (PLS-SEM) The values of Q^2 show the effect size (predictive relevance) of the endogenous constructs [42].

Medium Predictive Relevance

These constructs have a Q^2 of 28.9%–35.4% representing medium predictive relevance. This indicates model explains intermediate level of prediction for these specific Loyalty (LO) and Social Connection (SC) indicators This suggests that the exogenous variables contained in the model are relatively strong predictors of these endogenous variables, so then, (though not strongly) explain a fair amount of variance in those constructs.

Small Predictive Relevance:

These constructs exhibit small predictive relevance (Q^2 values between 1.4% and 7.1%). Or in other words, this also indicates a low discrimination of this model to predict those specific indicators. Low r^2 values of.18 for DTT and.29 for RWR suggest that the exogenous variables in the model are weak predictors of these constructs. This may indicate that more variables need to be included in the model or alternatively, different structure of the model should be reconsidered to capture variance in these constructs better. This information is relevant for model refinement and insight into how practical the model is. These learnings can be used to inform high-level strategy and areas of research, making sure the model is extensible, trustworthy, and useful in predicting important outcomes.

Societal Impact Of The Study

Digital marketing strategies for e-commerce companies → the societal implications of their economic dimensionsfreedigitalmarketingstrategiesforecommercecompa-niesSocietal Implications: Digital Marketing Strategies on E-Commerce Companies - The Economic Dimensions heidsdigitalmarketingstrategiesforecommercecompanies Below are few highlighted components of societal impact:

Accessibility and Convenience: Digital marketing has made access to goods & services more available than ever, allowing consumers to reach their products of choice, no matter where they are or whether they have any physical limits. People can shop from home with E-commerce platforms where they do not have to go to another place, so it saves time too. This wider availability increases consumer satisfaction and improves quality of life in general (Dallocchio et al., 2024).

Economic development and Job Opportunities: Digital marketing strategies has highlighted the growth of e commerce, which has generated many jobs in technology, logistics, ani other marketing sectors as well as even more jobs related to the customer service. E-commerce creates myriad job opportunities — for professional managers that handle R&D, who work in digital media, take care of website development and handling the requirements of digital marketing campaigns, deal with order fulfillment and customer support, etc. — which are all essential elements of e-commerce setup and growth. By encouraging growth in ancillary sectors such as payment processing, shipping and packaging, the growing e-commerce ecosystems also increase demand and cause an acceleration in job creation and entrepreneurship (Reddy & Nalla, 2024).

Enables Small Businesses and Entrepreneurs: Digital marketing is good for small businesses and entrepreneurs, because it makes them compete on a level playing field with the business giants by giving their smaller counterparts affordable and scalable tools to use to market themselves globally (Hendrawan et al., 2024). With e-commerce platforms, startups and micro-enterprises can make themselves available on the internet, promote their products or services well enough to compete with bigger corporations. Enabling of small entrepreneurship encourages innovation, competition and diversification of economic prospect in communities (Asikin et al., 2024).

Environmental Sustainability: Digital marketing and e-commerce can also be seen as eco-friendly in comparison with traditional methods of conducting retail business because they help to reduce the carbon footprint. Online transactions are generally more efficient than physical stores, as they consume fewer resources and energy in land for buildings, transportation, and inventory. Also, targeted advertising as well as personalized recommendations are made possible thanks to digital marketing which fits them into the low wastage principle by reducing mass marketing campaigns (Thiongo, 2024).

Promoting Social Impact: E-commerce businesses engage with users digitally using digital marketing methods and build a community around the brand. Via social media, online communities and engaging content brands create conversations, share information and promote causes creating a community of consumers who feel engaged and socially responsible. In addition, E-commerce platforms hold opportunities for charitable giving and cause marketing activities, where companies can empower to encourage its philanthropic endeavors as an effort in addressing social problems (Yuliastuti et al., 2024).

Digital Marketing for Diversity: Efforts to build an ecosystem of marketing that caters to diversity serve both digital inclusion and empowerment. When a marginalized entity engages in such activity, they are engaging in digital inclusion; further providing access to information, resources, and economic opportunities (Thoyyib & Wibowati, 2024). With the help of targeted advertising and localized content, e-commerce companies can reach underserved populations, reduce digital divides and enable socio-economic empowerment (Bari et al., 2024). Digital marketing supports inclusive economic development and social equity by empowering individuals to participate in online commerce and digital entrepreneurship (Nalla & Reddy, 2024) (Singh & Kaunert, 2025) (Singh et al., 2025).

9. CONCLUSION

Digital marketing strategies affect the performance of E-commerce companies not only but also on a social level (Singh et al., 2025) (Singh & Kaunert, 2025) (Singh & Kaunert, 2024). Their impact can be seen in multiple elements of daily life and socio-economic forces (Singh & Kaunert, 2025) (Singh & Kaunert, 2025). Digital marketing facilitates and fosters a more inclusive, sustainable, and prosperous society through accessibility, job creation, environmental sustainability, digital inclusion and empowerment (Singh et al., 2025) (Singh & Kaunert, 2025).

REFERENCES

Almestarihi, R., Ahmad, A. Y. A. B., Frangieh, R., Abu-AlSondos, I., Nser, K., & Ziani, A. (2024). Measuring the ROI of paid advertising campaigns in digital marketing and its effect on business profitability. *Uncertain Supply Chain Management*, 12(2), 1275–1284. DOI: 10.5267/j.uscm.2023.11.009

Apriani, A., Wahdiniawati, S. A., Perkasa, D. H., Magita, M., Meliantari, D., & Widayati, C. (2024). Digital Transformation of SMEs: Boosting Online Shopping Interest through E-Commerce Adoption. *Dinasti International Journal of Digital Business Management*, 5(3), 595–611.

Asikin, M. Z., Azzahra, A., & Afridi, F. K. (2024). Strategies for the Utilization of Information Technology in Micro, Small, and Medium Business Marketing. [AJEMB]. *American Journal of Economic and Management Business*, 3(5), 1–13. DOI: 10.58631/ajemb.v3i8.108

Asikin, M. Z., Fadilah, M. O., Saputro, W. E., Aditia, O., & Ridzki, M. M. (2024). The Influence Of Digital Marketing On Competitive Advantage And Performance of Micro, Small And Medium Enterprises. *International Journal of Social Service and Research*, 4(03), 963–970. DOI: 10.46799/ijssr.v4i03.749

Bari, M. H., Arif, N. U. M., Hasan, M. M., & Maraj, M. A. A. (2024). Comparative Analysis Of Digital Payment Platforms And E-Commerce Giants: A Five-Year Performance And Strategic Development Study Of Visa, Mastercard, Amazon, And Ebay. Global Mainstream Journal of Innovation, Engineering & Emerging Technology, 3(1), 1-10.

Bennet, D. (2024). Advancing e-commerce smart-pls as a catalyst for improved online shopping services. *International Transactions on Education Technology*, 2(2), 99–108.

Dallocchio, M., Lambri, M., Sironi, E., & Teti, E. (2024). The role of digitalization in cross-border e-commerce performance of Italian SMEs. *Sustainability (Basel)*, 16(2), 508. DOI: 10.3390/su16020508

Gau, A. M., & Saleh, N. (2024). Exploring e-Commerce Potential: Improving Sales Performance Through Product Innovation in The Agriculture Sector. *Jurnal Economic Resource*, 7(1), 47–56. DOI: 10.57178/jer.v7i1.836

Hendrawan, S. A., Chatra, A., Iman, N., Hidayatullah, S., & Suprayitno, D. (2024). Digital transformation in MSMEs: Challenges and opportunities in technology management. *Jurnal Informasi dan Teknologi*, 141-149.

Laila, N., Sucia Sukmaningrum, P., Saini Wan Ngah, W. A., Nur Rosyidi, L., & Rahmawati, I. (2024). An in-depth analysis of digital marketing trends and prospects in small and medium-sized enterprises: Utilizing bibliometric mapping. *Cogent Business & Management*, 11(1), 2336565. DOI: 10.1080/23311975.2024.2336565

Ma, X., & Gu, X. (2024). New marketing strategy model of E-commerce enterprises in the era of digital economy. *Heliyon*, 10(8), e29038. DOI: 10.1016/j.heliyon.2024.e29038 PMID: 38628774

Mardiani, E., Utami, E. Y., Suwarna, A. I., Hamizar, A., & Tubalawony, J. (2024). Quantitative Analysis of the Effect of Marketing Networks in Increasing Sales and Market Share in Indonesia Case Study on the E-commerce Industry. *Sciences du Nord Economics and Business*, 1(01), 11–16. DOI: 10.58812/sneb.v1i1.9

Nalla, L. N., & Reddy, V. M. (2024). AI-Driven Big Data Analytics for Enhanced Customer Journeys: A New Paradigm in E-Commerce. *International Journal of Advanced Engineering Technologies and Innovations*, 1(2), 719–740.

Reddy, V. M., & Nalla, L. N. (2024). Personalization in E-Commerce Marketing: Leveraging Big Data for Tailored Consumer Engagement. *Revista de Inteligencia Artificial en Medicina*, 15(1), 691–725.

Reddy, V. M., & Nalla, L. N. (2024). Optimizing E-Commerce Supply Chains Through Predictive Big Data Analytics: A Path to Agility and Efficiency. *International Journal of Machine Learning Research in Cybersecurity and Artificial Intelligence*, 15(1), 555–585.

Rose, D. E., Van Der Merwe, J., & Jones, J. (2024). Digital Marketing Strategy in Enhancing Brand Awareness and Profitability of E-Commerce Companies. *APTISI Transactions on Management*, 8(2), 160–166.

Semenda, O., Sokolova, Y., Korovina, O., Bratko, O., & Polishchuk, I. (2024). Using social media analysis to improve E-commerce marketing strategies. *International Review of Management and Marketing*, 14(4), 61–71. DOI: 10.32479/irmm.16196

Sharabati, A. A. A., Ali, A. A. A., Allahham, M. I., Hussein, A. A., Alheet, A. F., & Mohammad, A. S. (2024). The Impact of Digital Marketing on the Performance of SMEs: An Analytical Study in Light of Modern Digital Transformations. *Sustainability (Basel)*, 16(19), 8667. DOI: 10.3390/su16198667

Siahaan, A. M., Siboro, D. T., & Nainggolan, M. S. J. (2024). Strategies to Increase Profitability by Using Digital-Based Sales in Micro, Small and Medium Enterprise (MSMEs) in Medan City. *Management Studies and Entrepreneurship Journal*, 5(1), 514–523.

Singh, B., & Kaunert, C. (2024). Adventure in High Altitude of Mountainous Topographies and Health Impacts: Lensing Tourism Sustainability via Reducing Ecological and Sociocultural Footprint and Health Emergency and Medical Assistance Management. In Meraj, G., Hashimoto, S., & Kumar, P. (Eds.), *Navigating Natural Hazards in Mountainous Topographies. Disaster Risk Reduction*. Springer. DOI: 10.1007/978-3-031-65862-4_15

Singh, B., & Kaunert, C. (2025). Leveraging IoT for Patient Monitoring and Smart Healthcare: Connected Healthcare System. In B. S & S. Kadry (Eds.), *Revolutionizing Healthcare Systems Through Cloud Computing and IoT* (pp. 27-46). IGI Global. DOI: 10.4018/979-8-3693-7225-8.ch002

Singh, B., & Kaunert, C. (2025). Cloud Computing and IoMT in Disease Screening and Diagnosis: AI Approaches in Transmuting Healthier Homes. In B. S & S. Kadry (Eds.), *Revolutionizing Healthcare Systems Through Cloud Computing and IoT* (pp. 99-120). IGI Global. DOI: 10.4018/979-8-3693-7225-8.ch005

Singh, B., & Kaunert, C. (2025). Featuring Healthcare, Environment, and Human Rights: Applications of Artificial Intelligence in the Health Domain. In Chakraborty, S., & Satapathy, S. (Eds.), *Gender, Environment, and Human Rights: An Intersectional Exploration* (pp. 45–74). IGI Global. DOI: 10.4018/979-8-3693-6069-9.ch004

Singh, B., & Kaunert, C. (2025). Intelligent Machine Learning Solutions for Cybersecurity: Legal and Ethical Considerations in a Global Context. In Thangam, D. (Ed.), *Advancements in Intelligent Process Automation* (pp. 359–386). IGI Global. DOI: 10.4018/979-8-3693-5380-6.ch014

Singh, B., & Kaunert, C. (2025). Innovative Business Models in Digital and Virtual Reality for the Gig Economy: Space-Age Sustainable Development Projecting Smart Business Practices. In Taherdoost, H., Drazenovic, G., Madanchian, M., Khan, I., & Arshi, O. (Eds.), *Business Transformation in the Era of Digital Disruption* (pp. 127–156). IGI Global. DOI: 10.4018/979-8-3693-7056-8.ch005

Singh, B., Kaunert, C., & Singh, G. (2025). Scaling Legal Framework for Plastic Pollution and Advancing Cutting Edge Water Governance: Reducing and Eliminating Marine Pollution in Alignment With SDG 14 (Life Below Water). In Gaur, N., Sharma, E., Nguyen, T., Bilal, M., & Melkania, N. (Eds.), *Societal and Environmental Ramifications of Plastic Pollution* (pp. 197–222). IGI Global. DOI: 10.4018/979-8-3693-9163-1.ch010

Singh, B., Lal, S., Arora, M. K., & Kaunert, C. (2025). Mounting Legal-Driven Solutions for Plastic Pollution Focusing on Environment and Coastal Management: Eradicating Marine Pollution in Alignment With SDG 14 (Life Below Water). In Gaur, N., Sharma, E., Nguyen, T., Bilal, M., & Melkania, N. (Eds.), *Societal and Environmental Ramifications of Plastic Pollution* (pp. 223–252). IGI Global. DOI: 10.4018/979-8-3693-9163-1.ch011

Singh, B., Singh, A., Kaunert, C., Arora, M. K., Lal, S., & Ravesangar, K. (2025). Unleashing the Ethical and Legal Implications of E-Business Revolution: Consumer Privacy and Security Concerns in Phase of Digital Disruption. In Taherdoost, H., Drazenovic, G., Madanchian, M., Khan, I., & Arshi, O. (Eds.), *Business Transformation in the Era of Digital Disruption* (pp. 157–180). IGI Global. DOI: 10.4018/979-8-3693-7056-8.ch006

Sugiharto, B. H. (2024). The role of e-commerce for MSMEs as a digital marketing strategy in facing industrial revolution 4.0. *Management Studies and Business Journal*, 1(1), 99–107. DOI: 10.62207/80ndq458

Sulistyaningsih, E., Murti, W., & Ratnasih, C. (2024). Analysis of E-Marketing Strategy and Business Innovation in Optimizing Improvement of Service Quality and Its Effect on MSME Income. *ADI Journal on Recent Innovation*, 5(2), 155–167. DOI: 10.34306/ajri.v5i2.1045

Thiongo, M. (2024). Internationalizing E-commerce: Challenges and Opportunities for SMEs in Kenya as a Developing Country.

Thoyyib, M., & Wibowati, J. I. (2024). Evaluation of workshop and strategics of rights in the MSMEs in the digital age. *International Journal of Economic Literature*, 2(5), 1559–1570.

Verma, K. K., Mishra, J. K., Gautam, K. B., & Kumar, M. (2024). Role of Strategic Marketing on Competitive Advantage for E-Commerce Business in India: An Empirical Study. *Journal of Informatics Education and Research*, 4(1).

Wang, S. (2024). Research on the Digital Marketing Strategies in the E-commerce Logistics Service Mode under the Influence of Big Data. *Computer-Aided Design and Applications*, 21, 39–55.

Wang, S., Wang, B., Hu, A., & Zhang, X. (2024). Digital Marketing and Business Performance of Selected Micro-Enterprises in China. *Journal of Business and Management Studies*, 6(1), 134–151. DOI: 10.32996/jbms.2024.6.1.8

Wijayanto, G., Jushermi, J., Nursanti, A., Novandalina, A., & Rivai, Y. (2024). The Effect of E-commerce Platforms, Digital Marketing, and User Experience on Market Reach and Competitiveness of Indonesian MSMEs. *International Journal of Business, Law, and Education*, 5(1), 811–823. DOI: 10.56442/ijble.v5i1.492

Wu, C. W., Botella-Carrubi, D., & Blanco-González-Tejero, C. (2024). The empirical study of digital marketing strategy and performance in small and medium-sized enterprises (SMEs). *Technological Forecasting and Social Change*, 200, 123142. DOI: 10.1016/j.techfore.2023.123142

Yuliastuti, H., Putra, J. E., & Utomo, B. (2024). Digital Marketing, Entrepreneurial Orientation, and Business Capital on the Financial Performance of MSMEs in Indonesia. *International Journal of Business, Law, and Education*, 5(2), 1633–1645. DOI: 10.56442/ijble.v5i2.695

Zhang, Y. (2024). Research on China's agricultural product sales transformation: Online marketing mix strategy and performance on post pandemic area. *Frontiers in Sustainable Food Systems*, 7, 1297732. DOI: 10.3389/fsufs.2023.1297732

Chapter 13
Role of Sikhism and Buddhism in Addressing Violence and Enhancing Women's Mental Wellbeing for Enhancing World Peace and Sustainability

Gurveer Singh
https://orcid.org/0009-0008-3801-472X
GSSDGS Khalsa College, Patiala, India

Bhupinder Singh
https://orcid.org/0009-0006-4779-2553
Sharda University, India

Anjali Raghav
https://orcid.org/0009-0004-0248-7956
Sharda University, India

Saquib Ahmed
https://orcid.org/0009-0008-1891-6910
Sharda University, India

DOI: 10.4018/979-8-3693-9395-6.ch013

ABSTRACT

Violence against women continues to be a global phenomenon that asks societies to turn to solutions based on ethics, compassion, and justice. The leadership qualities rooted in the philosophies of Sikhism and Buddhism can provide deep reflections on tackling violence and all the essential elements that go into creating mental well-being in society for both genders, especially for women. Both religions highlight principles of compassion, equality, and non-violence as foundations of their tenets, ultimately creating frameworks for the reformation of society. Sikhism emboldened by the teachings of Sarbat da Bhala (welfare of all), gender equality, underlines the dignity and rights of women and encourages active resistance to oppression and violence. This chapter explores the teachings, historical contributions, and modern applications of Sikhism and Buddhism in addressing violence and fostering the mental well-being of women.

1. INTRODUCTION

Women around the world are faced with multiple challenges that affect their physical safety, their mental health, and their well-being as a whole. This is only one of many forms of gender-based violence that happen daily, including domestic violence, sexual assault, human trafficking, and institutional discrimination. Such violence has wider implications than physical harm; it deeply impacts women's psychological state, leading to depression, anxiety, post-traumatic stress disorder (PTSD), and other mental health issues. Through an attitude of the meditation and routines of calmness, Buddhism can submit assistance to attitude trauma knowledge yet also encourage psychological heartache. Meditation and the development of the (*Brahmaviharas)* (loving-kindness, compassion, empathetic joy, and equanimity) help women heal the emotional wounds of violence. This chapter highlights the Four Noble Truths in Buddhism and the Eightfold Path (Sahni et al., 2023), Buddhism way addresses the ultimate causes of suffering and they lead to freedom from suffering which is the last path, by emphasizing the causes of suffering and its eradication ultimately from the human psyche which automatically leads to holistic mental health. These intricacies are compounded by social stigmatization and insufficient support structures, making the path to healing and empowerment challenging. Women's mental health, an aspect of women's wellbeing that is often stigmatized and overlooked, is far from adequately addressed. These traditions provide holistic pathways to a more equitable and compassionate society by integrating spiritual insights with contemporary approaches (Bhutani & Singh, 2023).

Women in some of the global south regions with deeply patriarchal structures are cut out from proper mental healthcare. But it is the stigma around mental health that it take for granted that adds to the suffering of those who stay in their corners, unable to ask for help or express their pain. In this context, it is vital to focus on both violence and mental health issues to pave the way for a more equitable and compassionate world for women everywhere. The fact that religion and spirituality have historically constituted potent instruments for promoting change in our society is not new news alongside moral instruction, they are also about redemption. Grounded in human experience, spiritual traditions teach compassion, equality, and perseverance. They offer individuals frameworks to contemplate suffering, seek comfort, and unite against injustice. For women, these teachings can be especially empowering, providing hope and practical solutions for overcoming trauma and building mental toughness (Mitchell et al., 2022). Violence stemming from a lack of empowerment by religion mustn't overpower mental well-being, as there is great potential in the intersection of religion, spirituality, and women's empowerment to do the opposite.

Sikhism and *Buddhism* are among the world's spiritual traditions whose philosophies are remarkably progressive and teachings actionable. Sikhism was founded in the 15th century and is strongly associated with the advocacy of equality, justice, and community well-being. It denounces gender-based discrimination, asserting the inalienable dignity and rights of women. Sikhism offers not just social justice, but also spiritual tools to cope with issues of life through (*Seva)* and (*Naam Simran).* Figures such as (*Mata Sahib Kaur*) and (*Mai Bhago),* some of Sikh history's most inspiring women can lead the way towards empowerment and empowerment initiatives against gender-based violence.

Likewise, Buddhism's emphasis on mindfulness, Ahimsa, and compassion offers a deep framework for external violence and internal pain. Its core teachings about the Four Noble Truths and the Eightfold Path contain pragmatic instruction for navigating the trials of existence, and meditative practices like (*Metta Bhavana*) (loving-kindness meditation) have shown positive effects on mental health and emotional healing. Buddhism, seeking to alleviate suffering, is extremely relevant in working with the psychological trauma that violence creates. Drawing from the central tenets, historical illustrations, and modern-day applications of spiritual traditions, the article aspires to illuminate their ability to engender a more compassionate and equitable society. By embarking on this exploration, the article aims to join the global conversation on women's empowerment, mental health, and the transformative power of spirituality in effecting meaningful change (King, 2022).

2. PHILOSOPHICAL FOUNDATIONS OF SIKHISM AND BUDDHISM

Sikhism is a monotheistic faith, founded in 15th-century India by Guru Nanak, which promotes equality, justice, and service to humanity. It offers a spiritual framework that aims to challenge social injustices such as gender-based violence through a commitment to equality and a vision of socio-political life that promotes a pluralistic community. The core principles of *Sikhism* are Equality, *Seva* (selfless service), and *Sarbat da Bhala* (welfare of all) guide Sikhs around the world in overcoming disruptions facing them, their societies, and their communities.

2.1 Core Principles: Equality, *Seva*, and *Sarbat da Bhala*

Under *Sikhism*, equality of mankind prevails irrespective of sex, caste, or social status. Adding to this Guru Nanak's Dasa Mesh Kabir says that whether high or low caste everybody is the same in front of God. This focus on equality is based upon Sikh teaching, making *Sikhism* one of the most progressive faiths when it comes to gender roles. Another crucial aspect of *Sikhism* is *seva,* or selfless service, where individuals are encouraged to help the community and others around them. This means the welfare of all it's a concept that encourages the Sikhs to do for the good of the people rather than working for their interests not only do these principles tackle social issues, but they also provide a way for women who have been marginalized and oppressed to heal, empower, and become resilient together (Jaoudi, 2021).

2.2 Concept of *Miri-Piri:* Balancing Spiritual and Worldly Responsivities

The concept of Miri-Piri represents the balance between spiritual *(Piri)* and worldly *(Miri)* duties. It reflects the belief that the spiritual and the temporal are intertwined and must be harmonized. *Sikhism* sages say that man is not to be drawn from the world, but to engage in it hence with a sense of duty and responsibility. Especially by women, but that balances their diet family community society with their diet self-conscience focused on the other instead of society. They identify women as dual-role nurturers who could be not only a housewife but is an agent of change in both the spiritual and temporal worlds.

2.3 Gender Equality in Sikh Teachings and Practices

women empowerment, sikh women equality, gender equality, feminism, *Amrit*, gender justice, *khalsa, guru nanak, sikh* teachings. An equal society *Sikhism* has always advocated a society in which both men and women are treated equally. Guru Nanak from the outset challenged the norms that confined women in society. What do put Sikh scripture and teachings Sikh scripture and women's equal participation in Sikh scripture and teachings advocate a visit to worship places and Sikh scripture and teachings: These discourses are affirmations of social justice in Sikh scripture and teachings communities, ensuring women's equal participation in religious, social and economic spheres. The nature of Guruship itself (as defined within the Guru Granth Sahib instantiates that women have the same spiritual merit as men. Furthermore, historical figures such as Mata Sahib Kaur and Mai Bhago, who played key roles in Sikh history, exemplify empowerment. The important role and position of women in *Sikhism* are emphasized and *Sikhism* is a powerful spiritual ally in the struggle for gender equality, as it teaches to honor the interests and rights of all women in every sphere of life at home, in the family, in society and the world community (Ahmed & Nath, 2024).

Buddhism revolves around the teachings of Siddhartha Gautama (*the Buddha*), who lived in the 5th century BCE and developed a philosophy focusing on suffering and liberation. One of the core tenets of Buddhism is the acknowledgment that suffering is a part of existence, but that it can be transcended through practices of mindfulness, ethical behavior, and spiritual awareness. These Buddhist principles are compassion and non-violence and acknowledging that applying compassion and non-violence can help heal individuals as well as their collective societies from harm and trauma, and may promote mental health and even alleviate pain from all the systems that are going wrong in, such as violence against women, then resulting to peaceful means to solve this, and to provide sustainable structure.

3. CORE TEACHINGS: THE FOUR NOBLE TRUTHS AND THE EIGHTFOLD PATH

The core of *Buddhist* philosophy is the Four Noble Truths, which describe the nature of suffering and the way to end it. The first Noble Truth states that suffering is an inevitable, universal aspect of life; and that all, beings, experience it. The Second Noble Truth says that the cause of suffering is desire and clinging, and this is often bound with social injustice and trauma. Fortunately, the Third Noble Truth brings hope in the realization that suffering can be overcome. Lastly, the Fourth Noble Truth describes the Eightfold Path, a path consisting of ethical practices that lead to the end of suffering and a state of enlightenment. Her principles particularly resonate with the obstacles facing women in a society plagued by mental health issues and violence from others, as they provide a structure for change within individuals and a means for collective wellness (Singha & Yogesh, 2023).

3.1 *(Brahmaviharas)*: Loving-kindness, Compassion, Empathetic Joy, and Equanimity

The *Brahmaviharas* occupy a central place in Buddhist practice relating to ethical conduct and emotional well-being. There are four mental states, or attitudes, which are nurtured as a means to ease suffering and facilitate social harmony. The four *brahmavihara* (loving-kindness *(Metta),* compassion (Karuna), empathetic joy (Mudita), and equanimity *(upekkha)* are considered essential for personal mental health as well as social justice. Impacts such as increased domestic violence make these practices crucial, especially for women, to foster resilience during violence and trauma. Loving-kindness opens the heart, compassion tends to injuries of suffering, empathetic joy rejoices in others' happiness, and equanimity maintains balance amid distress. These features not only assist women in their personal development but also lay the foundation for tranquil and nurturing communities.

3.2 Focus on Mindfulness and Relief from Suffering

The practice of presence or awareness, adopted in various psychological treatments, or known more widely perhaps as mindfulness, is one of Buddhism's primary contributions to mental wellbeing. In my experience, being present and aware of your thoughts and feelings through mindfulness offers a method to process and tackle trauma and reduce stress by allowing those moments to unfold and be experienced in a safe, controlled way (Kapur et al., 2022). For women who undergo violence, mindfulness helps the emotional regulation, and recovery, establishing balance in their life and mind. Further, through help and loving-kindness in social relations, practices exist that urge us to resolve suffering, both within us and in our environment.

4. ADDRESSING VIOLENCE AGAINST WOMEN

Adequately combat violence against women, we need to be equipped with a full awareness of the culture, religion, and historical contexts that influence the attitudes and behaviors that perpetuate this violence. Both Sikhism and Buddhism provide unique viewpoints and structures to address this issue, with a focus on collective compassion, activism, and peaceful methods. They share some similar features with other faiths but also have their own unique beliefs and practices. The Khalsa, formed in 1699 by Guru Gobind Singh, represents these simple truths of equality, courage and selfless service. Sikh teachings promote the protection of those who may be marginalized, including women, who have faced persecution in the past. The Khalsa proves its fighting spirit from its opening lines embedded in its belief system when it states that there is no difference in caste or class and they are all created equal in the eyes of God, which in itself is a direct challenge to the belief systems that breed violence against women as an extension of the patriarchal society people live in. Women empowered within Sikhism are represented by historical figures such as Mai Bhago and leaders like Bibi Jagir Kaur, who held roles traditionally reserved for men in other religious practices. Not only did these women advocate for their rights, but they also challenged societal norms, motivating others to do the same (Mukhopadhyay & Kundu, 2023).

The issue, thus, requires Sikh communities to engage with its gendered nature as well as be involved in community support and activism. The siege sowed the seeds for organizations like Sikh Women's Aid, which now offers resources and support for victims of domestic abuse and sexual exploitation. Such organizations strive to break the silence and remove the stigma of abuse by educating people and facilitating dialogue about the problem. Campaigns around things like Domestic Violence Awareness Month, for example, try to highlight the prevalence of domestic violence in Sikh communities and ask members to "address these issues rather than be complicit with silence." Sikhs are taught that love and respect are at the core of their relationships, while Guru Gobind Singh's Hukams speak out against abuse of any kind towards women. Ahimsa (non-harming) is an important Buddhist concept that influences attitudes toward violence against women. This promise of non-violence is not only about preventing physical harm, it is about preventing emotional and psychological harm. The teaching of Buddhism encourages peace and cooperation, and compassion for all beings. The importance of Ahimsa in violence prevention at the societal level is demonstrated through multiple Buddhist-led initiatives around violence against women.

Such organization is the Women's Global Network for Reproductive Rights, who focus on gender equality through the lens of Buddhist advocacy and women's rights across the world. Whether it is through on-the-ground education programs or awareness campaigns there are case studies to provide insight on how Buddhists are fighting against violence towards women. Mindfulness and meditation initiatives not only empower women but also provide spaces where talking about gender-based violence can happen safely (Istratii et al., 2024). Such programs foster a culture of respect and understanding, where individuals are encouraged to reflect on their behavior and the potential effects they have on others. Insights from both Sikhism and Buddhism about offending violence against women: Both Sikhism and Buddhism teach about equality, community support, and non-violence. The Khalsa's role as defenders of justice in Sikhism parallels historical movements for women's empowerment in the faith. On the other hand, the emphasis on Ahimsa in Buddhism can serve as a guiding principle towards cultivating peaceful coexistence while tackling the question of violence in society. In doing so, each religion can make a vital contribution to the current global struggle against violence against women through community and other activist work relevant to contemporary social settings.

5. ENHANCING WOMEN'S MENTAL WELLBEING

Women's mental health is affected by the structures of society, cultural traditions, and personal experiences. Sikhism and Buddhism are two powerful frameworks that help us build resilience, heal, and empower ourselves. These traditions offer practical and spiritual tools, through their teachings and practices, which address the challenges encountered by women in their journey towards mental well-being (Peng et al., 2024). All have their own importance, but one of the best ways to cope with these is to cultivate our spirituality using the basic tenets of Sikhism, as it lays the foundation of mental strength and combined healing of the society and makes women strong-willed. By combining personal spiritual practices with community support, it takes a holistic approach that helps people find purpose and a sense of belonging.

5.1 Psychological Resilience through Naam Simran (Meditative Remembrance)

Naam Simran, the meditative practice of remembering God's name, is a central pillar of Sikh spiritual life. It is a means by which a human being must ensure to create a connection with Jay that is through repetition and create a connection with the good flow by which a person feels inner peace and makes the best without any emotional distress (Wanden-Berghe, 2021). Women who are trying to cope with trauma or stress can apply this practice as it serves as an excellent tool for psychological resilience, enabling them to deal with their challenges with more clarity and strength. The focus on surrendering to the divine will (Hukam) teaches us to learn to accept and rise above the challenge of life to tap into a potential source of mental peace and healing.

5.2 Role of Community and Collective Support in Healing

They contribute to the Sikh principle of Sangat (community) which helps in promoting mental health. The group support from the community, mostly through gatherings at Gurdwaras (Sikh temples), helps a woman experience a comfort zone and relieves her emotional stress. The activities fostered a sense of equality and mutual care, enhancing social bonds, such as Langar (community kitchen) and participation in religious congregations. This way of healing together creates an atmosphere that enables women to come together, feel strong, and get through mental health battles.

6. EMPOWERMENT THROUGH SIKH SPIRITUAL PRACTICES

The main teaching of Sikhism is to make both men & women independent and strong. The history of the religion is filled with women leaders, from Mai Bhago, who personified courage and resilience. The teachings of Sikhism motivate a woman to follow spirituality and moral values, with an emphasis on herself to empower herself. The practices of reciting Gurbani (Sikh hymns), engaging in Seva (selfless service), and getting inspired by the lives of Sikh Gurus, instill a sense of inner empowerment that enables women to rise to challenges with confidence and purpose (Schliesser, 2023). On the other Buddhism provides a route to mental health through mindfulness, compassion, and meditation. Its emphasis on reducing suffering and creating inner peace has established it as a potent resource in contemporary mental health treatments. Mindfulness, a practice that has ancient Buddhist roots, is the practice of being nonjudgmentally aware of the present moment. For trauma survivors: Women coping with the effects of trauma can use mindfulness as a therapeutic tool to help process emotions, decrease anxiety, and increase concentration. Once women create an attachment with what they are thinking and feeling, they can learn to bounce back and take charge of their mental health.

6.1 Transformative Power of Metta Bhavana (Loving-kindness meditation)

Metta Bhavana, or loving-kindness meditation, encourages practitioners to develop compassion toward self and others. For women struggling against sera acts of discrimination, this practice is a road of acceptance, a road of healing. It assists with turning negative feelings into goodwill, promoting forgiveness and self-esteem. At the same time, the focus on love specifically unconditional love closely mirrors the desired outcomes of mental health recovery, and thus makes it a powerful tool for addressing isolation and hopelessness.

6.2 Modern Applications of Buddhist Practices in Mental Health Therapies

Various Buddhist practices, especially mindfulness and loving-kindness meditation, are now incorporated into modern therapeutic models like Cognitive Behavioral Therapy (CBT) and Mindfulness-Based Stress Reduction (MBSR). These practices have been shown to reduce depression, anxiety, and post-traumatic stress disorder (PTSD) symptoms (Hemel, 2024). Such approaches can be incredibly beneficial for women with mental health conditions as they offer practical tips for growth, coping with stress, improving emotional regulation, and overall wellness.

7. INTERSECTION OF SIKHISM AND BUDDHISM IN WOMEN'S EMPOWERMENT

While Sikhism and Buddhism are two different religions that arose in different geographical contexts and have different beliefs, there are profound similarities that foster women's empowerment in both religions. The principles of compassion, equality, and non-violence inherent in this principle can be a good frame to tackle gender issues and build so much resiliency for women. Comparing these shared values shows that both individual people and society as a whole can be transformative.

7.1 Comparative Analysis of Shared Values Like Compassion, Equality and Non-Violence

Like Sikhism, Buddhism holds compassion as one of its central tenets. (*Sarbat da Bhala*) in Sikhism signifies the care of all in the world where people are expected to strive for the welfare of the entire society. Buddhism, for example, places great emphasis on karuna (compassion) and encourages practitioners to ease the suffering of others. Such motivators are put into action by a variety of initiatives and projects that encourage women to stay emotionally and morally healthy, so they can pull through the difficulties society throws their way. Another principle common to the two traditions is equality. Sikhism fiercely promotes gender equality and teaches through its scriptures and practices that women are equally entitled to participate spiritually and socially. These ideals align with Buddhism's rejection of hierarchical structures and emphasis on intrinsic human dignity, creating an environment in which inclusivity and opportunity for all, including women, are nurtured. Central to both religions is the principle of non-violence the aversion to all forms of harm, including gender-based violence as cultural underpinnings of peace and respect.

7.2 Synergistic Impact of Combining Spiritual Activism and Inner Healing

An empowering method that combines spiritual activism with inner healing. The core practice of Sikhism is (*Seva*) (selfless service), which, when combined with the focus on mindfulness and meditation of Buddhism, provides practitioners with a rounded approach to spirituality and self-awareness. Combined, these practices also encourage women to consider how to make contributions to society while feeling fulfilled at the individual level (Chavan, 2024). In this example, a Sikh woman doing Seva with a Buddhist mindfulness practice to grow her emotional resilience is balancing her inner and outer well-being together in synergy.

7.3 Collaborative Efforts Inspiring by these Traditions in addressing Gender-based Violence

Many organizations and communities follow the teachings of Sikhism and Buddhism to combat gender-based violence and provide education, advocacy, and support systems. Sikh-led efforts often emphasize collective action and community building, while Buddhist groups have been emphasizing trauma healing through meditation and compassion-based dialogue. Programs that are grounded in both traditions and work on these two levels can be mutually reinforcing, offering practical tools for recovery to women while also working towards societal change. The synthesis of Sikhism and Buddhism exposes the true interconnected nature of women's empowerment and makes it possible to develop successful strategies to overcome works' structural and psychogenic shivering enclosure. These traditions serve as roadmaps not only for the spiritual life but also for the achievement of equality, healing, and dignity for womanhood across the globe.

8. CONTEMPORARY APPLICATIONS AND CASE STUDIES

In overcoming the socio-spiritual difficulties that have targeted women, the values of Sikhism and Buddhism cannot remain bound by their religious structures. These two traditions inspire organizations and practices that translate these teachings into practical blueprints for social & internal change.

8.1 Examples of Sikh and Buddhist Organizations Advocating for Women's Rights

Some Sikh organizations work specifically on women empowerment and community empowerment through advocacy, education, and community support. The most famous models that promote social justice is the Kaur Movement, dedicated to addressing the social justice crisis it provides a platform to combat gender-based violence and speak our truth. It runs workshops and campaigns focused on issues ranging from domestic violence to women's rights to self-defense, drawing on Sikh values like (*Seva)* (selfless service) and (*Sarbat da Bhala*) (welfare of all). For example, (*Sakyadhita)* International Association of Buddhist Women is another Buddhist organization that has its role in empowering women across the world. Launched in 1987, (*Sakyadhita)* connects Buddhist women from various traditions to promote gender equity within religious communities and society more broadly (Valhgankar et al., 2021). The organization builds education, leadership development, and mindfulness practices so that women have equitable access to spiritual and social opportunities.

8.2 Incorporating Spiritual Principles into Contemporary Therapeutic Models

The impact of one Sikh practice, the meditative remembrance of the name of God called naam *(simran)*, is gaining recognition as a form of mindfulness meditation that cultivates emotional resilience and reduces stress, among many other benefits, in the secular understanding of mindfulness. In Sikh Gurdwaras, community-based practices, including counseling and support groups, address issues such as trauma and anxiety through spiritual guidance. Mindfulness-Based Stress Reduction (MBSR) and Mindfulness-Based Cognitive Therapy (MBCT) draw on Buddhism's influence. Meditation practices like Metta Bhavana, for example, have been incorporated into interventions designed for domestic violence survivors and others who have experienced trauma. For example, programs such as the Women's Mindfulness Initiative blend elements of Buddhist meditation and psychological counseling to teach women how to experience self-compassion, process their emotional pain, and recover from trauma.

8.3 Case Studies

One such case study is the Nan Tien Institute of Australia, a Buddhist-affiliated center that teaches courses and workshops on mindfulness and compassion-based practices for mental health. The United Sikhs, a global organization dedicated to serving the Sikh community and humanitarian needs worldwide, also acts as an advocate for women's empowerment, often marrying their spiritual foundations with contemporary principles of activism (Mwale, 2022). This highlights the significance of Sikhism and Buddhism to contemporary issues, especially concerning how they can be transformative with women's rights and mental well-being.

9. CHALLENGES AND LIMITATIONS

While Sikhism and Buddhism have the potential to transform and empower women and be beneficial to their mental health, various challenges and limitations create obstacles to the realization of their teachings in contemporary society. Such issues are meant to arise from misinterpretations, systemic resistance, and changing dynamics within modern society. A key issue is the distortion or selective use of religious teachings. In Sikhism, for instance, the universal principles enshrined in the Guru Granth Sahib can sometimes be ignored in favor of cultural traditions that continue to reinforce gender inequality. Likewise, Buddhism's teachings of compassion and non-attachment can be misconstrued to encourage passivity or compliance with unjust systems. Such distortions undermine the effect of such traditions as they relate to gender-based matters and more often than not prevent them from being an instrument of change (Singla & Malik, 2024).

9.1 Opposition from Patriarchal Structures

However, it should be noted that both Sikhism and Buddhism are practiced within patriarchal societies, as are many religious and cultural systems. Indeed, opposition to change tends to be founded in long-standing gender norms and power relations. In the ideal, through the practices of some Sikhs, women get barriers to leadership positions in Gurdwaras or religious institutions. With a monastic tradition closely tied to this concept of male and female monks, gender inequalities regarding fully ordained monks for women remain common throughout Buddhist monastic traditions, despite the greater Buddhist tenet of equality and compassion. Patriarchy attempts to hold up progress but these teachings cannot be hidden and their ability to empower women is limited (KC, 2024).

9.2 Connecting Ancient Religion with Modern Society

A major restriction regarding this is the difficulty of applying ancient spiritual teachings to today's social scenarios. However, there is a need to rework these principles for contemporary issues including gender-based violence, mental health as well as sustainable capitalism. It is rare that New Age spiritual practices, like meditation and community service, successfully infiltrate modern society through social movement organizations that focus on social activism or mental health support, instead of facing cultural and logistical barriers. Meeting the needs of the students in a way that merges the two can be challenging, especially on a wide scale.

10. RECOMMENDATIONS AND FUTURE DIRECTIONS

Sikhism and Buddhism provide profound teachings regarding gender equality and mental health improvement. The fundamental values of compassion, equality, and non-violence; principles, when incorporated into contemporary structures, can induce radical change (Hans & Theophil, 2024). The ensuing recommendations and directions for the future are to enable these teachings to realize maximum benefit for the empowerment of women and a just society.

10.1 Incorporating Sikh and Buddhist Teachings in Education and Social Policy

Embedding the teachings of Sikhism and Buddhism in education systems and social policies is one of the most powerful methods for harnessing their wisdom. Educational institutions can offer courses that underscore the egalitarian principles of Sikhism and the mindfulness practices of Buddhism. Character education does not have to be isolated from work that addresses interactions between people and communities, as Sikh values such as Sarbat da Bhala (welfare of all) can easily be integrated into such efforts (Habito, 2022). Likewise, core Buddhist concepts such as the Four Noble Truths and the Eightfold Path can foster resilience and emotional intelligence in youth. On an institutional level, not-for-profit, governments and social organizations might seek to implement frameworks inspired by these teachings to reduce the incidence of gender-based violence and facilitate mental health supports.

Community-based healing programs, drawn from Sikh traditions of Seva (self-less service) and Naam Simran (meditative remembrance), can be implemented to tackle the psychological and social dimensions of trauma. Martial arts of this nature can be combined with many principles of Buddhist-inspired policies about mindful and compassionate practices and could provide insight into psychological strategies ensuring mental health interventions are humane and inclusive (Kahkonen & da Silva, 2023).

10.2 Advocating for Interfaith Dialogues Towards Gender Equality and Positive Mental Health

Through interfaith dialogue, the universal values of Sikhism and Buddhism can be shared and integrated. Religious leaders, policy-makers, and activists should actively engage in such conversations, engineering processes that remove systemic barriers to gender equality and mental well-being. These conversations can encourage a less adversarial approach to spiritual teachings and modern social issues and ultimately result in a collaborative vision regarding advocacy and action. Interfaith workshops and conferences can also facilitate discussion about how groups and individuals from different sides of the aisle implement non-violence, compassion, and other principles in their lives (Milner et al., 2021). They can also encourage collaborative efforts to address these issues together such as domestic violence and workplace discrimination and in sharing best practices in trauma recovery and mental health needs.

10.3 The Intersection of Trauma Recovery and Spiritual Practice

Spirituality has tremendous potential in trauma recovery and therapy, as seen in the spiritual practice of Sikhism and Buddhism. The focus on community and collective healing in Sikhism can help create safe spaces for survivors of violence. Support groups that are built on the teachings of Sikhism act as pillars of strength, helping women regain the will to live and energize them to rebuild their lives with a sense of belonging and purpose. Contemporary Buddhist practices like mindfulness meditation and Metta Bhavana (loving-kindness meditation) have been quite effective with various therapeutic applications. Such methods could be incorporated into trauma recovery initiatives to assist women with developing self-compassion and emotional strength. Therapists and counselors can borrow from these traditions to create culturally appropriate practices that serve the particular needs of women with mental health difficulties (Ty, 2023).

11. CONCLUSION

Sikhism and Buddhism hold timeless wisdom that speaks to two of the major challenges confronting many women in the world today violence and mental health. Based on tenets of compassion, equality, and healing, these spiritual traditions provide transformative paradigms for nurturing individual and societal well-being (Singh & Kaunert, 2025). Their teachings serve not only as effective solutions to modern problems, but also as values that stretch across cultural, geographic, and temporal boundaries. Sikhism teaches Sarbat da Bhala (the well-being of all) and Naam Simran (meditative remembrance) and how these teachings enable individuals to face hardships through spiritual endurance and community support (Singh et al., 2025). This works to challenge patriarchal structures, which can lead to enlightened reforms within communities. Also, the Four Noble Truths and Eightfold Path of Buddhism provide practical tools for dealing with suffering, building mindfulness, and finding inner peace. Meditation techniques such as Metta Bhavana (loving-kindness meditation) and the Brahmaviharas allow people to turn pain into compassion and resilience. These teachings just may be applied to 21st-century educational curricula, policy-making, and mental health practices resulting in transformational change. The programs based on Sikh and Buddhist values can help women heal from the trauma, defend their rights, and be successful in their personal and work lives. Furthermore, such teachings can be instrumental in moving societies towards the eradication of gender injustices, which cannot only promote equity but also enduring peace and welfare. Also, potential requires more awareness taking action. Religious and secular leaders should join hands to reformulate and advocate this wisdom in ways that speak to contemporary sensibilities. Different faith perspectives can also emphasize their universal relevance and contribute to creating solidarity with others in meeting common challenges. All governments, educators, and health practitioners should emphasize embodying these philosophies, to ensure that the principles behind them inform policy and practice. Sikhism and Buddhism have the power to unite spiritual activism and practical solutions. By living by their teachings, we can help create a more level playing field a world where women are celebrated, violence is on the decline, and mental wellness is a given. It urges persons, communities, and institutions to invoke these philosophies, not just as ideals but as breathed precepts that can design our destiny.

REFERENCES

Ahmed, S. B., & Nath, A. (2024). *Breaking the Silence: Understanding Domestic Violence Among Muslim Women*. Notion Press.

Bhutani, S., & Singh, K. (2023). Sikhism and Its Contribution to Well-Being. In *Religious and Spiritual Practices in India: A Positive Psychological Perspective* (pp. 223–250). Springer Nature Singapore. DOI: 10.1007/978-981-99-2397-7_10

Chavan, S. (2024). *Culture, Identity & Change: The Evolution of Indian Society*. Sandeep Chavan.

Habito, R. (2022). Buddhist Praxis toward Global Healing—Cultivating Clarity, Wisdom, and Kinship. *Religions*, 13(4), 315. DOI: 10.3390/rel13040315

Hans, V., & Theophil, S. (2024). Religion in the Post Humanism World. *Sandeep, Religion in the Post Humanism World.*

Hemel, U. (2024). The Influence of Religions on Women's Health. In *Global Women's Health* (pp. 67–77). Springer. DOI: 10.1007/978-3-662-69700-9_6

Ilyas, M. (2024). The impact of armed conflict on education and children in Jammu and Kashmir: Implications for peace education. *Journal of Peace Education*, 1–21. DOI: 10.1080/17400201.2024.2433783

Istratii, R., Ali, P., & Feder, G. (2024). Integration of religious beliefs and faith-based resources in domestic violence services to migrant and ethnic minority communities: A scoping review. *Violence: An International Journal*, 5(1), 94–122. DOI: 10.1177/26330024241246810

Jaoudi, M. (2021). *Mindfulness as sustainability: Lessons from the world's religions*. State University of New York Press.

Kahkonen, S., & da Silva, R. (2023). Stretching the Peace: The Role of Kundalini Yoga in the Lives of Young People in Alexandra, South Africa. *Journal of Humanistic Psychology*. DOI: 10.1177/00221678231152636

Kapur, P., Misra, G., & Verma, N. K. (2022). *Psychological Perspectives on Identity, Religion and Well-Being: Empirical Findings from India*. Springer Nature. DOI: 10.1007/978-981-19-2844-4

KC, D. B. (2024). Targeted Intervention Program for the Preservation of the Traditional Himalayan Buddhist Culture and Customs: A Case Study of Ananda Sangh, Kathmandu. *NPRC Journal of Multidisciplinary Research, 1*(7), 43-52.

King, A. S. (2022). Hinduism: The culture of peace and the ethics of war. *The Wiley Blackwell Companion to Religion and Peace*, 195-215.

Millner, U. C., Maru, M., Ismail, A., & Chakrabarti, U. (2021). Decolonizing mental health practice: Reconstructing an Asian-centric framework through a social justice lens. *Asian American Journal of Psychology*, 12(4), 333–345. DOI: 10.1037/aap0000268

Mitchell, J., King, A. S., Hayward, S., Singh, J., Wilkes, G., Rey, J., & Timani, H. (2022). World Religions and Peace. *The Wiley Blackwell Companion to Religion and Peace*, 21-38.

Mukhopadhyay, M., & Kundu, A. (Eds.). (2023). *Academic Framework for 21st-Century Schooling: Promoting Global Peace and Harmony: Promoting Global Peace and Harmony*. IGI Global. DOI: 10.4018/978-1-6684-7005-3

Mwale, N. (2022). Religion and Sustainable Development: The Role of the Zambia Interfaith Networking Group (ZINGO) in Contemporary Times. In *Interfaith Networks and Development: Case Studies from Africa* (pp. 199–214). Springer International Publishing. DOI: 10.1007/978-3-030-89807-6_11

Peng, W., Zhang, L., Wen, F., Tang, X., Zeng, L., Chen, J., Galea, G., Wen, D., & Wang, Y. (2024). Trends and disparities in non-communicable diseases in the Western Pacific region. *The Lancet Regional Health. Western Pacific*, 43, 43. DOI: 10.1016/j.lanwpc.2023.100938 PMID: 38456093

Sahni, P. S., Singh, K., & Chopra, E. (2023). Role of Socio-spiritual Reformers in the Social Well-Being of Contemporary India. In *Religious and Spiritual Practices in India: A Positive Psychological Perspective* (pp. 251–272). Springer Nature Singapore. DOI: 10.1007/978-981-99-2397-7_11

Schliesser, C. (2023). *On the Significance of Religion for the SDGs: An Introduction*. Taylor & Francis. DOI: 10.4324/9781003332275

Singh, B., & Kaunert, C. (2025). Intelligent Machine Learning Solutions for Cybersecurity: Legal and Ethical Considerations in a Global Context. In Thangam, D. (Ed.), *Advancements in Intelligent Process Automation* (pp. 359–386). IGI Global. DOI: 10.4018/979-8-3693-5380-6.ch014

Singh, B., Kaunert, C., & Ravesangar, K. (2025). Artificial Intelligence and Employee Well-Being: Projecting Psychological and Physical Healthcare. In Yadav, P. (Ed.), *Human Resource Strategies in the Era of Artificial Intelligence* (pp. 109–134). IGI Global. DOI: 10.4018/979-8-3693-6412-3.ch005

Singha, R., & Yogesh Kanna, S. (2023). Mindfulness Promotes Health, Well-Being, and Sustainable Strategy to Eradicate Ill Effects from Tobacco. In *SDGs in the Asia and Pacific Region* (pp. 1–29). Springer International Publishing. DOI: 10.1007/978-3-030-91262-8_20-1

Singla, H., & Malik, P. (2024). Women Entrepreneurs and Wealth: Navigating Financial Well-Being in the Modern World. In *Emerging Perspectives on Financial Well-Being* (pp. 264-285). IGI Global.

Ty, R. (2023). A Grounded Theory of Spiritual Leadership and Social Transformation: A Case Study of Peacebuilding and Human Rights Advocacy Interventions. In *Asian Spiritualities and Social Transformation* (pp. 201–223). Springer Nature Singapore. DOI: 10.1007/978-981-99-2641-1_12

Vaingankar, J. A., Choudhary, N., Chong, S. A., Kumar, F. D. S., Abdin, E., Shafie, S., Chua, B. Y., van Dam, R. M., & Subramaniam, M. (2021). Religious affiliation in relation to positive mental health and mental disorders in a multi-ethnic Asian population. *International Journal of Environmental Research and Public Health*, 18(7), 3368. DOI: 10.3390/ijerph18073368 PMID: 33805121

Wanden-Berghe, J. G. (2021). Mahatma Gandhi's Sarvodaya (welfare for all) as a way to end violence and achieve happy, sustainable societies. In *Linking Sustainability and Happiness: Theoretical and Applied Perspectives* (pp. 65–81). Springer International Publishing.

Chapter 14
Smearing Machine Learning and Deep Learning in E-Commerce Transactions for Monetary Justice:
Crushing Financial Frauds and Fostering Strong Financial Institutions

Bhupinder Singh
https://orcid.org/0009-0006-4779-2553
Sharda University, India

Anjali Raghav
https://orcid.org/0009-0004-0248-7956
Sharda University, India

Saquib Ahmed
https://orcid.org/0009-0008-1891-6910
Sharda University, India

Manmeet Kaur Arora
https://orcid.org/0009-0002-5071-117X
Sharda University, India

Sahil Lal
https://orcid.org/0000-0001-9827-3717

DOI: 10.4018/979-8-3693-9395-6.ch014

Sharda University, India

ABSTRACT

Machine learning and deep learning techniques have emerged as powerful tools against several types of financial fraud. The banking and financial industry, a fundamental component of contemporary economies, is experiencing a significant upheaval due to the rise of digital transactions. This transition has resulted in an increase in financial fraud, necessitating a fundamental change in security standards. The use of advanced analytics, such as anomaly detection and pattern recognition, is examined to establish a strong defense against the continually changing strategies used by fraudulent entities in the ad click sector. Credit card management, a constant target for nefarious actions, necessitates an advanced strategy for fraud detection. This chapter examines AI-based document verification systems, highlighting their crucial role in safeguarding transactions reliant on document authentication. It addresses issues related to falsified documentation through novel methods, including the integration of blockchain technology with AI.

1. INTRODUCTION

Financial fraud presents a significant peril to the banking and financial sector, adversely impacting individuals, businesses, and entire economies. In recent years, the integration of which not only enhances security but also establishes an immutable ledger of transactions, mitigating risks associated with document-based frauds. Over the last few years, the e-commerce industry has grown incredibly to become a major player in how consumers interact with products and services (Havryk & Nazarova, 2024). Ecommerce has gone through significant but rapid changes in the way humans live their everyday lives, integrating online transactions which plays an important part for consumers globally as it offers convenience and accessibility. This explosive growth in e-commerce, however, has been accompanied by an explosion in financial fraud hurting both businesses and consumers. The Federal Trade commission reports annual losses from online fraud in the billions of dollars, so tools to detect and prevent fraud are more critical than ever. With advanced e-commerce platforms now in place, so too are the capabilities of fraudsters changing rapidly, calling for innovative solutions to address these dynamics.

The implementation and adaptation of machine learning and deep learning to detect and prevent financial fraud in e-commerce transactions are investigated. It will focus on different algorithms and methods used by banks and e-commerce platforms who fight efficiently against frauds. The exploration would also look at some use-cases of entities which were able to succeed with such technologies into its operations, thus gaining significant benefits like less fraudulent rates, better customer trust and better operational efficiency (Banerjee, 2024). The study will also delve into the challenges that may arise during implementation, including data privacy issues, regulatory requirements and the need to retrain models on an ongoing basis as fraudsters change their tactics. The financial sector has always struggled with financial fraud, as the threat only became more complicated thanks to ever-evolving cyber-attacks. This can include identity theft, credit card fraud, account takeovers, and other forms of fraudulent transactions; all conduct involving deceit misdirection or dishonesty. Fighting these fraudulent activities necessitates a combination of sophisticated technological solutions, a tighter regulatory environment coupled with collaborative engagement between financial organizations, governments and stakeholders in the technology industry (Singh & Nayyar, 2025).

These days, financial fraud can be reduced using some of the main solutions like Machine Learning (ML) and Deep Learning. Using these technologies, it is possible to proactively identify frauds by analyzing huge data sets, finding out the patterns in them and tagging under processing transactions as potential fraudulent activities. Unlike legacy rule-based systems, ML and DL models change as they are exposed to new data in real-time this is because models were specifically designed to detect fraud. This makes them particularly well suited to catching outliers that suggest fraud e.g. strange transaction activity.

Blockchain technology is yet another robust weapon in the hands of which ensures security of financial transactions. Through a decentralized, tamper-resistant ledger that guarantees transparency and immutability in records of transactions, blockchain obviates the possibility for malicious actors to alter data. When combined with artificial intelligence (AI) and big data analytics, these techologies kick up anti-fraud efforts a notch so financial institutions can identify in real time and respond to threats. A secure financial environment is needed to develop collaboration between regulatory bodies and financial organizations. Payment Card Industry Data Security Standard (PCI DSS) regulatory frameworks necessitate very robust security protocols, ensuring that organizations follow the utmost practices in preventing fraud. Combating financial fraud in the financial sector calls for an all-encompassing strategy. Through the power of ML, DL, blockchain, and high-stakes regulatory interventions fallouts be controlled to a huge extent from all kinds of fraudulent activity in the industry creating a safer eco-system for both small businesses and the consumers as such.

Figure 1. Shows the landscape of introduction section (Source- Self Prepared-Original)

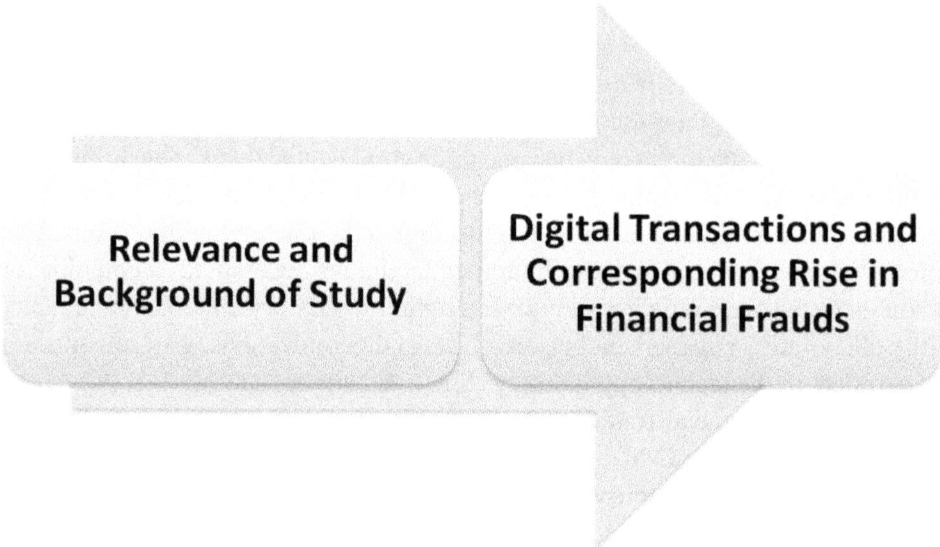

1.1 Relevance and Background of Study

The importance of this chapter is then to investigate how machine learning (ML) and deep learning (DL) can be considered essential in the prevention of financial fraud in the field of e-commerce. Most anti-fraud systems still rely on traditional fraud detection methods that use static rule-based systems, which are slow to respond to the up-to-the-minute tactics used by online criminals. Typically, these old methods yield significant rates of false positives and negatives both damaging to the customer experience and businesses top line. Whereas machine learning and deep learning are used to provide the next step in regards to fraud detection, which is a step change from previous algorithms that could not hope to analyze such a high volume of transaction data. Through mining large amounts of data, these technologies are able to operate by recognizing patterns and anomalies in data sets and this contributes into making e-commerce environments more secure as they improve the accuracy of fraud detection.

The impact of this study is not only theoretical, but also represents a valuable practical guideline for the e-commerce companies aiming to improve and enhance their fraud combat strategies. At a time when consumer trust is increasingly important, security and accuracy in financial transactions can be a powerful differentiator. And the businesses that take a proactive stance on adopting the machine learning and deep learning models will not only save themselves money but also improve their relationships with customers who want to know that their transactions whether they be peer-to-peer or business-to-business in nature are being securely carried out (Ali et al., 2024).

E-commerce cannot look to fight financial fraud with yesterday's strategies since e-commerce isn't buying in quite the same way. With this study, our purpose will be to shed light on the power of machine learning (ML) and deep learning (DL) in transforming e-commerce commerce into a fully secure space with peer integrity in financial transactions thereby supporting digital economy (Crepelle, 2024). This chapter is supposed to alert practitioners, policymakers and academics of the necessity for technological developments in fraud detection with a comprehensive overview on this important topic. It adds value to the more general discussion about where technology and financial overlap with each other and further demonstrates how state of the art technologies such as ML and DL can offer a radical change to finance business. Due to the increased sophistication of digital transactions, there is an increasingly important role for these technologies as regulatory frameworks grow to accommodate them (Hutiri et al., 2024).

1.2 Digital Transactions and Corresponding Rise in Financial Frauds

The last 10 years has seen a massive increase in the number of transactions that occur through digital processes so much that you could say digital is now normal and traditional is…well, quaint. With online shopping, mobile payments, and digital banking becoming more popular, an increasing number of people have been conducting financial transactions through electronic channels. This swift change to digital commerce hasn't just streamlined the buying experience but it has also increased complexity in terms of cyber threats and vulnerabilities. As a result, the number of financial frauds has surged and this is seen with credit card frauds, account takeovers, wire scams etc (Her, 2024).

A notable trend that has emerged in recent years is the perpetual rise of online fraud, which hundreds of reports have indicated (losses worth billions are reported every year). Scammers leverage weaknesses in e-commerce platforms, using more refined tricks to scam customers and financial institutions. Because of the anonymity and availability that the internet provides, fraudsters can operate from anywhere, it is hard for businesses to keep up with fraudulent activities in real time. As consumers rely more and more on their mobile devices for these transactions, the likelihood of security breaches increases; which can lead to them making financial details available to bad actors (Calzada, 2024). Digital fraud is constantly adapting as the way we use technology changes and to keep up with it we need fast action from businesses and financial institutions that can secure their systems. Failure to do so not only risks consumer faith, but also inflicts significant financial jeopardy; underscoring the dire imperative which must be addressed by innovative solutions that prevent financial fraud in a 24/7 digital commerce (Colbert, 2024).

2. FRAUD DETECTION: IMPACT OF FRAUD ON BUSINESSES AND CONSUMERS

Online fraud is a particularly destructive form of e-commerce crime, in part due to its ability to bypass the border guard dating all parts of the global economy. As more and more businesses around the world embraces e-commerce, the risks of fraud increase significantly that puts organizations and consumers at stake. Comprehending the significance of fraud detection for preserving financial systems, consumer interests and sustainability of e-commerce The effects of fraud on companies are significantly atrocious since it harms their long term financial viability, reputation, and daily function (Kishor et al., 2023). The consequences of financial losses from fraud can be hefty, with estimates suggesting that businesses lose 5% to fraudulent activities on average each year. Such financial leak can have multiple faces i.e. chargebacks, reversals along with operation disruption due fraudulent misconducts. This can be disastrous for small and medium-sized enterprises, which may find themselves in a position of insolvency or bankruptcy. Some of the largest companies who are making billions in revenue annually are not untouched either, and cases that make it to the media about them committing fraud amounting up to many millions of dollars only result in negative branding for them as well as a loss of trust from their consumers.

Reputation loss is another severe fall-out of fraud for companies. Fraudulent activities can do much more and damage the reputation of those companies that are prone to them as consumers may wonder how they could protect their confidential data. With the vast reach of information in the digital age, between social media and online reviews, negative publicity has long lasting effects on customer perception. The fraud can ruin the reputation of an organization and reduce trade; as a result, they will lose their target market. Likewise, those businesses that can show they have strong service to detect fraud will build a positive reputation among consumers as honest and reputable providers of goods and services meaning customers are more likely to do business with them over the long term.

It can not only have legal and financial repercussions, but it may also slow down or even shut down operations for business. E-commerce platforms spend a lot of resources on fraud control they need to have advanced levels of security, investigate disputes and deal with customer complaints. These efforts typically siphon resources way from core business activities, which can inhibit innovation and growth (Raghav et al., 2024). Associatively, expenses related to fraud mitigation require significant time and effort and lead to surge in operational charges that can be continued on to customers causing an hike in prices. The effect of fraud on consumers can be just as substantial. Financial fraud victims suffer high levels of emotional and psychological distress (Kaushik et al., 2024). The trust breach of a fraud takes over a personal security risk, mainly if plastic data is involved. For everyday users, the process of recovering their money that was lost or fixing unauthorized transactions could all be done in a quick and convenient manner, made much easier. But the very real cost of fraud can quickly erode personal savings, and that too from some of those who may perhaps least afford it.

All these issues contribute to the deterioration in consumer confidence in e-commerce as a whole. When online purchases feel unsafe to consumers due to rampant fraud, they may be inclined to defer to the trusted transaction methods of physical shopping. The current approach of e-commerce resistance is likely to impede the evolution of e-commerce and thereby curtail digital transformation in moment's industries. With the general public apprehensive about fraud since earlier this year after numerous scandals, companies will be increasingly interrogated on how they protect themselves, potentially making it even harder to earn customer trust. Of course, the key aspects closer to our hearts here are the detection of fraud. Robust fraud detection mechanisms are vital to reduce the potential risks of financial fraud. Machine learning and later deep learning technologies help a lot in improving the functionalities of detecting frauds. These technologies process huge volumes of transaction data in real-time to determine normal patterns and exceptions that may be fraudulent. Deploying these solutions will ensure that your business encounters the lowest of financial losses and also help create a better shopping experience for consumers. In addition, stronger detection practices can turn fraud detection into a benefit in customer relations. If customers trust that their financial dealings are secure, they are more likely to do repeat purchases which translate in long-term business profitability. By the same token, merchants that embrace fraud detection make a clear statement about protecting consumer interests and become attractive brand partners in a fiercely competitive marketplace.

So, while the need for fraud detection may be motivated by compliance and risk management imperatives, it also extends to the broader implications on business and consumers. The increased value of automated detection stratagems over manual investigation has been apparent in the harsh penalties financial, operational, and reputational recriminations of fraud. Enterprises can protect themselves from the widespread threats of fraud by using cutting-edge technologies and promoting a vigilant attitude, sustaining the health of e-commerce activities and financial eco-systems. As a result, they can improve consumer confidence, ensure e-commerce security on the rise and be used as driving force for expansion in digital economy today (Havryk & Nazarova, 2024).

Figure 2. Illuminates the types of financial frauds (Source- Self Prepared- Original)

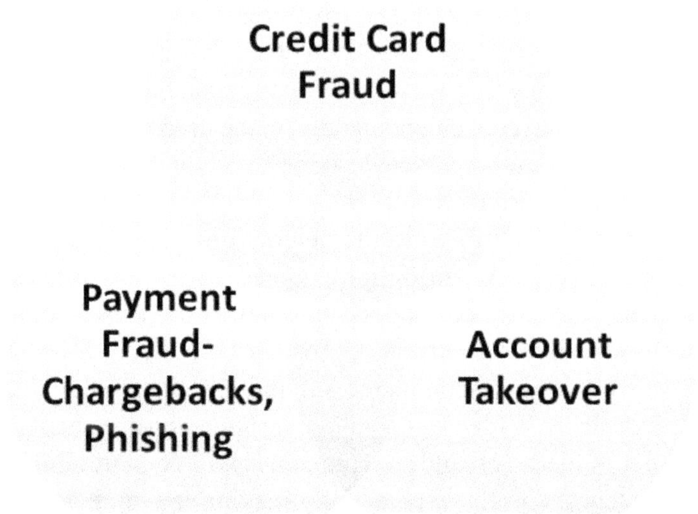

3. CURRENT STATISTICS ON FRAUD INCIDENTS IN E-COMMERCE: TRENDS IN FRAUDULENT ACTIVITIES AND EMERGING THREATS

The ecommerce surge has been dramatically different for the retail industry, offering consumers a level of convenience and ease of use unfathomable in earlier times. But this expansion has been accompanied by an alarming increase in the number of fraud cases, which means that businesses and consumers alike must also remain careful with new forms of crime. The ongoing statistics describe the emerging fraudulent activities, which highlight the twists and turns of the ever-developing e-commerce world (Ali et al., 2024). In 2022, fraud losses reached around $8.8 billion on an annual basis, much of that through e-commerce fraud, the Federal Trade Commission (FTC) reported. Since the COVID-19 crisis sped up e-commerce and hence changed more people to online shoppers, they have become even more lucrative targets for cybercriminals. Studies by the Identity Theft Resource Center (ITRC) show that between 2020 and 2021, online fraud rates have surged by an alarming 84%, emphasizing the urgency to develop effective methods of detecting and preventing this type of fraud (Stardust et al., 2023).

Payment fraud the number one category associated with e-commerce fraud, payment fraud covers an array of scams starting from credit card theft or account takeovers to phishing attempts. According to the 2022 Global Fraud and Risk Report, 58% of organizations saw an uptick in payment fraud efforts and almost 3 in 10 said those increases were significant. Cyber criminals use a variety of advanced methods, including social engineering and malware, to take advantage of loopholes across payment systems in stealing sensitive financial information (Dutta et al., 2024). A growing problem is friendly fraud, which occurs when consumers actually complete a legitimate sale but then dispute the charge to their credit card as unauthorized. This type of fraud is growing in popularity, as it goes to around 70% of chargebacks which the e-Commerce experienced. Although considered by many as a victimless crime, friendly fraud can take a significant toll on businesses, resulting in higher overheads and damaged relationships with payment processors.

Prevalence of new technologies and digital payment modes has added more to the changing nature of frauds Digital wallets and cryptocurrencies are just a couple examples of new opportunities that the burgeoning digital landscape has brought forth, with attackers who specifically target these platforms to take advantage of their borderline-anonymous world. Crypto-related scams targeted at new entrants to the markets and system breaches combined to make up a near $14 billion loss involved in fraudulent activity, according to figures included in the 2023 Crypt currency Crime Report by future.

Until now, bot attacks have not been rampant within e-commerce; however, with the growth of this sector, this may very well be a looming threat. The cybercriminals pen scripts to take advantage of e-commerce platforms, utilize account creation fraud, ticketing fraud and inventory abuse all automated entry points. Bot traffic now makes up a greater portion of web traffic than ever before, accounting for more than 30% of it in 2019 ridesharing companies like Lyft have reportedly had to deal with higher ratios. This is why companies need more sophisticated security solutions for protection against good human customers and bad bots that pose the biggest challenge in distinguishing between the two. New trends reveal the importance of consumer education and data security to be on the front line of the fight against e-commerce fraud. Phishing campaigns and the rise of mobile commerce and social media make consumers ever more at risk. More than half (53%) of consumers who participated in a survey by the Better Business Bureau were exposed to dishonest advertisements on the internet, pointing to the necessity for individuals everywhere to keep their radars up and learn as much as they can about scams.

There are recent e-commerce fraud findings paint a bleak picture that typifies the upward trend of fraud incidences and new threats. With the continued growth of e-commerce, businesses and consumers alike need to be vigilant about fraud detection, cybersecurity measures in place, making sure everyone is aware of what can happen with online transactions. Such added complexity underscores the importance of addressing these challenges to promote confidence in e-commerce, to maintain consumer trust and protect financial integrity on the digital marketplace. This future of fraud depends on stakeholders to stay aware of so that they can navigate through the choppy waters of e-commerce and protect themselves from an ever growing number of threats.

4. MACHINE LEARNING AND DEEP LEARNING: A PRIMER

Machine learning (ML) and deep learning (DL) are breakthrough technologies that have significantly affected the advancement of different industries through their capability to train and model data, giving intelligent decisions (Hutiri et al., 2024). Even though these words are sometimes used similarly, they are two separate but related domains in artificial intelligence (AI). Developers must understand the principles, methodologies and applications of these tools in order to use them effectively. AI, a subset of Artificial intelligence, that mostly involves Machine Learning(A detailed piece on ML coming soon) which is the practice in data where methodologies and techniques are aimed at enabling computers to learn from data and make accurate predictions. The basic idea is to let the machines learn from its exposure to an external environment, and as a result improve upon their learning by trial and error without being explicitly programmed. ML can be broadly classified into three types: supervised, unsupervised and reinforcement learning.

So, in Supervised Learning, we have the labeled data basically where for an input we know which output should come. The workings of melody are that given your inputs, it tries to predict output taking the error of its predictions against ground truth/input into consideration. Examples of supervised learning are spam detection, fraud detection, and image recognition. Typical algorithms used in supervised learning are linear regression, decision trees, and support vector machines. By contrast Unsupervised Learning works with unlabeled data, the algorithm needs to identify some pattern/relationship within the data, without outputs being already defined. It is ideal for cluster analysis, spotting anomalies and threading through the noise finding relatively few dimensions on which to split. Supervised learning algorithm: None (no labels) unsupervised learning algorithm: k-Means, hierarchical clustering (De Felice et al., 2023).

Reinforcement Learning is an exciting and dynamic way for the agent to learn interacting with his environment while continually learning to perform certain actions. Based on what the agent does, it then gets rewarded or punished punishing, and therefore learn a strategy over time that is optimal. Applications of reinforcement learning in robotics, gaming and autonomous vehicles have seen marked success. Inspired by biological neuron behavior, deep learning an advancement in the machine learning subfield extends this basic concept using neural networks with more layers. In a way, these networks mimic the neurons in our brain where information is being processed through interconnected nodes (Crepelle, 2024). These exhibit state-of-the-art performance in large-scale data processing due to their ability to automatically extract highly hierarchical features from raw input data and contribute special success in image and speech recognition.

The most prominent deep learning model is the artificial neural network (ANN), which consists of connected layers of nodes. By letting each of these nodes process the input data and feed it through to the next layer, we allow the network to learn complex representations. Deep learning models are typically very resource-intensive and are usually trained on large datasets. Frameworks like TensorFlow and PyTorch have made it easier to create deep learning models. Machine learning and deep learning have a wide range of applications. ML algorithms in healthcare analyze patient data to predict disease outcomes, aid in diagnosis and personalize treatment plans. They are used for fraud detection, algorithmic trading, and credit scoring in finance. In e-commerce, ML and DL are used for recommendation systems to customer service through chatbots to supply chain management.

While both have high potential for transformation, ML and DL are not free of other challenges and limitations. Insufficient or biased data can also result in inaccurate predictions, hence data quality and quantity are essentials for an accurate model. Moreover, it is not always clear how complex models make predictions especially in high-stakes applications where decisions need to be justified. There is also the issue of ethical concerns around deploying AI technologies. The deployment of our machine learning and deep learning systems must take into account issues such as data privacy, algorithmic bias (the risk that these AIs will make discriminatory decisions), and the possibility that they might render people jobless as machines are able to do a larger segment of laborious tasks.

Machine learning and deep learning are some of the most powerful tools that are shaping industries and paving a new way forward in many fields. So, naturally they hold the promise of being able to make our systems learn and take intelligent decisions from data making things more productive, resulting in better outcomes and creating new opportunities. Now that machine learning and deep learning are moving from bench to production, knowledge of such principles, methodology and ethical practices would be crucial for organizations to gain more advantages from this domain at the same time minimize any downside of it (Lal at al., 2024).

5. TRADITIONAL METHODS VS. MACHINE LEARNING/ DL APPROACHES IN STRENGTHS AND WEAKNESSES OF TRADITIONAL FRAUD DETECTION METHODS

Businesses are calling in fraud detection howitzers for quite some time and it has been one of the key focus areas given the pace at which e-commerce has re-invented itself. Numerous security systems are built on top of traditional fraud detection methods, which suffer from various limitations that ML and DL models overcome. Knowing the pros and cons of these conventional methods will shed some light on why you should move to newer tech.

5.1 Traditional Fraud Detection Method Strengths

Rule-based systems and statistical techniques have been traditionally used for the detection of frauds. Simplicity and ease of implementation are two of their main benefits. Organizations can design simple rules based on well-known fraud patterns to achieve that are, like highlights transactions above certain limit or tracking several but similar transaction from one account in a short time (Arora et al., 2024). It helps to quickly spot outright frauds and can work well in low transaction volume situations. Many traditional methods are less computationally expensive and can function in real time with a small amount of data. The point of these methods is to provide a realistic solution for small businesses and organizations that may not be able to spend large amounts on technology or infrastructure.

5.2 Traditional Fraud Detection Methods are Limited

Traditional fraud detection methods are far from perfect and have several shortcomings as well. A big handicap is that they work based on a set of predefined rules and heuristics which can cover only the known fraud patterns (Kaushik et al., 2024). However, as these systems are largely rule-based and unable to learn from the patterns of fraud which evolve so quickly, organisations may find themselves ill-equipped to detect new and sophisticated forms of fraud. Because this approach is so inflexible, it can cause a high false positive rate typically resulting in transactions that are actually clean being identified as potential frauds and will ultimately lead to customer frustration and lost sales.

Traditional methods usually do not provide capabilities for handling vast volumes of data which could be highily complex. Given the growing volume and variety of e-commerce transactions, it is necessary to identify even subtle (dynamic) patterns. Machine learning and deep learning algorighms are more efficient than these methods where data is too huge to find hidden correlations. The traditional setups may not properly utilize historical data to enhance their detection efficiency. ML and DL techniques on the other hand use bigger datasets at their disposal to train models on historical transactions which will then help find anomalies and predict fraudulent activities with higher precision (Raghav et al., 2024).

The reliance on traditional fraud detection methods makes sense for their own simplicity and ease of implementation, but those are able to address neither the complexities nor dynamics that present-day e-commerce industry faces when it comes to fraud. Despite being reliable, the limits of these methods make them less appealing to businesses to try machine learning and deep learning. With powerful technology at their disposal, businesses can fine-tune and optimise fraud detection to reduce false positives, fight back against a moving target of new fraud behaviours in the digital economy.

6. BLOCKCHAIN TECHNOLOGY FOR FINANCIAL TRANSACTION SECURITY: ROLE OF AI AND BIG DATA IN ENHANCING FRAUD DETECTION

During a time when digital transition of monetary transactions has indeed offered immense benefits; the trust deficit in money management gets even wider and thus is gaining currency with regards to the vital issues of making secure, transparent, as efficient transaction systems. Blockchain technology, which is decentralized and can also be called as unalterable system, poses a paradigm shift in securing financial transactions against various forms of military aggression (Calzada, 2024). Through integration with artificial intelligence (AI) and big data analytics, blockchain can dramatically elevate the fraud detection system, one of the growing faces of financial fraud solutions today.

Blockchain technology are essentially a shared database with the added feature of built-in safeguards & security there is no centralised data storage, which makes it impossible for any single entity or hacker to take over. This characteristic guarantees data integrity and increases the visibility. Classified into blocks, each transaction is then chained together one after the other, to create a chain of this data i.e., Blockchain. A separate block is brought together on the chain, preventing it from making any deceptive efforts. The blockchain to make the verification of transactions more secure, by not having to depend on centralised authority which are for the most part compromised (Das et al., 2023). Blockchain is decentralized, giving you a lot less single points of failure such as the servers to gain access to your ledger; hence the security risks like cyber-attacks and fraud are reduced.

Blockchain may provide a robust environment around financial transactions, but combining it with AI and big data analytics pushes fraud detection to the next level. The classification of the AIs can take a split second to guess at large swaths of transaction data that is fed through them, which renders organizations capable of finding if everything in place is working correctly (sasi et al., 2023). This whole process is always driven by Big data. Financial transactions create huge data sets and the ability to process this data rapidly and efficiently is vital for fraud detection that can take place in real-time. Applying AI-driven analytics to these large data sets, they can filter out the noise and reveal actionable insights in significant correlations and more subtle trends that might otherwise escape human analysis. Machine learning models are able to predict suspicious transactions based on past transaction, meaning the algorithm evolves to predict new ways of detecting fraud (Askanius et al., 2023).

AI features including neural networks and natural language processing (NLP) help fraud detection efforts go a long way as they are able to tackle increasingly complex analysis of transaction data. This is contrasted by neural networks' ability to learn complex patterns in transaction behavior, and NLP's capability to sift through messy unstructured data (i.e. customer inputs in claims forms; fuming visitors on social media) for indications of a downside risk. Blockchain-AI-Machine Learning, big data As a consequence of an interwoven network, blockchain-enablement's provide more transparency and trust in financial transactions (Khedekar, 2023). Built on a system that keeps an immutable record of every transaction, blockchain enables stakeholders to follow the path of each transaction from its very first point in business to where it ends up. Not only does this transparency help fight fraud, it is also comforting to consumers who will know that their financial transactions take place in a secure environment (Angel & Calo, 2024). AI can help drive the auditing process by monitoring transactions on an ongoing basis and raising alerts in case anything unusual is observed. This proactive approach allows for immediate responses by the organizations thereby reducing its impact on operations.

While this might put blockchain ahead when integrated with AI and big data for fraud detection, it is nevertheless not a seamless task (Afina et al., 2024). These technologies are complex hence require specific skills and expertise which can act as a barrier for some of these organisations. Likewise, the scalability of blockchain networks (being forced to process hundreds or thousands of transactions per second as is common in financial markets) could also become a problem.

The blockchain technology when integrated with AI and big data analytics can be a potent way to make financial transactions more safe and secure while lowering fraud detection also]init capabilities. With the help of these technologies, organizations can develop stronger security shields and enhance trust in the financial ecosystem. With a changing digital climate, these may also be the kind of revolutionary methods that need adoption to preserve secure financial transactions. This may also raise the issue of data privacy, with blockchain being completely transparent and accessible by anybody. Compliance with regulations, such as the General Data Protection Regulation (GDPR), is a key consideration in deploying these technologies (Harrison & Todes, 2024).

7. CONCLUSION AND FUTURE SCOPE

The payments is an area where financial fraud in e-commerce transactions becomes more pre-eminent and the use of machine learning (ML) and deep learning (DL) together with its integration into payments processes is a new horizon for banks. Traditional detection methods are falling short as fraudulent activities become more sophisticated and advanced techniques leveraging complex pattern recognition and threat adaptation are required to safeguard against the threat landscape. Both ML and DL algorithms have proven to be exceptionally good at processing massive datasets quickly, uncovering inconsistencies and predicting potential fraud before it reaches businesses and consumers.

The future of ML and DL in fighting financial fraud, however, seems very bright. Further improvements in algorithm development, combined with a depth of big data coming online, will also make it possible to improve detection accuracy and reduce false positives so that end users have the best experience possible. In the future, explainable AI (XAI) will be even more important: it enables stakeholders to understand how such models arrive at decisions and therefore trust in automated systems. The cooperation among financial institutions, e-commerce platforms and technology vendors also means more powerful fraud prevention tools are being built. The advent of ML and Deep learning algorithms backed with e-commerce across sectors is going to leave a significant impact on the kind of frauds while offering a safer and more reliable market place that would be beneficial for all the stakeholders.

REFERENCES

Afina, Y., Buchser, M., Krasodomski, A., Rowe, J., Sun, N., & Wilkinson, R. (2024). Towards a global approach to digital platform regulation.

Ali, M., Shahroz, M., Mushtaq, M. F., Alfarhood, S., Safran, M., & Ashraf, I. (2024). Hybrid Machine Learning Model for Efficient Botnet Attack Detection in IoT Environment. *IEEE Access : Practical Innovations, Open Solutions*, 12, 40682–40699. DOI: 10.1109/ACCESS.2024.3376400

Ali, M., Shahroz, M., Mushtaq, M. F., Alfarhood, S., Safran, M., & Ashraf, I. (2024). Hybrid Machine Learning Model for Efficient Botnet Attack Detection in IoT Environment. *IEEE Access : Practical Innovations, Open Solutions*, 12, 40682–40699. DOI: 10.1109/ACCESS.2024.3376400

Angel, M. P., & Calo, R. (2024). Distinguishing Privacy Law. *Columbia Law Review*, 124(2), 507–562.

Arora, M. K., Lal, S., Singh, B., & Olyaee, M. (2024). Through an Energy Lens: Examining SDGs From a Policy Perspective. In Riswandi, B., Singh, B., Kaunert, C., & Vig, K. (Eds.), *AI Applications for Clean Energy and Sustainability* (pp. 320–343). IGI Global., DOI: 10.4018/979-8-3693-6567-0.ch016

Askanius, T., Kavada, A., Mattoni, A., Uldam, J., & Kaun, A. (2023). *Activist strategies for confronting and harnessing digital power*. State of Power.

Banerjee, R. (2024). *Corporate Frauds: Now Bigger, Broader and Bolder*. Penguin Random House India Private Limited.

Calzada, I. (2024). Democratic Erosion of Data-Opolies: Decentralized Web3 Technological Paradigm Shift Amidst AI Disruption. *Big Data and Cognitive Computing*, 2024(8), 26. DOI: 10.3390/bdcc8030026

Calzada, I. (2024). Democratic Erosion of Data-Opolies: Decentralized Web3 Technological Paradigm Shift Amidst AI Disruption. *Big Data and Cognitive Computing*, 2024(8), 26. DOI: 10.3390/bdcc8030026

Colbert, C. (2024). *Technology is Dead: The Path to a More Human Future*. CRC Press. DOI: 10.1201/9781003089902

Crepelle, A. (2024). Tribes and AI: Possibilities for Tribal Sovereignty. *SSRN*, 25(1), 1–47. DOI: 10.2139/ssrn.4971212

Das, A., Wu, Y., Pradeep, N., Ghonge, M. M., & Pal, O. (Eds.). (2023). *Unleashing the Potentials of Blockchain Technology for Healthcare Industries*. Elsevier.

De Felice, F., Rehman, M., Petrillo, A., & Baffo, I. (2023). A metaworld: Implications, opportunities and risks of the metaverse. *IET Collaborative Intelligent Manufacturing*, 5(3), e12079. DOI: 10.1049/cim2.12079

Dutta, P. K., Singh, B., Towfeek, A.-S. K., Adamopoulou, J. P., Bardavouras, A. N., Bamwerinde, W., Turyasingura, B., & Ayiga, N. (2024). IoT Revolutionizes Humidity Measurement and Management in Smart Cities to Enhance Health and Wellness. *Mesopotamian Journal of Artificial Intelligence in Healthcare*, 2024, 110–117. DOI: 10.58496/MJAIH/2024/013

Harrison, P., & Todes, A. (2024). *The Promise of Planning: Global Aspirations and South African Experience Since 2008*. Taylor & Francis. DOI: 10.4324/9781003104438

Havryk, A., & Nazarova, T. (2024). Artificial intelligence and its role in the labor market and financial sector itself: US point of view. *International Science Journal of Management. Economics & Finance*, 3(3), 1–9.

Her, R. S. (2024). Thoughts and Practice of Good Enterprises. In *The Economy of Goodness* (pp. 351–443). Springer Nature Singapore. DOI: 10.1007/978-981-97-6363-4_12

Hutiri, W., Papakyriakopoulos, O., & Xiang, A. (2024, June). Not My Voice! A Taxonomy of Ethical and Safety Harms of Speech Generators. In *The 2024 ACM Conference on Fairness, Accountability, and Transparency* (pp. 359-376).

Kaushik, T. K., Singh, A., Raghav, A., Singh, B., Arora, M. K., & Lal, S. (2024). Untapping Artificial Intelligence in Environmental and Sustainable Progression: Projecting Legal and Ethical Considerations. In B. Singh, C. Kaunert, K. Vig, & S. Dutta (Eds.), *Maintaining a Sustainable World in the Nexus of Environmental Science and AI* (pp. 109-130). IGI Global. DOI: 10.4018/979-8-3693-6336-2.ch005

Khedekar, D. (2023). *Communicating Precarity and Resistance Under Surveillance: Fragile Organizing in Private Online Groups* (Doctoral dissertation, University of Colorado at Boulder).

Kishor, R., Patle, B., & Bhojane, P. (2023). The AI vantage: An exposition of global dynamics. *Journal of Mechatronics and Artificial Intelligence in Engineering*, 4(2), 58–82. DOI: 10.21595/jmai.2023.23389

Lal, S., Arora, M. K., Riswandi, B. A., Singh, N., & Singh, B. (2024). Melding Artificial Intelligence and Remote Sensing Data for Real-Time Monitoring of Marine Biodiversity. In Riswandi, B., Singh, B., Kaunert, C., & Vig, K. (Eds.), *AI Applications for Clean Energy and Sustainability* (pp. 299–319). IGI Global., DOI: 10.4018/979-8-3693-6567-0.ch015

Raghav, A., Singh, B., & Jermsittiparsert, K. (2024). Role of Artificial Intelligence and Machine Learning in Clean and Blue Energy for Enhancing Efficiency and Sustainability. In Riswandi, B., Singh, B., Kaunert, C., & Vig, K. (Eds.), *AI Applications for Clean Energy and Sustainability* (pp. 366–386). IGI Global., DOI: 10.4018/979-8-3693-6567-0.ch018

Raghav, A., Singh, B., Jermsittiparsert, K., Raghav, R., & Yadav, U. (2024). Artificial Intelligence in Environmental and Climate Changes: A Sustainable Future. In Singh, B., Kaunert, C., Vig, K., & Dutta, S. (Eds.), *Maintaining a Sustainable World in the Nexus of Environmental Science and AI* (pp. 485–506). IGI Global. DOI: 10.4018/979-8-3693-6336-2.ch019

Sasi, T., Lashkari, A. H., Lu, R., Xiong, P., & Iqbal, S. (2023). A comprehensive survey on IoT attacks: Taxonomy, detection mechanisms and challenges. *Journal of Information and Intelligence*.

Singh, B., & Nayyar, A. (2025). Satelliting traditional to smart healthcare advancement using artificial intelligence: A paradigm shift routing futuristic slant redefining. In *Revolutionizing Medical Systems using Artificial Intelligence* (pp. 265–283). Academic Press. DOI: 10.1016/B978-0-443-32862-6.00014-6

Stardust, Z., Blunt, D., Garcia, G., Lee, L., D'Adamo, K., & Kuo, R. (2023). High risk hustling: Payment processors, sexual proxies, and discrimination by design. *CUNY Law Review*, 26, 57.

Chapter 15
The Integration of AI in Performance Appraisal: Balancing Automation With Human Judgment

Thean Pheng Lim
https://orcid.org/0009-0002-4051-9491
Tunku Abdul Rahman University of Management and Technology, Malaysia

Kamalesh Ravesangar
https://orcid.org/0009-0004-2154-184X
Tunku Abdul Rahman University of Management and Technology, Malaysia

ABSTRACT

Integrating artificial intelligence into human resource management practices, particularly in performance appraisal, transforms how organisations evaluate and manage employee performance. AI-driven systems offer enhanced accuracy and efficiency through continuous data collection and analysis. Yet, human judgement remains indispensable in capturing the nuances of employee behaviour, interpersonal dynamics, and organisational culture. This chapter explores the balance between AI-driven automation and human oversight in performance appraisal, emphasising the need for a hybrid model that leverages both strengths. This chapter examines AI's role in performance management, focusing on its advantages and limitations. It also offers a conceptual model to integrate artificial intelligence with human judgment. This framework highlights the critical role of human judgment, ensuring that AI enhances rather than supplants human decision-making processes. By leveraging the complementary strengths of AI and human insight, organisations can develop equitable and efficient evaluation systems.

DOI: 10.4018/979-8-3693-9395-6.ch015

1 INTRODUCTION

In recent years, the rapid advancement of Artificial Intelligence (AI) has significantly impacted various domains, including human resource management (HRM) (Nawaz et al., 2024). Organisations increasingly use AI to streamline HR processes, enhance decision-making, and improve employee performance (Budhwar et al., 2022). Among the HR functions most significantly affected by AI is performance appraisal, a critical process for assessing employee contributions and directing professional development (Buck & Morrow, 2018).

1.1 The Traditional Performance Appraisal Process

Historically, performance appraisals have been executed annually or semi-annually, emphasising past performance through subjective assessments by supervisors or managers (DeNisi & Pritchard, 2006). Although these evaluations offer significant feedback, they are frequently hindered by problems, such as prejudice, inconsistency, and the failure to encompass the entirety of an employee's daily efforts (Grund & Przemeck, 2012; Na-Nan et al., 2020).

In its traditional form, performance appraisal denotes the systematic assessment of an employee's performance against predetermined criteria (Rajapakse, 2024). It functions as an instrument for evaluating accomplishments, pinpointing areas for improvement, and informing decisions on promotions, remuneration, or training. This technique has always encountered criticism for its retroactive nature and limited breadth (Leavitt et al., 2024). Managers may judge personnel influenced by recent occurrences, resulting in recency bias, or permit a singular, exceptional characteristic to affect their overall evaluation (the halo effect) (Cantarelli, 2023). Furthermore, employees frequently obtain feedback belatedly, hindering their ability to implement timely enhancements and diminishing the appraisal's efficacy in promoting immediate development (O'Pry & Schumacher, 2012).

1.2 The Rise of AI in Performance Appraisal

Artificial Intelligence, by its capacity to process extensive datasets instantaneously, provides a remedy for numerous difficulties. In contrast to conventional assessments, AI-driven performance appraisal solutions allow organisations to gather and analyse ongoing performance data, rendering the review process more dynamic, objective, and actionable (Nyathani, 2023). Artificial intelligence technologies, like machine learning and natural language processing (NLP), enable human resources departments to evaluate employee performance with enhanced accuracy, reducing the subjectivity that frequently skews manual assessments (Chukwuka & Dibie, 2024).

For example, AI performs functions that may include evaluating employees' work schedules, productivity, and interaction with others, which human evaluators may fail to notice. An AI system can analyse numerical data like sales data, project completion percentage, etc., and non-numerical data regarding other colleagues' feedback, perceived self or others' behavioural competence or leadership competence, or other qualitative observations. Moreover, AI-based approaches will help plan the recruiting and evaluations of employees by examining subordinates' behaviours more comprehensively to identify better their needs and objectives (Chang, 2020). This data-driven approach ensures that the employees are being appraised holistically regarding the reporting period and not on rumours or some specific incidences their superiors may have felt crossed their eyes at some point.

While using AI has many advantages, such as reduced bias and increased objectivity, there are also major ethical and practical concerns when applying it to performance appraisal (Glikson & Woolley, 2020). One advantage is the ability of the AI appraisal system to remove existing human biases, including but not limited to favouritism or implicit bias. However, prejudice can exist in the AI appraisal system; problems in the data or the algorithm may lead to biased employee evaluation if not adequately moderated (Park et al., 2021). This remains a significant issue: how to make the AI appraisal system transparent and fair while maintaining the possibility for automated evaluations and adequate human check-and-balance for complex or context-dependent performance aspects (Budhwar et al., 2022).

In addition, the AI appraisal system enables prescriptive analytics based on past performance. It highlights what an employee is capable of doing in the future (Huang et al., 2023). By studying these behaviours, the AI appraisal system can help the HR manager select those with leadership potential or, on the contrary, those who may need extra encouragement. However, this predictive capability must be used cautiously since the results will limit chances for employees who are evaluated solely with respect to past performance records without considering their progress or improvements. Despite such concerns, the AI appraisal system has infiltrated the performance evaluation process with the ability to increase efficacy, size, and effectiveness (Nyathani, 2023). AI appraisal systems can also enhance the appraisal process by reducing the burden on HR practitioners and managers, allowing them to focus more on the developmental part of appraisal rather than on the bureaucratic aspects.

2 THE ROLE OF AI IN PERFORMANCE APPRAISAL

Performance appraisal has always been an essential function of human resource management. It is a tool for reviewing employees' performance, identifying their strengths and weaknesses, and determining their promotion, bonus, and reward destiny. This method has long relied on human discretion but is constrained by factors such as bias, subjectivity, and irreprehensible consistency (Hristov et al., 2022). AI tools can solve these challenges, bringing a revolutionary change in organisational personnel assessment techniques (Nyathani, 2023).

Artificial intelligence is gradually being adopted in performance appraisals to mitigate the reliance on subjective ratings. Algorithms replace most human-directed activities and enrich the holistic performance management system through automation, analytics, and real-time feedback (Malik et al., 2020). While big data analysis is conducted in real-time, AI may offer more detailed assessments that include metrics and behaviours, which will help managers make better decisions (Chowdhury et al., 2023).

In this section, we explore the current use of AI in performance management practices, essential uses that make AI beneficial, and how bias is eliminated whilst increasing objectivity in performance appraisal.

2.1 AI is Transforming Performance Appraisal: Key Applications

The integration of AI into performance appraisal systems brings a set of improvements that compensate for the drawbacks of traditional approaches. AI performance appraisal systems allow organisations to go beyond average evaluation, thus allowing constant evaluation, which in turn provides better outcomes. They include continuous feedback, real-time analysis, predictive analytics, and personalised development plans.

Yanamala (2023) addressed one of the key areas in which AI contributed to changing the traditional performance management process from the annual/semi-annual review to the continuous feedback mode. Conventional performance appraisal provided feedback at certain intervals, meaning improvement was limited only to those set intervals within a given year. AI solves this by actively tracking the performance metrics and feeding back instantly to the employees, thereby encouraging high performance. These systems will pull performance information from many sources, such as work management, communication, and job accomplishments, from a broad worker perspective (Chukwuka & Dibie, 2024). Frequent feedback helps the workers receive immediate results, mind the changes needed, and, overall, produce better results in a flow that is more efficient and flexible (Awan et al., 2020).

In addition, Chukwuka & Dibie (2024) pointed out that an AI-based performance appraisal system could analyse the data in real-time. They refer to performance-related big data from numerous sources, unlike relying on hearsay or random experiences (Faqihi & Miah, 2023). These may include the rates of job completion, cooperation indicators, communication patterns and project contributions. AI systems employ such data to give supervisors a comprehensive view of an employee's performance and work satisfaction levels, thus ensuring that the assessments provide consistent behavioural patterns instead of one-off incidents (Pan & Froese, 2023). As a result, real-time performance appraisal systems reduce the chances of human errors or prejudices that compromise the assessment results.

Apart from this, the predictive capability of AI is instrumental in performance management. Using prior data, predictive analytics aims at predicting future performance to allow managers to note possible weaknesses or strengths of their employees (Basu et al., 2023). While AI cannot handle uncertainty (for example, the presence of COVID-19) or the unpredictability of human behaviour, it is still possible to provide humans with relevant data and make them control AI's potential – in this case, humans as gatekeepers (Chowdhury et al., 2023). Using data from the past, AI-driven performance appraisal systems may inform an employee on the likelihood of accomplishing set goals in the future, likely skill gaps that may exist, or even illustrate the need for additional support or professional development (Halid et al., 2024). These observations are useful in anticipatory performance appraisal, allowing organisations to effectively plan talent management development measures and succession planning. Predictive analytics enhances the assessment criteria and helps managers, at some level, make informed decisions on matters related to employees.

Moreover, AI directly aids in the personalisation of the learning intervention for employees by analysing data on employee strengths, career gaps, learning preferences, and performance history. This makes it possible for AI systems to recommend training in equal and specific measures that target individual needs (Budhwar et al., 2022). Training programmes are given to employees to help reduce performance gaps and when weaknesses are noticed, coaching is then offered to the employees. The provided approach ensures that employees have the essential services to enhance their professional direction and allow for a more productive and engaged human resource capital (Casey et al., 2021). When employees feel their personal self is valued, they are willing to transform themselves and thus increase productivity, contributing immensely to the strategic plan. People and the organisation improve employee and collective welfare through continuous learning as organisations design progressive enhancement processes using AI for constructing personalisation training programmes (Dixit & Jatav, 2024).

Therefore, integrating AI into organisational performance appraisal enhances performance through continuous feedback, real-time data processing, predictive analysis, and personalised training programmes. This dynamic methodology minimises bias, provides accurate performance metrics, and aligns employees' skills development with business goals.

2.2 Enhancing Objectivity and Reducing Bias in AI-Driven Appraisals

One of AI's first benefits in performance appraisal is its capability to reduce bias. Human assessors often agree with biases such as preferential processing, whereby recent performance overshadows previous performance, and the halo effect, in which one positive feature dominates the evaluation. AI reduces the impacts of such elements as it relies on data, not subjective perceptions (Park et al., 2021). AI reduces these challenges using data objectivity, algorithmic auditing, and consistent and transparent assessment.

AI systems do not allow for biases because appraisals on employee performance are provided after analysing the measurable performance indicators (Yanamala, 2022). This prepares the foundation for an impartial performance appraisal whereby calls on promotion, award, or career progression opportunities revolve around the merit's column instead of the assessment tributary. For example, when an AI system is used to review the performance of employees, then the system considers factors such as the rate of project completion, revenues generated or the rating of customer satisfaction. The AI system will reward an employee in the customer service department who relentlessly solves many client issues and receives outstanding feedback due to these measurable factors. This method ensures that employees' relationships with supervisors or biases do not influence the assessment results. Thus, deciding on a promotion or developmental chance would focus only on measurable outcomes, making the process fairer and merit-based (Nyathani, 2023).

However, as emphasised by Varsha (2023), there is a need to acknowledge that AI systems are susceptible to bias. Like any other form of machine learning, AI learns knowledge from previous data patterns, reflecting the bias the past data might already have (Ntoutsi et al., 2020). If previous evaluations in an organisation have benefitted some groups of employees and to the disadvantage of others, the AI system may inadvertently continue to do the same. For instance, suppose the data shows that employees in a particular department, for example, sales, are constantly receiving better performance ratings than employees in other departments but fail to exhibit objectively more outstanding performance. The AI system may later promote the sales personnel for increased incentives and rewards or even provide them with training opportunities, which keeps prejudice and overlooks high performers in other departments. This bias would block all further attempts to diversify and incline the representatives, ultimately perpetuating existing business discrimination. AI systems need to be audited regularly by organisations so that all possible biases can be found and addressed as well. Algorithmic auditing helps AI-generated appraisals be free from bias and align with the organisation's inclusion and fairness policies (El-Ghoul et al., 2024). As AI-based systems suggest, organisations can ensure no escalation of existing disparities by constantly monitoring and tweaking these systems.

The objectivity provided by AI surpasses bias mitigation, enabling fair and transparent evaluation (Park et al., 2021). AI systems can elucidate the generation of performance ratings, the metrics evaluated, and the contribution of various data points to the final assessment. This degree of transparency is essential for fostering employee confidence in the evaluation process (Chowdhury et al., 2023). When employees comprehend the assessment criteria and the reasoning behind their ratings, they are more likely to see the system as equitable and to respond more favourably to feedback. Transparency empowers employees by alleviating concerns about bias and comprehending expectations for improvement (Zhou et al., 2023). For instance, an AI system may evaluate an employee's performance using quantifiable metrics such as work completion rate, customer evaluation, and response times. After the assessment, the AI will furnish a comprehensive analysis, elucidating the contribution of each measure to the overall result. Employees saw that a high work completion rate enhanced their score, while a diminished customer evaluation score marginally decreased it. This openness enables the employee to comprehend their evaluation, identify particular areas for development, and grasp the rationale behind their final score, establishing confidence in the process and motivating them to respond to criticism.

Concisely, AI makes performance appraisals less skewed by biases while providing merit-based evaluations. However, it may carry over some of the bias from the previous data, suggesting that organisations need to refresh the system continuously. To achieve equity and fairness, organisations need to frequently review the AI system algorithm to ensure they are free from bias.

3 BALANCING AI AND HUMAN JUDGMENT IN PERFORMANCE APPRAISAL

The integration of AI in performance appraisal systems alters how organisations assess employee performance. AI improves the evaluation process with analytics and reliable data, thus offering efficiency, objectivity and constant insight. However, when such systems are implemented, the issues of human monitoring become an important factor. Human decision-making is vital for understanding the underlying intention behind the employees' behaviour, the environment and moderation in the appraisal process. Maintaining a balance between automation offered by AI and human supervision ensures that appraisals are fair, conclusive and meaningful.

3.1 The Role of Human Judgment in AI-Enhanced Performance Appraisal

In using AI-integrated appraisals, human interventions are critically important for maintaining fairness and unbiased values. That is because AI has several benefits, including speed, use of data, and objectivity, none of which allow it to understand the complexity of objective, qualitative aspects of human work. This is the point at which human assessors come into play, providing important context and comprehension that AI cannot offer. Incorporating the present arrangements that allow AI to process vast amounts of data with human insight will ensure a more enlightened and comprehensive evaluation (Vincent, 2021).

The fundamental emphasis of AI in performance appraisals is on objective indicators, such as job completion rates, reaction times, and attendance, which provide real-time feedback and ongoing monitoring possibilities. However, AI systems are not always good at determining the relative weightage, which evaluates the subjective part of the performance (Tambe et al., 2019). For instance, leadership skills, cooperation, and creativity are often crucial in judging an employee's performance. These attributes are inherently difficult to describe solely through quantitative data. Jarrahi (2018) suggests that this is true even for the most complex forms of analysis, which are characterised by uncertainty and subjectivity, at least, though human involvement in making these sorts of judgments is inevitable. For example, an AI system may classify an individual as failing based on quantitative measures, such as missed deadlines or heightened complaints.

Nonetheless, even quantitative data occasionally fails to represent the entire tale. External variables affecting employee performance, such as personal concerns or changes in job responsibilities, may not be adequately addressed by AI. In this scenario, human judgement must assess the broader context, considering the employee's condition and providing a more holistic view of their performance.

Furthermore, a qualitative assessment is crucial in recognising opportunities for development and enhancement, an aspect that artificial intelligence may neglect (Pan & Froese, 2023). Managers may provide tailored feedback considering an employee's strengths, weaknesses, and career advancement. For instance, although AI can recognise patterns of inefficiency in work management, a human assessor can ascertain if this inefficiency arises from a skill deficiency, lack of motivation or any other underlying factors that AI cannot interpret. Human feedback can thus be more tailored and constructive, helping employees to grow and develop in ways that data-driven algorithms cannot address. An experimental research by (Biswas et al., 2024) indicated that managers possessing robust interpersonal communication skills and transformational leadership styles are more adept at transmitting performance-related information to employees. The effective communication of information cultivates good attitudes of human managers, enhancing pleasant impressions among employees compared to the AI system. The research emphasises how these leadership characteristics improve communication quality and the whole evaluation process, fostering superior management-employee interactions.

Another area in which AI and human decision-making coexist is to reduce prejudice. Although using facts instead of individuals' judgments is one way AI can minimise weaknesses, prejudice might still exist. Algorithms depend on the characteristics of the data used to train the model, which means the algorithm will be flawed if the data is deficient or insufficient (Bogani et al., 2023). This is because there is always a possibility of bias that may be produced from the AI-generated appraisals. Thus, we need humans to act as a reviewer to rectify them. A human reviewer will realise if an AI system discriminatively penalises certain groups of employees based on biased performance indicators. The reviewer can then modify the system appropriately.

The combination of AI-based systems and human judgement in performance appraisals allows organisations to create a moderate method that utilises the benefits of artificial intelligence while also incorporating human cognition. AI appraisal systems can process large, time-consuming data while humans can evaluate more subjective and complex performance criteria. Through this endeavour, the criterion of fairness and accuracy in performance evaluation within an organisation will improve, and a less harsh and more enlightened approach to employee evaluation will be accomplished.

In conclusion, while AI benefits performance appraisal by increasing objectivity and productivity, human factors are still crucial for interpretational wisdom, qualitative evaluation, and ethical scrutiny. Therefore, the most effective performance appraisal systems must combine AI's algorithm dependability with the complex knowledge and fairness inherent in human reasoning.

3.2 The Risks of Over-Reliance on AI in Performance Appraisal

While adopting AI in performance appraisal has advantages in reducing inaccuracies and time wastage, it also has some drawbacks. A prominent concern is the risk of dehumanising the appraisal process (Burbach, 2018). Performance appraisal is a comprehensive process that includes evaluating the output from the work done and the evaluation of the person doing it. When organisations over-rely on AI systems, they need to remember the human elements and start treating the employees as performance indicators or ratios to be achieved.

Another concern is that AI can misunderstand certain actions or ignore important context. (Park et al., 2021). For instance, AI can view reduced working hours or declining performance as negative indicators while not considering actual problems employees face, such as personal illnesses, family issues or workplace dynamics that affect performance. As such, a human assessor may perceive these contextual factors and adjust the evaluation accordingly, which is more considerate and accurate.

Also, if we rely too much on AI, performance reviews can wind up being too easy. While AI excels at processing numerical data, it often needs human interpretation when dealing with more complex human behaviours like creativity, empathy, and interpersonal connections. An unfair or inadequate performance review that fails to consider this complexity (Edwin et al., 2024) might discourage employees rather than motivate them to do better.

3.3 Humanising Performance Appraisals: Maintaining Empathy and Connection

Empathy is critical in human resource management, especially when the employee and the appraiser are under pressure during the appraisal process (Alam & Singh, 2021). Employees might need more appreciation and feel isolated while getting feedback from a purely AI-based system. Human contact in performance appraisals may help create a sense of belonging because it lets the employees know they are valued as persons and not only as cogs in the company's wheel. The organisation's personal touch helps employees better perceive feedback and be responsive.

Human evaluators supplement AI's data-driven insights with empathy in a well-rounded approach, leading to a more thorough evaluation process. An employee's poor performance might be caused by factors beyond their control, such as problems in their personal or familial lives. AI could be the only thing that notices a drop in output. On the other hand, human evaluators can better empathise, understand, and help when needed; they can also recognise when a performance issue is temporary and point the way toward improvement. When performance reviews are infused with empathy, they enhance the work experience, foster trust, and encourage participation. Workers are more likely to stay involved, make substantial contributions, and show loyalty to the company if they see evaluations as fair and compassionate.

There is room for both human and AI judgment in a performance appraisal system; in fact, the two may work together to create something more equitable and effective (Vincent, 2021). Insights and data abound with artificial intelligence, which can track performance metrics over time, spot trends, and flag potential problems. Human evaluators may then put the results into perspective and make well-informed decisions by considering quantitative and qualitative performance factors. AI alone cannot determine an employee's positive contributions to team dynamics or leadership potential; for example, AI can recognise that an individual consistently fulfils project deadlines. A hybrid approach, which combines AI with human understanding of context, emotion, and behaviour, ensures a more accurate and fair assessment.

In addition, combining AI with human judgment may establish a feedback loop in the performance evaluation process. Managers may review AI reports and adjust the ratings based on their knowledge of the employee's work environment and their own observations. By gradually improving the evaluation process, this iterative strategy guarantees that objective and subjective factors are considered.

In conclusion, AI has numerous advantages for performance reviews, such as objectivity, efficiency, and real-time data access, but it must involve human judgment. A fair and balanced evaluation process may be achieved by combining AI with human oversight; this way, data-driven insights can be supplemented by human empathy, understanding of context, and qualitative analysis. Organisations may create a caring and accurate system of performance reviews by reducing the risks of AI over-reliance and enabling constant two-way communication between AI and human supervisors.

4 CONCEPTUAL MODEL: INTEGRATING AI AND HUMAN EVALUATION IN PERFORMANCE APPRAISAL

Performance was always subjective, tainted by human prejudice and limited by our brains. On incorporating AI in HR, this process changes to have more holistic, nuanced and unbiased performance metrics. It will also be able to analyse big data that human reviewers might overlook, as well as work quality and productivity and even more abstract factors such as teamwork and innovation (Ali et al., 2019). Thus, leveraging NLP and machine learning, AI is capable of evaluating things like employee feedback in a team environment, participation in tests of the work environment and differences made in the scheme of the work atmosphere. Interestingly, AI takes performance appraisals to a whole new level, as it can track an employee's performance continuously rather than through an appraisal (Hunkenschroer & Luetge, 2022). This kind of continuous evaluation helps in dynamically viewing the development of an employee and managing trends and patterns that result in much more informed assessments of one's strengths and areas of improvement. The AI will predict career progression for an employee within the business to intervene and support their development or redirect their career for mutual benefit. It is employee-centered and puts the strategy of talent management in line with overall business objectives. This

AI measuring of employee performance metrics, therefore, makes the workplace fair and justifies standardisation of the various assessments and subjective biases so that appraisals are merit-based on actual performances. Of importance, this will be very key to establishing a culture of trust and meritocracy within the business (Hmoud, 2021). Nevertheless, there are challenges associated with integrating AI into the evaluation process. AI decision-making algorithms also need auditing to prevent perpetuating current biases and uphold ethical standards. More importantly, there is a need for clarity on how these AI systems work; the way some AI tools are just too opaque might make employees sceptical and unresponsive. The use of AI in measuring employee performance is a way through which organisations can move toward data-driven talent management that is equitable and predictive (Cao & Yao, 2020). This also can enable the HR team to draw on data to give employees feedback about what they have been contributing to and what could be done better (Guan et al., 2022). The more we know how AI influences performance appraisal, the more we realise that a truly ethical and responsible introduction of AI can really positively impact personal and corporate performance in a digitising world.

4.1 Hybrid Appraisal Model Combining AI-Generated Data and Human Judgement

Employee performance appraisal was historically deeply implicated in the subjective experiences of human bias and the finite and imperfect capacities of human rational faculties. In the realm of Human Resources, Artificial Intelligence (AI) is gradually starting to change this dynamic by enabling an easier, more detailed, and objective assessment of performance measures.

Studies demonstrate that the introduction of a computer or decisions made by humans can affect employee perceptions. Employee selection studies show that AI-based interviews tend to be perceived as being less fair and just by potential employees than their human counterparts, as they feel they cannot fully showcase their abilities to potential employers during these AI assessments (e.g., Acikgoz et al., 2020; Langer et al., 2019). Furthermore, the rising trend of the literature shows that people tend to trust the recommendations given by other humans more than the ones given by an algorithm, even though the algorithms may be more accurate. This attitude extends to AI in that employees have found that performance appraisals carried out by AI facilitate a consideration inferior to those performed by managers- instead of their individualities being considered, only several performance appraisals are left (Newman et al., 2020). On the contrary, AI has often been seen as a more objective and less biased means of generating decisions (Langer et al. 2020). Providing performance feedback through computer means has drawn significant attention from researchers. From the literature, employee reactions are expected to vary and are tied to myriad factors. For example, earlier studies on computer-mediated feedback revealed that employees were likely to react more favourably to computer-mediated feedback than to manager feedback because computer-mediated feedback was seen to be more neutral, objective, and threatening compared to direct communication with a manager.

Furthermore, where the subject matter concerns a simple query, employees may prefer a chatbot to sort out HR-related queries, as the responses would arrive quickly (Mozafari et al., 2020). However, it must be understood that there are also downsides to computer-based feedback. In most cases, employees would regard the engagement with managers as fairer and more personal (Stone et al., 2015), while interaction with a chatbot may appear too cold, impersonal, and lacking emotion (Rese et al., 2020). Consequently, chatbots may lead to employees feeling under-appreciated within the organisation. In addition, they answer simple issues more effectively; in the same way, as customers may react negatively if chatbots fail to assist them (Nicolescu & Tudorache, 2022), employees are unlikely to be favourably disposed toward chatbots in more complicated discussions about performance. Furthermore, like the consumers' experience (Crolic et al., 2022), AI chatbots almost completely inhibit employees' emotional connection to the organisation, especially when negative feedback and experience are concerned. To sum up, performance appraisal communication represents a chance for managers to inspire employees to improve their performance; however, how employees' motivations are affected when an AI-enabled chatbot undertakes this process is uncertain.

In summary, AI improves objectivity in performance appraisals but frequently encounters employee mistrust owing to its perceived deficiency in fairness and personal engagement. Although effective for basic feedback or HR inquiries, AI's impersonal characteristics may impede emotional connection and motivation, underscoring the necessity to reconcile AI's neutrality with human contact in appraisals.

4.2 AI-Driven Metrics and Human Judgement

The evolution of artificial intelligence has led firms to use AI-centric performance appraisal systems. Some companies have begun creating tailored proprietary AI systems. For example, IBM uses its home-grown AI system, Watson, to predict employees' future performance (Greene 2018). IBM claims that this implementation has realised significant economies, such as lowering the staff of human resources by 30% (Rosenbaum 2019). Furthermore, ready-to-use AI-driven performance appraisal systems are being made available by companies like Enaible and ButterFly. Ai. Even though it constitutes a tiny portion of AI performance appraisals at present, this sector is expected to continue growing, say the industry analysts (Holsinger et al. 2019). AI systems are particularly attractive to managers because they believe they provide a simple, cost-effective, and efficient way to evaluate their workforce (Cheng & Hackett 2021). AI enables firms to do objective ratings of many more jobs collectively than before. Abstractly, AI can, therefore, improve the judgments made by individual managers along two important dimensions: performance appraisal across many different data types in an objective fashion and an automatic system of establishing weights for each worker based upon known measures that influence job performance, such as economic conditions and competitive actions. Besides utilising historical data, the AI system is also on track to assess real-time performance indicators. This includes metrics such as the number of assigned tasks, deadline speed, and complexity of ongoing projects. In real-time tracking of these performance indicators, AI can evaluate the current overload on an individual and correlate it to the likely impact on that person's mental well-being (Knight, 2020). The system is built to flag any deviation from the norm in performance. For example, should a person start performing at a pace lower than usual or exhibit fewer communicative interactions with peers, such variations would typically be interpreted by the AI system as indications of heightened work-related stress. Development in real-time integration with historical data would permit AI to give a much better evaluation of the individual's present state of mental health.

AI technology's predictive analytics becomes the differentiator that empowers firms with the retention and recruitment of employees. Contrary to typical historical-based assessments of past achievements, AI engines have the capability to analyse historical data with performance patterns, which allows them to identify areas of development for an employee and provide insights into an employee's potential for future success (Castelo et al., 2019). Specifically, AI provides firms with tools to intensify proactive performance management and move from the traditional historical models. The AI approach is to project future success and the employees' areas that they still may need to work on based on tendencies and patterns identified based on previous employee activities that the employees participated in. This futuristic insight leverages capacity development for leading training intervention proactively, and by doing so, workers can be nurtured and equipped for future roles and functions. Hence, predictive approaches, when evaluating employee performance, are regarded as the talent managers' tools and succession planners. Organisations will be able to distinguish their high-potentials and preparedness status so that individuals can move to leadership positions while simultaneously creating personalised programs for future leaders' growth. AI is an impressive approach to making employees more flexible and well-prepared to solve future problems. Additionally, predictive analytics assist organisations in optimising the use of their available resources by identifying areas requiring additional training or support (Berger et al., 2021). This targeted approach cultivates the best approach to talent development, with a corresponding enhancement of organisational-wide resource benefits from such programs.

The role of artificial intelligence in less structured managerial tasks facilitates higher-order collaboration between AI and human managers. Our study indicates that AI performs, on some occasions, better than human managers in generating higher-quality structured feedback, demonstrating a positive "deployment effect" of AI feedback. In contrast, human managers are good at producing favourable employee impressions, implying a negative "disclosure effect" of AI feedback (Achchab et al., 2021). This provides a collaborative opportunity for AI and human managers to derive more excellent value by transmitting AI-generated feedback to employees. In such a context, organisations can thus be leveraged by AI as an invaluable managerial assistant doing data analysis and delivering feedback content to complement human managers' interactions with their teams alongside his/her oversight. Employees recognise human managers as their most important source of feedback, treating it as digital backing (Tong et al., 2021).

4.3 Synthesis of Data and Judgment for Holistic Appraisal

Artificial intelligence significantly boosts modern organisations and has transformed many business operations, especially HRM. It can assess performance by collecting, processing, and analysing large data sets. Integrating quantitative and qualitative information makes AI a powerful tool for providing insights, enhancing decision-making, and enabling organisational success (Wilkinson, 2021). Employee evaluation has been critical to talent management in today's competitive business environment. The combination of qualitative and quantitative data has proved advantageous in improving the precision and efficacy of the appraisal system, and accurately establishing the performance of individual employees contributes to an organisation overall (Riaz & Ghanghas, 2024). Apparent and substantiated findings from the Society for Human Resource Management (SHRM) indicate that organisations utilising both subjective and objective performances create a 30% improvement in the accuracy of performance assessments (Saeij, 2020). The combined evaluation helps understand an employee's abilities, skills, and performance well so suitable decisions on promotions, training, and developmental opportunities may be taken. A case study published in the Harvard Business Review illustrated how, in adopting a mixed-methods approach to the evaluation of employees, a company improved employee retention by 20% during the first year (Smith, 2019). Pulling together qualitative insights gleaned from supervisor assessments with quantitative data like sales performance or completion rates of projects allowed the company to accurately identify high-potential employees and develop customised development plans fostering their growth within the company. This approach was not limited to elevating employee satisfaction and positively touching upon the organisation's financial performance, reiterating the solid benefit of adopting qualitative and quantitative analyses to assist in evaluation. Adopting a comprehensive strategy has enhanced organisational performance more than the previously defined methods of integrating qualitative and quantitative indicators. A survey published in the Harvard Business Review indicates that organisations using qualitative and conventional quantitative measures improved their overall performance by an incredible 24 stories (Profit C Team, 2023). Qualitative evaluations- the input of co-workers and managers' assessments provide insight into cooperation, leadership characteristics, and general contributions to team development, which results in a clearer sense of an employee's performance.

Moreover, the Society for Human Resource Management conducted a survey showing that 90% of HR professionals believe that a holistic performance appraisal process fosters greater employee engagement and satisfaction (Yu, 2018). By adopting a system that emphasises qualitative factors such as communication ability and adaptability and quantitative measures such as sales performance and project completion rates, organisations can develop a much more complex assessment of employee performance. This process yields individualised development plans, heightened employee enthusiasm, and better overall results for organisations. The impact is on creating a profound effect in the joint evaluation of performance qualitatively and quantitatively towards building an organisational culture of improvement.

4.4 Feedback Loop: Adjusting AI Models Based on Human Feedback

A recent field of artificial intelligence application involves analysing individual employees' positions and performance feedback. Through big data analytics and self-learning technologies, AI-enabled applications may track employee work activities, stress their performance appraisal, and suggest improvements that could increase productivity. Enable, a pioneering platform, has developed an AI system that is claimed to track employee work remotely. The AI measures each employee's typical workflow, assigns him/her a “productivity score,” and identifies areas for improving efficiency within the workflow. This AI feedback system has been licensed by the Dubai customs agency and Omnicom Media Group, and it is claimed to be far into discussions with Delta Airlines and CVS Health. MetLife, a large insurance company, has also created and implemented an AI training program that analyses service employees' customer interactions and recommends improvements. Further, new employees at Unilever receive feedback on their performance via AI programs (Heaven, 2020).

The potential of artificial intelligence for performance feedback at the workplace has garnered considerable attention. On the one hand, AI-fueled by advanced data analytics could closely monitor employee behaviour, say minute-by-minute, evaluate productivity with unprecedented precision, and give fine-tuned job-enhancement recommendations while maintaining scrutiny and objectivity. These capabilities promise massive employee performance improvements (Heaven, 2020; Colangelo, 2020). On the other hand, introducing AI systems, especially without explicit policies and guidelines that govern their deployment, might sway the power balance towards employers and alienate employees from their work (Bughin & Manyika, 2019). The appearance of an AI feedback model could significantly affect how employees view AI as a manager and how the surveillance of employees at the workplace by machines and algorithms might decrease the trust among employees and reduce team and organisational work engagement, ultimately hindering performance (Cheatham, Javanmardian, & Samandari, 2019).

In summary, the question of how AI feedback influences employee performance leaves us with a trade-off. If companies inform employees about AI-based feedback, they risk losing part of their AI-driven performance improvement. Yet, at least from some legal and ethical perspectives, employees do have a right to know that machines and algorithms monitor them and their behaviour and decisions, which might, in turn, lead to a necessity for companies to be transparent about the AI utilisation in their company, for example judicial cases and regulators have already expressed strong judgements towards the duty of companies to inform employees about algorithms and specifically AI that decide important work-related outcomes (MacCarthy, 2020; O'Keefe, Moss, Martinez, & Rose, 2019). However, no scientific evidence tells us how this trade-off manifests itself and balances out, and the trade-off has never been systematically analysed in academic literature. Thus, research still needs to answer whether AI feedback influences employee performance and, if so, how companies can potentially reduce its adverse effects if they disclose their AI use policy to their workforce.

5 OPPORTUNITIES AND CHALLENGES

Implementing Artificial Intelligence (AI) in assessing employee performance offers numerous opportunities and benefits. As for formal performance appraisals in traditional settings, typically, these are handled by managers with feedback that could affect the entire career trajectory of employees (Tambe et al., 2019). Managers' responsibilities are already widespread, including but not limited to performance appraisal, identifying appropriate training opportunities, evaluating contributions of individual team members, giving performance-related feedback, establishing future objectives and other related tasks. Under these circumstances, managers with the burden of making such judgments regarding many employees may experience considerable stress, leading to human errors: the seeping in of personal biases, judgement based on scant information, and even selective favouritism. Traditional performance appraisals rely on limited data and a set pattern of performance indicators determined in the review form (Tong et al., 2021). In stark contrast, AI-powered performance appraisals mine massive datasets and create predictions based on the current assessment and an employee's performance history and career progression from day one. This holistic approach is vital for grasping the employees' potential and designing relevant goals. It also helps managers pinpoint promotion-worthy candidates and allocate rewards more equitably (Nasr et al., 2019).

The counterargument for AI performance management is that human resources are the sole data footing on which it would operate without favour or prejudice to anyone and assemble the facts from more than one angle of view to reduce the chances of inaccurate data (Reim et al., 2020). AI would enhance managers' ability to give objective feedback, creating win-win situations for the company and employees.

Shifting from conventional periodic performance appraisal to continuous review practices provides numerous advantages. Assessment of performance allows skills to be improved consistently and follow the improvements or corrections quickly; therefore, it nurtures a responsive and flexible organisational culture. Data can be constantly collected from different sources, such as employee communications or calendar activities, with the help of AI (Alrashedi & Abbod, 2020). This enables real-time employee performance assessment, allowing for timely managerial decisions and fast feedback. It also reduces the time spent preparing performance appraisals because the employee does not need to recall and validate information from various sources. Artificial intelligence has created many tools with greater accuracy and impartiality for assessing employee performance. Some examples are sentiment analysis for assessing employee engagement and satisfaction and predictive analytics for forecasting future performance based on historical performance metrics (Logg et al., 2019). AI-backed, organizationally developed systems facilitate employee performance monitoring; hence, the feedback and coaching would be more fine-tuned to the necessity. Retaining talents of quality has become the bane of the majority of organisations, where conducting a good performance evaluation is of utmost importance for retention of the same. AI-augmented tools introduced into the performance appraisal process provide accurate and credible feedback and thus encourage employees to know precisely where they are succeeding and where some improvements and career training might be further needed (Wisniewski et al., 2020). The former can help enhance engagement and satisfaction levels through a more targeted focus on coaching and development, hopefully leading to higher retention levels thereafter.

Implementing AI into performance appraisal should bring unprecedented benefits, yet it will face hurdles and barriers that need to be tackled effectively. The most common constraints that impede the application of AI in performance systems relate to data and technological constraints, the entire organisation prepared for such implementation, and ethical concerns and privacy issues related to the employee's information. The proper and successful implementation of AI hinges on having enough related, high-quality data available. If performance data are sometimes incomplete, unstructured, or incorrect, the results may not be trustworthy, and there is cause to doubt AI analyses (Tambe et al., 2019). Apart from that, AI technology used in performance appraisal heavily relies on the smooth integration of these AI systems into the organisation. The system integration enhances inter-communication with the rest of the organisation's systems and could enhance the process of collecting and analysing data.

More so, the establishment and functioning of AI-based appraisal systems require a substantial amount of funding (Bibi, 2019). Conjuring means negotiating the costs of acquiring technology, training human resources teams and managers, and providing technical support, which is terribly impossible for organisations with weak budgets. Its execution comes down to competency in data analytics, data sciences, and the use of AI technologies (Chakraborty et al., 2020). Where these technical skills do not exist within the Human Resource teams or senior managers, training has to be provided to those managers or recruitment of workers competent in such areas. Also, some employees and managers may be unwilling to welcome the use of technology in the performance appraisal process. Acceptance and support of broader organisational culture often present a challenge to the successful implementation of AI technology (Thakre et al., 2021). Such transformations as the introduction of AI into performance appraisals must coincide with the contemporary organisation's culture. Instead, organisations should build a culture that favours the adoption of new technologies and innovation.

A prime hindrance from within the organisation includes the use of sensitive information about other employees being used for performance appraisals. Specific financial means must be acquired to use AI effectively in performance appraisals from the perspective of funding budget services (Rožman et al., 2022). The very nature of AI-induced decisions may confuse participants within organisations, leading to discomfort and loss of faith in the appraisal system.

5.1 Actionable Strategies

The growth of human resources by implementing technology tools is an essential factor in the integration of HR technology (AI) in the assessment of human resources (HR). Gulliford and Dixon (2019) state that the integration of human capital in the age of artificial intelligence means that organisations must consider options from providing their employees with training and development opportunities in AI to integrating information technology and HR functions, as well as creating frameworks for analysing the effective integration of AI through interpreting analytical results and systematic approaches that drive decision-making based on data-driven insights. The use of artificial intelligence technology in performance appraisal may require complex project management. This implies that project management skills training is needed for human resource teams to successfully plan, deliver and monitor projects (Arslan et al., 2021).

AI-powered human resource solutions are outcomes of the partnership between the human resources (HR) department and the information technology (IT) department (Achchab & Temsamani, 2021). The HR department will provide the needs and performance factors of an organisation, whereas the IT department provides technical aspects of organising and implementing AI technologies (Arora & Siradhana, 2022). Planning and designing an AI-aided performance appraisal (PE) system are the roles of these teams together. Evaluation criteria and organisational goals will be input by the HR department. The IT department, in turn, could provide the tech and algorithms needed to execute the system. Technical support and maintenance services will be ongoing for the appraisal system after implementation, and both teams should work in synchronisation. Together, they will ensure the seamless running of systems, avoid data loss and rapid rectification for technical blunders. Performance appraisal needs organisations to establish KPIs that are associated directly with the right use of AI. These KPIs could have the employee perception, efficiency that is processed on an individual level and efficacy of assessment. Employee feedback will be useful in identifying deficiencies and personalisation of the system according to organisation needs. The organisation must periodically evaluate how its performance appraisal strategy with AI integrates into the business delivery. If technology is different from strategising of the business, then there should be corrective measures and changes (Dabbous et al., 2021)

6 FUTURE PROSPECTS

The most remarkable thing about performance management through AI is the steadily developing systems of automated performance appraisal. AI technologies can collect information from massive amounts of data to give more impartial and precise evaluations concerning employee performance. This could decrease bias, which is meant to allow promotion and reward processes based on a merit system. This would allow for recognition of the area of development as well. The risk lies in the complete automation of the appraisal process. Furthermore, excessive dependence on AI will lessen the role of human judgement and empathy, thereby stunting the development of workers and cutting off the chances of engaging their colleagues. Thus, effective balance is necessary between automating this process and maintaining human involvement to ensure that a performance appraisal still retains total objectivity and, at the same time, a human meaning (Glikson & Woolley, 2020).

AI-enhanced coaching systems help employees with personalised guidance and support, which are suitable in harmony with their special needs and aspirations (Grabmann & Schermuly, 2021). These systems are able to analyse the performance metrics, identify strengths and weaknesses, and suggest recommendations to improve them. AI coaches provide instant feedback and motivation, building new skills, boosting employee confidence, and facilitating their potential growth. Personalised learning platforms use appropriate artificial intelligence to customise training programs in line with each learner's style, pace, and progress (Maity, 2019). These platforms will find what is missing in the knowledge and change the learning content for these areas of weakness. Personalised learning platforms provide context and context in-depth learning experiences for individual employees, thereby increasing the efficacy and efficiency of skill acquisition.

Moreover, Natural Language Processing (NLP) can be used as a tool to read feedback from employees, identify trends, and understand the deeper meaning of the organisational culture (Johnson et al., 2020). Analysis of survey feedback, appraisals and other textual data lets us in on NLP-based findings about the sentiment of employees, areas for improvement and the effects of HR initiatives. As a form of analytics, predictive analytics uses historical data to predict patterns and trend forecasted results in the future for organisations. Predictive analytics, based on examining employee performance metrics and attendance logs, among other significant variables, allows organisations to identify potential low-performers or quitters (Cao & Yao, 2020). Armed with this information, an organisation can sequence and operationalise steps to pre-empt probable shortfalls while implementing an advanced intervention to reduce mass leakages. As the progression of the technological age advances, a drastic change in the process of performing performance appraisal should be expected. AI-based coaching, advanced learning management systems, natural language processing, and predictive analytics will give companies the EDGE to tailor performance assessments effectively and efficiently (Newman et al., 2020). Introducing this technology in an organisation will elevate engagement, fairness, and performance.

7 CONCLUSION

Even though AI can benefit your performance appraisal systems immensely, one must recognise its limitations and strike a balance between such and human intelligence. While AI can analyse information quickly and without bias, it may not pick up on the nuances of employee behaviour or more extensive context clues to performance. In addition, AI algorithms can further affirm or exacerbate existing biases if not painstakingly constructed and overseen. Second, AI cannot replicate the creativity of human evaluators or their ability to feel empathy with regard to interpersonal skills. Human check-ups are done more frequently in AI-based performance appraisals to determine where human judgment should take precedence over machine judgment. This will help the organisation treat AI as an assisting solution to human judgement because human judgement will continue to be the final decision. The principle behind AI use in HRM raises considerable ethical concerns. AI software is designed to eradicate bias and promote fairness and justice. Yet, at the same time, care should be taken not to err in the field of employee data privacy. Without such guarantees, AI applications should not expect much transparency and accountability to generate the required degree of trust and indisputable ethics. In short, AI has a great opportunity for performance appraisals mechanised with data-driven and somewhat unbiased measurements. However, it does not remotely suggest that AI can easily replace human judgment. When automation is combined with human contributions correctly, organisations can capitalise on both — and deliver a complete and unbiased performance appraisal process more effectively. These mandates establishing clear standards for AI application, investing in employee training, and ongoing appraisal to use these technologies more efficiently while favouring human judgement on things that matter the most. In addition, we need to identify on an ongoing basis the ethical considerations and challenges of employing AI in human resource management so that its potential benefits can be realised while avoiding possible undesired outcomes.

REFERENCES

Achchab, S., & Temsamani, Y. K. (2021). Artificial Intelligence Use in Human Resources Management: Strategy and Operation's Impact. 2021 IEEE 2nd International Conference on Pattern Recognition and Machine Learning (PRML), 311–315. https://api.semanticscholar.org/CorpusID:237328919

Acikgoz, Y., Davison, K. H., Compagnone, M., & Laske, M. (2020). Justice perceptions of artificial intelligence in selection. International Journal of Selection and Assessment. DOI: 10.1111/ijsa.12306

Alam, M., & Singh, P. (2021). Performance feedback interviews as affective events: An exploration of the impact of emotion regulation of negative performance feedback on supervisor–employee dyads. *Human Resource Management Review*, 31(2), 100740. DOI: 10.1016/j.hrmr.2019.100740

Ali, Al Shawabkeh, Salameh, & Al Amro. (2019). Performance predicting in hiring process and performance appraisals using machine learning. IEEE Conference Publication https://ieeexplore.ieee.org/abstract/document/8809154

Alrashedi, A. and Abbod, M. (2020). The effect of using artificial intelligence on performance of appraisal system: a case study for University of Jeddah staff in Saudi Arabia. DOI: 10.1007/978-3-030-55180-3_11

Arora, R. G., & Siradhana, N. K. (2022). HR Transformation Through Artificial Intelligence: An Insight Through Literature Survey. *International Journal of Information Systems and Social Change*, 13(1), 1–16. DOI: 10.4018/IJISSC.309736

Arslan, A., Cooper, C. D., Khan, Z., Golgeci, I., & Ali, I. (2021). Artificial intelligence and human workers interaction at team level: a conceptual assessment of the challenges and potential HRM strategies. International Journal of Manpower. https://api.semanticscholar.org/CorpusID:237728755

Awan, S. H., Habib, N., Shoaib Akhtar, C., & Naveed, S. (2020). Effectiveness of Performance Management System for Employee Performance Through Engagement. *SAGE Open*, 10(4). DOI: 10.1177/2158244020969383

Basu, S., Majumdar, B., Mukherjee, K., Munjal, S., & Palaksha, C. (2023). Artificial Intelligence–HRM Interactions and Outcomes: A Systematic Review and Causal Configurational Explanation. *Human Resource Management Review*, 33(1), 100893. DOI: 10.1016/j.hrmr.2022.100893

Berger, B., Adam, M., Rühr, A., & Benlian, A. (2021). Watch me improve – Algorithm aversion and demonstrating the ability to learn. *Business & Information Systems Engineering*, 63(1), 55–68. DOI: 10.1007/s12599-020-00678-5

Bibi, M. (2019). Execution of artificial intelligence approach in human resource management functions: Benefits and challenges in Pakistan. *Sarhad Journal of Management Sciences*, 5(1), 113–124. DOI: 10.31529/sjms.2018.5.1.8

Biswas, M. I., Talukder, M. S., & Khan, A. R. (2024). Who do you choose? Employees' perceptions of artificial intelligence versus humans in performance feedback. *China Accounting and Finance Review*, 26(4), 512–532. DOI: 10.1108/CAFR-08-2023-0095

Bogani, R., Theodorou, A., Arnaboldi, L., & Wortham, R. H. (2023). Garbage in, toxic data out: A proposal for ethical artificial intelligence sustainability impact statements. *AI and Ethics*, 3(4), 1135–1142. DOI: 10.1007/s43681-022-00221-0 PMID: 36281314

Buck, B., & Morrow, J. (2018). AI, performance management and engagement: Keeping your best their best. *Strategic HR Review*, 17(5), 261–262. DOI: 10.1108/SHR-10-2018-145

Budhwar, P., Malik, A., De Silva, M. T. T., & Thevisuthan, P. (2022). Artificial intelligence – challenges and opportunities for international HRM: A review and research agenda. *International Journal of Human Resource Management*, 33(6), 1065–1097. DOI: 10.1080/09585192.2022.2035161

Bughin, J., & Manyika, J. (2019). Your AI efforts Won't succeed unless they benefit employees. Harvard Business Review https://hbr.org/2019/07/your-ai-efforts-wont-succeed-unless-they-benefit-employees

Burbach, R. (2018). *Strategic evaluation of e-HRM. In e-HRM*. Routledge.

Cantarelli, P. (2023). People Administration. In Management and Performance in Mission Driven Organizations (pp. 77-89). Springer Nature Switzerland. DOI: 10.1007/978-3-031-40490-0_5

Cao, J., & Yao, J. (2020). Linking different artificial intelligence functions to employees' psychological appraisals and work. *Proceedings - Academy of Management*, 2020(1), 19876. DOI: 10.5465/AMBPP.2020.105

Casey, T., Turner, N., Hu, X., & Bancroft, K. (2021). Making safety training stickier: A richer model of safety training engagement and transfer. *Journal of Safety Research*, 78, 303–313. DOI: 10.1016/j.jsr.2021.06.004 PMID: 34399927

Castelo, N., Bos, M. W., & Lehmann, D. R. (2019). Task-dependent algorithm aversion. *JMR, Journal of Marketing Research*, 56(5), 809–825. DOI: 10.1177/0022243719851788

Chakraborty, S., Giri, A., Aich, A., & Biswas, S. (2020). Evaluating Influence of Artificial Intelligence on Human Resource Management Using PLS-SEM. *International Journal of Science & Technology Research*, 9(3), 58765880.

Chang, K. (2020). Artificial intelligence in personnel management: The development of APM model. *The Bottom Line (New York, N.Y.)*, 33(4), 377–388. DOI: 10.1108/BL-08-2020-0055

Cheatham, B., Javanmardian, K., & Samandari, H. (2019). Confronting AI risks. McKinsey Quarterly. Available from https://www.mckinsey.com/business-functions/mckinsey-analytics/our-insights/confronting-the-risksof-artificial-intelligence#

Cheng, M. M., & Hackett, R. D. (2021). A critical review of algorithms in HRM: Definition, theory, and practice. *Human Resource Management Review*, 31(1), 100698. DOI: 10.1016/j.hrmr.2019.100698

Chowdhury, S., Dey, P., Joel-Edgar, S., Bhattacharya, S., Rodriguez-Espindola, O., Abadie, A., & Truong, L. (2023). Unlocking the value of artificial intelligence in human resource management through AI capability framework. *Human Resource Management Review*, 33(1), 100899. DOI: 10.1016/j.hrmr.2022.100899

Chukwuka, E. J., & Dibie, K. E. (2024). Strategic Role of Artificial Intelligence (AI) on Human Resource Management (HR) Employee Performance Evaluation Function. *International Journal of Entrepreneurship and Business Innovation*, 7(2), 269–282. DOI: 10.52589/IJEBI-HET5STYK

Colangelo, M. (2020). Mass adoption of AI in financial services expected within two years. Forbes. Available from https://www.forbes.com/sites/cognitiveworld/2020/02/20/mass-adoption-of-ai-in-financial-services-expectedwithin-two-years/#58e29b667d71

Crolic, C., Thomaz, F., Hadi, R., & Stephen, A. T. (2022). Blame the Bot: Anthropomorphism and Anger in Customer–Chatbot Interactions. *Journal of Marketing*, 86(1), 132–148. DOI: 10.1177/00222429211045687

Dabbous, A., Barakat, K. A., & Sayegh, M. M. (2021). Enabling organizational use of artificial intelligence: an employee perspective. Journal of Asia Business Studies. https://api.semanticscholar.org/CorpusID:233932158

DeNisi, A. S., & Pritchard, R. D. (2006). Performance Appraisal, Performance Management and Improving Individual Performance: A Motivational Framework. *Management and Organization Review*, 2(2), 253–277. DOI: 10.1111/j.1740-8784.2006.00042.x

Dixit, A. S., & Jatav, S. (2024). Evolving needs of learners and role of artificial intelligence (AI) in training and development (T&D): T&D professionals' perspective. Journal of Management Development. DOI: 10.1108/JMD-01-2024-0009

Edwin, E. I., Ugwu, C. C. O., & Obumnaeme, I. K. (2024). Implementation of Artificial Intelligence on Personnel Management in a Dynamic Society. *Management*, 12(2), 41–52.

El-Ghoul, M., Almassri, M. M., El-Habibi, M. F., Al-Qadi, M. H., Abou Eloun, A., Abu-Nasser, B. S., & Abu-Naser, S. S. (2024). AI in HRM: Revolutionizing Recruitment, Performance Management, and Employee Engagement. *International Journal of Academic Applied Research (Ijaar)*, 8(9), 16–23.

Faqihi, A., & Miah, S. J. (2023). Artificial Intelligence-Driven Talent Management System: Exploring the Risks and Options for Constructing a Theoretical Foundation. *Journal of Risk and Financial Management*, 16(1), 31. DOI: 10.3390/jrfm16010031

Glikson, E., & Woolley, A. W. (2020). Human Trust in Artificial Intelligence: Review of Empirical Research. *The Academy of Management Annals*, 14(2), 627–660. DOI: 10.5465/annals.2018.0057

Grabmann, C., & Schermuly, C. C. (2021). Coaching With Artificial Intelligence: Concepts and Capabilities. *Human Resource Development Review*, 20(1), 106–126. DOI: 10.1177/1534484320982891

Greene, T. (2018). IBM is using its AI to predict how employees will perform. Retrieved from https://thenextweb.com/artificial-intelligence/2018/07/10/ibm-is-using-its-ai-topredict-how-employees-will-perform/

Grund, C., & Przemeck, J. (2012). Subjective performance appraisal and inequality aversion. *Applied Economics*, 44(17), 2149–2155. DOI: 10.1080/00036846.2011.560109

Guan, H., Liye, D., & Zhao, A. (2022). Ethical risk factors and mechanisms in artificial intelligence decision making. *Behavioral Sciences (Basel, Switzerland)*, 12(9), 343. DOI: 10.3390/bs12090343 PMID: 36135147

Gulliford, F., & Dixon, A. P. (2019). AI: the HR revolution. Strategic HR Review. https://api.semanticscholar.org/CorpusID:159308484

Halid, H., Ravesangar, K., Mahadzir, S. L., & Halim, S. N. A. (2024). Artificial Intelligence (AI) in Human Resource Management (HRM). In Machado, C. (Ed.), *Building the Future with Human Resource Management* (pp. 37–70). Springer International Publishing. DOI: 10.1007/978-3-031-52811-8_2

Heaven, W. D. (2020). This startup is using AI to give workers a "productivity score". MIT Technology Review. Available from https://www.technologyreview.com/2020/06/04/1002671/startup-ai-workers-productivityscore-bias-machine-learning-business-covid/?mod=djemAIPro

Hmoud, B. (2021) The adoption of artificial intelligence in human resource management and the role of human resources. Questa Soft https://www.ceeol.com/search/articledetail?id=940529

Holsinger, L. (2019). Performance Transformation in the Future of Work. Mercer. https://www.mercer.com/our-thinking/career/performance-transformation-in-the-futureof-work.html

Hristov, I., Camilli, R., & Mechelli, A. (2022). Cognitive biases in implementing a performance management system: Behavioral strategy for supporting managers' decision-making processes. *Management Research Review*, 45(9), 1110–1136. DOI: 10.1108/MRR-11-2021-0777

Huang, X., Yang, F., Zheng, J., Feng, C., & Zhang, L. (2023). Personalized human resource management via HR analytics and artificial intelligence: Theory and implications. Asia Pacific Management Review, 28(4), 598-610. https://doi.org/https://doi.org/10.1016/j.apmrv.2023.04.004

Hunkenschroer, A. L., & Luetge, C. (2022). Ethics of AI-Enabled Recruiting and Selection: A Review and Research agenda. *Journal of Business Ethics*, 178(4), 977–1007. DOI: 10.1007/s10551-022-05049-6

Jarrahi, M. H. (2018). Artificial intelligence and the future of work: Human-AI symbiosis in organizational decision making. *Business Horizons*, 61(4), 577–586. DOI: 10.1016/j.bushor.2018.03.007

Johnson, R., Stone, D., & Lukaszewski, K. (2020). The benefits of ehrm and ai for talent acquisition. *Journal of Tourism Futures*, 7(1), 40–52. DOI: 10.1108/JTF-02-2020-0013

Knight, R. (2020). How to Do Performance Reviews — Remotely. Harvard Business Review. https://hbr.org/2020/06/how-to-do-performance-reviews-remotely

Langer, M., König, C. J., & Hemsing, V. (2020). Is anybody listening? The impact of automatically evaluated job interviews on impression management and applicant reactions. *Journal of Managerial Psychology*, 35(4), 271–284. DOI: 10.1108/JMP-03-2019-0156

Langer, M., König, C. J., & Papathanasiou, M. (2019). Highly automated job interviews: Acceptance under the influence of stakes. *International Journal of Selection and Assessment*, 27(3), 217234. DOI: 10.1111/ijsa.12246

Leavitt, K., Barnes, C. M., & Shapiro, D. L. (2022). The Role of Human Managers within Algorithmic Performance Management Systems: A Process Model of Employee Trust in Managers through Reflexivity. Academy of Management Review. DOI: 10.5465/amr.2022.0058

Logg, J. M., Minson, J. A., & Moore, D. A. (2019). Algorithm appreciation: People prefer algorithmic to human judgment. *Organizational Behavior and Human Decision Processes*, 151(151), 90–103. DOI: 10.1016/j.obhdp.2018.12.005

MacCarthy, M. (2020). AI needs more regulation, not less. Brookings Institution. https://www.brookings.edu/research/ai-needs-more-regulation-not-less/

Maity, S. (2019). Identifying opportunities for artificial intelligence in the evolution of training and development practices. *Journal of Management Development*, 651663(8), 651–663. Advance online publication. DOI: 10.1108/JMD-03-2019-0069

Malik, A., Srikanth, N., & Budhwar, P. (2020). Digitisation, artificial intelligence (AI) and HRM. Human resource management: Strategic and international perspectives, 88, 103.

Mozafari, N., Weiger, W. H., & Hammerschmidt, M. (2020). The Chatbot Disclosure Dilemma: Desirable and Undesirable Effects of Disclosing the Non-Human Identity of Chatbots.

Na-Nan, K., Kanthong, S., Joungtrakul, J., & Smith, I. D. (2020). Mediating Effects of Job Satisfaction and Organizational Commitment between Problems with Performance Appraisal and Organizational Citizenship Behavior. *Journal of Open Innovation*, 6(3), 64. DOI: 10.3390/joitmc6030064

Nasr, M., Shaaban, E., & Samir, A. (2019). A proposed Model for Predicting Employees' Performance Using Data Mining Techniques: Egyptian Case Study. *International Journal of Computer Science and Information Security*, 17(1), 31–40. DOI: 10.5815/ijcsis.2019.01.04

Nawaz, N., Arunachalam, H., Pathi, B. K., & Gajenderan, V. (2024). The adoption of artificial intelligence in human resources management practices. *International Journal of Information Management Data Insights*, 4(1), 100208. DOI: 10.1016/j.jjimei.2023.100208

Newman, D., Fast, N., & Harmon, D. (2020). When eliminating bias isn't fair: Algorithmic reductionism and procedural justice in human resource decisions. *Organizational Behavior and Human Decision Processes*, 160, 149–167. DOI: 10.1016/j.obhdp.2020.03.008

Nicolescu, L., & Tudorache, M. T. (2022). HumanComputer Interaction in Customer Service: The Experience with AI Chatbots—A Systematic Literature Review. *Electronics (Basel)*, 11(10), 10. Advance online publication. DOI: 10.3390/electronics11101579

Ntoutsi, E., Fafalios, P., Gadiraju, U., Iosifidis, V., Nejdl, W., Vidal, M.-E., Ruggieri, S., Turini, F., Papadopoulos, S., Krasanakis, E., Kompatsiaris, I., Kinder-Kurlanda, K., Wagner, C., Karimi, F., Fernandez, M., Alani, H., Berendt, B., Kruegel, T., Heinze, C., & Staab, S. (2020). Bias in data-driven artificial intelligence systems—An introductory survey. *Wiley Interdisciplinary Reviews. Data Mining and Knowledge Discovery*, 10(3), e1356. DOI: 10.1002/widm.1356

Nyathani, R. (2023). AI in performance management: redefining performance appraisals in the digital age. Journal of Artificial Intelligence & Cloud Computing. DOI: 10.47363/JAICC/2023

O'keefe, J., Moss, D., Martinez, T., & Rose, P. (2019). Professional perspective AI regulation and risks to employers. https://bna.com/copyright-permission-request/

O'Pry, S. C., & Schumacher, G. (2012). New teachers' perceptions of a standards-based performance appraisal system. *Educational Assessment, Evaluation and Accountability*, 24(4), 325–350. DOI: 10.1007/s11092-012-9148-4

Pan, Y., & Froese, F. J. (2023). An interdisciplinary review of AI and HRM: Challenges and future directions. *Human Resource Management Review*, 33(1), 100924. DOI: 10.1016/j.hrmr.2022.100924

Park, H., Ahn, D., Hosanagar, K., & Lee, J. (2021). Human-AI Interaction in Human Resource Management: Understanding Why Employees Resist Algorithmic Evaluation at Workplaces and How to Mitigate Burdens Proceedings of the 2021 CHI Conference on Human Factors in Computing Systems. DOI: 10.1145/3411764.3445304

Profit, C. (2023) Use of artificial intelligence in performance reviews. Best OKR Software by Profit.co https://www.profit.co/article/performance-management/useof-artificial-intelligence-in-performance-reviews/

Rajapakse, V. (2024). Performance Management Process: Performance Reviewing. In Employee Performance Management for Improved Workplace Motivation (pp. 57-90). IGI Global. DOI: 10.4018/979-8-3693-4387-6.ch003

Reddy Yanamala, K. K. (2022). Integrating Machine Learning and Human Feedback for Employee Performance Evaluation. *Journal of Advanced Computing Systems*, 2(1), 1–10. DOI: 10.69987/JACS.2022.20101

Reddy Yanamala, K. K. (2023). AI and the Future of Cognitive Decision-Making in HR. Applied Research in Artificial Intelligence and Cloud Computing, 6(9), 31-46. https://researchberg.com/index.php/araic/article/view/204

Reim, W., Åström, J., & Eriksson, O. (2020). Implementation of Artificial Intelligence (AI): A Roadmap for Business Model Innovation. *AI*, 1(2), 180191. DOI: 10.3390/ai1020011

Rese, A., Ganster, L., & Baier, D. (2020). Chatbots in retailers' customer communication: How to measure their acceptance? *Journal of Retailing and Consumer Services*, 56, 102176. DOI: 10.1016/j.jretconser.2020.102176

Riaz & Ghanghas. (2024). Artificial Intelligence in Employee Performance Evaluation and Its Managerial Implication. *Journal of Informatics Education and Research.*, 4(1), 299–307. DOI: 10.52783/jier.v4i1.559

Rosenbaum, E. (2019). IBM artificial intelligence can predict with 95% accuracy which workers are about to quit their jobs. Retrieved from https://www.cnbc.com/2019/04/03/ibm-ai-can-predict-with-95-percent-accuracy-whichemployees-will-quit.html

Rožman, M., Oreški, D., & Tominc, P. (2022). Integrating artificial intelligence into a talent management model to increase the work engagement and performance of enterprises. *Frontiers in Psychology*, 13, 1014434. Advance online publication. DOI: 10.3389/fpsyg.2022.1014434 PMID: 36506984

Saeij, M. (2020). *Why Implementing AI and ML is a Must for Credit Managers.* Barclays.

Smith, C. L. (2019). An employee's best friend? How AI can boost employee engagement and performance. *Strategic HR Review*, 18(1), 17–20. DOI: 10.1108/SHR-11-2018-0092

Stone, D. L., Deadrick, D. L., Lukaszewski, K. M., & Johnson, R. (2015). The influence of technology on the future of human resource management. *Human Resource Management Review*, 25(2), 216–231. DOI: 10.1016/j.hrmr.2015.01.002

Tambe, P., Cappelli, P., & Yakubovich, V. (2019). Artificial Intelligence in Human Resources Management: Challenges and a Path Forward. *California Management Review*, 61(4), 15–42. DOI: 10.1177/0008125619867910

Thakre, G., Wankhede, P., Patle, S., Joshi, S., & Chauhan, A. (2021). Implementation of Machine Learning Model for Employee Retention Prediction. *International Journal of Scientific Research in Science and Technology*, 8(3), 503–508. DOI: 10.32628/IJSRST2183122

Tong, S., Jia, N., Luo, X., & Fang, Z. (2021). The Janus face of artificial intelligence feedback: Deployment versus disclosure effects on employee performance. *Strategic Management Journal*, 42(9), 1600–1631. Advance online publication. DOI: 10.1002/smj.3322

Varsha, P. S. (2023). How can we manage biases in artificial intelligence systems – A systematic literature review. *International Journal of Information Management Data Insights*, 3(1), 100165. DOI: 10.1016/j.jjimei.2023.100165

Vincent, V. U. (2021). Integrating intuition and artificial intelligence in organizational decision-making. *Business Horizons*, 64(4), 425–438. DOI: 10.1016/j.bushor.2021.02.008

Wilkinson, S. (2021). Machine Learning for Performance Management. Cimlogic. [online] Retrieved from https://www.cimlogic.co.uk/article/machine-learning-for-performance- management/

Wisniewski, B., Zierer, K., & Hattie, J. (2020). The power of feedback revisited: A meta-analysis of educational feedback research. *Frontiers in Psychology*, 10, 3087. DOI: 10.3389/fpsyg.2019.03087 PMID: 32038429

Yu, M. C. (2018). Viewing expert judgment in individual assessments through the Lens Model: Testing the limits of expert information processing. PhD, University of Minnesota.

Zhou, Y., Wang, L., & Chen, W. (2023). The dark side of AI-enabled HRM on employees based on AI algorithmic features. *Journal of Organizational Change Management*, 36(7), 1222–1241. DOI: 10.1108/JOCM-10-2022-0308

Chapter 16
Trends of Artificial Intelligence in Human Resources Management Using Bibliometric Analysis

Wei Chien Ng
https://orcid.org/0000-0003-1293-6781
Universiti Sains Malaysia, Malaysia

Kamalesh Ravesangar
https://orcid.org/0009-0004-2154-184X
Tunku Abdul Rahman University of Management and Technology, Malaysia

Guat Guan Toh
Tunku Abdul Rahman University of Management and Technology, Malaysia

Yu Qing Soong
Tunku Abdul Rahman University of Management and Technology, Malaysia

ABSTRACT

Human resource management (HRM) is essential in organizations, as employees drive productivity and growth. To improve HRM, many practitioners are implementing artificial intelligence (AI). This chapter explores AI's significant impact on HRM through a bibliometric and visualization analysis of 676 research articles from the Scopus database, covering studies from 1991 to September 2024. Key areas examined include leading authors, countries, institutions, journals, and research

DOI: 10.4018/979-8-3693-9395-6.ch016

themes using VOSviewer. Findings reveal China, the United States, and India as top contributors, with Human Resource Management Review publishing the highest number of articles (10) and Aston University having the most contributions (15). No single author dominated, with a maximum of six articles published by one individual. This study also suggests future research directions, offering valuable insights for researchers and organizational leaders to leverage AI for enhanced HRM practices.

INTRODUCTION

A large number of organizations in various sectors today are implementing or have an interest in implementing artificial intelligence (AI) (Füller et al., 2022). Industries such as telecommunications, engineering, financial services, customer service, healthcare, pharmaceuticals, and educational institutions are at the forefront of adopting AI tools and technologies (Perifanis & Kitsios, 2023). The fast pace of digitization, and AI's acceptance in particular, is changing the face of business (Javaid et al., 2022). AI has changed how organizations operate and has become part of corporate strategy. Human Resources Management (HRM) departments are affected in a similar way. The HRM role has changed in many dimensions, creating a redefined impact on both micro-organizational and macro-economic levels (Hmoud & Varallyai, 2023). As a result, there has been a clear transformation in the HRM role, with an increase in focus on strategic aspects. AI in HRM can provide organizations better capacity, more value-adding insights, and analytical support, ultimately allowing personnel management to be more effective.

AI is an initiative technological advancement with implications for the workplace. We must understand the impact of AI development on research (Tambe et al., 2019). Once AI proliferates, it could eliminate many jobs in an already unequal social structure, or it could lead to advances in job quality or number of jobs that exist rather than simply eliminate them. With these conditions, it is apparent that AI will have a vast influence on the future of human resource management (HRM). The promise of AI integration into HRM is significant and can generate numerous impressive outcomes (Radonjić et al., 2022). The interdisciplinary character of AI IN HRM goes far beyond the typically understood scope of standard HRM practices. While AI-driven HR solutions depend mainly on technological developments, their application and implications must be illuminated by the social sciences. Scholars across disciplines have significantly contributed to the emergence of artificial intelligence and human resource management (Saini & Tarkar, 2022). For example, in computer science, researchers have developed AI algorithms meant to aid in addressing problems encountered by practitioners in human resource management (HRM). While there is a myriad of research on the intersection of AI and HRM across many fields, it must be recognized that each field has contributed their expertise, frequently overlooking the advantages of an interdisciplinary approach. It is surprising that many departments in various organisations are utilising AI-driven tools in their daily efforts, but Human Resources (HR) departments, as reported by Glawat et al., have struggled mightily when attempting to utilise the AI in HRM technologies (2022).

Historically, the integration of technology and human resource management can be classified into four phases. First, human resource managers employed human resource management information systems to support planning, management, decision-making, and control activities in order to minimise business employment costs (Verma & Bandi, 2019). In the 1990s, electronic human resource management appeared - the strategic application of information technology in human resource practices. This innovation increased employee involvement in human resource departments and influenced their work behaviours. By the early 21st century, organisations began engaging in virtual human resource management - the network technology-enabled new framework prioritising partnerships and information technology to support the acquisition, development, and use of intellectual capital. With the digital age underway, new information technologies emerged - particularly big data - resulting in the advent of big data human resource management - the use of big data to drive organizational human resource, change employee experience, and create value within the organization (Vrontis et al., 2023). The emergence of big data technology has effectively changed a significant portion of the internal and external conditions of enterprises, with important implications for their survival and growth (Zhang & Chen, 2024). Human resources are the basis for this survival and growth. Therefore, it is essential to examine human resource management through the lens of big data. Researchers have already begun looking into this area, with Ameer et al. (2020) commenting that human resource management with big data has provided quality upgrades to the traditional relationship model of information that creates competitive advantage for enterprises. Verma and Bandi (2019) also defined Big Data HRM and reviewed evidence regarding its influence on the quality of human resource services and the innovativeness of small-medium enterprises.

Human beings are inherently visual thinkers, famously captured in the adage, a picture is worth a thousand words. A study by 3M Corporation in 1997 showed that the human brain processes visual information 60,000 times faster than text. Data visualization is a graphical means to represent information, the process of taking data and converting it into a visual image. This can be accomplished with many optical elements, using graphs, charts, dashboards, or even maps. Studies (Khan, 2021) used COVID-19 data and the SEIR prediction model to present the data. Data visualization is more than just a visual attraction, the ultimate goal of data visualization is to simplify complex and/or large datasets and communicate the critical elements of a dataset through visualization (Ameer et al., 2020). Data visualization and visualization overall is located somewhere at the intersection of information science, communication, and design. Visual analytic tools, such as Power BI, Tableau, Excel, and Python (Wang et al., 2021) which allow users to visualize large datasets into actionable insights for business. These tools allow decision/ business users to engage with the data by looking for new patterns, relationships within the data, and using evidence to make informed decisions based on data. In terms of human resource management, data visualization can provide an organization with a good advantage. Good human resource analytics and visualization aids the organization in meeting business targets and needs, reducing human risk, obtaining a competitive advantage, and improving return on investment of the people. However, it is important to understand what the perceptions are of how the practitioner interprets HR data visualization and makes decisions on that interpretation (Gong et al., 2022).

That is why the introduction of artificial intelligence (AI) into the human resource management (HRM) brings a number of issues and dilemmas. The other issue is ethical concern like the algorithm being an issue and impact on employee's privacy. From the viewpoint of eliminating bias and making the decision-making process fair it required transparency, accountability and fairness from AI systems. Also, where AI takes over some tasks or undertakes the tasks on behalf of the employees, there are genuine concerns associated with the loss of employment and changing roles of CHROs (Jayawarden, et.al, 2020). Such challenges can be addressed only through a transformation of roles and responsibilities, development of human capital and change of management relationships where human and AI coexist. AI integration in the context of the HRM is predicted to grow and diversify in the next years. New developments in AI should be expected to enhance the future of HRM, including the processes of workforce planning as well as the support of strategic decision-making (Budhwar, et.al, 2022). First of all, for the efficient combination of human insights and artificial intelligence it is possible to improve the organisational performance; however, these two approaches should be used bearing in mind the following disadvantages. Despite the optimistic trends for the future, organisations need not relax because the problems will persist. With the help of the mentioned impact AI eliminates different works, enhances decision-making, and enhances the overall experience of employees in the field of HRM. Of course, there are some obstacles in the way of those organisations that incorporate the use of AI in HRM, but in theory, the organisations success is likely to be higher because the organisations use AI to attract the best employees. However, they can also streamline HR operations and enhance overall productivity (Jose, et.al, 2019). Although this transformation is promising, it requires careful consideration and adaptation.

The first part of a bibliometric analysis exploring Human Resource Management (HRM) in the context of Artificial Intelligence (AI), as shown (Kaushal et al., 2023), sets the stage for the work while describing the importance and context of the study. It has more recently, as noted (Mathushan et al., 2023), become an area of interest to organizational researchers. AI, the authors note, provides organizations and HR professionals with unique opportunities but significant challenges, as it relates to an evolving AI-based 21st century workplace. In work highlighting the need to study the changing context for HRM in light of AI, Khan (2020) emphasized the importance of understanding the shifting terrain around HRM. Therefore, this bibliometric and visualisation analysis will address the significant body of literature that has been developed in this important area. The intent of this analysis is to use bibliometric tools and techniques to identify not only trends arising in the literature, but also HRM challenges in the age of AI. Consequently, this study addresses the following research questions (RQs):

1. What is the publication trend based on the number of articles by year of AI in HRM?
2. What are the leading publications, outlets and key articles on AI in HRM?
3. Who are the leading contributors in terms of authors, countries, and institutions for AI in HRM?
4. What are the main research themes and future research direction of AI in HRM?

The remainder of this study is presented as follows. First, the literature summary of AI in HRM is presented. This is followed by a description of bibliometric methodology used in this study. Subsequently, this study analyses and presents the findings from the bibliometric analysis of AI in HRM research. Finally, it outlines the future research avenues in the field of AI in HRM.

DATA SOURCE AND METHODS

Data Source

The rationale for deciding on the articles for this review was performed in September 2024 employing the search strategy described by Kumar and his colleagues (2021). This strategy encompasses four stages such as database search, scholarly filtration, language filtration, and subject filtration. At the first step, the articles were retrieved only from the Scopus database. Kumar et al. (2021) have substantiated Scopus due to its rigorous indexing guidelines which in appeal only the scientifically and academically creditworthy articles along with the abundance of bibliometrics. Scopus is deemed as an acceptable source for building up a sizeable pool of literature for the purpose of reviewing (Paul et al., 2021) and is often recommended for bibliographic analyses (Donthu et al., 2021). Furthermore, it is accepted that Scopus is a proper source of bibliometric data (Baas, 2020). The dependability of the metrics provided by Scopus and other databases, including Web of Science, is striking (Archambault et al., 2009), though Scopus covers more sources and is a more comprehensive and high-quality database for bibliometric reviews (Paul et al., 2021).

For this reason, the keywords used in this case were: "artificial intelligence*" joined with "human resource management" and "HRM". The search was restricted to articles and conference proceedings to and including the year 2024. The first database search produced a total of 1717 articles. The second part of the study was scholarly filtration, whereby only the journal articles met the inclusion criteria. These types of publications were chosen because they generally stand a chance of having passed through novelty evaluation and peer review, which are critical for capturing as much diverse knowledge as possible and for ensuring that any reporting of insights is of high quality. After this filtration process another 1138 articles were removed leading to final select of 579 articles to be examined.

In the third stage, language limitation was implemented regarding only English articles were selected compared with the second stage. This choice was made for two main reasons: first, the researchers are native English speakers; second, it is impossible to translate articles due to the large dataset's characteristic of bibliometric reviews. They called for more studies examining the potential impact of multiple or cross effects within the associations by linking together the factors under review. Due to this filtration, 25 articles were eliminated out of 554 articles for further analysis. Filtration by subject was conducted in stage 4. Since AI in HRM is interdisciplinary by nature, the study decided to incorporate all disciplines in the analysis in case anything of value was missed. Therefore, the final selection included only 554 articles out of the articles available for the current study after passing through all the phases of the filtering process.

Figure 1. Search and filtration steps for bibliometric review

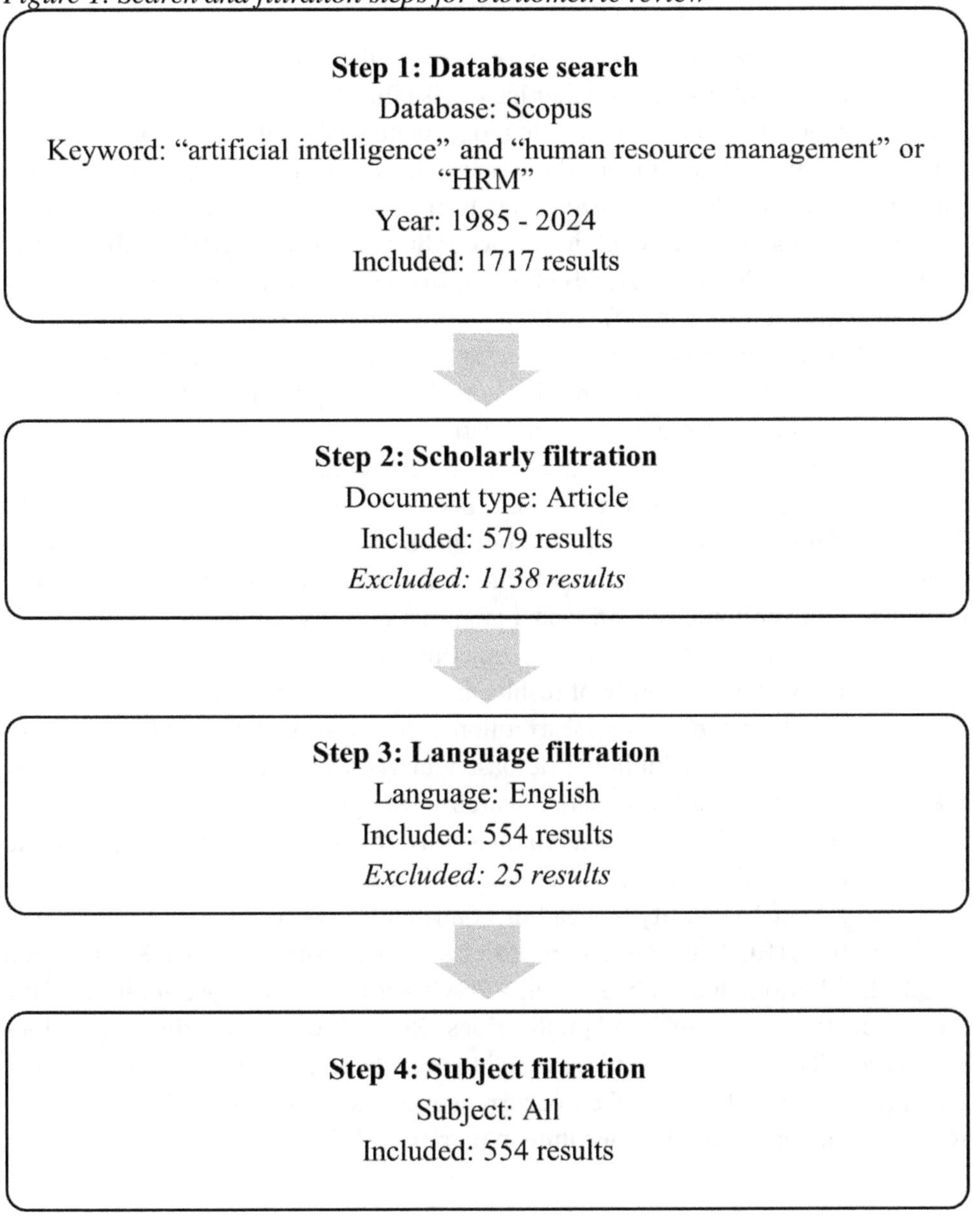

Methods

Bibliometric analysis is used as a tool to assess the scientific outputs of authors, institutions or countries, on the other hand, visualized analysis simply presents the data in graphical form thus highlighting main features for enhanced understanding. It is this visualization technique which makes it easy for users to quickly filter and interpret a study on the generalized aspects of data. One of the most popular tools for semi-visual analysis is VOSviewer, according to (Li et al., 2022). Bibliometric analysis successfully identifies and contributes to the specification of promising topics and key researchers of a specific field. It involves study of publication information, citing behaviour, authors' identities, the most common words and the institutions and countries to which they belong (Li et al., 2022). Application such as VOSviewer are used to develop graphical visualizations of the density, co-citation, trends, and relationships in bibliometric data, which help researchers and policymakers in understanding the current research trends and developments in the different fields. Therefore, for the purpose of carrying out this bibliometric analysis, this study selected VOSviewer as the tool for visualisation. VOSviewer is one of the first tools considered for bibliometric and visual analysis; recently, Chhtrapati et al. (2021) and McAllister et al. (2022) confirmed that this tool is popular among scholars due to its simplicity and readability of results and is selected for this study.

This review therefore undertook a bibliometric assessment of the AI in the HRM. In this study, a series of bibliometric based analysis was done using 554 articles that formed part of the bibliometric search in Scopus, which had been retained. Therefore, in answering this research questions, this study undertook publication, global citation, and social network analyses in order to describe the publication trends (RQ1) and to identify the leading contributor in terms of authors, countries, and institutions (RQ2) and outlets and articles that have shaped AI in HRM research (RQ3). In addition, this study adopted VOSviewer to enrich the exploration of the leading contributors (RQ2) and publications (RQ3) through co-authorship and local citation. The same software was used to map the intellectual structure of AI in HRM (RQ4) through keyword co-occurrence analysis, which can also help future research to identify avenues for future exploration (RQ5).

RESULTS

Publication Trends (RQ1) 1985-2024

Figure 2. Publication trends of AI in HRM research from 1985 to 2024

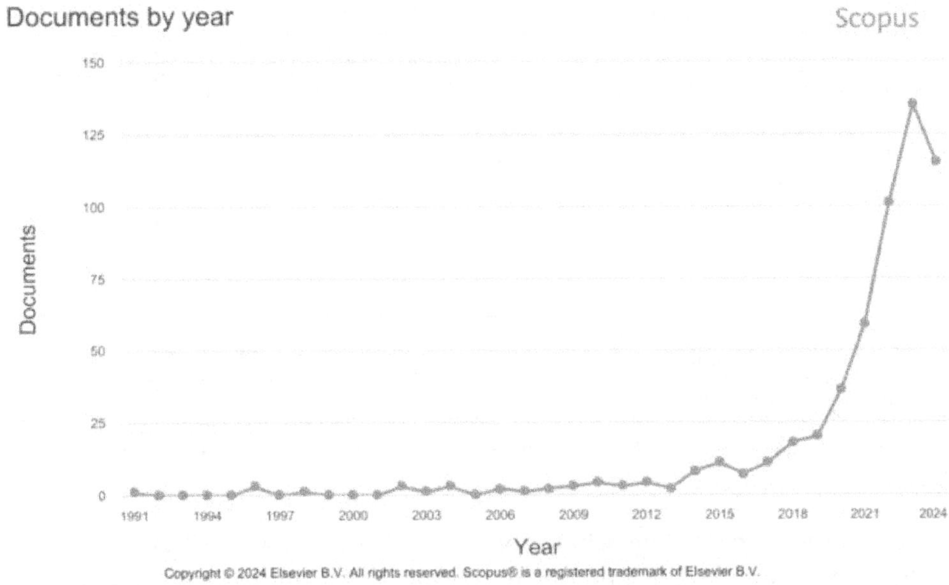

The data shows a significant upward trend in the number of documents published over time, particularly from 2020 onwards. The publication count remained relatively low and stable from 1991 to 2016, with annual figures mostly in the single digits, indicating limited interest or activity in this area of research during those years. A gradual increase began around 2017, but the most notable surge occurred after 2020. In 2021, the number of publications rose to 59, followed by a sharp increase in 2022 and 2023, reaching 101 and 135 documents, respectively. As of September 2024, there are 115 articles published which demonstrate an overall growing interest and engagement in the field, suggesting that the research of AI in HRM has become a rapidly emerging area of study in recent years.

Publication Outlet (RQ2)

Table 1. Leading publication outlets contributing to the research of AI in HRM

	Source Title	CiteScore 2023	SJR 2023 (Ranking)	h-index	Number of Articles
1	Human Resource Management Review	20.2	3.302 (Q1)	121	10
2	Sustainability (Switzerland)	6.8	0.672 (Q1)	169	9
3	Technological Forecasting and Social Change	21.3	3.12 (Q1)	179	7
4	International Journal of Human Resource Management	11.7	2.078 (Q1)	139	7
5	IEEE Access	9.8	0.96 (Q1)	242	7
6	Organizational Dynamics	4.6	0.675 (Q1)	74	6
7	Mobile Information Systems	N/A	Delisted	46	6
8	IEEE Transactions on Engineering Management	10.3	1.201 (Q1)	112	6
9	Asia Pacific Journal of Human Resources	7.2	1.243 (Q1)	42	6

Note: The leading publication outlets with 6 or more articles published in the research of technology in GCED.

Table 1 shows the leading publication outlets that contribute to the research of AI in HRM. In terms of number of articles published, *Human Resource Management Review* published the most articles with 10 followed by *Sustainability (Switzerland)* with 9 articles, *Technological Forecasting and Social Change, International Journal of Human Resource Management* and *IEEE Access* with 7 articles respectively.

CiteScore is a metric that reflects the average number of citations received per document published in a journal over a specific period (usually four years). A higher CiteScore indicates that the journal's articles are more frequently cited, suggesting greater influence or impact in the academic community. Based on the CiteScore 2023, *Technological Forecasting and Social Change* scored the highest with 21.3 followed by Human Resource Management Review with 20.2 and International Journal of Human Resource Management with 11.7.

The SCImago Journal Rank (SJR) measures the scientific influence of journals by accounting for both the number of citations received by a journal and the prestige of the journals where the citations come from. It reflects the quality and reputation of the publication outlet. The "Q1" ranking signifies that the journal is in the top 25% of journals in its category, indicating high quality. Based on Table 1, all journals listed achieved Q1 except for *Mobile Information Systems* which was delisted.

Among the journals, *Human Resource Management Review* scored the highest SJR 2023 with 3.302.

The h-index is a metric that measures both the productivity and citation impact of the publications within a journal. A higher h-index indicates that the journal has published a large number of highly cited papers. For h-index, *IEEE Access* has the highest h-index of 242 followed by *Technological Forecasting and Social Change* (h-index = 179), and *International Journal of Human Resource Management* (h-index = 139).

Publication Performance (RQ2)

Table 2. Leading articles of AI in HRM research from 1991 to 2024

Rank	Article Title	Author(s) and Year	Global Citations
1	Artificial intelligence in human resources management: Challenges and A path forward	Tambe et al. (2019)	489
2	Artificial intelligence, robotics, advanced technologies and human resource management: a systematic review	Vrontis et al. (2023)	417
3	An Internet of Things-enabled BIM platform for on-site assembly services in prefabricated construction	Li et al. (2018)	310
4	A fuzzy AHP approach to personnel selection problem	Güngör et al. (2009)	305
5	Intelligent Agent Transparency in Human-Agent Teaming for Multi-UxV Management	Mercado et al. (2016)	256
6	Human resources for Big Data professions: A systematic classification of job roles and required skill sets	De Mauro et al. (2018)	243
7	Unlocking the value of artificial intelligence in human resource management through AI capability framework	Chowdhury et al. (2023)	214
8	Smartphone-based construction workers' activity recognition and classification	Akhavian and Behzadan (2016)	205
9	An experimental investigation of the impact of computer-based decision aids on decision making strategies	Todd and Benbasat (1991)	205
10	An Internet of Things Based Smart Waste Management System Using LoRa and Tensorflow Deep Learning Model	Sheng et al. (2020)	167

Note: Top 10 articles with the highest number of global citations based on Scopus since year 1991 to 2024.

Table 2 presents the top 10 most cited articles in AI and HRM research from 1991 to 2024, ranked by their global citation counts according to Scopus. The most influential article, authored by Tambe et al. (2019), has received 489 citations, followed closely Vrontis et al. (2023) with 417 citations. The articles cover diverse topics, including AI challenges in HRM, systematic reviews, applications in construction, and AI's role in decision-making and personnel selection. The publication years range from 1991 to 2023, indicating both longstanding and recent interest in the field. These articles highlight the leading research contributions and demonstrate the growing impact of AI in HRM studies over time.

Authors (RQ3)

Leading Authors

Table 3. Leading authors for research of AI in HRM

	Author Name	Affiliation	Country	Number of Articles
1	Budhwar, P.	Aston Business School	United Kingdom	6
2	Malik, A.	The University of Newcastle, Australia	Australia	6
3	Cagan, J.	College of Engineering	United States	5
4	Carlson, D.A.	Northwestern Medicine	United States	4
5	Demir, M.	Ira A. Fulton Schools of Engineering	United States	4
6	Dutta, D.	Indian Institute of Management Bangalore	India	4
7	Etemadi, M.	Northwestern University Feinberg	United States	4
8	Gyory, J.T.	College of Engineering	United States	4
9	Kar, A.K.	Indian Institute of Technology Delhi	India	4
10	Kou, W.	Northwestern Medicine	United States	4
11	Lukaszewski, K.M.	Wright State University	United States	4
12	McComb, C.	College of Engineering	United States	4
13	McNeese, N.J.	Clemson University	United States	4
14	Nawaz, N.	Kingdom University	Bahrain	4
15	Pandolfino, J.E.	Northwestern Medicine	United States	4
16	Prikshat, V.	CQUniversity Australia	Australia	4
17	Stone, D.L.	Virginia Polytechnic Institute and State University	United States	4

Note: Leading authors with four or more published articles in the research AI in HRM.

Table 4 below depicts the top authors in the research of AI in HRM. About the most productive authors the following can be stated: Budhwar, P. affiliated with Aston Business School, United Kingdom., and Malik, A. of The University of Newcastle, Australia They have published the most number of articles for the research of AI in HRM that is 6. However, the review has discovered that there is no individual author who dominates this area of research which opens up a good niche for the researchers to lead the research.

Co-Authorship Analysis

Co-authorship analysis provides some important understanding of the nature and the level of connectedness in terms of researching among scholars, which looks like a web of many researchers collaborating in the given field of the study (Donthu et al., 2021). For the co-authorship analysis here is the two-visualisation developed using VOSviewer which are the network visualisation and the overlay visualisation. Visualization in VOSviewer is a graphical rendering of the bibliometric data so as to map the relations within and between authors, keywords, institutions or countries. Co-occurrence analysis enables one to pinpoint commonalities, groups, and the degree of associations between these components and provide researchers with understandings of how different subjects or objects relate within a given area of study (Van Eck & Waltman, 2023). Regarding the network visualisation, the points are actually elements and the size of the point meaning the importance or frequency of it. Connections between nodes present collaborations via shared interests or citations, a nautical rope between several points referring to the intensity of the interactions. Nodes gathered together and frequently coloured govern groups of interconnected elements and define important subcategories or topics. Facilitated by this visualization, researchers can quickly pick trends, multi-sited collaborations, and dominant trends in a research area.

Overlay in VOSviewer is one of the graphical presentation methods which describes the dynamics of the features such as the keywords, author and the institutions in the bibliometric data. Unlike net iconisation that involves representation of the connection between objects, overlay visualisation incorporates one extra dimension of information in terms of colour shades associated with the object that has temporal or other variable information such as the average year of publication or citation (Van Eck & Waltman, 2023). For example, older elements can be seen blue and less recent elements can be illustrated in yellow so that researchers can determine emerging or declining topics. Using this graph, one can easily grasp the dynamics of research areas and even define what has been lately changed in the field.

Figure 3. Network visualisation on co-authorship analysis produced using VOSviewer in the research of AI in HRM

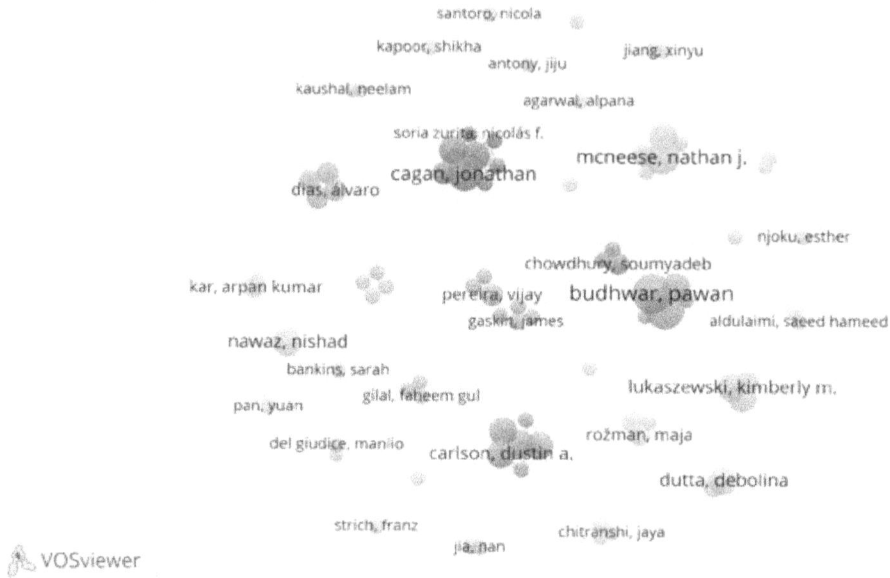

Figure 3 shows co-authorship analysis produced using VOSviewer in the research of AI in HRM. There are a few major clusters found throughout the co-authorship analysis. For example, Cluster 1 in red shows that there are collaborations between Balon, C., Cagan, J., Gyory, J. T., Kotovsky, K., Martin, J., Mccomb, C., Soria Zurita, N. F., and Stump, G while Cluster 2 in green shows that there are collaborations between Chiappetta, J. C., Christofi, M., Gaskin, J., Ogbeibu, S., Oseghale, R., Pereira, V., and Vrontis, D.

Figure 4. Overlay visualisation on co-authorship analysis produced using VOSviewer in the research of AI in HRM

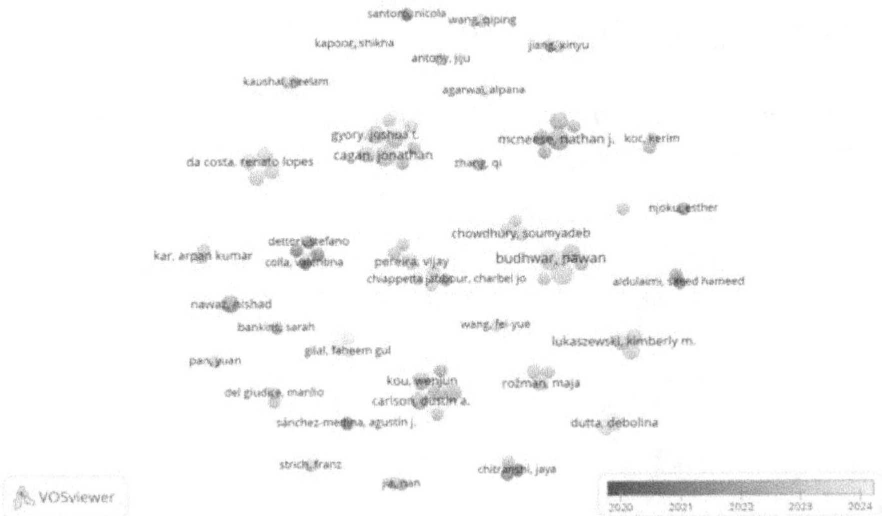

For overlay visualisation in Figure 4 can also be used to show pioneering and uprising researchers in the research area of AI in HRM. For example, researchers such as Gilal, F. G., and Dutta, D. are the uprising researchers for AI in HRM as the nodes are shown in yellow. Researchers such as Dettori, S., and Colla, V. with the nodes shown in blue has established themselves as the pioneers in the research for AI in HRM.

Countries (RQ3)

Leading Countries

Figure 5. Leading contributing countries in the research of AI in HRM

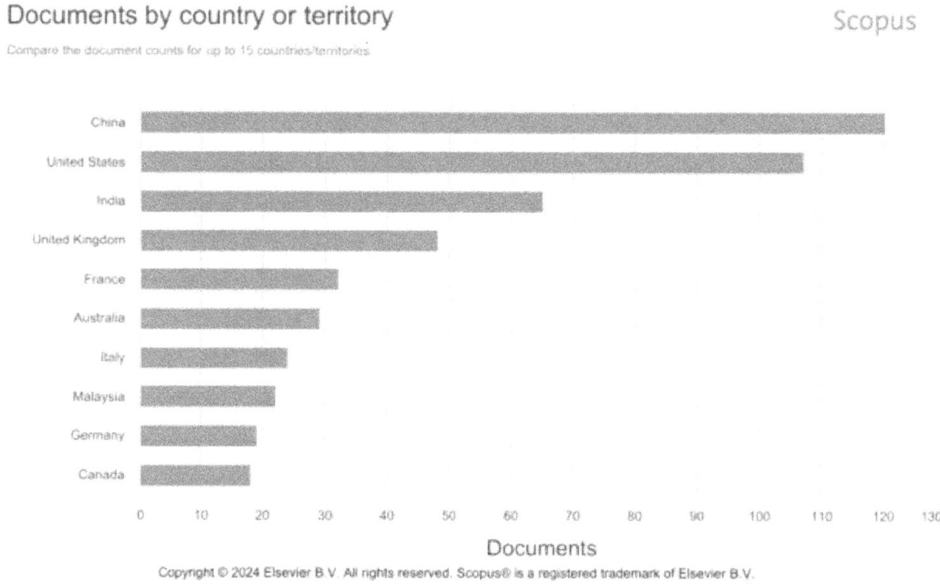

Figure 5 shows Leading contributing countries in the research of AI in HRM. From the review of articles from 1991 to 2024, China is the leading country in AI and HRM research with 120 documents, followed closely by the United States with 107 documents. India, the United Kingdom, and France complete the top five, contributing 65, 48, and 32 articles, respectively. This dominance reflects these countries' significant investments in AI research, technological advancements, and a strong focus on integrating AI in HRM practices. Other countries such as Australia, Italy, Malaysia, Germany, and Canada also contribute notably but to a lesser extent, indicating a broader global interest in this field. While China and the United States have a clear lead, the presence of a diverse range of countries, from Europe, Asia, and other continents, demonstrates the global reach and interdisciplinary interest in AI applications within HRM. This wide-ranging contribution from different countries underlines the growing importance of AI in HRM across varied geographical regions, economies, and technological infrastructures.

Leading Country Collaborations

For leading country collaboration, there are also two visualisations will be created using VOSviewer such as network visualisation and overlay visualisation. Figure 6 shows the Network visualisation for leading country collaborations while Figure 7 shows the overlay visualisation for leading country collaborations.

Figure 6. Network visualisation for leading country collaborations in the research of AI in HRM

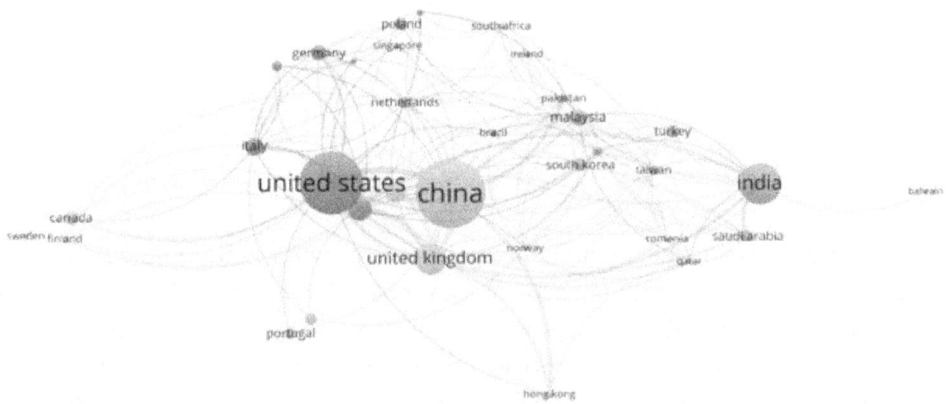

Figure 6 shows the leading country collaborations analysis in the research of AI in HRM, produced using VOSviewer. Based on Figure 6, there are seven clusters of countries collaborations identified. The first major cluster in red involves Austria, Brazil, France, Germany, Indonesia, Italy, Poland, Russia Federation and the United States. The second major cluster in green involves Malaysia, Norway, Qatar, Romania, South Korea, Taiwan, Turkey. It is followed by the third cluster in blue that consists of Ireland, Netherlands, Pakistan, Singapore, South Africa, and United Arab Emirates, the fourth cluster in yellow that consists of Australia, Canada, Finland, Sweden, and the United Kingdom, fifth cluster in purple that consists of Bahrain, India, and Saudi Arab, sixth cluster in orange that consists of China and Hong Kong, and seventh cluster in orange that consists of Portugal and Spain.

Figure 7. Network visualisation for leading country collaborations in the research of AI in HRM

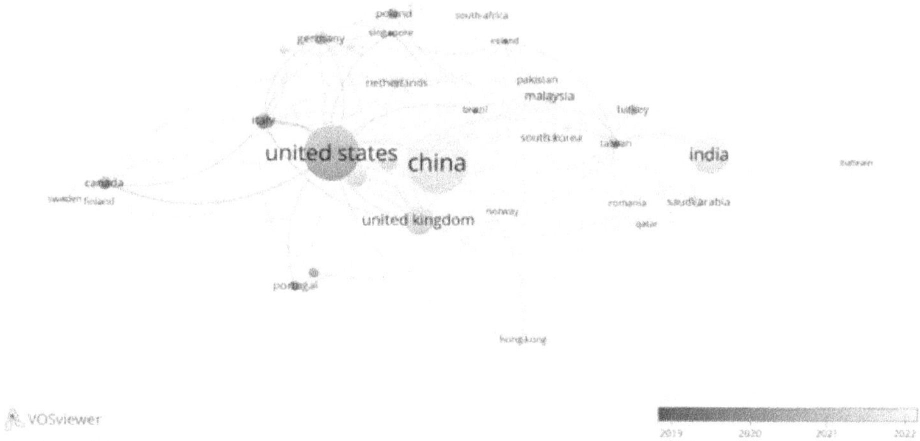

For the overlay visualisation for country collaboration, the review found that countries such as Italy, Portugal, and Canada (nodes in blue) have been pioneering the research of AI in HRM. Interestingly, countries such as China, India, and Malaysia (nodes in yellow) are the uprising countries in the research of AI in HRM as these countries contributed a great amount of research articles related to AI in HRM in recent years.

Institutions (RQ3)

Table 4. Leading institutions in research of AI in HRM

	Affiliation	Country	No of Articles
1	Aston University	United Kingdom	15
2	The University of Newcastle, Australia	Australia	7
3	Symbiosis International Deemed University	India	7
4	Clemson University	United States	6
5	Carnegie Mellon University	United States	6
6	Universidade de Lisboa	Portugal	6
7	NEOMA Business School	France	6
8	Arizona State University	United States	5
9	RMIT University	Australia	5

continued on following page

Table 4. Continued

	Affiliation	Country	No of Articles
10	Indian Institute of Technology Delhi	India	5
11	Indian Institute of Management Bangalore	India	5
12	College of Engineering	United States	5
13	TBS Business School	France	5

Note: Leading institutions with five or more published articles in the research of AI in HRM.

Table 5 identifies the leading institutions in AI and HRM research, with Aston University in the United Kingdom at the top, contributing 15 articles, making it the most prolific institution in this field. The University of Newcastle, Australia, and Symbiosis International Deemed University, India, follow with 7 articles each. Several institutions from the United States, such as Clemson University, Carnegie Mellon University, and Arizona State University, also feature prominently with 6 or 5 articles each, indicating a significant contribution from the US. Institutions from other countries like Portugal (Universidade de Lisboa), France (NEOMA Business School and TBS Business School), and India (Indian Institute of Technology Delhi and Indian Institute of Management Bangalore) are also active contributors, demonstrating a diverse, global interest in AI research within HRM. This spread across different countries highlights the widespread academic engagement in integrating AI into HRM practices.

Themes (RQ4)

To answer RQ4, network visualisation and overlay visualisation are also produced using VOSviewer.

Figure 8. Network visualisation for themes in the research of AI in HRM

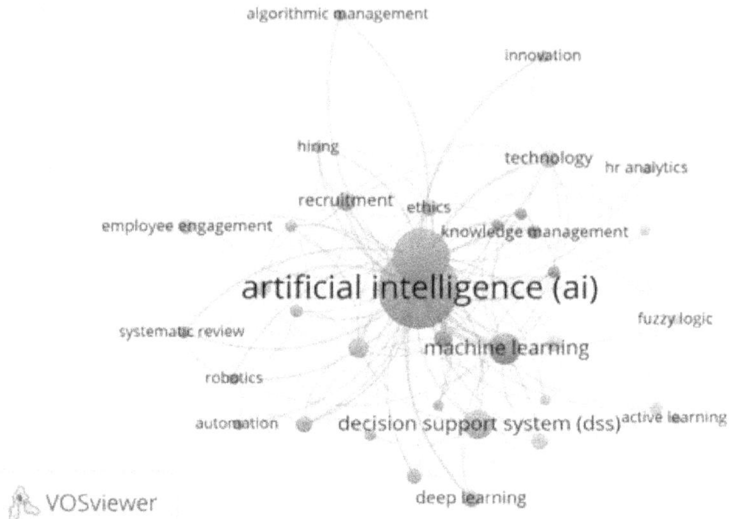

The study found 9 clusters based on the keywords co-occurrence network analysis for network visualization as shown in Figure 8. All notes and the theme for each cluster is summarised in Table 6. Cluster 1 with the colour red colour specifies 6 nodes, with the emphasis on "Generative AI for Decision-Making and Knowledge in Higher Education for HRM". In Cluster 1, *"machine learning"* is the primary keyword (Total link strength = 48, Occurrences = 38). It is followed by *"decision making"* (Total link strength = 19, Occurrences = 13) and *"knowledge management"* (Total link strength = 10, Occurrences = 8). In the context of keyword co-occurrence in VOSviewer, total link strength refers to the cumulative strength of the connections between a specific keyword and all the other keywords it co-occurs with in the dataset meanwhile occurrences in a keyword co-occurrence analysis refers to the number of times a specific keyword appears in the dataset (Van Eck & Waltman, 2023).

Cluster 2 with green shown 6 nodes that emphasis on "Ethical E-HRM in Recruitment and Selection". In Cluster 2, *"artificial intelligence (ai)"* is the primary keyword (Total link strength = 256, Occurrences = 246). It is followed by *"industry 4.0"* (Total link strength = 14, Occurrences = 12) and *"robotics"* (Total link strength = 11, Occurrences = 6). Cluster 3 with blue colour shown 5 nodes that emphasis on "Robotics and AI in Industry 4.0 for HRM". In Cluster 3, *"recruitment"* is the primary keyword (Total link strength = 32, Occurrences = 15). It is followed by *"human resource"* (Total link strength = 28, Occurrences = 16) and *"ethics"* (Total link strength = 20, Occurrences = 10).

Cluster 4 in yellow colour shows 5 nodes that focus on "Fuzzy Logic and HR Analytics in Active Learning for Project Management". In Cluster 4, *"project management"* is the primary keyword (Total link strength = 10, Occurrences = 7). It is followed by *"fuzzy logic"* (Total link strength = 6, Occurrences = 6) and *"information systems"* (Total link strength = 11, Occurrences = 5). Cluster 5 in purple colour shows 5 nodes that focus on "Deep Learning and IoT in DSS for Personnel Selection and Risk Management". In Cluster 5, *"decision support system (dss)"* is the primary keyword (Total link strength = 22, Occurrences = 35). It is followed by *"deep learning"* (Total link strength = 13, Occurrences = 13) and *"internet of things"* (Total link strength = 8, Occurrences = 9). Cluster 6 in sky blue colour shows 3 nodes that focus on "Big Data and Data Mining for Business Intelligence in HRM". In Cluster 6, *"data mining"* is the primary keyword (Total link strength = 20, Occurrences = 10). It is followed by *"big data"* (Total link strength = 13, Occurrences = 10) and *"business intelligence"* (Total link strength = 8, Occurrences = 5).

Cluster 7 in orange colour shows 2 nodes that focus on "Innovation and Technology in HRM". In Cluster 7, *"technology"* is the primary keyword (Total link strength = 26, Occurrences = 13). It is followed by *"innovation"* (Total link strength = 7, Occurrences = 6). Cluster 8 in brown colour shows 3 nodes that focus on "Algorithmic Management in HRM". In Cluster 8, *"human resource management (hrm)"* is the primary keyword (Total link strength = 174, Occurrences = 122). It is followed by *"algorithmic management"* (Total link strength = 6, Occurrences = 5). Cluster 9 in pink colour shows 3 nodes that focus on "Talent Management for Enhanced Employee Engagement". In Cluster 9, *"talent management"* is the primary keyword (Total link strength = 19, Occurrences = 9). It is followed by *"employee engagement"* (Total link strength = 8, Occurrences = 10).

From the network visualisation in the research of AI in HRM, this review found that keyword *"artificial intelligence (ai)"* has the highest total link strength of 256, followed by *"human resource management (hrm)* that has total link strength of 174, "*machine learning*" that has total link strength of 48, "*recruitment*" that has total link strength of 32, and "*human resource*" that has total link strength of 28. Figure 9 shows the overlay visualisation for themes in the research of AI in HRM. The review found that keywords such as *"ethics"*, *"hiring"*, *"chatgpt"*, *"generative artificial intelligence"*, and *"employee engagement"* are the most frequently appearing keywords in the research.

Table 5. Authors keywords and themes for AI in HRM research

Cluster 1: Generative AI for Decision-Making and Knowledge in Higher Education for HRM	**Cluster 2: Ethical E-HRM in Recruitment and Selection**	**Cluster 3: Robotics and AI in Industry 4.0 for HRM**
● Chatgpt	● E-HRM	● Artificial Intelligence (AI)
● Decision-making	● Ethics	● Automation
● Generative artificial intelligence	● Hiring	● Industry 4.0
● Higher education	● Human resources	● Robotics
● Knowledge management	● Recruitment	● Systematic review
● Machine learning	● Selection	
Cluster 4: Fuzzy Logic and HR Analytics in Active Learning for Project Management	Cluster 5: Deep Learning and IoT in DSS for Personnel Selection and Risk Management	Cluster 6: Big Data and Data Mining for Business Intelligence in HRM
● Active learning	● Decision support system (DSS)	● Big data
● Fuzzy logic	● Deep learning	● Business intelligence
● HR analytics	● Internet of things	● Data mining
● Information systems	● Personnel selection	
● Project management	● Risk management	
Cluster 7: Innovation and Technology in HRM	Cluster 8: Algorithmic Management in HRM	Cluster 9: Talent Management for Enhanced Employee Engagement
● Innovation	● Algorithmic management	● Employee engagement
● Technology	● Human resource management	● Talent management

Figure 9. Overlay visualisation for themes in the research of AI in HRM

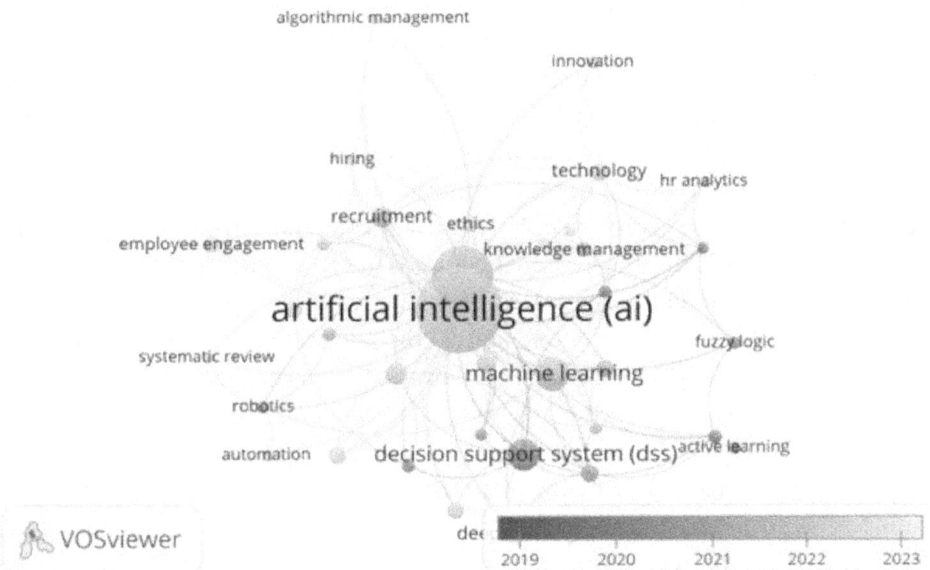

CONCLUSION

In conclusion, the widespread adoption of AI across various sectors, including telecommunications, healthcare, and education, is reshaping the landscape of business operations, particularly in HRM. Such changes make the operations of the HR departments more enhanced in decision-making, riches in insights, and more efficiency in managing personnel, hence the shift and focus toward realizing more strategic roles in any HR organizations' operations. Nevertheless, potential of AI as a tool to qualify jobs and enhance the functioning of HR departments brings with it challenges in the form of robotics that push job displacement, which is why an interdisciplinary approach that would involve the usage of new technologies and social sciences, as well. This paper compares the traditional and integrated systems of Human Resource Management Technologies, specifically concluding on the incorporation of big data into management systems, and the impact of these changes on the growth and competitiveness of an organization. Furthermore, with tools such as Power BI and Tableau, HR professionals can parse thousands of datasets, find insights, and use that information to help improve organizational performance. For the maximum usability of AI in HRM, more focus is required to address interdisciplinary co-operation on the application of AI in areas of HRM and to ensure the successful implementation of AI in HRM solutions would return positive benefits to organizations and employees both.

Consequently, by applying bibliometric analysis on 554 articles included in the study, the study was able to systematically scrutinise structural patterns in terms of publication and citation activities as well as global contributions by authors, countries, and institutions. For the purpose of selecting high quality and relevant research for the study, four stages of data filtration and refinement were conducted which included database search, scholarly filtration, language filtration followed by the subject filtration. Thus, the systematic approach enabled to identify the specific findings for the presented line of research, exploring the nature of AI in HRM per se and its relevance. The results pointed out that the AI increase is exponential where there is a significant leap in research works after 2020 and especially in the last two years. It depicts increasing trends of interest and participation in this cross-privileged field as a result of global sensitization. Several leading publications such as Human Resource Management Review and Sustainability have risen to this position meaning academics are starting to focus on the part played by AI in remaking the HR practice. By using method of analysis based on the number of contributors, it became obvious that China, the USA, as well as India are among the leaders in AI in HRM research due to scientific development and AI funds these countries invest in.

The co-authorship analysis of AI in HRM highlighted the relationships between scholars and organizations; Aston University was identified as the most productive organization in AI research. Contrary to existing studies, this research identified no defining author in the field, which may signal a chance for the further development of the topic and the formation of the subsequent direction of debates on AI in the context of HRM. Furthermore, utilizing VOSviewer to analyse the co- occurrences of the keywords, several major theme areas of AI applications in the HRM research have been discovered. We observed that various areas in the field of HR can benefit from AI, including topics like generative AI, ethical e-HRM, robotics in Industry 4.0, or big data-driven HRM. Further, the study enhances the awareness of ethical concern, recruitment selection criteria and the integrated application of AI in HRM decision making and knowledge management. In sum, this investigation not only presents the mapping of the AI in HRM research frontiers but also offers implications for subsequent research. This present study is beneficial for academic scholars and practitioners interested in discovering new insights about the transformative role of AI in HRM as it provides the trends, contributors, and themes emerging in the field. Therefore, the study indicates that the integration of AI into the concept of HRM will progress over expanding technology, data science and analysis, and teamwork in varied disciplines in the progression of HRM into the future.

REFERENCES

Akhavian, R., & Behzadan, A. H. (2016). Smartphone-based construction workers' activity recognition and classification. *Automation in Construction*, 71, 198–209. DOI: 10.1016/j.autcon.2016.08.015

Ameer, M., Rahul, S. P., & Manne, S. (2020). Human resource analytics using power bi visualization tool. *Quantitative Science Studies*, 1(1), 377–386.

Budhwar, P., Malik, A., De Silva, M. T., & Thevisuthan, P. (2022). Artificial intelligence–challenges and opportunities for international HRM: A review and research agenda. *International Journal of Human Resource Management*, 33(6), 1065–1097. DOI: 10.1080/09585192.2022.2035161

Chhtrapati, D., Chaudhari, S. P., Mevada, D., Bhatt, A., & Trivedi, D. (2021). Research productivity and network visualization on digital evidence: A bibliometric study. *Science & Technology Libraries*, 40(4), 358–372. DOI: 10.1080/0194262X.2021.1948486

Chowdhury, S., Dey, P., Joel-Edgar, S., Bhattacharya, S., Rodriguez-Espindola, O., Abadie, A., & Truong, L. (2023). Unlocking the value of artificial intelligence in human resource management through AI capability framework. *Human Resource Management Review*, 33(1), 100899. DOI: 10.1016/j.hrmr.2022.100899

De Mauro, A., Greco, M., Grimaldi, M., & Ritala, P. (2018). Human resources for Big Data professions: A systematic classification of job roles and required skill sets. *Information Processing & Management*, 54(5), 807–817. DOI: 10.1016/j.ipm.2017.05.004

Donthu, N., Kumar, S., Mukherjee, D., Pandey, N., & Lim, W. M. (2021). How to conduct a bibliometric analysis: An overview and guidelines. *Journal of Business Research*, 133, 285–296. DOI: 10.1016/j.jbusres.2021.04.070

Füller, J., Hutter, K., Wahl, J., Bilgram, V., & Tekic, Z. (2022). How AI revolutionizes innovation management–Perceptions and implementation preferences of AI-based innovators. *Technological Forecasting and Social Change*, 178, 121598. DOI: 10.1016/j.techfore.2022.121598

Gong, T., Jiang, Y., Saldivia, L. E., & Agard, C. (2022). Using Sankey diagrams to visualize drag and drop action sequences in technology-enhanced items. *Behavior Research Methods*, 54(1), 117–132. DOI: 10.3758/s13428-021-01615-4 PMID: 34109559

Güngör, Z., Serhadlıoğlu, G., & Kesen, S. E. (2009). A fuzzy AHP approach to personnel selection problem. *Applied Soft Computing*, 9(2), 641–646. DOI: 10.1016/j.asoc.2008.09.003

Hmoud, B., & Varallyai, L. (2023). Role of Artificial Intelligence in Human Resource Management in the Middle East Countries. *KnE Social Sciences*, 435–448-435–448.

Javaid, M., Haleem, A., Singh, R. P., Suman, R., & Gonzalez, E. S. (2022). Understanding the adoption of Industry 4.0 technologies in improving environmental sustainability. *Sustainable Operations and Computers*, 3, 203–217. DOI: 10.1016/j.susoc.2022.01.008

Jayawardena NS, Behl A, Thaichon P, Quach S (2022). Artificial intelligence (AI)-based market intelligence and customer insights. *Artificial Intelligence for Marketing Management*, 120-41.

Jose, S. (2019). Innovation in recruitment and talent acquisition: A study on technologies and strategies adopted for talent management in IT sector. *International Journal of Marketing and Human Resource Management*, 10(2), 1–8. DOI: 10.34218/IJMHRM.10.3.2019.001

Kaushal, N., Kaurav, R. P. S., Sivathanu, B., & Kaushik, N. (2023). Artificial intelligence and HRM: Identifying future research Agenda using systematic literature review and bibliometric analysis. *Management Review Quarterly*, 73(2), 455–493. DOI: 10.1007/s11301-021-00249-2

Khan, S. (2020). Artificial Intelligence Virtual Assistants (Chatbots) are Innovative Investigators. *IJCSNS, 20*(2).

Kumar, S., Pandey, N., Lim, W. M., Chatterjee, A. N., & Pandey, N. (2021). What do we know about transfer pricing? Insights from bibliometric analysis. *Journal of Business Research*, 134, 275–287. DOI: 10.1016/j.jbusres.2021.05.041

Li, C. Z., Xue, F., Li, X., Hong, J., & Shen, G. Q. (2018). An Internet of Things-enabled BIM platform for on-site assembly services in prefabricated construction. *Automation in Construction*, 89, 146–161. DOI: 10.1016/j.autcon.2018.01.001

Li, J., Rothrauff, B., Chen, S., Zhao, S., Wu, Z., Chen, Q., & He, J. (2022). Trends in anterior cruciate ligament repair: A bibliometric and visualized analysis. *Orthopaedic Journal of Sports Medicine*, 10(10). DOI: 10.1177/23259671221132564 PMID: 36338352

Mathushan, P., Gamage, A. S., & Wachissara, V. (2023). Human Resource Management and Artificial Intelligence: A Bibliometric Exploration. [former Vidyodaya Journal of Management]. *Journal of Business Research and Insights*, 9(I).

McAllister, J. T., Lennertz, L., & Atencio Mojica, Z. (2022). Mapping a discipline: A guide to using VOSviewer for bibliometric and visual analysis. *Science & Technology Libraries*, 41(3), 319–348. DOI: 10.1080/0194262X.2021.1991547

Mercado, J. E., Rupp, M. A., Chen, J. Y., Barnes, M. J., Barber, D., & Procci, K. (2016). Intelligent agent transparency in human–agent teaming for multi-UxV management. *Human Factors*, 58(3), 401–415. DOI: 10.1177/0018720815621206 PMID: 26867556

Paul, J., Lim, W. M., O'Cass, A., Hao, A. W., & Bresciani, S. (2021). Scientific procedures and rationales for systematic literature reviews (SPAR-4-SLR). *International Journal of Consumer Studies*, 45(4), O1–O16. DOI: 10.1111/ijcs.12695

Perifanis, N.-A., & Kitsios, F. (2023). Investigating the influence of artificial intelligence on business value in the digital era of strategy: A literature review. *Information (Basel)*, 14(2), 85. DOI: 10.3390/info14020085

Radonjić, A., Duarte, H., & Pereira, N. (2022). Artificial intelligence and HRM: HR managers' perspective on decisiveness and challenges. *European Management Journal.*

Saini, H., & Tarkar, P. (2022). Artificial intelligence in human resource practices with challenges and future directions. In *Handbook of Research on Innovative Management Using AI in Industry 5.0* (pp. 222–230). IGI Global. DOI: 10.4018/978-1-7998-8497-2.ch015

Sheng, T. J., Islam, M. S., Misran, N., Baharuddin, M. H., Arshad, H., Islam, M. R., Chowdhury, M. E. H., Rmili, H., & Islam, M. T. (2020). An internet of things based smart waste management system using LoRa and tensorflow deep learning model. *IEEE Access : Practical Innovations, Open Solutions*, 8, 148793–148811. DOI: 10.1109/ACCESS.2020.3016255

Tambe, P., Cappelli, P., & Yakubovich, V. (2019). Artificial intelligence in human resources management: Challenges and a path forward. *California Management Review*, 61(4), 15–42. DOI: 10.1177/0008125619867910

Todd, P., & Benbasat, I. (1991). An experimental investigation of the impact of computer-based decision aids on decision making strategies. *Information Systems Research*, 2(2), 87–115. DOI: 10.1287/isre.2.2.87

Van Eck, N. J., & Waltman, L. (2023). VOSviewer manual. Manual for VOSviewer version. 1.6. 8.

Verma, R., & Bandi, S. (2019). Artificial intelligence & human resource management in Indian IT sector. Proceedings of 10th international conference on digital strategies for organizational success. DOI: 10.2139/ssrn.3319897

Wang, X., Zhang, J., Yao, K., & Qin, J. (2021). ResumeVis Interactive Visualization of Resumes Based on Multi-Source Data. *International Journal of Web Services Research*, 18(2), 40–53. DOI: 10.4018/IJWSR.2021040103

Zhang, J., & Chen, Z. (2024). Exploring human resource management digital transformation in the digital age. *Journal of the Knowledge Economy*, 15(1), 1482–1498. DOI: 10.1007/s13132-023-01214-y

Compilation of References

Accenture. (2023). How AI is reshaping financial services: A new era of innovation and growth. Retrieved from https://www.accenture.com/us-en/insights/financial-services/artificial-intelligence

Achchab, S., & Temsamani, Y. K. (2021). Artificial Intelligence Use in Human Resources Management: Strategy and Operation's Impact. 2021 IEEE 2nd International Conference on Pattern Recognition and Machine Learning (PRML), 311–315. https://api.semanticscholar.org/CorpusID:237328919

Acikgoz, Y., Davison, K. H., Compagnone, M., & Laske, M. (2020). Justice perceptions of artificial intelligence in selection. International Journal of Selection and Assessment. DOI: 10.1111/ijsa.12306

Adams, R., & Brown, C. (2022). Enhancing judicial efficiency with AI tools: A case study approach. *Judicial Review Quarterly*, 29(3), 150–172.

Adwan, A. (2024). Can companies in digital marketing benefit from artificial intelligence in content creation? *International Journal of Data and Network Science*, 8(2), 797–808. DOI: 10.5267/j.ijdns.2023.12.024

Afina, Y., Buchser, M., Krasodomski, A., Rowe, J., Sun, N., & Wilkinson, R. (2024). Towards a global approach to digital platform regulation.

Agbo, F. J., Oyelere, S. S., Suhonen, J., & Adewumi, S. (2019, November). A systematic review of computational thinking approach for programming education in higher education institutions. In *Proceedings of the 19th Koli Calling International Conference on Computing Education Research* (pp. 1-10). DOI: 10.1145/3364510.3364521

Aguinis, H., Beltran, J. R., & Cope, A. (2024). How to use generative AI as a human resource management assistant. *Organizational Dynamics*, 53(1), 101029. DOI: 10.1016/j.orgdyn.2024.101029

Ahmed, S. B., & Nath, A. (2024). *Breaking the Silence: Understanding Domestic Violence Among Muslim Women*. Notion Press.

Ahn, M. J., & Chen, Y. C. (2020, June). Artificial intelligence in government: potentials, challenges, and the future. In *Proceedings of the 21st Annual International Conference on Digital Government Research* (pp. 243-252). DOI: 10.1145/3396956.3398260

Ahonen, E., & Farén, E. (2024). Gender biases in AI-Mitigation strategies contributing to fairness.

Akhavian, R., & Behzadan, A. H. (2016). Smartphone-based construction workers' activity recognition and classification. *Automation in Construction*, 71, 198–209. DOI: 10.1016/j.autcon.2016.08.015

Akpuokwe, C. U., Adeniyi, A. O., Bakare, S. S., & Eneh, N. E. (2024). The impact of judicial reforms on legal systems: A review in African countries. *International Journal of Applied Research in Social Sciences*, 6(3), 198–211. DOI: 10.51594/ijarss.v6i3.850

Akter, S., McCarthy, G., Sajib, S., Michael, K., Dwivedi, Y. K., D'Ambra, J., & Shen, K. N. (2021). Algorithmic bias in data-driven innovation in the age of AI. *International Journal of Information Management*, 60, 102387. DOI: 10.1016/j.ijinfomgt.2021.102387

Al-Alawi, A. I., Naureen, M., AlAlawi, E. I., & Al-Hadad, A. A. N. (2021). The role of artificial intelligence in recruitment process decision-making. *Information (Basel)*, 9(11), 269.

Alam, M., & Singh, P. (2021). Performance feedback interviews as affective events: An exploration of the impact of emotion regulation of negative performance feedback on supervisor–employee dyads. *Human Resource Management Review*, 31(2), 100740. DOI: 10.1016/j.hrmr.2019.100740

Alhasan, T. K. (2025). Integrating AI Into Arbitration: Balancing Efficiency With Fairness and Legal Compliance. *Conflict Resolution Quarterly*, crq.21470. DOI: 10.1002/crq.21470

Alhosani, K., & Alhashmi, S. M. (2024). Opportunities, challenges, and benefits of AI innovation in government services: A review. *Discover Artificial Intelligence*, 4(1), 18. DOI: 10.1007/s44163-024-00111-w

Ali, Al Shawabkeh, Salameh, & Al Amro. (2019). Performance predicting in hiring process and performance appraisals using machine learning. IEEE Conference Publication https://ieeexplore.ieee.org/abstract/document/8809154

Ali, M., Shahroz, M., Mushtaq, M. F., Alfarhood, S., Safran, M., & Ashraf, I. (2024). Hybrid Machine Learning Model for Efficient Botnet Attack Detection in IoT Environment. *IEEE Access : Practical Innovations, Open Solutions*, 12, 40682–40699. DOI: 10.1109/ACCESS.2024.3376400

Allal-Chérif, O., Aránega, A. Y., & Sánchez, R. C. (2021). Intelligent recruitment: How to identify, select, and retain talents from around the world using artificial intelligence. *Technological Forecasting and Social Change*, 169, 120822. DOI: 10.1016/j.techfore.2021.120822

Allden, N., & Harris, L. (2013). Building a positive candidate experience: Towards a networked model of e-recruitment. *The Journal of Business Strategy*, 34(5), 36–47. DOI: 10.1108/JBS-11-2012-0072

Almestarihi, R., Ahmad, A. Y. A. B., Frangieh, R., Abu-AlSondos, I., Nser, K., & Ziani, A. (2024). Measuring the ROI of paid advertising campaigns in digital marketing and its effect on business profitability. *Uncertain Supply Chain Management*, 12(2), 1275–1284. DOI: 10.5267/j.uscm.2023.11.009

Alrashedi, A. and Abbod, M. (2020). The effect of using artificial intelligence on performance of appraisal system: a case study for University of Jeddah staff in Saudi Arabia. DOI: 10.1007/978-3-030-55180-3_11

Alsaif, A., & Sabih Aksoy, M. (2023). AI-HRM: artificial intelligence in human resource management: a literature review. *Journal of Computing and Communication*, 2(2), 1–7. DOI: 10.21608/jocc.2023.307053

Amankwah-Amoah, J., Abdalla, S., Mogaji, E., Elbanna, A., & Dwivedi, Y. K. (2024). The impending disruption of creative industries by generative AI: Opportunities, challenges, and research agenda. *International Journal of Information Management*, 79, 102759. DOI: 10.1016/j.ijinfomgt.2024.102759

Ameer, M., Rahul, S. P., & Manne, S. (2020). Human resource analytics using power bi visualization tool. *Quantitative Science Studies*, 1(1), 377–386.

Andrada, G., Clowes, R. W., & Smart, P. R. (2023). Varieties of transparency: Exploring agency within AI systems. *AI & Society*, 38(4), 1321–1331. DOI: 10.1007/s00146-021-01326-6 PMID: 35035112

Andrews, L., & Bucher, H. (2022). Automating Discrimination: AI Hiring Practices and Gender Inequality. *Cardozo Law Review*, 44, 145.

Angel, M. P., & Calo, R. (2024). Distinguishing Privacy Law. *Columbia Law Review*, 124(2), 507–562.

Angel, M., Havens, J. C., & Winfield, A. F. T. (2017). ETHICALLY ALIGNED DESIGN A Vision for Prioritizing Human Wellbeing with Artificial Intelligence and.... In *ResearchGate*. IEEE. https://www.researchgate.net/publication/378975517_ETHICALLY_ALIGNED_DESIGN_A_Vision_for_Prioritizing_Human_Wellbeing_with_Artificial_Intelligence_and_Autonomous_Systems

Angwin, J., Larson, J., Mattu, S., & Kirchner, L. (2016). *Machine Bias*. ProPublica; ProPublica. https://www.propublica.org/article/machine-bias-risk-assessments-in-criminal-sentencing

Antoni, L., Guniš, J., Gurský, P., Horvát, Š., Krajči, S., Krídlo, O., & Andrejková, G. (2020). Data Science and its position in university education within National Project IT Academy-Education for 21st Century. *The Quarterly Journal of Economics*, 118(4), 1279–1333.

Apiola, M., & Sutinen, E. (2021). Design science research for learning software engineering and computational thinking: Four cases. *Computer Applications in Engineering Education*, 29(1), 83–101. DOI: 10.1002/cae.22291

Applegarth, D. M., Lewis, R. A., & Rief, R. M. (2023). Imperfect tools: A research note on developing, applying, and increasing understanding of criminal justice risk assessments. *Criminal Justice Policy Review*, 34(4), 319–336. DOI: 10.1177/08874034231180505

Apriani, A., Wahdiniawati, S. A., Perkasa, D. H., Magita, M., Meliantari, D., & Widayati, C. (2024). Digital Transformation of SMEs: Boosting Online Shopping Interest through E-Commerce Adoption. *Dinasti International Journal of Digital Business Management*, 5(3), 595–611.

Arora, A., Kumar, S., Bansal, D., & Bansal, S. (2024). A Study of Awareness and Perception Regarding MOOC Courses with Special Reference to NPTEL. *Prabandhan: Indian Journal Of Management*, 17(4), 43–57. DOI: 10.17010/pijom/2024/v17i4/173427

Arora, M. K., Lal, S., Singh, B., & Olyaee, M. (2024). Through an Energy Lens: Examining SDGs From a Policy Perspective. In Riswandi, B., Singh, B., Kaunert, C., & Vig, K. (Eds.), *AI Applications for Clean Energy and Sustainability* (pp. 320–343). IGI Global., DOI: 10.4018/979-8-3693-6567-0.ch016

Arora, R. G., & Siradhana, N. K. (2022). HR Transformation Through Artificial Intelligence: An Insight Through Literature Survey. *International Journal of Information Systems and Social Change*, 13(1), 1–16. DOI: 10.4018/IJISSC.309736

Arslan, A., Cooper, C. D., Khan, Z., Golgeci, I., & Ali, I. (2021). Artificial intelligence and human workers interaction at team level: a conceptual assessment of the challenges and potential HRM strategies. International Journal of Manpower. https://api.semanticscholar.org/CorpusID:237728755

Ashley, K. D. (2017). *Artificial Intelligence and Legal Analytics*. Cambridge University Press. DOI: 10.1017/9781316761380

Asikin, M. Z., Azzahra, A., & Afridi, F. K. (2024). Strategies for the Utilization of Information Technology in Micro, Small, and Medium Business Marketing. [AJEMB]. *American Journal of Economic and Management Business*, 3(5), 1–13. DOI: 10.58631/ajemb.v3i8.108

Asikin, M. Z., Fadilah, M. O., Saputro, W. E., Aditia, O., & Ridzki, M. M. (2024). The Influence Of Digital Marketing On Competitive Advantage And Performance of Micro, Small And Medium Enterprises. *International Journal of Social Service and Research*, 4(03), 963–970. DOI: 10.46799/ijssr.v4i03.749

Askanius, T., Kavada, A., Mattoni, A., Uldam, J., & Kaun, A. (2023). *Activist strategies for confronting and harnessing digital power*. State of Power.

Awan, S. H., Habib, N., Shoaib Akhtar, C., & Naveed, S. (2020). Effectiveness of Performance Management System for Employee Performance Through Engagement. *SAGE Open*, 10(4). DOI: 10.1177/2158244020969383

Baker, C., & Moore, A. (2023). Case management solutions through AI: Enhancing judicial productivity? *Judicial Management Review*, 14(1), 45–63.

Baker, R. S., & Hawn, A. (2022). Algorithmic bias in education. *International Journal of Artificial Intelligence in Education*, •••, 1–41.

Balasubramaniam, N., Kauppinen, M., Rannisto, A., Hiekkanen, K., & Kujala, S. (2023). Transparency and explainability of AI systems: From ethical guidelines to requirements. *Information and Software Technology*, 159, 107197. DOI: 10.1016/j.infsof.2023.107197

Banerjee, R. (2024). *Corporate Frauds: Now Bigger, Broader and Bolder*. Penguin Random House India Private Limited.

Barcelos, T. S., & Silveira, I. F. (2012, October). Teaching computational thinking in initial series an analysis of the confluence among mathematics and computer sciences in elementary education and its implications for higher education. In *2012 XXXVIII Conferencia Latinoamericana En Informatica (CLEI)* (pp. 1-8). IEEE. DOI: 10.1109/CLEI.2012.6427135

Barghi, B., Gallardo-Gallardo, E., & Fernandez, V. (2022). An overview of chatbots usage in recruitment and selection practices. *MCIS 2022 Proceedings*.

Bari, M. H., Arif, N. U. M., Hasan, M. M., & Maraj, M. A. A. (2024). Comparative Analysis Of Digital Payment Platforms And E-Commerce Giants: A Five-Year Performance And Strategic Development Study Of Visa, Mastercard, Amazon, And Ebay. Global Mainstream Journal of Innovation, Engineering & Emerging Technology, 3(1), 1-10.

Barocas, S., Hardt, M., & Narayanan, A. (2019). Fairness and Machine Learning. Fairness, Accountability, and Transparency in Machine Learning. https://fairmlbook .org/

Barocas, S., & Selbst, A. D. (2016). *Big Data's Disparate Impact*. DOI: 10.2139/ ssrn.2477899

Basu, S., Majumdar, B., Mukherjee, K., Munjal, S., & Palaksha, C. (2023). Artificial Intelligence–HRM Interactions and Outcomes: A Systematic Review and Causal Configurational Explanation. *Human Resource Management Review*, 33(1), 100893. DOI: 10.1016/j.hrmr.2022.100893

Bati, K., Yetişir, M. I., Çalişkan, I., Güneş, G., & Gül Saçan, E. (2018). Teaching the concept of time: A steam-based program on computational thinking in science education. *Cogent Education*, 5(1), 1507306. DOI: 10.1080/2331186X.2018.1507306

Becher, S., & Alarie, B. (2025). LexOptima: The promise of AI-enabled legal systems. *University of Toronto Law Journal*, 75(1), 73–121. DOI: 10.3138/utlj-2024-0002

Belenguer, L. (2022). AI bias: Exploring discriminatory algorithmic decision-making models and the application of possible machine-centric solutions adapted from the pharmaceutical industry. *AI and Ethics*, 2(4), 771–787. DOI: 10.1007/s43681-022-00138-8 PMID: 35194591

Bellamy, R. K., Dey, K., Hind, M., Hoffman, S. C., Houde, S., Kannan, K., Lohia, P., Martino, J., Mehta, S., Mojsilovic, A., Nagar, S., Ramamurthy, K. N., Richards, J., Saha, D., Sattigeri, P., Singh, M., Varshney, K. R., & Zhang, Y. (2019). AI Fairness 360: An extensible toolkit for detecting and mitigating algorithmic bias. *IBM Journal of Research and Development*, 63(4/5), 4–1. DOI: 10.1147/JRD.2019.2942287

Benjamin, R. (2023). *Race After Technology: Abolitionist Tools for the New Jim Code*. Politybooks.com; Polity. https://www.politybooks.com/bookdetail?book_slug =race-after-technology-abolitionist-tools-for-the-new-jim-code--9781509526390

Bennet, D. (2024). Advancing e-commerce smart-pls as a catalyst for improved online shopping services. *International Transactions on Education Technology*, 2(2), 99–108.

Bennett Moses, L., & Chan, J. (2016). Algorithmic prediction in policing: Assumptions, evaluation, and accountability. *Policing and Society*, 28(7), 806–822. DOI: 10.1080/10439463.2016.1253695

Benyekhlef, K., & Zhu, J. (2024). The judicial system and the work of judges and lawyers in the application of law and sanctions assisted by AI. In *Handbook of Artificial Intelligence at Work* (pp. 250–275). Edward Elgar Publishing. DOI: 10.4337/9781800889972.00021

Berch, V., Lankevych, A., Naturkach, R., Bysaha, Y., & Prodan, V. (2024). The role of digital technologies in building an inclusive and transparent society: An analysis of the legal mechanisms of democratic governance. *Amazonia Investiga*, 13(79), 177–188. DOI: 10.34069/AI/2024.79.07.14

Berger, B., Adam, M., Rühr, A., & Benlian, A. (2021). Watch me improve – Algorithm aversion and demonstrating the ability to learn. *Business & Information Systems Engineering*, 63(1), 55–68. DOI: 10.1007/s12599-020-00678-5

Berryhill, J., Heang, K. K., Clogher, R., & McBride, K. (2019). Hello, World: Artificial intelligence and its use in the public sector.

Bhalla, N., Brooks, L., & Leach, T. (2023). Ensuring a 'responsible' AI future in India: RRI as an approach for identifying the ethical challenges from an Indian perspective. *AI and Ethics*. Advance online publication. DOI: 10.1007/s43681-023-00370-w

Bharadwaj, S., Khan, N. A., & Yameen, M. (2022). Unbundling employer branding, job satisfaction, organizational identification and employee retention: A sequential mediation analysis. *Asia-Pacific Journal of Business Administration*, 14(3), 309–334. DOI: 10.1108/APJBA-08-2020-0279

Bharati, R. K. (2024). AI and the right to fair trial: Legal standards and technological advances. *International Journal of Science Academic Research*, 5(7), 7865–7867. http://www.scienceijsar.com

Bhatia, V., Rawat, P., Kumar, A., & Shah, R. R. (2019). End-to-end resume parsing and finding candidates for a job description using bert. *arXiv preprint arXiv:1910.03089*.

Bhutani, S., & Singh, K. (2023). Sikhism and Its Contribution to Well-Being. In *Religious and Spiritual Practices in India: A Positive Psychological Perspective* (pp. 223–250). Springer Nature Singapore. DOI: 10.1007/978-981-99-2397-7_10

Bibi, M. (2019). Execution of artificial intelligence approach in human resource management functions: Benefits and challenges in Pakistan. *Sarhad Journal of Management Sciences*, 5(1), 113–124. DOI: 10.31529/sjms.2018.5.1.8

Binns, R. (2018). Fairness in Machine Learning: Lessons from Political Philosophy. In *Proceedings of the 2018 Conference on Fairness, Accountability, and Transparency* (pp. 149-158). DOI: 10.1145/3287560.3287598

Binns, R. (2021). The ethical implications of AI in judicial decision-making. *AI & Society*, 36(4), 1235–1245.

Binns, R., Van Kleek, M., Veale, M., Lyngs, U., Zhao, J., & Shadbolt, N. (2018). "It's Reducing a Human Being to a Percentage." *Proceedings of the 2018 CHI Conference on Human Factors in Computing Systems - CHI '18*. DOI: 10.1145/3173574.3173951

Bishnoi, R., Kaur, R., Kaur, N., Kaur, H., Kaur, A., & Johal, A. (2024). Utilizing Artificial Intelligence in Legal System with Special Reference of India. *Educational Administration: Theory and Practice*, 30(5), 2217–2223.

Biswas, M. I., Talukder, M. S., & Khan, A. R. (2024). Who do you choose? Employees' perceptions of artificial intelligence versus humans in performance feedback. *China Accounting and Finance Review*, 26(4), 512–532. DOI: 10.1108/CAFR-08-2023-0095

Bogani, R., Theodorou, A., Arnaboldi, L., & Wortham, R. H. (2023). Garbage in, toxic data out: A proposal for ethical artificial intelligence sustainability impact statements. *AI and Ethics*, 3(4), 1135–1142. DOI: 10.1007/s43681-022-00221-0 PMID: 36281314

Bokolo, B. G., & Liu, Q. (2024). Artificial Intelligence in Social Media Forensics: A Comprehensive Survey and Analysis. *Electronics (Basel)*, 13(9), 1671. DOI: 10.3390/electronics13091671

Bondarouk, T., & Brewster, C. (2016). Conceptualising the future of HRM and technology research. *International Journal of Human Resource Management*, 27(21), 2652–2671. DOI: 10.1080/09585192.2016.1232296

Borenstein, J., & Howard, A. (2021). Emerging challenges in AI and the need for AI ethics education. *AI and Ethics*, 1(1), 61–65. DOI: 10.1007/s43681-020-00002-7 PMID: 38624388

Bough, B., & Gunter, A. (2022). Marketing and financial services in the age of artificial intelligence. ResearchGate. https://www.researchgate.net/publication/350843589_Marketing_and_Financial_Services_in_the_Age_of_Artificial_Intelligence

Bowers, K., & Johnson, S. (2024). Facing the future of crime: A framework for police use of technology. *The Political Quarterly*, 95(3), 480–488. DOI: 10.1111/1467-923X.13426

Brayne, S. (2020). *Predict and Surveil*. Google Books; Oxford University Press. https://books.google.co.in/books?hl=en&lr=&id=01AAEAAAQBAJ&oi=fnd&pg=PP1&dq=%E2%80%A2+Brayne

Brown, E., & Ballucci, D. (2024). Specialized knowledge: Understanding crime analysts' roles and responsibilities and the impact of their work. *Criminology & Criminal Justice*, 24(1), 3–19. DOI: 10.1177/17488958221095980

Buck, B., & Morrow, J. (2018). AI, performance management and engagement: Keeping your best their best. *Strategic HR Review*, 17(5), 261–262. DOI: 10.1108/SHR-10-2018-145

Budhwar, P., Malik, A., De Silva, M. T., & Thevisuthan, P. (2022). Artificial intelligence–challenges and opportunities for international HRM: A review and research agenda. *International Journal of Human Resource Management*, 33(6), 1065–1097. DOI: 10.1080/09585192.2022.2035161

Bughin, J., & Manyika, J. (2019). Your AI efforts Won't succeed unless they benefit employees. Harvard Business Review https://hbr.org/2019/07/your-ai-efforts-wont-succeed-unless-they-benefit-employees

Buitrago-Flórez, F., Danies, G., Restrepo, S., & Hernández, C. (2021). Fostering 21st Century Competences through Computational Thinking and Active Learning: A Mixed Method Study. *International Journal of Instruction*, 14(3), 737–754. DOI: 10.29333/iji.2021.14343a

Bulchand-Gidumal, J., William Secin, E., O'Connor, P., & Buhalis, D. (2024). Artificial intelligence's impact on hospitality and tourism marketing: Exploring key themes and addressing challenges. *Current Issues in Tourism*, 27(14), 2345–2362. DOI: 10.1080/13683500.2023.2229480

Buolamwini, J., & Gebru, T. (2018). *Gender Shades: Intersectional Accuracy Disparities in Commercial Gender Classification*. PMLR. https://proceedings.mlr.press/v81/buolamwini18a.html

Burbach, R. (2018). *Strategic evaluation of e-HRM. In e-HRM*. Routledge.

Business Insider Intelligence. (2022). The impact of AI on banking and finance: Trends to watch.

Cachat-Rosset, G., & Klarsfeld, A. (2023). Diversity, equity, and inclusion in artificial intelligence: An evaluation of guidelines. *Applied Artificial Intelligence*, 37(1), 2176618. Advance online publication. DOI: 10.1080/08839514.2023.2176618

Calzada, I. (2024). Democratic Erosion of Data-Opolies: Decentralized Web3 Technological Paradigm Shift Amidst AI Disruption. *Big Data and Cognitive Computing*, 2024(8), 26. DOI: 10.3390/bdcc8030026

Campbell, K. (2020). Gender and technology: Social context and intersectionality. *Handbook of research in educational communications and technology: Learning design*, 115-204.

Cantarelli, P. (2023). People Administration. In Management and Performance in Mission Driven Organizations (pp. 77-89). Springer Nature Switzerland. DOI: 10.1007/978-3-031-40490-0_5

Cao, J., & Yao, J. (2020). Linking different artificial intelligence functions to employees' psychological appraisals and work. *Proceedings - Academy of Management*, 2020(1), 19876. DOI: 10.5465/AMBPP.2020.105

Capgemini Research Institute. (2022). How AI is transforming customer engagement in banking.

Carter, L., & Lewis, M. (2023). AI-driven legal analytics: Revolutionizing case outcomes? *The Journal of Legal Analysis*, 9(3), 77–94.

Casey, T., Turner, N., Hu, X., & Bancroft, K. (2021). Making safety training stickier: A richer model of safety training engagement and transfer. *Journal of Safety Research*, 78, 303–313. DOI: 10.1016/j.jsr.2021.06.004 PMID: 34399927

Caskey, S. (2021). AI-enabled marketing in finance: Current applications. Emerj. Retrieved from https://emerj.com/ai-marketing-in-finance/

Castelo, N., Bos, M. W., & Lehmann, D. R. (2019). Task-dependent algorithm aversion. *JMR, Journal of Marketing Research*, 56(5), 809–825. DOI: 10.1177/0022243719851788

Castets-Renard, C. (2021). Human rights and algorithmic impact assessment for predictive policing. In Micklitz, H.-W., Pollicino, O., Reichman, A., Simoncini, A., Sartor, G., & De Gregorio, G. (Eds.), *Constitutional challenges in the algorithmic society* (pp. 93–110). Cambridge University Press. DOI: 10.1017/9781108914857.007

Cath, C. (2018). Governing artificial intelligence: Ethical, legal and technical opportunities and challenges. *Philosophical Transactions. Series A, Mathematical, Physical, and Engineering Sciences*, 376(2133), 20180080. DOI: 10.1098/rsta.2018.0080 PMID: 30322996

Chakraborty, S., Giri, A., Aich, A., & Biswas, S. (2020). Evaluating Influence of Artificial Intelligence on Human Resource Management Using PLS-SEM. *International Journal of Science & Technology Research*, 9(3), 58765880.

Chang, K. (2020). Artificial intelligence in personnel management: The development of APM model. *The Bottom Line (New York, N.Y.)*, 33(4), 377–388. DOI: 10.1108/BL-08-2020-0055

Charlwood, A., & Guenole, N. (2022). Can HR adapt to the paradoxes of artificial intelligence? *Human Resource Management Journal*, 32(4), 729–742. DOI: 10.1111/1748-8583.12433

Chavan, S. (2024). *Culture, Identity & Change: The Evolution of Indian Society*. Sandeep Chavan.

Cheatham, B., Javanmardian, K., & Samandari, H. (2019). Confronting AI risks. McKinsey Quarterly. Available from https://www.mckinsey.com/business-functions/mckinsey-analytics/our-insights/confronting-the-risksof-artificial-intelligence#

Cheng, M. M., & Hackett, R. D. (2021). A critical review of algorithms in HRM: Definition, theory, and practice. *Human Resource Management Review*, 31(1), 100698. DOI: 10.1016/j.hrmr.2019.100698

Chen, Y., Jensen, S., Albert, L. J., Gupta, S., & Lee, T. (2023). Artificial intelligence (AI) student assistants in the classroom: Designing chatbots to support student success. *Information Systems Frontiers*, 25(1), 161–182. DOI: 10.1007/s10796-022-10291-4

Chen, Z. (2023). Ethics and discrimination in artificial intelligence-enabled recruitment practices. *Humanities & Social Sciences Communications*, 10(567), 567. Advance online publication. DOI: 10.1057/s41599-023-02079-x

Cheuk, T. (2021). Can AI be racist? Color-evasiveness in the application of machine learning to science assessments. *Science Education*, 105(5), 825–836. Advance online publication. DOI: 10.1002/sce.21671

Chhtrapati, D., Chaudhari, S. P., Mevada, D., Bhatt, A., & Trivedi, D. (2021). Research productivity and network visualization on digital evidence: A bibliometric study. *Science & Technology Libraries*, 40(4), 358–372. DOI: 10.1080/0194262X.2021.1948486

Chiao, V. (2019). Fairness, accountability and transparency: Notes on algorithmic decision-making in criminal justice. *International Journal of Law in Context*, 15(2), 126–139. DOI: 10.1017/S1744552319000077

Chinu, B., & Bansal, U. (2024). Explainable AI: To reveal the logic of black-box models. *New Generation Computing*, 42(1), 53–87. DOI: 10.1007/s00354-022-00201-2

Chouldechova, A., & G'Sell, M. (2017, June 30). *Fairer and more accurate, but for whom?* ArXiv.org; Cornel University. DOI: 10.48550/arXiv.1707.00046

Chouldechova, A. (2017). Fair Prediction with Disparate Impact: A Study of Bias in Recidivism Prediction Instruments. *Big Data*, 5(2), 153–163. DOI: 10.1089/big.2016.0047 PMID: 28632438

Chowdhury, S., Dey, P., Joel-Edgar, S., Bhattacharya, S., Rodriguez-Espindola, O., Abadie, A., & Truong, L. (2023). Unlocking the value of artificial intelligence in human resource management through AI capability framework. *Human Resource Management Review*, 33(1), 100899. DOI: 10.1016/j.hrmr.2022.100899

Chui, M., Manyika, J., & Miremadi, M. (2022). *The state of AI in 2022: Trends and insights for financial services firms*. McKinsey Global Institute.

Chukwuka, E. J., & Dibie, K. E. (2024). Strategic Role of Artificial Intelligence (AI) on Human Resource Management (HR) Employee Performance Evaluation Function. *International Journal of Entrepreneurship and Business Innovation*, 7(2), 269–282. DOI: 10.52589/IJEBI-HET5STYK

Coeckelbergh, M. (2020). *AI Ethics*. The MIT Press. https://www.researchgate.net/publication/339103412_AI_Ethics

Colangelo, M. (2020). Mass adoption of AI in financial services expected within two years. Forbes. Available from https://www.forbes.com/sites/cognitiveworld/2020/02/20/mass-adoption-of-ai-in-financial-services-expectedwithin-two-years/#58e29b667d71

Colbert, C. (2024). *Technology is Dead: The Path to a More Human Future*. CRC Press. DOI: 10.1201/9781003089902

Cole, S. A., & Lynch, M. (2006). The Social and Legal Construction of Suspects. *Annual Review of Law and Social Science*, 2(1), 39–60. DOI: 10.1146/annurev.lawsocsci.2.081805.110001

Cooper, R. G. (2024). The AI transformation of product innovation. *Industrial Marketing Management*, 119, 62–74. DOI: 10.1016/j.indmarman.2024.03.008

Corbett-Davies, S., & Goel, S. (2018). The Measure and Mismeasure of Fairness: A Critical Review of Fair Machine Learning. *ArXiv (Cornell University), 24.* / arxiv.1808.00023DOI: 10.48550

Costanza-Chock, S. (2020). *Design justice: Community-led practices to build the worlds we need.* The MIT Press. DOI: 10.7551/mitpress/12255.001.0001

Crawford, K., & Calo, R. (2016). There is a blind spot in AI research. *Nature*, 538(7625), 311–313. DOI: 10.1038/538311a PMID: 27762391

Crawford, K., & Schultz, J. (2013, October 1). *Big Data and Due Process: Toward a Framework to Redress Predictive Privacy Harms.* https://papers.ssrn.com/sol3/papers.cfm?abstract_id=2325784

Crepelle, A. (2024). Tribes and AI: Possibilities for Tribal Sovereignty. *SSRN*, 25(1), 1–47. DOI: 10.2139/ssrn.4971212

Crolic, C., Thomaz, F., Hadi, R., & Stephen, A. T. (2022). Blame the Bot: Anthropomorphism and Anger in Customer–Chatbot Interactions. *Journal of Marketing*, 86(1), 132–148. DOI: 10.1177/00222429211045687

Cummings, M. (2024). *Scholars@Duke publication: Automation bias in intelligent time critical decision support systems.* Duke University. https://scholars.duke.edu/publication/1108365

Czerkawski, B. C., & Lyman, E. W.III. (2015). Exploring issues about computational thinking in higher education. *TechTrends*, 59(2), 57–65. DOI: 10.1007/s11528-015-0840-3

Dabbous, A., Barakat, K. A., & Sayegh, M. M. (2021). Enabling organizational use of artificial intelligence: an employee perspective. Journal of Asia Business Studies. https://api.semanticscholar.org/CorpusID:233932158

Dallocchio, M., Lambri, M., Sironi, E., & Teti, E. (2024). The role of digitalization in cross-border e-commerce performance of Italian SMEs. *Sustainability (Basel)*, 16(2), 508. DOI: 10.3390/su16020508

Darmawanto, A. T. (2023). The Influence of PDRB, Unemployment and Human Development Index on Poverty in Kalimantan Province. *Syntax Idea*, 5(12), 2335–2354.

Das, A., Wu, Y., Pradeep, N., Ghonge, M. M., & Pal, O. (Eds.). (2023). *Unleashing the Potentials of Blockchain Technology for Healthcare Industries.* Elsevier.

Dastin, J. (2018). Amazon scrapped a secret AI recruiting tool after it showed bias against women. Ethics of Data and Analytics. Auerbach Publications.

Datta, P. (2023). The promise and challenges of the fourth industrial revolution (4IR). *Journal of Information Technology Teaching Cases*, 13(1), 2–15. DOI: 10.1177/20438869211056938

De Felice, F., Rehman, M., Petrillo, A., & Baffo, I. (2023). A metaworld: Implications, opportunities and risks of the metaverse. *IET Collaborative Intelligent Manufacturing*, 5(3), e12079. DOI: 10.1049/cim2.12079

de Fine Licht, K., & de Fine Licht, J. (2020). Artificial intelligence, transparency, and public decision-making. *AI & Society*, 35(4), 917–926. DOI: 10.1007/s00146-020-00960-w

de Manuel, A., Delgado, J., Parra Jounou, I., Ausín, T., Casacuberta, D., Cruz, M., Guersenzvaig, A., Moyano, C., Rodríguez-Arias, D., Rueda, J., & Puyol, A. (2023). Ethical assessments and mitigation strategies for biases in AI-systems used during the COVID-19 pandemic. *Big Data & Society*, 10(1), 20539517231179199. Advance online publication. DOI: 10.1177/20539517231179199

De Mauro, A., Greco, M., Grimaldi, M., & Ritala, P. (2018). Human resources for Big Data professions: A systematic classification of job roles and required skill sets. *Information Processing & Management*, 54(5), 807–817. DOI: 10.1016/j.ipm.2017.05.004

Deloitte. (2025). How artificial intelligence is transforming the financial services industry. Retrieved from https://www.deloitte.com/ng/en/services/risk-advisory/services/how-artificial-intelligence-is-transforming-the-financial-services-industry.html

DeNisi, A. S., & Pritchard, R. D. (2006). Performance Appraisal, Performance Management and Improving Individual Performance: A Motivational Framework. *Management and Organization Review*, 2(2), 253–277. DOI: 10.1111/j.1740-8784.2006.00042.x

Denning, P. J., & Tedre, M. (2021). Computational thinking: A disciplinary perspective. *Informatics in Education*, 20(3), 361.

Dhar, S., & Bahl, N. (2022). Harassment of Women at Workplace in India Amounting to Psychological Scourge: A Socio-Legal Insight. *Agathos*, 13(2), 151–161.

Dixit, A. S., & Jatav, S. (2024). Evolving needs of learners and role of artificial intelligence (AI) in training and development (T&D): T&D professionals' perspective. Journal of Management Development. DOI: 10.1108/JMD-01-2024-0009

Donthu, N., Kumar, S., Mukherjee, D., Pandey, N., & Lim, W. M. (2021). How to conduct a bibliometric analysis: An overview and guidelines. *Journal of Business Research*, 133, 285–296. DOI: 10.1016/j.jbusres.2021.04.070

Drage, E., & Mackereth, K. (2022). Does AI debias recruitment? Race, gender, and AI's "eradication of difference". *Philosophy & Technology*, 35(4), 89. DOI: 10.1007/s13347-022-00543-1 PMID: 36246553

Dulebohn, J. H., & Stone, D. L. (2018). *The Brave New World of EHRM 2.0*. IAP.

Durai, S., Manoharan, G., Priya, T. S., Jayanthi, R., Razak, A., & Ashtikar, S. P. (2024). Quantifying the Impacts of Artificial Intelligence Implementations in Marketing. In *Smart and Sustainable Interactive Marketing* (pp. 120–144). IGI Global. DOI: 10.4018/979-8-3693-1339-8.ch008

Dutta, P. K., Singh, B., Towfeek, A.-S. K., Adamopoulou, J. P., Bardavouras, A. N., Bamwerinde, W., Turyasingura, B., & Ayiga, N. (2024). IoT Revolutionizes Humidity Measurement and Management in Smart Cities to Enhance Health and Wellness. *Mesopotamian Journal of Artificial Intelligence in Healthcare*, 2024, 110–117. DOI: 10.58496/MJAIH/2024/013

Dwivedi, Y. K., Hughes, L., Ismagilova, E., Aarts, G., Coombs, C., Crick, T., Duan, Y., Dwivedi, R., Edwards, J., Eirug, A., Galanos, V., Ilavarasan, P. V., Janssen, M., Jones, P., Kar, A. K., Kizgin, H., Kronemann, B., Lal, B., Lucini, B., & Williams, M. D. (2021). Artificial Intelligence (AI): Multidisciplinary perspectives on emerging challenges, opportunities, and agenda for research, practice and policy. *International Journal of Information Management*, 57, 101994. DOI: 10.1016/j.ijinfomgt.2019.08.002

Dwork, C. (2008). Differential Privacy: A Survey of Results. *Lecture Notes in Computer Science*, 4978, 1–19. DOI: 10.1007/978-3-540-79228-4_1

Edwin, E. I., Ugwu, C. C. O., & Obumnaeme, I. K. (2024). Implementation of Artificial Intelligence on Personnel Management in a Dynamic Society. *Management*, 12(2), 41–52.

Ejjami, R. (2024). AI-driven justice: Evaluating the impact of artificial intelligence on legal systems. *Int. J. Multidiscip. Res*, 6(3), 1–29.

El-Ghoul, M., Almassri, M. M., El-Habibi, M. F., Al-Qadi, M. H., Abou Eloun, A., Abu-Nasser, B. S., & Abu-Naser, S. S. (2024). AI in HRM: Revolutionizing Recruitment, Performance Management, and Employee Engagement. *International Journal of Academic Applied Research (Ijaar)*, 8(9), 16–23.

El-Ghoul, M., Almassri, M. M., El-Habibi, M. F., Al-Qadi, M. H., Abou Eloun, A., Abu-Nasser, B. S., & Abu-Naser, S. S. (2024). AI in HRM: Revolutionizing Recruitment, Performance Management, and Employee Engagement. *International Journal of Academic Applied Research*, 8(9), 16–29.

Enholm, I. M., Papagiannidis, E., Mikalef, P., & Krogstie, J. (2022). Artificial intelligence and business value: A literature review. *Information Systems Frontiers*, 24(5), 1709–1734. DOI: 10.1007/s10796-021-10186-w

Ernst & Young (EY). (2025). How artificial intelligence is reshaping the financial services industry. Retrieved from https://www.ey.com/en_gr/insights/financial-services/how-artificial-intelligence-is-reshaping-the-financial-services-industry

Eubanks, V. (2018, July 2). *Book Review: Automating Inequality: How High-Tech Tools Profile, Police and Punish the Poor by Virginia Eubanks*. LSE Review of Books. https://blogs.lse.ac.uk/lsereviewofbooks/2018/07/02/book-review-automating-inequality-how-high-tech-tools-profile-police-and-punish-the-poor-by-virginia-eubanks/

Eubanks, B. (2022). *Artificial intelligence for HR: Use AI to support and develop a successful workforce*. Kogan Page Publishers.

European Banking Authority (EBA) Report on Artificial Intelligence in Financial Services (2023).

European Commission. (2021). *Proposal for a Regulation laying down harmonised rules on artificial intelligence*. European Commission. https://eur-lex.europa.eu/legal-content/EN/TXT/HTML/?uri=CELEX:52021PC0206

Evans, K., & Lee, J. (2022). The rise of algorithmic justice: Implications for human rights. *International Journal of Human Rights*, 26(5), 789–805.

Ezeugwa, F. A., Olaniyi, O. O., Ugonnia, J. C., Arigbabu, A. S., & Joeaneke, P. C. (2024). Artificial Intelligence, Big Data, and Cloud Infrastructures: Policy Recommendations for Enhancing Women's Participation in the Tech-Driven Economy. *Journal of Engineering Research and Reports*, 26(6), 1–16. DOI: 10.9734/jerr/2024/v26i61158

Faqihi, A., & Miah, S. J. (2023). Artificial Intelligence-Driven Talent Management System: Exploring the Risks and Options for Constructing a Theoretical Foundation. *Journal of Risk and Financial Management*, 16(1), 31. DOI: 10.3390/jrfm16010031

Faruque, M. O., Chowdhury, S., Rabbani, G., & Nure, A. (2024). Technology adoption and digital transformation in small businesses: Trends, challenges, and opportunities. *International Journal For Multidisciplinary Research, 6*.

Fernandes, A. B. A., & Machado, C. F. (2022). E-recruitment and the impact of digital age on recruitment: A critical literature review. *Organizational innovation in the digital age*, 199-209.

Fernández-Martínez, C., & Fernández, A. (2020). AI and recruiting software: Ethical and legal implications. *Paladyn : Journal of Behavioral Robotics*, 11(1), 199–216. DOI: 10.1515/pjbr-2020-0030

Ferrara, E. (2023). Fairness and bias in artificial intelligence: A brief survey of sources, impacts, and mitigation strategies. *JMIR Preprints*, 21, 48399. https://doi.org/DOI: 10.2196/preprints.48399

Financial Times Special Report on Artificial Intelligence in Banking and Finance (2022).

Finextra Research Ltd. (2023). AI in banking: Use cases and implications for the future.

Forrester Research, Inc. (2023). The future of AI in financial services: Trends and predictions for 2025.

Frennert, S. (2021). Gender blindness: On health and welfare technology, AI and gender equality in community care. *Nursing Inquiry*, 28(4), e12419. DOI: 10.1111/nin.12419 PMID: 33979011

Fritts, M., & Cabrera, F. (2021). AI recruitment algorithms and the dehumanization problem. *Ethics and Information Technology*, 23(4), 791–801. DOI: 10.1007/s10676-021-09615-w

Füller, J., Hutter, K., Wahl, J., Bilgram, V., & Tekic, Z. (2022). How AI revolutionizes innovation management–Perceptions and implementation preferences of AI-based innovators. *Technological Forecasting and Social Change*, 178, 121598. DOI: 10.1016/j.techfore.2022.121598

Galanaki, E., & Papalexandris, A. (2020). Human resource management and artificial intelligence: The future is here. *Handbook of research on human resources strategies for the new millennial workforce*, 88-105.

Galante, N., Cotroneo, R., Furci, D., Lodetti, G., & Casali, M. B. (2023). Applications of artificial intelligence in forensic sciences: Current potential benefits, limitations, and perspectives. *International Journal of Legal Medicine*, 137(2), 445–458. DOI: 10.1007/s00414-022-02928-5 PMID: 36507961

Garcia, P., & Kim, S. (2023). Algorithmic bias in legal decision-making: Addressing the challenges of fairness. *AI Ethics Journal*, 5(1), 15–30.

García-Peñalvo, F. J., & Mendes, A. J. (2018). Exploring the computational thinking effects in pre-university education. *Computers in Human Behavior*, 80, 407–411. DOI: 10.1016/j.chb.2017.12.005

Garg, N., & Singh, B. (2022). Sustainable Development-Adopting a Balanced Approach between Development and Development Induced Changes. *ECS Transactions*, 107(1), 15–31. DOI: 10.1149/10701.0015ecst

Garrick, A., Johnson, W. D., & Arendt, S. W. (2024). Breaking barriers: Strategies for fostering inclusivity in the workplace. *International Journal of Academic Research in Business & Social Sciences*, 14(2), 115–121. DOI: 10.6007/IJARBSS/v14-i2/20799

Gartner. (2025). AI in marketing: The future of smart marketing. Retrieved from https://www.gartner.com/en/marketing/topics/ai-in-marketing

Gau, A. M., & Saleh, N. (2024). Exploring e-Commerce Potential: Improving Sales Performance Through Product Innovation in The Agriculture Sector. *Jurnal Economic Resource*, 7(1), 47–56. DOI: 10.57178/jer.v7i1.836

Gaubienė, N. (2024). Can Artificial Intelligence Engage in the Practice of Law as the Art of Good and Justice?. *Filosofija. Sociologija, 35*(2 Special).

Gawali, P., & Sony, R. (2020). The role of artificial intelligence in improving the criminal justice system: Indian perspective. *Legal Issues in the Digital Age*, 3(3), 78–96. DOI: 10.17323/2713-2749.2020.3.78.96

Geffner, C. J. (2023). *Building a New Leadership Ladder: Transforming Male-dominated Organizations to Support Women on the Rise*. MIT Press. DOI: 10.7551/mitpress/14386.001.0001

Gentzel, M. (2021). Biased face recognition technology used by government: A problem for liberal democracy. *Philosophy & Technology*, 34(4), 1639–1663. DOI: 10.1007/s13347-021-00478-z PMID: 34603941

Ghallab, M. (2019). Responsible AI: Requirements and challenges. *AI Perspectives*, 1(3), 3. Advance online publication. DOI: 10.1186/s42467-019-0003-z

Glikson, E., & Woolley, A. W. (2020). Human Trust in Artificial Intelligence: Review of Empirical Research. *The Academy of Management Annals*, 14(2), 627–660. DOI: 10.5465/annals.2018.0057

Gökçe, S., & Yenmez, A. A. (2023). Ingenuity of scratch programming on reflective thinking towards problem solving and computational thinking. *Education and Information Technologies*, 28(5), 5493–5517. DOI: 10.1007/s10639-022-11385-x

Golder, S., O'Connor, K., Wang, Y., Stevens, R., & Gonzalez-Hernandez, G. (2022). Best practices on big data analytics to address sex-specific biases in our understanding of the etiology, diagnosis, and prognosis of diseases. *Annual Review of Biomedical Data Science*, 5(1), 251–267. DOI: 10.1146/annurev-biodatasci-122120-025806 PMID: 35562851

Gong, T., Jiang, Y., Saldivia, L. E., & Agard, C. (2022). Using Sankey diagrams to visualize drag and drop action sequences in technology-enhanced items. *Behavior Research Methods*, 54(1), 117–132. DOI: 10.3758/s13428-021-01615-4 PMID: 34109559

Goodman, B., & Flaxman, S. (2017). European Union Regulations on Algorithmic Decision-Making and a "Right to Explanation.". *AI Magazine*, 38(3), 50–57. DOI: 10.1609/aimag.v38i3.2741

Google Cloud. (2025). AI in finance: Applications, examples & benefits. Retrieved from https://cloud.google.com/discover/finance-ai?hl=en

Gordon, J. S. (2021). AI and law: Ethical, legal, and socio-political implications. *AI & Society*, 36(2), 403–404. DOI: 10.1007/s00146-021-01194-0

Grabmann, C., & Schermuly, C. C. (2021). Coaching With Artificial Intelligence: Concepts and Capabilities. *Human Resource Development Review*, 20(1), 106–126. DOI: 10.1177/1534484320982891

Greene, T. (2018). IBM is using its AI to predict how employees will perform. Retrieved from https://thenextweb.com/artificial-intelligence/2018/07/10/ibm-is-using-its-ai-topredict-how-employees-will-perform/

Greig, A., & Flood, M. (2020). Work with men and boys for gender equality: a review of field formation, the evidence base and future directions. *UN-Women Discussion Paper Series. New York: United Nations Entity for Gender Equality and the Empowerment of Women.*

Gross, S., Kim, M., Schlosser, J., Mohtadi, C., Lluch, D., & Schneider, D. (2014, April). Fostering computational thinking in engineering education: Challenges, examples, and best practices. In *2014 IEEE Global Engineering Education Conference (EDUCON)* (pp. 450-459). IEEE. DOI: 10.1109/EDUCON.2014.6826132

Grund, C., & Przemeck, J. (2012). Subjective performance appraisal and inequality aversion. *Applied Economics*, 44(17), 2149–2155. DOI: 10.1080/00036846.2011.560109

Guan, H., Liye, D., & Zhao, A. (2022). Ethical risk factors and mechanisms in artificial intelligence decision making. *Behavioral Sciences (Basel, Switzerland)*, 12(9), 343. DOI: 10.3390/bs12090343 PMID: 36135147

Guembe, B., Azeta, A., Misra, S., Osamor, V. C., Fernández-Sanz, L., & Pospelova, V. (2022). The emerging threat of AI-driven cyber attacks: A review. *Applied Artificial Intelligence*, 36(1), 2037254. Advance online publication. DOI: 10.1080/08839514.2022.2037254

Guenole, N., & Feinzig, S. (2018). *The business case for AI in HR: With insights and tips on getting started*. IBM Publishing.

Guha, A., Grewal, D., & Atlas, S. (2024). Generative AI and Marketing Education: What the Future Holds. *Journal of Marketing Education*, 46(1), 6–17. DOI: 10.1177/02734753231215436

Gulliford, F., & Dixon, A. P. (2019). AI: the HR revolution. Strategic HR Review. https://api.semanticscholar.org/CorpusID:159308484

Güngör, Z., Serhadlıoğlu, G., & Kesen, S. E. (2009). A fuzzy AHP approach to personnel selection problem. *Applied Soft Computing*, 9(2), 641–646. DOI: 10.1016/j.asoc.2008.09.003

Gunning, D., Stefik, M., Choi, J., Miller, T., Stumpf, S., & Yang, G.-Z. (2019). XAI—Explainable artificial intelligence. *Science Robotics*, 4(37), eaay7120. Advance online publication. DOI: 10.1126/scirobotics.aay7120 PMID: 33137719

Gursoy, D., & Cai, R. (2025). Artificial intelligence: An overview of research trends and future directions. *International Journal of Contemporary Hospitality Management*, 37(1), 1–17. DOI: 10.1108/IJCHM-03-2024-0322

Habito, R. (2022). Buddhist Praxis toward Global Healing—Cultivating Clarity, Wisdom, and Kinship. *Religions*, 13(4), 315. DOI: 10.3390/rel13040315

Hagendorff, T., & Wezel, K. (2020). 15 challenges for AI: Or what AI (currently) can't do. *AI & Society*, 35(2), 355–365. DOI: 10.1007/s00146-019-00886-y

Halid, H., Ravesangar, K., Mahadzir, S. L., & Halim, S. N. A. (2024). Artificial Intelligence (AI) in Human Resource Management (HRM). In *Building the Future with Human Resource Management* (pp. 37-70). Springer.

Halid, H., Ravesangar, K., Mahadzir, S. L., & Halim, S. N. A. (2024). Artificial Intelligence (AI) in Human Resource Management (HRM). In Machado, C. (Ed.), *Building the Future with Human Resource Management* (pp. 37–70). Springer International Publishing. DOI: 10.1007/978-3-031-52811-8_2

Hall, J., & Wright, G. (2022). The future of justice: AI's role in transforming legal systems worldwide. *Global Journal of Comparative Law*, 11(2), 99–121.

Hamadaqa, M. H. M., Alnajjar, M., Ayyad, M. N., Al-Nakhal, M. A., Abunasser, B. S., & Abu-Naser, S. S. (2024). Leveraging Artificial Intelligence for Strategic Business Decision-Making: Opportunities and Challenges.

Hans, V., & Theophil, S. (2024). Religion in the Post Humanism World. *Sandeep, Religion in the Post Humanism World.*

Hardyns, W., & Rummens, A. (2018). Predictive policing as a new tool for law enforcement? Recent developments and challenges. *European Journal on Criminal Policy and Research*, 24(2), 201–218. DOI: 10.1007/s10610-017-9361-2

Harrison, P., & Todes, A. (2024). *The Promise of Planning: Global Aspirations and South African Experience Since 2008*. Taylor & Francis. DOI: 10.4324/9781003104438

Hasan, A., Brown, S., Davidovic, J., Lange, B., & Regan, M. (2022). Algorithmic bias and risk assessments: Lessons from practice. *Digital Society : Ethics, Socio-Legal and Governance of Digital Technology*, 1(2), 14. DOI: 10.1007/s44206-022-00017-z

Havryk, A., & Nazarova, T. (2024). Artificial intelligence and its role in the labor market and financial sector itself: US point of view. *International Science Journal of Management. Economics & Finance*, 3(3), 1–9.

HBR Analytics Services. (2022). The role of AI in transforming customer experiences in banking and finance. *Harvard Business Review.*

Heaven, W. D. (2020). This startup is using AI to give workers a "productivity score". MIT Technology Review. Available from https://www.technologyreview.com/2020/06/04/1002671/startup-ai-workers-productivityscore-bias-machine-learning-business-covid/?mod=djemAIPro

Hemel, U. (2024). The Influence of Religions on Women's Health. In *Global Women's Health* (pp. 67–77). Springer. DOI: 10.1007/978-3-662-69700-9_6

Hendrawan, S. A., Chatra, A., Iman, N., Hidayatullah, S., & Suprayitno, D. (2024). Digital transformation in MSMEs: Challenges and opportunities in technology management. *Jurnal Informasi dan Teknologi*, 141-149.

Henz, P. (2021). Ethical and legal responsibility for Artificial Intelligence. *Discover Artificial Intelligence*, 1(2), 2. Advance online publication. DOI: 10.1007/s44163-021-00002-4

Her, R. S. (2024). Thoughts and Practice of Good Enterprises. In *The Economy of Goodness* (pp. 351–443). Springer Nature Singapore. DOI: 10.1007/978-981-97-6363-4_12

Hewage, A. (2023). Exploring the applicability of artificial intelligence in recruitment and selection processes: A focus on the recruitment phase. *Journal of Human Resource and Sustainability Studies*, 11(3), 603–634. DOI: 10.4236/jhrss.2023.113034

Hilb, M. (2020). Toward artificial governance? The role of artificial intelligence in shaping the future of corporate governance. *The Journal of Management and Governance*, 24(4), 851–870. DOI: 10.1007/s10997-020-09519-9

Hill, D., O'Connor, C. D., & Slane, A. (2022). Police use of facial recognition technology: The potential for engaging the public through co-constructed policy-making. *International Journal of Police Science & Management*, 24(3), 325–335. DOI: 10.1177/14613557221089558

Hitch, D. (2024). Artificial intelligence augmented qualitative analysis: The way of the future? *Qualitative Health Research*, 34(7), 595–606. DOI: 10.1177/10497323231217392 PMID: 38064244

Hmoud, B. (2021) The adoption of artificial intelligence in human resource management and the role of human resources. Questa Soft https://www.ceeol.com/search/articledetail?id=940529

Hmoud, B., & Varallyai, L. (2023). Role of Artificial Intelligence in Human Resource Management in the Middle East Countries. *KnE Social Sciences*, 435–448-435–448.

Hollanek, T. (2023). AI transparency: A matter of reconciling design with critique. *AI & Society*, 38(5), 2071–2079. DOI: 10.1007/s00146-020-01110-y

Holsinger, L. (2019). Performance Transformation in the Future of Work. Mercer. https://www.mercer.com/our-thinking/career/performance-transformation-in-the-futureof-work.html

Horodyski, P. (2023). Applicants' perception of artificial intelligence in the recruitment process. *Computers in Human Behavior Reports*, 11, 100303. DOI: 10.1016/j.chbr.2023.100303

Horodyski, P. (2023). Recruiter's perception of artificial intelligence (AI)-based tools in recruitment. *Computers in Human Behavior Reports*, 10, 100298. DOI: 10.1016/j.chbr.2023.100298

Hristov, I., Camilli, R., & Mechelli, A. (2022). Cognitive biases in implementing a performance management system: Behavioral strategy for supporting managers' decision-making processes. *Management Research Review*, 45(9), 1110–1136. DOI: 10.1108/MRR-11-2021-0777

Hsu, T. C., & Liang, Y. S. (2021). Simultaneously improving computational thinking and foreign language learning: Interdisciplinary media with plugged and unplugged approaches. *Journal of Educational Computing Research*, 59(6), 1184–1207. DOI: 10.1177/0735633121992480

Huang, X., Yang, F., Zheng, J., Feng, C., & Zhang, L. (2023). Personalized human resource management via HR analytics and artificial intelligence: Theory and implications. Asia Pacific Management Review, 28(4), 598-610. https://doi.org/https://doi.org/10.1016/j.apmrv.2023.04.004

Hunkenschroer, A. L., & Luetge, C. (2022). Ethics of AI-Enabled Recruiting and Selection: A Review and Research agenda. *Journal of Business Ethics*, 178(4), 977–1007. DOI: 10.1007/s10551-022-05049-6

Hutchins, N. M., Biswas, G., Maróti, M., Lédeczi, Á., Grover, S., Wolf, R., Blair, K. P., Chin, D., Conlin, L., Basu, S., & McElhaney, K. (2020). C2STEM: A system for synergistic learning of physics and computational thinking. *Journal of Science Education and Technology*, 29(1), 83–100. DOI: 10.1007/s10956-019-09804-9

Hutiri, W., Papakyriakopoulos, O., & Xiang, A. (2024, June). Not My Voice! A Taxonomy of Ethical and Safety Harms of Speech Generators. In *The 2024 ACM Conference on Fairness, Accountability, and Transparency* (pp. 359-376).

Hyatt, J., & Chanenson, S. L. (2016). The use of risk assessment at sentencing: Implications for research and policy (Villanova Law/Public Policy Research Paper No. 2017-1040). *SSRN*. https://ssrn.com/abstract=2961288

Ibegbulam, C., Olowonubi, F., Fatounde, P., & Oyegunwa, P. (2023). Artificial intelligence in the era of 4IR: Drivers, challenges, and opportunities. *Engineering Science & Technology Journal*, 4(6), 473–488. DOI: 10.51594/estj.v4i6.668

IBM Institute for Business Value. (2023). Banking on AI: How financial institutions can leverage artificial intelligence to drive growth and efficiency.

Idris, R., Faisal-E-Alam, M., Castanho, R. A., & Loures, L. (2024). Bridging the gender gap in STEM fields: Empowering women for economic and social development in Malaysia. *WSEAS Transactions On Business And Economics*, 21, 617–629. DOI: 10.37394/23207.2024.21.51

Ilyas, M. (2024). The impact of armed conflict on education and children in Jammu and Kashmir: Implications for peace education. *Journal of Peace Education*, 1–21. DOI: 10.1080/17400201.2024.2433783

Intelion Systems. (2023). *AI Recruitment Statistics*. LinkedIn. https://www.linkedin.com/pulse/ai-recruitment-statistics-intelion-systems/

Istratii, R., Ali, P., & Feder, G. (2024). Integration of religious beliefs and faith-based resources in domestic violence services to migrant and ethnic minority communities: A scoping review. *Violence: An International Journal*, 5(1), 94–122. DOI: 10.1177/26330024241246810

Jansen, F., Sánchez-Monedero, J., & Dencik, L. (2021). Biometric identity systems in law enforcement and the politics of (voice) recognition: The case of SiiP. *Big Data & Society*, 8(2). Advance online publication. DOI: 10.1177/20539517211063604

Jaoudi, M. (2021). *Mindfulness as sustainability: Lessons from the world's religions*. State University of New York Press.

Jarrahi, M. H. (2018). Artificial intelligence and the future of work: Human-AI symbiosis in organizational decision making. *Business Horizons*, 61(4), 577–586. DOI: 10.1016/j.bushor.2018.03.007

Javaid, M., Haleem, A., Singh, R. P., Suman, R., & Gonzalez, E. S. (2022). Understanding the adoption of Industry 4.0 technologies in improving environmental sustainability. *Sustainable Operations and Computers*, 3, 203–217. DOI: 10.1016/j.susoc.2022.01.008

Javed, K., & Li, J. (2025). Bias in adjudication: Investigating the impact of artificial intelligence, media, financial and legal institutions in pursuit of social justice. *PLoS One*, 20(1), e0315270. DOI: 10.1371/journal.pone.0315270 PMID: 39752385

Jayawardena NS, Behl A, Thaichon P, Quach S (2022). Artificial intelligence (AI)-based market intelligence and customer insights. *Artificial Intelligence for Marketing Management*, 120-41.

Jimenez-Gomez, C. E., Cano-Carrillo, J., & Lanas, F. F. (2020). Artificial intelligence in government. *Computer*, 53(10), 23–27. DOI: 10.1109/MC.2020.3010043

Johansson, J., & Herranen, S. (2019). The application of artificial intelligence (AI) in human resource management: Current state of AI and its impact on the traditional recruitment process. In.

John-Mathews, J. M., Cardon, D., & Balagué, C. (2022). From reality to world. A critical perspective on AI fairness. *Journal of Business Ethics*, 178(4), 945–959. DOI: 10.1007/s10551-022-05055-8

Johnson, K., & Smith, L. (2022). Predictive analytics in the courtroom: A new era for justice? *The Journal of Law and Technology*, 15(2), 45–67.

Johnson, R., Stone, D., & Lukaszewski, K. (2020). The benefits of ehrm and ai for talent acquisition. *Journal of Tourism Futures*, 7(1), 40–52. DOI: 10.1108/JTF-02-2020-0013

Jose, S. (2019). Innovation in recruitment and talent acquisition: A study on technologies and strategies adopted for talent management in IT sector. *International Journal of Marketing and Human Resource Management*, 10(2), 1–8. DOI: 10.34218/IJMHRM.10.3.2019.001

Journals, I. A. E. S. (2024). The use of artificial intelligence in interrogations: Voluntary confession. *IAES International Journal of Robotics and Automation*, 13(2), 113–121. DOI: 10.11591/ijra.v13i2.pp113-121

Kabir, M. S., & Alam, M. N. (2023). The role of AI technology for legal research and decision making. *Journal Title*, 10, 2395–0056.

Kahkonen, S., & da Silva, R. (2023). Stretching the Peace: The Role of Kundalini Yoga in the Lives of Young People in Alexandra, South Africa. *Journal of Humanistic Psychology*. DOI: 10.1177/00221678231152636

Kanade, V. (2022). *What Is Artificial Intelligence (AI)? Definition, Types, Goals, Challenges, and Trends in 2022.* Spiceworks https://www.spiceworks.com/tech/artificial-intelligence/articles/what-is-ai/

Kannan, R. (2024). Revolutionizing the Tourism Industry through Artificial Intelligence: A Comprehensive Review of AI Integration, Impact on Customer Experience, Operational Efficiency, and Future Trends. *International Journal for Multidimensional Research Perspectives,* 2(2), 1-14.

Kapur, P., Misra, G., & Verma, N. K. (2022). *Psychological Perspectives on Identity, Religion and Well-Being: Empirical Findings from India.* Springer Nature. DOI: 10.1007/978-981-19-2844-4

Karnani, A. K. (2024). AI empowerment in democratic governance: enhancing participation and efficiency. *Journal of Data Acquisition and Processing*, 39(1), 993.

Karnani, A. K. (2024). AI empowerment in democratic governance: Enhancing participation and efficiency. *Journal of Data Acquisition and Processing*, 39(1), 993.

Kaur, N., & Kaur, M. (2024). Role of artificial intelligence in the Indian courts. *International Journal of Law. Policy and Social Review*, 6(1), 17–20.

Kaushal, N., Kaurav, R. P. S., Sivathanu, B., & Kaushik, N. (2023). Artificial intelligence and HRM: Identifying future research Agenda using systematic literature review and bibliometric analysis. *Management Review Quarterly*, 73(2), 455–493. DOI: 10.1007/s11301-021-00249-2

Kaushik, T. K., Singh, A., Raghav, A., Singh, B., Arora, M. K., & Lal, S. (2024). Untapping Artificial Intelligence in Environmental and Sustainable Progression: Projecting Legal and Ethical Considerations. In B. Singh, C. Kaunert, K. Vig, & S. Dutta (Eds.), *Maintaining a Sustainable World in the Nexus of Environmental Science and AI* (pp. 109-130). IGI Global. DOI: 10.4018/979-8-3693-6336-2.ch005

KC, D. B. (2024). Targeted Intervention Program for the Preservation of the Traditional Himalayan Buddhist Culture and Customs: A Case Study of Ananda Sangh, Kathmandu. *NPRC Journal of Multidisciplinary Research, 1*(7), 43-52.

Kehl, D., Guo, P., & Kessler, S. (2017). *Algorithms in the criminal justice system: Assessing the use of risk assessments in sentencing*. Responsive Communities Initiative, Berkman Klein Center for Internet & Society, Harvard Law School. http://nrs.harvard.edu/urn-3:HUL.InstRepos:3374604

Kesharwani, S. (2023). Interrelationship Between E-satisfaction, E-trust and E-loyalty in the Banking Industry. *Global Journal of Enterprise Information System*, 15(3), 9–16.

Khalifa, M., & Sabry, M. (2024, January). The Challenges of The Artificial Intelligence of Law in The Context of Technological Development. In *2024 ASU International Conference in Emerging Technologies for Sustainability and Intelligent Systems (ICETSIS)* (pp. 1-5). IEEE. DOI: 10.1109/ICETSIS61505.2024.10459547

Khan, D., & Lucas, M. (2023). The impact of technology on the criminal justice system.

Khan, S. (2020). Artificial Intelligence Virtual Assistants (Chatbots) are Innovative Investigators. *IJCSNS, 20*(2).

Khanal, S., Zhang, H., & Taeihagh, A. (2024). Building an AI ecosystem in a small nation: Lessons from Singapore's journey to the forefront of AI. *Humanities & Social Sciences Communications*, 11(1), 866. DOI: 10.1057/s41599-024-03289-7

Khattri, U., Sharma, P., Adarsh, A., & Kour, G. D. (2025). How Can Artificial Intelligence Enable Sustainable Development Goals? Leveraging Technology for a Sustainable Future. In *Renewable Energy and the Economic Welfare of Society* (pp. 423-450). IGI Global Scientific Publishing.

Khedekar, D. (2023). *Communicating Precarity and Resistance Under Surveillance: Fragile Organizing in Private Online Groups* (Doctoral dissertation, University of Colorado at Boulder).

King, A. S. (2022). Hinduism: The culture of peace and the ethics of war. *The Wiley Blackwell Companion to Religion and Peace*, 195-215.

Kishor, R., Patle, B., & Bhojane, P. (2023). The AI vantage: An exposition of global dynamics. *Journal of Mechatronics and Artificial Intelligence in Engineering*, 4(2), 58–82. DOI: 10.21595/jmai.2023.23389

Klucin, F. (2020). *The use of artificial intelligence in the recruitment process*

Knight, R. (2020). How to Do Performance Reviews — Remotely. Harvard Business Review. https://hbr.org/2020/06/how-to-do-performance-reviews-remotely

Köbis, N., Starke, C., & Rahwan, I. (2022). The promise and perils of using artificial intelligence to fight corruption. *Nature Machine Intelligence*, 4(5), 418–424. DOI: 10.1038/s42256-022-00489-1

Kolade, T. M., Aideyan, N. T., Oyekunle, S. M., Ogungbemi, O. S., Dapo-Oyewole, D. L., & Olaniyi, O. O. (2024). Artificial Intelligence and Information Governance: Strengthening Global Security, through Compliance Frameworks, and Data Security. *Available atSSRN* 5044032. DOI: 10.9734/ajrcos/2024/v17i12528

Kostka, G., Steinacker, L., & Meckel, M. (2021). Between security and convenience: Facial recognition technology in the eyes of citizens in China, Germany, the United Kingdom, and the United States. *Public Understanding of Science (Bristol, England)*, 30(6), 671–690. DOI: 10.1177/09636625211001555 PMID: 33769157

Koulu, R. (2020). Proceduralizing control and discretion: Human oversight in artificial intelligence policy. *Maastricht Journal of European and Comparative Law*, 27(6), 720–735. DOI: 10.1177/1023263X20978649

KPMG. (2023). The impact of artificial intelligence on financial services: Opportunities and challenges ahead. Retrieved from https://home.kpmg/xx/en/home/insights/2023/01/the-impact-of-artificial-intelligence-on-financial-services.html

Kshetri, N., Dwivedi, Y. K., Davenport, T. H., & Panteli, N. (2024). Generative artificial intelligence in marketing: Applications, opportunities, challenges, and research agenda. *International Journal of Information Management*, 75, 102716. DOI: 10.1016/j.ijinfomgt.2023.102716

Kucharčíková, A., Mičiak, M., Tokarčíková, E., & Štaffenová, N. (2023). The investments in human capital within the human capital management and the impact on the enterprise's performance. *Sustainability (Basel)*, 15(6), 5015. DOI: 10.3390/su15065015

Kulal, A., Rahiman, H. U., Suvarna, H., Abhishek, N., & Dinesh, S. (2024). Enhancing public service delivery efficiency: Exploring the impact of AI. *Journal of Open Innovation*, 10(3), 100329. DOI: 10.1016/j.joitmc.2024.100329

Kulkarni, S. B., & Che, X. (2019). Intelligent software tools for recruiting. *Journal of International Technology and Information Management*, 28(2), 2–16. DOI: 10.58729/1941-6679.1398

Kumar, D., & Suthar, N. (2024). Ethical and legal challenges of AI in marketing: An exploration of solutions. *Journal of Information. Communication and Ethics in Society*, 22(1), 124–144. DOI: 10.1108/JICES-05-2023-0068

Kumar, S., Pandey, N., Lim, W. M., Chatterjee, A. N., & Pandey, N. (2021). What do we know about transfer pricing? Insights from bibliometric analysis. *Journal of Business Research*, 134, 275–287. DOI: 10.1016/j.jbusres.2021.05.041

Kumar, S., & Patel, A. K. (2019). An analysis of cointegration between nifty index, dollar/INR and crude oil price. *Journal of Advanced Research in Dynamical and Control Systems*, 11(12), 151–159. DOI: 10.5373/JARDCS/V11I12/20193223

Kumar, V., Ashraf, A. R., & Nadeem, W. (2024). AI-powered marketing: What, where, and how? *International Journal of Information Management*, 77, 102783. DOI: 10.1016/j.ijinfomgt.2024.102783

Kundi, B., El Morr, C., Gorman, R., & Dua, E. (2023). Artificial intelligence and bias: A scoping review. *AI & Society*, 199–215.

Kunz, W. H., & Wirtz, J. (2024). Corporate digital responsibility (CDR) in the age of AI: Implications for interactive marketing. *Journal of Research in Interactive Marketing*, 18(1), 31–37. DOI: 10.1108/JRIM-06-2023-0176

Łabuz, M. (2025). A Teleological Interpretation of the Definition of DeepFakes in the EU Artificial Intelligence Act—A Purpose-Based Approach to Potential Problems With the Word "Existing". *Policy and Internet.*

Lahoti, Y. (2023). Impact of artificial intelligence on Human Resource Management. *Journal for ReAttach Therapy and Developmental Diversities*, 6(1), 1655–1664. DOI: 10.53555/jrtdd.v6i1.2839

Laila, N., Sucia Sukmaningrum, P., Saini Wan Ngah, W. A., Nur Rosyidi, L., & Rahmawati, I. (2024). An in-depth analysis of digital marketing trends and prospects in small and medium-sized enterprises: Utilizing bibliometric mapping. *Cogent Business & Management*, 11(1), 2336565. DOI: 10.1080/23311975.2024.2336565

Langer, M., König, C. J., & Hemsing, V. (2020). Is anybody listening? The impact of automatically evaluated job interviews on impression management and applicant reactions. *Journal of Managerial Psychology*, 35(4), 271–284. DOI: 10.1108/JMP-03-2019-0156

Langer, M., König, C. J., & Papathanasiou, M. (2019). Highly automated job interviews: Acceptance under the influence of stakes. *International Journal of Selection and Assessment*, 27(3), 217234. DOI: 10.1111/ijsa.12246

Laqueur, H. S., & Copus, R. W. (2024). An algorithmic assessment of parole decisions. *Journal of Quantitative Criminology*, 40(1), 151–188. DOI: 10.1007/s10940-022-09563-8

Laurim, V., Arpaci, S., Prommegger, B., & Krcmar, H. (2021). Computer, whom should i hire?–acceptance criteria for artificial intelligence in the recruitment process.

Leavitt, K., Barnes, C. M., & Shapiro, D. L. (2022). The Role of Human Managers within Algorithmic Performance Management Systems: A Process Model of Employee Trust in Managers through Reflexivity. Academy of Management Review. DOI: 10.5465/amr.2022.0058

Leavy, S., O'Sullivan, B., & Siapera, E. (2020). Data, Power and Bias in Artificial Intelligence. *ArXiv, abs/2008.07341.*

Lee, Y., Bradford, B., & Posch, K. (2024). The Effectiveness of Big Data-Driven Predictive Policing: Systematic Review. *Justice Evaluation Journal*, 1–34. https://doi.org/DOI: 10.1080/24751979.2024.2371781

Lee, C. L., Yam, S., Susilawati, C., & Blake, A. (2024). The future property workforce: Challenges and opportunities for property professionals in the changing landscape. *Buildings (Basel, Switzerland)*, 14(1), 224. DOI: 10.3390/buildings14010224

Lee, I., Grover, S., Martin, F., Pillai, S., & Malyn-Smith, J. (2020). Computational thinking from a disciplinary perspective: Integrating computational thinking in K-12 science, technology, engineering, and mathematics education. *Journal of Science Education and Technology*, 29(1), 1–8. DOI: 10.1007/s10956-019-09803-w

Lee, M., & Chen, Y. (2023). AI and access to justice: Enhancing legal services through technology. *Harvard Law Review*, 136(3), 789–812.

Li, B., Chen, Y., Liu, L., & Zheng, B. (2023). Users' intention to adopt artificial intelligence-based chatbot: A meta-analysis. *Service Industries Journal*, 43(15-16), 1117–1139. DOI: 10.1080/02642069.2023.2217756

Li, C. Z., Xue, F., Li, X., Hong, J., & Shen, G. Q. (2018). An Internet of Things-enabled BIM platform for on-site assembly services in prefabricated construction. *Automation in Construction*, 89, 146–161. DOI: 10.1016/j.autcon.2018.01.001

Li, J., Rothrauff, B., Chen, S., Zhao, S., Wu, Z., Chen, Q., & He, J. (2022). Trends in anterior cruciate ligament repair: A bibliometric and visualized analysis. *Orthopaedic Journal of Sports Medicine*, 10(10). DOI: 10.1177/23259671221132564 PMID: 36338352

Li, L., Mu, X., Li, S., & Peng, H. (2020). A review of face recognition technology. *IEEE Access : Practical Innovations, Open Solutions*, 8, 139110–139120. DOI: 10.1109/ACCESS.2020.3011028

Limantė, A. (2023). Bias in facial recognition technologies used by law enforcement: Understanding the causes and searching for a way out. *Nordic Journal of Human Rights*, 42(2), 115–134. DOI: 10.1080/18918131.2023.2277581

Lim, D. (2025). Determinants of Socially Responsible AI Governance. *Duke Law & Technology Review*, 25(1), 183–232.

Lim, W. H., Wong, C., Jain, S. R., Ng, C. H., Tai, C. H., Devi, M. K., Samarasekera, D. D., Iyer, S. G., & Chong, C. S. (2021). The unspoken reality of gender bias in surgery: A qualitative systematic review. *PLoS One*, 16(2), e0246420. DOI: 10.1371/journal.pone.0246420 PMID: 33529257

Lin, T. A., & Chen, P. H. C. (2022). Artificial intelligence in a structurally unjust society. Feminist Philosophy Quarterly, 8(3/4).

Liu, H. P., Perera, S. M., & Klein, J. W. (2017). Using model-based learning to promote computational thinking education. *Emerging research, practice, and policy on computational thinking*, 153-172.

Li, Z. (2024). Ethical frontiers in artificial intelligence: Navigating the complexities of bias, privacy, and accountability. *International Journal of Engineering and Management Research*, 14(3), 109–116.

Lockwood, J., & Mooney, A. (2017). Computational Thinking in Education: Where does it fit? A systematic literary review. *arXiv preprint arXiv:1703.07659*.

Lodi, M., & Martini, S. (2021). Computational thinking, between Papert and Wing. *Science & Education*, 30(4), 883–908. DOI: 10.1007/s11191-021-00202-5

Logg, J. M., Minson, J. A., & Moore, D. A. (2019). Algorithm appreciation: People prefer algorithmic to human judgment. *Organizational Behavior and Human Decision Processes*, 151(151), 90–103. DOI: 10.1016/j.obhdp.2018.12.005

MacCarthy, M. (2020). AI needs more regulation, not less. Brookings Institution. https://www.brookings.edu/research/ai-needs-more-regulation-not-less/

Madaio, M. A., Stark, L., Wortman Vaughan, J., & Wallach, H. (2020, April). Co-designing checklists to understand organizational challenges and opportunities around fairness in AI. In *Proceedings of the 2020 CHI conference on human factors in computing systems* (pp. 1-14). DOI: 10.1145/3313831.3376445

Madaoui, N. (2024). The impact of artificial intelligence on legal systems: Challenges and opportunities. *Problems of Legality*, 1(164), 285–303. DOI: 10.21564/2414-990X.164.289266

Maity, S. (2019). Identifying opportunities for artificial intelligence in the evolution of training and development practices. *Journal of Management Development*, 651663(8), 651–663. Advance online publication. DOI: 10.1108/JMD-03-2019-0069

Malik, A., Srikanth, N., & Budhwar, P. (2020). Digitisation, artificial intelligence (AI) and HRM. *Human resource management: Strategic and international perspectives, 88*, 103.

Mandalapu, V., Elluri, L., Vyas, P., & Roy, N. (2023). Crime prediction using machine learning and deep learning: A systematic review and future directions. *IEEE Access : Practical Innovations, Open Solutions*, 1(1), 1–1. DOI: 10.1109/ACCESS.2023.3286344

Mannix, E., & Neale, M. A. (2005). What differences make a difference? The promise and reality of diverse teams in organizations. *Psychological Science in the Public Interest*, 6(2), 31–55. DOI: 10.1111/j.1529-1006.2005.00022.x PMID: 26158478

Mäntymäki, M., Minkkinen, M., Birkstedt, T., & Viljanen, M. (2022). Putting AI ethics into practice: The hourglass model of organizational AI governance. *arXiv preprint arXiv:2206.00335*.

Mardiani, E., Utami, E. Y., Suwarna, A. I., Hamizar, A., & Tubalawony, J. (2024). Quantitative Analysis of the Effect of Marketing Networks in Increasing Sales and Market Share in Indonesia Case Study on the E-commerce Industry. *Sciences du Nord Economics and Business*, 1(01), 11–16. DOI: 10.58812/sneb.v1i1.9

Marler, J. H., & Fisher, S. L. (2013). An evidence-based review of e-HRM and strategic human resource management. *Human Resource Management Review*, 23(1), 18–36. DOI: 10.1016/j.hrmr.2012.06.002

Marquis, Y., Oladoyinbo, T. O., Olabanji, S. O., Olaniyi, O. O., & Ajayi, S. A. (2024). Proliferation of AI tools: A multifaceted evaluation of user perceptions and emerging trend. *Asian Journal of Advanced Research and Reports*, 18(1), 30–55. DOI: 10.9734/ajarr/2024/v18i1596

Martinez, L., & Torres, F. (2021). Exploring the role of machine learning in judicial processes. *The Journal of Legal Studies*, 30(2), 150–175.

Martin, K. D., & Zimmermann, J. (2024). Artificial intelligence and its implications for data privacy. *Current Opinion in Psychology*, 58, 101829. DOI: 10.1016/j.copsyc.2024.101829 PMID: 38954851

Marwala, T., & Mpedi, L. G. (2024). Artificial intelligence and the law. In *Artificial Intelligence and the Law* (pp. 1–25). Springer Nature Singapore.

Marwala, T., & Mpedi, L. G. (2024). Criminal justice system and AI. In *Artificial intelligence and the law* (pp. 1–15). Palgrave Macmillan. DOI: 10.1007/978-981-97-2827-5_3

Mathushan, P., Gamage, A. S., & Wachissara, V. (2023). Human Resource Management and Artificial Intelligence: A Bibliometric Exploration. [former Vidyodaya Journal of Management]. *Journal of Business Research and Insights*, 9(I).

Ma, X., & Gu, X. (2024). New marketing strategy model of E-commerce enterprises in the era of digital economy. *Heliyon*, 10(8), e29038. DOI: 10.1016/j.heliyon.2024.e29038 PMID: 38628774

McAllister, J. T., Lennertz, L., & Atencio Mojica, Z. (2022). Mapping a discipline: A guide to using VOSviewer for bibliometric and visual analysis. *Science & Technology Libraries*, 41(3), 319–348. DOI: 10.1080/0194262X.2021.1991547

McAra-Hunter, D. (2024). How AI hype impacts the LGBTQ+ community. *AI and Ethics*, 4(3), 1–20. DOI: 10.1007/s43681-024-00423-8

McColl, R., & Michelotti, M. (2019). Sorry, could you repeat the question? Exploring video-interview recruitment practice in HRM. *Human Resource Management Journal*, 29(4), 637–656. DOI: 10.1111/1748-8583.12249

McKinsey & Company. (2025). Building the AI bank of the future. Retrieved from https://www.mckinsey.com/~/media/mckinsey/industries/financial%20services/our%20insights/building%20the%20ai%20bank%20of%20the%20future/building-the-ai-bank-of-the-future.pdf

Medaglia, R., Gil-Garcia, J. R., & Pardo, T. A. (2023). Artificial intelligence in government: Taking stock and moving forward. *Social Science Computer Review*, 41(1), 123–140. DOI: 10.1177/08944393211034087

Meijer, A., & Wessels, M. (2019). Predictive Policing: Review of Benefits and Drawbacks. *International Journal of Public Administration*, 42(12), 1031–1039. DOI: 10.1080/01900692.2019.1575664

Mensah, G. B., Mijwil, M. M., Abotaleb, M., Ali, G., & Dutta, P. K. (2009). High Performance Medicine: Involving Artificial Intelligence Models in Enhancing Medical Laws and Medical Negligence Matters A Case Study of Act, 2009 (Act 792) in Ghana.

Mercado, J. E., Rupp, M. A., Chen, J. Y., Barnes, M. J., Barber, D., & Procci, K. (2016). Intelligent agent transparency in human–agent teaming for multi-UxV management. *Human Factors*, 58(3), 401–415. DOI: 10.1177/0018720815621206 PMID: 26867556

Mercan, G., & Selçuk, Z. V. (2024). Artificial intelligence (AI) activities in legal practices. *International Journal of Eurasian Education and Culture*, 9(25), 131–144. DOI: 10.35826/ijoecc.1824

Meterko, V., & Cooper, G. (2022). Cognitive biases in criminal case evaluation: A review of the research. *Journal of Police and Criminal Psychology*, 37(1), 101–122. DOI: 10.1007/s11896-020-09425-8

Mikalef, P., Conboy, K., Lundström, J. E., & Popovič, A. (2022). Thinking responsibly about responsible AI and 'the dark side' of AI. *European Journal of Information Systems*, 31(3), 257–268. DOI: 10.1080/0960085X.2022.2026621

Miller, D., & Thompson, H. (2021). AI in the courtroom: The future of legal practice? *Legal Technology Journal*, 12(4), 67–89.

Millner, U. C., Maru, M., Ismail, A., & Chakrabarti, U. (2021). Decolonizing mental health practice: Reconstructing an Asian-centric framework through a social justice lens. *Asian American Journal of Psychology*, 12(4), 333–345. DOI: 10.1037/aap0000268

Min, A. (2023). Artificial intelligence and bias: Challenges, implications, and remedies. *Journal of Social Research*, 2(11), 3808–3817. DOI: 10.55324/josr.v2i11.1477

Mishra, A. K., Tyagi, A. K., Dananjayan, S., Rajavat, A., Rawat, H., & Rawat, A. (2024). Revolutionizing Government Operations: The Impact of Artificial Intelligence in Public Administration. *Conversational Artificial Intelligence*, 607-634.

Mitchell, J., King, A. S., Hayward, S., Singh, J., Wilkes, G., Rey, J., & Timani, H. (2022). World Religions and Peace. *The Wiley Blackwell Companion to Religion and Peace*, 21-38.

Mittal, V., Mehta, P., Relan, D., & Gabrani, G. (2020). Methodology for resume parsing and job domain prediction. *Journal of Statistics and Management Systems*, 23(7), 1265–1274. DOI: 10.1080/09720510.2020.1799583

Mohamed, N. (2023). Current trends in AI and ML for cybersecurity: A state-of-the-art survey. *Cogent Engineering*, 10(2), 2272358. Advance online publication. DOI: 10.1080/23311916.2023.2272358

Mohsin, K. (2021). Artificial Intelligence in Forensic Science. SSRN Electronic Journal. DOI: 10.2139/ssrn.3910244

Mökander, J. (2023). Auditing of AI: Legal, ethical and technical approaches. *Digital Society : Ethics, Socio-Legal and Governance of Digital Technology*, 2(3), 49. DOI: 10.1007/s44206-023-00074-y

Montiel, H., & Gomez-Zermeño, M. G. (2021). Educational challenges for computational thinking in k–12 education: A systematic literature review of "scratch" as an innovative programming tool. *Computers*, 10(6), 69. DOI: 10.3390/computers10060069

Morganson, V. J., Jones, M. P., & Major, D. A. (2010). Understanding women's underrepresentation in science, technology, engineering, and mathematics: The role of social coping. *The Career Development Quarterly*, 59(2), 169–179. DOI: 10.1002/j.2161-0045.2010.tb00060.x

Mozafari, N., Weiger, W. H., & Hammerschmidt, M. (2020). The Chatbot Disclosure Dilemma: Desirable and Undesirable Effects of Disclosing the Non-Human Identity of Chatbots.

Mugari, I., & Obioha, E. E. (2021). Predictive policing and crime control in the United States of America and Europe: Trends in a decade of research and the future of predictive policing. *Social Sciences (Basel, Switzerland)*, 10(6), 234. DOI: 10.3390/socsci10060234

Mukhopadhyay, M., & Kundu, A. (Eds.). (2023). *Academic Framework for 21st-Century Schooling: Promoting Global Peace and Harmony: Promoting Global Peace and Harmony*. IGI Global. DOI: 10.4018/978-1-6684-7005-3

Mwale, N. (2022). Religion and Sustainable Development: The Role of the Zambia Interfaith Networking Group (ZINGO) in Contemporary Times. In *Interfaith Networks and Development: Case Studies from Africa* (pp. 199–214). Springer International Publishing. DOI: 10.1007/978-3-030-89807-6_11

Nadjia, M. (2024). The Impact of Artificial Intelligence on Legal Systems: Challenges and Opportunities. *R30-02144*, 285.

Naidu, G., & Krishnan, V. (2025). Artificial Intelligence-Powered Legal Document Processing for Medical Negligence Cases: A Critical Review. *International Journal of Intelligence Science*, 15(1), 10–55. DOI: 10.4236/ijis.2025.151002

Nair, M. M., Deshmukh, A., & Tyagi, A. K. (2024). Artificial intelligence for cyber security: Current trends and future challenges. *Automated Secure Computing for Next-Generation Systems*, 83-114.

Nalla, L. N., & Reddy, V. M. (2024). AI-Driven Big Data Analytics for Enhanced Customer Journeys: A New Paradigm in E-Commerce. *International Journal of Advanced Engineering Technologies and Innovations*, 1(2), 719–740.

Na-Nan, K., Kanthong, S., Joungtrakul, J., & Smith, I. D. (2020). Mediating Effects of Job Satisfaction and Organizational Commitment between Problems with Performance Appraisal and Organizational Citizenship Behavior. *Journal of Open Innovation*, 6(3), 64. DOI: 10.3390/joitmc6030064

Nan, Z., Yuping, C., & Kongjue, Z. (2024). The Future of Marketing Analytics: Trends and Emerging Technologies. *International Journal of Advances in Business and Management Research*, 1(3), 23–32. DOI: 10.62674/ijabmr.2024.v1i03.003

Nasr, M., Shaaban, E., & Samir, A. (2019). A proposed Model for Predicting Employees' Performance Using Data Mining Techniques: Egyptian Case Study. *International Journal of Computer Science and Information Security*, 17(1), 31–40. DOI: 10.5815/ijcsis.2019.01.04

National Judicial Academy. (2021). *Introduction of artificial intelligence in the judicial system*. Retrieved from https://www.nja.gov.in/Concluded_Programmes/2021-22/P-1281_PPTs/2.Introduction%20of%20Artificial%20Intelligence%20in%20the%20Judicial%20System.pdf

Nawaz, N. (2020). *How far have we come with the study of artificial intelligence for recruitment process. SSRN.*

Nawaz, N., Arunachalam, H., Pathi, B. K., & Gajenderan, V. (2024). The adoption of artificial intelligence in human resources management practices. *International Journal of Information Management Data Insights*, 4(1), 100208. DOI: 10.1016/j.jjimei.2023.100208

Nayak, A., Patnaik, A., Satpathy, I., Khang, A., & Patnaik, B. (2024). The Power of Artificial Intelligence in Talent Recruitment Revolution: Creating a Smarter Workforce. In *AI-Oriented Competency Framework for Talent Management in the Digital Economy* (pp. 54–75). CRC Press. DOI: 10.1201/9781003440901-4

Nazer, L. H., Zatarah, R., Waldrip, S., Ke, J. X. C., Moukheiber, M., Khanna, A. K., Hicklen, R. S., Moukheiber, L., Moukheiber, D., Ma, H., & Mathur, P. (2023). Bias in artificial intelligence algorithms and recommendations for mitigation. *PLOS Digital Health*, 2(6), e0000278. DOI: 10.1371/journal.pdig.0000278 PMID: 37347721

Ness, S., Singh, N., Volkivskyi, M., & Phia, W. J. (2024). The Application of AI and Computer Science in the Context of International Law and Governance "Opportunities and Challenges". *American Journal of Computing and Engineering*, 7(1), 26–36. DOI: 10.47672/ajce.1878

Neumann, O., Guirguis, K., & Steiner, R. (2022). Exploring artificial intelligence adoption in public organizations: A comparative case study. *Public Management Review*, 26(1), 114–141. DOI: 10.1080/14719037.2022.2048685

Newman, D., Fast, N., & Harmon, D. (2020). When eliminating bias isn't fair: Algorithmic reductionism and procedural justice in human resource decisions. *Organizational Behavior and Human Decision Processes*, 160, 149–167. DOI: 10.1016/j.obhdp.2020.03.008

Nguyen, T., & Patel, S. (2022). Data privacy concerns with AI applications in judicial settings: An analysis. *International Data Privacy Journal*, 12(4), 201–220.

Nicolescu, L., & Tudorache, M. T. (2022). HumanComputer Interaction in Customer Service: The Experience with AI Chatbots—A Systematic Literature Review. *Electronics (Basel)*, 11(10), 10. Advance online publication. DOI: 10.3390/electronics11101579

Nishant, R., Schneckenberg, D., & Ravishankar, M. (2024). The formal rationality of artificial intelligence-based algorithms and the problem of bias. *Journal of Information Technology*, 39(1), 19–40. DOI: 10.1177/02683962231176842

Njuki, J., et al. (2023). A review of evidence on gender equality, women's empowerment, and food systems. Science and innovations for food systems transformation, 165.

Novelli, C., Taddeo, M., & Floridi, L. (2024). Accountability in artificial intelligence: What it is and how it works. *AI & Society*, 39(4), 1871–1882. DOI: 10.1007/s00146-023-01635-y

Ntoutsi, E., Fafalios, P., Gadiraju, U., Iosifidis, V., Nejdl, W., Vidal, M.-E., Ruggieri, S., Turini, F., Papadopoulos, S., Krasanakis, E., Kompatsiaris, I., Kinder-Kurlanda, K., Wagner, C., Karimi, F., Fernandez, M., Alani, H., Berendt, B., Kruegel, T., Heinze, C., & Staab, S. (2020). Bias in data-driven artificial intelligence systems—An introductory survey. *Wiley Interdisciplinary Reviews. Data Mining and Knowledge Discovery*, 10(3), e1356. DOI: 10.1002/widm.1356

Nyathani, R. (2023). AI in performance management: redefining performance appraisals in the digital age. Journal of Artificial Intelligence & Cloud Computing. DOI: 10.47363/JAICC/2023

O'Connor, J., & Lee, T. (2024). The impact of AI on human rights in judicial processes: A critical review. *Human Rights Law Review*, 24(2), 145–168.

O'Connor, S., & Liu, H. (2024). Gender bias perpetuation and mitigation in AI technologies: Challenges and opportunities. *AI & Society*, 39(4), 2045–2057. DOI: 10.1007/s00146-023-01675-4

O'keefe, J., Moss, D., Martinez, T., & Rose, P. (2019). Professional perspective AI regulation and risks to employers. https://bna.com/copyright-permission-request/

O'Pry, S. C., & Schumacher, G. (2012). New teachers' perceptions of a standards-based performance appraisal system. *Educational Assessment, Evaluation and Accountability*, 24(4), 325–350. DOI: 10.1007/s11092-012-9148-4

Obermeyer, Z., Powers, B., Vogeli, C., & Mullainathan, S. (2019). Dissecting racial bias in an algorithm used to manage the health of populations. *Science*, 366(6464), 447–453. DOI: 10.1126/science.aax2342 PMID: 31649194

Odilla, F. (2023). Bots against corruption: Exploring the benefits and limitations of AI-based anti-corruption technology. *Crime, Law, and Social Change*, 80(4), 353–396. DOI: 10.1007/s10611-023-10091-0 PMID: 37359505

OECD. (2019). *The OECD Artificial Intelligence (AI) Principles*. OECD. https://oecd.ai/en/ai-principles

Ogundipe, D. O., Babatunde, S. O., & Abaku, E. A. (2024). AI and product management: A theoretical overview from idea to market. *International Journal of Management & Entrepreneurship Research*, 6(3), 950–969. DOI: 10.51594/ijmer.v6i3.965

Ogunleye, O. S. (2024). Using Artificial Intelligence to Enhance E-Government Services Delivery Through Data Science and Machine Learning. In *Machine Learning and Data Science Techniques for Effective Government Service Delivery* (pp. 1–28). IGI Global.

Okeleke, P. A., Ajiga, D., Folorunsho, S. O., & Ezeigweneme, C. (2024). Predictive analytics for market trends using AI: A study in consumer behavior. *International Journal of Engineering Research Updates*, 7(1), 36–49. DOI: 10.53430/ijeru.2024.7.1.0032

Okorie, G. N., Udeh, C. A., & Adaga, E. M. (2024). Digital marketing in the age of iot: A review of trends and impacts. *International Journal of Management & Entrepreneurship Research*, 6(1), 104–131. DOI: 10.51594/ijmer.v6i1.712

Olan, F., Arakpogun, E. O., Suklan, J., Nakpodia, F., Damij, N., & Jayawickrama, U. (2022). Artificial intelligence and knowledge sharing: Contributing factors to organizational performance. *Journal of Business Research*, 145, 605–615. DOI: 10.1016/j.jbusres.2022.03.008

Olateju, O., Okon, S. U., Olaniyi, O. O., Samuel-Okon, A. D., & Asonze, C. U. (2024). Exploring the concept of explainable AI and developing information governance standards for enhancing trust and transparency in handling customer data. *Available atSSRN*. DOI: 10.2139/ssrn.4879025

O'Reilly Media, Inc. & Harvard Business Publishing Corporate Learning. (Eds.). (2022). Artificial Intelligence in Financial Services: A Practical Guide.

Orhan, K., Gülbeş, M. M., Jadhav, A., & Jagtap, R. (2024). Medico-Legal Problems of Artificial Intelligence. In *Artificial Intelligence in Dentistry* (pp. 259–282). Springer International Publishing.

Outeda, C. C. (2024). The EU's AI act: A framework for collaborative governance. *Internet of Things : Engineering Cyber Physical Human Systems*, 27, 101291. DOI: 10.1016/j.iot.2024.101291

Pal, R., Shaikh, S., Satpute, S., & Bhagwat, S. (2022). Resume classification using various machine learning algorithms. ITM Web of Conferences, Panerai, F. (2018). *Artificial Intelligence Needs Human Ingenuity and Moral*. Medium. https://medium.com/@fiammapanerai/artificial-intelligence-needs-human-ingenuity-and-moral-a6f0bcad8ca0

Pan, Y., & Froese, F. J. (2023). An interdisciplinary review of AI and HRM: Challenges and future directions. *Human Resource Management Review*, 33(1), 100924. DOI: 10.1016/j.hrmr.2022.100924

Papadakis, S. (2020). Evaluating a teaching intervention for teaching STEM and programming concepts through the creation of a weather-forecast app for smart mobile devices. In *Handbook of research on tools for teaching computational thinking in P-12 education* (pp. 31–53). IGI Global. DOI: 10.4018/978-1-7998-4576-8.ch002

Park, H., Ahn, D., Hosanagar, K., & Lee, J. (2021). Human-AI Interaction in Human Resource Management: Understanding Why Employees Resist Algorithmic Evaluation at Workplaces and How to Mitigate Burdens Proceedings of the 2021 CHI Conference on Human Factors in Computing Systems. DOI: 10.1145/3411764.3445304

Pasquale, F. (2015). The Black Box Society: The Secret Algorithms That Control Money and Information. In *JSTOR*. Harvard University Press. https://www.jstor.org/stable/j.ctt13x0hch

Paul, J., Lim, W. M., O'Cass, A., Hao, A. W., & Bresciani, S. (2021). Scientific procedures and rationales for systematic literature reviews (SPAR-4-SLR). *International Journal of Consumer Studies*, 45(4), O1–O16. DOI: 10.1111/ijcs.12695

Peng, W., Zhang, L., Wen, F., Tang, X., Zeng, L., Chen, J., Galea, G., Wen, D., & Wang, Y. (2024). Trends and disparities in non-communicable diseases in the Western Pacific region. *The Lancet Regional Health. Western Pacific*, 43, 43. DOI: 10.1016/j.lanwpc.2023.100938 PMID: 38456093

Perifanis, N.-A., & Kitsios, F. (2023). Investigating the influence of artificial intelligence on business value in the digital era of strategy: A literature review. *Information (Basel)*, 14(2), 85. DOI: 10.3390/info14020085

Pollak, M., & Ebner, M. (2019). The missing link to computational thinking. *Future Internet*, 11(12), 263. DOI: 10.3390/fi11120263

Pollock, L., Mouza, C., Guidry, K. R., & Pusecker, K. (2019, February). Infusing computational thinking across disciplines: Reflections & lessons learned. In *Proceedings of the 50th ACM Technical Symposium on Computer Science Education* (pp. 435-441). DOI: 10.1145/3287324.3287469

Porkodi, S., & Raman, A. M. (2024). Success of cloud computing adoption over an era in human resource management systems: a comprehensive meta-analytic literature review. *Management Review Quarterly*, 1-35.

Power, D. J., Heavin, C., & O'Connor, Y. (2021). Balancing privacy rights and surveillance analytics: A decision process guide. *Journal of Business Analytics*, 4(2), 155–170. DOI: 10.1080/2573234X.2021.1920856

Prem, E. (2023). From ethical AI frameworks to tools: A review of approaches. *AI and Ethics*, 3(3), 699–716. DOI: 10.1007/s43681-023-00258-9

Priel, D. (2019). Law as a social construction and conceptual legal theory. *Articles & Book Chapters*, 2751. https://digitalcommons.osgoode.yorku.ca/scholarly_works/275

Profit, C. (2023) Use of artificial intelligence in performance reviews. Best OKR Software by Profit.co https://www.profit.co/article/performance-management/useof-artificial-intelligence-in-performance-reviews/

Psycharis, S., Kalovrektis, K., Sakellaridi, E., Korres, K., & Mastorodimos, D. (2018). Unfolding the curriculum: physical computing, computational thinking and computational experiment in STEM's transdisciplinary approach. *European Journal of Engineering and Technology Research*, 19-24.

Psycharis, S. (2018). STEAM in education: A literature review on the role of computational thinking, engineering epistemology and computational science. computational steam pedagogy (CSP). *Scientific Culture*, 4(2), 51–72.

Pulimood, S. M., Pearson, K., & Bates, D. C. (2016, February). A study on the impact of multidisciplinary collaboration on computational thinking. In *Proceedings of the 47th ACM technical symposium on computing science education* (pp. 30-35). DOI: 10.1145/2839509.2844636

Putra, G. A. (2024). The Journey of Marketing Research in Driving Successful Marketing Strategies. *Advances in Business & Industrial Marketing Research*, 2(1), 26–35. DOI: 10.60079/abim.v2i1.241

PwC. (2021). *The new global imperative to modernise justice systems*. Retrieved from https://www.pwc.com/gx/en/industries/government-public-services/public-sector-research-centre/global-imperative-modernise-justice-systems.html

PWC. (2023). AI and the future of financial services: A roadmap for success. Retrieved from https://www.pwc.com/gx/en/services/consulting/artificial-intelligence.html

Qin, H. (2009, March). Teaching computational thinking through bioinformatics to biology students. In *Proceedings of the 40th ACM technical symposium on Computer science education* (pp. 188-191). DOI: 10.1145/1508865.1508932

Raaj, S. (2024). Education, research and innovation in India: The shifting paradigms. *Journal of Higher Education Theory and Practice*, 24(1), 75.

Radonjić, A., Duarte, H., & Pereira, N. (2022). Artificial intelligence and HRM: HR managers' perspective on decisiveness and challenges. *European Management Journal*.

Raghav, A., Singh, B., Jermsittiparsert, K., Raghav, R., & Yadav, U. (2024). Artificial Intelligence in Environmental and Climate Changes: A Sustainable Future. In Singh, B., Kaunert, C., Vig, K., & Dutta, S. (Eds.), *Maintaining a Sustainable World in the Nexus of Environmental Science and AI* (pp. 485–506). IGI Global. DOI: 10.4018/979-8-3693-6336-2.ch019

Raghavan, M., Barocas, S., Kleinberg, J., & Levy, K. (2020). Mitigating bias in algorithmic hiring: Evaluating claims and practices. *Journal of Surgical Education*, 78(4), 1175–1181. PMID: 33250429

Rajapakse, V. (2024). Performance Management Process: Performance Reviewing. In Employee Performance Management for Improved Workplace Motivation (pp. 57-90). IGI Global. DOI: 10.4018/979-8-3693-4387-6.ch003

Raji, M. A., Olodo, H. B., Oke, T. T., Addy, W. A., Ofodile, O. C., & Oyewole, A. T. (2024). E-commerce and consumer behavior: A review of AI-powered personalization and market trends. *GSC Advanced Research and Reviews, 18*(3), 66-77.

Raji, I. D., Smart, A., White, R. N., Mitchell, M., Gebru, T., Hutchinson, B., Smith-Loud, J., Theron, D., & Barnes, P. (2020). Closing the AI Accountability Gap: Defining an End-to-End Framework for Internal Algorithmic Auditing. DOI: 10.1145/3351095.3372873

Ramos, R., Rita, P., & Vong, C. (2024). Mapping research in marketing: Trends, influential papers and agenda for future research. *Spanish Journal of Marketing - ESIC*, 28(2), 187–206. DOI: 10.1108/SJME-10-2022-0221

Ransbotham, S., Mitra, S., & Puryear, J. (2022). Artificial intelligence in marketing: The next frontier for financial institutions? *MIT Sloan Management Review*.

Raso, F., Hilligoss, H., Krishnamurthy, V., Bavitz, C., & Kim, L. Y. (2018). *Artificial intelligence & human rights: Opportunities & risks*. Berkman Klein Center Research Publication No. 2018-6. https://doi.org/DOI: 10.2139/ssrn.3259344

Ratten, V. (2024). Artificial intelligence, digital trends and globalization: Future research trends. *FIIB Business Review*, 13(3), 286–293. DOI: 10.1177/23197145231222774

Rawas, S. (2024). AI: The future of humanity. *Discover Artificial Intelligence*, 4(1), 25. DOI: 10.1007/s44163-024-00118-3

Rebolledo, V. G. (2025). Impact of the artificial intelligence on international relations: Towards a global algorithms governance.

Reddy Yanamala, K. K. (2023). AI and the Future of Cognitive Decision-Making in HR. Applied Research in Artificial Intelligence and Cloud Computing, 6(9), 31-46. https://researchberg.com/index.php/araic/article/view/204

Reddy Yanamala, K. K. (2022). Integrating Machine Learning and Human Feedback for Employee Performance Evaluation. *Journal of Advanced Computing Systems*, 2(1), 1–10. DOI: 10.69987/JACS.2022.20101

Reddy, V. M., & Nalla, L. N. (2024). Optimizing E-Commerce Supply Chains Through Predictive Big Data Analytics: A Path to Agility and Efficiency. *International Journal of Machine Learning Research in Cybersecurity and Artificial Intelligence*, 15(1), 555–585.

Reddy, V. M., & Nalla, L. N. (2024). Personalization in E-Commerce Marketing: Leveraging Big Data for Tailored Consumer Engagement. *Revista de Inteligencia Artificial en Medicina*, 15(1), 691–725.

Reim, W., Åström, J., & Eriksson, O. (2020). Implementation of Artificial Intelligence (AI): A Roadmap for Business Model Innovation. *AI*, 1(2), 180191. DOI: 10.3390/ai1020011

Rese, A., Ganster, L., & Baier, D. (2020). Chatbots in retailers' customer communication: How to measure their acceptance? *Journal of Retailing and Consumer Services*, 56, 102176. DOI: 10.1016/j.jretconser.2020.102176

Resnik, D. B., & Hosseini, M. (2024). The ethics of using artificial intelligence in scientific research: New guidance needed for a new tool. *AI and Ethics*. Advance online publication. DOI: 10.1007/s43681-024-00493-8

Reverberi, C., Rigon, T., Solari, A., Hassan, C., Cherubini, P., Antonelli, G., Awadie, H., Bernhofer, S., Carballal, S., Dinis-Ribeiro, M., Fernández-Clotett, A., Esparrach, G. F., Gralnek, I., Higasa, Y., Hirabayashi, T., Hirai, T., Iwatate, M., Kawano, M., Mader, M., & Cherubini, A. (2022). Experimental evidence of effective human–AI collaboration in medical decision-making. *Scientific Reports*, 12(1), 14952. DOI: 10.1038/s41598-022-18751-2 PMID: 36056152

Riaz & Ghanghas. (2024). Artificial Intelligence in Employee Performance Evaluation and Its Managerial Implication. *Journal of Informatics Education and Research.*, 4(1), 299–307. DOI: 10.52783/jier.v4i1.559

Ribeiro, M. T., Singh, S., & Guestrin, C. (2016). "Why Should I Trust You?": Explaining the Predictions of Any Classifier. *ARVIS, 1*. DOI: 10.1145/2939672.2939778

Richardson, R., Schultz, J., & Crawford, K. (2019, February 13). *Dirty Data, Bad Predictions: How Civil Rights Violations Impact Police Data, Predictive Policing Systems, and Justice*. https://ssrn.com/abstract=3333423

Rizzi, A., Kessler, A., & Menajovsky, J. (2021). The Stories Algorithms Tell: Bias and Financial Inclusion at the Data Margins. *Center for Financial Inclusion, Accion* (2021), 35.

Roberts, T., & Green, J. (2022). The role of AI in international law: Challenges and opportunities. *International Journal of Law and Information Technology*, 30(1), 34–56.

Robinson, H., & Clark, D. (2024). AI's influence on sentencing decisions: An exploratory study. *Criminal Justice Ethics*, 43(2), 89–105.

Rodrigues, R. (2020). Legal and human rights issues of AI: Gaps, challenges and vulnerabilities. *Journal of Responsible Technology*, 4, 100005. DOI: 10.1016/j.jrt.2020.100005

Romero, M., Lepage, A., & Lille, B. (2017). Computational thinking development through creative programming in higher education. *International Journal of Educational Technology in Higher Education*, 14(1), 1–15. DOI: 10.1186/s41239-017-0080-z

Rosário, A. T. (2024). Generative ai and generative pre-trained transformer applications: Challenges and opportunities. *Making Art With Generative AI Tools*, 45-71.

Rose, D. E., Van Der Merwe, J., & Jones, J. (2024). Digital Marketing Strategy in Enhancing Brand Awareness and Profitability of E-Commerce Companies. *APTISI Transactions on Management*, 8(2), 160–166.

Rosenbaum, E. (2019). IBM artificial intelligence can predict with 95% accuracy which workers are about to quit their jobs. Retrieved from https://www.cnbc.com/2019/04/03/ibm-ai-can-predict-with-95-percent-accuracy-whichemployees-will-quit.html

Roy, P. K., Chowdhary, S. S., & Bhatia, R. (2020). A Machine Learning approach for automation of Resume Recommendation system. *Procedia Computer Science*, 167, 2318–2327. DOI: 10.1016/j.procs.2020.03.284

Rožman, M., Oreški, D., & Tominc, P. (2022). Integrating artificial intelligence into a talent management model to increase the work engagement and performance of enterprises. *Frontiers in Psychology*, 13, 1014434. Advance online publication. DOI: 10.3389/fpsyg.2022.1014434 PMID: 36506984

Ryberg, J. (2024). Criminal justice and artificial intelligence: How should we assess the performance of sentencing algorithms? *Philosophy & Technology*, 37(1), 9. DOI: 10.1007/s13347-024-00694-3

Sachoulidou, A. (2024). Harnessing AI for law enforcement: Solutions and boundaries from the forthcoming AI Act. *New Journal of European Criminal Law*, 15(2), 117–125. DOI: 10.1177/20322844241260114

Saeij, M. (2020). *Why Implementing AI and ML is a Must for Credit Managers.* Barclays.

Saini, H., & Tarkar, P. (2022). Artificial intelligence in human resource practices with challenges and future directions. In *Handbook of Research on Innovative Management Using AI in Industry 5.0* (pp. 222–230). IGI Global. DOI: 10.4018/978-1-7998-8497-2.ch015

Sanyaolu, E., & Atsaboghena, R. (2022). Role of Artificial Intelligence in Human Resource Management: Overview of its benefits and challenges. *ResearchGate*, (December), 1–8.

Sarirete, A., Balfagih, Z., Brahimi, T., Lytras, M. D., & Visvizi, A. (2022). Artificial intelligence and machine learning research: Towards digital transformation at a global scale. *Journal of Ambient Intelligence and Humanized Computing*, 13(7), 3319–3321. DOI: 10.1007/s12652-021-03168-y

Saritepeci, M. (2020). Developing computational thinking skills of high school students: Design-based learning activities and programming tasks. *The Asia-Pacific Education Researcher*, 29(1), 35–54. DOI: 10.1007/s40299-019-00480-2

Sasi, T., Lashkari, A. H., Lu, R., Xiong, P., & Iqbal, S. (2023). A comprehensive survey on IoT attacks: Taxonomy, detection mechanisms and challenges. *Journal of Information and Intelligence.*

Sayyed, H. (2024). Artificial intelligence and criminal liability in India: Exploring legal implications and challenges. *Cogent Social Sciences*, 10(1), 2343195. Advance online publication. DOI: 10.1080/23311886.2024.2343195

Schliesser, C. (2023). *On the Significance of Religion for the SDGs: An Introduction.* Taylor & Francis. DOI: 10.4324/9781003332275

Schwartz, R., Schwartz, R., Vassilev, A., Greene, K., Perine, L., Burt, A., & Hall, P. (2022). Towards a standard for identifying and managing bias in artificial intelligence (Vol. 3, p. 00). US Department of Commerce, National Institute of Standards and *Technology.*

Selenko, E., Bankins, S., Shoss, M., Warburton, J., & Restubog, S. L. D. (2022). Artificial intelligence and the future of work: A functional-identity perspective. *Current Directions in Psychological Science*, 31(3), 272–279. DOI: 10.1177/09637214221091823

Semenda, O., Sokolova, Y., Korovina, O., Bratko, O., & Polishchuk, I. (2024). Using social media analysis to improve E-commerce marketing strategies. *International Review of Management and Marketing*, 14(4), 61–71. DOI: 10.32479/irmm.16196

Shams, R. A., Zowghi, D., & Bano, M. (2023). AI and the quest for diversity and inclusion: A systematic literature review. *AI and Ethics*, 1–28.

Sharabati, A. A. A., Ali, A. A. A., Allahham, M. I., Hussein, A. A., Alheet, A. F., & Mohammad, A. S. (2024). The Impact of Digital Marketing on the Performance of SMEs: An Analytical Study in Light of Modern Digital Transformations. *Sustainability (Basel)*, 16(19), 8667. DOI: 10.3390/su16198667

Sharma, A. (2018). *How AI reinvented hiring practice at L'Ore'al.* People Matters. https://www.peoplematters.in/article/techhr-2018/how-the-worlds-largest-cosmetic-company-transformed-its-hiring-practice-with-ai-19006

Sheng, T. J., Islam, M. S., Misran, N., Baharuddin, M. H., Arshad, H., Islam, M. R., Chowdhury, M. E. H., Rmili, H., & Islam, M. T. (2020). An internet of things based smart waste management system using LoRa and tensorflow deep learning model. *IEEE Access : Practical Innovations, Open Solutions*, 8, 148793–148811. DOI: 10.1109/ACCESS.2020.3016255

Sheshadri, T., Shelly, R., Sharma, K., Sharma, T., & Basha, M. (2024). An Empirical Study on Integration of Artificial Intelligence and Marketing Management to Transform Consumer Engagement in Selected PSU Banks (PNB and Canara Banks). *Naturalista Campano*, 28(1), 463–471.

Shin, D., Hameleers, M., Park, Y. J., Kim, J. N., Trielli, D., Diakopoulos, N., Helberger, N., Lewis, S. C., Westlund, O., & Baumann, S. (2022). Countering algorithmic bias and disinformation and effectively harnessing the power of AI in media. *Journalism & Mass Communication Quarterly*, 99(4), 887–907. DOI: 10.1177/10776990221129245

Shivanjali, S. R., & Kumar, M. (2024). Exploring Stem Learners' Perceptions of Artificial Intelligence in Personalizing Metacognitive Strategy Development. *Journal of the Indian Academy of Applied Psychology*, 299.

Siahaan, A. M., Siboro, D. T., & Nainggolan, M. S. J. (2024). Strategies to Increase Profitability by Using Digital-Based Sales in Micro, Small and Medium Enterprise (MSMEs) in Medan City. *Management Studies and Entrepreneurship Journal*, 5(1), 514–523.

Singh, A. K., & Kushwaha, A. (n.d.). Unmasking the Transformative Impact: Artificial Intelligence in India's Judiciary System.

Singh, B., & Kaunert, C. (2025). Cloud Computing and IoMT in Disease Screening and Diagnosis: AI Approaches in Transmuting Healthier Homes. In B. S & S. Kadry (Eds.), *Revolutionizing Healthcare Systems Through Cloud Computing and IoT* (pp. 99-120). IGI Global. DOI: 10.4018/979-8-3693-7225-8.ch005

Singh, B., & Kaunert, C. (2025). Leveraging IoT for Patient Monitoring and Smart Healthcare: Connected Healthcare System. In B. S & S. Kadry (Eds.), *Revolutionizing Healthcare Systems Through Cloud Computing and IoT* (pp. 27-46). IGI Global. DOI: 10.4018/979-8-3693-7225-8.ch002

Singha, R., & Yogesh Kanna, S. (2023). Mindfulness Promotes Health, Well-Being, and Sustainable Strategy to Eradicate Ill Effects from Tobacco. In *SDGs in the Asia and Pacific Region* (pp. 1–29). Springer International Publishing. DOI: 10.1007/978-3-030-91262-8_20-1

Singh, B., & Kaunert, C. (2024). Adventure in High Altitude of Mountainous Topographies and Health Impacts: Lensing Tourism Sustainability via Reducing Ecological and Sociocultural Footprint and Health Emergency and Medical Assistance Management. In Meraj, G., Hashimoto, S., & Kumar, P. (Eds.), *Navigating Natural Hazards in Mountainous Topographies. Disaster Risk Reduction*. Springer. DOI: 10.1007/978-3-031-65862-4_15

Singh, B., & Kaunert, C. (2024). Future of Digital Marketing: Hyper-Personalized Customer Dynamic Experience with AI-Based Predictive Models. In *Revolutionizing the AI-Digital Landscape* (pp. 189–203). Productivity Press. DOI: 10.4324/9781032688305-14

Singh, B., & Kaunert, C. (2025). Exploring Effective Strategies for Combatting Cybercrime and Intersection of IoT, Deep Learning: Legal Standpoints on Progressive Data Analytics. In Kumar, R., Srivastava, S., & Elngar, A. (Eds.), *Human Impact on Security and Privacy: Network and Human Security, Social Media, and Devices* (pp. 141–172). IGI Global. https://doi.org/10.4

Singh, B., & Kaunert, C. (2025). Featuring Healthcare, Environment, and Human Rights: Applications of Artificial Intelligence in the Health Domain. In Chakraborty, S., & Satapathy, S. (Eds.), *Gender, Environment, and Human Rights: An Intersectional Exploration* (pp. 45–74). IGI Global. DOI: 10.4018/979-8-3693-6069-9.ch004

Singh, B., & Kaunert, C. (2025). Innovative Business Models in Digital and Virtual Reality for the Gig Economy: Space-Age Sustainable Development Projecting Smart Business Practices. In Taherdoost, H., Drazenovic, G., Madanchian, M., Khan, I., & Arshi, O. (Eds.), *Business Transformation in the Era of Digital Disruption* (pp. 127–156). IGI Global. DOI: 10.4018/979-8-3693-7056-8.ch005

Singh, B., & Kaunert, C. (2025). Intelligent Machine Learning Solutions for Cybersecurity: Legal and Ethical Considerations in a Global Context. In Thangam, D. (Ed.), *Advancements in Intelligent Process Automation* (pp. 359–386). IGI Global. DOI: 10.4018/979-8-3693-5380-6.ch014

Singh, B., Kaunert, C., & Ravesangar, K. (2025). Artificial Intelligence and Employee Well-Being: Projecting Psychological and Physical Healthcare. In Yadav, P. (Ed.), *Human Resource Strategies in the Era of Artificial Intelligence* (pp. 109–134). IGI Global. DOI: 10.4018/979-8-3693-6412-3.ch005

Singh, B., Kaunert, C., & Singh, G. (2025). Scaling Legal Framework for Plastic Pollution and Advancing Cutting Edge Water Governance: Reducing and Eliminating Marine Pollution in Alignment With SDG 14 (Life Below Water). In Gaur, N., Sharma, E., Nguyen, T., Bilal, M., & Melkania, N. (Eds.), *Societal and Environmental Ramifications of Plastic Pollution* (pp. 197–222). IGI Global. DOI: 10.4018/979-8-3693-9163-1.ch010

Singh, B., & Nayyar, A. (2025). Satelliting traditional to smart healthcare advancement using artificial intelligence: A paradigm shift routing futuristic slant redefining. In *Revolutionizing Medical Systems using Artificial Intelligence* (pp. 265–283). Academic Press. DOI: 10.1016/B978-0-443-32862-6.00014-6

Singh, R., & Kumar, P. (2024). Navigating ethical dilemmas in AI-assisted judicial decision-making processes. *Ethics and Information Technology*, 26(1), 55–70.

Singla, H., & Malik, P. (2024). Women Entrepreneurs and Wealth: Navigating Financial Well-Being in the Modern World. In *Emerging Perspectives on Financial Well-Being* (pp. 264-285). IGI Global.

Sırakaya, M., Alsancak Sırakaya, D., & Korkmaz, Ö. (2020). The impact of STEM attitude and thinking style on computational thinking determined via structural equation modeling. *Journal of Science Education and Technology*, 29(4), 561–572. DOI: 10.1007/s10956-020-09836-6

Skrobotov, A. (2021). The perceptions of recruitment practitioners on the adoption of artificial intelligence in recruitment and selection. *International Journal of Human Resource Management*, 43, 1–25.

Smith, C. L. (2019). An employee's best friend? How AI can boost employee engagement and performance. *Strategic HR Review*, 18(1), 17–20. DOI: 10.1108/SHR-11-2018-0092

Smith, M., & Miller, S. (2022). The ethical application of biometric facial recognition technology. *AI & Society*, 37(1), 167–175. DOI: 10.1007/s00146-021-01199-9 PMID: 33867693

Soleimani, M., Intezari, A., Taskin, N., & Pauleen, D. (2021). Cognitive biases in developing biased Artificial Intelligence recruitment system.

Stahl, B. C., Brooks, L., Hatzakis, T., Santiago, N., & Wright, D. (2023). Exploring ethics and human rights in artificial intelligence – A Delphi study. *Technological Forecasting and Social Change*, 191, 122502. DOI: 10.1016/j.techfore.2023.122502

Stardust, Z., Blunt, D., Garcia, G., Lee, L., D'Adamo, K., & Kuo, R. (2023). High risk hustling: Payment processors, sexual proxies, and discrimination by design. *CUNY Law Review*, 26, 57.

Starke, C., Baleis, J., Keller, B., & Marcinkowski, F. (2022). Fairness perceptions of algorithmic decision-making: A systematic review of the empirical literature. *Big Data & Society*, 9(2). Advance online publication. DOI: 10.1177/20539517221115189

Statista Research Department. (2023). Global market size of artificial intelligence in the banking sector from 2019 to 2025.

Statista. (2017). *Global Recruiting Trends: Key Benefits of Artificial Intelligence 2017*. Statista. https://www.statista.com/statistics/831693/recruitment-trends-benefits-of-artificial-intelligence/

Steyvers, M., & Kumar, A. (2024). Three challenges for AI-assisted decision-making. *Perspectives on Psychological Science*, 19(5), 722–734. DOI: 10.1177/17456916231181102 PMID: 37439761

Stinson, C. (2022). Algorithms are not neutral. *AI and Ethics*, 2(4), 763–770. DOI: 10.1007/s43681-022-00136-w PMID: 35128540

Stone, D. L., Deadrick, D. L., Lukaszewski, K. M., & Johnson, R. (2015). The influence of technology on the future of human resource management. *Human Resource Management Review*, 25(2), 216–231. DOI: 10.1016/j.hrmr.2015.01.002

Sugiharto, B. H. (2024). The role of e-commerce for MSMEs as a digital marketing strategy in facing industrial revolution 4.0. *Management Studies and Business Journal*, 1(1), 99–107. DOI: 10.62207/80ndq458

Sulistyaningsih, E., Murti, W., & Ratnasih, C. (2024). Analysis of E-Marketing Strategy and Business Innovation in Optimizing Improvement of Service Quality and Its Effect on MSME Income. *ADI Journal on Recent Innovation*, 5(2), 155–167. DOI: 10.34306/ajri.v5i2.1045

Supriadi, A. (2024). The Impact of Artificial Intelligence (AI) on Marketing Strategy. *Management Studies and Business Journal*, 1(1), 146–153. DOI: 10.62207/pspbtk28

Sushina, T., & Sobenin, A. (2020). Artificial intelligence in the criminal justice system: Leading trends and possibilities. *Proceedings of the 3rd International Scientific Conference Social and Cultural Transformations in the Context of Modern Globalism*. DOI: 10.2991/assehr.k.200526.062

Taherdoost, H., & Madanchian, M. (2024). AI advancements: Comparison of innovative techniques. *AI*, 5(1), 38–54. DOI: 10.3390/ai5010003

Tallberg, J., Erman, E., Furendal, M., Geith, J., Klamberg, M., & Lundgren, M. (2023). The global governance of artificial intelligence: Next steps for empirical and normative research. *International Studies Review*, 25(3), viad040. Advance online publication. DOI: 10.1093/isr/viad040

Tambe, P., Cappelli, P., & Yakubovich, V. (2019). Artificial Intelligence in Human Resources Management: Challenges and a Path Forward. *California Management Review*, 61(4), 15–42. DOI: 10.1177/0008125619867910

Taylor, I. (2023). Justice by algorithm: The limits of AI in criminal sentencing. *Criminal Justice Ethics*, 42(3), 193–213. DOI: 10.1080/0731129X.2023.2275967

Taylor, S., & Williams, A. (2023). Machine learning and legal outcomes: An empirical study. *Journal of Empirical Legal Studies*, 20(1), 98–115.

Tedre, M., & Denning, P. J. (2016, November). The long quest for computational thinking. In *Proceedings of the 16th Koli Calling international conference on computing education research* (pp. 120-129).

Thakkar, S. (2024). The Impact of AI On Financial Inclusion In Emerging Markets. *International Journal Of Computer Engineering And Technology*, 15(5), 266–277.

Thakre, G., Wankhede, P., Patle, S., Joshi, S., & Chauhan, A. (2021). Implementation of Machine Learning Model for Employee Retention Prediction. *International Journal of Scientific Research in Science and Technology*, 8(3), 503–508. DOI: 10.32628/IJSRST2183122

Thiongo, M. (2024). Internationalizing E-commerce: Challenges and Opportunities for SMEs in Kenya as a Developing Country.

Thomas, J., & Davis, F. (2021). The intersection of technology and law: AI's transformative potential in courts. *Technology and Society Journal*, 15(2), 112–130.

Thoyyib, M., & Wibowati, J. I. (2024). Evaluation of workshop and strategics of rights in the MSMEs in the digital age. *International Journal of Economic Literature*, 2(5), 1559–1570.

Todd, P., & Benbasat, I. (1991). An experimental investigation of the impact of computer-based decision aids on decision making strategies. *Information Systems Research*, 2(2), 87–115. DOI: 10.1287/isre.2.2.87

Tong, S., Jia, N., Luo, X., & Fang, Z. (2021). The Janus face of artificial intelligence feedback: Deployment versus disclosure effects on employee performance. *Strategic Management Journal*, 42(9), 1600–1631. Advance online publication. DOI: 10.1002/smj.3322

Toptal. (2025). Financial implications of using AI in marketing. Retrieved from https://www.toptal.com/marketing/digital/ai-marketing

Trotta, A., Ziosi, M., & Lomonaco, V. (2023). The future of ethics in AI: Challenges and opportunities. *AI & Society*, 38(2), 439–441. DOI: 10.1007/s00146-023-01644-x

Tsamados, A., Aggarwal, N., Cowls, J., Morley, J., Roberts, H., Taddeo, M., & Floridi, L. (2022). The ethics of algorithms: Key problems and solutions. *AI & Society*, 37(1), 215–230. DOI: 10.1007/s00146-021-01154-8

Tsamados, A., Floridi, L., & Taddeo, M. (2024). Human control of AI systems: From supervision to teaming. *AI and Ethics*. Advance online publication. DOI: 10.1007/s43681-024-00489-4

Tsortanidou, X., Daradoumis, T., & Barberá, E. (2019). Connecting moments of creativity, computational thinking, collaboration and new media literacy skills. *Information and Learning Science*, 120(11/12), 704–722. DOI: 10.1108/ILS-05-2019-0042

Tynan, P. (2024). The integration and implications of artificial intelligence in forensic science. *Forensic Science, Medicine, and Pathology*, 20(3), 1103–1105. Advance online publication. DOI: 10.1007/s12024-023-00772-6 PMID: 38175310

Ty, R. (2023). A Grounded Theory of Spiritual Leadership and Social Transformation: A Case Study of Peacebuilding and Human Rights Advocacy Interventions. In *Asian Spiritualities and Social Transformation* (pp. 201–223). Springer Nature Singapore. DOI: 10.1007/978-981-99-2641-1_12

Ulenaers, J. (2020). The impact of artificial intelligence on the right to a fair trial: Towards a robot judge? *Asian Journal of Law and Economics*, 11(2), 20200008. DOI: 10.1515/ajle-2020-0008

Umamaheswari, D. D. (2024). Role of Artificial Intelligence in Marketing Strategies and Performance. *Migration Letters : An International Journal of Migration Studies*, 21(S4), 1589–1599.

UNESCO. (2024). *AI and the rule of law: Capacity building for judicial systems.* Retrieved from https://www.unesco.org/en/artificial-intelligence/rule-law/mooc-judges

Upadhyay, A. K., & Khandelwal, K. (2018). Applying artificial intelligence: Implications for recruitment. *Strategic HR Review*, 17(5), 255–258. DOI: 10.1108/SHR-07-2018-0051

Urquhart, L., & Miranda, D. (2021). Policing faces: The present and future of intelligent facial surveillance. *Information & Communications Technology Law*, 31(2), 194–219. DOI: 10.1080/13600834.2021.1994220

Vaingankar, J. A., Choudhary, N., Chong, S. A., Kumar, F. D. S., Abdin, E., Shafie, S., Chua, B. Y., van Dam, R. M., & Subramaniam, M. (2021). Religious affiliation in relation to positive mental health and mental disorders in a multi-ethnic Asian population. *International Journal of Environmental Research and Public Health*, 18(7), 3368. DOI: 10.3390/ijerph18073368 PMID: 33805121

Valovicova, Ľ., Ondruška, J., Zelenický, Ľ., Chytrý, V., & Medová, J. (2020). Enhancing computational thinking through interdisciplinary STEAM activities using tablets. *Mathematics*, 8(12), 2128. DOI: 10.3390/math8122128

Van Eck, N. J., & Waltman, L. (2023). VOSviewer manual. Manual for VOSviewer version. 1.6. 8.

Van Esch, P., Black, J. S., & Ferolie, J. (2019). Marketing AI recruitment: The next phase in job application and selection. *Computers in Human Behavior*, 90, 215–222. DOI: 10.1016/j.chb.2018.09.009

Van Noordt, C., & Misuraca, G. (2022). Artificial intelligence for the public sector: Results of landscaping the use of AI in government across the European Union. *Government Information Quarterly*, 39(3), 101714. DOI: 10.1016/j.giq.2022.101714

van Norren, D. E. (2023). The ethics of artificial intelligence, UNESCO and the African Ubuntu perspective. *Journal of Information. Communication and Ethics in Society*, 21(1), 112–128. DOI: 10.1108/JICES-04-2022-0037

Vargas-Murillo, A. R., Turriate-Guzman, A. M., Delgado-Chávez, C. A., & Sanchez-Paucar, F. (2024). Transforming Justice: Implications of Artificial Intelligence in Legal Systems. *Academic Journal of Interdisciplinary Studies, 13.*

Varsha, P. S. (2023). How can we manage biases in artificial intelligence systems – A systematic literature review. *International Journal of Information Management Data Insights*, 3(1), 100165. DOI: 10.1016/j.jjimei.2023.100165

Vedapradha, R., Hariharan, R., & Shivakami, R. (2019). Artificial intelligence: A technological prototype in recruitment. *Journal of Service Science and Management*, 12(3), 382–390. DOI: 10.4236/jssm.2019.123026

Velasco, C. (2022). Cybercrime and artificial intelligence: An overview of the work of international organizations on criminal justice and the international applicable instruments. *ERA Forum*, 23, 109–126. https://doi.org/DOI: 10.1007/s12027-022-00702-z

Verhoeven, T. (2020). Digitalisierung im Recruiting. *Wie sich Recruiting durch künstliche Intelligenz, Algorithmen und Bots verändert.*

Verma, R., & Bandi, S. (2019). Artificial intelligence & human resource management in Indian IT sector. Proceedings of 10th international conference on digital strategies for organizational success. DOI: 10.2139/ssrn.3319897

Verma, K. K., Mishra, J. K., Gautam, K. B., & Kumar, M. (2024). Role of Strategic Marketing on Competitive Advantage for E-Commerce Business in India: An Empirical Study. *Journal of Informatics Education and Research*, 4(1).

Vincent, V. U. (2021). Integrating intuition and artificial intelligence in organizational decision-making. *Business Horizons*, 64(4), 425–438. DOI: 10.1016/j.bushor.2021.02.008

Vinnykova, N. (2022). Digtial technologies in combating global corruption. *The Journal of VN Karazin Kharkiv National University.Issues of Political Science*, 41, 30–39.

Vishwakarma, L. P., & Singh, R. K. (2023). An analysis of the challenges to human resource in implementing artificial intelligence. In *The Adoption and Effect of Artificial Intelligence on Human Resources Management, Part B* (pp. 81-109). Emerald Publishing Limited. DOI: 10.1108/978-1-80455-662-720230006

von Braun, J., Archer, M. S., Reichberg, G. M., & Sánchez Sorondo, M. (2021). AI, robotics, and humanity: Opportunities, risks, and implications for ethics and policy. In von Braun, J., Archer, M. S., Reichberg, G. M., & Sánchez Sorondo, M. (Eds.), *Robotics, AI, and humanity* (pp. 1–20). Springer., DOI: 10.1007/978-3-030-54173-6_1

Wachter, S., & Mittelstadt, B. (2018, October 5). *A Right to Reasonable Inferences: Re-Thinking Data Protection Law in the Age of Big Data and AI*. Papers. DOI: 10.31228/osf.io/mu2kf

Wachter, S., Mittelstadt, B., & Floridi, L. (2016). Why a Right to Explanation of Automated Decision-Making Does Not Exist in the General Data Protection Regulation. *International Data Privacy Law*, 7(2), 76–99. DOI: 10.1093/idpl/ipx005

Waheed, A., Xiaoming, M., Waheed, S., Ahmad, N., & Tian-tian, S. (2020). E-HRM implementation, adoption and its predictors: A case of small and medium enterprises of Pakistan. *International Journal of Information Technology and Management*, 19(2-3), 162–180. DOI: 10.1504/IJITM.2020.106217

Wanden-Berghe, J. G. (2021). Mahatma Gandhi's Sarvodaya (welfare for all) as a way to end violence and achieve happy, sustainable societies. In *Linking Sustainability and Happiness: Theoretical and Applied Perspectives* (pp. 65–81). Springer International Publishing.

Wang, C., Shen, J., & Chao, J. (2022). Integrating computational thinking in STEM education: A literature review. *International Journal of Science and Mathematics Education*, 20(8), 1949–1972. DOI: 10.1007/s10763-021-10227-5

Wang, S. (2024). Research on the Digital Marketing Strategies in the E-commerce Logistics Service Mode under the Influence of Big Data. *Computer-Aided Design and Applications*, 21, 39–55.

Wang, S., Wang, B., Hu, A., & Zhang, X. (2024). Digital Marketing and Business Performance of Selected Micro-Enterprises in China. *Journal of Business and Management Studies*, 6(1), 134–151. DOI: 10.32996/jbms.2024.6.1.8

Wang, X., Wu, Y. C., Zhou, M., & Fu, H. (2024). Beyond surveillance: Privacy, ethics, and regulations in face recognition technology. *Frontiers in Big Data*, 7, 1337465. Advance online publication. DOI: 10.3389/fdata.2024.1337465 PMID: 39027377

Wang, X., Zhang, J., Yao, K., & Qin, J. (2021). ResumeVis Interactive Visualization of Resumes Based on Multi-Source Data. *International Journal of Web Services Research*, 18(2), 40–53. DOI: 10.4018/IJWSR.2021040103

Weintrop, D., Beheshti, E., Horn, M., Orton, K., Jona, K., Trouille, L., & Wilensky, U. (2016). Defining computational thinking for mathematics and science classrooms. *Journal of Science Education and Technology*, 25(1), 127–147. DOI: 10.1007/s10956-015-9581-5

White, E., & Black, N. (2021). Automation in legal research: Opportunities and risks for practitioners. *Legal Studies Review*, 30(4), 234–250.

Wijayanto, G., Jushermi, J., Nursanti, A., Novandalina, A., & Rivai, Y. (2024). The Effect of E-commerce Platforms, Digital Marketing, and User Experience on Market Reach and Competitiveness of Indonesian MSMEs. *International Journal of Business, Law, and Education*, 5(1), 811–823. DOI: 10.56442/ijble.v5i1.492

Wilkinson, S. (2021). Machine Learning for Performance Management. Cimlogic. [online] Retrieved from https://www.cimlogic.co.uk/article/machine-learning-for-performance- management/

Wisniewski, B., Zierer, K., & Hattie, J. (2020). The power of feedback revisited: A meta-analysis of educational feedback research. *Frontiers in Psychology*, 10, 3087. DOI: 10.3389/fpsyg.2019.03087 PMID: 32038429

World Economic Forum (WEF). (2023). Artificial intelligence and the future of financial services: A global perspective.

World Economic Forum. (2021). Global Gender Gap Report 2021. Retrieved from https://www.weforum.org/reports/global-gender-gap-report-2021

World Economic Forum. (2023). Global Gender Gap Report 2023. Retrieved from https://www.weforum.org/reports/global-gender-gap-report-2023/

Woxsen University. (2021). *Exploring the use of AI in legal decision making: Benefits and ethical implications*. Retrieved from https://woxsen.edu.in/research/white-papers/exploring-the-use-of-ai-in-legal-decision-making-benefits-and-ethical-implications/

Wrigley-Asante, C., Ackah, C. G., & Frimpong, L. K. (2023). Gender differences in academic performance of students studying Science Technology Engineering and Mathematics (STEM) subjects at the University of Ghana. *SN Social Sciences*, 3(1), 12. DOI: 10.1007/s43545-023-00608-8 PMID: 36686568

Wu, C. W., Botella-Carrubi, D., & Blanco-González-Tejero, C. (2024). The empirical study of digital marketing strategy and performance in small and medium-sized enterprises (SMEs). *Technological Forecasting and Social Change*, 200, 123142. DOI: 10.1016/j.techfore.2023.123142

Wu, Z., Shen, S., Li, H., Zhou, H., & Lu, C. (2021). A basic framework for privacy protection in personalized information retrieval: An effective framework for user privacy protection. [JOEUC]. *Journal of Organizational and End User Computing*, 33(6), 1–26. DOI: 10.4018/JOEUC.292526

Xu, Y., Liu, X., Cao, X., Huang, C., Liu, E., Qian, S., Liu, X., Wu, Y., Dong, F., Qiu, C.-W., Qiu, J., Hua, K., Su, W., Wu, J., Xu, H., Han, Y., Fu, C., Yin, Z., Liu, M., & Zhang, J. (2021). Artificial intelligence: A powerful paradigm for scientific research. *Innovation (Cambridge (Mass.))*, 2(4), 100179. DOI: 10.1016/j.xinn.2021.100179 PMID: 34877560

Yadav, A., Mayfield, C., Zhou, N., Hambrusch, S., & Korb, J. T. (2014). Computational thinking in elementary and secondary teacher education. *ACM Transactions on Computing Education*, 14(1), 1–16. DOI: 10.1145/2576872

Yadong, C. (2024). Analysis of Artificial Intelligence Judicial Cases. In *Blue Book on AI and Rule of Law in the World (2022)* (pp. 347–365). Springer Nature Singapore. DOI: 10.1007/978-981-97-1060-7_8

Yadong, C. (2024). Special Reports on the Development of Artificial Intelligence Rule of Law. In *Blue Book on AI and Rule of Law in the World* (pp. 367–422). Springer Nature Singapore. DOI: 10.1007/978-981-97-1060-7_9

Yau, K.-L. A., Saad, N. M., & Chong, Y.-W. (2021). Artificial intelligence marketing (AIM) for enhancing customer relationships. *Applied Sciences (Basel, Switzerland)*, 11(18), 8562. DOI: 10.3390/app11188562

Yilmaz Ince, E., & Koc, M. (2021). The consequences of robotics programming education on computational thinking skills: An intervention of the Young Engineer's Workshop (YEW). *Computer Applications in Engineering Education*, 29(1), 191–208. DOI: 10.1002/cae.22321

Yu, M. C. (2018). Viewing expert judgment in individual assessments through the Lens Model: Testing the limits of expert information processing. PhD, University of Minnesota.

Yuliastuti, H., Putra, J. E., & Utomo, B. (2024). Digital Marketing, Entrepreneurial Orientation, and Business Capital on the Financial Performance of MSMEs in Indonesia. *International Journal of Business, Law, and Education*, 5(2), 1633–1645. DOI: 10.56442/ijble.v5i2.695

Zafar, A. (2024). Balancing the scale: Navigating ethical and practical challenges of artificial intelligence (AI) integration in legal practices. *Discover Artificial Intelligence*, 4(1), 27. DOI: 10.1007/s44163-024-00121-8

Zaidan, E., & Ibrahim, I. A. (2024). AI governance in a complex and rapidly changing regulatory landscape: A global perspective. *Humanities & Social Sciences Communications*, 11(1), 1121. DOI: 10.1057/s41599-024-03560-x

Završnik, A. (2020). Criminal justice, artificial intelligence systems, and human rights. *ERA Forum, 20*(3), 567–583. DOI: 10.1007/s12027-020-00602-0

Zengler, T., & Kauffman, R.J. (2023). The intersection of AI and finance: Opportunities for innovation and growth.

Zhang, J., & Chen, Z. (2024). Exploring human resource management digital transformation in the digital age. *Journal of the Knowledge Economy*, 15(1), 1482–1498. DOI: 10.1007/s13132-023-01214-y

Zhang, Y. (2024). Research on China's agricultural product sales transformation: Online marketing mix strategy and performance on post pandemic area. *Frontiers in Sustainable Food Systems*, 7, 1297732. DOI: 10.3389/fsufs.2023.1297732

Zhang, Y., Wu, M., Tian, G. Y., Zhang, G., & Lu, J. (2021). Ethics and privacy of artificial intelligence: Understandings from bibliometrics. *Knowledge-Based Systems*, 222, 106994. DOI: 10.1016/j.knosys.2021.106994

Zhao, X., & Patel, R. (2024). Ethical frameworks for AI in the judiciary: A comparative analysis. *Law and Ethics of Human Rights*, 18(2), 200–225.

Zhou, Y., Wang, L., & Chen, W. (2023). The dark side of AI-enabled HRM on employees based on AI algorithmic features. *Journal of Organizational Change Management*, 36(7), 1222–1241. DOI: 10.1108/JOCM-10-2022-0308

Zhu, T., Ye, D., Wang, W., Zhou, W., & Philip, S. Y. (2020). More than privacy: Applying differential privacy in key areas of artificial intelligence. *IEEE Transactions on Knowledge and Data Engineering*, 34(6), 2824–2843. DOI: 10.1109/TKDE.2020.3014246

Zint, M., Michel, J. O., Valentine, T., & Collins, S. (2024). *Collaborating with Students to Advance Climate Change Education at the University of Michigan.* Insights and Recommendations.

Zirar, A., Ali, S. I., & Islam, N. (2023). Worker and workplace Artificial Intelligence (AI) coexistence: Emerging themes and research agenda. *Technovation, 124*, 102747. Camilleri, M. A. (2020). A Taxonomy of Online Marketing Methods. *Hajarian, M., Camilleri, MA, Díaz, P. & Aedo, I.(2020). A Taxonomy of Online Marketing Methods.* In Camilleri, M. A. (Ed.), *Strategic Corporate Communication in the Digital Age*. Emerald.

Zuwanda, Z. S., Lubis, A. F., Solapari, N., Sakmaf, M. S., & Triyantoro, A. (2024). Ethical and Legal Analysis of Artificial Intelligence Systems in Law Enforcement with a Study of Potential Human Rights Violations in Indonesia. *The Easta Journal Law and Human Rights*, 2(03), 176–185. DOI: 10.58812/eslhr.v2i03.283

About the Contributors

Christian Kaunert is Professor of International Security at Dublin City University, Ireland. He is also Professor of Policing and Security, as well as Director of the International Centre for Policing and Security at the University of South Wales. In addition, he is Jean Monnet Chair, Director of the Jean Monnet Centre of Excellence and Director of the Jean Monnet Network on EU Counter-Terrorism (www.eucter.net). Previously, he served as Academic Director and Professor at the Institute for European Studies, Vrije Universiteit Brussel, a Professor of International Politics, Head of Discipline in Politics, and the Director of the European Institute for Security and Justice, a Jean Monnet Centre for Excellence, at the University of Dundee. Prof Kaunert has researched and taught in many international universities, such as University of Shandong, Jinan, China, IBEI Barcelona, Spain, Diplomatic Academy Yerevan, Armenia – United Nations Development Mission, University of Cairo, Egypt, Collegio Carlo Alberto, Turin, Italy, Ecole nationale d'administration Paris, European Institute of Public Administration Maastricht, Netherlands, European Studies Institute (ESI) at Moscow, University of Porto, Portugal, etc. He was previously Senior Lecturer at the University of Dundee, Marie Curie Senior Research Fellow at the European University Institute Florence, and Senior Lecturer in EU Politics & International Relations, University of Salford. Christian has been invited expert for the European Institute for Public Administration (EIPA), the Counter-Terrorism Committee of the European Parliament, the European Union Institute for Security Studies (an agency of the EU), the United Nations Development Programme (UNDP) and the North Atlantic Treaty Organisation (NATO). Over his career, he has been awarded seven prestigious Marie Curie Fellowships, four Jean Monnet Chairs, and, finally, three Jean Monnet Centre of Excellence, as well as one Jean Monnet Network of Excellence 'EUCTER'. Additionally, he was awarded a large Horizon 2020 research grant on Terrorist Radicalisation processes – Mindb4Act. He is currently Editor of the Journal of Contemporary European Studies, was also previously an elected member of the national (UK) Executive Committee of the University Association for Contemporary European Studies (UACES).

Anjali Raghav is a Research Scholar at the School of Law, Sharda University, Greater Noida. She is a graduate in Law and has completed her Master's in Law from Sharda School of Law, Sharda University. She has over 3 years of experience as a criminal practising lawyer. Anjali has attended 21+ national and international conferences, webinars, seminars, and symposiums, along with paper presentations, and has participated in 4+ faculty development programs. She has over 25+ publications in various esteemed journals and books. Anjali is an active member at the Family Dispute Resolution Clinic, Meditation Centre, Greater Noida. She has a keen interest in the areas of Criminal Law, Intellectual Property Rights, Artificial Intelligence, Machine Learning, and Blockchain Technology.

Bhupinder Singh is working as Professor at Sharda University, India. Also, Honorary Professor in University of South Wales UK and Santo Tomas University Tunja, Colombia. His areas of publications as Smart Healthcare, Medicines, fuzzy logics, artificial intelligence, robotics, machine learning, deep learning, federated learning, IoT, PV Glasses, metaverse and many more. He has 3 books, 139 paper publications, 163 paper presentations in international/national conferences and seminars, participated in more than 40 workshops/FDP's/QIP's, 25 courses from international universities of repute, organized more than 59 events with international and national academicians and industry people's, editor-inchief and co-editor in journals, developed new courses. He has given talks at international universities, resource person in international conferences such as in Nanyang Technological University Singapore, Tashkent State University of Law Uzbekistan; KIMEP University Kazakhstan, All'ah meh Tabatabi University Iran, the Iranian Association of International Criminal law, Iran and Hague Center for International Law and Investment, The Netherlands, Northumbria University Newcastle UK, Taylor's University Malaysia, AFM Krakow University Poland, European Institute for Research and Development Georgia, Business and Technology University Georgia, Texas A & M University US name a few. His leadership, teaching, research and industry experience is of 16 years and 3 Months. His research interests are health law, criminal law, research methodology and emerging multidisciplinary areas as Blockchain Technology, IoT, Machine Learning, Artificial Intelligence, Genome-editing, Photovoltaic PV Glass, SDG's and many more.

Budi Agus Riswandi is a professor of law in the field of intellectual property rights and cyberlaw and Dean of the Faculty of Law, Universitas Islam Indonesia. He teaches Intellectual Property Law at the Faculty of Law, Universitas Islam

Indonesia. In addition, he also teaches at various Law Faculties in Indonesia. He usually conducts research focusing on the field of intellectual property rights and cyberlaw and publications in the form of books, journals in the field of Green Energies, intellectual property rights and cyberlaw. He is also usually appointed as a speaker in various scientific activities such as seminars or conferences both at national and international levels, especially in the field of intellectual property rights and renewable energies. He is also registered as an advocate with the Indonesian Advocates Association and a registered Intellectual Property Consultant at the Directorate General of Intellectual Property of the Ministry of Law and Human Rights of the Republic of Indonesia as well as the Coordinator of the Intellectual Property Consultants Association of Yogyakarta Special Region. In addition, he is also the Chairman of the Indonesian Intellectual Property Centre Association.

***

Saquib Ahmed is a legal professional and accomplished academic, currently a Research Scholar at the Sharda School of Law, Sharda University, Greater Noida, India. He has a strong educational background and a bachelor's degree. from Aligarh Muslim University and Master of Law from Jamia Millia Islamia, where he developed his knowledge in Corporate Law, Intellectual Property Rights, Competition law etc.. He has a robust portfolio of publications in esteemed journals and books, reflecting his dedication to contributing to the body of knowledge in his fields of interest. His research has been recognized on various platforms, as evidenced by his participation in national and international conferences, seminars, webinars, and symposiums. Also, in his academic and research pursuits, Saquib is a skilled editor, having successfully overseen the editorial process of several publications and he is also editorial team member of the Sharda Law Review. Mr Ahmed has been active in organizing various programs like Moot Court Competition, Conferences, Faculty Development Programs and Quiz Competitions.

Amit Kumar Arora is serving as an Assistant Professor in KIET School of Management, KIET Group of Institutions, Ghaziabad. He is pursuing his Ph.D from IGNOU, New Delhi. He is an Associate Member of Cost and Management Accountants (ACMA), UGC-NET, M.B.A (Finance), M.Com, M.A. (Eco.), P.hD(P). He is having more than 15 Years of academic and corporate experience. His areas of interest are Costing, Accountancy, Finance and Economics. He is the author of two text book titled Management of Working Capital and Financial Management. His various papers have been published in reputed research journals including Journal of ICAI-CMA.

Manmeet Kaur Arora is a Research Scholar at the School of Law, Sharda University, Greater Noida. She is a graduate of Law and has completed her Master's in Law from Amity University, Noida. Manmeet Kaur is a qualified Company Secretary Executive Programme. She has over 8+ years of Industry Experience and 1 year of experience as an Associate at a reputed IPR Law Firm. Manmeet Kaur has attended 20+ National & International Conferences, Webinars, Seminars, Symposiums, and Paper Presentations and participated in 5+ Faculty Development programs. She has over 50+ publications in various esteemed Journals and Books. She is active at the Family Dispute Resolution Clinic, Meditation Centre, Greater Noida. Manmeet Kaur has a keen interest in the areas of Corporate Law, Intellectual Property Rights, Insolvency, Artificial Intelligence, Machine Learning, and Blockchain Technology.

Saurabh Chandra is an accomplished legal scholar and currently serves as an Associate Professor & Assistant Dean at the School of Law, Bennett University, India. With a robust academic foundation, he earned his Bachelor of Arts and Bachelor of Laws (B.A. LL.B.) from the prestigious Aligarh Muslim University (A.M.U.). He further specialized in Business Laws, completing his Master of Laws (LL.M.) at the renowned National Law School of India University (NLSIU), Bangalore. Dr. Chandra's academic journey culminated in a Doctorate in Law (Ph.D.) from the esteemed National Law University (NLU) Delhi.Dr. Saurabh Chandra also holds a master's degree in Management with specialization in Human Resources in Management and another in Journalism and Mass Communication. With 16 years of teaching experience, he has established himself as an expert in Business Laws, with numerous publications to his credit. Dr. Saurabh Chandra is an expert in Business Laws, with a profound understanding of the intricate legal frameworks that govern the business world.Dr. Chandra brings a wealth of experience in Academic Administration, having successfully held various key administrative positions.

Madhurima Dasgupta is currently pursuing a post-doctorate in the Sociology of Gender from Abo-Akademi University, Finland. She is the Head of the Department of Gender Studies and Social Studies at Ashadi Wisdom Campus, Sri Lanka. She holds a Ph.D. from Jadavpur University, ranked 4th by NIRF in 2023, and is UGC-NET qualified in Sociology. With over 11 years of teaching and research experience, she has been a sought-after resource person and keynote speaker at numerous international conferences. Dr. Dasgupta has published around 40 papers in UGC CARE and Web of Science journals and authored notable books. She has been recognized among the top 100 professors in India by Foxclues Ltd.

Souvik Dhar is currently working as Assistant Professor of Law. He has completed his Ph.D. in Law from Amity University Noida. He has successfully passed both the UGC-NET and WB-SET examinations. He has a diverse academic experience. Furthermore, he worked as a Research Investigator at the Centre for Child Rights, WB NUJS, contributing to a UNICEF project focusing on the 'Evaluation of the POCSO Act, 2012 in West Bengal'. His educational qualifications include a B.A. LL.B. from the Department of Law, University of Calcutta, and an LL.M. in Business Laws from Amity Law School, Amity University, Kolkata. Dr. Dhar has also practiced as an Advocate handling cases in consumer rights, banking, civil, and criminal law. He has actively participated, delivered special lectures as resource person. His scholarly contributions comprise numerous articles in reputable journals (including UGC-Care listed journals) and edited books covering diverse legal issues. He is the author and co-author of several books on various legal subjects. He has a total of over 30 publications which includes 15 books. His area of interest includes Health Law, Criminal Law, Corporate Law, and Human Rights Law.

Sheikh Inam Ul Mansoor (BA.LLB Hon's, LLM, CCPT WIPO, PhD International Trade Law) is a highly accomplished academician presently working as an Assistant Professor of Law at the School of Law, Dayananda Sagar University in Bangalore, India. With a strong background in law and a passion for academia, Dr. Sheikh has made significant contributions to the field through his extensive research and publications. Pursued his BA. LLB (Hon's) from the University of Kashmir, LLM from JNU Jaipur and Ph.D. International Trade Law from LPU Punjab. Prior to his academic career, Dr. Sheikh served as an Advocate and Solicitor at the Jammu and Kashmir High Court and other subordinate courts in Jammu and Kashmir. This experience as a legal practitioner has provided him with valuable insights into the practical application of law and enhanced his understanding of legal dynamics. As an Assistant Professor Law at Dayananda Sagar University, Dr. Sheikh Inam Ul Mansoor continues to make significant contributions to the legal field through his research, teaching, and involvement in various professional activities.

Puneet Kumar is a strong advocate of innovative learning as well as teaching in rapidly changing educational environment. He has a rich experience of more than 29 years in academics, research, teaching, training & consultancy. He is an expert in institutionalizing pedagogy innovation and bringing about changes in all aspects of education which effect faculty and students.As an accomplished educationist entrepreneur he has turned around campuses and has given new dimensions to education. He was also closely associated with conceiving and in giving shape to some of the educational institutions like Pt. Deen Dayal Upadhyay Management College (Meerut), Cosmic Business School (New Delhi) and K R Mangalam

Global Institute of Management (New Delhi). In the past he has also convened and coordinated various academic activities for the benefit of students and academicians, some of these include International Conference in the year 2017 and 2018. He has to his credit plenty of publications in refereed Journals of repute. His area of expertise is financial management and capital markets.

Sahil Lal is a Research Scholar at School of Law, Sharda University. He pursued his graduation from National Law University, Lucknow and completed his Master's in Law from Gujarat National Law University, Gandhinagar. Sahil has completed a certificate course on 'AI & Law' from Lund University, Sweden and on 'Cyber Law' from Indian Law Institute, New Delhi. Sahil Lal is a qualified UGC-NET & JRF candidate. He has a 10+ year Industry Experience and is an active member of Family Dispute Resolution Clinic, Mediation Center, Greater Noida. Sahil has attended 20+ International & National Conferences along with Paper Presentation and has also participated in more than 5+ Faculty Development Programme. Mr. Sahil has more than 50+ publications in various esteemed Journals & Books. Mr. Sahil has a keen interest in area of Artificial Intelligence, Machine Learning, Robotics, Block-Chain Technology and Intellectual Property Rights.

Thean PhengLim is a lecturer and Deputy Head at Tunku Abdul Rahman University of Management and Technology, Penang Branch. He holds a bachelor's degree in management and a master's degree in information technology (technopreneurship) from Universiti Sains Malaysia. He is also a member of the Malaysian Institute of Management and an affiliate of the Chartered Management Institute, UK. Lim has more than 15 years of working experience in the business and education industry. Beginning his career as a Business and Financial Consultant, Lim was involved in various consultancy projects with multinational enterprises such as Chee Wah Corporation Berhad and International Business Machines Corporation (IBM). In academics, he has vast experience supervising dissertations for bachelor's degree students, industry consultancy projects and lecturing in courses related to Operations Management, Entrepreneurship and Information Technology.

Ng Wei Chien (PhD) is a Senior Lecturer and Coordinator for Operations Management, Business Analytics & Marketing Section in School of Management (Universiti Sains Malaysia). He obtained his PhD in Industrial Analytics from Universiti Sains Malaysia. He is a certified TRIZ level 1 instructor and International MATRIZ level 3 practitioner. NG has published numerous articles in international journals and conference proceedings. He specializes in Business Analytics, TRIZ, Six Sigma, FMEA and Operations Management.

Kamalesh Ravesangar is an academician with over ten years of experience in teaching Certificate, Diploma, Degree, and supervision for MBA(coursework mode) students from various social and cultural backgrounds at private colleges and universities. Currently, she works as Senior Lecturer at Tunku Abdul Rahman University of Management & Technology in Malaysia. Moreover, she has a total of three years of experience in industries related to educational, manufacturing, recruitment, and engineering. She is also a Professional Member of Malaysian Institute of Human Resource Management (MIHRM). A subject matter expert in human resource management, human resource development, management and organizational behavior studies. She has published articles and reviewed articles in online journal publications. She holds a Phd (doctorate) and a Master's degree in Organizational Behavior and Human Resource Management. She is also peer-reviewer for a few journals in the field of Business, Management, HRM. Besides, she has been awarded " Certificate of Recognition & Excellence in Reviewing by Asian Journal of Economics, Business & Accounting and Journal of Global Economics, Management and Business Research & Institute of Industry and Academic Research Incorporated (IIARI).

Mohammad Saleem is currently serving his duties as an Assistant Professor at Faculty of Law, Marwadi University, Rajkot, Gujarat. He is also pursuing his Ph.D. in Law from Vellore Institute of Technology School of Law, Chennai, Tamil Nadu. He also holds a Post-Graduate Diploma in Cyber Laws from Bhartiya Vidyapeeth, Pune. Mr. Saleem hails from Lucknow, the capital city of Uttar Pradesh. After his schooling from Lucknow Public College, he joined National P.G. College for his graduation in B.Sc. and afterwards joined the Faculty of Law, University of Lucknow, Lucknow, U.P. to pursue his undergraduate degree in law (LL.B.). Afterwards, he joined the Faculty of Law, Aligarh Muslim University, Aligarh, U.P. to pursue his masters in law (LL.M.). He has a specialization in Constitutional Law and also secured Distinction in LL.M. He cleared the UGC NET exam in December, 2019 and started his teaching career in 2020. He has authored a book with title, "Words of Hate: A Statutory Analysis of Hate Speech in India". He has participated and presented research papers in various seminars and conference at national and international level and published various research papers on diverse topics of law in national and international journals. His academic interest lies in Constitutional Law, Comparative Constitutional Law, Human Rights, Civil Liberties, legal philosophy and legal reforms, through which he seeks to empower the marginalized and downtrodden class of persons of the society. His research areas include rights related to women and children, freedom of speech and expression, preventive detention laws, election laws, democracy and everyday political developments at national and international level.

Karun Sanjaya is an Assistant Professor at Symbiosis Law School, Nagpur and a Research Scholar at VIT School of Law, Vellore Institute of Technology, Chennai, India. He specialises in the area of Intellectual Property Laws. He is a recipient of many awards, including the prestigious Justice V.R. Krishna Iyer Memorial Merit Awards in the years 2019 and 2022. He has published over sixty research items and is a keen researcher in diverse areas of law, including intellectual property law.

Yu QingSoong is a PhD candidate at Universiti Sains Malaysia, where she also completed her Master of Arts and Bachelor of Management degrees. She is currently a lecturer at Tunku Abdul Rahman University of Management and Technology, specializing in finance. Her research expertise lies in finance, corporate governance, sustainability, and TRIZ methodology.

Surendra Tiwari is presently working with Institute of Technology and Science, Ghaziabad. He is PhD in Business Administration from Dr. B. R. Ambedkar University, Agra and has qualified many certifications from premier B schools and prestigious International University like IIT, John Hopkins- USA and University of Leeds-UK. Dr. Tiwari has two and half decade of rich academic and industry experience in the area of Marketing and Strategic Management. He has International and National patents to his credit and has authored books, research papers and articles in the journals of international repute. He is a member of various professional bodies and provides training and consulting services to organizations. He is actively engaged in bridging the corporate world and academia in the area of Consumer Behavior, Marketing Communication, Client Service, UX/UI Management and Strategic Marketing.

Showkat Wani has good publications in SAGE, IGI Global and other reputed journals like Springer. He has completed many research targets, including four PhD Research Scholars and eight P.G. Dissertations who had already completed their research and were awarded. Dr. Wani has so far written 30 Research articles and attended 48 Conferences. Dr. Wani has also edited one book.

Index

A

B

C

D

E

F

G

H

I

J

L

M

P

R

S

T

V

www.ingramcontent.com/pod-product-compliance
Lightning Source LLC
LaVergne TN
LVHW060007031026
849161LV00025B/2219
* 9 7 9 8 3 6 9 3 9 3 9 5 6 *